C#:
The Complete Reference

About the Author

Herbert Schildt is the world's leading programming author. He is an authority on the C, C++, Java, and C# languages, and is a master Windows programmer. His programming books have sold more than 3 million copies worldwide and have been translated into all major foreign languages. He is the author of numerous bestsellers, including *C++: The Complete Reference*, *Java 2: The Complete Reference*, *C#: A Beginner's Guide*, *Java 2: A Beginner's Guide*, *Windows 2000 Programming from the Ground Up*, and *C: The Complete Reference*. Schildt holds a Master's Degree in computer science from the University of Illinois. He can be reached at his consulting office at (217) 586-4683.

C#:
The Complete Reference

Herbert Schildt

McGraw-Hill/Osborne

New York Chicago San Francisco
Lisbon London Madrid Mexico City
Milan New Delhi San Juan
Seoul Singapore Sydney Toronto

McGraw-Hill/Osborne
2600 Tenth Street
Berkeley, California 94710
U.S.A.

To arrange bulk purchase discounts for sales promotions, premiums, or fund-raisers, please contact **McGraw-Hill**/Osborne at the above address. For information on translations or book distributors outside the U.S.A., please see the International Contact Information page immediately following the index of this book.

C#: The Complete Reference

1234567890 DOC DOC 0198765432
ISBN 0-07-213485-2

Publisher
  Brandon A. Nordin

Vice President & Associate Publisher
  Scott Rogers

Acquisitions Editor
  Ann Sellers

Project Editors
  Lisa Theobald and Madhu Prasher

Acquisitions Coordinator
  Tim Madrid

Technical Editor
  Paul Garland

Copy Editors
  Jan Jue and Lisa Theobald

Proofreader
  Pamela Vevea

Indexer
  Sheryl Schildt

Computer Designers
  George Toma Charbak and Carie Abrew

Illustrators
  Michael Mueller, Lyssa Wald

Series Design
  Peter F. Hancik

This book was composed with Corel VENTURA™ Publisher.

Contents at a Glance

Contents

Part I
The C# Language

Part II

Exploring the C# Library

Part III

Applying C#

Preface

We programmers are a demanding bunch, always looking for ways to improve the performance, efficiency, and portability of the programs that we write. We also demand much from the tools we use, especially when it comes to programming languages. There are many programming languages, but only a few are great. A great programming language must be powerful, yet flexible. Its syntax must be terse, but clear. It must facilitate the creation of correct code while not getting in our way. It must support state-of-the-art features, but not trendy dead ends. Finally, a great programming language must have one more almost intangible quality: it must feel right when we use it. C# is such a language.

Created by Microsoft to support its .NET Framework, C# builds on a rich programming heritage. Its chief architect was longtime programming guru Anders Hejlsberg. C# is directly descended from two of the world's most successful computer languages: C and C++. From C, it derives its syntax, many of its keywords, and operators. It builds upon and improves the object model defined by C++. C# is also closely related to another very successful language: Java. Sharing a common ancestry, but differing in many important ways, C# and Java are more like cousins. For example, both support distributed programming and both use intermediate code to achieve portability, but the details differ.

Building on the strong foundation that it inherits, C# adds several important innovations that advance the art of programming. For example, C# includes delegates, properties, indexers, and events as language elements. It also adds syntax that supports attributes. Furthermore, C# streamlines the creation of components, eliminating the troubles associated with COM. One other point: like Java, C# offers a significant amount of runtime error checking, security, and managed execution. However, unlike Java, C# also gives you access to pointers. Thus, C# combines the raw power of C++ with the type safety of Java. Furthermore, the tradeoffs between power and safety are carefully balanced and nearly transparent.

Throughout the history of computing, programming languages have evolved to accommodate changes in the computing environment and changes in the way that we think about and approach the job of programming. C# is no exception. In the ongoing process of refinement, adaptation, and innovation, C# is currently at the forefront. It is a language that no professional programmer can afford to ignore.

What's Inside

One of the most challenging aspects of writing about C# is knowing when to stop! The C# language, by itself, is big. The C# class library is even bigger. To help manage this large amount of material, the book is divided into these three parts:

- Part I: The C# Language
- Part II: Exploring the C# Library
- Part III: Applying C#

Part I provides a comprehensive discussion of the C# language. This is the largest part in the book, and it describes the keywords, syntax, and features that define the C# language. I/O, file handling, reflection, and the preprocessor are also described in Part I.

Part II explores the C# class library, which is also the .NET Framework class library. This library is huge! Because of space limitations, it is not possible to cover the entire .NET Framework class library in one book. Instead, Part II focuses on the core library, which is contained in the **System** namespace. This is the part of the library that relates most specifically to C#. Also covered are collections, multithreading, and networking. These are the parts of the library that nearly every C# programmer will use.

Part III contains examples that apply C#. Chapter 24 shows how to build software components, Chapter 25 describes the construction of Windows applications using the Windows Forms library, and Chapter 26 develops a recursive-descent parser for numerical expressions.

A Book for All Programmers

No previous programming experience is required to use this book. If you already know C++ or Java, you will be able to advance quite rapidly, because C# has much in common with those languages. If you don't have any previous programming experience, you will still be able to learn C# from this book, but you will need to work carefully through the examples in each chapter.

Required Software

To compile and run the programs in this book, you will need Visual Studio .NET 7 (or later) and the .NET Framework must be installed on your computer.

Don't Forget: Code on the Web

Remember, the source code for all of the programs in this book is available free of charge on the Web at **www.osborne.com**.

For Further Study

C#: The Complete Reference is your gateway to the Herb Schildt series of programming books. Here are some others that you will find of interest.

For a carefully-paced introduction to C#, try

C#: A Beginner's Guide

To learn about C++, you will find these books especially helpful:

C++: The Complete Reference

C++: A Beginner's Guide

Teach Yourself C++

C++ from the Ground Up

STL Programming from the Ground Up

The C/C++ Programming Annotated Archives

To learn about Java programming, we recommend the following:

Java 2: A Beginner's Guide

Java 2: The Complete Reference

Java 2: Programmer's Reference

If you want to learn about the C language, which is the foundation of all modern programming, you will find the following titles of interest:

C: The Complete Reference

Teach Yourself C

When you need solid answers, fast, turn to Herbert Schildt, the recognized authority on programming.

The Complete Reference

Part I

The C# Language

Part I discusses the elements of the C# language, including its keywords, syntax, and operators. Also described are several foundational C# techniques, such as I/O and reflection, which are tightly linked with the C# language.

Chapter 1

The Creation of C#

C# represents the next step in the ongoing evolution of programming languages. Its creation was deeply rooted in the process of refinement and adaptation that has characterized computer language development for the past several years. Like all successful languages that came before, C# builds upon the past while advancing the art of programming.

Created by Microsoft to support development for its .NET Framework, C# leverages time-tested features with cutting-edge innovations. It provides a highly usable, efficient way to write programs for the modern enterprise computing environment, which includes Windows, the Internet, components, and so on. In the process, C# has redefined the programming landscape.

The purpose of this chapter is to place C# into its historical context, including the forces that drove its creation, its design philosophy, and how it was influenced by other computer languages. The chapter also explains how C# relates to the .NET Framework.

C#'s Family Tree

Computer languages do not exist in a void. Rather, they relate to one another, with each new language influenced in one form or another by the ones that came before. In a process akin to cross-pollination, features from one language are adapted by another, a new innovation is integrated into an existing context, or an older construct is removed. In this way, languages evolve and the art of programming advances. C# is no exception.

C# inherits a rich programming legacy. It is directly descended from two of the world's most successful computer languages: C and C++. It is closely related to another: Java. Understanding the nature of these relationships is crucial to understanding C#. Thus, we begin our examination of C# by placing it in the historical context of these three languages.

C: The Beginning of the Modern Age of Programming

The creation of C marks the beginning of the modern age of programming. C was invented by Dennis Ritchie in the 1970s on a DEC PDP-11 that used the UNIX operating system. While some earlier languages, most notably Pascal, had achieved significant success, it was C that established the paradigm that still charts the course of programming today.

C grew out of the *structured programming* revolution of the 1960s. Prior to structured programming, large programs were difficult to write because the program logic tended to degenerate into what is known as "spaghetti code," a tangled mass of jumps, calls, and returns that is difficult to follow. Structured languages addressed this problem by adding well-defined control statements, subroutines with local variables, and other improvements. Using structured languages, it became possible to write moderately large programs.

Although there were other structured languages at the time, C was the first to combine power, elegance, and expressiveness successfully. Its terse yet easy-to-use syntax, coupled with its philosophy that the programmer (not the language) was in charge, quickly won many converts. It can be a bit hard to understand from today's perspective, but C was a breath of fresh air that programmers had long awaited. As a result, C became the most widely used structured programming language of the 1980s.

However, even the venerable C language had its limits. One of the most troublesome was its inability to handle large programs. The C language hits a barrier once a project reaches a certain size, and after that point, C programs are difficult to understand and maintain. Precisely where this limit is reached depends upon the program, the programmer, and the tools at hand, but it can be encountered with as few as 5,000 lines of code.

The Creation of OOP and C++

By the late 1970s, the size of many projects was near or at the limits of what structured programming methodologies and the C language could handle. To solve this problem, a new way to program began to emerge, called *object-oriented programming* (OOP). Using OOP, a programmer could handle much larger programs. The trouble was that C, the most popular language at the time, did not support OOP. The desire for an object-oriented version of C ultimately led to the creation of C++.

C++ was invented by Bjarne Stroustrup beginning in 1979 at Bell Laboratories in Murray Hill, New Jersey. He initially called the new language "C with Classes." However, in 1983 the name was changed to C++. C++ contains the entire C language. Thus, C is the foundation upon which C++ is built. Most of the additions that Stroustrup made to C were designed to support object-oriented programming. In essence, C++ is the object-oriented version of C. By building upon the foundation of C, Stroustrup provided a smooth migration path to OOP. Instead of having to learn an entirely new language, a C programmer needed to learn only a few new features before reaping the benefits of the object-oriented methodology.

C++ simmered in the background during much of the 1980s, undergoing extensive development. By the beginning of the 1990s, C++ was ready for mainstream use, and its popularity exploded. By the end of the decade, it had become the most widely used programming language. Today, C++ is still the preeminent language for the development of high-performance, system level code.

It is critical to understand that the invention of C++ was not an attempt to create a new programming language. Instead, it was an enhancement to an already highly successful language. This approach to language development—beginning with an existing language and moving it forward—established a trend that continues today.

The Internet and Java Emerge

The next major advance in programming languages is Java. Work on Java, which was originally called Oak, began in 1991 at Sun Microsystems. The main driving force behind Java's design was James Gosling. Patrick Naughton, Chris Warth, Ed Frank, and Mike Sheridan also played a role.

Java is a structured, object-oriented language with a syntax and philosophy derived from C++. The innovative aspects of Java were driven not so much by advances in the art of programming (although some certainly were), but rather by changes in the computing environment. Prior to the mainstreaming of the Internet, most programs were written, compiled, and targeted for a specific CPU and a specific operating system. While it has always been true that programmers like to reuse their code, the ability to easily port a program from one environment to another had yet to be achieved, and portablility had taken a backseat to more pressing problems. However, with the rise of the Internet, in which many different types of CPUs and operating systems are connected, the old problem of portability reemerged. To solve the problem of portability, a new language was needed, and this new language was Java.

Although the single most important aspect of Java (and the reason for its rapid acceptance) is its ability to create cross-platform, portable code, it is interesting to note that the original impetus for Java was not the Internet, but rather the need for a platform-independent language that could be used to create software for embedded controllers. In 1993, it became clear that the issues of cross-platform portability found when creating code for embedded controllers are also encountered when attempting to create code for the Internet. Remember: the Internet is a vast, distributed computing universe in which many different types of computers live. The same techniques that solved the portability problem on a small scale could be applied to the Internet on a large scale.

Java achieved portability by translating a program's source code into an intermediate language called *bytecode.* This bytecode was then executed by the Java Virtual Machine (JVM). Therefore, a Java program could run in any environment for which a JVM was available. Also, since the JVM is relatively easy to implement, it was readily available for a large number of environments.

Java's use of bytecode differed radically from both C and C++, which were nearly always compiled to executable machine code. Machine code is tied to a specific CPU and operating system. Thus, if you wanted to run a C/C++ program on a different system, it needed to be recompiled to machine code specifically for that environment. Therefore, to create a C/C++ program that would run in a variety of environments, several different executable versions of the program were needed. Not only was this impractical, it was expensive. Java's use of an intermediate language was an elegant, cost-effective solution. It is also a solution that C# would adapt for its own purposes.

As mentioned, Java is descended from C and C++. Its syntax is based on C, and its object model is evolved from C++. Although Java code is neither upwardly nor downwardly compatible with C or C++, its syntax is sufficiently similar that the large pool of existing C/C++ programmers could move to Java with very little effort. Furthermore, because Java built upon and improved an existing paradigm, Gosling, et al., were free to focus their attentions on the new and innovative features. Just as Stroustrup did not need to "reinvent the wheel" when creating C++, Gosling did not need to create an entirely new language when developing Java. Moreover, with the creation of Java, C and C++ became the accepted substrata upon which new computer languages are built.

The Creation of C#

While Java has successfully addressed many of the issues surrounding portability in the Internet environment, there are still features that it lacks. One is *cross-language interoperability*, also called *mixed-language programming.* This is the ability for the code produced by one language to work easily with the code produced by another. Cross-language interoperability is needed for the creation of large, distributed software systems. It is also desirable for programming software components because the most valuable component is one that can be used by the widest variety of computer languages, in the greatest number of operating environments.

Another feature lacking in Java is full integration with the Windows platform. Although Java programs can be executed in a Windows environment (assuming that the Java Virtual Machine has been installed), Java and Windows are not closely coupled. Since Windows is the most widely used operating system in the world, lack of direct support for Windows is a drawback to Java.

To answer these and other needs, Microsoft developed C#. C# was created at Microsoft late in the 1990s and was part of Microsoft's overall .NET strategy. It was first released in its alpha version in the middle of 2000. C#'s chief architect was Anders Hejlsberg, one of the world's leading language experts with several notable accomplishments to his credit. For example, in the 1980s he was the original author of the highly successful and influential Turbo Pascal, whose streamlined implementation set the standard for all future compilers.

C# is directly related to C, C++, and Java. This is not by accident. These are three of the most widely used—and most widely liked—programming languages in the world. Furthermore, nearly all professional programmers today know C and C++, and most know Java. By building C# upon a solid, well-understood foundation, C# offers an easy migration path from these languages. Since it was neither necessary nor desirable for Hejlsberg to "reinvent the wheel," he was free to focus on specific improvements and innovations.

The family tree for C# is shown in Figure 1-1. The grandfather of C# is C. From C, C# derives its syntax, many of its keywords, and its operators. C# builds upon and improves the object model defined by C++. If you know C or C++, then you will feel at home with C#.

C# and Java have a bit more complicated relationship. As explained, Java is also descended from C and C++. It too shares the C/C++ syntax and object model. Like Java, C# is designed to produce portable code. However, C# is not descended from Java. Instead, C# and Java are more like cousins, sharing a common ancestry, but differing in many important ways. The good news, though, is that if you know Java, then many C# concepts will be familiar. Conversely, if in the future you need to learn Java, then many of the things you learn about C# will carry over.

C# contains many innovative features that we will examine at length throughout the course of this book, but some of its most important relate to its built-in support for software components. In fact, C# has been characterized as being a component-oriented language because it contains integral support for the writing of software components.

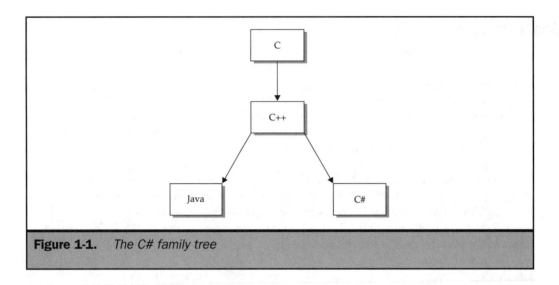

Figure 1-1. *The C# family tree*

For example, C# includes features that directly support the constituents of components, such as properties, methods, and events. However, C#'s ability to work in a mixed-language environment is perhaps its most important component-oriented feature.

How C# Relates to the .NET Framework

Although C# is a computer language that can be studied on its own, it has a special relationship to its runtime environment, the .NET Framework. The reason for this is twofold. First, C# was initially designed by Microsoft to create code for the .NET Framework. Second, the libraries used by C# are the ones defined by the .NET Framework. Thus, even though it is possible to separate C# the language from the .NET environment, the two are closely linked. Because of this, it is important to have a general understanding of the .NET Framework and why it is important to C#.

What Is the .NET Framework?

The .NET Framework defines an environment that supports the development and execution of highly-distributed, component-based applications. It enables differing computer languages to work together and provides for security, program portability, and a common programming model for the Windows platform. It is important to state, however, that the .NET Framework is not inherently limited to Windows (although this is the only environment that is currently available), which means that programs written for it might be portable to non-Windows environments in the future.

As it relates to C#, the .NET Framework defines two very important entities. The first is the *Common Language Runtime* (CLR). This is the system that manages the execution of your program. Along with other benefits, the CLR is the part of the .NET Framework that enables programs to be portable, supports mixed-language programming, and provides for security.

The second entity is the .NET *class library.* This library gives your program access to the runtime environment. For example, if you want to perform I/O, such as displaying something on the screen, you will use the .NET class library to do it. If you are new to programming, then the term *class* may be new. Although it is explained in detail later in this book, for now a brief definition will suffice: a class is an object-oriented construct that helps organize programs. As long as a program restricts itself to the features defined by the .NET class library, it can run anywhere that the .NET runtime system is supported. Since C# automatically uses the .NET class library, C# programs are automatically portable to all .NET environments.

How the Common Language Runtime Works

The CLR manages the execution of .NET code. Here is how it works: When you compile a C# program, the output of the compiler is not executable code. Instead, it is a file that contains a special type of pseudocode called *Microsoft Intermediate Language* (MSIL). MSIL defines a set of portable instructions that are independent of any specific CPU. In essence, MSIL defines a portable assembly language. One other point: although MSIL is similar in concept to Java's bytecode, the two are not the same.

It is the job of the CLR to translate the intermediate code into executable code when a program is run. Thus, any program compiled to MSIL can be run in any environment for which the CLR is implemented. This is part of how the .NET Framework achieves portability.

Microsoft Intermediate Language is turned into executable code using a *JIT compiler.* "JIT" stands for "Just-In-Time." The process works like this: When a .NET program is executed, the CLR activates the JIT compiler. The JIT compiler converts MSIL into native code on a demand basis as each part of your program is needed. Thus, your C# program actually executes as native code even though it is initially compiled into MSIL. This means that your program runs nearly as fast as it would if it had been compiled to native code in the first place, but it gains the portability benefits of MSIL.

In addition to MSIL, one other thing is output when you compile a C# program: *metadata*. Metadata describes the data used by your program and enables your code to interact with other code. The metadata is contained in the same file as the MSIL.

Managed vs. Unmanaged Code

In general, when you write a C# program, you are creating what is called *managed code.* Managed code is executed under the control of the Common Language Runtime as just described. Because it is running under the control of the CLR, managed code is subject to certain constraints—and derives several benefits. The constraints are easily described and met: the compiler must produce an MSIL file targeted for the CLR (which C# does) and use the .NET Framework libraries (which C# does). The benefits of managed code are many, including modern memory management, the ability to mix languages, better security, support for version control, and a clean way for software components to interact.

The opposite of managed code is unmanaged code. Unmanaged code does not execute under the Common Language Runtime. Thus, all Windows programs prior to the creation of the .NET Framework use unmanaged code. It is possible for managed code and unmanaged code to work together, so the fact that C# generates managed code does not restrict its ability to operate in conjunction with preexisting programs.

The Common Language Specification

Although all managed code gains the benefits provided by the CLR, if your code will be used by other programs written in different languages, then for maximum usability, it should adhere to the *Common Language Specification* (CLS). The CLS describes a set of features that different languages have in common. CLS compliance is especially important when creating software components that will be used by other languages. The CLS includes a subset of the *Common Type System* (CTS). The CTS defines the rules concerning data types. Of course, C# supports both the CLS and the CTS.

The
Complete
Reference

Chapter 2

An Overview of C#

By far, the hardest thing about learning a programming language is the fact that no element exists in isolation. Instead, the components of the language work together. This interrelatedness makes it difficult to discuss one aspect of C# without involving others. Often, the discussion of one feature implies prior knowledge of another. To help overcome this problem, this chapter provides a brief overview of several C# features, including the general form of a C# program, some basic control statements, and operators. It does not go into too many details, but rather concentrates on the general concepts common to any C# program. Most of the topics discussed here are examined in greater detail in the remaining chapters of Part I.

Object-Oriented Programming

At the center of C# is *object-oriented programming* (OOP). The object-oriented methodology is inseparable from C#, and all C# programs are to at least some extent object oriented. Because of its importance to C#, it is useful to understand OOP's basic principles before you write even a simple C# program.

OOP is a powerful way to approach the job of programming. Programming methodologies have changed dramatically since the invention of the computer, primarily to accommodate the increasing complexity of programs. For example, when computers were first invented, programming was done by toggling in the binary machine instructions using the computer's front panel. As long as programs were just a few hundred instructions long, this approach worked. As programs grew, assembly language was invented so that a programmer could deal with larger, increasingly complex programs, using symbolic representations of the machine instructions. As programs continued to grow, high-level languages such as FORTRAN and COBOL were introduced that gave the programmer more tools with which to handle complexity. When these early languages began to reach their breaking point, structured programming was invented.

Consider this: At each milestone in the development of programming, techniques and tools were created to allow the programmer to deal with increasingly greater complexity. Each step of the way, the new approach took the best elements of the previous methods and moved forward. The same is true of object-oriented programming. Prior to OOP, many projects were nearing (or exceeding) the point where the structured approach no longer worked. A better way to handle complexity was needed, and object-oriented programming was the solution.

Object-oriented programming took the best ideas of structured programming and combined them with several new concepts. The result was a different and better way of organizing a program. In the most general sense, a program can be organized in one of two ways: around its code (what is happening) or around its data (what is being affected). Using only structured programming techniques, programs are typically organized around code. This approach can be thought of as "code acting on data."

Object-oriented programs work the other way around. They are organized around data, with the key principle being "data controlling access to code." In an object-oriented language, you define the data and the code that is permitted to act on that data. Thus, a data type defines precisely the operations that can be applied to that data.

To support the principles of object-oriented programming, all OOP languages, including C#, have three traits in common: encapsulation, polymorphism, and inheritance. Let's examine each.

Encapsulation

Encapsulation is a programming mechanism that binds together code and the data it manipulates, and that keeps both safe from outside interference and misuse. In an object-oriented language, code and data can be bound together in such a way that a self-contained *black box* is created. Within the box are all necessary data and code. When code and data are linked together in this fashion, an *object* is created. In other words, an object is the device that supports encapsulation.

Within an object, code, data, or both may be *private* to that object or *public*. Private code or data is known to and accessible by only another part of the object. That is, private code or data cannot be accessed by a piece of the program that exists outside the object. When code or data is public, other parts of your program can access it even though it is defined within an object. Typically, the public parts of an object are used to provide a controlled interface to the private elements.

C#'s basic unit of encapsulation is the *class*. A class defines the form of an object. It specifies both the data and the code that will operate on that data. C# uses a class specification to construct *objects*. Objects are instances of a class. Thus, a class is essentially a set of plans that specify how to build an object.

The code and data that constitute a class are called *members* of the class. Specifically, the data defined by the class is referred to as *member variables* or *instance variables.* The code that operates on that data is referred to as *member methods* or just *methods. Method* is C#'s term for a subroutine. If you are familiar with C/C++, it may help to know that what a C# programmer calls a *method*, a C/C++ programmer calls a *function.* Because C# is a direct descendent of C++, the term *function* is also commonly used when referring to a C# method.

Polymorphism

Polymorphism (from the Greek, meaning "many forms") is the quality that allows one interface to access a general class of actions. A simple example of polymorphism is found in the steering wheel of an automobile. The steering wheel (the interface) is the same no matter what type of actual steering mechanism is used. That is, the steering wheel works the same whether your car has manual steering, power steering, or rack-and-pinion steering. Thus, turning the steering wheel left causes the car to go left no matter what type of steering is used. The benefit of the uniform interface is, of course, that once you know how to operate the steering wheel, you can drive any type of car.

The same principle can also apply to programming. For example, consider a *stack* (which is a first-in, last-out list). You might have a program that requires three different types of stacks. One stack is used for integer values, one for floating-point values, and one for characters. In this case, the algorithm that implements each stack is the same, even though the data being stored differs. In a non-object-oriented language, you would be required to create three different sets of stack routines, with each set using different names. However, because of polymorphism, in C# you can create one general set of stack routines that works for all three specific situations. This way, once you know how to use one stack, you can use them all.

More generally, the concept of polymorphism is often expressed by the phrase "one interface, multiple methods." This means that it is possible to design a generic interface to a group of related activities. Polymorphism helps reduce complexity by allowing the same interface to be used to specify a *general class of action*. It is the compiler's job to select the *specific action* (that is, method) as it applies to each situation. You, the programmer, don't need to do this selection manually. You need only remember and utilize the general interface.

Inheritance

Inheritance is the process by which one object can acquire the properties of another object. This is important because it supports the concept of hierarchical classification. If you think about it, most knowledge is made manageable by hierarchical (that is, top-down) classifications. For example, a Red Delicious apple is part of the classification *apple,* which in turn is part of the *fruit* class, which is under the larger class *food.* That is, the *food* class possesses certain qualities (edible, nutritious, and so on) which also, logically, apply to its subclass, *fruit.* In addition to these qualities, the *fruit* class has specific characteristics (juicy, sweet, and so on) that distinguish it from other food. The *apple* class defines those qualities specific to an apple (grows on trees, not tropical, and so on). A Red Delicious apple would, in turn, inherit all the qualities of all preceding classes and would define only those qualities that make it unique.

Without the use of hierarchies, each object would have to explicitly define all of its characteristics. Using inheritance, an object need only define those qualities that make it unique within its class. It can inherit its general attributes from its parent. Thus, it is the inheritance mechanism that makes it possible for one object to be a specific instance of a more general case.

A First Simple Program

It is now time to look at an actual C# program. We will begin by compiling and running the short program shown here:

```
/*
   This is a simple C# program.

   Call this program Example.cs.
*/

using System;

class Example {

  // A C# program begins with a call to Main().
  public static void Main() {
    Console.WriteLine("A simple C# program.");
  }
}
```

At the time of this writing, the only available C# development environment is Visual Studio .NET. Using Visual Studio .NET, there are two ways to edit, compile, and run a C# program. First, you can use the command-line compiler, **csc.exe**. Second, you can use the Visual Studio Integrated Development Environment (IDE). Both methods are described here. (If you are using a different compiler, follow the instructions provided with it.)

Using csc.exe, the C# Command-Line Compiler

Although the Visual Studio IDE is what you will probably be using for your commercial projects, the C# command-line compiler is the easiest way to compile and run most of the sample programs shown in this book. To create and run programs using the C# command-line compiler, you will follow these three steps:

1. Enter the program using a text editor.
2. Compile the program.
3. Run the program.

Entering the Program

The programs shown in this book are available from Osborne's web site: **www.osborne.com**. However, if you want to enter the programs by hand, you are free to do so. In this case, you must enter the program into your computer using a text editor, such as Notepad. Remember, you must create text-only files, not formatted word- processing files, because the format information in a word processor file will confuse the C# compiler. When entering the program, call the file **Example.cs**.

Compiling the Program

To compile the program, execute the C# compiler, **csc.exe**, specifying the name of the source file on the command line, as shown here:

```
C:\>csc Example.cs
```

The **csc** compiler creates a file called **Example.exe** that contains the MSIL version of the program. Although MSIL is not executable code, it is still contained in an **exe** file. The Common Language Runtime automatically invokes the JIT compiler when you attempt to execute **Example.exe**. Be aware, however, that if you try to execute **Example.exe** (or any other **exe** file that contains MSIL) on a computer for which the .NET Framework is not installed, the program will not execute because the CLR will be missing.

Note *Prior to running **csc.exe**, you may need to run the batch file **vcvars32.bat**, which is typically found in the //Program Files/Microsoft Visual Studio .NET/Vc7/Bin directory. Alternatively, you can activate a command-prompt session that is already initialized for C# by selecting a Visual Studio .NET Command Prompt from the list of tools shown under the Microsoft Visual Studio .NET entry in the Start | Programs menu of the task bar.*

Running the Program

To actually run the program, just type its name on the command line, as shown here:

```
C:\>Example
```

When the program is run, the following output is displayed:

```
A simple C# program.
```

Using the Visual Studio IDE

Beginning with Visual Studio .NET version 7, the Visual Studio IDE can compile C# programs. To edit, compile, and run a C# program using the Visual Studio version 7 IDE, you will follow these steps. (If you have a different version of Visual Studio, you may need to follow different steps.)

1. Create a new, empty C# project by selecting File | New | Project.

2. Select Visual C# Projects, and then select Empty Project, as shown here:

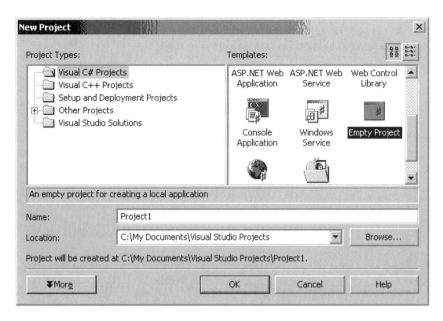

3. After the project is created, right-click on the project name in the Solution Explorer window. Then, using the pop-up context menu, select Add. Next, select Add New Item. Your screen will look like this:

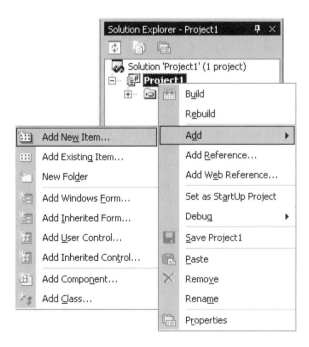

4. When you see the Add New Item dialog box, select Local Project Items. Finally, select Code File. Your screen will look like this:

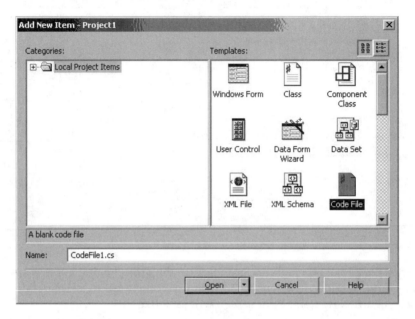

5. Enter the program and save the file using the name **Example.cs**. (Remember, you can download the programs in this book from **www.osborne.com**.) When done, your screen will look like that shown in Figure 2-1.

6. Compile the program by selecting Build | Build Solution.

7. Run the program by selecting Debug | Start Without Debugging.

When you run the program, you will see the window shown in Figure 2-2.

To compile and run the sample programs in this book, you don't need to create a new project for each one. Instead, you can use the same C# project. Just delete the current file and add the new file. Then, recompile and run.

As explained, for the short programs shown in the first part of this book, using the **csc** command-line compiler is a much simpler approach. Of course, the choice is yours.

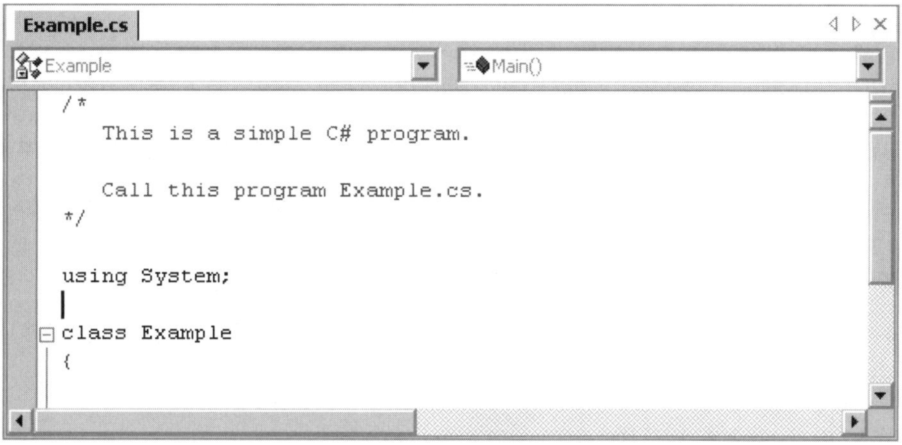

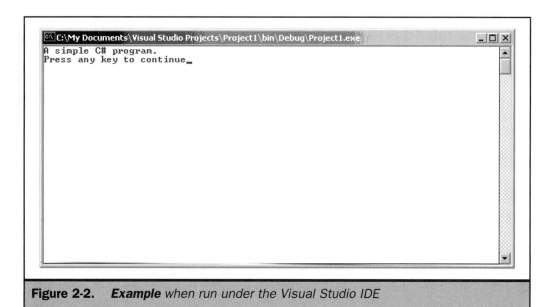

Figure 2-1. *Example.cs* *Project screen*

Figure 2-2. *Example* *when run under the Visual Studio IDE*

The First Sample Program, Line by Line

Although **Example.cs** is quite short, it includes several key features that are common to all C# programs. Let's closely examine each part of the program, beginning with its name.

The name of a C# program is arbitrary. Unlike some computer languages (most notably, Java) in which the name of a program file is very important, this is not the case for C#. You were told to call the sample program **Example.cs** so that the instructions for compiling and running the program would apply, but as far as C# is concerned, you could have called the file by another name. For example, the preceding sample program could have been called **Sample.cs**, **Test.cs**, or even **X.cs**.

By convention, C# programs use the **.cs** file extension, and this is a convention that you should follow. Also, many programmers call a file by the name of the principal class defined within the file. This is why the filename **Example.cs** was chosen. Since the names of C# programs are arbitrary, names won't be specified for most of the sample programs in this book. Just use names of your own choosing.

The program begins with the following lines:

```
/*
    This is a simple C# program.

    Call this program Example.cs.
*/
```

This is a *comment*. Like most other programming languages, C# lets you enter a remark into a program's source file. The contents of a comment are ignored by the compiler. Instead, a comment describes or explains the operation of the program to anyone who is reading its source code. In this case, the comment describes the program and reminds you to call the source file **Example.cs**. Of course, in real applications, comments generally explain how some part of the program works or what a specific feature does.

C# supports three styles of comments. The one shown at the top of the program is called a *multiline comment*. This type of comment must begin with /* and end with */. Anything between these two comment symbols is ignored by the compiler. As the name suggests, a multiline comment can be several lines long.

The next line in the program is

```
using System;
```

This line indicates that the program is using the **System** namespace. In C#, a *namespace* defines a declarative region. Although we will look at namespaces in detail later, a namespace provides a way to keep one set of names separate from another. In essence, names declared in one namespace will not conflict with the same names declared in another. The namespace used by the program is **System**, which is the namespace reserved for items associated with the .NET Framework class library, which is the library used by C#. The **using** keyword simply states that the program is using the names in the given namespace.

The next line of code in the program is shown here:

```
class Example {
```

This line uses the keyword **class** to declare that a new class is being defined. As mentioned, the class is C#'s basic unit of encapsulation. **Example** is the name of the class. The class definition begins with the opening curly brace ({) and ends with the closing curly brace (}). The elements between the two braces are members of the class. For the moment, don't worry too much about the details of a class except to note that in C#, all program activity occurs within one. This is one reason why all C# programs are (at least a little bit) object oriented.

The next line in the program is the *single-line comment,* shown here:

```
// A C# program begins with a call to Main().
```

This is the second type of comment supported by C#. A *single-line comment* begins with a // and ends at the end of the line. As a general rule, programmers use multiline comments for longer remarks and single-line comments for brief, line-by-line descriptions.

The next line of code is shown here:

```
   public static void Main() {
```

This line begins the **Main( )** method. As mentioned earlier, in C#, a subroutine is called a method. As the comment preceding it suggests, this is the line at which the program will begin executing. All C# applications begin execution by calling **Main( )**. (This is similar to the way C/C++ programs begin execution at **main( )**.) The complete meaning of each part of this line cannot be given now, since it involves a detailed understanding of several other C# features. However, since many of the examples in this book will use this line of code, let's take a brief look at it now.

The **public** keyword is an *access* specifier. An access specifier determines how other parts of a program can access a member of a class. When a class member is preceded by **public**, then that member can be accessed by code outside the class in which it is declared. (The opposite of **public** is **private**, which prevents a member from being used by code defined outside of its class.) In this case, **Main( )** is declared as **public** because it will be called by code outside of its class (the operating system) when the program is started.

Note *At the time of this writing, C# does not actually require **Main( )** to be declared as **public**. However, this is the way that many of the examples supplied by Visual Studio .NET declare it. It is also the way that many C# programmers prefer. For these reasons, this book will also declare **Main( )** as **public**. Don't be surprised, though, if you see it declared a bit differently.*

The keyword **static** allows **Main( )** to be called before an object of its class has been created. This is necessary since **Main( )** is called at program startup. The keyword **void** simply tells the compiler that **Main( )** does not return a value. As you will see, methods can also return values. The empty parentheses that follow **Main** indicate that no information is passed to **Main( )**. As you will see, it is possible to pass information into **Main( )** or into any other method. The last character on the line is the {. This signals the start of **Main( )**'s body. All of the code that comprises a method will occur between the method's opening curly brace and its closing curly brace.

The next line of code is shown here. Notice that it occurs inside **Main( )**.

```
Console.WriteLine("A simple C# program.");
```

This line outputs the string "A simple C# program." followed by a new line on the screen. Output is actually accomplished by the built-in method **WriteLine( )**. In this case, **WriteLine( )** displays the string that is passed to it. Information that is passed to a method is called an *argument*. In addition to strings, **WriteLine( )** can be used to display other types of information, too. The line begins with **Console**, which is the name of a predefined class that supports console I/O. By connecting **Console** with **WriteLine( )**, you are telling the compiler that **WriteLine( )** is a member of the **Console** class. The fact that C# uses an object to define console output is further evidence of its object-oriented nature.

Notice that the **WriteLine( )** statement ends with a semicolon, as does the **using System** statement earlier in the program. All statements in C# end with a semicolon. The reason that several other lines in the program do not end in a semicolon is that they are not, technically, statements.

The first } in the program ends **Main( )**, and the last } ends the **Example** class definition.

One last point: C# is case-sensitive. Forgetting this can cause serious problems. For example, if you accidentally type **main** instead of **Main**, or **writeline** instead of **WriteLine**, the preceding program will be incorrect. Furthermore, although the C# compiler *will* compile classes that do not contain a **Main( )** method, it has no way to execute them. So, if you had mistyped **Main**, the compiler would still compile your program. However, you would also see an error message that states that **Example.exe** does not have an entry point defined.

Handling Syntax Errors

If you have not yet done so, enter, compile, and run the preceding program. As you may know from your previous programming experience, it is quite easy to accidentally type something incorrectly when entering code into your computer. Fortunately, if you enter something incorrectly, the compiler will report a *syntax error* message when it tries to compile it. The C# compiler attempts to make sense out of your source code no matter what you have written. For this reason, the error that is reported may not always reflect the actual cause of the problem. In the preceding program, for example, an accidental omission of the opening curly brace after the **Main( )** method generates the following sequence of errors when compiled by the **csc** command-line compiler. (Similar errors are generated when compiling using the IDE.)

```
Example.cs(12,28): error CS1002: ; expected
Example.cs(13,22): error CS1519: Invalid token '(' in class, struct, or
  interface member declaration
Example.cs(15,1): error CS1022: Type or namespace definition, or end-of-file
  expected
```

Clearly, the first error message is completely wrong, because what is missing is not a semicolon, but a curly brace. The second two messages are equally confusing.

The point of this discussion is that when your program contains a syntax error, don't necessarily take the compiler's messages at face value. They may be misleading. You may need to "second guess" an error message in order to find the problem. Also, look at the last few lines of code immediately preceding the one in which the error was reported. Sometimes an error will not be reported until several lines after the point at which the error really occurred.

A Small Variation

Although all of the programs in this book will use it, the statement

```
using System;
```

at the start of the first example program is not technically needed. It is, however, a valuable convenience. The reason it's not necessary is that in C# you can always *fully qualify* a name with the namespace to which it belongs. For example, the line

```
Console.WriteLine("A simple C# program.");
```

can be rewritten as

```
System.Console.WriteLine("A simple C# program.");
```

Thus, the first example could be recoded as shown here:

```
// This version does not include the using System statement.

class Example {

  // A C# program begins with a call to Main().
  public static void Main() {

    // Here, Console.WriteLine is fully qualified.
    System.Console.WriteLine("A simple C# program.");
  }
}
```

Since it is quite tedious to always specify the **System** namespace whenever a member of that namespace is used, most C# programmers include the **using System** statement at the top of their programs, as will all of the programs in this book. It is important to understand, however, that you can explicitly qualify a name with its namespace if needed.

A Second Simple Program

Perhaps no other construct is as important to a programming language as the assignment of a value to a variable. A *variable* is a named memory location that can be assigned a value. Further, the value of a variable can be changed during the execution of a program. That is, the content of a variable is changeable, not fixed.

The following program creates two variables called **x** and **y**.

```
// This program demonstrates variables.

using System;

class Example2 {
  public static void Main() {
    int x; // this declares a variable
    int y; // this declares another variable
```

```
    x = 100; // this assigns 100 to x

    Console.WriteLine("x contains " + x);

    y = x / 2;

    Console.Write("y contains x / 2: ");
    Console.WriteLine(y);
  }
}
```

When you run this program, you will see the following output:

```
x contains 100
y contains x / 2: 50
```

This program introduces several new concepts. First, the statement

```
int x; // this declares a variable
```

declares a variable called **x** of type integer. In C#, all variables must be declared before they are used. Further, the kind of values that the variable can hold must also be specified. This is called the *type* of the variable. In this case, **x** can hold integer values. These are whole numbers. In C#, to declare a variable to be of type integer, precede its name with the keyword **int**. Thus, the preceding statement declares a variable called **x** of type **int**.

The next line declares a second variable called **y**.

```
int y; // this declares another variable
```

Notice that it uses the same format as the first except that the name of the variable is different.

In general, to declare a variable, you will use a statement like this:

type var-name;

Here, *type* specifies the type of variable being declared, and *var-name* is the name of the variable. In addition to **int**, C# supports several other data types.

The following line of code assigns **x** the value 100:

```
x = 100; // this assigns 100 to x
```

In C#, the assignment operator is the single equal sign. It copies the value on its right side into the variable on its left.

The next line of code outputs the value of **x** preceded by the string "x contains ".

```
Console.WriteLine("x contains " + x);
```

In this statement, the plus sign causes the value of **x** to be displayed after the string that precedes it. This approach can be generalized. Using the **+** operator, you can chain together as many items as you want within a single **WriteLine( )** statement.

The next line of code assigns **y** the value of **x** divided by 2:

```
y = x / 2;
```

This line divides the value in **x** by 2 and then stores that result in **y**. Thus, after the line executes, **y** will contain the value 50. The value of **x** will be unchanged. Like most other computer languages, C# supports a full range of arithmetic operators, including those shown here:

+	Addition
−	Subtraction
*	Multiplication
/	Division

Here are the next two lines in the program:

```
Console.Write("y contains x / 2: ");
Console.WriteLine(y);
```

Two new things are occurring here. First, the built-in method **Write( )** is used to display the string "y contains x / 2: ". This string is *not* followed by a new line. This means that when the next output is generated, it will start on the same line. The **Write( )** method is just like **WriteLine( )**, except that it does not output a new line after each call. Second, in the call to **WriteLine( )**, notice that **y** is used by itself. Both **Write( )** and **WriteLine( )** can be used to output values of any of C#'s built-in types.

One more point about declaring variables before we move on: It is possible to declare two or more variables using the same declaration statement. Just separate their names by commas. For example, **x** and **y** could have been declared like this:

```
int x, y; // both declared using one statement
```

Another Data Type

In the preceding program, a variable of type **int** was used. However, a variable of type **int** can hold only whole numbers. Thus, it cannot be used when a fractional component is required. For example, an **int** variable can hold the value 18, but not the value 18.3. Fortunately, **int** is only one of several data types defined by C#. To allow numbers with fractional components, C# defines two floating-point types: **float** and **double**, which represent single- and double-precision values, respectively. Of the two, **double** is probably the most commonly used.

To declare a variable of type **double**, use a statement similar to that shown here:

```
double result;
```

Here, **result** is the name of the variable, which is of type **double**. Because **result** has a floating-point type, it can hold values such as 122.23, 0.034, or –19.0.

To better understand the difference between **int** and **double**, try the following program:

```
/*
   This program illustrates the differences
   between int and double.
*/

using System;

class Example3 {
  public static void Main() {
    int ivar;      // this declares an int variable
    double dvar;   // this declares a floating-point variable

    ivar = 100;    // assign ivar the value 100

    dvar = 100.0; // assign dvar the value 100.0

    Console.WriteLine("Original value of ivar: " + ivar);
    Console.WriteLine("Original value of dvar: " + dvar);

    Console.WriteLine(); // print a blank line

    // now, divide both by 3
    ivar = ivar / 3;
    dvar = dvar / 3.0;

    Console.WriteLine("ivar after division: " + ivar);
    Console.WriteLine("dvar after division: " + dvar);
```

```
   }
}
```

The output from this program is shown here:

```
Original value of ivar: 100
Original value of dvar: 100

ivar after division: 33
dvar after division: 33.3333333333333
```

As you can see, when **ivar** is divided by 3, a whole-number division is performed, and the outcome is 33—the fractional component is lost. However, when **dvar** is divided by 3, the fractional component is preserved.

As the program shows, when you want to specify a floating-point value in a program, it must include a decimal point. If you don't, it will be interpreted as an integer. For example, in C#, the value 100 is an integer, but the value 100.0 is a floating-point value.

There is one other new thing to notice in the program. To print a blank line, simply call **WriteLine( )** without any arguments.

The floating-point data types are often used when working with real-world quantities where fractional components are commonly needed. For example, this program computes the area of a circle. It uses the value 3.1416 for pi.

```
// Compute the area of a circle.

using System;

class Circle {
  static void Main() {
    double radius;
    double area;

    radius = 10.0;
    area = radius * radius * 3.1416;

    Console.WriteLine("Area is " + area);
  }
}
```

The output from the program is shown here:

```
Area is 314.16
```

THE C# LANGUAGE

Clearly, the computation of a circle's area could not be satisfactorily achieved without the use of floating-point data.

Two Control Statements

Inside a method, execution proceeds from one statement to the next, top to bottom. However, it is possible to alter this flow through the use of the various program control statements supported by C#. Although we will look closely at control statements later, two are briefly introduced here because we will be using them to write sample programs.

The if Statement

You can selectively execute part of a program through the use of C#'s conditional statement: the **if**. The **if** statement works in C# much like the IF statement in any other language. For example, it is syntactically identical to the **if** statements in C, C++, and Java. Its simplest form is shown here:

if(*condition*) *statement*;

Here, *condition* is a Boolean (that is, true or false) expression. If *condition* is true, then the statement is executed. If *condition* is false, then the statement is bypassed. Here is an example:

```
if(10 < 11) Console.WriteLine("10 is less than 11");
```

In this case, since 10 is less than 11, the conditional expression is true, and **WriteLine( )** will execute. However, consider the following:

```
if(10 < 9) Console.WriteLine("this won't be displayed");
```

In this case, 10 is not less than 9. Thus, the call to **WriteLine( )** will not take place.

C# defines a full complement of relational operators that can be used in a conditional expression. They are shown here:

Operator	Meaning
<	Less than
<=	Less than or equal
>	Greater than
>=	Greater than or equal
= =	Equal to
!=	Not equal

Here is a program that illustrates the **if** statement:

```
// Demonstrate the if.

using System;

class IfDemo {
  public static void Main() {
    int a, b, c;

    a = 2;
    b = 3;

    if(a < b) Console.WriteLine("a is less than b");

    // this won't display anything
    if(a == b) Console.WriteLine("you won't see this");

    Console.WriteLine();

    c = a - b; // c contains -1

    Console.WriteLine("c contains -1");
    if(c >= 0) Console.WriteLine("c is non-negative");
    if(c < 0) Console.WriteLine("c is negative");

    Console.WriteLine();

    c = b - a; // c now contains 1
    Console.WriteLine("c contains 1");
    if(c >= 0) Console.WriteLine("c is non-negative");
    if(c < 0) Console.WriteLine("c is negative");

  }
}
```

The output generated by this program is shown here:

```
a is less than b

c contains -1
c is negative
```

```
c contains 1
c is non-negative
```

Notice one other thing in this program. The line

```
int a, b, c;
```

declares three variables, **a**, **b**, and **c**, by use of a comma-separated list. As mentioned earlier, when you need two or more variables of the same type, they can be declared in one statement. Just separate the variable names by commas.

The for Loop

You can repeatedly execute a sequence of code by creating a *loop*. C# supplies a powerful assortment of loop constructs. The one we will look at here is the **for** loop. If you are familiar with C, C++, or Java, then you will be pleased to know that the **for** loop in C# works the same way it does in those languages. The simplest form of the **for** loop is shown here:

for(*initialization*; *condition*; *iteration*) *statement*;

In its most common form, the *initialization* portion of the loop sets a loop control variable to an initial value. The *condition* is a Boolean expression that tests the loop control variable. If the outcome of that test is true, the **for** loop continues to iterate. If it is false, the loop terminates. The *iteration* expression determines how the loop control variable is changed each time the loop iterates. Here is a short program that illustrates the **for** loop:

```
// Demonstrate the for loop.

using System;

class ForDemo {
  public static void Main() {
    int count;

    for(count = 0; count < 5; count = count+1)
      Console.WriteLine("This is count: " + count);

    Console.WriteLine("Done!");
  }
}
```

The output generated by the program is shown here:

```
This is count: 0
This is count: 1
This is count: 2
This is count: 3
This is count: 4
Done!
```

In this example, **count** is the loop control variable. It is set to zero in the initialization portion of the **for**. At the start of each iteration (including the first one), the conditional test **count < 5** is performed. If the outcome of this test is true, the **WriteLine( )** statement is executed, and then the iteration portion of the loop is executed. This process continues until the conditional test is false, at which point execution picks up at the bottom of the loop.

As a point of interest, in professionally written C# programs you will almost never see the iteration portion of the loop written as shown in the preceding program. That is, you will seldom see statements like this:

```
count = count + 1;
```

The reason is that C# includes a special increment operator that performs this operation more efficiently. The increment operator is **++** (that is, two consecutive plus signs). The increment operator increases its operand by one. By use of the increment operator, the preceding statement can be written like this:

```
count++;
```

Thus, the **for** in the preceding program will usually be written like this:

```
for(count = 0; count < 5; count++)
```

You might want to try this. As you will see, the loop still runs exactly the same as it did before.

C# also provides a decrement operator, which is specified as **– –**. This operator decreases its operand by one.

Using Blocks of Code

Another key element of C# is the *code block*. A code block is a grouping of two or more statements. This is done by enclosing the statements between opening and closing curly braces. Once a block of code has been created, it becomes a logical unit that can be used any place that a single statement can. For example, a block can be a target for **if** and **for** statements. Consider this **if** statement:

```
if(w < h) {
  v = w * h;
  w = 0;
}
```

Here, if **w** is less than **h**, then both statements inside the block will be executed. Thus, the two statements inside the block form a logical unit, and one statement cannot execute without the other also executing. The key point here is that whenever you need to logically link two or more statements, you do so by creating a block. Code blocks allow many algorithms to be implemented with greater clarity and efficiency.

Here is a program that uses a block of code to prevent a division by zero:

```
// Demonstrate a block of code.

using System;

class BlockDemo {
  public static void Main() {
    int i, j, d;

    i = 5;
    j = 10;

    // the target of this if is a block
    if(i != 0) {
      Console.WriteLine("i does not equal zero");
      d = j / i;
      Console.WriteLine("j / i is " + d);
    }
  }
}
```

The output generated by this program is shown here:

```
i does not equal zero
j / i is 2
```

In this case, the target of the **if** statement is a block of code and not just a single statement. If the condition controlling the **if** is true (as it is in this case), the three statements inside the block will be executed. Try setting **i** to zero and observe the result.

Here is another example. It uses a block of code to compute the sum and the product of the numbers from 1 to 10.

```
// Compute the sum and product of the numbers from 1 to 10.

using System;

class ProdSum {
  static void Main() {
    int prod;
    int sum;
    int i;

    sum = 0;
    prod = 1;

    for(i=1; i <= 10; i++) {
      sum = sum + i;
      prod = prod * i;
    }
    Console.WriteLine("Sum is " + sum);
    Console.WriteLine("Product is " + prod);

  }
}
```

The output is shown here:

```
Sum is 55
Product is 3628800
```

Here, the block enables one loop to compute both the sum and the product. Without the use of the block, two separate **for** loops would have been required.

One last point: Code blocks do not introduce any runtime inefficiencies. In other words, the { and } do not consume any extra time during the execution of a program. In fact, because of their ability to simplify the coding of certain algorithms, the use of code blocks generally increases speed and efficiency.

Semicolons and Positioning

In C#, the semicolon signals the end of a statement. That is, each individual statement must end with a semicolon.

As you know, a block is a set of logically connected statements that is surrounded by opening and closing braces. A block is *not* terminated with a semicolon. Since a block is a group of statements, with a semicolon after each statement, it makes sense that a block is not terminated by a semicolon; instead, the end of the block is indicated by the closing brace.

C# does not recognize the end of the line as the end of a statement—only a semicolon terminates a statement. For this reason, it does not matter where on a line you put a statement. For example, to C#,

```
x = y;
y = y + 1;
Console.WriteLine(x + " " + y);
```

is the same as

```
x = y;   y = y + 1;   Console.WriteLine(x + " " + y);
```

Furthermore, the individual elements of a statement can also be put on separate lines. For example, the following is perfectly acceptable:

```
Console.WriteLine("This is a long line of output" +
                  x + y + z +
                  "more output");
```

Breaking long lines in this fashion is often used to make programs more readable. It can also help prevent excessively long lines from wrapping.

Indentation Practices

You may have noticed in the previous examples that certain statements were indented. C# is a free-form language, meaning that it does not matter where you place statements relative to each other on a line. However, over the years, a common and accepted indentation style has developed that allows for very readable programs. This book follows that style, and it is recommended that you do so as well. Using this style, you indent one level after each opening brace and move back out one level after each closing brace. Certain statements encourage some additional indenting; these will be covered later.

abstract	as	base	bool	break
byte	case	catch	char	checked
class	const	continue	decimal	default
delegate	do	double	else	enum
event	explicit	extern	false	finally
fixed	float	for	foreach	goto
if	implicit	in	int	interface
internal	is	lock	long	namespace
new	null	object	operator	out
override	params	private	protected	public
readonly	ref	return	sbyte	sealed
short	sizeof	stackalloc	static	string
struct	switch	this	throw	true
try	typeof	uint	ulong	unchecked
unsafe	ushort	using	virtual	volatile
void	while			

Table 2-1.   *The C# Keywords*

The C# Keywords

There are currently 77 keywords defined in the C# language (see Table 2-1). These keywords, combined with the syntax of the operators and separators, form the definition of the C# language. These keywords cannot be used as names for a variable, class, or method.

Identifiers

In C#, an identifier is a name assigned to a method, a variable, or any other user-defined item. Identifiers can be from one to several characters long. Variable names may start with any letter of the alphabet or an underscore. Next may be a letter, a digit, or an underscore. The underscore can be used to enhance the readability of a variable name, as in **line_count**. Uppercase and lowercase are different; that is, to C#, **myvar** and **MyVar** are separate names. Here are some examples of acceptable identifiers:

Test	x	y2	MaxLoad
up	_top	my_var	sample23

Remember, you can't start an identifier with a digit. Thus, **12x** is invalid, for example. Good programming practice dictates that you use identifier names that reflect the meaning or usage of the items being named.

Although you cannot use any of the C# keywords as identifier names, C# does allow you to precede a keyword with an @, allowing it to be a legal identifier. For example, **@for** is a valid identifier. In this case, the identifier is actually **for** and the @ is ignored. Here is a program that illustrates the use of an @ identifier:

```
// Demonstrate an @ identifier.

using System;

class IdTest {
  static void Main() {
    int @if; // use if as an identifier

    for(@if = 0; @if < 10; @if++)
      Console.WriteLine("@if is " + @if);
  }
}
```

The output shown here proves the **@if** is properly interpreted as an identifier:

```
@if is 0
@if is 1
@if is 2
@if is 3
@if is 4
@if is 5
@if is 6
@if is 7
@if is 8
@if is 9
```

Frankly, using @-qualified keywords for identifiers is not recommended, except for special purposes. Also, the @ can precede any identifier, but this is considered bad practice.

The C# Class Libraries

The sample programs shown in this chapter make use of two of C#'s built-in methods: **WriteLine( )** and **Write( )**. As mentioned, these methods are members of the **Console** class, which is part of the **System** namespace, which is defined by the .NET Framework's class libraries. As explained earlier in this chapter, the C# environment relies on the .NET Framework class libraries to provide support for such things as I/O, string handling, networking, and GUIs. Thus, C# as a totality is a combination of the C# language itself, plus the .NET standard classes. As you will see, the class libraries provide much of the functionality that is part of any C# program. Indeed, part of becoming a C# programmer is learning to use these standard classes. Throughout Part I, various elements of the .NET library classes and methods are described. Part II examines the .NET library in detail.

The
Complete
Reference

Chapter 3

Data Types, Literals, and Variables

This chapter examines three fundamental elements of C#: data types, literals, and variables. In general, the types of data that a language provides define the class of problems to which it can be applied. As you might expect, C# offers a rich set of built-in data types, which makes C# suitable for a wide range of applications. You can create variables of any of these types, and you can specify constants of each type, which in the language of C# are called *literals*.

Why Data Types Are Important

Data types are especially important in C# because it is a strongly typed language. This means that all operations are type-checked by the compiler for type compatibility. Illegal operations will not be compiled. Thus, strong type-checking helps prevent errors and enhances reliability. To enable strong type-checking, all variables, expressions, and values have a type. There is no concept of a "typeless" variable, for example. Furthermore, the type of a value determines what operations are allowed on it. An operation allowed on one type might not be allowed on another.

C#'s Value Types

C# contains two general categories of built-in data types: *value types* and *reference types*. C#'s reference types are defined by classes, and a discussion of classes is deferred until later. However, at the core of C# are its 13 value types, which are shown in Table 3-1. These are built-in types that are defined by keywords in the C# language, and they are available for use by any C# program.

The term *value type* indicates that variables of these types contain their values directly. (This differs from reference types, in which a variable contains a reference to the actual value.) Thus, the value types act much like the data types found in other programming languages, such as C++. The value types are also known as *simple types*.

C# strictly specifies a range and behavior for each value type. Because of portability requirements, C# is uncompromising on this account. For example, an **int** is the same in all execution environments. There is no need to rewrite code to fit a specific platform. While strictly specifying the size of the value types may cause a small loss of performance in some environments, it is necessary in order to achieve portability.

Integers

C# defines nine integer types: **char**, **byte**, **sbyte**, **short**, **ushort**, **int**, **uint**, **long**, and **ulong**. However, the **char** type is primarily used for representing characters, and it is

Type	Meaning
bool	Represents true/false values
byte	8-bit unsigned integer
char	Character
decimal	Numeric type for financial calculations
double	Double-precision floating point
float	Single-precision floating point
int	Integer
long	Long integer
sbyte	8-bit signed integer
short	Short integer
uint	An unsigned integer
ulong	An unsigned long integer
ushort	An unsigned short integer

Table 3-1.   *The C# Value Types*

discussed later in this chapter. The remaining eight integer types are used for numeric calculations. Their bit-width and ranges are shown here:

Type	Width in Bits	Range
byte	8	0 to 255
sbyte	8	−128 to 127
short	16	−32,768 to 32,767
ushort	16	0 to 65,535
int	32	−2,147,483,648 to 2,147,483,647
uint	32	0 to 4,294,967,295
long	64	−9,223,372,036,854,775,808 to 9,223,372,036,854,775,807
ulong	64	0 to 18,446,744,073,709,551,615

As the table shows, C# defines both signed and unsigned versions of the various integer types. The difference between signed and unsigned integers is in the way the high-order bit of the integer is interpreted. If a signed integer is specified, then the C# compiler will generate code that assumes that the high-order bit of an integer is to be used as a *sign flag*. If the sign flag is 0, then the number is positive; if it is 1, then the number is negative. Negative numbers are almost always represented using the *two's complement* approach. In this method, all bits in the number (except the sign flag) are reversed, and then 1 is added to this number. Finally, the sign flag is set to 1.

Signed integers are important for a great many algorithms, but they have only half the absolute magnitude of their unsigned relatives. For example, as a **short**, here is 32,767:

0 1 1 1 1 1 1 1 1 1 1 1 1 1 1 1

For a signed value, if the high-order bit were set to 1, the number would then be interpreted as –1 (assuming the two's complement format). However, if you declared this to be a **ushort**, then when the high-order bit was set to 1, the number would become 65,535.

Probably the most commonly used integer type is **int**. Variables of type **int** are often employed to control loops, to index arrays, and for general-purpose integer math. When you need an integer that has a range greater than **int**, you have many options. If the value you want to store is unsigned, you can use **uint**. For large signed values, use **long**. For large unsigned values, use **ulong**. For example, here is a program that computes the distance from the Earth to the sun, in inches. Because this value is so large, the program uses a **long** variable to hold it.

```csharp
// Compute the distance from the Earth to the sun, in inches.

using System;

class Inches {
  public static void Main() {
    long inches;
    long miles;

    miles = 93000000; // 93,000,000 miles to the sun

    // 5,280 feet in a mile, 12 inches in a foot
    inches = miles * 5280 * 12;

    Console.WriteLine("Distance to the sun: " +
                      inches + " inches.");

  }
}
```

Here is the output from the program:

```
Distance to the sun: 5892480000000 inches.
```

Clearly, the result could not have been held in an **int** or **uint** variable.

The smallest integer types are **byte** and **sbyte**. The **byte** type is an unsigned value between 0 and 255. Variables of type **byte** are especially useful when working with raw binary data, such as a bytestream of data produced by some device. For small signed integers, use **sbyte**. Here is an example that uses a variable of type **byte** to control a **for** loop that produces the summation of the number 100:

```
// Use byte.

using System;

class Use_byte {
  public static void Main() {
    byte x;
    int sum;

    sum = 0;
    for(x = 1; x <= 100; x++)
      sum = sum + x;

    Console.WriteLine("Summation of 100 is " + sum);
  }
}
```

The output from the program is shown here:

```
Summation of 100 is 5050
```

Since the **for** loop runs only from 0 to 100, which is well within the range of a **byte**, there is no need to use a larger type variable to control it.

When you need an integer that is larger than a **byte** or **sbyte**, but smaller than an **int** or **uint**, use **short** or **ushort**.

Floating-Point Types

The floating-point types can represent numbers that have fractional components. There are two kinds of floating-point types, **float** and **double**, which represent single- and double-precision numbers, respectively. The type **float** is 32 bits wide and has a range of 1.5E–45 to 3.4E+38. The **double** type is 64 bits wide and has a range of 5E–324 to 1.7E+308.

Of the two, **double** is the most commonly used. One reason for this is that many of the math functions in C#'s class library (which is the .NET Framework library) use **double** values. For example, the **Sqrt( )** method (which is defined by the standard **System.Math** class) returns a **double** value that is the square root of its **double** argument. Here, **Sqrt( )** is used to compute the radius of a circle given the circle's area:

```
// Find the radius of a circle given its area.

using System;

class FindRadius {
  public static void Main() {
    Double r;
    Double area;

    area = 10.0;

    r = Math.Sqrt(area / 3.1416);

    Console.WriteLine("Radius is " + r);
  }
}
```

The output from the program is shown here:

```
Radius is 1.78412203012729
```

One other point about the preceding example. As mentioned, **Sqrt( )** is a member of the **Math** class. Notice how **Sqrt( )** is called; it is preceded by the name **Math**. This is similar to the way **Console** precedes **WriteLine( )**. Although not all standard methods are called by specifying their class name first, several are, as the next example shows.

The following program demonstrates several of C#'s trigonometric functions, which are also part of C#'s math library. They also operate on **double** data. The program displays the sine, cosine, and tangent for the angles (measured in radians) from 0.1 to 1.0.

```
//  Demonstrate Math.Sin(), Math.Cos(), and Math.Tan().

using System;

class Trigonometry {
  public static void Main() {
    Double theta; // angle in radians

    for(theta = 0.1; theta <= 1.0; theta = theta + 0.1) {
      Console.WriteLine("Sine of " + theta + "  is " +
                   Math.Sin(theta));
      Console.WriteLine("Cosine of " + theta + "  is " +
                   Math.Cos(theta));
      Console.WriteLine("Tangent of " + theta + "  is " +
                   Math.Tan(theta));
      Console.WriteLine();
    }

  }
}
```

Here is a portion of the program's output:

```
Sine of 0.1  is 0.0998334166468282
Cosine of 0.1  is 0.995004165278026
Tangent of 0.1  is 0.100334672085451

Sine of 0.2  is 0.198669330795061
Cosine of 0.2  is 0.980066577841242
Tangent of 0.2  is 0.202710035508673

Sine of 0.3  is 0.29552020666134
Cosine of 0.3  is 0.955336489125606
Tangent of 0.3  is 0.309336249609623
```

To compute the sine, cosine, and tangent, the standard library methods **Math.Sin( )**, **Math.Cos( )**, and **Math.Tan( )** are used. Like **Math.Sqrt( )**, the trigonometric methods are called with a **double** argument, and they return a **double** result. The angles must be specified in radians.

The decimal Type

Perhaps the most interesting C# numeric type is **decimal**, which is intended for use in monetary calculations. The **decimal** type utilizes 128 bits to represent values within the range 1E–28 to 7.9E+28. As you may know, normal floating-point arithmetic is subject to a variety of rounding errors when it is applied to decimal values. The **decimal** type eliminates these errors and can accurately represent up to 28 decimal places (or 29 places in some cases). This ability to represent decimal values without rounding errors makes it especially useful for computations that involve money.

Here is a program that uses a **decimal** type in a financial calculation. The program computes the discounted price given the original price and a discount percentage.

```
// Use the decimal type to compute a discount.

using System;

class UseDecimal {
  public static void Main() {
    decimal price;
    decimal discount;
    decimal discounted_price;

    // compute discounted price
    price = 19.95m;
    discount = 0.15m; // discount rate is 15%

    discounted_price = price - ( price * discount);

    Console.WriteLine("Discounted price: $" + discounted_price);
  }
}
```

The output from this program is shown here:

```
Discounted price: $16.9575
```

In the program, notice that the decimal constants are followed by the **m** suffix. This is necessary because without the suffix, these values would be interpreted as standard floating-point constants, which are not compatible with the **decimal** data type. You can assign an integer value, such as 10, to a **decimal** variable without the use of the **m** suffix, though. (We will look more closely at how to specify numeric constants later in this chapter.)

Here is another example that uses the **decimal** type. It computes the future value of an investment that has a fixed rate of return over a period of years.

```
/*
   Use the decimal type to compute the future value
   of an investment.
*/

using System;

class FutVal {
  public static void Main() {
    decimal amount;
    decimal rate_of_return;
    int years, i;

    amount = 1000.0m;
    rate_of_return = 0.07m;
    years = 10;

    Console.WriteLine("Original investment: $" + amount);
    Console.WriteLine("Rate of return: " + rate_of_return);
    Console.WriteLine("Over " + years + " years");

    for(i = 0; i < years; i++)
      amount = amount + (amount * rate_of_return);

    Console.WriteLine("Future value is $" + amount);
  }
}
```

Here is the output:

```
Original investment: $1000
Rate of return: 0.07
Over 10 years
Future value is $1967.15135728956532249
```

Notice that the result is accurate to several decimal places—more than you would probably want! Later in this chapter you will see how to format such output in a more appealing fashion.

Characters

In C#, characters are not 8-bit quantities like they are in many other computer languages, such as C++. Instead, C# uses a 16-bit character type called *Unicode.* Unicode defines a character set that is large enough to represent all of the characters found in all human languages. Although many languages, such as English, French, or German, use relatively small alphabets, some languages, such as Chinese, use very large character sets that cannot be represented using just 8 bits. To accommodate the character sets of all languages, 16-bit values are required. Thus, in C#, **char** is an unsigned 16-bit type having a range of 0 to 65,535. The standard 8-bit ASCII character set is a subset of Unicode and ranges from 0 to 127. Thus, the ASCII characters are still valid C# characters.

A character variable can be assigned a value by enclosing the character inside single quotes. For example, this assigns X to the variable **ch**:

```
char ch;
ch = 'X';
```

You can output a **char** value using a **WriteLine( )** statement. For example, this line outputs the value in **ch**:

```
Console.WriteLine("This is ch: " + ch);
```

Although **char** is defined by C# as an integer type, it cannot be freely mixed with integers in all cases. This is because there are no automatic type conversions from integer to **char**. For example, the following fragment is invalid:

```
char ch;

ch = 10; // error, won't work
```

The reason the preceding code will not work is that 10 is an integer value, and it won't automatically convert to a **char**. If you attempt to compile this code, you will see an error message. Later in this chapter you will see a way around this restriction.

The bool Type

The **bool** type represents true/false values. C# defines the values true and false using the reserved words **true** and **false**. Thus, a variable or expression of type **bool** will be one of these two values. Furthermore, there is no conversion defined between **bool** and integer values. For example, 1 does not convert to true, and 0 does not convert to false.

Here is a program that demonstrates the **bool** type:

```
// Demonstrate bool values.

using System;

class BoolDemo {
  public static void Main() {
    bool b;

    b = false;
    Console.WriteLine("b is " + b);
    b = true;
    Console.WriteLine("b is " + b);

    // a bool value can control the if statement
    if(b) Console.WriteLine("This is executed.");

    b = false;
    if(b) Console.WriteLine("This is not executed.");

    // outcome of a relational operator is a bool value
    Console.WriteLine("10 > 9 is " + (10 > 9));
  }
}
```

The output generated by this program is shown here:

```
b is False
b is True
This is executed.
10 > 9 is True
```

There are three interesting things to notice about this program. First, as you can see, when a **bool** value is output by **WriteLine( )**, "True" or "False" is displayed. Second, the value of a **bool** variable is sufficient, by itself, to control the **if** statement. There is no need to write an **if** statement like this:

```
if(b == true) ...
```

Third, the outcome of a relational operator, such as **<**, is a **bool** value. This is why the expression **10 > 9** displays the value "True." Further, the extra set of parentheses around **10 > 9** is necessary because the **+** operator has a higher precedence than the **>**.

Some Output Options

Up to this point, when data has been output using a **WriteLine( )** statement, it has been displayed using the default format provided by C#. However, C# defines a sophisticated formatting mechanism that gives you detailed control over how data is displayed. Although formatted I/O is covered in detail later in this book, it is useful to introduce some formatting options at this time. Using these options, you will be able to specify the way values look when output via a **WriteLine( )** statement. Doing so enables you to produce more appealing output. Keep in mind that the C# formatting mechanism supports many more features than described here.

When outputting lists of data, you have been separating each part of the list with a plus sign, as shown here:

```
Console.WriteLine("You ordered " + 2 + " items at $" + 3 + " each.");
```

While very convenient, outputting numeric information in this way does not give you any control over how that information appears. For example, for a floating-point value, you can't control the number of decimal places displayed. Consider the following statement:

```
Console.WriteLine("Here is 10/3: " + 10.0/3.0);
```

It generates this output:

```
Here is 10/3: 3.33333333333333
```

While this might be fine for some purposes, displaying so many decimal places could be inappropriate for others. For example, in financial calculations, you will usually want to display two decimal places.

To control how numeric data is formatted, you will need to use a second form of **WriteLine( )**, shown here, which allows you to embed formatting information:

WriteLine(*"format string"*, *arg0*, *arg1*, ... , *argN*);

In this version, the arguments to **WriteLine( )** are separated by commas and not + signs. The *format string* contains two items: regular, printing characters that are displayed as-is, and format specifiers. Format specifiers take this general form:

{*argnum*, *width*: *fmt*}

Here, *argnum* specifies the number of the argument (starting from zero) to display. The minimum width of the field is specified by *width*, and the format is specified by *fmt*.

During execution, when a format specifier is encountered in the format string, the corresponding argument, as specified by *argnum*, is substituted and displayed. Thus, it is the position of a format specification within the format string that determines where its matching data will be displayed. Both *width* and *fmt* are optional. Therefore, in its simplest form, a format specifier simply indicates which argument to display. For example, {0} indicates *arg0*, {1} specifies *arg1*, and so on.

Let's begin with a simple example. The statement

```
Console.WriteLine("February has {0} or {1} days.", 28, 29);
```

produces the following output:

```
February has 28 or 29 days.
```

As you can see, the value 28 is substituted for {0}, and 29 is substituted for {1}. Thus, the format specifiers identify the location at which the subsequent arguments, in this case 28 and 29, are displayed within the string. Furthermore, notice that the additional values are separated by commas, not + signs.

Here is a variation of the preceding statement that specifies minimum field widths:

```
Console.WriteLine("February has {0,10} or {1,5} days.", 28, 29);
```

It produces the following output:

```
February has         28 or     29 days.
```

As you can see, spaces have been added to fill out the unused portions of the fields. Remember, a minimum field width is just that: the *minimum* width. Output can exceed that width if needed.

Of course, the arguments associated with a format command need not be constants. For example, this program displays a table of squares and cubes. It uses format commands to output the values.

```
// Use format commands.

using System;
```

```
class DisplayOptions {
  public static void Main() {
    int i;

    Console.WriteLine("Value\tSquared\tCubed");

    for(i = 1; i < 10; i++)
      Console.WriteLine("{0}\t{1}\t{2}",
                        i, i*i, i*i*i);
  }
}
```

The output is shown here:

```
Value   Squared Cubed
1       1       1
2       4       8
3       9       27
4       16      64
5       25      125
6       36      216
7       49      343
8       64      512
9       81      729
```

In the preceding examples, no formatting was applied to the values themselves. Of course, the purpose of using format specifiers is to control the way the data looks. The types of data most commonly formatted are floating-point and decimal values. One of the easiest ways to specify a format is to describe a template that **WriteLine( )** will use. To do this, show an example of the format that you want, using #s to mark the digit positions. You can also specify the decimal point and commas. For example, here is a better way to display 10 divided by 3:

```
Console.WriteLine("Here is 10/3: {0:#.##}", 10.0/3.0);
```

The output from this statement is shown here:

```
Here is 10/3: 3.33
```

In this example, the template is #.##, which tells **WriteLine( )** to display two decimal places. It is important to understand, however, that **WriteLine( )** will display more than one digit to the left of the decimal point, if necessary, so as not to misrepresent the value.

Here is another example. This statement

```
Console.WriteLine("{0:###,###.##}", 123456.56);
```

generates this output:

```
123,456.56
```

If you want to display values using a dollars and cents format, use the **C** format specifier. For example:

```
decimal balance;

balance = 12323.09m;
Console.WriteLine("Current balance is {0:C}", balance);
```

The output from this sequence is shown here:

```
Current balance is $12,323.09
```

The **C** format can be used to improve the output from the price discount program shown earlier:

```
/*
   Use the C format specifier to output dollars and cents.
*/

using System;

class UseDecimal {
  public static void Main() {
    decimal price;
    decimal discount;
    decimal discounted_price;
```

```
// compute discounted price
price = 19.95m;
discount = 0.15m; // discount rate is 15%

discounted_price = price - ( price * discount);

Console.WriteLine("Discounted price: {0:C}", discounted_price);

    }
}
```

Here is the way the output now looks:

```
Discounted price: $16.96
```

Literals

In C#, *literals* refer to fixed values that are represented in their human-readable form. For example, the number 100 is a literal. Literals are also commonly called *constants*. For the most part, literals and their usage are so intuitive that they have been used in one form or another by all the preceding sample programs. Now the time has come to explain them formally.

C# literals can be of any value type. The way each literal is represented depends upon its type. As explained earlier, character constants are enclosed between single quotes. For example, 'a' and '%' are both character constants.

Integer literals are specified as numbers without fractional components. For example, 10 and –100 are integer constants. Floating-point constants require the use of the decimal point followed by the number's fractional component. For example, 11.123 is a floating-point constant. C# also allows you to use scientific notation for floating-point numbers.

Since C# is a strongly typed language, literals, too, have a type. Naturally, this raises the following question: What is the type of a numeric literal? For example, what is the type of 12, 123987, or 0.23? Fortunately, C# specifies some easy-to-follow rules that answer these questions.

First, for integer literals, the type of the literal is the smallest integer type that will hold it, beginning with **int**. Thus, an integer literal is either of type **int**, **uint**, **long**, or **ulong**, depending upon its value. Second, floating-point literals are of type **double**.

If C#'s default type is not what you want for a literal, you can explicitly specify its type by including a suffix. To specify a **long** literal, append an *l* or an *L*. For example, 12 is an **int**, but 12L is a **long**. To specify an unsigned integer value, append a *u* or *U*.

Thus, 100 is an **int**, but 100U is a **uint**. To specify an unsigned, long integer, use *ul* or *UL*. For example, 984375UL is of type **ulong**.

To specify a **float** literal, append an *F* or *f* to the constant. For example, 10.19F is of type **float**.

To specify a **decimal** literal, follow its value with an *m* or *M*. For example, 9.95M is a **decimal** literal.

Although integer literals create an **int**, **uint**, **long**, or **ulong** value by default, they can still be assigned to variables of type **byte**, **sbyte**, **short**, or **ushort** as long as the value being assigned can be represented by the target type. An integer literal can always be assigned to a **long** variable.

Hexadecimal Literals

As you probably know, in programming it is sometimes easier to use a number system based on 16 instead of 10. The base 16 number system is called *hexadecimal* and uses the digits 0 through 9 plus the letters A through F, which stand for 10, 11, 12, 13, 14, and 15. For example, the hexadecimal number 10 is 16 in decimal. Because of the frequency with which hexadecimal numbers are used, C# allows you to specify integer constants in hexadecimal format. A hexadecimal literal must begin with 0x (a zero followed by an *x*). Here are some examples:

```
count = 0xFF; // 255 in decimal
incr = 0x1a;  // 26 in decimal
```

Character Escape Sequences

Enclosing character constants in single quotes works for most printing characters, but a few characters, such as the carriage return, pose a special problem when a text editor is used. In addition, certain other characters, such as the single and double quotes, have special meaning in C#, so you cannot use them directly. For these reasons, C# provides several *escape sequences*, sometimes referred to as *backslash character constants*, shown in Table 3-2. These sequences are used in place of the characters that they represent.

For example, this assigns **ch** the tab character:

```
ch = '\t';
```

The next example assigns a single-quote to **ch**:

```
ch = '\'';
```

Escape Sequence	Description
\a	Alert (bell)
\b	Backspace
\f	Form feed
\n	New line (linefeed)
\r	Carriage return
\t	Horizontal tab
\v	Vertical tab
\0	Null
\'	Single quote
\"	Double quote
\\	Backslash

Table 3-2. *Character Escape Sequences*

String Literals

C# supports one other type of literal: the string. A *string* is a set of characters enclosed by double quotes. For example,

```
"this is a test"
```

is a string. You have seen examples of strings in many of the **WriteLine( )** statements in the preceding sample programs.

In addition to normal characters, a string literal can also contain one or more of the escape sequences just described. For example, consider the following program. It uses the **\n, \t,** and **\"** escape sequences.

```
// Demonstrate escape sequences in strings.

using System;

class StrDemo {
```

```
public static void Main() {
  Console.WriteLine("Line One\nLine Two\nLine Three");
  Console.WriteLine("One\tTwo\tThree");
  Console.WriteLine("Four\tFive\tSix");

  // embed quotes
  Console.WriteLine("\"Why?\", he asked.");
  }
}
```

The output is shown here:

```
Line One
Line Two
Line Three
One     Two     Three
Four    Five    Six
"Why?", he asked.
```

Notice how the **\n** escape sequence is used to generate a new line. You don't need to use multiple **WriteLine( )** statements to get multiline output. Just embed **\n** within a longer string at the points at which you want the new lines to occur. Also note how a quotation mark is generated inside a string.

In addition to the form of string literal just described, you can also specify a *verbatim string literal.* A verbatim string literal begins with an @, which is followed by a quoted string. The contents of the quoted string are accepted without modification and can span two or more lines. Thus, you can include newlines, tabs, and so on, but you don't need to use the escape sequences. The only exception is that to obtain a double-quote ("), you must use two double-quotes in a row (""). Here is a program that demonstrates verbatim string literals:

```
// Demonstrate verbatim string literals.

using System;

class Verbatim {
  public static void Main() {
    Console.WriteLine(@"This is a verbatim
string literal
that spans several lines.
");
```

```
     Console.WriteLine(@"Here is some tabbed output:
1    2    3    4
5    6    7    8
");
     Console.WriteLine(@"Programmers say, ""I like C#.""");
   }
}
```

The output from this program is shown here:

```
This is a verbatim
string literal
that spans several lines.

Here is some tabbed output:
1       2       3       4
5       6       7       8


Programmers say, "I like C#."
```

The important point to notice about the preceding program is that the verbatim string literals are displayed precisely as they are entered into the program.

The advantage of verbatim string literals is that you can specify output in your program exactly as it will appear on the screen. However, in the case of multiline strings, the wrapping will cause the indentation of your program to be obscured. For this reason, the programs in this book will make only limited use of verbatim string literals. That said, they are still a wonderful benefit for many formatting situations.

One last point: Don't confuse strings with characters. A character literal, such as 'X', represents a single letter of type **char**. A string containing only one letter, such as "X", is still a string.

A Closer Look at Variables

Variables were introduced in Chapter 2. As you learned earlier, variables are declared using this form of statement:

type var-name;

where *type* is the data type of the variable and *var-name* is its name. You can declare a variable of any valid type, including the value types just described. When you create a variable, you are creating an instance of its type. Thus, the capabilities of a variable are determined by its type. For example, a variable of type **bool** cannot be used to store floating-point values. Furthermore, the type of a variable cannot change during its lifetime. An **int** variable cannot turn into a **char** variable, for example.

All variables in C# must be declared prior to their use. This is necessary because the compiler must know what type of data a variable contains before it can properly compile any statement that uses the variable. It also enables C# to perform strict type-checking.

C# defines several different kinds of variables. The kind that we have been using are called *local variables* because they are declared within a method.

Initializing a Variable

You must give a variable a value prior to using it. One way to do this is through an assignment statement, as you have already seen. Another way is by giving it an initial value when it is declared. To do this, follow the variable's name with an equal sign and the value being assigned. The general form of initialization is shown here:

type var = value;

Here, *value* is the value that is given to *var* when *var* is created. The value must be compatible with the specified type.

Here are some examples:

```
int count = 10; // give count an initial value of 10
char ch = 'X';  // initialize ch with the letter X
float f = 1.2F; // f is initialized with 1.2
```

When declaring two or more variables of the same type using a comma-separated list, you can give one or more of those variables an initial value. For example:

```
int a, b = 8, c = 19, d; // b and c have initializations
```

In this case, only **b** and **c** are initialized.

Dynamic Initialization

Although the preceding examples have used only constants as initializers, C# allows variables to be initialized dynamically, using any expression valid at the time the variable is declared. For example, here is a short program that computes the hypotenuse of a right triangle given the lengths of its two opposing sides.

```
// Demonstrate dynamic initialization.
```

```
using System;

class DynInit {
  public static void Main() {
    double s1 = 4.0, s2 = 5.0; // length of sides

    // dynamically initialize hypot
    double hypot = Math.Sqrt( (s1 * s1) + (s2 * s2) );

    Console.Write("Hypotenuse of triangle with sides " +
                  s1 + " by " + s2 + " is ");

    Console.WriteLine("{0:#.###}.", hypot);

  }
}
```

Here is the output:

```
Hypotenuse of triangle with sides 4 by 5 is 6.403.
```

Here, three local variables—**s1**, **s2**, and **hypot**—are declared. The first two, **s1** and **s2**, are initialized by constants. However, **hypot** is initialized dynamically to the length of the hypotenuse. Notice that the initialization involves calling **Math.Sqrt( )**. As explained, you can use any expression valid at the time of the declaration. Since a call to **Math.Sqrt( )** (or any other library method) is valid at this point, it can be used in the initialization of **hypot**. The key point here is that the initialization expression can use any element valid at the time of the initialization, including calls to methods, other variables, or literals.

The Scope and Lifetime of Variables

So far, all of the variables that we have been using were declared at the start of the **Main( )** method. However, C# allows a local variable to be declared within any block. A block is begun with an opening curly brace and ended by a closing curly brace. A block defines a *declaration space*, or *scope*. Thus, each time you start a new block, you are creating a new scope. A scope determines what objects are visible to other parts of your program. It also determines the lifetime of those objects.

The most important scopes in C# are those defined by a class and those defined by a method. A discussion of class scope (and variables declared within it) is deferred until later in this book, when classes are described. For now, we will examine only the scopes defined by or within a method.

The scope defined by a method begins with its opening curly brace. However, if that method has parameters, they too are included within the method's scope.

As a general rule, variables declared inside a scope are not visible (that is, accessible) to code that is defined outside that scope. Thus, when you declare a variable within a scope, you are localizing that variable and protecting it from unauthorized access and/or modification. Indeed, the scope rules provide the foundation for encapsulation.

Scopes can be nested. For example, each time you create a block of code, you are creating a new, nested scope. When this occurs, the outer scope encloses the inner scope. This means that objects declared in the outer scope will be visible to code within the inner scope. However, the reverse is not true. Objects declared within the inner scope will not be visible outside it.

To understand the effect of nested scopes, consider the following program:

```
// Demonstrate block scope.

using System;

class ScopeDemo {
  public static void Main() {
    int x; // known to all code within Main()

    x = 10;
    if(x == 10) { // start new scope

      int y = 20; // known only to this block

      // x and y both known here.
      Console.WriteLine("x and y: " + x + " " + y);
      x = y * 2;
    }
    // y = 100; // Error! y not known here

    // x is still known here.
    Console.WriteLine("x is " + x);
  }
}
```

As the comments indicate, the variable **x** is declared at the start of **Main( )**'s scope and is accessible to all subsequent code within **Main( )**. Within the **if** block, **y** is declared. Since a block defines a scope, **y** is visible only to other code within its block. This is why outside of its block, the line **y = 100;** is commented out. If you remove the leading comment symbol, a compile-time error will occur, because **y** is not visible outside of its block. Within the **if** block, **x** can be used because code within a block (that is, a nested scope) has access to variables declared by an enclosing scope.

Within a block, variables can be declared at any point, but are valid only after they are declared. Thus, if you define a variable at the start of a method, it is available to all of the code within that method. Conversely, if you declare a variable at the end of a block, it is effectively useless, because no code will have access to it.

Here is another important point to remember: Variables are created when their scope is entered and destroyed when their scope is left. This means that a variable will not hold its value once it has gone out of scope. Therefore, variables declared within a method will not hold their values between calls to that method. Also, a variable declared within a block will lose its value when the block is left. Thus, the lifetime of a variable is confined to its scope.

If a variable declaration includes an initializer, then that variable will be reinitialized each time the block in which it is declared is entered. For example, consider this program:

```
// Demonstrate lifetime of a variable.

using System;

class VarInitDemo {
  public static void Main() {
    int x;

    for(x = 0; x < 3; x++) {
      int y = -1; // y is initialized each time block is entered
      Console.WriteLine("y is: " + y); // this always prints -1
      y = 100;
      Console.WriteLine("y is now: " + y);
    }
  }
}
```

The output generated by this program is shown here:

```
y is: -1
y is now: 100
```

```
y is: -1
y is now: 100
y is: -1
y is now: 100
```

As you can see, **y** is always reinitialized to –1 each time the **for** loop is entered. Even though it is subsequently assigned the value 100, this value is lost.

There is one quirk to C#'s scope rules that may surprise you: Although blocks can be nested, no variable declared within an inner scope can have the same name as a variable declared by an enclosing scope. For example, the following program, which tries to declare two separate variables with the same name, will not compile.

```
/*
   This program attempts to declare a variable
   in an inner scope with the same name as one
   defined in an outer scope.

   *** This program will not compile. ***
*/

using System;

class NestVar {
  public static void Main() {
    int count;

    for(count = 0; count < 10; count = count+1) {
      Console.WriteLine("This is count: " + count);

      int count; // illegal!!!
      for(count = 0; count < 2; count++)
        Console.WriteLine("This program is in error!");
    }
  }
}
```

If you come from a C/C++ background, then you know that there is no restriction on the names that you give variables declared in an inner scope. Thus, in C/C++ the declaration of **count** within the block of the outer **for** loop is completely valid. However, in C/C++, such a declaration hides the outer variable. The designers of C# felt that this *name hiding* could easily lead to programming errors and disallowed it.

Type Conversion and Casting

In programming, it is common to assign one type of variable to another. For example, you might want to assign an **int** value to a **float** variable, as shown here:

```
int i;
float f;

i = 10;
f = i; // assign an int to a float
```

When compatible types are mixed in an assignment, the value of the right side is automatically converted to the type of the left side. Thus, in the preceding fragment, the value in **i** is converted into a **float** and then assigned to **f**. However, because of C#'s strict type-checking, not all types are compatible, and thus, not all type conversions are implicitly allowed. For example, **bool** and **int** are not compatible. Fortunately, it is still possible to obtain a conversion between incompatible types by using a *cast*. A cast performs an explicit type conversion. Both automatic type conversion and casting are examined here.

Automatic Conversions

When one type of data is assigned to another type of variable, an *automatic* type conversion will take place if

- The two types are compatible.
- The destination type is larger than the source type.

When these two conditions are met, a *widening conversion* takes place. For example, the **int** type is always large enough to hold all valid **byte** values, and both **int** and **byte** are integer types, so an automatic conversion can be applied.

For widening conversions, the numeric types, including integer and floating-point types, are compatible with each other. For example, the following program is perfectly valid since **long** to **double** is a widening conversion that is automatically performed.

```
// Demonstrate automatic conversion from long to double.

using System;

class LtoD {
  public static void Main() {
    long L;
```

```
    double D;

    L = 100123285L;
    D = L;

    Console.WriteLine("L and D: " + L + " " + D);
  }
}
```

Although there is an automatic conversion from **long** to **double**, there is no automatic conversion from **double** to **long** since this is not a widening conversion. Thus, the following version of the preceding program is invalid:

```
// *** This program will not compile. ***

using System;

class LtoD {
  public static void Main() {
    long L;
    double D;

    D = 100123285.0;
    L = D; // Illegal!!!

    Console.WriteLine("L and D: " + L + " " + D);

  }
}
```

In addition to the restrictions just described, there are no automatic conversions between **decimal** and **float** or **double**, or from the numeric types to **char** or **bool**. Also, **char** and **bool** are not compatible with each other.

Casting Incompatible Types

Although the automatic type conversions are helpful, they will not fulfill all programming needs, because they apply only to widening conversions between compatible types. For all other cases you must employ a cast. A *cast* is an instruction to the compiler to convert one type into another. Thus, it requests an explicit type conversion. A cast has this general form:

(target-type) expression

Here, *target-type* specifies the desired type to convert the specified expression to. For example, if you want the type of the expression **x/y** to be **int**, you can write

```
double x, y;
// ...
(int) (x / y)
```

Here, even though **x** and **y** are of type **double**, the cast converts the outcome of the expression to **int**. The parentheses surrounding **x / y** are necessary. Otherwise, the cast to **int** would apply only to the **x**, and not to the outcome of the division. The cast is necessary here because there is no automatic conversion from **double** to **int**.

When a cast involves a *narrowing conversion*, information might be lost. For example, when casting a **long** into an **int**, information will be lost if the **long**'s value is greater than the range of an **int**, because its high-order bits are removed. When a floating-point value is cast to an integer type, the fractional component will also be lost due to truncation. For example, if the value 1.23 is assigned to an integer, the resulting value will simply be 1. The 0.23 is lost.

The following program demonstrates some type conversions that require casts. It also shows some situations in which the casts cause data to be lost.

```
// Demonstrate casting.

using System;

class CastDemo {
  public static void Main() {
    double x, y;
    byte b;
    int i;
    char ch;
    uint u;
    short s;
    long l;

    x = 10.0;
    y = 3.0;

    // cast an int into a double
    i = (int) (x / y); // cast double to int, fractional component lost
    Console.WriteLine("Integer outcome of x / y: " + i);
    Console.WriteLine();
```

```csharp
// cast an int into a byte, no data lost
i = 255;
b = (byte) i;
Console.WriteLine("b after assigning 255: " + b +
                  " -- no data lost.");

// cast an int into a byte, data lost
i = 257;
b = (byte) i;
Console.WriteLine("b after assigning 257: " + b +
                  " -- data lost.");
Console.WriteLine();

// cast a uint into a short, no data lost
u = 32000;
s = (short) u;
Console.WriteLine("s after assigning 32000: " + s +
                  " -- no data lost.");

// cast a uint into a short, data lost
u = 64000;
s = (short) u;
Console.WriteLine("s after assigning 64000: " + s +
                  " -- data lost.");
Console.WriteLine();

// cast a long into a uint, no data lost
l = 64000;
u = (uint) l;
Console.WriteLine("u after assigning 64000: " + u +
                  " -- no data lost.");

// cast a long into a uint, data lost
l = -12;
u = (uint) l;
Console.WriteLine("u after assigning -12: " + u +
                  " -- data lost.");
Console.WriteLine();

// cast an int into a char
b = 88; // ASCII code for X
ch = (char) b;
Console.WriteLine("ch after assigning 88: " + ch);
```

```
    }
}
```

The output from the program is shown here:

```
Integer outcome of x / y: 3

b after assigning 255: 255 -- no data lost.
b after assigning 257: 1 -- data lost.

s after assigning 32000: 32000 -- no data lost.
s after assigning 64000: -1536 -- data lost.

u after assigning 64000: 64000 -- no data lost.
u after assigning -12: 4294967284 -- data lost.

ch after assigning 88: X
```

Let's look at each assignment. The cast of **(x / y)** to **int** results in the truncation of the fractional component, and information is lost.

No loss of information occurs when **b** is assigned the value 255 because a **byte** can hold the value 255. However, when the attempt is made to assign **b** the value 257, information loss occurs because 257 exceeds a **byte**'s range. In both cases the casts are needed because there is no automatic conversion from **int** to **byte**.

When the **short** variable **s** is assigned the value 32,000 through the **uint** variable **u**, no data is lost because a **short** can hold the value 32,000. However, in the next assignment, **u** has the value 64,000, which is outside the range of a **short**, and data is lost. In both cases the casts are needed because there is no automatic conversion from **uint** to **short**.

Next, **u** is assigned the value 64,000 through the **long** variable **l**. In this case, no data is lost because 64,000 is within the range of a **uint**. However, when the value –12 is assigned to **u**, data is lost because a **uint** cannot hold negative numbers. In both cases the casts are needed because there is no automatic conversion from **long** to **uint**.

Finally, no information is lost, but a cast is needed when assigning a **byte** value to a **char**.

Type Conversion in Expressions

In addition to occurring within an assignment, type conversions also take place within an expression. In an expression, you can freely mix two or more different types of data as long as they are compatible with each other. For example, you can mix **short** and

long within an expression because they are both numeric types. When different types of data are mixed within an expression, they are converted to the same type, on an operation-by-operation basis.

The conversions are accomplished through the use of C#'s *type promotion rules.* Here is the algorithm that they define for binary operations:

IF one operand is a **decimal**, THEN the other operand is promoted to **decimal** (unless it is of type **float** or **double**, in which case an error results).

ELSE IF one operand is a **double**, the second is promoted to **double**.

ELSE IF one operand is a **float**, the second is promoted to **float**.

ELSE IF one operand is a **ulong**, the second is promoted to **ulong** (unless it is of type **sbyte**, **short**, **int**, or **long**, in which case an error results).

ELSE IF one operand is a **long**, the second is promoted to **long**.

ELSE IF one operand is a **uint** and the second is of type **sbyte**, **short**, or **int**, both are promoted to **long**.

ELSE IF one operand is a **uint**, the second is promoted to **uint**.

ELSE both operands are promoted to **int**.

There are a couple of important points to be made about the type promotion rules. First, not all types can be mixed in an expression. Specifically, there is no implicit conversion from **float** or **double** to **decimal**, and it is not possible to mix **ulong** with any signed integer type. To mix these types requires the use of an explicit cast.

Second, pay special attention to the last rule. It states that if none of the preceding rules apply, then all other operands are promoted to **int**. Therefore, in an expression, all **char**, **sbyte**, **byte**, **ushort**, and **short** values are promoted to **int** for the purposes of calculation. This is called *integer promotion.* It also means that the outcome of all arithmetic operations will be no smaller than **int**.

It is important to understand that type promotions apply only to the values operated upon when an expression is evaluated. For example, if the value of a **byte** variable is promoted to **int** inside an expression, outside the expression, the variable is still a **byte**. Type promotion only affects the evaluation of an expression.

Type promotion can, however, lead to somewhat unexpected results. For example, when an arithmetic operation involves two **byte** values, the following sequence occurs. First, the **byte** operands are promoted to **int**. Then the operation takes place, yielding an **int** result. Thus, the outcome of an operation involving two **byte** values will be an **int**. This is not what you might intuitively expect. Consider the following program:

```
// A promotion surprise!
```

```
using System;

class PromDemo {
  public static void Main() {
    byte b;

    b = 10;
    b = (byte) (b * b); // cast needed!!

    Console.WriteLine("b: "+ b);
  }
}
```

Somewhat counterintuitively, a cast to **byte** is needed when assigning **b * b** back to **b**! The reason is because in **b * b**, the value of **b** is promoted to **int** when the expression is evaluated. Thus, **b * b** results in an **int** value, which cannot be assigned to a **byte** variable without a cast. Keep this in mind if you get unexpected type-incompatibility error messages on expressions that would otherwise seem perfectly OK.

This same sort of situation also occurs when performing operations on **char**s. For example, in the following fragment, the cast back to **char** is needed because of the promotion of **ch1** and **ch2** to **int** within the expression

```
char ch1 = 'a', ch2 = 'b';

ch1 = (char) (ch1 + ch2);
```

Without the cast, the result of adding **ch1** to **ch2** would be **int**, which can't be assigned to a **char**.

Type promotions also occur when a unary operation, such as the unary –, takes place. For the unary operations, operands smaller than **int** (**byte**, **sbyte**, **short**, and **ushort**) are promoted to **int**. Also, a **char** operand is converted to **int**. Furthermore, if a **uint** value is negated, it is promoted to **long**.

Using Casts in Expressions

A cast can be applied to a specific portion of a larger expression. This gives you fine-grained control over the way type conversions occur when an expression is evaluated. For example, consider the following program. It displays the square roots of the numbers from 1 to 10. It also displays the whole number portion and the fractional part of each result, separately. To do so, it uses a cast to convert the result of **Math.Sqrt( )** to **int**.

```
// Using casts in an expression.

using System;

class CastExpr {
  public static void Main() {
    double n;

     for(n = 1.0; n <= 10; n++) {
       Console.WriteLine("The square root of {0} is {1}",
                    n, Math.Sqrt(n));

       Console.WriteLine("Whole number part: {0}" ,
                    (int) Math.Sqrt(n));

       Console.WriteLine("Fractional part: {0}",
                    Math.Sqrt(n) - (int) Math.Sqrt(n) );
       Console.WriteLine();
    }

  }
}
```

Here is the output from the program:

```
The square root of 1 is 1
Whole number part: 1
Fractional part: 0

The square root of 2 is 1.4142135623731
Whole number part: 1
Fractional part: 0.414213562373095

The square root of 3 is 1.73205080756888
Whole number part: 1
Fractional part: 0.732050807568877

The square root of 4 is 2
Whole number part: 2
Fractional part: 0
```

```
The square root of 5 is 2.23606797749979
Whole number part: 2
Fractional part: 0.23606797749979

The square root of 6 is 2.44948974278318
Whole number part: 2
Fractional part: 0.449489742783178

The square root of 7 is 2.64575131106459
Whole number part: 2
Fractional part: 0.645751311064591

The square root of 8 is 2.82842712474619
Whole number part: 2
Fractional part: 0.82842712474619

The square root of 9 is 3
Whole number part: 3
Fractional part: 0

The square root of 10 is 3.16227766016838
Whole number part: 3
Fractional part: 0.16227766016838
```

As the output shows, the cast of **Math.Sqrt( )** to **int** results in the whole number component of the value. In this expression,

```
Math.Sqrt(n) - (int) Math.Sqrt(n)
```

the cast to **int** obtains the whole number component, which is then subtracted from the complete value, yielding the fractional component. Thus, the outcome of the expression is **double**. Only the value of the second call to **Math.Sqrt( )** is cast to **int**.

Chapter 4

Operators

C# provides an extensive set of operators that gives the programmer detailed control over the construction and evaluation of expressions. C# has four general classes of operators: *arithmetic, bitwise, relational,* and *logical.* These are examined in this chapter. Also discussed are the assignment operator and the **?** operator. C# also defines several other operators that handle certain special situations. These special operators are examined later in this book, when the features to which they apply are discussed.

Arithmetic Operators

C# defines the following arithmetic operators:

Operator	Meaning
+	Addition
−	Subtraction (also unary minus)
*	Multiplication
/	Division
%	Modulus
++	Increment
− −	Decrement

The operators **+, −, *,** and **/** all work the same way in C# as they do in any other computer language (or in algebra, for that matter). These can be applied to any built-in numeric data type.

Although the actions of arithmetic operators are well known to all readers, a few special situations warrant some explanation. First, remember that when **/** is applied to an integer, any remainder will be truncated; for example, 10/3 will equal 3 in integer division. You can obtain the remainder of this division by using the modulus operator, **%**. It works in C# the way that it does in other languages: It yields the remainder of an integer division. For example, 10 % 3 is 1. In C#, the % can be applied to both integer and floating-point types. Thus, 10.0 % 3.0 is also 1. (This differs from C/C++, which allow modulus operations only on integer types.) The following program demonstrates the modulus operator:

```
// Demonstrate the % operator.

using System;

class ModDemo {
  public static void Main() {
```

```
    int iresult, irem;
    double dresult, drem;

    iresult = 10 / 3;
    irem = 10 % 3;

    dresult = 10.0 / 3.0;
    drem = 10.0 % 3.0;

    Console.WriteLine("Result and remainder of 10 / 3: " +
                      iresult + " " + irem);
    Console.WriteLine("Result and remainder of 10.0 / 3.0: " +
                      dresult + " " + drem);
  }
}
```

The output from the program is shown here:

```
Result and remainder of 10 / 3: 3 1
Result and remainder of 10.0 / 3.0: 3.33333333333333 1
```

As you can see, the % yields a remainder of 1 for both integer and floating-point operations.

Increment and Decrement

Introduced in Chapter 2, the **++** and the **− −** are the increment and decrement operators. As you will see, they have some special properties that make them quite interesting. Let's begin by reviewing precisely what the increment and decrement operators do.

The increment operator adds 1 to its operand, and the decrement operator subtracts 1. Therefore,

```
x = x + 1;
```

is the same as

```
x++;
```

and

```
x = x - 1;
```

is the same as

```
x--;
```

Both the increment and decrement operators can either precede (prefix) or follow (postfix) the operand. For example, this

```
x = x + 1;
```

can be written as

```
++x; // prefix form
```

or as

```
x++; // postfix form
```

In the foregoing example, there is no difference whether the increment is applied as a prefix or a postfix. However, when an increment or decrement is used as part of a larger expression, there is an important difference. When an increment or decrement operator *precedes* its operand, C# will perform the operation prior to obtaining the operand's value for use by the rest of the expression. If the operator *follows* its operand, then C# will obtain the operand's value before incrementing or decrementing it. Consider the following:

```
x = 10;
y = ++x;
```

In this case, **y** will be set to 11. However, if the code is written as

```
x = 10;
y = x++;
```

then **y** will be set to 10. In both cases, **x** is still set to 11; the difference is when it happens.

There are significant advantages in being able to control when the increment or decrement operation takes place. Consider the following program, which generates a series of numbers:

```
/*
   Demonstrate the difference between prefix
   postfix forms of ++.
```

```
*/
using System;

class PrePostDemo {
  public static void Main() {
    int x, y;
    int i;

    x = 1;
    Console.WriteLine("Series generated using y = x + x++;");
    for(i = 0; i < 10; i++) {

      y = x + x++; // postfix ++

      Console.WriteLine(y + " ");
    }
    Console.WriteLine();

    x = 1;
    Console.WriteLine("Series generated using y = x + ++x;");
    for(i = 0; i < 10; i++) {

      y = x + ++x; // prefix ++

      Console.WriteLine(y + " ");
    }
    Console.WriteLine();

  }
}
```

The output is shown here:

```
Series generated using y = x + x++;
2
4
6
8
10
12
14
16
```

```
18
20

Series generated using y = x + ++x;
3
5
7
9
11
13
15
17
19
21
```

As the output confirms, the statement

```
y = x + x++;
```

adds the value of **x** to **x** and assigns that result to **y**. It then increments **x**. However, the statement

```
y = x + ++x;
```

obtains the value of **x**, then increments **x**, and then adds that value to the original value of **x**. The result is assigned to **y**. As the output shows, simply changing x++ to ++ x changes the number series from even to odd.

One other point about the preceding example: Don't let expressions like

```
x + ++x
```

intimidate you. Although having two operators back-to-back is a bit unsettling at first glance, the compiler keeps it all straight. Just remember, this expression simply adds the value of **x** to the value of **x** incremented.

Relational and Logical Operators

In the terms *relational operator* and *logical operator*, *relational* refers to the relationships that values can have with one another, and *logical* refers to the ways in which true and false values can be connected together. Since the relational operators produce true or false results, they often work with the logical operators. For this reason they will be discussed together here.

The relational operators are as follows:

Operator	Meaning
==	Equal to
!=	Not equal to
>	Greater than
<	Less than
>=	Greater than or equal to
<=	Less than or equal to

The logical operators are shown next:

Operator	Meaning
&	AND
|	OR
^	XOR (exclusive OR)
||	Short-circuit OR
&&	Short-circuit AND
!	NOT

The outcome of the relational and logical operators is a **bool** value.

In C#, all objects can be compared for equality or inequality using == and !=. However, the comparison operators, <, >, <=, or >=, can be applied only to those types that support an ordering relationship. Therefore, all of the relational operators can be applied to all numeric types. However, values of type **bool** can only be compared for equality or inequality, since the **true** and **false** values are not ordered. For example, **true > false** has no meaning in C#.

For the logical operators, the operands must be of type **bool**, and the result of a logical operation is of type **bool**. The logical operators, **&**, **|**, **^**, and **!**, support the basic logical operations AND, OR, XOR, and NOT, according to the following truth table:

p	q	p & q	p	q	p ^ q	!p
False	False	False	False	False	True
True	False	False	True	True	False
False	True	False	True	True	True
True	True	True	True	False	False

As the table shows, the outcome of an exclusive OR operation is true when exactly one and only one operand is true.

Here is a program that demonstrates several of the relational and logical operators:

```
// Demonstrate the relational and logical operators.

using System;

class RelLogOps {
  public static void Main() {
    int i, j;
    bool b1, b2;

    i = 10;
    j = 11;
    if(i < j) Console.WriteLine("i < j");
    if(i <= j) Console.WriteLine("i <= j");
    if(i != j) Console.WriteLine("i != j");
    if(i == j) Console.WriteLine("this won't execute");
    if(i >= j) Console.WriteLine("this won't execute");
    if(i > j) Console.WriteLine("this won't execute");

    b1 = true;
    b2 = false;
    if(b1 & b2) Console.WriteLine("this won't execute");
    if(!(b1 & b2)) Console.WriteLine("!(b1 & b2) is true");
```

```
    if(b1 | b2) Console.WriteLine("b1 | b2 is true");
    if(b1 ^ b2) Console.WriteLine("b1 ^ b2 is true");
  }
}
```

The output from the program is shown here:

```
i < j
i <= j
i != j
!(b1 & b2) is true
b1 | b2 is true
b1 ^ b2 is true
```

The logical operators provided by C# perform the most commonly used logical operations. However, there are several other operations defined by the rules for formal logic. These other logical operations can be constructed using the logical operators supported by C#. Thus, C# supplies a set of logical operators sufficient to construct any other logical operation. For example, another logical operation is *implication*. Implication is a binary operation in which the outcome is false only when the left operand is true and the right operand is false. (The implication operation reflects the idea that true cannot imply false.) Thus, the truth table for the implication operator is shown here:

p	q	p implies q
True	True	True
True	False	False
False	False	True
False	True	True

The implication operation can be constructed using a combination of the ! and the | operator, as shown here:

!p | q

The following program demonstrates this implementation:

```
// Create an implication operator in C#.

using System;
```

```
class Implication {
public static void Main() {
bool p=false, q=false;
    int i, j;

    for(i = 0; i < 2; i++) {
      for(j = 0; j < 2; j++) {
        if(i==0) p = true;
        if(i==1) p = false;
        if(j==0) q = true;
        if(j==1) q = false;

        Console.WriteLine("p is " + p + ", q is " + q);
        if(!p | q) Console.WriteLine(p + " implies " + q +
                  " is " + true);
        Console.WriteLine();
      }
    }
  }
}
```

The output is shown here:

```
p is True, q is True
True implies True is True

p is True, q is False

p is False, q is True
False implies True is True

p is False, q is False
False implies False is True
```

Short-Circuit Logical Operators

C# supplies special *short-circuit* versions of its AND and OR logical operators that can be used to produce more efficient code. To understand why, consider the following. In an AND operation, if the first operand is false, the outcome is false no matter what value the second operand has. In an OR operation, if the first operand is true, the outcome of the operation is true no matter what the value of the second operand. Thus, in these two cases there is no need to evaluate the second operand. By not evaluating the second operand, time is saved and more efficient code is produced.

The short-circuit AND operator is **&&** and the short-circuit OR operator is **||**. As described earlier, their normal counterparts are **&** and **|**. The only difference between the normal and short-circuit versions is that the normal operands will always evaluate each operand, but short-circuit versions will evaluate the second operand only when necessary.

Here is a program that demonstrates the short-circuit AND operator. The program determines if the value in **d** is a factor of **n**. It does this by performing a modulus operation. If the remainder of **n / d** is zero, then **d** is a factor. However, since the modulus operation involves a division, the short-circuit form of the AND is used to prevent a divide-by-zero error.

```
// Demonstrate the short-circuit operators.

using System;

class SCops {
  public static void Main() {
    int n, d;

    n = 10;
    d = 2;
    if(d != 0 && (n % d) == 0)
      Console.WriteLine(d + " is a factor of " + n);

    d = 0; // now, set d to zero

    // Since d is zero, the second operand is not evaluated.
    if(d != 0 && (n % d) == 0)
      Console.WriteLine(d + " is a factor of " + n);

    /* Now, try the same thing without short-circuit operator.
       This will cause a divide-by-zero error.  */
    if(d != 0 & (n % d) == 0)
      Console.WriteLine(d + " is a factor of " + n);
  }
}
```

To prevent a divide-by-zero error, the **if** statement first checks to see if **d** is equal to zero. If it is, the short-circuit AND stops at that point and does not perform the modulus division. Thus, in the first test, **d** is 2 and the modulus operation is performed.

The second test fails because **d** is set to zero, and the modulus operation is skipped, avoiding a divide-by-zero error. Finally, the normal AND operator is tried. This causes both operands to be evaluated, which leads to a runtime error when the division by zero occurs.

Since the short-circuit operators are, in some cases, more efficient than their normal counterparts, you might be wondering why C# still offers the normal AND and OR operators. The answer is that in some cases you will want both operands of an AND or OR operation to be evaluated because of the side effects produced. Consider the following:

```
// Side-effects can be important.

using System;

class SideEffects {
  public static void Main() {
    int i;

    i = 0;

    /* Here, i is still incremented even though
       the if statement fails. */
    if(false & (++i < 100))
      Console.WriteLine("this won't be displayed");
    Console.WriteLine("if statement executed: " + i); // displays 1

    /* In this case, i is not incremented because
       the short-circuit operator skips the increment. */
    if(false && (++i < 100))
      Console.WriteLine("this won't be displayed");
    Console.WriteLine("if statement executed: " + i); // still 1 !!
  }
}
```

As the comments indicate, in the first **if** statement, **i** is incremented whether the **if** succeeds or not. However, when the short-circuit operator is used, the variable **i** is not incremented when the first operand is false. The lesson here is that if your code expects the right-hand operand of an AND or OR operation to be evaluated, you must use C#'s non–short-circuit forms of these operations.

One other point: The short-circuit AND is also known as the *conditional-AND*, and the short-circuit OR is also called the *conditional-OR*.

The Assignment Operator

You have been using the assignment operator since Chapter 2. Now it is time to take a formal look at it. The *assignment operator* is the single equal sign, =. The assignment operator works in C# much as it does in any other computer language. It has this general form:

var = *expression*;

Here, the type of *var* must be compatible with the type of *expression*.

The assignment operator does have one interesting attribute that you may not be familiar with: It allows you to create a chain of assignments. For example, consider this fragment:

```
int x, y, z;

x = y = z = 100; // set x, y, and z to 100
```

This fragment sets the variables **x**, **y**, and **z** to 100 using a single statement. This works because the = is an operator that yields the value of the right-hand expression. Thus, the value of **z = 100** is 100, which is then assigned to **y**, which in turn is assigned to **x**. Using a "chain of assignment" is an easy way to set a group of variables to a common value.

Compound Assignments

C# provides special compound assignment operators that simplify the coding of certain assignment statements. Let's begin with an example. The assignment statement shown here:

```
x = x + 10;
```

can be written using a compound assignment as

```
x += 10;
```

The operator pair **+=** tells the compiler to assign to **x** the value of **x** plus 10.
Here is another example. The statement

```
x = x - 100;
```

is the same as

```
x -= 100;
```

Both statements assign to **x** the value of **x** minus 100.

There are compound assignment operators for all the binary operators (that is, those that require two operands). The general form of the shorthand is

var op = expression;

Thus, the arithmetic and logical assignment operators are

+=	−=	*=	/=
%=	&=	| =	^=

Because the compound assignment statements are shorter than their noncompound equivalents, the compound assignment operators are also sometimes called the *shorthand assignment* operators.

The compound assignment operators provide two benefits. First, they are more compact than their "longhand" equivalents. Second, they can result in more efficient executable code (because the operand is evaluated only once). For these reasons, you will often see the compound assignment operators used in professionally written C# programs.

The Bitwise Operators

C# provides a set of *bitwise* operators that expand the types of problems to which C# can be applied. The bitwise operators act directly upon the bits of their operands. They are defined only for integer operands. They cannot be used on **bool, float,** or **double.**

They are called the *bitwise* operators because they are used to test, set, or shift the bits that comprise an integer value. Bitwise operations are important to a wide variety of systems-level programming tasks, such as when status information from a device must be interrogated or constructed. Table 4-1 lists the bitwise operators.

The Bitwise AND, OR, XOR, and NOT Operators

The bitwise operators AND, OR, XOR, and NOT are &, |, ^, and ~. They perform the same operations as their Boolean logic equivalents described earlier. The difference is

Operator	Result
&	Bitwise AND
|	Bitwise OR
^	Bitwise exclusive OR (XOR)
>>	Shift right
<<	Shift left
~	One's complement (unary NOT)

Table 4-1.   *The Bitwise Operators*

that the bitwise operators work on a bit-by-bit basis. The following table shows the outcome of each operation using 1's and 0's:

p	q	p & q	p | q	p ^ q	~p
0	0	0	0	0	1
1	0	0	1	1	0
0	1	0	1	1	1
1	1	1	1	0	0

In terms of its most common usage, you can think of the bitwise AND as a way to turn bits off. That is, any bit that is 0 in either operand will cause the corresponding bit in the outcome to be set to 0. For example,

```
    1101 0011
    1010 1010
&  _____
    1000 0010
```

The following program demonstrates the & by using it to convert odd numbers into even numbers. It does this by turning off bit zero. For example, the number 9 in binary is 0000 1001. When bit zero is turned off, this number becomes 8, or 0000 1000 in binary.

```
//  Use bitwise AND to make a number even.

using System;

class MakeEven {
  public static void Main() {
    ushort num;
    ushort i;

    for(i = 1; i <= 10; i++) {
      num = i;

      Console.WriteLine("num: " + num);

      num = (ushort) (num & 0xFFFE); // num & 1111 1110

      Console.WriteLine("num after turning off bit zero: "
                        +  num + "\n");
    }
  }
}
```

The output from this program is shown here:

```
num: 1
num after turning off bit zero: 0

num: 2
num after turning off bit zero: 2

num: 3
num after turning off bit zero: 2

num: 4
num after turning off bit zero: 4

num: 5
num after turning off bit zero: 4
```

```
num: 6
num after turning off bit zero: 6

num: 7
num after turning off bit zero: 6

num: 8
num after turning off bit zero: 8

num: 9
num after turning off bit zero: 8

num: 10
num after turning off bit zero: 10
```

The value 0xFFFE used in the AND statement is the decimal representation of 1111 1110.
Thus, the AND operation leaves all bits in **ch** unchanged except for bit zero, which is
set to zero. Thus, any even number is unchanged, but odd numbers are made even by
reducing their values by 1.

The AND operator is also useful when you want to determine whether a bit is on or
off. For example, this program determines if a number is odd:

```
// Use bitwise AND to determine if a number is odd.

using System;

class IsOdd {
  public static void Main() {
    ushort num;

    num = 10;

    if((num & 1) == 1)
      Console.WriteLine("This won't display.");

    num = 11;

    if((num & 1) == 1)
      Console.WriteLine(num + " is odd.");

  }
}
```

The output is shown here:

```
11 is odd.
```

In the **if** statements, the value of **num** is ANDed with 1. If bit zero in **num** is set, the result of **num & 1** is 1; otherwise, the result is zero. Therefore, the **if** statement can succeed only when the number is odd.

You can use the bit-testing capability of the bitwise **&** to create a program that uses the bitwise **&** to show the bits of a **byte** value in binary format. Here is one approach:

```
// Display the bits within a byte.

using System;

class ShowBits {
  public static void Main() {
    int t;
    byte val;

    val = 123;
    for(t=128; t > 0; t = t/2) {
      if((val & t) != 0) Console.Write("1 ");
      if((val & t) == 0) Console.Write("0 ");
    }
  }
}
```

The output is shown here:

```
0 1 1 1 1 0 1 1
```

The **for** loop successively tests each bit in **val**, using the bitwise AND, to determine if it is on or off. If the bit is on, the digit **1** is displayed; otherwise, **0** is displayed.

The bitwise OR, as the reverse of AND, can be used to turn bits on. Any bit that is set to 1 in either operand will cause the corresponding bit in the variable to be set to 1. For example,

```
1101 0011
1010 1010
| ─────────
1111 1011
```

You can make use of the OR to change the make-even program shown earlier into a make-odd program, as shown here:

```
//  Use bitwise OR to make a number odd.

using System;

class MakeOdd {
  public static void Main() {
    ushort num;
    ushort i;

    for(i = 1; i <= 10; i++) {
      num = i;

      Console.WriteLine("num: " + num);

      num = (ushort) (num | 1); // num | 0000 0001

      Console.WriteLine("num after turning on bit zero: "
                        +  num + "\n");
    }
  }
}
```

The output from this program is shown here:

```
num: 1
num after turning on bit zero: 1

num: 2
num after turning on bit zero: 3

num: 3
num after turning on bit zero: 3

num: 4
num after turning on bit zero: 5

num: 5
num after turning on bit zero: 5

num: 6
num after turning on bit zero: 7
```

```
num: 7
num after turning on bit zero: 7

num: 8
num after turning on bit zero: 9

num: 9
num after turning on bit zero: 9

num: 10
num after turning on bit zero: 11
```

The program works by ORing each character with the value 1, which is 0000 0001 in binary. Thus, 1 is the value that produces a value in binary in which only bit zero is set. When this value is ORed with any other value, it produces a result in which the low-order bit is set and all other bits remain unchanged. Thus, a value that is even will be increased by one, becoming odd.

An exclusive OR, usually abbreviated XOR, will set a bit on if, and only if, the bits being compared are different, as illustrated here:

```
    0 1 1 1 1 1 1 1
    1 0 1 1 1 0 0 1
^ ─────────────────
    1 1 0 0 0 1 1 0
```

The XOR operator has an interesting property that makes it a simple way to encode a message. When some value X is XORed with another value Y, and then that result is XORed with Y again, X is produced. That is, given the sequence

```
R1 = X ^ Y;
R2 = R1 ^ Y;
```

R2 is the same value as X. Thus, the outcome of a sequence of two XORs using the same value produces the original value. You can use this principle to create a simple cipher program in which some integer is the key that is used to both encode and decode a message by XORing the characters in that message. To encode, the XOR operation is applied the first time, yielding the ciphertext. To decode, the XOR is applied a second time, yielding the plaintext. Here is a simple example that uses this approach to encode and decode a short message:

```
// Use XOR to encode and decode a message.

using System;
```

```
class Encode {
  public static void Main() {
    char ch1 = 'H';
    char ch2 = 'i';
    char ch3 = '!';

    int key = 88

    Console.WriteLine("Original message: "+
                       ch1 + ch2 + ch3);

    // encode the message
    ch1 = (char) (ch1 ^ key);
    ch2 = (char) (ch2 ^ key);
    ch3 = (char) (ch3 ^ key);

    Console.WriteLine("Encoded message: "+
                       ch1 + ch2 + ch3);

    // decode the message
    ch1 = (char) (ch1 ^ key);
    ch2 = (char) (ch2 ^ key);
    ch3 = (char) (ch3 ^ key);

    Console.WriteLine("Decoded message: "+
                       ch1 + ch2 + ch3);
  }
}
```

Here is the output:

```
Original message: Hi!
Encoded message: ly
Decoded message: Hi!
```

As you can see, the result of two XORs using the same key produces the decoded message.

The unary one's complement (NOT) operator reverses the state of all the bits of the operand. For example, if some integer called **A** has the bit pattern 1001 0110, then ~**A** produces a result with the bit pattern 0110 1001.

The following program demonstrates the NOT operator by displaying a number and its complement in binary:

```
// Demonstrate the bitwise NOT.
```

```
using System;

class NotDemo {
  public static void Main() {
    sbyte b = -34;
    int t;
    for(t=128; t > 0; t = t/2) {
      if((b & t) != 0) Console.Write("1 ");
      if((b & t) == 0) Console.Write("0 ");
    }
    Console.WriteLine();

    // reverse all bits
    b = (sbyte) ~b;

    for(t=128; t > 0; t = t/2) {
      if((b & t) != 0) Console.Write("1 ");
      if((b & t) == 0) Console.Write("0 ");
    }
  }
}
```

Here is the output:

```
1 1 0 1 1 1 1 0
0 0 1 0 0 0 0 1
```

The Shift Operators

In C# it is possible to shift the bits that comprise a value to the left or to the right by a specified amount. C# defines the two bit-shift operators shown here:

<<   Left shift

>>   Right shift

The general forms for these operators are shown here:

value << num-bits
value >> num-bits

Here, *value* is the value being shifted by the number of bit positions specified by *num-bits*.

A left shift causes all bits within the specified value to be shifted left one position and a zero bit to be brought in on the right. A right shift causes all bits to be shifted right one position. In the case of a right shift on an unsigned value, a zero is brought in on the left. In the case of a right shift on a signed value, the sign bit is preserved. Recall that negative numbers are represented by setting the high-order bit of an integer value to 1. Thus, if the value being shifted is negative, each right shift brings in a 1 on the left. If the value is positive, each right shift brings in a 0 on the left.

For both left and right shifts, the bits shifted out are lost. Thus, a shift is not a rotate and there is no way to retrieve a bit that has been shifted out.

Here is a program that graphically illustrates the effect of a left and right shift. First, an integer is given an initial value of 1, which means that its low-order bit is set. Then, eight shifts are performed on the integer. After each shift, the lower eight bits of the value are shown. The process is then repeated, except that a 1 is put in the eighth bit position, and right shifts are performed.

```csharp
// Demonstrate the shift << and >> operators.

using System;

class ShiftDemo {
  public static void Main() {
    int val = 1;
    int t;
    int i;
    for(i = 0; i < 8; i++) {
      for(t=128; t > 0; t = t/2) {
        if((val & t) != 0) Console.Write("1 ");
        if((val & t) == 0) Console.Write("0 ");
      }
      Console.WriteLine();
      val = val << 1; // left shift
    }
    Console.WriteLine();

    val = 128;
    for(i = 0; i < 8; i++) {
      for(t=128; t > 0; t = t/2) {
        if((val & t) != 0) Console.Write("1 ");
        if((val & t) == 0) Console.Write("0 ");
      }
      Console.WriteLine();
      val = val >> 1; // right shift
    }
  }
}
```

The output from the program is shown here:

```
0 0 0 0 0 0 0 1
0 0 0 0 0 0 1 0
0 0 0 0 0 1 0 0
0 0 0 0 1 0 0 0
0 0 0 1 0 0 0 0
0 0 1 0 0 0 0 0
0 1 0 0 0 0 0 0
1 0 0 0 0 0 0 0

1 0 0 0 0 0 0 0
0 1 0 0 0 0 0 0
0 0 1 0 0 0 0 0
0 0 0 1 0 0 0 0
0 0 0 0 1 0 0 0
0 0 0 0 0 1 0 0
0 0 0 0 0 0 1 0
0 0 0 0 0 0 0 1
```

Since binary is based on powers of 2, the shift operators can be used as a very fast way to multiply or divide an integer by 2. A shift left doubles a value. A shift right halves it. Of course, this works only as long as you are not shifting bits off one end or the other. Here is an example:

```
// Use the shift operators to multiply and divide by 2.

using System;

class MultDiv {
  public static void Main() {
    int n;

    n = 10;

    Console.WriteLine("Value of n: " + n);

    // multiply by 2
    n = n << 1;
    Console.WriteLine("Value of n after n = n * 2: " + n);
```

```
    // multiply by 4
    n = n << 2;
    Console.WriteLine("Value of n after n = n * 4: " + n);

    // divide by 2
    n = n >> 1;
    Console.WriteLine("Value of n after n = n / 2: " + n);

    // divide by 4
    n = n >> 2;
    Console.WriteLine("Value of n after n = n / 4: " + n);
    Console.WriteLine();

    // reset n
    n = 10;
    Console.WriteLine("Value of n: " + n);

    // multiply by 2, 30 times
    n = n << 30; // data is lost
    Console.WriteLine("Value of n after left-shifting 30 places: " + n);

  }
}
```

The output is shown here:

```
Value of n: 10
Value of n after n = n * 2: 20
Value of n after n = n * 4: 80
Value of n after n = n / 2: 40
Value of n after n = n / 4: 10

Value of n: 10
Value of n after left-shifting 30 places: -2147483648
```

Notice the last line in the output. When the value 10 is left-shifted 30 times (that is, when it is multiplied by 2^{30}), information is lost because bits are shifted out of the range of an **int**. In this case, the garbage value produced is negative because a 1 bit is shifted into the high-order bit, which is used as a sign bit, causing the number to be interpreted as negative. This illustrates why you must be careful when using the shift operators to multiply or divide a value by 2. (See Chapter 3 for an explanation of signed vs. unsigned data types.)

Bitwise Compound Assignments

All of the binary bitwise operators can be used in compound assignments. For example, the following two statements both assign to **x** the outcome of an XOR of **x** with the value 127:

```
x = x ^ 127;
x ^= 127;
```

The ? Operator

One of C#'s most fascinating operators is the **?**. The **?** operator is often used to replace certain types of if-then-else constructions. The **?** is called a *ternary operator* because it requires three operands. It takes the general form

Exp1 ? Exp2 : Exp3;

where *Exp1* is a **bool** expression, and *Exp2* and *Exp3* are expressions. The type of *Exp2* and *Exp3* must be the same. Notice the use and placement of the colon.

The value of a **?** expression is determined like this: *Exp1* is evaluated. If it is true, then *Exp2* is evaluated and becomes the value of the entire **?** expression. If *Exp1* is false, then *Exp3* is evaluated, and its value becomes the value of the expression. Consider this example, which assigns **absval** the absolute value of **val**:

```
absval = val < 0 ? -val : val; // get absolute value of val
```

Here, **absval** will be assigned the value of **val** if **val** is zero or greater. If **val** is negative, then **absval** will be assigned the negative of that value (which yields a positive value).

Here is another example of the **?** operator. This program divides two numbers, but will not allow a division by zero.

```
// Prevent a division by zero using the ?.

using System;

class NoZeroDiv {
  public static void Main() {
    int result;
    int i;
    for(i = -5; i < 6; i++) {
      result = i != 0 ? 100 / i : 0;
      if(i != 0)
```

```
        Console.WriteLine("100 / " + i + " is " + result);
    }
  }
}
```

The output from the program is shown here:

```
100 / -5 is -20
100 / -4 is -25
100 / -3 is -33
100 / -2 is -50
100 / -1 is -100
100 / 1 is 100
100 / 2 is 50
100 / 3 is 33
100 / 4 is 25
100 / 5 is 20
```

Pay special attention to this line from the program:

```
result = i != 0 ? 100 / i : 0;
```

Here, **result** is assigned the outcome of the division of 100 by **i**. However, this division takes place only if **i** is not zero. When **i** is zero, a placeholder value of zero is assigned to **result**.

You don't actually have to assign the value produced by the **?** to some variable. For example, you could use the value as an argument in a call to a method. Or, if the expressions are all of type **bool**, the **?** can be used as the conditional expression in a loop or **if** statement. For example, here is the preceding program rewritten a bit more efficiently. It produces the same output as before.

```
// Prevent a division by zero using the ?.

using System;

class NoZeroDiv2 {
  public static void Main() {
    int i;
    for(i = -5; i < 6; i++)
      if(i != 0 ? true : false)
```

```
        Console.WriteLine("100 / " + i +
                          " is " + 100 / i);
    }
}
```

Notice the **if** statement. If **i** is zero, then the outcome of the **if** is false, the division by zero is prevented, and no result is displayed. Otherwise the division takes place.

Spacing and Parentheses

An expression in C# can have tabs and spaces in it to make it more readable. For example, the following two expressions are the same, but the second is easier to read:

```
x=10/y*(127/x);
```

```
x = 10 / y * (127/x);
```

Parentheses increase the precedence of the operations contained within them, just like in algebra. Use of redundant or additional parentheses will not cause errors or slow down the execution of the expression. You are encouraged to use parentheses to make clear the exact order of evaluation, both for yourself and for others who may have to figure out your program later. For example, which of the following two expressions is easier to read?

```
x = y/3-34*temp+127;
```

```
x = (y/3) - (34*temp) + 127;
```

Operator Precedence

Table 4-2 shows the order of precedence for all C# operators, from highest to lowest. This table includes several operators that will be discussed later in this book.

Highest

()	[]	.	++(postfix)	--(postfix)	checked	new	sizeof	typeof	unchecked
!	~		(cast)	+(unary)	-(unary)	++(prefix)		--(prefix)	

```
*  /   %
+  -
<<  >>
<  >  <=  >=  is
==  !=
&
^
|
&&
||
?:
=  op=
```

Lowest

Table 4-2.   *The Precedence of the C# Operators*

The Complete Reference

Chapter 5

Program Control Statements

This chapter discusses C#'s program control statements. There are three categories of program control statements: *selection* statements, which are the **if** and the **switch**; *iteration* statements, which consist of the **for**, **while**, **do-while**, and **foreach** loops; and *jump* statements, which include **break**, **continue**, **goto**, **return**, and **throw**. Except for **throw**, which is part of C#'s exception-handling mechanism and is discussed in Chapter 13, the others are examined here.

The if Statement

Chapter 2 introduced the **if** statement. It is examined in detail here. The complete form of the **if** statement is

> if(*condition*) *statement*;
> else *statement*;

where the targets of the **if** and **else** are single statements. The **else** clause is optional. The targets of both the **if** and **else** can be blocks of statements. The general form of the **if** using blocks of statements is

> if(*condition*)
> {
>   *statement sequence*
> }
> else
> {
>   *statement sequence*
> }

If the conditional expression is true, the target of the **if** will be executed; otherwise, if it exists, the target of the **else** will be executed. At no time will both of them be executed. The conditional expression controlling the **if** must produce a **bool** result.

Here is a simple example that uses an **if** and **else** statement to report if a number is positive or negative:

```
// Determine if a value is positive or negative.

using System;

class PosNeg {
  public static void Main() {
    int i;

    for(i=-5; i <= 5; i++) {
      Console.Write("Testing " + i + ": ");
```

```
        if(i < 0) Console.WriteLine("negative");
        else Console.WriteLine("positive");
    }


  }
}
```

The output is shown here:

```
Testing -5: negative
Testing -4: negative
Testing -3: negative
Testing -2: negative
Testing -1: negative
Testing 0: positive
Testing 1: positive
Testing 2: positive
Testing 3: positive
Testing 4: positive
Testing 5: positive
```

In this example, if **i** is less than zero, then the target of the **if** is executed. Otherwise, the target of the **else** is executed. In no case are both executed.

Nested ifs

A *nested if* is an **if** statement that is the target of another **if** or **else**. Nested **if**s are very common in programming. The main thing to remember about nested **if**s in C# is that an **else** statement always refers to the nearest **if** statement that is within the same block as the **else** and not already associated with an **else**. Here is an example:

```
if(i == 10) {
  if(j < 20) a = b;
  if(k > 100) c = d;
  else a = c; // this else refers to if(k > 100)
}
else a = d; // this else refers to if(i == 10)
```

As the comments indicate, the final **else** is not associated with **if(j<20)**, because it is not in the same block (even though it is the nearest **if** without an **else**). Rather, the final **else** is associated with **if(i==10)**. The inner **else** refers to **if(k>100)**, because it is the closest **if** within the same block.

The following program demonstrates a nested **if**. In the positive/negative program shown earlier, zero is reported as positive. However, for some applications, zero is considered signless. The following version of the program reports zero as being neither positive nor negative.

```
// Determine if a value is positive, negative, or zero.

using System;

class PosNegZero {
  public static void Main() {
    int i;

    for(i=-5; i <= 5; i++) {

      Console.Write("Testing " + i + ": ");

      if(i < 0) Console.WriteLine("negative");
      else if(i == 0) Console.WriteLine("no sign");
        else Console.WriteLine("positive");
    }

  }
}
```

Here is the output:

```
Testing -5: negative
Testing -4: negative
Testing -3: negative
Testing -2: negative
Testing -1: negative
Testing 0: no sign
Testing 1: positive
Testing 2: positive
Testing 3: positive
Testing 4: positive
Testing 5: positive
```

The if-else-if Ladder

A common programming construct that is based upon the nested **if** is the *if-else-if ladder*. It looks like this:

if(*condition*)
  statement;
else if(*condition*)
  statement;
else if(*condition*)
  statement;
  .
  .
  .
else
  statement;

The conditional expressions are evaluated from the top downward. As soon as a true condition is found, the statement associated with it is executed, and the rest of the ladder is bypassed. If none of the conditions is true, then the final **else** statement will be executed. The final **else** often acts as a default condition. That is, if all other conditional tests fail, then the last **else** statement is performed. If there is no final **else** and all other conditions are false, then no action will take place.

The following program demonstrates the **if-else-if** ladder. It finds the smallest single-digit factor (other than 1) for a given value.

```
// Determine smallest single-digit factor.

using System;

class Ladder {
  public static void Main() {
    int num;

    for(num = 2; num < 12; num++) {
      if((num % 2) == 0)
        Console.WriteLine("Smallest factor of " + num + " is 2.");
      else if((num % 3) == 0)
        Console.WriteLine("Smallest factor of " + num + " is 3.");
      else if((num % 5) -- 0)
        Console.WriteLine("Smallest factor of " + num + " is 5.");
      else if((num % 7) == 0)
        Console.WriteLine("Smallest factor of " + num + " is 7.");
      else
        Console.WriteLine(num + " is not divisible by 2, 3, 5, or 7.");
    }
```

```
    }
}
```

The program produces the following output:

```
Smallest factor of 2 is 2.
Smallest factor of 3 is 3.
Smallest factor of 4 is 2.
Smallest factor of 5 is 5.
Smallest factor of 6 is 2.
Smallest factor of 7 is 7.
Smallest factor of 8 is 2.
Smallest factor of 9 is 3.
Smallest factor of 10 is 2.
11 is not divisible by 2, 3, 5, or 7.
```

As you can see, the default **else** is executed only if none of the preceding **if** statements succeed.

The switch Statement

The second of C#'s selection statements is the **switch**. The **switch** provides for a multiway branch. Thus, it enables a program to select among several alternatives. Although a series of nested **if** statements can perform multiway tests, for many situations the **switch** is a more efficient approach. It works like this: The value of an expression is successively tested against a list of constants. When a match is found, the statement sequence associated with that match is executed. The general form of the **switch** statement is

```
switch(expression) {
    case constant1:
        statement sequence
        break;
    case constant2:
        statement sequence
        break;
    case constant3:
        statement sequence
        break;
        .
        .
        .
```

```
    default:
        statement sequence
        break;
}
```

The **switch** expression must be of an integer type, such as **char**, **byte**, **short**, or **int**, or of type **string** (which is described later in this book). Thus, floating-point expressions, for example, are not allowed. Frequently, the expression controlling the **switch** is simply a variable. The **case** constants must be literals of a type compatible with the expression. No two **case** constants in the same **switch** can have identical values.

The **default** statement sequence is executed if no **case** constant matches the expression. The **default** is optional; if it is not present, no action takes place if all matches fail. When a match is found, the statements associated with that **case** are executed until the **break** is encountered.

The following program demonstrates the **switch**:

```csharp
// Demonstrate the switch.

using System;

class SwitchDemo {
  public static void Main() {
    int i;

    for(i=0; i<10; i++)
      switch(i) {
        case 0:
          Console.WriteLine("i is zero");
          break;
        case 1:
          Console.WriteLine("i is one");
          break;
        case 2:
          Console.WriteLine("i is two");
          break;
        case 3:
          Console.WriteLine("i is three");
          break;
        case 4:
          Console.WriteLine("i is four");
          break;
        default:
```

```
        Console.WriteLine("i is five or more");
        break;
    }

  }
}
```

The output produced by this program is shown here:

```
i is zero
i is one
i is two
i is three
i is four
i is five or more
i is five or more
i is five or more
i is five or more
i is five or more
```

As you can see, each time through the loop, the statements associated with the **case** constant that matches **i** are executed. All others are bypassed. When **i** is five or greater, no **case** constants match, so the **default** statement is executed.

In the preceding example, the **switch** was controlled by an **int** variable. As explained, you can control a **switch** with any integer type, including **char**. Here is an example that uses a **char** expression and **char** case constants:

```
// Use a char to control the switch.

using System;

class SwitchDemo2 {
  public static void Main() {
    char ch;

    for(ch='A'; ch<= 'E'; ch++)
      switch(ch) {
        case 'A':
          Console.WriteLine("ch is A");
          break;
        case 'B':
          Console.WriteLine("ch is B");
```

```
        break;
      case 'C':
        Console.WriteLine("ch is C");
        break;
      case 'D':
        Console.WriteLine("ch is D");
        break;
      case 'E':
        Console.WriteLine("ch is E");
        break;
    }
  }
}
```

The output from this program is shown here:

```
ch is A
ch is B
ch is C
ch is D
ch is E
```

Notice that this example does not include a **default** statement. Remember, the **default** is optional. When not needed, it can be left out.

In C#, it is an error for the statement sequence associated with one **case** to continue on into the next **case**. This is called the "no fall-through" rule. This is why **case** sequences end with a **break** statement. (You can avoid fall-through in other ways, such as by using the **goto** discussed later in this chapter, but **break** is by far the most commonly used approach.) When encountered within the statement sequence of a **case**, the **break** statement causes program flow to exit from the entire **switch** statement and resume at the next statement outside the **switch**. The **default** statement must also not "fall through," and it too usually ends with a **break**.

The no fall-through rule is one point on which C# differs from C, C++, and Java. In those languages, one **case** may continue on (that is, fall through) into the next **case**. There are two reasons that C# instituted the no fall-through rule for **case**s. First, it allows the compiler to freely rearrange the order of the **case** statements, perhaps for purposes of optimization. Such a rearrangement would not be possible if one **case** could flow into the next. Second, requiring each **case** to explicitly end prevents a programmer from accidentally allowing one **case** to flow into the next.

Although you cannot allow one **case** sequence to fall through into another, you can have two or more **case** statements refer to the same code sequence, as shown in this example:

```
// Empty cases can fall through.
```

```
using System;

class EmptyCasesCanFall {
  public static void Main() {
    int i;

    for(i=1; i < 5; i++)
      switch(i) {
        case 1:
        case 2:
        case 3: Console.WriteLine("i is 1, 2 or 3");
          break;
        case 4: Console.WriteLine("i is 4");
          break;
      }

  }
}
```

The output is shown here:

```
i is 1, 2 or 3
i is 1, 2 or 3
i is 1, 2 or 3
i is 4
```

In this example, if **i** has the value 1, 2, or 3, then the first **WriteLine( )** statement executes. If it is 4, then the second **WriteLine( )** statement executes. The stacking of **case**s does not violate the no fall-through rule, because the **case** statements all use the same statement sequence.

Stacking **case** statements is a commonly employed technique when several **case**s share common code. This technique prevents the unnecessary duplication of code sequences.

Nested switch Statements

It is possible to have a **switch** as part of the statement sequence of an outer **switch**. This is called a *nested switch*. The **case** constants of the inner and outer **switch** can contain common values and no conflicts will arise. For example, the following code fragment is perfectly acceptable:

```
switch(ch1) {
```

```
case 'A': Console.WriteLine("This A is part of outer switch.");
  switch(ch2) {
    case 'A':
      Console.WriteLine("This A is part of inner switch");
      break;
    case 'B': // ...
  } // end of inner switch
  break;
case 'B': // ...
```

The for Loop

You have been using a simple form of the **for** loop since Chapter 2. Here, it is examined in detail. You might be surprised at just how powerful and flexible the **for** loop is. Let's begin by reviewing the basics, starting with the most traditional forms of the **for**.

The general form of the **for** loop for repeating a single statement is

for(*initialization*; *condition*; *iteration*) *statement*;

For repeating a block, the general form is

for(*initialization*; *condition*; *iteration*)
{
   statement sequence
}

The *initialization* is usually an assignment statement that sets the initial value of the *loop control variable*, which acts as the counter that controls the loop. The *condition* is an expression of type **bool** that determines whether the loop will repeat. The *iteration* expression defines the amount by which the loop control variable will change each time the loop is repeated. Notice that these three major sections of the loop must be separated by semicolons. The **for** loop will continue to execute as long as the condition tests true. Once the condition becomes false, the loop will exit, and program execution will resume on the statement following the **for**.

The **for** loop can proceed in a positive or negative fashion, and it can change the loop control variable by any amount. For example, the following program prints the numbers 100 to –100, in decrements of 5:

```
// A negatively running for loop.

using System;

class DecrFor {
```

```
public static void Main() {
  int x;

  for(x = 100; x > -100; x -= 5)
    Console.WriteLine(x);
}
}
```

An important point about **for** loops is that the conditional expression is always tested at the top of the loop. This means that the code inside the loop may not be executed at all if the condition is false to begin with. Here is an example:

```
for(count=10; count < 5; count++)
  x += count; // this statement will not execute
```

This loop will never execute because its control variable, **count**, is greater than 5 when the loop is first entered. This makes the conditional expression, **count<5**, false from the outset; thus, not even one iteration of the loop will occur.

The **for** loop is most useful when you will be iterating a known number of times. For example, the following program uses two **for** loops to find the prime numbers between 2 and 20. If the number is not prime, then its largest factor is displayed.

```
/*
   Determine if a number is prime.  If it is not,
   then display its largest factor.
*/

using System;

class FindPrimes {
  public static void Main() {
    int num;
    int i;
    int factor;
    bool isprime;


    for(num = 2; num < 20; num++) {
      isprime = true;
      factor = 0;
```

```
      // see if num is evenly divisible
      for(i=2; i <= num/2; i++) {
        if((num % i) == 0) {
          // num is evenly divisible -- not prime
          isprime = false;
          factor = i;
        }
      }

      if(isprime)
        Console.WriteLine(num + " is prime.");
      else
        Console.WriteLine("Largest factor of " + num +
                          " is " + factor);
    }
  }
}
```

The output from the program is shown here:

```
2 is prime.
3 is prime.
Largest factor of 4 is 2
5 is prime.
Largest factor of 6 is 3
7 is prime.
Largest factor of 8 is 4
Largest factor of 9 is 3
Largest factor of 10 is 5
11 is prime.
Largest factor of 12 is 6
13 is prime.
Largest factor of 14 is 7
Largest factor of 15 is 5
Largest factor of 16 is 8
17 is prime.
Largest factor of 18 is 9
19 is prime.
```

Some Variations on the for Loop

The **for** is one of the most versatile statements in the C# language because it allows a wide range of variations. They are examined here.

Using Multiple Loop Control Variables

The **for** loop allows you to use two or more variables to control the loop. When using multiple loop control variables, the initialization and increment statements for each variable are separated by commas. For example:

```
// Use commas in a for statement.

using System;

class Comma {
  public static void Main() {
    int i, j;

    for(i=0, j=10; i < j; i++, j--)
      Console.WriteLine("i and j: " + i + " " + j);
  }
}
```

The output from the program is shown here:

```
i and j:  0 10
i and j:  1 9
i and j:  2 8
i and j:  3 7
i and j:  4 6
```

Here, commas separate the two initialization statements and the two iteration expressions. When the loop begins, both **i** and **j** are initialized. Each time the loop repeats, **i** is incremented and **j** is decremented. Multiple loop control variables are often convenient and can simplify certain algorithms. You can have any number of initialization and iteration statements, but in practice, more than two make the **for** loop unwieldy.

Here is a practical use of the multiple loop control variables in a **for** statement. This program uses two loop control variables within a single **for** loop to find the largest and smallest factor of a number, in this case 100. Pay special attention to the termination condition. It relies on both loop control variables.

```
/*
   Use commas in a for statement to find
   the largest and smallest factor of a number.
*/

using System;

class Comma {
  public static void Main() {
    int i, j;
    int smallest, largest;
    int num;

    num = 100;

    smallest = largest = 1;

    for(i=2, j=num/2; (i <= num/2) & (j >= 2); i++, j--) {

      if((smallest == 1) & ((num % i) == 0))
        smallest = i;

      if((largest == 1) & ((num % j) == 0))
        largest = j;

    }

    Console.WriteLine("Largest factor: " + largest);
    Console.WriteLine("Smallest factor: " + smallest);
  }
}
```

Here is the output from the program:

```
Largest factor: 50
Smallest factor: 2
```

Through the use of two loop control variables, a single **for** loop can find both the smallest and the largest factor of a number. The control variable i is used to search for the smallest factor. It is initially set to 2 and incremented until its value exceeds one half of **num**. The control variable j is used to search for the largest factor. Its value is initially set to one half the **num** and decremented until it is less than 2. The loop runs until both **i** and **j** are at their termination values. When the loop ends, both factors will have been found.

The Conditional Expression

The conditional expression controlling a **for** loop can be any valid expression that produces a **bool** result. It does not need to involve the loop control variable. For example, in the next program, the **for** loop is controlled by the value of **done**.

```
// Loop condition can be any bool expression.

using System;

class forDemo {
  public static void Main() {
     int i, j;
     bool done = false;

     for(i=0, j=100; !done; i++, j--) {

       if(i*i >= j) done = true;

       Console.WriteLine("i, j: " + i + " " + j);
     }

   }
}
```

The output is shown here:

```
i, j: 0 100
i, j: 1 99
i, j: 2 98
i, j: 3 97
i, j: 4 96
i, j: 5 95
i, j: 6 94
i, j: 7 93
i, j: 8 92
i, j: 9 91
i, j: 10 90
```

In this example, the **for** loop iterates until the **bool** variable **done** is true. This variable is set to true inside the loop when **i** squared is greater than or equal to **j**.

Missing Pieces

Some interesting **for** loop variations are created by leaving pieces of the loop definition empty. In C#, it is possible for any or all of the initialization, condition, or iteration portions of the **for** loop to be blank. For example, consider the following program:

```
// Parts of the for can be empty.

using System;

class Empty {
  public static void Main() {
    int i;

    for(i = 0; i < 10; ) {
      Console.WriteLine("Pass #" + i);
      i++; // increment loop control var
    }
  }
}
```

Here, the iteration expression of the **for** is empty. Instead, the loop control variable **i** is incremented inside the body of the loop. This means that each time the loop repeats, **i** is tested to see whether it equals 10, but no further action takes place. Of course, since **i** is incremented within the body of the loop, the loop runs normally, displaying the following output:

```
Pass #0
Pass #1
Pass #2
Pass #3
Pass #4
Pass #5
Pass #6
Pass #7
Pass #8
Pass #9
```

In the next example, the initialization portion is also moved out of the **for**:

```
// Move more out of the for loop.

using System;
```

```
class Empty2 {
  public static void Main() {
    int i;

    i = 0; // move initialization out of loop
    for(; i < 10; ) {
      Console.WriteLine("Pass #" + i);
      i++; // increment loop control var
    }
  }
}
```

In this version, **i** is initialized before the loop begins, rather than as part of the **for**. Normally, you will want to initialize the loop control variable inside the **for**. Placing the initialization outside of the loop is generally done only when the initial value is derived through a complex process that does not lend itself to containment inside the **for** statement.

The Infinite Loop

You can create an *infinite loop* (a loop that never terminates) using the **for** by leaving the conditional expression empty. For example, the following fragment shows the way many C# programmers create an infinite loop:

```
for(;;) // intentionally infinite loop
{
  //...
}
```

This loop will run forever. Although there are some programming tasks, such as operating system command processors, that require an infinite loop, most "infinite loops" are really just loops with special termination requirements. Near the end of this chapter you will see how to halt a loop of this type. (Hint: It's done using the **break** statement.)

Loops with No Body

In C#, the body associated with a **for** loop (or any other loop) can be empty. This is because a *null statement* is syntactically valid. Bodyless loops are often useful. For example, the following program uses a bodyless loop to sum the numbers 1 through 5:

```
// The body of a loop can be empty.
```

```
using System;

class Empty3 {
  public static void Main() {
    int i;
    int sum = 0;

    // sum the numbers through 5
    for(i = 1; i <= 5; sum += i++) ;

    Console.WriteLine("Sum is " + sum);
  }
}
```

The output from the program is shown here:

```
Sum is 15
```

Notice that the summation process is handled entirely within the **for** statement, and no body is needed. Pay special attention to the iteration expression:

```
sum += i++
```

Don't be intimidated by statements like this. They are common in professionally written C# programs and are easy to understand if you break them down into their parts. In words, this statement says "add to **sum** the value of **sum** plus **i**, then increment **i**." Thus, it is the same as this sequence of statements:

```
sum = sum + i;
i++;
```

Declaring Loop Control Variables Inside the for Loop

Often the variable that controls a **for** loop is needed only for the purposes of the loop and is not used elsewhere. When this is the case, it is possible to declare the variable inside the initialization portion of the **for**. For example, the following program computes both the summation and the factorial of the numbers 1 through 5. It declares its loop control variable **i** inside the **for**:

```
// Declare loop control variable inside the for.

using System;

class ForVar {
  public static void Main() {
    int sum = 0;
    int fact = 1;

    // compute the factorial of the numbers through 5
    for(int i = 1; i <= 5; i++) {
      sum += i;  // i is known throughout the loop
      fact *= i;
    }

    // but, i is not known here.

    Console.WriteLine("Sum is " + sum);
    Console.WriteLine("Factorial is " + fact);
  }
}
```

When you declare a variable inside a **for** loop, there is one important point to remember: the scope of that variable ends when the **for** statement does. (That is, the scope of the variable is limited to the **for** loop.) Outside the **for** loop, the variable will cease to exist. Thus, in the preceding example, **i** is not accessible outside the **for** loop. If you need to use the loop control variable elsewhere in your program, you will not be able to declare it inside the **for** loop.

Before moving on, you might want to experiment with your own variations on the **for** loop. As you will find, it is a fascinating statement.

The while Loop

Another of C#'s loops is the **while**. The general form of the **while** loop is

while(*condition*) *statement*;

where *statement* can be a single statement or a block of statements, and *condition* defines the condition that controls the loop, and it may be any valid Boolean expression. The statement is performed while the condition is true. When the condition becomes false, program control passes to the line immediately following the loop.

Here is a simple example in which a **while** is used to compute the order of magnitude of an integer:

```
// Compute the order of magnitude of an integer

using System;

class WhileDemo {
  public static void Main() {
    int num;
    int mag;

    num = 435679;
    mag = 0;

    Console.WriteLine("Number: " + num);

    while(num > 0) {
      mag++;
      num = num / 10;
    };

    Console.WriteLine("Magnitude: " + mag);
  }
}
```

The output is shown here:

```
Number: 435679
Magnitude: 6
```

The **while** loop works like this: The value of **num** is tested. If **num** is greater than zero, the **mag** counter is incremented, and **num** is divided by 10. As long as the value in **num** is greater than zero, the loop repeats. When **num** is zero, the loop terminates and **mag** contains the order of magnitude of the original value.

As with the **for** loop, the **while** checks the conditional expression at the top of the loop, which means that the loop code may not execute at all. This eliminates the need for performing a separate test before the loop. The following program illustrates this characteristic of the **while** loop. It computes the integer powers of 2 from 0 to 9.

```
// Compute integer powers of 2.

using System;

class Power {
```

```
public static void Main() {
  int e;
  int result;

  for(int i=0; i < 10; i++) {
    result = 1;
    e = i;

    while(e > 0) {
      result *= 2;
      e--;
    }

    Console.WriteLine("2 to the " + i +
                      " power is " + result);
  }
 }
}
```

The output from the program is shown here:

```
2 to the 0 power is 1
2 to the 1 power is 2
2 to the 2 power is 4
2 to the 3 power is 8
2 to the 4 power is 16
2 to the 5 power is 32
2 to the 6 power is 64
2 to the 7 power is 128
2 to the 8 power is 256
2 to the 9 power is 512
```

Notice that the **while** loop executes only when **e** is greater than 0. Thus, when **e** is zero, as it is in the first iteration of the **for** loop, the **while** loop is skipped.

The do-while Loop

The third C# loop is the **do-while**. Unlike the **for** and the **while** loops, in which the condition is tested at the top of the loop, the **do-while** loop checks its condition at the bottom of the loop. This means that a **do-while** loop will always execute at least once. The general form of the **do-while** loop is

```
do {
    statements;
} while(condition);
```

Although the braces are not necessary when only one statement is present, they are often used to improve readability of the **do-while** construct, thus preventing confusion with the **while**. The **do-while** loop executes as long as the conditional expression is true.

The following program uses a **do-while** loop to display the digits of an integer in reverse order:

```
// Display the digits of an integer in reverse order.

using System;

class DoWhileDemo {
  public static void Main() {
    int num;
    int nextdigit;

    num = 198;

    Console.WriteLine("Number: " + num);

    Console.Write("Number in reverse order: ");

    do {
      nextdigit = num % 10;
      Console.Write(nextdigit);
      num = num / 10;
    } while(num > 0);

    Console.WriteLine();
  }
}
```

The output is shown here:

```
Number: 198
Number in reverse order: 891
```

Here is how the loop works. With each iteration, the rightmost digit is obtained by finding the remainder of an integer division by 10. This digit is then displayed. Next, the value in **num** is divided by 10. Since this is an integer division, it results in the rightmost digit being removed. This process repeats until **num** is zero.

The foreach Loop

The **foreach** loop cycles through the elements of a *collection*. A collection is a group of objects. C# defines several types of collections, of which one is an array. The **foreach** loop is examined in Chapter 7, when arrays are discussed.

Using break to Exit a Loop

It is possible to force an immediate exit from a loop, bypassing any code remaining in the body of the loop and the loop's conditional test, by using the **break** statement. When a **break** statement is encountered inside a loop, the loop is terminated, and program control resumes at the next statement following the loop. Here is a simple example:

```
// Using break to exit a loop.

using System;

class BreakDemo {
  public static void Main() {

    // use break to exit this loop
    for(int i=-10; i <= 10; i++) {
      if(i > 0) break; // terminate loop when i is positive
      Console.Write(i + " ");
    }
    Console.WriteLine("Done");
  }
}
```

This program generates the following output:

```
-10 -9 -8 -7 -6 -5 -4 -3 -2 -1 0 Done
```

As you can see, although the **for** loop is designed to run from –10 to 10, the **break** statement causes it to terminate early, when **i** becomes positive.

The **break** statement can be used with any of C#'s loops, including intentionally infinite loops. For example, here is the previous program recoded to use a **do-while** loop:

```
// Using break to exit a do-while loop.

using System;

class BreakDemo2 {
  public static void Main() {
    int i;

    i = -10;
    do {
      if(i > 0) break;
      Console.Write(i + " ");
      i++;
    } while(i <= 10);

    Console.WriteLine("Done");
  }
}
```

Here is a more practical example of **break**. This program finds the smallest factor of a number.

```
// Find the smallest factor of a value.

using System;

class FindSmallestFactor {
  public static void Main() {
    int factor = 1;
    int num = 1000;

    for(int i=2; i < num/2; i++) {
      if((num%i) == 0) {
        factor = i;
        break; // stop loop when factor is found
      }
```

```
    }
    Console.WriteLine("Smallest factor is " + factor);
  }
}
```

The output is shown here:

```
Smallest factor is 2
```

The **break** stops the **for** loop as soon as a factor is found. The use of **break** in this situation prevents the loop from trying any other values once a factor has been found, thus preventing inefficiency.

When used inside a set of nested loops, the **break** statement will break out of only the innermost loop. For example:

```
// Using break with nested loops.

using System;

class BreakNested {
  public static void Main() {

    for(int i=0; i<3; i++) {
      Console.WriteLine("Outer loop count: " + i);
      Console.Write("    Inner loop count: ");

      int t = 0;
      while(t < 100) {
        if(t == 10) break; // terminate loop if t is 10
        Console.Write(t + " ");
        t++;
      }
      Console.WriteLine();
    }
    Console.WriteLine("Loops complete.");
  }
}
```

This program generates the following output:

```
Outer loop count: 0
    Inner loop count: 0 1 2 3 4 5 6 7 8 9
Outer loop count: 1
    Inner loop count: 0 1 2 3 4 5 6 7 8 9
Outer loop count: 2
    Inner loop count: 0 1 2 3 4 5 6 7 8 9
Loops complete.
```

As you can see, the **break** statement in the inner loop causes only the termination of that loop. The outer loop is unaffected.

Here are two other points to remember about **break**. First, more than one **break** statement may appear in a loop, but be careful. Too many **break** statements have the tendency to destructure your code. Second, the **break** that terminates a **switch** statement affects only that **switch** statement and not any enclosing loops.

Using continue

It is possible to force an early iteration of a loop, bypassing the loop's normal control structure. This is accomplished using **continue**. The **continue** statement forces the next iteration of the loop to take place, skipping any code in between. Thus, **continue** is essentially the complement of **break**. For example, the following program uses **continue** to help print the even numbers between 0 and 100.

```
// Use continue.

using System;

class ContDemo {
  public static void Main() {
    // print even numbers between 0 and 100
    for(int i = 0; i <= 100; i++) {
      if((i%2) != 0) continue; // iterate
      Console.WriteLine(i);
    }
  }
}
```

Only even numbers are printed, because an odd number will cause the loop to iterate early, bypassing the call to **WriteLine( )**.

In **while** and **do-while** loops, a **continue** statement will cause control to go directly to the conditional expression and then continue the looping process. In the case of the

for, the iteration expression of the loop is evaluated, then the conditional expression is executed, and then the loop continues.

Good uses of **continue** are rare. One reason is that C# provides a rich set of loop statements that fit most applications. However, for those special circumstances in which early iteration is needed, the **continue** statement provides a structured way to accomplish it.

return

The **return** statement causes a method to return. It can also be used to return a value. It is examined in Chapter 6.

The goto

The **goto** is C#'s unconditional jump statement. When encountered, program flow jumps to the location specified by the **goto**. The statement fell out of favor with programmers many years ago because it encouraged the creation of "spaghetti code." However, the **goto** is still occasionally—and sometimes effectively—used. This book will not make a judgment regarding its validity as a form of program control. It should be stated, however, that there are no programming situations that require the use of the **goto** statement—it is not an item necessary for making the language complete. Rather, it is a convenience that, if used wisely, can be of benefit in certain programming situations. As such, the **goto** is not used in this book outside of this section. The chief concern most programmers have about the **goto** is its tendency to clutter a program and render it nearly unreadable. However, there are times when the use of the **goto** can clarify program flow rather than confuse it.

The **goto** requires a label for operation. A *label* is a valid C# identifier followed by a colon. Furthermore, the label must be in the same method as the **goto** that uses it. For example, a loop from 1 to 100 could be written using a **goto** and a label, as shown here:

```
x = 1;
loop1:
  x++;
  if(x < 100) goto loop1;
```

The **goto** can also be used to jump to a **case** or **default** statement within a **switch**. Technically, the **case** and **default** statements of a **switch** are labels. Thus, they can be targets of a **goto**. However, the **goto** statement must be executed from within the **switch**. That is, you cannot use the **goto** to jump into a **switch** statement. Here is an example that illustrates **goto** with a **switch**:

```
// Use goto with a switch.
```

```
using System;

class SwitchGoto {
  public static void Main() {

    for(int i=1; i < 5; i++) {
      switch(i) {
        case 1:
          Console.WriteLine("In case 1");
          goto case 3;
        case 2:
          Console.WriteLine("In case 2");
          goto case 1;
        case 3:
          Console.WriteLine("In case 3");
          goto default;
        default:
          Console.WriteLine("In default");
          break;
      }

      Console.WriteLine();
    }

//    goto case 1; // Error! Can't jump into a switch.
  }
}
```

The output from the program is shown here:

```
In case 1
In case 3
In default

In case 2
In case 1
In case 3
In default

In case 3
In default

In default
```

Inside the **switch**, notice how the **goto** is used to jump to other **case** statements or the **default** statement. Furthermore, notice that the **case** statements do not end with a **break**. Since the **goto** prevents one **case** from falling through to the next, the "no fall-through" is not violated, and there is no need for a **break** statement. As explained, it is not possible to use the **goto** to jump into a **switch**. If you remove the comment symbols from the start of this line

```
//    goto case 1; // Error! Can't jump into a switch.
```

the program will not compile. Frankly, using a **goto** with a **switch** can be useful in some special-case situations, but it is not recommended style in general.

One good use for the **goto** is to exit from a deeply nested routine. Here is a simple example:

```
// Demonstrate the goto.

using System;

class Use_goto {
  public static void Main() {
    int i=0, j=0, k=0;

    for(i=0; i < 10; i++) {
      for(j=0; j < 10; j++ ) {
        for(k=0; k < 10; k++) {
          Console.WriteLine("i, j, k: " + i + " " + j + " " + k);
          if(k == 3) goto stop;
        }
      }
    }

stop:
    Console.WriteLine("Stopped! i, j, k: " + i + ", " + j + " " + k);

  }
}
```

The output from the program is shown here:

```
i, j, k: 0 0 0
i, j, k: 0 0 1
i, j, k: 0 0 2
i, j, k: 0 0 3
Stopped! i, j, k: 0, 0 3
```

Eliminating the **goto** would force the use of three **if** and **break** statements. In this case, the **goto** simplifies the code. While this is a contrived example used for illustration, you can probably imagine situations in which a **goto** might be beneficial.

Chapter 6

Introducing Classes, Objects, and Methods

This chapter introduces the class. The class is the essence of C# because it defines the nature of an object. It is the foundation upon which the entire C# language is built. As such, the class forms the basis for object-oriented programming in C#. Within a class are defined data and code that acts upon that data. The code is contained in methods. Because classes, objects, and methods are fundamental to C#, they are introduced in this chapter. Having a basic understanding of these features will allow you to write more sophisticated programs and better understand certain key C# elements described in following chapters.

Class Fundamentals

Since all C# program activity occurs within a class, we have been using classes since the start of this book. Of course, only extremely simple classes have been used, and we have not taken advantage of the majority of their features. As you will see, classes are substantially more powerful than the limited ones presented so far.

Let's begin by reviewing the basics. A class is a template that defines the form of an object. It specifies both the data and the code that will operate on that data. C# uses a class specification to construct *objects*. Objects are *instances* of a class. Thus, a class is essentially a set of plans that specify how to build an object. It is important to be clear on one issue: A class is a logical abstraction. It is not until an object of that class has been created that a physical representation of that class exists in memory.

One other point: Recall that the methods and variables that constitute a class are called *members* of the class.

The General Form of a Class

When you define a class, you declare the data that it contains and the code that operates on it. While very simple classes might contain only code or only data, most real-world classes contain both.

In general terms, data is contained in instance variables defined by the class, and code is contained in methods. It is important to state at the outset, however, that C# defines several specific flavors of data and code members, which include instance variables, static variables, constants, methods, constructors, destructors, indexers, events, operators, and properties. For now, we will limit our discussion of the class to its essential elements: instance variables and methods. Later in this chapter constructors and destructors are discussed. The other types of members are described in subsequent chapters.

A class is created by use of the keyword **class**. The general form of a **class** definition that contains only instance variables and methods is shown here:

```
class classname {
    // declare instance variables
    access type var1;
    access type var2;
```

```
    // ...
    access type varN;

    // declare methods
    access ret-type method1(parameters) {
        // body of method
    }
    access ret-type method2(parameters) {
        // body of method
    }
        // ...
    access ret-type methodN(parameters) {
        // body of method
    }
}
```

Notice that each variable and method is preceded with *access*. Here, *access* is an access specifier, such as **public**, which specifies how the member can be accessed. As mentioned in Chapter 2, class members can be private to a class or more accessible. The access specifier determines what type of access is allowed. The access specifier is optional and if absent, then the member is private to the class. Members with private access can be used only by other members of their class. For the examples in this chapter, all members will be specified as **public**, which means that they can be used by all other code—even code defined outside the class. We will return to the topic of access specifiers in Chapter 8.

Although there is no syntactic rule that enforces it, a well-designed class should define one and only one logical entity. For example, a class that stores names and telephone numbers will not normally also store information about the stock market, average rainfall, sunspot cycles, or other unrelated information. The point here is that a well-designed class groups logically connected information. Putting unrelated information into the same class will quickly destructure your code.

Up to this point, the classes that we have been using have had only one method: **Main( )**. Soon you will see how to create others. Notice, however, that the general form of a class does not specify a **Main( )** method. A **Main( )** method is required only if that class is the starting point for your program.

Defining a Class

To illustrate classes, we will be evolving a class that encapsulates information about buildings, such as houses, stores, offices, and so on. This class is called **Building**, and it will store three items of information about a building: the number of floors, the total area, and the number of occupants.

The first version of **Building** is shown here. It defines three instance variables: **floors**, **area**, and **occupants**. Notice that **Building** does not contain any methods. Thus, it is currently a data-only class. (Subsequent sections will add methods to it.)

```
class Building {
  public int floors;    // number of floors
  public int area;      // total square footage of building
  public int occupants; // number of occupants
}
```

The instance variables defined by **Building** illustrate the way that instance variables are declared in general. The general form for declaring an instance variable is shown here:

access type var-name;

Here, *access* specifies the access, *type* specifies the type of variable, and *var-name* is the variable's name. Thus, aside from the access specifier, you declare an instance variable in the same way that you declare local variables. For **Building**, the variables are preceded by the **public** access modifier. As explained, this allows them to be accessed by code outside of **Building**.

A **class** definition creates a new data type. In this case, the new data type is called **Building**. You will use this name to declare objects of type **Building**. Remember that a **class** declaration is only a type description; it does not create an actual object. Thus, the preceding code does not cause any objects of type **Building** to come into existence.

To actually create a **Building** object, you will use a statement like the following:

```
Building house = new Building(); // create object of type Building
```

After this statement executes, **house** will be an instance of **Building**. Thus, it will have "physical" reality. For the moment, don't worry about the details of this statement.

Each time you create an instance of a class, you are creating an object that contains its own copy of each instance variable defined by the class. Thus, every **Building** object will contain its own copies of the instance variables **floors**, **area**, and **occupants**. To access these variables, you will use the *dot* (.) operator. The dot operator links the name of an object with the name of a member. The general form of the dot operator is shown here:

object.member

Thus, the object is specified on the left, and the member is put on the right. For example, to assign the **floors** variable of **house** the value 2, use the following statement:

```
house.floors = 2;
```

In general, you can use the dot operator to access both instance variables and methods.

Here is a complete program that uses the **Building** class:

```
// A program that uses the Building class.

using System;

class Building {
  public int floors;    // number of floors
  public int area;      // total square footage of building
  public int occupants; // number of occupants
}

// This class declares an object of type Building.
class BuildingDemo {
  public static void Main() {
    Building house = new Building(); // create a Building object
    int areaPP; // area per person

    // assign values to fields in house
    house.occupants = 4;
    house.area = 2500;
    house.floors = 2;

    // compute the area per person
    areaPP = house.area / house.occupants;

    Console.WriteLine("house has:\n   " +
                  house.floors + " floors\n   " +
                  house.occupants + " occupants\n   " +
                  house.area + " total area\n   " +
                  areaPP + " area per person");
  }
}
```

This program consists of two classes: **Building** and **BuildingDemo**. Inside **BuildingDemo**, the **Main( )** method creates an instance of **Building** called **house**. Then the code within **Main( )** accesses the instance variables associated with **house**, assigning them values and using those values. It is important to understand that **Building** and **BuildingDemo** are two separate classes. The only relationship they have to each other is that one class creates an instance of the other. Although they are separate classes, code inside **BuildingDemo** can access the members of **Building** because they are declared **public**. If they had not been given the **public** access specifier, their access would have been limited to the **Building** class, and **BuildingDemo** would not have been able to use them.

Assume that you call the preceding file **UseBuilding.cs**. Compiling this program creates a file called **UseBuilding.exe**. Both the **Building** and **BuildingDemo** classes are automatically part of the executable file. The program displays the following output:

```
house has:
  2 floors
  4 occupants
  2500 total area
  625 area per person
```

Actually, it is not necessary for the **Building** and the **BuildingDemo** class to actually be in the same source file. You could put each class in its own file, called **Building.cs** and **BuildingDemo.cs**, for example. Just tell the C# compiler to compile both files and link them together. For example, you could use this command line to compile the program if you split it into two pieces as just described:

```
csc Building.cs BuildingDemo.cs
```

If you are using the Visual Studio IDE, you will need to add both files to your project and then build.

Before moving on, let's review a fundamental principle: each object has its own copies of the instance variables defined by its class. Thus, the contents of the variables in one object can differ from the contents of the variables in another. There is no connection between the two objects except for the fact that they are both objects of the same type. For example, if you have two **Building** objects, each has its own copy of **floors**, **area**, and **occupants**, and the contents of these can differ between the two objects. The following program demonstrates this fact:

```
// This program creates two Building objects.

using System;
```

```
class Building {
  public int floors;     // number of floors
  public int area;       // total square footage of building
  public int occupants; // number of occupants
}

// This class declares two objects of type Building.
class BuildingDemo {
  public static void Main() {
    Building house = new Building();
    Building office = new Building();

    int areaPP; // area per person

    // assign values to fields in house
    house.occupants = 4;
    house.area = 2500;
    house.floors = 2;

    // assign values to fields in office
    office.occupants = 25;
    office.area = 4200;
    office.floors = 3;

    // compute the area per person in house
    areaPP = house.area / house.occupants;

    Console.WriteLine("house has:\n  " +
                      house.floors + " floors\n  " +
                      house.occupants + " occupants\n  " +
                      house.area + " total area\n  " +
                      areaPP + " area per person");

    Console.WriteLine();

    // compute the area per person in office
    areaPP = office.area / office.occupants;
```

```
        Console.WriteLine("office has:\n   " +
                  office.floors + " floors\n   " +
                  office.occupants + " occupants\n   " +
                  office.area + " total area\n   " +
                  areaPP + " area per person");
    }
}
```

The output produced by this program is shown here:

```
house has:
  2 floors
  4 occupants
  2500 total area
  625 area per person

office has:
  3 floors
  25 occupants
  4200 total area
  168 area per person
```

As you can see, **house**'s data is completely separate from the data contained in **office**. Figure 6-1 depicts this situation.

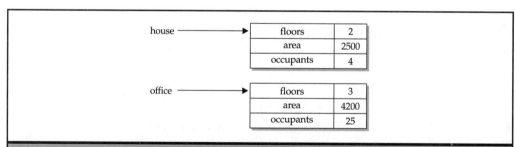

Figure 6-1.   *One object's instance variables are separate from another's*

How Objects Are Created

In the preceding programs, the following line was used to declare an object of type **Building**:

```
Building house = new Building();
```

This declaration performs two functions. First, it declares a variable called **house** of the class type **Building**. This variable does not define an object. Instead, it is simply a variable that can *refer to* an object. Second, the declaration creates an actual, physical copy of the object and assigns to **house** a reference to that object. This is done by using the **new** operator. Thus, after the line executes, **house** refers to an object of type **Building**.

The **new** operator dynamically allocates (that is, allocates at runtime) memory for an object and returns a reference to it. This reference is, more or less, the address in memory of the object allocated by **new**. This reference is then stored in a variable. Thus, in C#, all class objects must be dynamically allocated.

The two steps combined in the preceding statement can be rewritten like this to show each step individually:

```
Building house; // declare reference to object
house = new Building(); // allocate a Building object
```

The first line declares **house** as a reference to an object of type **Building**. Thus, **house** is a variable that can refer to an object, but it is not an object itself. At this point, **house** contains the value **null**, which means that it does not refer to an object. The next line creates a new **Building** object and assigns a reference to it to **house**. Now, **house** is linked with an object.

The fact that class objects are accessed through a reference explains why classes are called *reference types.* The key difference between value types and reference types is what a variable of each type means. For a variable of a value type, the variable, itself, contains the value. For example, given

```
int x;
x = 10;
```

x contains the value 10 because x is a variable of type **int**, which is a value type. However, in the case of

```
Building house = new Building();
```

house does not, itself, contain the object. Instead, it contains a reference to the object.

Reference Variables and Assignment

In an assignment operation, reference variables act differently than do variables of a value type, such as **int**. When you assign one value type variable to another, the situation is straightforward. The variable on the left receives a *copy* of the *value* of the variable on the right. When you assign an object reference variable to another, the situation is a bit more complicated because you are changing the object to which the reference variable refers. The effect of this difference can cause some counterintuitive results. For example, consider the following fragment:

```
Building house1 = new Building();
Building house2 = house1;
```

At first glance, it is easy to think that **house1** and **house2** refer to different objects, but this is not the case. Instead, **house1** and **house2** will both refer to the *same* object. The assignment of **house1** to **house2** simply makes **house2** refer to the same object as does **house1**. Thus, the object can be acted upon by either **house1** or **house2**. For example, after the assignment

```
house1.area = 2600;
```

executes, both of these **WriteLine( )** statements

```
Console.WriteLine(house1.area);
Console.WriteLine(house2.area);
```

display the same value: 2600.

Although **house1** and **house2** both refer to the same object, they are not linked in any other way. For example, a subsequent assignment to **house2** simply changes the object to which **house2** refers. For example:

```
Building house1 = new Building();
Building house2 = house1;
Building house3 = new Building();

house2 = house3; // now house2 and house3 refer to the same object.
```

After this sequence executes, **house2** refers to the same object as **house3**. The object referred to by **house1** is unchanged.

Methods

As explained, instance variables and methods are two of the primary constituents of classes. So far, the **Building** class contains data, but no methods. Although data-only classes are perfectly valid, most classes will have methods. *Methods* are subroutines that manipulate the data defined by the class and, in many cases, provide access to that data. Typically, other parts of your program will interact with a class through its methods.

A method contains one or more statements. In well-written C# code, each method performs only one task. Each method has a name, and it is this name that is used to call the method. In general, you can give a method whatever name you please. However, remember that **Main( )** is reserved for the method that begins execution of your program. Also, don't use C#'s keywords for method names.

When denoting methods in text, this book has used and will continue to use a convention that has become common when writing about C#. A method will have parentheses after its name. For example, if a method's name is **getval**, then it will be written **getval( )** when its name is used in a sentence. This notation will help you distinguish variable names from method names in this book.

The general form of a method is shown here:

```
access ret-type name(parameter-list) {
   // body of method
}
```

Here, *access* is an access modifier that determines what other parts of a program can call the method. As explained earlier, the access modifier is optional. If not present, then the method is private to the class in which it is declared. For now, we will declare all methods as **public** so that they can be called by any other code in the program. The *ret-type* specifies the type of data returned by the method. This can be any valid type, including class types that you create. If the method does not return a value, its return type must be **void**. The name of the method is specified by *name*. This can be any legal identifier other than those already used by other items within the current scope. The *parameter-list* is a sequence of type and identifier pairs separated by commas. Parameters are essentially variables that receive the value of the arguments passed to the method when it is called. If the method has no parameters, then the parameter list will be empty.

Adding a Method to the Building Class

As just explained, the methods of a class typically manipulate and provide access to the data of the class. With this in mind, recall that **Main( )** in the preceding examples computed the area-per-person by dividing the total area by the number of occupants.

While technically correct, this is not the best way to handle this computation. The calculation of area-per-person is something that is best handled by the **Building** class itself. The reason for this conclusion is easy to understand: The area-per-person of a building is dependent upon the values in the **area** and **occupants** fields, which are encapsulated by **Building**. Thus, it is possible for the **Building** class to perform this calculation on its own. Furthermore, by adding this calculation to **Building**, you prevent each program that uses **Building** from having to perform this calculation manually. This prevents the unnecessary duplication of code. Finally, by adding a method to **Building** that computes the area-per-person, you are enhancing its object-oriented structure by encapsulating the quantities that relate directly to a building inside **Building**.

To add a method to **Building**, specify it within **Building**'s declaration. For example, the following version of **Building** contains a method called **areaPerPerson( )** that displays the area-per-person for a building:

```
// Add a method to Building.

using System;

class Building {
  public int floors;    // number of floors
  public int area;      // total square footage of building
  public int occupants; // number of occupants

  // Display the area per person.
  public void areaPerPerson() {
    Console.WriteLine("  " + area / occupants +
                      " area per person");
  }
}

// Use the areaPerPerson() method.
class BuildingDemo {
  public static void Main() {
    Building house = new Building();
    Building office = new Building();


    // assign values to fields in house
    house.occupants = 4;
    house.area = 2500;
    house.floors = 2;
```

```
    // assign values to fields in office
    office.occupants = 25;
    office.area = 4200;
    office.floors = 3;


    Console.WriteLine("house has:\n  " +
                  house.floors + " floors\n  " +
                  house.occupants + " occupants\n  " +
                  house.area + " total area");
    house.areaPerPerson();

    Console.WriteLine();

    Console.WriteLine("office has:\n  " +
                  office.floors + " floors\n  " +
                  office.occupants + " occupants\n  " +
                  office.area + " total area");
    office.areaPerPerson();
  }
}
```

This program generates the following output, which is the same as before:

```
house has:
  2 floors
  4 occupants
  2500 total area
  625 area per person

office has:
  3 floors
  25 occupants
  4200 total area
  168 area per person
```

Let's look at the key elements of this program, beginning with the **areaPerPerson( )** method itself. The first line of **areaPerPerson( )** is

```
public void areaPerPerson() {
```

This line declares a method called **areaPerPerson** that has no parameters. It is specified as **public**, so it can be used by all other parts of the program. Its return type is **void**. Thus, **areaPerPerson( )** does not return a value to the caller. The line ends with the opening curly brace of the method body.

The body of **areaPerPerson( )** consists solely of this statement:

```
Console.WriteLine("   " + area / occupants +
                    " area per person");
```

This statement displays the area-per-person of a building by dividing **area** by **occupants**. Since each object of type **Building** has its own copy of **area** and **occupants**, when **areaPerPerson( )** is called, the computation uses the calling object's copies of those variables.

The **areaPerPerson( )** method ends when its closing curly brace is encountered. This causes program control to transfer back to the caller.

Next, look closely at this line of code from inside **Main( )**:

```
house.areaPerPerson();
```

This statement invokes the **areaPerPerson( )** method on **house**. That is, it calls **areaPerPerson( )** relative to the **house** object, using the object's name followed by the dot operator. When a method is called, program control is transferred to the method. When the method terminates, control is transferred back to the caller, and execution resumes with the line of code following the call.

In this case, the call to **house.areaPerPerson( )** displays the area-per-person of the building defined by **house**. In similar fashion, the call to **office.areaPerPerson( )** displays the area-per-person of the building defined by **office**. Each time **areaPerPerson( )** is invoked, it displays the area-per-person for the specified object.

There is something very important to notice inside the **areaPerPerson( )** method: The instance variables **area** and **occupants** are referred to directly, without preceding them with an object name or the dot operator. When a method uses an instance variable that is defined by its class, it does so directly, without explicit reference to an object and without use of the dot operator. This makes sense if you think about it. A method is always invoked relative to some object of its class. Once this invocation has occurred, the object is known. Thus, within a method, there is no need to specify the object a second time. This means that **area** and **occupants** inside **areaPerPerson( )** implicitly refer to the copies of those variables found in the object that invokes **areaPerPerson( )**.

Returning from a Method

In general, there are two conditions that cause a method to return. The first, as the **areaPerPerson( )** method in the preceding example shows, is when the method's closing curly brace is encountered. The second is when a **return** statement is executed. There are two forms of **return**: one for use in **void** methods (those that do not return a value) and one for returning values. The first form is examined here. The next section explains how to return values.

In a **void** method, you can cause the immediate termination of a method by using this form of **return**:

```
return ;
```

When this statement executes, program control returns to the caller, skipping any remaining code in the method. For example, consider this method:

```
public void myMeth() {
  int i;

  for(i=0; i<10; i++) {
    if(i == 5) return; // stop at 5
    Console.WriteLine();
  }
}
```

Here, the **for** loop will only run from 0 to 5, because once **i** equals 5, the method returns.

It is permissible to have multiple **return** statements in a method, especially when there are two or more routes out of it. For example,

```
public void myMeth() {
  // ...
  if(done) return;
  // ...
  if(error) return;
}
```

Here, the method returns if it is done or if an error occurs. Be careful, however. Having too many exit points in a method can destructure your code, so avoid using them casually.

To review: A **void** method can return in one of two ways—its closing curly brace is reached, or a **return** statement is executed.

Returning a Value

Although methods with a return type of **void** are not rare, most methods will return a value. In fact, the ability to return a value is one of the most useful features of a method. You have already seen an example of a return value: when we used the **Math.Sqrt( )** function to obtain a square root in Chapter 3.

Return values are used for a variety of purposes in programming. In some cases, such as with **Math.Sqrt( )**, the return value contains the outcome of some calculation. In other cases, the return value may simply indicate success or failure. In still others, it may contain a status code. Whatever the purpose, using method return values is an integral part of C# programming.

Methods return a value to the calling routine using this form of **return**:

return *value*;

Here, *value* is the value returned.

You can use a return value to improve the implementation of **areaPerPerson( )**. Instead of displaying the area-per-person, a better approach is to have **areaPerPerson( )** return this value. Among the advantages to this approach is that you can use the value for other calculations. The following example modifies **areaPerPerson( )** to return the area-per-person rather than displaying it:

```
// Return a value from areaPerPerson().

using System;

class Building {
  public int floors;    // number of floors
  public int area;      // total square footage of building
  public int occupants; // number of occupants

  // Return the area per person.
  public int areaPerPerson() {
    return area / occupants;
  }
}

// Use the return value from areaPerPerson().
class BuildingDemo {
  public static void Main() {
    Building house = new Building();
    Building office = new Building();
    int areaPP; // area per person

    // assign values to fields in house
    house.occupants = 4;
    house.area = 2500;
```

```
        house.floors = 2;

        // assign values to fields in office
        office.occupants = 25;
        office.area = 4200;
        office.floors = 3;

        // obtain area per person for house
        areaPP = house.areaPerPerson();

        Console.WriteLine("house has:\n   " +
                        house.floors + " floors\n   " +
                        house.occupants + " occupants\n   " +
                        house.area + " total area\n   " +
                        areaPP + " area per person");


        Console.WriteLine();

        // obtain area per person for office
        areaPP = office.areaPerPerson();

        Console.WriteLine("office has:\n   " +
                        office.floors + " floors\n   " +
                        office.occupants + " occupants\n   " +
                        office.area + " total area\n   " +
                        areaPP + " area per person");
    }
}
```

The output is the same as shown earlier.

In the program, notice that when **areaPerPerson( )** is called, it is put on the right side of an assignment statement. On the left is a variable that will receive the value returned by **areaPerPerson( )**. Thus, after

```
areaPP = house.areaPerPerson();
```

executes, the area-per-person of the **house** object is stored in **areaPP**.

Notice that **areaPerPerson( )** now has a return type of **int**. This means that it will return an integer value to the caller. The return type of a method is important because the type of data returned by a method must be compatible with the return type specified by the method. Thus, if you want a method to return data of type **double**, then its return type must be type **double**.

Although the preceding program is correct, it is not written as efficiently as it could be. Specifically, there is no need for the **areaPP** variable. A call to **areaPerPerson( )** can be used in the **WriteLine( )** statement directly, as shown here:

```
Console.WriteLine("house has:\n   " +
                  house.floors + " floors\n   " +
                  house.occupants + " occupants\n   " +
                  house.area + " total area\n   " +
                  house.areaPerPerson() + " area per person");
```

In this case, when **WriteLine( )** is executed, **house.areaPerPerson( )** is called automatically, and its value will be passed to **WriteLine( )**. Furthermore, you can use a call to **areaPerPerson( )** whenever the area-per-person of a **Building** object is needed. For example, this statement compares the per-person areas of two buildings:

```
if(b1.areaPerPerson() > b2.areaPerPerson())
  Console.WriteLine("b1 has more space for each person");
```

Using Parameters

It is possible to pass one or more values to a method when the method is called. As explained, a value passed to a method is called an *argument*. Inside the method, the variable that receives the argument is called a *parameter*. Parameters are declared inside the parentheses that follow the method's name. The parameter declaration syntax is the same as that used for variables. A parameter is within the scope of its method, and aside from its special task of receiving an argument, it acts like any other local variable.

Here is a simple example that uses a parameter. Inside the **ChkNum** class, the method **isPrime( )** returns **true** if the value that it is passed is prime. It returns **false** otherwise. Therefore, **isPrime( )** has a return type of **bool**.

```
// A simple example that uses a parameter.

using System;

class ChkNum {
  // Return true if x is prime.
  public bool isPrime(int x) {
    for(int i=2; i < x/2 + 1; i++)
```

```
      if((x %i) == 0) return false;

    return true;
  }
}

class ParmDemo {
  public static void Main() {
    ChkNum ob = new ChkNum();

    for(int i=1; i < 10; i++)
      if(ob.isPrime(i)) Console.WriteLine(i + " is prime.");
      else Console.WriteLine(i + " is not prime.");

  }
}
```

Here is the output produced by the program:

```
1 is prime.
2 is prime.
3 is prime.
4 is not prime.
5 is prime.
6 is not prime.
7 is prime.
8 is not prime.
9 is not prime.
```

In the program, **isPrime( )** is called nine times, and each time a different value is passed. Let's look at this process closely. First, notice how **isPrime( )** is called. The argument is specified between the parentheses. When **isPrime( )** is called the first time, it is passed value 1. Thus, when **isPrime( )** begins executing, the parameter **x** receives the value 1. In the second call, 2 is the argument, and **x** then has the value 2. In the third call, the argument is 3, which is the value that **x** receives, and so on. The point is that the value passed as an argument when **isPrime( )** is called is the value received by its parameter, **x**.

A method can have more than one parameter. Simply declare each parameter, separating one from the next with a comma. For example, here the **ChkNum** class is expanded by adding a method called **lcd( )**, which returns the least common denominator for the two values it is passed:

```
// Add a method that takes two arguments.

using System;

class ChkNum {
  // Return true if x is prime.
  public bool isPrime(int x) {
    for(int i=2; i < x/2 + 1; i++)
      if((x %i) == 0) return false;

    return true;
  }

  // Return the least common denominator.
  public int lcd(int a, int b) {
    int max;

    if(isPrime(a) | isPrime(b)) return 1;

    max = a < b ? a : b;

    for(int i=2; i < max/2 + 1; i++)
      if(((a%i) == 0) & ((b%i) == 0)) return i;

    return 1;
  }
}

class ParmDemo {
  public static void Main() {
    ChkNum ob = new ChkNum();
    int a, b;

    for(int i=1; i < 10; i++)
      if(ob.isPrime(i)) Console.WriteLine(i + " is prime.");
      else Console.WriteLine(i + " is not prime.");

    a = 7;
    b = 8;
    Console.WriteLine("Least common denominator for " +
                   a + " and " + b + " is " +
```

```
                              ob.lcd(a, b));

    a = 100;
    b = 8;
    Console.WriteLine("Least common denominator for " +
                      a + " and " + b + " is " +
                      ob.lcd(a, b));

    a = 100;
    b = 75;
    Console.WriteLine("Least common denominator for " +
                      a + " and " + b + " is " +
                      ob.lcd(a, b));

  }
}
```

Notice that when **lcd( )** is called, the arguments are also separated by commas. The output from the program is shown here:

```
1 is prime.
2 is prime.
3 is prime.
4 is not prime.
5 is prime.
6 is not prime.
7 is prime.
8 is not prime.
9 is not prime.
Least common denominator for 7 and 8 is 1
Least common denominator for 100 and 8 is 2
Least common denominator for 100 and 75 is 5
```

When using multiple parameters, each parameter specifies its own type, which can differ from the others. For example, this is perfectly valid:

```
int myMeth(int a, double b, float c) {
  // ...
```

Adding a Parameterized Method to Building

You can use a parameterized method to add a new feature to the **Building** class: the ability to compute the maximum number of occupants for a building assuming that each occupant must have a certain minimal space. This new method is called **maxOccupant( )**. It is shown here:

```
/* Return the maximum number of occupants if each
   is to have at least the specified minimum area. */
public int maxOccupant(int minArea) {
  return area / minArea;
}
```

When **maxOccupant( )** is called, the parameter **minArea** receives the minimum space needed for each occupant. The method divides the total area of the building by this value and returns the result.

The entire **Building** class that includes **maxOccupant( )** is shown here:

```
/*
   Add a parameterized method that computes the
   maximum number of people that can occupy a
   building assuming each needs a specified
   minimum space.
*/

using System;

class Building {
  public int floors;    // number of floors
  public int area;      // total square footage of building
  public int occupants; // number of occupants

  // Return the area per person.
  public int areaPerPerson() {
    return area / occupants;
  }

  /* Return the maximum number of occupants if each
     is to have at least the specified minimum area. */
  public int maxOccupant(int minArea) {
    return area / minArea;
  }
}

// Use maxOccupant().
class BuildingDemo {
```

```
public static void Main() {
  Building house = new Building();
  Building office = new Building();

  // assign values to fields in house
  house.occupants = 4;
  house.area = 2500;
  house.floors = 2;

  // assign values to fields in office
  office.occupants = 25;
  office.area = 4200;
  office.floors = 3;

  Console.WriteLine("Maximum occupants for house if each has " +
                    300 + " square feet: " +
                    house.maxOccupant(300));

  Console.WriteLine("Maximum occupants for office if each has " +
                    300 + " square feet: " +
                    office.maxOccupant(300));
  }
}
```

The output from the program is shown here:

```
Maximum occupants for house if each has 300 square feet: 8
Maximum occupants for office if each has 300 square feet: 14
```

Avoiding Unreachable Code

When creating methods, you must avoid causing a situation in which a portion of code cannot, under any circumstances, be executed. This is called *unreachable code,* and it is considered incorrect in C#. The compiler will issue a warning message if you create a method that contains unreachable code. For example:

```
public void m() {
  char a, b;

  // ...
```

```
   if(a==b) {
     Console.WriteLine("equal");
     return;
   } else {
     Console.WriteLine("not equal");
     return;
   }
   Console.WriteLine("this is unreachable");
}
```

Here, the method **m( )** will always return before the final **WriteLine( )** statement is executed. If you try to compile this method, you will receive a warning. In general, unreachable code constitutes a mistake on your part, so it is a good idea to take unreachable code warnings seriously.

Constructors

In the preceding examples, the instance variables of each **Building** object had to be set manually using of a sequence of statements, such as:

```
house.occupants = 4;
house.area = 2500;
house.floors = 2;
```

An approach like this would never be used in professionally written C# code. Aside from being error prone (you might forget to set one of the fields), there is simply a better way to accomplish this task: the constructor.

A *constructor* initializes an object when it is created. It has the same name as its class and is syntactically similar to a method. However, constructors have no explicit return type. The general form of constructor is shown here:

access class-name( ) {
   // constructor code
}

Typically, you will use a constructor to give initial values to the instance variables defined by the class, or to perform any other startup procedures required to create a fully formed object. Also, usually, *access* is **public** because constructors are normally called from outside their class.

All classes have constructors, whether you define one or not, because C# automatically provides a default constructor that initializes all member variables to zero (for value types) or null (for reference types). However, once you define your own constructor, the default constructor is no longer used.

Here is a simple example that uses a constructor:

```
// A simple constructor.

using System;

class MyClass {
  public int x;

  public MyClass() {
    x = 10;
  }
}

class ConsDemo {
  public static void Main() {
    MyClass t1 = new MyClass();
    MyClass t2 = new MyClass();

    Console.WriteLine(t1.x + " " + t2.x);
  }
}
```

In this example, the constructor for **MyClass** is

```
public MyClass() {
  x = 10;
}
```

Notice that the constructor is specified as **public**. This is because the constructor will be called from code defined outside of its class. This constructor assigns the instance variable **x** of **MyClass** the value 10. This constructor is called by **new** when an object is created. For example, in the line

```
MyClass t1 = new MyClass();
```

the constructor **MyClass( )** is called on the **t1** object, giving **t1.x** the value 10. The same is true for **t2**. After construction, **t2.x** has the value 10. Thus, the output from the program is

```
10 10
```

Parameterized Constructors

In the preceding example, a parameterless constructor was used. While this is fine for some situations, most often you will need a constructor that accepts one or more parameters. Parameters are added to a constructor in the same way that they are added to a method: just declare them inside the parentheses after the constructor's name. For example, here **MyClass** is given a parameterized constructor:

```
// A parameterized constructor.

using System;

class MyClass {
  public int x;

  public MyClass(int i) {
    x = i;
  }
}

class ParmConsDemo {
  public static void Main() {
    MyClass t1 = new MyClass(10);
    MyClass t2 = new MyClass(88);

    Console.WriteLine(t1.x + " " + t2.x);
  }
}
```

The output from this program is shown here:

```
10 88
```

In this version of the program, the **MyClass( )** constructor defines one parameter called **i**, which is used to initialize the instance variable, **x**. Thus, when the line

```
MyClass t1 = new MyClass(10);
```

executes, the value 10 is passed to **i**, which is then assigned to **x**.

Adding a Constructor to the Building Class

We can improve the **Building** class by adding a constructor that automatically initializes the **floors**, **area**, and **occupants** fields when an object is constructed. Pay special attention to how **Building** objects are created.

```
// Add a constructor to Building.

using System;

class Building {
  public int floors;     // number of floors
  public int area;       // total square footage of building
  public int occupants;  // number of occupants

  public Building(int f, int a, int o) {
    floors = f;
    area = a;
    occupants = o;
  }

  // Return the area per person.
  public int areaPerPerson() {
    return area / occupants;
  }

  /* Return the maximum number of occupants if each
     is to have at least the specified minimum area. */
  public int maxOccupant(int minArea) {
    return area / minArea;
  }
}

// Use the parameterized Building constructor.
class BuildingDemo {
  public static void Main() {
    Building house = new Building(2, 2500, 4);
```

```
Building office = new Building(3, 4200, 25);

Console.WriteLine("Maximum occupants for house if each has " +
                  300 + " square feet: " +
                  house.maxOccupant(300));

Console.WriteLine("Maximum occupants for office if each has " +
                  300 + " square feet: " +
                  office.maxOccupant(300));
  }
}
```

The output from this program is the same as for the previous version.

Both **house** and **office** were initialized by the **Building( )** constructor when they were created. Each object is initialized as specified in the parameters to its constructor. For example, in the following line,

```
Building house = new Building(2, 2500, 4);
```

the values 2, 2500, and 4 are passed to the **Building( )** constructor when **new** creates the object. Thus, **house**'s copy of **floors**, **area**, and **occupants** will contain the values 2, 2500, and 4, respectively.

The new Operator Revisited

Now that you know more about classes and their constructors, let's take a closer look at the **new** operator. The **new** operator has this general form:

class-var = new *class-name*( );

Here, *class-var* is a variable of the class type being created. The *class-name* is the name of the class that is being instantiated. The class name followed by parentheses specifies the constructor for the class. If a class does not define its own constructor, **new** will use the default constructor supplied by C#. Thus, **new** can be used to create an object of any class type.

Since memory is finite, it is possible that **new** will not be able to allocate memory for an object because insufficient memory exists. If this happens, a runtime exception will occur. (You will learn how to handle this and other exceptions in Chapter 13.) For the sample programs in this book, you won't need to worry about running out of memory, but you will need to consider this possibility in real-world programs that you write.

Using new with Value Types

At this point, you might be asking why you don't need to use **new** for variables of the value types, such as **int** or **float**? In C#, a variable of a value type contains its own value. Memory to hold this value is automatically allocated by the compiler when a program is compiled. Thus, there is no need to explicitly allocate this memory using **new**. Conversely, a reference variable stores a reference to an object. The memory to hold this object is allocated dynamically, during execution.

Not making the fundamental types, such **int** or **char**, into reference types greatly improves the performance of your program. When using a reference type, there is a layer of indirection that adds overhead to each object access that is avoided by a value type.

As a point of interest, it is permitted to use **new** with the value types, as shown here:

```
int i = new int();
```

Doing so invokes the default constructor for type **int**, which initializes **i** to zero. For example:

```
// Use new with a value type.

using System;

class newValue {
  public static void Main() {
    int i = new int(); // initialize i to zero

    Console.WriteLine("The value of i is: " + i);
  }
}
```

The output from this program is

```
The value of i is: 0
```

As the output verifies, **i** is initialized to zero. Remember, without the use of **new**, **i** would be uninitialized, and it would be an error to attempt to use it in the **WriteLine( )** statement without explicitly giving it a value.

In general, invoking **new** for a value type invokes the default constructor for that type. It does not, however, dynamically allocate memory. Frankly, most programmers do not use **new** with the value types.

Garbage Collection and Destructors

As you have seen, objects are dynamically allocated from a pool of free memory by using the **new** operator. Of course, memory is not infinite, and the free memory can be exhausted. Thus, it is possible for **new** to fail because there is insufficient free memory to create the desired object. For this reason, one of the key components of any dynamic allocation scheme is the recovery of free memory from unused objects, making that memory available for subsequent reallocation. In many programming languages, the release of previously allocated memory is handled manually. For example, in C++, you use the **delete** operator to free memory that was allocated. However, C# uses a different, more trouble-free approach: *garbage collection.*

C#'s garbage collection system reclaims objects automatically—occurring transparently, behind the scenes, without any programmer intervention. It works like this: When no references to an object exist, that object is assumed to be no longer needed, and the memory occupied by the object is released. This recycled memory can then be used for a subsequent allocation.

Garbage collection occurs only sporadically during the execution of your program. It will not occur simply because one or more objects exist that are no longer used. Because garbage collection takes time, the C# runtime system does it only when needed, or at other appropriate times. Thus, you can't know precisely when garbage collection will take place.

Destructors

It is possible to define a method that will be called just prior to an object's final destruction by the garbage collector. This method is called a *destructor,* and it can be used to ensure that an object terminates cleanly. For example, you might use a destructor to make sure that an open file owned by that object is closed.

Destructors have this general form:

```
~class-name( ) {
   // destruction code
}
```

Here, *class-name* is the name of the class. Thus, a destructor is declared like a constructor except that it is preceded with a ~ (tilde). Notice it has no return type.

To add a destructor to a class, you simply include it as a member. It is called whenever an object of its class is about to be recycled. Inside the destructor you will specify those actions that must be performed before an object is destroyed.

It is important to understand that the destructor is called just prior to garbage collection. It is not called when an object goes out of scope, for example. (This differs from destructors in C++, which *are* called when an object goes out of scope.) This means that you cannot know precisely when a destructor will be executed. However, all destructors will be called before a program terminates.

The following program demonstrates a destructor. It works by creating and destroying a large number of objects. During this process, at some point the garbage collector will be activated, and the destructors for the objects will be called.

```csharp
// Demonstrate a destructor.

using System;

class Destruct {
  public int x;

  public Destruct(int i) {
    x = i;
  }

  // called when object is recycled
  ~Destruct() {
    Console.WriteLine("Destructing " + x);
  }

  // generates an object that is immediately destroyed
  public void generator(int i) {
    Destruct o = new Destruct(i);
  }

}

class DestructDemo {
  public static void Main() {
    int count;

    Destruct ob = new Destruct(0);

    /* Now, generate a large number of objects.  At
       some point, garbage collection will occur.
       Note: you might need to increase the number
       of objects generated in order to force
       garbage collection. */

    for(count=1; count < 100000; count++)
```

```
        ob.generator(count);

    Console.WriteLine("Done");
  }
}
```

Here is how the program works. The constructor sets the instance variable **x** to a known value. In this example, **x** is used as an object ID. The destructor displays the value of **x** when an object is recycled. Of special interest is **generator( )**. This method creates and then promptly destroys a **Destruct** object. The **DestructDemo** class creates an initial **Destruct** object called **ob**. Then using **ob**, it creates 100,000 objects by calling **generator( )** on **ob**. This has the net effect of creating and destroying 100,000 objects. At various points in the middle of this process, garbage collection will take place. Precisely how often or when is dependent upon several factors, such as the initial amount of free memory, the operating system, and so on. However, at some point, you will start to see the messages generated by the destructor. If you don't see the messages prior to program termination (that is, before you see the "Done" message), try increasing the number of objects being generated by upping the count in the **for** loop.

Because of the nondeterministic way in which destructors are called, they should not be used to perform actions that must occur at a specific point in your program. One other point: It is possible to request garbage collection. This is described in Part II, when C#'s class library is discussed. However, manually initiating garbage collection is not recommended for most circumstances, because it can lead to inefficiencies. Also, because of the way the garbage collector works, even if you explicitly request garbage collection, there is no way to know precisely when a specific object will be recycled.

The this Keyword

Before concluding this chapter, it is necessary to introduce **this**. When a method is called, it is automatically passed an implicit argument that is a reference to the invoking object (that is, the object on which the method is called). This reference is called **this**. To understand **this**, first consider a program that creates a class called **Rect** that encapsulates the width and height of a rectangle and includes a method called **area( )** that returns its area.

```
using System;

class Rect {
  public int width;
  public int height;
```

```
  public Rect(int w, int h) {
    width = w;
    height = h;
  }

  public int area() {
    return width * height;
  }
}

class UseRect {
  public static void Main() {
    Rect r1 = new Rect(4, 5);
    Rect r2 = new Rect(7, 9);

    Console.WriteLine("Area of r1: " + r1.area());

    Console.WriteLine("Area of r2: " + r2.area());

  }
}
```

As you know, within a method, the other members of a class can be accessed directly, without any object or class qualification. Thus, inside **area( )**, the statement

```
return width * height;
```

means that the copies of **width** and **height** associated with the invoking object will be multiplied together and the result returned. However, the same statement can also be written like this:

```
return this.width * this.height;
```

Here, **this** refers to the object on which **area( )** was called. Thus, **this.width** refers to that object's copy of **width**, and **this.height** refers to that object's copy of **height**. For example, if **area( )** had been invoked on an object called **x**, then **this** in the preceding statement would have been referring to **x**. Writing the statement without using **this** is really just shorthand.

Here is the entire **Rect** class written using the **this** reference:

```
using System;
```

```
class Rect {
  public int width;
  public int height;

  public Rect(int w, int h) {
    this.width = w;
    this.height = h;
  }

  public int area() {
    return this.width * this.height;
  }
}

class UseRect {
  public static void Main() {
    Rect r1 = new Rect(4, 5);
    Rect r2 = new Rect(7, 9);

    Console.WriteLine("Area of r1: " + r1.area());

    Console.WriteLine("Area of r2: " + r2.area());

  }
}
```

Actually, no C# programmer would use **this** as just shown, because nothing is gained, and the standard form is easier. However, **this** has some important uses. For example, the C# syntax permits the name of a parameter or a local variable to be the same as the name of an instance variable. When this happens, the local name *hides* the instance variable. You can gain access to the hidden instance variable by referring to it through **this**. For example, while not recommended style, the following is a syntactically valid way to write the **Rect( )** constructor:

```
public Rect(int width, int height) {
  this.width = width;
  this.height = height;
}
```

In this version, the names of the parameters are the same as the names of the instance variables, thus hiding them; **this** is used to "uncover" the instance variables.

The Complete Reference

Chapter 7

Arrays and Strings

169

This chapter returns to the subject of C#'s data types. It discusses arrays and the **string** type. The **foreach** loop is also examined.

Arrays

An *array* is a collection of variables of the same type that are referred to by a common name. In C#, arrays can have one or more dimensions, although the one-dimensional array is the most common. Arrays are used for a variety of purposes because they offer a convenient means of grouping together related variables. For example, you might use an array to hold a record of the daily high temperature for a month, a list of stock prices, or your collection of programming books.

The principal advantage of an array is that it organizes data in such a way that it can be easily manipulated. For example, if you have an array containing the dividends for a selected group of stocks, it is easy to compute the average income by cycling through the array. Also, arrays organize data in such a way that it can be easily sorted.

Although arrays in C# can be used just like arrays in other programming languages, they have one special attribute: they are implemented as objects. This fact is one reason that a discussion of arrays was deferred until objects had been introduced. By implementing arrays as objects, several important advantages are gained, not the least of which is that unused arrays can be garbage-collected.

One-Dimensional Arrays

A *one-dimensional array* is a list of related variables. Such lists are common in programming. For example, you might use a one-dimensional array to store the account numbers of the active users on a network. Another array might store the current batting averages for a baseball team.

To declare a one-dimensional array, you will use this general form:

type[ ] *array-name* = new *type*[*size*];

Here, *type* declares the base type of the array. The base type determines the data type of each element that comprises the array. Notice the square brackets that follow *type*. They indicate that a one-dimensional array is being declared. The number of elements that the array will hold is determined by *size*. Since arrays are implemented as objects, the creation of an array is a two-step process. First, you declare an array reference variable. Second, you allocate memory for the array, assigning a reference to that memory to the array variable. Thus, arrays in C# are dynamically allocated using the **new** operator.

Note   *If you come from a C or C++ background, pay special attention to the way arrays are declared. Specifically, the square brackets follow the type name, not the array name.*

Here is an example. The following creates an **int** array of ten elements and links it to an array reference variable named **sample**.

```
int[] sample = new int[10];
```

This declaration works just like an object declaration. The **sample** variable holds a reference to the memory allocated by **new**. This memory is large enough to hold ten elements of type **int**.

As with objects, it is possible to break the preceding declaration in two. For example:

```
int[] sample;
sample = new int[10];
```

In this case, when **sample** is first created, it refers to no physical object. It is only after the second statement executes that **sample** is linked with an array.

An individual element within an array is accessed by use of an index. An *index* describes the position of an element within an array. In C#, all arrays have zero as the index of their first element. Because **sample** has ten elements, it has index values of 0 through 9. To index an array, specify the number of the element you want, surrounded by square brackets. Thus, the first element in **sample** is **sample[0]**, and the last element is **sample[9]**. For example, the following program loads **sample** with the numbers 0 through 9:

```
// Demonstrate a one-dimensional array.

using System;

class ArrayDemo {
  public static void Main() {
    int[] sample = new int[10];
    int i;

    for(i = 0; i < 10; i = i+1)
      sample[i] = i;

    for(i = 0; i < 10; i = i+1)
      Console.WriteLine("sample[" + i + "]: " +
                        sample[i]);
  }
}
```

The output from the program is shown here:

```
sample[0]: 0
sample[1]: 1
sample[2]: 2
sample[3]: 3
sample[4]: 4
sample[5]: 5
sample[6]: 6
sample[7]: 7
sample[8]: 8
sample[9]: 9
```

Conceptually, the **sample** array looks like this:

0	1	2	3	4	5	6	7	8	9
sample [0]	sample [1]	sample [2]	sample [3]	sample [4]	sample [5]	sample [6]	sample [7]	sample [8]	sample [9]

Arrays are common in programming because they let you deal easily with large numbers of related variables. For example, the following program finds the average of the set of values stored in the **nums** array by cycling through the array using a **for** loop:

```
// Compute the average of a set of values.

using System;

class Average {
  public static void Main() {
    int[] nums = new int[10];
    int avg = 0;

    nums[0] = 99;
    nums[1] = 10;
    nums[2] = 100;
    nums[3] = 18;
    nums[4] = 78;
    nums[5] = 23;
    nums[6] = 63;
```

```
    nums[7] = 9;
    nums[8] = 87;
    nums[9] = 49;

    for(int i=0; i < 10; i++)
      avg = avg + nums[i];

    avg = avg / 10;

    Console.WriteLine("Average: " + avg);
  }
}
```

The output from the program is shown here:

```
Average: 53
```

Initializing an Array

In the preceding program, the **nums** array was given values by hand, using ten separate assignment statements. While that is perfectly correct, there is an easier way to accomplish this. Arrays can be initialized when they are created. The general form for initializing a one-dimensional array is shown here:

type[ ] *array-name* = { *val1, val2, val3, ..., valN* };

Here, the initial values are specified by *val1* through *valN*. They are assigned in sequence, left to right, in index order. C# automatically allocates an array large enough to hold the intializers that you specify. There is no need to explicitly use the **new** operator. For example, here is a better way to write the **Average** program:

```
// Compute the average of a set of values.

using System;

class Average {
  public static void Main() {
    int[] nums = { 99, 10, 100, 18, 78, 23,
                   63, 9, 87, 49 };
    int avg = 0;;

    for(int i=0; i < 10; i++)
      avg = avg + nums[i];
```

```
    avg = avg / 10;

    Console.WriteLine("Average: " + avg);
  }
}
```

As a point of interest, although not needed, you can use **new** when initializing an array. For example, this is a proper, but redundant, way to initialize **nums** in the foregoing program:

```
int[] nums = new int[] { 99, 10, 100, 18, 78, 23,
                         63, 9, 87, 49 };
```

While redundant here, the **new** form of array initialization is useful when you are assigning a new array to an already existent array reference variable. For example:

```
int[] nums;
nums = new int[] { 99, 10, 100, 18, 78, 23,
                   63, 9, 87, 49 };
```

In this case, **nums** is declared in the first statement and initialized by the second.

One last point: It is permissible to explicitly specify the array size when initializing an array, but the size must agree with the number of initializers. For example, here is another way to initialize **nums**:

```
int[] nums = new int[10] { 99, 10, 100, 18, 78, 23,
                           63, 9, 87, 49 };
```

In this declaration, the size of **nums** is explicitly stated as 10.

Boundaries Are Enforced

Array boundaries are strictly enforced in C#; it is a runtime error to overrun or underrun the end of an array. If you want to confirm this for yourself, try the following program that purposely overruns an array:

```
// Demonstrate an array overrun.

using System;

class ArrayErr {
```

```
public static void Main() {
  int[] sample = new int[10];
  int i;

  // generate an array overrun
  for(i = 0; i < 100; i = i+1)
    sample[i] = i;
}
}
```

As soon as **i** reaches 10, an **IndexOutOfRangeException** is generated and the program is terminated.

Multidimensional Arrays

Although the one-dimensional array is the most commonly used array in programming, multidimensional arrays are certainly not rare. A *multidimensional array* is an array that has two or more dimensions, and an individual element is accessed through the combination of two or more indices.

Two-Dimensional Arrays

The simplest form of the multidimensional array is the two-dimensional array. In a two-dimensional array, the location of any specific element is specified by two indices. If you think of a two-dimensional array as a table of information, one index indicates the row, the other indicates the column.

To declare a two-dimensional integer array called **table** of size 10, 20, you would write

```
int[,] table = new int[10, 20];
```

Pay careful attention to the declaration. Notice that the two dimensions are separated from each other by a comma. In the first part of the declaration, the syntax

```
[,]
```

indicates that a two-dimensional array reference variable is being created. When memory is actually allocated for the array using **new**, this syntax is used:

```
int[10, 20]
```

This creates a 10×20 array, and again, the comma separates the dimensions.

To access an element in a two-dimensional array, you must specify both indices, separating the two with a comma. For example, to assign location 3, 5 of array **table** the value 10, you would use

```
table[3, 5] = 10;
```

Here is a complete example. It loads a two-dimensional array with the numbers 1 through 12 and then displays the contents of the array.

```
// Demonstrate a two-dimensional array.

using System;

class TwoD {
  public static void Main() {
    int t, i;
    int[,] table = new int[3, 4];

    for(t=0; t < 3; ++t) {
      for(i=0; i < 4; ++i) {
        table[t,i] = (t*4)+i+1;
        Console.Write(table[t,i] + " ");
      }
      Console.WriteLine();
    }
  }
}
```

In this example, **table[0, 0]** will have the value 1, **table[0, 1]** the value 2, **table[0, 2]** the value 3, and so on. The value of **table[2, 3]** will be 12. Conceptually, the array will look like that shown in Figure 7-1.

Note	*If you come from a C, C++, or Java background, be careful when declaring or accessing multidimensional arrays. In these other languages, array dimensions and indices are specified within their own set of brackets. C# separates dimensions using commas.*

Arrays of Three or More Dimensions

C# allows arrays with more than two dimensions. Here is the general form of a multidimensional array declaration:

type[, ...,] *name* = new *type*[*size1, size2, ..., sizeN*];

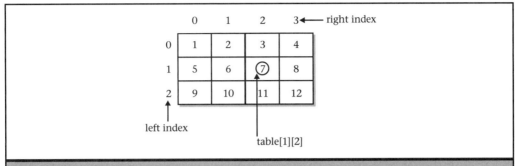

Figure 7-1. *A conceptual view of the **table** array created by the **TwoD** program*

For example, the following declaration creates a 4×10×3 three-dimensional integer array:

```
int[,,] multidim = new int[4, 10, 3];
```

To assign element 2, 4, 1 of **multidim** the value 100, use this statement:

```
multidim[2, 4, 1] = 100;
```

Here is a program that uses a three-dimensional array that holds a 3×3×3 matrix of values. It then sums the values on one of the diagonals through the cube.

```
// Sum the values on a diagonal of a 3x3x3 matrix.

using System;

class ThreeDMatrix {
  public static void Main() {
    int[,,] m = new int[3, 3, 3];
    int sum = 0;
    int n = 1;

    for(int x=0; x < 3; x++)
      for(int y=0; y < 3; y++)
        for(int z=0; z < 3; z++)
          m[x, y, z] = n++;
```

```
    sum = m[0,0,0] + m[1,1,1] + m[2, 2, 2];

    Console.WriteLine("Sum of first diagonal: " + sum);
  }
}
```

The output is shown here:

```
Sum of first diagonal: 42
```

Initializing Multidimensional Arrays

A multidimensional array can be initialized by enclosing each dimension's initializer list within its own set of curly braces. For example, the general form of array initialization for a two-dimensional array is shown here:

type[,] array_name = {
  { *val, val, val, ..., val* },
  { *val, val, val, ..., val* },
 .
 .
 .
  { *val, val, val, ..., val* }
};

Here, *val* indicates an initialization value. Each inner block designates a row. Within each row, the first value will be stored in the first position of the array, the second value in the second position, and so on. Notice that commas separate the initializer blocks and that a semicolon follows the closing }.

For example, the following program initializes an array called **sqrs** with the numbers 1 through 10 and their squares.

```
// Initialize a two-dimensional array.

using System;

class Squares {
  public static void Main() {
    int[,] sqrs = {
      { 1, 1 },
      { 2, 4 },
      { 3, 9 },
```

```
        { 4, 16 },
        { 5, 25 },
        { 6, 36 },
        { 7, 49 },
        { 8, 64 },
        { 9, 81 },
        { 10, 100 }
      };
      int i, j;

      for(i=0; i < 10; i++) {
        for(j=0; j < 2; j++)
          Console.Write(sqrs[i,j] + " ");
        Console.WriteLine();
      }
    }
}
```

Here is the output from the program:

```
1 1
2 4
3 9
4 16
5 25
6 36
7 49
8 64
9 81
10 100
```

Jagged Arrays

In the preceding examples, when you created a two-dimensional array, you were creating what C# calls a *rectangular array*. Thinking of two-dimensional arrays as tables, a rectangular array is a two-dimensional array in which the length of each row is the same for the entire array. However, C# also allows you to create a special type of two-dimensional array called a *jagged array*. A jagged array is an *array of arrays* in which the length of each array can differ. Thus, a jagged array can be used to create a table in which the lengths of the rows are not the same.

Jagged arrays are declared by using sets of square brackets to indicate each dimension. For example, to declare a two-dimensional jagged array, you will use this general form:

type[ ] [ ] *array-name* = new *type*[*size*][ ];

Here, *size* indicates the number of rows in the array. The rows, themselves, have not been allocated. Instead, the rows are allocated individually. This allows for the length of each row to vary. For example, the following code allocates memory for the first dimension of **jagged** when it is declared. It then allocates the second dimensions manually.

```
int[][] jagged = new int[3][];
jagged[0] = new int[4];
jagged[1] = new int[3];
jagged[2] = new int[5];
```

After this sequence executes, **jagged** looks like this:

jagged [0][0]	jagged [0][1]	jagged [0][2]	jagged [0][3]

jagged [1][0]	jagged [1][1]	jagged [1][2]

jagged [2][0]	jagged [2][1]	jagged [2][2]	jagged [2][3]	jagged [2][4]

It is easy to see how jagged arrays got their name!

Once a jagged array has been created, an element is accessed by specifying each index within its own set of brackets. For example, to assign the value 10 to element 2, 1 of **jagged**, you would use this statement:

```
jagged[2][1] = 10;
```

Note that this differs from the syntax that is used to access an element of a rectangular array.

The following program demonstrates the creation of a jagged two-dimensional array:

```
// Demonstrate jagged arrays.

using System;
```

```
class Jagged {
  public static void Main() {
    int[][] jagged = new int[3][];
    jagged[0] = new int[4];
    jagged[1] = new int[3];
    jagged[2] = new int[5];

    int i;

    // store values in first array
    for(i=0; i < 4; i++)
      jagged[0][i] = i;

    // store values in second array
    for(i=0; i < 3; i++)
      jagged[1][i] = i;

    // store values in third array
    for(i=0; i < 5; i++)
      jagged[2][i] = i;


    // display values in first array
    for(i=0; i < 4; i++)
      Console.Write(jagged[0][i] + " ");

    Console.WriteLine();

    // display values in second array
    for(i=0; i < 3; i++)
      Console.Write(jagged[1][i] + " ");

    Console.WriteLine();

    // display values in third array
    for(i=0; i < 5; i++)
      Console.Write(jagged[2][i] + " ");

    Console.WriteLine();
  }
}
```

The output is shown here:

```
0 1 2 3
0 1 2
0 1 2 3 4
```

Jagged arrays are not used by all applications, but they can be effective in some situations. For example, if you need a very large two-dimensional array that is sparsely populated (that is, one in which not all of the elements will be used), then an irregular array might be a perfect solution.

One last point: Since jagged arrays are arrays of arrays, there is no requirement that each array be of the same kind. For example, the following creates an array of two-dimensional arrays:

```
int[][,] jagged = new int[3][,];
```

The next statement assigns **jagged[0]** a reference to a 4 by 2 array:

```
jagged[0] = new int[4, 2];
```

The following statement assigns a value to **jagged[0][1,0]**:

```
jagged[0][1,0] = i;
```

Assigning Array References

Like other objects, when you assign one array reference variable to another, you are simply changing the object to which the variable refers. You are not causing a copy of the array to be made, nor are you causing the contents of one array to be copied to the other. For example, consider this program:

```
// Assigning array reference variables.

using System;

class AssignARef {
  public static void Main() {
    int i;

    int[] nums1 = new int[10];
```

```
    int[] nums2 = new int[10];

    for(i=0; i < 10; i++) nums1[i] = i;

    for(i=0; i < 10; i++) nums2[i] = -i;

    Console.Write("Here is nums1: ");
    for(i=0; i < 10; i++)
      Console.Write(nums1[i] + " ");
    Console.WriteLine();

    Console.Write("Here is nums2: ");
    for(i=0; i < 10; i++)
      Console.Write(nums2[i] + " ");
    Console.WriteLine();

    nums2 = nums1; // now nums2 refers to nums1

    Console.Write("Here is nums2 after assignment: ");
    for(i=0; i < 10; i++)
      Console.Write(nums2[i] + " ");
    Console.WriteLine();

   // now operate on nums1 array through nums2
   nums2[3] = 99;

    Console.Write("Here is nums1 after change through nums2: ");
    for(i=0; i < 10; i++)
      Console.Write(nums1[i] + " ");
    Console.WriteLine();
  }
}
```

The output from the program is shown here:

```
Here is nums1: 0 1 2 3 4 5 6 7 8 9
Here is nums2: 0 -1 -2 -3 -4 -5 -6 -7 -8 -9
Here is nums2 after assignment: 0 1 2 3 4 5 6 7 8 9
Here is nums1 after change through nums2: 0 1 2 99 4 5 6 7 8 9
```

As the output shows, after the assignment of **nums1** to **nums2**, both array reference variables refer to the same object.

Using the Length Property

A number of benefits result because C# implements arrays as objects. One comes from the fact that each array has associated with it a **Length** property that contains the number of elements that the array can hold. Thus, each array carries with it a field that contains the array's length. Here is a program that demonstrates this property:

```
// Use the Length array property.

using System;

class LengthDemo {
  public static void Main() {
    int[] nums = new int[10];

    Console.WriteLine("Length of nums is " + nums.Length);

    // use Length to initialize nums
    for(int i=0; i < nums.Length; i++)
      nums[i] = i * i;

    // now use Length to display nums
    Console.Write("Here is nums: ");
    for(int i=0; i < nums.Length; i++)
      Console.Write(nums[i] + " ");

    Console.WriteLine();
  }
}
```

This program displays the following output:

```
Length of nums is 10
Here is nums: 0 1 4 9 16 25 36 49 64 81
```

In **LengthDemo** notice the way that **nums.Length** is used by the **for** loops to govern the number of iterations that take place. Since each array carries with it its own length, you can use this information rather than manually keeping track of an array's size. Keep in mind that the value of **Length** has nothing to do with the number of elements that are actually in use. It contains the number of elements that the array is capable of holding.

When the length of a multidimensional array is obtained, the total number of elements that can be held by the array is returned. For example:

```
// Use the Length array property on a 3-D array.

using System;

class LengthDemo3D {
  public static void Main() {
    int[,,] nums = new int[10, 5, 6];

    Console.WriteLine("Length of nums is " + nums.Length);

  }
}
```

The output is shown here:

```
Length of nums is 300
```

As the output verifies, **Length** obtains the number of elements that **nums** can hold, which is 300 (10×5×6) in this case. It is not possible to obtain the length of a specific dimension.

The inclusion of the **Length** property simplifies many algorithms by making certain types of array operations easier—and safer—to perform. For example, the following program uses **Length** to reverse the contents of an array by copying it back-to-front into another array:

```
// Reverse an array.

using System;

class RevCopy {
  public static void Main() {
    int i,j;
    int[] nums1 = new int[10];
    int[] nums2 = new int[10];

    for(i=0; i < nums1.Length; i++) nums1[i] = i;

    Console.Write("Original contents: ");
```

```
    for(i=0; i < nums2.Length; i++)
      Console.Write(nums1[i] + " ");

    Console.WriteLine();

    // reverse copy nums1 to nums2
    if(nums2.Length >= nums1.Length) // make sure nums2 is long enough
      for(i=0, j=nums1.Length-1; i < nums1.Length; i++, j--)
        nums2[j] = nums1[i];

    Console.Write("Reversed contents: ");
    for(i=0; i < nums2.Length; i++)
      Console.Write(nums2[i] + " ");

    Console.WriteLine();
  }
}
```

Here is the output:

```
Original contents: 0 1 2 3 4 5 6 7 8 9
Reversed contents: 9 8 7 6 5 4 3 2 1 0
```

Here, **Length** helps perform two important functions. First, it is used to confirm that the target array is large enough to hold the contents of the source array. Second, it provides the termination condition of the **for** loop that performs the reverse copy. Of course, in this simple example, the size of the arrays is easily known, but this same approach can be applied to a wide range of more challenging situations.

Using Length with Jagged Arrays

A special case occurs when **Length** is used with jagged arrays. In this situation, it is possible to obtain the length of each individual array. For example, consider the following program, which simulates the CPU activity on a network with four nodes:

```
// Demonstrate Length with jagged arrays.

using System;

class Jagged {
  public static void Main() {
```

```
    int[][] network_nodes = new int[4][];
    network_nodes[0] = new int[3];
    network_nodes[1] = new int[7];
    network_nodes[2] = new int[2];
    network_nodes[3] = new int[5];


    int i, j;

    // fabricate some fake CPU usage data
    for(i=0; i < network_nodes.Length; i++)
      for(j=0; j < network_nodes[i].Length; j++)
        network_nodes[i][j] = i * j + 70;


    Console.WriteLine("Total number of network nodes: " +
                  network_nodes.Length + "\n");

    for(i=0; i < network_nodes.Length; i++) {
      for(j=0; j < network_nodes[i].Length; j++) {
        Console.Write("CPU usage at node " + i +
                  " CPU " + j + ": ");
        Console.Write(network_nodes[i][j] + "% ");
        Console.WriteLine();
      }
      Console.WriteLine();
    }

  }
}
```

The output is shown here:

```
Total number of network nodes: 4

CPU usage at node 0 CPU 0: 70%
CPU usage at node 0 CPU 1: 70%
CPU usage at node 0 CPU 2: 70%

CPU usage at node 1 CPU 0: 70%
CPU usage at node 1 CPU 1: 71%
```

```
CPU usage at node 1 CPU 2: 72%
CPU usage at node 1 CPU 3: 73%
CPU usage at node 1 CPU 4: 74%
CPU usage at node 1 CPU 5: 75%
CPU usage at node 1 CPU 6: 76%

CPU usage at node 2 CPU 0: 70%
CPU usage at node 2 CPU 1: 72%

CPU usage at node 3 CPU 0: 70%
CPU usage at node 3 CPU 1: 73%
CPU usage at node 3 CPU 2: 76%
CPU usage at node 3 CPU 3: 79%
CPU usage at node 3 CPU 4: 82%
```

Pay special attention to the way **Length** is used on the jagged array **network_nodes**. Recall, a two-dimensional jagged array is an array of arrays. Thus, when the expression

```
network_nodes.Length
```

is used, it obtains the number of *arrays* stored in **network_nodes**, which is 4 in this case. To obtain the length of any individual array in the jagged array, you will use an expression such as this,

```
network_nodes[0].Length
```

which, in this case, obtains the length of the first array.

The foreach Loop

In Chapter 5 it was mentioned that C# defines a loop called **foreach**, but a discussion of that statement was deferred until later. The time for that discussion has now come.

The **foreach** loop is used to cycle through the elements of a *collection*. A collection is a group of objects. C# defines several types of collections, of which one is an array. The general form of **foreach** is shown here:

foreach(*type var-name* in *collection*) *statement*;

Here, *type var-name* specifies the type and name of an *iteration variable* that will receive the values of the elements from the collection as the **foreach** iterates. The collection being cycled through is specified by *collection*, which, for this discussion, is an array.

Thus, *type* must be the same as (or compatible with) the base type of the array. One important point to remember is that the iteration variable is read-only as far as the array is concerned. Thus, you can't change the contents of the array by assigning the iteration variable a new value.

Here is a simple example that uses **foreach**. It creates an array of integers and gives it some initial values. It then displays those values, computing the summation in the process.

```
// Use the foreach loop.

using System;

class ForeachDemo {
  public static void Main() {
    int sum = 0;
    int[] nums = new int[10];

    // give nums some values
    for(int i = 0; i < 10; i++)
      nums[i] = i;

    // use foreach to display and sum the values
    foreach(int x in nums) {
      Console.WriteLine("Value is: " + x);
      sum += x;
    }
    Console.WriteLine("Summation: " + sum);
  }
}
```

The output from the program is shown here:

```
Value is: 0
Value is: 1
Value is: 2
Value is: 3
Value is: 4
Value is: 5
Value is: 6
Value is: 7
Value is: 8
Value is: 9
Summation: 45
```

As this output shows, the **foreach** cycles through an array in sequence from the lowest index to the highest.

Although the **foreach** loop iterates until all elements in an array have been examined, it is possible to terminate a **foreach** loop early by using a **break** statement. For example, this program sums only the first five elements of **nums**:

```
// Use break with a foreach.

using System;

class ForeachDemo {
  public static void Main() {
    int sum = 0;
    int[] nums = new int[10];

    // give nums some values
    for(int i = 0; i < 10; i++)
      nums[i] = i;

    // use foreach to display and sum the values
    foreach(int x in nums) {
      Console.WriteLine("Value is: " + x);
      sum += x;
      if(x == 4) break; // stop the loop when 4 is obtained
    }
    Console.WriteLine("Summation of first 5 elements: " + sum);
  }
}
```

This is the output produced:

```
Value is: 0
Value is: 1
Value is: 2
Value is: 3
Value is: 4
Summation of first 5 elements: 10
```

As is evident, the **foreach** loop stops after the fifth element has been obtained.

The **foreach** also works on multidimensional arrays. It returns those elements in row order, from first to last.

```
// Use foreach on a two-dimensional array.

using System;

class ForeachDemo2 {
  public static void Main() {
    int sum = 0;
    int[,] nums = new int[3,5];

    // give nums some values
    for(int i = 0; i < 3; i++)
      for(int j=0; j < 5; j++)
        nums[i,j] = (i+1)*(j+1);

    // use foreach to display and sum the values
    foreach(int x in nums) {
      Console.WriteLine("Value is: " + x);
      sum += x;
    }
    Console.WriteLine("Summation: " + sum);
  }
}
```

The output from this program is shown here:

```
Value is: 1
Value is: 2
Value is: 3
Value is: 4
Value is: 5
Value is: 2
Value is: 4
Value is: 6
Value is: 8
Value is: 10
Value is: 3
Value is: 6
Value is: 9
Value is: 12
Value is: 15
Summation: 90
```

Since the **foreach** can only cycle through an array sequentially, from start to finish, you might think that its use is limited. However, this is not true. A large number of algorithms require exactly this mechanism, of which one of the most common is searching. For example, the following program uses a **foreach** loop to search an array for a value. It stops if the value is found.

```csharp
// Search an array using foreach.

using System;

class Search {
  public static void Main() {
    int[] nums = new int[10];
    int val;
    bool found = false;

    // give nums some values
    for(int i = 0; i < 10; i++)
      nums[i] = i;

    val = 5;

    // use foreach to search nums for key
    foreach(int x in nums) {
      if(x == val) {
        found = true;
        break;
      }
    }

    if(found)
      Console.WriteLine("Value found!");
  }
}
```

Other types of **foreach** applications include such things as computing an average, finding the minimum or maximum of a set, looking for duplicates, and so on. As you will see later in this book, the **foreach** is especially useful when operating on other types of collections.

Strings

From a day-to-day programming standpoint, one of the most important of C#'s data types is **string**. **string** defines and supports character strings. In many other programming languages a string is an array of characters. This is not the case with C#. In C#, strings are objects. Thus, **string** is a reference type. Although **string** is a built-in data type in C#, a discussion of **string** needed to wait until classes and objects had been introduced.

Actually, you have been using the **string** class since Chapter 2, but you did not know it. When you create a string literal, you are actually creating a **string** object. For example, in the statement

```
Console.WriteLine("In C#, strings are objects.");
```

the string "In C#, strings are objects." is automatically made into a **string** object by C#. Thus, the use of the **string** class has been "below the surface" in the preceding programs. In this section you will learn to handle them explicitly.

Constructing Strings

The easiest way to construct a **string** is to use a string literal. For example, here **str** is a **string** reference variable that is assigned a reference to a string literal:

```
string str = "C# strings are powerful.";
```

In this case, **str** is initialized to the character sequence "C# strings are powerful."

You can also create a **string** from a **char** array. For example:

```
char[] charray = {'t', 'e', 's', 't'};
string str = new string(charray);
```

Once you have created a **string** object, you can use it anywhere that a quoted string is allowed. For example, you can use a **string** object as an argument to **WriteLine( )**, as shown in this example:

```
// Introduce string.

using System;
```

```
class StringDemo {
  public static void Main() {

    char[] charray = {'A', ' ', 's', 't', 'r', 'i', 'n', 'g', '.' };
    string str1 = new string(charray);
    string str2 = "Another string.";

    Console.WriteLine(str1);
    Console.WriteLine(str2);
  }
}
```

The output from the program is shown here:

```
A string.
Another string.
```

Operating on Strings

The **string** class contains several methods that operate on strings. Table 7-1 shows a few.

The **string** type also includes the **Length** property, which contains the length of the string.

To obtain the value of an individual character of a string, you simply use an index. For example:

```
string str = "test";
Console.WriteLine(str[0]);
```

This displays t, the first character of "test". Like arrays, string indexes begin at zero. One important point, however, is that you cannot assign a new value to a character within a string using an index. An index can only be used to obtain a character.

To test two strings for equality, you can use the = = operator. Normally, when the = = operator is applied to object references, it determines if both references refer to the same object. This differs for objects of type **string**. When the = = is applied to two **string** references, the contents of the strings, themselves, are compared for equality. The same is true for the != operator: when comparing **string** objects, the contents of the strings are compared. However, the other relational operators, such as < or >=, compare the references, just like they do for other types of objects.

Method	Description
static string Copy(string *str*)	Returns a copy of *str*.
int CompareTo(string *str*)	Returns less than zero if the invoking string is less than *str*, greater than zero if the invoking string is greater than *str*, and zero if the strings are equal.
int IndexOf(string *str*)	Searches the invoking string for the substring specified by *str*. Returns the index of the first match, or –1 on failure.
int LastIndexOf(string *str*)	Searches the invoking string for the substring specified by *str*. Returns the index of the last match, or –1 on failure.
string ToLower( )	Returns a lowercase version of the invoking string.
string ToUpper( )	Returns an uppercase version of the invoking string.

Table 7-1. *Common String Handling Methods*

Here is a program that demonstrates several string operations:

```
// Some string operations.

using System;

class StrOps {
  public static void Main() {
    string str1 =
      "When it comes to  .NET programming, C# is #1.",
    string str2 = string.Copy(str1);
    string str3 = "C# strings are powerful.";
    string strUp, strLow;
    int result, idx;

    Console.WriteLine("str1: " + str1);
```

```
    Console.WriteLine("Length of str1: " +
                      str1.Length);

    // create upper- and lowercase versions of str1
    strLow = str1.ToLower();
    strUp =  str1.ToUpper();
    Console.WriteLine("Lowercase version of str1:\n    " +
                      strLow);
    Console.WriteLine("Uppercase version of str1:\n    " +
                      strUp);

    Console.WriteLine();

    // display str1, one char at a time.
    Console.WriteLine("Display str1, one char at a time.");
    for(int i=0; i < str1.Length; i++)
      Console.Write(str1[i]);
    Console.WriteLine("\n");

    // compare strings
    if(str1 == str2)
      Console.WriteLine("str1 == str2");
    else
      Console.WriteLine("str1 != str2");

    if(str1 == str3)
      Console.WriteLine("str1 == str3");
    else
      Console.WriteLine("str1 != str3");

    result = str1.CompareTo(str3);
    if(result == 0)
      Console.WriteLine("str1 and str3 are equal");
    else if(result < 0)
      Console.WriteLine("str1 is less than str3");
    else
      Console.WriteLine("str1 is greater than str3");

    Console.WriteLine();

    // assign a new string to str2
    str2 = "One Two Three One";
```

```
    // search string
    idx = str2.IndexOf("One");
    Console.WriteLine("Index of first occurrence of One: " + idx);
    idx = str2.LastIndexOf("One");
    Console.WriteLine("Index of last occurrence of One: " + idx);

  }
}
```

This program generates the following output:

```
str1: When it comes to .NET programming, C# is #1.
Length of str1: 44
Lowercase version of str1:
    when it comes to .net programming, c# is #1.
Uppercase version of str1:
    WHEN IT COMES TO .NET PROGRAMMING, C# IS #1.

Display str1, one char at a time.
When it comes to .NET programming, C# is #1.

str1 == str2
str1 != str3
str1 is greater than str3

Index of first occurrence of One: 0
Index of last occurrence of One: 14
```

You can concatenate (join together) two strings using the + operator. For example, this statement:

```
string str1 = "One";
string str2 = "Two";
string str3 = "Three";
string str4 = str1 + str2 + str3;
```

initializes **str4** with the string "OneTwoThree".

One other point: The **string** keyword is an *alias* for (that is, maps directly to) the **System.String** class defined by the .NET Framework class library. Thus, the fields and methods defined by **string** are those of the **System.String** class, which includes more than the sampling described here. **System.String** is examined in detail in Part II.

Arrays of Strings

Like any other data type, strings can be assembled into arrays. For example:

```
// Demonstrate string arrays.

using System;

class StringArrays {
  public static void Main() {
    string[] str = { "This", "is", "a", "test." };

    Console.WriteLine("Original array: ");
    for(int i=0; i < str.Length; i++)
      Console.Write(str[i] + " ");
    Console.WriteLine("\n");

    // change a string
    str[1] = "was";
    str[3] = "test, too!";

    Console.WriteLine("Modified array: ");
    for(int i=0; i < str.Length; i++)
      Console.Write(str[i] + " ");
  }
}
```

Here is the output from this program:

```
Original array:
This is a test.

Modified array:
This was a test, too!
```

Here is a more interesting example. The following program displays an integer value using words. For example, the value 19 would display as "one nine".

```
// Display the digits of an integer using words.

using System;

class ConvertDigitsToWords {
```

```
public static void Main() {
    int num;
    int nextdigit;
    int numdigits;
    int[] n = new int[20];

    string[] digits = { "zero", "one", "two",
                        "three", "four", "five",
                        "six", "seven", "eight",
                        "nine" };

    num = 1908;

    Console.WriteLine("Number: " + num);

    Console.Write("Number in words: ");

    nextdigit = 0;
    numdigits = 0;

    /* Get individual digits and store in n.
       These digits are stored in reverse order. */
    do {
        nextdigit = num % 10;
        n[numdigits] = nextdigit;
        numdigits++;
        num = num / 10;
    } while(num > 0);
    numdigits--;

    // display words
    for( ; numdigits >= 0; numdigits--)
        Console.Write(digits[n[numdigits]] + " ");

    Console.WriteLine();
  }
}
```

The output is shown here:

```
Number: 1908
Number in words: one nine zero eight
```

In the program, the **string** array **digits** holds in order the word equivalents of the digits from zero to nine. The program converts an integer into words by first obtaining each digit of the value, beginning with the rightmost, and storing those digits, in reverse order, in the **int** array called **n**. Then, this array is cycled through from back to front. In the process, each integer value in **n** is used as an index into **digits**, with the corresponding string being displayed.

Strings Are Immutable

Here is something that might surprise you: The contents of a **string** object are immutable. That is, once created, the character sequence comprising that string cannot be altered. This restriction allows C# to implement strings more efficiently. Even though this probably sounds like a serious drawback, it isn't. When you need a string that is a variation on one that already exists, simply create a new string that contains the desired changes. Since unused string objects are automatically garbage-collected, you don't even need to worry about what happens to the discarded strings.

It must be made clear, however, that **string** reference variables may, of course, change the object to which they refer. It is just that the contents of a specific **string** object cannot be changed after it is created.

To fully understand why immutable strings are not a hindrance, we will use another of **string**'s methods: **Substring( )**. The **Substring( )** method returns a new string that contains a specified portion of the invoking string. Because a new **string** object is manufactured that contains the substring, the original string is unaltered, and the rule of immutability is still intact. The form of **Substring( )** that we will be using is shown here:

string Substring(int *start*, int *len*)

Here, *start* specifies the beginning index, and *len* specifies the length of the substring.

Here is a program that demonstrates **Substring( )** and the principle of immutable strings:

```
// Use Substring().

using System;

class SubStr {
  public static void Main() {
    string orgstr = "C# makes strings easy.";

    // construct a substring
    string substr = orgstr.Substring(5, 12);

    Console.WriteLine("orgstr: " + orgstr);
    Console.WriteLine("substr: " + substr);
```

```
    }
}
```

Here is the output from the program:

```
orgstr: C# makes strings easy.
substr: kes strings
```

As you can see, the original string **orgstr** is unchanged and **substr** contains the substring.

One more point: Although the immutability of **string** objects is not usually a restriction or hindrance, there may be times when it would be beneficial to be able to modify a string. To allow this, C# offers a class called **StringBuilder**, which is in the **System.Text** namespace. It creates string objects that can be changed. For most purposes, however, you will want to use **string**, not **StringBuilder**.

Strings Can Be Used in switch Statements

A **string** can be used to control a **switch** statement. It is the only non-**int** type that can be used in the **switch**. The fact that strings can be used in **switch** statements makes it possible to handle some situations quite easily. For example, the following program displays the digit equivalent of the words "one," "two," and "three":

```
// A string can control a switch statement.

using System;

class StringSwitch {
  public static void Main() {
    string[] strs = { "one", "two", "three", "two", "one" };

    foreach(string s in strs) {
      switch(s) {
        case "one":
          Console.Write(1);
          break;
        case "two":
          Console.Write(2);
          break;
        case "three":
```

```
        Console.Write(3);
        break;
    }
  }
  Console.WriteLine();

  }
}
```

The output is shown here:

```
12321
```

Chapter 8

A Closer Look at Methods and Classes

T his chapter resumes the examination of classes and methods. It begins by explaining how to control access to the members of a class. It then discusses the passing and returning of objects, method overloading, the various forms of **Main( )**, recursion, and the use of the keyword **static**.

Controlling Access to Class Members

In its support for encapsulation, the class provides two major benefits. First, it links data with code. You have been taking advantage of this aspect of the class since Chapter 6. Second, it provides the means by which access to members can be controlled. It is this second feature that is examined here.

Although C#'s approach is a bit more sophisticated, in essence, there are two basic types of class members: public and private. A public member can be freely accessed by code defined outside of its class. This is the type of class member that we have been using up to this point. A private member can be accessed only by methods defined by its class. It is through the use of private members that access is controlled.

Restricting access to a class' members is a fundamental part of object-oriented programming because it helps prevent the misuse of an object. By allowing access to private data only through a well-defined set of methods, you can prevent improper values from being assigned to that data—by performing a range-check, for example. It is not possible for code outside the class to set the value of a private member directly. You can also control precisely how and when the data within an object is used. Thus, when correctly implemented, a class creates a "black box" that can be used, but the inner workings of which are not open to tampering.

C#'s Access Specifiers

Member access control is achieved through the use of four *access specifiers*: **public**, **private**, **protected**, and **internal**. In this chapter we will be concerned with **public** and **private**. The **protected** modifier applies only when inheritance is involved and is described in Chapter 9. The **internal** modifier applies mostly to the use of an *assembly*, which for C# loosely means a program. The **internal** modifier is examined in Chapter 16.

When a member of a class is modified by the **public** specifier, that member can be accessed by any other code in your program. This includes methods defined inside other classes.

When a member of a class is specified as **private**, then that member can be accessed only by other members of its class. Thus, methods in other classes are not able to access a **private** member of another class. As explained in Chapter 6, if no access specifier is used, a class member is private to its class by default. Thus, the **private** specifier is optional when creating private class members.

An access specifier precedes the rest of a member's type specification. That is, it must begin a member's declaration statement. Here are some examples:

```
public string errMsg;
private double bal;
private bool isError(byte status) { // ...
```

To understand the difference between **public** and **private**, consider the following program:

```
// Public vs private access.

using System;

class MyClass {
  private int alpha; // private access explicitly specified
  int beta;          // private access by default
  public int gamma;  // public access

  /* Methods to access alpha and beta.  It is OK for a
     member of a class to access a private member
     of the same class.
  */
  public void setAlpha(int a) {
    alpha = a;
  }

  public int getAlpha() {
    return alpha;
  }

  public void setBeta(int a) {
    beta = a;
  }

  public int getBeta() {
    return beta;
  }
}

class AccessDemo {
  public static void Main() {
    MyClass ob = new MyClass();

    /* Access to alpha and beta is allowed only
```

```
      through methods. */
   ob.setAlpha(-99);
   ob.setBeta(19);
   Console.WriteLine("ob.alpha is " + ob.getAlpha());
   Console.WriteLine("ob.beta is " + ob.getBeta());

   // You cannot access alpha or beta like this:
// ob.alpha = 10; // Wrong! alpha is private!
// ob.beta = 9;   // Wrong! beta is private!

   // It is OK to directly access gamma because it is public.
   ob.gamma = 99;
   }
}
```

As you can see, inside the **MyClass** class, **alpha** is specified as **private**, **beta** is private by default, and **gamma** is specified as **public**. Because **alpha** and **beta** are private, they cannot be accessed by code outside of their class. Therefore, inside the **AccessDemo** class, neither can be used directly. Each must be accessed through public methods, such as **setAlpha( )** and **getAlpha( )**. For example, if you were to remove the comment symbol from the beginning of the following line,

```
// ob.alpha = 10; // Wrong! alpha is private!
```

you would not be able to compile this program because of the access violation. Although access to **alpha** by code outside of **MyClass** is not allowed, methods defined within **MyClass** can freely access it, as the **setAlpha( )** and **getAlpha( )** methods show. The same is true for **beta**.

The key point is this: A private member can be used freely by other members of its class, but it cannot be accessed by code outside its class.

Applying Public and Private Access

The proper use of public and private access is a key component of successful object-oriented programming. Although there are no hard and fast rules, here are some general principles that serve as guidelines:

1. Members of a class that are used only within the class itself should be private.

2. Instance data that must be within a specific range should be private, with access provided through public methods that can perform range checks.

3. If changing a member can cause an effect that extends beyond the member itself (that is, affects other aspects of the object), that member should be private, and access to it should be controlled.

4. Members that can cause harm to an object when improperly used should be private. Access to these members should be through public methods that prevent improper usage.

5. Methods that get and set the values of private data must be public.

6. Public instance variables are permissible when there is no reason for them to be private.

Of course, there are many nuances that the preceding rules do not address, and special cases cause one or more rules to be violated. But in general, if you follow these rules, you will be creating resilient objects that are not easily misused.

Controlling Access: A Case Study

To better understand the "how and why" behind access control, a case study is useful. One of the quintessential examples of object-oriented programming is a class that implements a stack. As you probably know, a stack is a data structure that implements a first-in, last-out list. Its name comes from the analogy of a stack of plates on a table. The first plate on the table is the last one to be used.

A stack is a classic example of object-oriented programming because it combines storage for information along with the methods that access that information. Thus, a stack is a *data engine* that enforces the first-in, last-out usage. Such a combination is an excellent choice for a class in which the members that provide storage for the stack are private, and public methods provide access. By encapsulating the underlying storage, it is not possible for code that uses the stack to access the elements out of order.

A stack defines two basic operations: *push* and *pop*. A push puts a value onto the top of the stack. A pop removes a value from the top of the stack. Thus, a pop is consumptive; once a value has been popped off the stack, it has been removed and cannot be accessed again.

The example shown here creates a class called **Stack** that implements a stack. The underlying storage for the stack is provided by a private array. The push and pop operations are available through the public methods of the **Stack** class. Thus, the public methods enforce the first-in, last-out mechanism. As shown here, the **Stack** class stores characters, but the same mechanism could be used to store any type of data:

```
// A stack class for characters.

using System;

class Stack {
```

```csharp
// these members are private
char[] stck; // holds the stack
int tos;     // index of the top of the stack

// Construct an empty Stack given its size.
public Stack(int size) {
  stck = new char[size]; // allocate memory for stack
  tos = 0;
}

// Push characters onto the stack.
public void push(char ch) {
  if(tos==stck.Length) {
    Console.WriteLine(" -- Stack is full.");
    return;
  }

  stck[tos] = ch;
  tos++;
}

// Pop a character from the stack.
public char pop() {
  if(tos==0) {
    Console.WriteLine(" -- Stack is empty.");
    return (char) 0;
  }

  tos--;
  return stck[tos];
}

// Return true if the stack is full.
public bool full() {
  return tos==stck.Length;
}

// Return true if the stack is empty.
public bool empty() {
  return tos==0;
}
```

```
  // Return total capacity of the stack.
  public int capacity() {
    return stck.Length;
  }

  // Return number of objects currently on the stack.
  public int getNum() {
    return tos;
  }
}
```

Let's examine this class closely. The **Stack** class begins by declaring these two instance variables:

```
// these members are private
char[] stck; // holds the stack
int tos;     // index of the top of the stack
```

The **stck** array provides the underlying storage for the stack, which in this case holds characters. Notice that no array is allocated. The allocation of the actual array is handled by the **Stack** constructor. The **tos** member holds the index of the top of the stack.

Both the **tos** and **stck** members are private. This enforces the first-in, last-out stack mechanism. If public access to **stck** were allowed, then the elements on the stack could be accessed out of order. Also, since **tos** holds the index of the top element in the stack, manipulations of **tos** by code outside the **Stack** class must be prevented in order to avoid corruption of the stack. Access to **stck** and **tos** are available, indirectly, to the user of **Stack** through the various public methods described shortly.

The stack constructor is shown next:

```
// Construct an empty Stack given its size.
public Stack(int size) {
  stck = new char[size]; // allocate memory for stack
  tos = 0;
}
```

The constructor is passed the desired size of the stack. It allocates the underlying array and sets **tos** to zero. Thus, a zero value in **tos** indicates that the stack is empty.

The public **push( )** method puts an element onto the stack. It is shown here:

```
// Push characters onto the stack.
public void push(char ch) {
```

```
  if(tos==stck.Length) {
    Console.WriteLine(" -- Stack is full.");
    return;
  }

  stck[tos] = ch;
  tos++;
}
```

The element to be pushed onto the stack is passed in **ch**. Before the element is added to the stack, a check is made to ensure that there is still room in the underlying array. This is done by making sure that **tos** does not exceed the length of **stck**. If there is still room, the element is stored in **stck** at the index specified by **tos**, and then **tos** is incremented. Thus, **tos** always contains the index of the next free element in **stck**.

To remove an element from the stack, call the public method **pop( )**. It is shown here:

```
// Pop a character from the stack.
public char pop() {
  if(tos==0) {
    Console.WriteLine(" -- Stack is empty.");
    return (char) 0;
  }

  tos--;
  return stck[tos];
}
```

Here, the value of **tos** is checked. If it is zero, the stack is empty. Otherwise, **tos** is decremented, and the element at that index is returned.

Although a **push( )** and **pop( )** are the only methods needed to implement a stack, some others are quite useful, and the **Stack** class defines four more. These are **full( )**, **empty( )**, **capacity( )**, and **getNum( )**, and they provide information about the state of the stack. They are shown here:

```
// Return true if the stack is full.
public bool full() {
  return tos==stck.Length;
}

// Return true if the stack is empty.
public bool empty() {
  return tos==0;
```

```
    }

    // Return total capacity of the stack.
    public int capacity() {
      return stck.Length;
    }

    // Return number of objects currently on the stack.
    public int getNum() {
      return tos;
    }
```

The **full( )** method returns **true** when the stack is full and **false** otherwise. The **empty( )** method returns **true** when the stack is empty, and **false** otherwise. To obtain the total capacity of the stack (that is, the total number of elements it can hold), call **capacity( )**. To obtain the number of elements currently stored on the stack, call **getNum( )**. These methods are useful because the information they provide requires access to **tos**, which is private. They are also examples of how public methods can provide safe access to private members.

The following program demonstrates the stack:

```
// Demonstrate the Stack class.

using System;

class StackDemo {
  public static void Main() {
    Stack stk1 = new Stack(10);
    Stack stk2 = new Stack(10);
    Stack stk3 = new Stack(10);
    char ch;
    int i;

    // Put some characters into stk1.
    Console.WriteLine("Push A through Z onto stk1.");
    for(i=0; !stk1.full(); i++)
      stk1.push((char) ('A' + i));

    if(stk1.full()) Console.WriteLine("stk1 is full.");

    // Display the contents of stk1.
    Console.Write("Contents of stk1: ");
```

```
   while( !stk1.empty() ) {
     ch = stk1.pop();
     Console.Write(ch);
   }

   Console.WriteLine();

   if(stk1.empty()) Console.WriteLine("stk1 is empty.\n");

   // put more characters into stk1
   Console.WriteLine("Again push A through Z onto stk1.");
   for(i=0; !stk1.full(); i++)
     stk1.push((char) ('A' + i));

   /* Now, pop from stk1 and push the element in stk2.
      This causes stk2 to hold the elements in
      reverse order. */
   Console.WriteLine("Now, pop chars from stk1 and push " +
                      "them onto stk2.");
   while( !stk1.empty() ) {
     ch = stk1.pop();
     stk2.push(ch);
   }

   Console.Write("Contents of stk2: ");
   while( !stk2.empty() ) {
     ch = stk2.pop();
     Console.Write(ch);
   }

   Console.WriteLine("\n");

   // put 5 characters into stack
   Console.WriteLine("Put 5 characters on stk3.");
   for(i=0; i < 5; i++)
     stk3.push((char) ('A' + i));

   Console.WriteLine("Capacity of stk3: " + stk3.capacity());
   Console.WriteLine("Number of objects in stk3: " +
                      stk3.getNum());

  }
}
```

The output from the program is shown here:

```
Push A through Z onto stk1.
stk1 is full.
Contents of stk1: JIHGFEDCBA
stk1 is empty.

Again push A through Z onto stk1.
Now, pop chars from stk1 and push them onto stk2.
Contents of stk2: ABCDEFGHIJ

Put 5 characters on stk3.
Capacity of stk3: 10
Number of objects in stk3: 5
```

Pass Objects to Methods

Up to this point, the examples in this book have been using value types, such as **int** or **double**, as parameters to methods. However, it is both correct and common to pass objects to methods. For example, consider the following program:

```
// Objects can be passed to methods.

using System;

class MyClass {
  int alpha, beta;

  public MyClass(int i, int j) {
    alpha = i;
    beta = j;
  }

  /* Return true if ob contains the same values
     as the invoking object. */
  public bool sameAs(MyClass ob) {
    if((ob.alpha == alpha) & (ob.beta == beta))
      return true;
    else return false;
  }

  // Make a copy of ob.
```

```
    public void copy(MyClass ob) {
      alpha = ob.alpha;
      beta  = ob.beta;
    }

    public void show() {
      Console.WriteLine("alpha: {0}, beta: {1}",
                         alpha, beta);
    }
  }

  class PassOb {
    public static void Main() {
      MyClass ob1 = new MyClass(4, 5);
      MyClass ob2 = new MyClass(6, 7);

      Console.Write("ob1: ");
      ob1.show();

      Console.Write("ob2: ");
      ob2.show();

      if(ob1.sameAs(ob2))
        Console.WriteLine("ob1 and ob2 have the same values.");
      else
        Console.WriteLine("ob1 and ob2 have different values.");

      Console.WriteLine();

      // now, make ob1 a copy of ob2
      ob1.copy(ob2);

      Console.Write("ob1 after copy: ");
      ob1.show();

      if(ob1.sameAs(ob2))
        Console.WriteLine("ob1 and ob2 have the same values.");
      else
        Console.WriteLine("ob1 and ob2 have different values.");

    }
  }
```

This program generates the following output:

```
ob1: alpha: 4, beta: 5
ob2: alpha: 6, beta: 7
ob1 and ob2 have different values.

ob1 after copy: alpha: 6, beta: 7
ob1 and ob2 have the same values.
```

The **sameAs( )** and **copy( )** methods each take an object as an argument. The **sameAs( )** method compares the values of **alpha** and **beta** in the invoking object with the values of **alpha** and **beta** in the object passed as an argument in **ob**. The method returns **true** only if the two objects contain the same values for these instance variables. The **copy( )** method assigns the values of **alpha** and **beta** in the object passed in **ob** to **alpha** and **beta** in the invoking object. In both cases, notice that the parameter **ob** specifies **MyClass** as its type. As this example shows, syntactically, object types are passed to methods in the same way as are the value types.

How Arguments Are Passed

As the preceding example demonstrated, passing an object to a method is a straightforward task. However, there are some nuances that the example did not show. In certain cases, the effects of passing an object will be different than those experienced when passing nonobject arguments. To see why, let's review the two ways in which an argument can be passed to a subroutine.

The first way is *call-by-value.* This method copies the *value* of an argument into the formal parameter of the subroutine. Therefore, changes made to the parameter of the subroutine have no effect on the argument used in the call. The second way an argument can be passed is *call-by-reference.* In this method, a reference to an argument (not the value of the argument) is passed to the parameter. Inside the subroutine, this reference is used to access the actual argument specified in the call. This means that changes made to the parameter will affect the argument used to call the subroutine. As you will see, C# can use both methods.

When you pass a value type, such as **int** or **double**, to a method, it is passed by value. Thus, what occurs to the parameter that receives the argument has no effect outside the method. For example, consider the following program:

```
// Simple types are passed by value.

using System;

class Test {
```

```
/* This method causes no change to the arguments
   used in the call. */
public void noChange(int i, int j) {
  i = i + j;
  j = -j;
}
}

class CallByValue {
  public static void Main() {
    Test ob = new Test();

    int a = 15, b = 20;

    Console.WriteLine("a and b before call: " +
                      a + " " + b);

    ob.noChange(a, b);

    Console.WriteLine("a and b after call: " +
                      a + " " + b);
  }
}
```

The output from this program is shown here:

```
a and b before call: 15 20
a and b after call: 15 20
```

As you can see, the operations that occur inside **noChange( )** have no effect on the values of **a** and **b** used in the call.

When you pass an object reference to a method, the situation is a bit more complicated. Technically, the object reference, itself, is passed by value. Thus, a copy of the reference is made and changes to the parameter will not affect the argument. (For example, making the parameter refer to a new object will not change the object to which the argument refers.) However—and this is a big however—changes *made to the object* being referred to by the parameter *will* affect the object referred to by the argument. Let's see why.

Recall that when you create a variable of a class type, you are only creating a reference to an object. Thus, when you pass this reference to a method, the parameter that receives it will refer to the same object as that referred to by the argument. This effectively means that objects are passed to methods by use of call-by-reference.

Changes to the object inside the method *do* affect the object used as an argument. For example, consider the following program:

```
// Objects are passed by reference.

using System;

class Test {
  public int a, b;

  public Test(int i, int j) {
    a = i;
    b = j;
  }

  /* Pass an object. Now, ob.a and ob.b in object
     used in the call will be changed. */
  public void change(Test ob) {
    ob.a = ob.a + ob.b;
    ob.b = -ob.b;
  }
}

class CallByRef {
  public static void Main() {
    Test ob = new Test(15, 20);

    Console.WriteLine("ob.a and ob.b before call: " +
                      ob.a + " " + ob.b);

    ob.change(ob);

    Console.WriteLine("ob.a and ob.b after call: " +
                      ob.a + " " + ob.b);
  }
}
```

This program generates the following output:

```
ob.a and ob.b before call: 15 20
ob.a and ob.b after call: 35 -20
```

As you can see, in this case, the actions inside **change( )** have affected the object used as an argument.

To review: When an object reference is passed to a method, the reference itself is passed by use of call-by-value. Thus, a copy of that reference is made. However, since the value being passed refers to an object, the copy of that value will still refer to the same object as its corresponding argument.

Using ref and out Parameters

As just explained, value types, such as **int** or **char**, are passed by value to a method. This means that changes to the parameter that receives a value type will not affect the actual argument used in the call. You can, however, alter this behavior. Through the use of the **ref** and **out** keywords, it is possible to pass any of the value types by reference. Doing so allows a method to change the argument used in the call.

Before going into the mechanics of using **ref** and **out**, it is useful to understand why you might want to pass a value type by reference. In general, there are two reasons: to allow a method to alter the contents of its arguments or to allow a method to return more than one value. Let's look at each reason in detail.

Often you will want a method to be able to operate on the actual arguments that are passed to it. The quintessential example of this is a **swap( )** method that exchanges the values of its two arguments. Since value types are passed by value, it is not possible to write a method that swaps the value of two **int**s, for example, using C#'s default call-by-value parameter passing mechanism. The **ref** modifier solves this problem.

As you know, a **return** statement enables a method to return a value to its caller. However, a method can return *only one* value each time it is called. What if you need to return two or more pieces of information? For example, what if you want to create a method that decomposes a floating-point number into its integer and fractional parts? To do this requires that two pieces of information be returned: the integer portion and the fractional component. This method cannot be written using only a single return value. The **out** modifier solves this problem.

Using ref

The **ref** parameter modifier causes C# to create a call-by-reference, rather than a call-by-value. The **ref** modifier is used when the method is declared and when it is called. Let's begin with a simple example. The following program creates a method called **sqr( )** that returns in-place the square of its integer argument. Notice the use and placement of **ref**.

```
// Use ref to pass a value type by reference.

using System;
```

```
class RefTest {
  /* This method changes its argument.
     Notice the use of ref. */
  public void sqr(ref int i) {
    i = i * i;
  }
}

class RefDemo {
  public static void Main() {
    RefTest ob = new RefTest();

    int a = 10;

    Console.WriteLine("a before call: " + a);

    ob.sqr(ref a); // notice the use of ref

    Console.WriteLine("a after call: " + a);
  }
}
```

Notice that **ref** precedes the entire parameter declaration in the method and that it precedes the name of the argument when the method is called. The output from this program, shown here, confirms that the value of the argument, **a**, was indeed modified by **sqr( )**:

```
a before call: 10
a after call: 100
```

Using **ref**, it is now possible to write a method that exchanges the values of its two value-type arguments. For example, here is a program that contains a method called **swap( )** that exchanges the values of the two integer arguments with which it is called:

```
// Swap two values.

using System;

class Swap {
  // This method now changes its arguments.
  public void swap(ref int a, ref int b) {
    int t;
```

```
      t = a;
      a = b;
      b = t;
   }
}

class SwapDemo {
  public static void Main() {
    Swap ob = new Swap();

    int x = 10, y = 20;

    Console.WriteLine("x and y before call: " + x + " " + y);

    ob.swap(ref x, ref y);

    Console.WriteLine("x and y after call: " + x + " " + y);
  }
}
```

The output from this program is shown here:

```
x and y before call: 10 20
x and y after call: 20 10
```

Here is one important point to understand about **ref**: An argument passed by **ref** must be assigned a value prior to the call. The reason is that the method that receives such an argument assumes that the parameter refers to a valid value. Thus, using **ref**, you cannot use a method to give an argument an initial value.

Using out

Sometimes you will want to use a reference parameter to receive a value from a method, but not pass in a value. For example, you might have a method that performs some function, such as opening a network socket, that returns a success/fail code in a reference parameter. In this case, there is no information to pass into the method, but there is information to pass back out. The problem with this scenario is that a **ref** parameter must be initialized to a value prior to the call. Thus, to use a **ref** parameter would require giving the argument a dummy value just to satisfy this constraint. Fortunately, C# provides a better alternative: the **out** parameter.

An **out** parameter is similar to a **ref** parameter with this one exception: It can only be used to pass a value out of a method. It is not necessary (or useful) to give the variable used as an **out** parameter an initial value prior to calling the method. The method will give the variable a value. Furthermore, inside the method, an **out** parameter is always considered *unassigned*, that is, it is assumed to have no initial value. Instead, the method *must* assign the parameter a value prior to the method's termination. Thus, after the call to the method, an **out** parameter will contain a value.

Here is an example that uses an **out** parameter. In the class **Decompose**, the **parts( )** method decomposes a floating-point number into its integer and fractional parts. Notice how each component is returned to the caller.

```
// Use out.

using System;

class Decompose {

  /* Decompose a floating-point value into its
     integer and fractional parts. */
  public int parts(double n, out double frac) {
    int whole;

    whole = (int) n;
    frac = n - whole; // pass fractional part back through frac
    return whole; // return integer portion
  }
}

class UseOut {
  public static void Main() {
    Decompose ob = new Decompose();
    int i;
    double f;

    i = ob.parts(10.125, out f);

    Console.WriteLine("Integer portion is " + i);
    Console.WriteLine("Fractional part is " + f);
  }
}
```

The output from the program is shown here:

```
Integer portion is 10
Fractional part is 0.125
```

The **parts( )** method returns two pieces of information. First, the integer portion of **n** is returned as **parts( )**'s return value. Second, the fractional portion of **n** is passed back to the caller through the **out** parameter **frac**. As this example shows, by using **out**, it is possible for one method to return two values.

Of course, you are not limited to only one **out** parameter. A method can return as many pieces of information as necessary through **out** parameters. Here is an example that uses two **out** parameters. The method **isComDenom( )** performs two functions. First, it determines if two integers have a common denominator. It returns **true** if they do and **false** otherwise. Second, if they do have a common denominator, **isComDenom( )** returns the least and greatest common denominators in **out** parameters.

```
// Use two out parameters.

using System;

class Num {
  /* Determine if x and v have a common denominator.
     If so, return least and greatest common denominators in
     the out parameters. */
  public bool isComDenom(int x, int y,
                         out int least, out int greatest) {
    int i;
    int max = x < y ? x : y;
    bool first = true;

    least = 1;
    greatest = 1;

    // find least and greatest common denominators
    for(i=2; i <= max/2 + 1; i++) {
      if( ((y%i)==0) & ((x%i)==0) ) {
        if(first) {
          least = i;
          first = false;
        }
```

```
        greatest = i;
      }
    }

    if(least != 1) return true;
    else return false;
  }
}

class DemoOut {
  public static void Main() {
    Num ob = new Num();
    int lcd, gcd;

    if(ob.isComDenom(231, 105, out lcd, out gcd)) {
      Console.WriteLine("Lcd of 231 and 105 is " + lcd);
      Console.WriteLine("Gcd of 231 and 105 is " + gcd);
    }
    else
      Console.WriteLine("No common denominator for 35 and 49.");

    if(ob.isComDenom(35, 51, out lcd, out gcd)) {
      Console.WriteLine("Lcd of 35 and 51 " + lcd);
      Console.WriteLine("Gcd of 35 and 51 is " + gcd);
    }
    else
      Console.WriteLine("No common denominator for 35 and 51.");

  }
}
```

In **Main( )**, notice that **lcd** and **gcd** are not assigned values prior to the call to **isComDenom( )**. This would be an error if the parameters had been **ref** rather than **out**. The method returns either **true** or **false**, depending upon whether the two integers have a common denominator. If they do, the least and greatest common denominators are returned in the **out** parameters. The output from this program is shown here:

```
Lcd of 231 and 105 is 3
Gcd of 231 and 105 is 21
No common denominator for 35 and 51.
```

Using ref and out on Reference Parameters

The use of **ref** and **out** is not limited to value parameters. They can also be used on reference parameters, such as when an object reference is passed. When **ref** or **out** modifies a reference parameter, it causes the reference, itself, to be passed by reference. This allows a method to change the object to which the reference refers. Consider the following program, which uses **ref** reference parameters to exchange the objects to which two references are referring:

```
// Swap two references.

using System;

class RefSwap {
  int a, b;

  public RefSwap(int i, int j) {
    a = i;
    b = j;
  }

  public void show() {
    Console.WriteLine("a: {0}, b: {1}", a, b);
  }

  // This method changes its arguments.
  public void swap(ref RefSwap ob1, ref RefSwap ob2) {
    RefSwap t;

    t = ob1;
    ob1 = ob2;
    ob2 = t;
  }
}

class RefSwapDemo {
  public static void Main() {
    RefSwap x = new RefSwap(1, 2);
    RefSwap y = new RefSwap(3, 4);

    Console.Write("x before call: ");
    x.show();
```

```
      Console.Write("y before call: ");
      y.show();

      Console.WriteLine();

      // exchange the objects to which x and y refer
      x.swap(ref x, ref y);

      Console.Write("x after call: ");
      x.show();

      Console.Write("y after call: ");
      y.show();

    }
  }
```

The output from this program is shown here:

```
x before call: a: 1, b: 2
y before call: a: 3, b: 4

x after call: a: 3, b: 4
y after call: a: 1, b: 2
```

In this example, the method **swap( )** exchanges the objects to which the two arguments
to **swap( )** refer. Before calling **swap( )**, **x** refers to an object that contains the values 1
and 2, and **y** refers to an object that contains the values 3 and 4. After the call to **swap( )**, **x**
refers to the object that contains the values 3 and 4, and **y** refers to the object that contains
the values 1 and 2. If **ref** parameters had not been used, then the exchange inside **swap( )**
would have had no effect outside **swap( )**. You might want to prove this by removing
ref from **swap( )**.

Using a Variable Number of Arguments

When you create a method, you usually know in advance the number of arguments
that you will be passing to it, but this is not always the case. Sometimes you will want
to create a method that can be passed an arbitrary number of arguments. For example,
consider a method that finds the smallest of a set of values. Such a method might be
passed as few as two values, or three, or four, and so on. In all cases, you want that
method to return the smallest value. Such a method cannot be created using normal

parameters. Instead, you must use a special type of parameter that stands for an arbitrary number of parameters. This is done by creating a **params** parameter.

The **params** modifier is used to declare an array parameter that will be able to receive zero or more arguments. The number of elements in the array will be equal to the number of arguments passed to the method. Your program then accesses the array to obtain the arguments.

Here is an example that uses **params** to create a method called **minVal( )**, which returns the minimum value from a set of values:

```
// Demonstrate params.

using System;

class Min {
  public int minVal(params int[] nums) {
    int m;

    if(nums.Length == 0) {
      Console.WriteLine("Error: no arguments.");
      return 0;
    }

    m = nums[0];
    for(int i=1; i < nums.Length; i++)
      if(nums[i] < m) m = nums[i];

    return m;
  }
}

class ParamsDemo {
  public static void Main() {
    Min ob = new Min();
    int min;
    int a = 10, b = 20;

    // call with two values
    min = ob.minVal(a, b);
    Console.WriteLine("Minimum is " + min);

    // call with 3 values
    min = ob.minVal(a, b, -1);
```

```
    Console.WriteLine("Minimum is " + min);

    // call with 5 values
    min = ob.minVal(18, 23, 3, 14, 25);
    Console.WriteLine("Minimum is " + min);

    // can call with an int array, too
    int[] args = { 45, 67, 34, 9, 112, 8 };
    min = ob.minVal(args);
    Console.WriteLine("Minimum is " + min);
  }
}
```

The output from the program is shown here:

```
Minimum is 10
Minimum is -1
Minimum is 3
Minimum is 8
```

Each time **minVal( )** is called, the arguments are passed to it via the **nums** array. The length of the array equals the number of elements. Thus, you can use **minVal( )** to find the minimum of any number of values.

Although you can pass a **params** parameter any number of arguments, they all must be of a type compatible with the array type specified by the parameter. For example, calling **minVal( )** like this:

```
    min = ob.minVal(1, 2.2);
```

is illegal because there is no automatic conversion from **double** (2.2) to **int**, which is the type of **nums** in **minVal( )**.

When using **params**, you need to be careful about boundary conditions because a **params** parameter can accept any number of arguments—*even zero*! For example, it is syntactically valid to call **minVal( )** as shown here:

```
min = ob.minVal(); // no arguments
min = ob.minVal(3); // 1 argument
```

This is why there is a check in **minVal( )** to confirm that at least one element is in the **nums** array before there is an attempt to access that element. If the check were not there, then a runtime exception would result if **minVal( )** were called with no arguments.

(Later in this book when exceptions are discussed, you will see a better way to handle these types of errors.) Furthermore, the code in **minVal( )** was written in such a way as to permit calling **minVal( )** with one argument. In that situation, the lone argument is returned.

A method can have normal parameters and a variable-length parameter. For example, in the following program, the method **showArgs( )** takes one **string** parameter and then a **params** integer array:

```
// Use regular parameter with a params parameter.

using System;

class MyClass {
  public void showArgs(string msg, params int[] nums) {
    Console.Write(msg + ": ");

    foreach(int i in nums)
      Console.Write(i + " ");

    Console.WriteLine();
  }
}

class ParamsDemo2 {
  public static void Main() {
    MyClass ob = new MyClass();

    ob.showArgs("Here are some integers",
                1, 2, 3, 4, 5);

    ob.showArgs("Here are two more",
                17, 20);

  }
}
```

This program displays the following output:

```
Here are some integers: 1 2 3 4 5
Here are two more: 17 20
```

In cases where a method has regular parameters and a **params** parameter, the **params** parameter must be the last one in the parameter list. Furthermore, in all situations, there must be only one **params** parameter.

Returning Objects

A method can return any type of data, including class types. For example, the following version of the **Rect** class includes a method called **enlarge( )** that creates a rectangle that is proportionally the same as the invoking rectangle, but larger by a specified factor:

```
// Return an object.

using System;

class Rect {
  int width;
  int height;

  public Rect(int w, int h) {
    width = w;
    height = h;
  }

  public int area() {
    return width * height;
  }

  public void show() {
    Console.WriteLine(width + " " + height);
  }

  /* Return a rectangle that is a specified
     factor larger than the invoking rectangle. */
  public Rect enlarge(int factor) {
    return new Rect(width * factor, height * factor);
  }
}

class RetObj {
  public static void Main() {
    Rect r1 = new Rect(4, 5);
```

```
      Console.Write("Dimensions of r1: ");
      r1.show();
      Console.WriteLine("Area of r1: " + r1.area());

      Console.WriteLine();

      // create a rectangle that is twice as big as r1
      Rect r2 = r1.enlarge(2);

      Console.Write("Dimensions of r2: ");
      r2.show();
      Console.WriteLine("Area of r2 " + r2.area());
   }
}
```

The output is shown here:

```
Dimensions of r1: 4 5
Area of r1: 20

Dimensions of r2: 8 10
Area of r2 80
```

When an object is returned by a method, it remains in existence until there are no more references to it. At that point it is subject to garbage collection. Thus, an object won't be destroyed just because the method that created it terminates.

One application of object return types is the *class factory*. A class factory is a method that is used to construct objects of its class. In some situations you may not want to give users of a class access to the class' constructor because of security concerns, or because object construction depends upon certain external factors. In such cases, a class factory is used to construct objects. Here is a simple example:

```
// Use a class factory.

using System;

class MyClass {
   int a, b; // private

   // Create a class factory for MyClass.
   public MyClass factory(int i, int j) {
```

```
    MyClass t = new MyClass();

    t.a = i;
    t.b = j;

    return t; // return an object
  }

  public void show() {
    Console.WriteLine("a and b: " + a + " " + b);
  }

}

class MakeObjects {
  public static void Main() {
    MyClass ob = new MyClass();
    int i, j;

    // generate objects using the factory
    for(i=0, j=10; i < 10; i++, j--) {
      MyClass anotherOb = ob.factory(i, j); // make an object
      anotherOb.show();
    }

    Console.WriteLine();
  }
}
```

The output is shown here:

```
a and b: 0 10
a and b: 1 9
a and b: 2 8
a and b: 3 7
a and b: 4 6
a and b: 5 5
a and b: 6 4
a and b: 7 3
a and b: 8 2
a and b: 9 1
```

Let's look closely at this example. **MyClass** does not define a constructor, so only the default constructor is available. Thus, it is not possible to set the values of **a** and **b** using a constructor. However, the class factory **factory( )** can create objects in which **a** and **b** are given values. Moreover, since **a** and **b** are private, using **factory( )** is the only way to set these values.

In **Main( )**, a **MyClass** object is instantiated, and its factory method is used inside the **for** loop to create ten other objects. The line of code that does this is shown here:

```
MyClass anotherOb = ob.factory(i, j); // get an object
```

With each iteration, an object reference called **anotherOb** is created, and it is assigned a reference to the object constructed by the factory. At the end of each iteration of the loop, **anotherOb** goes out of scope, and the object to which it refers is recycled.

Returning an Array

Since in C# arrays are implemented as objects, a method can also return an array. (This differs from C++ in which arrays are not valid as return types.) For example, in the following program, the method **findfactors( )** returns an array that holds the factors of the argument that it is passed:

```
// Return an array.

using System;

class Factor {
  /* Return an array containing the factors of num.
     On return, numfactors will contain the number of
     factors found. */
  public int[] findfactors(int num, out int numfactors) {
    int[] facts = new int[80]; // size of 80 is arbitrary
    int i, j;

    // find factors and put them in the facts array
    for(i=2, j=0; i < num/2 + 1; i++)
      if( (num%i)==0 ) {
        facts[j] = i;
        j++;
      }

    numfactors = j;
    return facts;
```

```
    }
}

class FindFactors {
  public static void Main() {
    Factor f = new Factor();
    int numfactors;
    int[] factors;

    factors = f.findfactors(1000, out numfactors);

    Console.WriteLine("Factors for 1000 are: ");
    for(int i=0; i < numfactors; i++)
      Console.Write(factors[i] + " ");

    Console.WriteLine();
  }
}
```

The output is shown here:

```
Factors for 1000 are:
2 4 5 8 10 20 25 40 50 100 125 200 250 500
```

In **Factor**, **findfactors( )** is declared like this:

```
public int[] findfactors(int num, out int numfactors) {
```

Notice how the **int** array return type is specified. This syntax can be generalized.
Whenever a method returns an array, specify it in a similar fashion, adjusting the
type and dimensions as needed. For example, the following declares a method called
someMeth( ) that returns a two-dimensional array of **double**:

```
public double[,] someMeth() { // ...
```

Method Overloading

In this section, you will learn about one of C#'s most exciting features: method
overloading. In C#, two or more methods within the same class can share the same
name, as long as their parameter declarations are different. When this is the case, the

methods are said to be *overloaded,* and the process is referred to as *method overloading.*
Method overloading is one of the ways that C# implements polymorphism.

In general, to overload a method, simply declare different versions of it. The compiler
takes care of the rest. You must observe one important restriction: the type and/or number
of the parameters of each overloaded method must differ. It is not sufficient for two
methods to differ only in their return types. They must differ in the types or number of
their parameters. (Return types do not provide sufficient information in all cases for C# to
decide which method to use.) Of course, overloaded methods *may* differ in their return
types, too. When an overloaded method is called, the version of the method whose
parameters match the arguments is executed.

Here is a simple example that illustrates method overloading:

```csharp
// Demonstrate method overloading.

using System;

class Overload {
  public void ovlDemo() {
    Console.WriteLine("No parameters");
  }

  // Overload ovlDemo for one integer parameter.
  public void ovlDemo(int a) {
    Console.WriteLine("One parameter: " + a);
  }

  // Overload ovlDemo for two integer parameters.
  public int ovlDemo(int a, int b) {
    Console.WriteLine("Two parameters: " + a + " " + b);
    return a + b;
  }

  // Overload ovlDemo for two double parameters.
  public double ovlDemo(double a, double b) {
    Console.WriteLine("Two double parameters: " +
                       a + " "+ b);
    return a + b;
  }
}

class OverloadDemo {
  public static void Main() {
```

```
      Overload ob = new Overload();
      int resI;
      double resD;

      // call all versions of ovlDemo()
      ob.ovlDemo();
      Console.WriteLine();

      ob.ovlDemo(2);
      Console.WriteLine();

      resI = ob.ovlDemo(4, 6);
      Console.WriteLine("Result of ob.ovlDemo(4, 6): " +
                         resI);
      Console.WriteLine();


      resD = ob.ovlDemo(1.1, 2.32);
      Console.WriteLine("Result of ob.ovlDemo(1.1, 2.32): " +
                         resD);
  }
}
```

This program generates the following output:

```
No parameters

One parameter: 2

Two parameters: 4 6
Result of ob.ovlDemo(4, 6): 10

Two double parameters: 1.1 2.32
Result of ob.ovlDemo(1.1, 2.32): 3.42
```

As you can see, **ovlDemo( )** is overloaded four times. The first version takes no parameters, the second takes one integer parameter, the third takes two integer parameters, and the fourth takes two **double** parameters. Notice that the first two versions of **ovlDemo( )** return **void** and the second two return a value. This is perfectly valid, but as explained, overloading is not affected one way or the other by the return type of a method. Thus, attempting to use these two versions of **ovlDemo( )** will cause an error:

```
// One ovlDemo(int) is OK.
public void ovlDemo(int a) {
  Console.WriteLine("One parameter: " + a);
}

/* Error! Two ovlDemo(int)s are not OK even though
   return types differ. */
public int ovlDemo(int a) {
  Console.WriteLine("One parameter: " + a);
  return a * a;
}
```

As the comments suggest, the difference in their return types is an insufficient difference for the purposes of overloading.

As you will recall from Chapter 3, C# provides certain automatic type conversions. These conversions also apply to parameters of overloaded methods. For example, consider the following:

```
/* Automatic type conversions can affect
   overloaded method resolution. */

using System;

class Overload2 {
  public void f(int x) {
    Console.WriteLine("Inside f(int): " + x);
  }

  public void f(double x) {
    Console.WriteLine("Inside f(double): " + x);
  }
}

class TypeConv {
  public static void Main() {
    Overload2 ob = new Overload2();

    int i = 10;
    double d = 10.1;
```

```
   byte b = 99;
   short s = 10;
   float f = 11.5F;


   ob.f(i); // calls ob.f(int)
   ob.f(d); // calls ob.f(double)

   ob.f(b); // calls ob.f(int) -- type conversion
   ob.f(s); // calls ob.f(int) -- type conversion
   ob.f(f); // calls ob.f(double) -- type conversion
  }
}
```

The output from the program is shown here:

```
Inside f(int): 10
Inside f(double): 10.1
Inside f(int): 99
Inside f(int): 10
Inside f(double): 11.5
```

In this example, only two versions of **f( )** are defined: one that has an **int** parameter and one that has a **double** parameter. However, it is possible to pass **f( )** a **byte**, **short**, or **float** value. In the case of **byte** and **short**, C# automatically converts them to **int**. Thus, **f(int)** is invoked. In the case of **float**, the value is converted to **double** and **f(double)** is called.

It is important to understand, however, that the automatic conversions apply only if there is no direct match between a parameter and an argument. For example, here is the preceding program with the addition of a version of **f( )** that specifies a **byte** parameter:

```
// Add f(byte).

using System;

class Overload2 {
  public void f(byte x) {
    Console.WriteLine("Inside f(byte): " + x);
  }

  public void f(int x) {
    Console.WriteLine("Inside f(int): " + x);
```

```
  }

  public void f(double x) {
    Console.WriteLine("Inside f(double): " + x);
  }
}

class TypeConv {
  public static void Main() {
    Overload2 ob = new Overload2();

    int i = 10;
    double d = 10.1;

    byte b = 99;
    short s = 10;
    float f = 11.5F;


    ob.f(i); // calls ob.f(int)
    ob.f(d); // calls ob.f(double)

    ob.f(b); // calls ob.f(byte) -- now, no type conversion

    ob.f(s); // calls ob.f(int) -- type conversion
    ob.f(f); // calls ob.f(double) -- type conversion
  }
}
```

Now when the program is run, the following output is produced:

```
Inside f(int): 10
Inside f(double): 10.1
Inside f(byte): 99
Inside f(int): 10
Inside f(double): 11.5
```

In this version, since there is a version of **f( )** that takes a **byte** argument, when **f( )** is called with a **byte** argument, **f(byte)** is invoked and the automatic conversion to **int** does not occur.

Both **ref** and **out** participate in overload resolution. For example, the following defines two distinct and separate methods:

```
public void f(int x) {
  Console.WriteLine("Inside f(int): " + x);
}

public void f(ref int x) {
  Console.WriteLine("Inside f(ref int): " + x);
}
```

Thus,

```
ob.f(i)
```

invokes **f(int x)**, but

```
ob.f(ref i)
```

invokes **f(ref int x)**.

Method overloading supports polymorphism because it is one way that C# implements the "one interface, multiple methods" paradigm. To understand how, consider the following. In languages that do not support method overloading, each method must be given a unique name. However, frequently you will want to implement essentially the same method for different types of data. Consider the absolute value function. In languages that do not support overloading, there are usually three or more versions of this function, each with a slightly different name. For instance, in C, the function **abs( )** returns the absolute value of an integer, **labs( )** returns the absolute value of a long integer, and **fabs( )** returns the absolute value of a floating-point value. Since C does not support overloading, each function has to have its own name, even though all three functions do essentially the same thing. This makes the situation more complex, conceptually, than it actually is. Although the underlying concept of each function is the same, you still have three names to remember. This situation does not occur in C#, because each absolute value method can use the same name. Indeed, C#'s standard class library includes an absolute value method, called **Abs( )**. This method is overloaded by C#'s **System.Math** class to handle the numeric types. C# determines which version of **Abs( )** to call based upon the type of argument.

A principal value of overloading is that it allows related methods to be accessed by use of a common name. Thus, the name **Abs** represents the *general action* that is being performed. It is left to the compiler to choose the right *specific* version for a particular circumstance. You, the programmer, need only remember the general operation being performed. Through the application of polymorphism, several names have been reduced to one. Although this example is fairly simple, if you expand the concept, you can see how overloading can help manage greater complexity.

When you overload a method, each version of that method can perform any activity you desire. There is no rule stating that overloaded methods must relate to one another.

However, from a stylistic point of view, method overloading implies a relationship. Thus, while you can use the same name to overload unrelated methods, you should not. For example, you could use the name **sqr** to create methods that return the *square* of an integer and the *square root* of a floating-point value. But these two operations are fundamentally different. Applying method overloading in this manner defeats its original purpose. In practice, you should only overload closely related operations.

C# defines the term *signature*, which is the name of a method plus its parameter list. Thus, for the purposes of overloading, no two methods within the same class can have the same signature. Notice that a signature does not include the return type since it is not used by C# for overload resolution. Also, a signature does not include a **params** parameter if one is present. Thus, **params** does not participate in overload resolution.

Overloading Constructors

Like methods, constructors can also be overloaded. Doing so allows you to construct objects in a variety of ways. For example, consider the following program:

```
// Demonstrate an overloaded constructor.

using System;

class MyClass {
  public int x;

  public MyClass() {
    Console.WriteLine("Inside MyClass().");
    x = 0;
  }

  public MyClass(int i) {
    Console.WriteLine("Inside MyClass(int).");
    x = i;
  }

  public MyClass(double d) {
    Console.WriteLine("Inside MyClass(double).");
    x = (int) d;
  }

  public MyClass(int i, int j) {
    Console.WriteLine("Inside MyClass(int, int).");
    x = i * j;
```

```
    }
}

class OverloadConsDemo {
  public static void Main() {
    MyClass t1 = new MyClass();
    MyClass t2 = new MyClass(88);
    MyClass t3 = new MyClass(17.23);
    MyClass t4 = new MyClass(2, 4);

    Console.WriteLine("t1.x: " + t1.x);
    Console.WriteLine("t2.x: " + t2.x);
    Console.WriteLine("t3.x: " + t3.x);
    Console.WriteLine("t4.x: " + t4.x);
  }
}
```

The output from the program is shown here:

```
Inside MyClass().
Inside MyClass(int).
Inside MyClass(double).
Inside MyClass(int, int).
t1.x: 0
t2.x: 88
t3.x: 17
t4.x: 8
```

MyClass( ) is overloaded four ways, each constructing an object differently. The proper constructor is called based upon the parameters specified when **new** is executed. By overloading a class' constructor, you give the user of your class flexibility in the way objects are constructed.

One of the most common reasons that constructors are overloaded is to allow one object to initialize another. For example, here is an enhanced version of the **Stack** class developed earlier that allows one stack to be constructed from another:

```
// A stack class for characters.

using System;

class Stack {
```

```csharp
// these members are private
char[] stck; // holds the stack
int tos;     // index of the top of the stack

// Construct an empty Stack given its size.
public Stack(int size) {
  stck = new char[size]; // allocate memory for stack
  tos = 0;
}

// Construct a Stack from a stack.
public Stack(Stack ob) {
  // allocate memory for stack
  stck = new char[ob.stck.Length];

  // copy elements to new stack
  for(int i=0; i < ob.tos; i++)
    stck[i] = ob.stck[i];

  // set tos for new stack
  tos = ob.tos;
}

// Push characters onto the stack.
public void push(char ch) {
  if(tos==stck.Length) {
    Console.WriteLine(" -- Stack is full.");
    return;
  }

  stck[tos] = ch;
  tos++;
}

// Pop a character from the stack.
public char pop() {
  if(tos==0) {
    Console.WriteLine(" -- Stack is empty.");
    return (char) 0;
  }

  tos--;
```

```csharp
    return stck[tos];
  }

  // Return true if the stack is full.
  public bool full() {
    return tos==stck.Length;
  }

  // Return true if the stack is empty.
  public bool empty() {
    return tos==0;
  }

  // Return total capacity of the stack.
  public int capacity() {
    return stck.Length;
  }

  // Return number of objects currently on the stack.
  public int getNum() {
    return tos;
  }
}

// Demonstrate the Stack class.
class StackDemo {
  public static void Main() {
    Stack stk1 = new Stack(10);
    char ch;
    int i;

    // Put some characters into stk1.
    Console.WriteLine("Push A through Z onto stk1.");
    for(i=0; !stk1.full(); i++)
      stk1.push((char) ('A' + i));

    // Create a copy of stck1
    Stack stk2 = new Stack(stk1);

    // Display the contents of stk1.
    Console.Write("Contents of stk1: ");
    while( !stk1.empty() ) {
```

```
      ch = stk1.pop();
      Console.Write(ch);
    }

    Console.WriteLine();

    Console.Write("Contents of stk2: ");
    while ( !stk2.empty() ) {
      ch = stk2.pop();
      Console.Write(ch);
    }

    Console.WriteLine("\n");

  }
}
```

The output is shown here:

```
Push A through Z onto stk1.
Contents of stk1: JIHGFEDCBA
Contents of stk2: JIHGFEDCBA
```

In **StackDemo**, the first stack, **stk1**, is constructed and filled with characters. This stack is then used to construct the second stack, **stk2**. This causes the following **Stack** constructor to be executed:

```
// Construct a Stack from a stack
public Stack(Stack ob) {
  // allocate memory for stack
  stck = new char[ob.stck.Length];

  // copy elements to new stack
  for(int i=0; i < ob.tos; i++)
    stck[i] = ob.stck[i];

  // set tos for new stack
  tos = ob.tos;
}
```

Inside this constructor, an array is allocated that is long enough to hold the elements contained in the stack passed in **ob**. Then, the contents of **ob**'s array are copied to the new array, and **tos** is set appropriately. After the constructor finishes, the new stack and the original stack are separate, but identical.

Invoking an Overloaded Constructor Through this

When working with overloaded constructors, it is sometimes useful for one constructor to invoke another. In C#, this is accomplished by using another form of the **this** keyword. The general form is shown here:

constructor-name(*parameter-list1*) : this(*parameter-list2*) {
  // ... body of constructor, which may be empty
}

When the constructor is executed, the overloaded constructor that matches the parameter list specified by *parameter-list2* is first executed. Then, if there are any statements inside the original constructor, they are executed. Here is an example:

```
// Demonstrate invoking a constructor through this.

using System;

class XYCoord {
  public int x, y;

  public XYCoord() : this(0, 0) {
    Console.WriteLine("Inside XYCoord()");
  }

  public XYCoord(XYCoord obj) : this(obj.x, obj.y) {
    Console.WriteLine("Inside XYCoord(obj)");
  }

  public XYCoord(int i, int j) {
    Console.WriteLine("Inside XYCoord(int, int)");
    x = i;
    y = j;
  }
}

class OverloadConsDemo {
  public static void Main() {
```

```
    XYCoord t1 = new XYCoord();
    XYCoord t2 = new XYCoord(8, 9);
    XYCoord t3 = new XYCoord(t2);

    Console.WriteLine("t1.x, t1.y: " + t1.x + ", " + t1.y);
    Console.WriteLine("t2.x, t2.y: " + t2.x + ", " + t2.y);
    Console.WriteLine("t3.x, t3.y: " + t3.x + ", " + t3.y);
  }
}
```

The output from the program is shown here:

```
Inside XYCoord(int, int)
Inside XYCoord()
Inside XYCoord(int, int)
Inside XYCoord(int, int)
Inside XYCoord(obj)
t1.x, t1.y: 0, 0
t2.x, t2.y: 8, 9
t3.x, t3.y: 8, 9
```

Here is how the program works. In the **XYCoord** class, the only constructor that actually initializes the **x** and **y** fields is **XYCoord(int, int)**. The other two constructors simply invoke **XYCoord(int, int)** through **this**. For example, when object **t1** is created, its constructor, **XYCoord( )**, is called. This causes **this(0, 0)** to be executed, which in this case translates into a call to **XYCoord(0, 0)**. The creation of **t2** works in similar fashion.

One reason why invoking overloaded constructors through **this** can be useful is that it can prevent the unnecessary duplication of code. In the foregoing example, there is no reason for all three constructors to duplicate the same initialization sequence, which the use of **this** avoids. Another advantage is that you can create constructors with implied "default arguments" that are used when these arguments are not explicitly specified. For example, you could create another **XYCoord** constructor as shown here:

```
public XYCoord(int x) : this(x, x) { }
```

This constructor automatically defaults the **y** coordinate to the same value as the **x** coordinate. Of course, it is wise to use such "default arguments" carefully because their misuse could easily confuse users of your classes.

The Main( ) Method

Up to this point, you have been using one form of **Main( )**. However, there are several overloaded forms of **Main( )**. Some can be used to return a value, and some can receive arguments. Each is examined here.

Returning Values from Main( )

When a program ends, you can return a value to the calling process (often the operating system) by returning a value from **Main( )**. To do so, you can use this form of **Main( )**.

    public static int Main( )

Notice that instead of being declared **void**, this version of **Main( )** has a return type of **int**.

Usually, the return value from **Main( )** indicates whether the program ended normally or due to some abnormal condition. By convention, a return value of 0 usually indicates normal termination. All other values indicate some type of error occurred.

Passing Arguments to Main( )

Many programs accept what are called *command-line* arguments. A command-line argument is the information that directly follows the program's name on the command line when it is executed. For C# programs, these arguments are then passed to the **Main( )** method. To receive the arguments, you must use one of these forms of **Main( )**:

    public static void Main(string[ ] *args*)
    public static int Main(string[ ] *args*)

The first form returns **void**; the second can be used to return an integer value, as described in the preceding section. For both, the command-line arguments are stored as strings in the **string** array passed to **Main( )**.

For example, the following program displays all of the command-line arguments that it is called with:

```
// Display all command-line information.

using System;

class CLDemo {
  public static void Main(string[] args) {
    Console.WriteLine("There are " + args.Length +
                      " command-line arguments.");

    Console.WriteLine("They are: ");
```

```
      for(int i=0; i<args.Length; i++)
        Console.WriteLine(args[i]);
  }
}
```

If **CLDemo** is executed like this:

```
CLDemo one two three
```

you will see the following output:

```
There are 3 command-line arguments.
They are:
one
two
three
```

To get a taste of the way that command-line arguments can be used, consider the next program. It encodes or decodes messages. The message to be encoded or decoded is specified on the command line. The encryption method is very simple: to encode a word, each letter is incremented by 1. Thus, A becomes B, and so on. To decode, each letter is decremented.

```
// Encode or decode a message.

using System;

class Cipher {
  public static int Main(string[] args) {

    // see if arguments are present
    if(args.Length < 2) {
      Console.WriteLine("Usage: encode/decode word1 [word2...wordN]");
      return 1; // return failure code
    }

    // if args present, first arg must be encode or decode
    if(args[0] != "encode" & args[0] != "decode") {
      Console.WriteLine("First arg must be encode or decode.");
      return 1; // return failure code
    }

    // encode or decode message
```

```
    for(int n=1; n < args.Length; n++) {
      for(int i=0; i < args[n].Length; i++) {
        if(args[0]=="encode")
          Console.Write((char) (args[n][i] + 1) );
        else
          Console.Write((char) (args[n][i] - 1) );
      }
      Console.Write(" ");
    }

    Console.WriteLine();

    return 0;
  }
}
```

To use the program, specify either the "encode" or "decode" command followed by the phrase that you want to encrypt or decrypt. Assuming the program is called Cipher, here are two sample runs:

```
C:>Cipher encode one two
pof uxp

C:>Cipher decode pof uxp
one two
```

There are two interesting things in this program. First, notice how the program checks that a command-line argument is present before it continues execution. This is very important and can be generalized. When a program relies on there being one or more command-line arguments, it must always confirm that the proper arguments have been supplied. Failure to do this can lead to program malfunctions. Also, since the first command-line argument must be either "encode" or "decode", the program also checks this before proceeding.

Second, notice how the program returns a termination code. If the required command line is not present, then 1 is returned, indicating abnormal termination. Otherwise, 0 is returned when the program ends.

Recursion

In C#, a method can call itself. This process is called *recursion*, and a method that calls itself is said to be *recursive*. In general, recursion is the process of defining something in terms of itself and is somewhat similar to a circular definition. The key component of a recursive method is that it contains a statement that executes a call to itself. Recursion is a powerful control mechanism.

The classic example of recursion is the computation of the factorial of a number. The factorial of a number N is the product of all the whole numbers between 1 and N. For example, 3 factorial is 1×2×3, or 6. The following program shows a recursive way to compute the factorial of a number. For comparison purposes, a nonrecursive equivalent is also included.

```csharp
// A simple example of recursion.

using System;

class Factorial {
  // This is a recursive function.
  public int factR(int n) {
    int result;

    if(n==1) return 1;
    result = factR(n-1) * n;
    return result;
  }

  // This is an iterative equivalent.
  public int factI(int n) {
    int t, result;

    result = 1;
    for(t=1; t <= n; t++) result *= t;
    return result;
  }
}

class Recursion {
  public static void Main() {
    Factorial f = new Factorial();

    Console.WriteLine("Factorials using recursive method.");
    Console.WriteLine("Factorial of 3 is " + f.factR(3));
    Console.WriteLine("Factorial of 4 is " + f.factR(4));
    Console.WriteLine("Factorial of 5 is " + f.factR(5));
    Console.WriteLine();
```

```
    Console.WriteLine("Factorials using iterative method.");
    Console.WriteLine("Factorial of 3 is " + f.factI(3));
    Console.WriteLine("Factorial of 4 is " + f.factI(4));
    Console.WriteLine("Factorial of 5 is " + f.factI(5));
  }
}
```

The output from this program is shown here:

```
Factorials using recursive method.
Factorial of 3 is 6
Factorial of 4 is 24
Factorial of 5 is 120

Factorials using iterative method.
Factorial of 3 is 6
Factorial of 4 is 24
Factorial of 5 is 120
```

The operation of the nonrecursive method **factI( )** should be clear. It uses a loop starting at 1 and progressively multiplies each number by the moving product.

The operation of the recursive **factR( )** is a bit more complex. When **factR( )** is called with an argument of 1, the method returns 1; otherwise, it returns the product of **factR(n–1)*n**. To evaluate this expression, **factR( )** is called with **n–1**. This process repeats until **n** equals 1 and the calls to the method begin returning. For example, when the factorial of 2 is calculated, the first call to **factR( )** will cause a second call to be made with an argument of 1. This call will return 1, which is then multiplied by 2 (the original value of **n**). The answer is then 2. You might find it interesting to insert **WriteLine( )** statements into **factR( )** that show at what level each call is and what the intermediate results are.

When a method calls itself, new local variables and parameters are allocated storage on the system stack, and the method code is executed with these new variables from the start. A recursive call does not make a new copy of the method. Only the arguments are new. As each recursive call returns, the old local variables and parameters are removed from the stack, and execution resumes at the point of the call inside the method. Recursive methods could be said to "telescope" out and back.

Here is another example of recursion. The **displayRev( )** method uses recursion to display its string argument backwards.

```
// Display a string in reverse by using recursion.
```

```
using System;

class RevStr {

  // Display a string backwards.
  public void displayRev(string str) {
    if(str.Length > 0)
      displayRev(str.Substring(1, str.Length-1));
    else
      return;

    Console.Write(str[0]);
  }
}

class RevStrDemo {
  public static void Main() {
    string s = "this is a test";
    RevStr rsOb = new RevStr();

    Console.WriteLine("Original string: " + s);

    Console.Write("Reversed string: ");
    rsOb.displayRev(s);

    Console.WriteLine();
  }
}
```

Here is the output:

```
Original string: this is a test
Reversed string: tset a si siht
```

Each time **displayRev( )** is called, it first checks to see if **str** has a length greater than zero. If it does, it recursively calls **displayRev( )** with a new string that consists of **str** minus its first character. This process repeats until a zero-length string is passed. This causes the recursive calls to start unraveling. As they do, the first character of **str** in each call is displayed. This results in the string being displayed in reverse order.

Recursive versions of many routines may execute a bit more slowly than the iterative equivalent because of the added overhead of the additional method calls. Too many recursive calls to a method could cause a stack overrun. Because storage for parameters and local variables is on the system stack, and each new call creates a new copy of these variables, it is possible that the stack could be exhausted. If this occurs, the C# runtime system will cause an exception. However, you probably will not have to worry about this unless a recursive routine runs wild.

The main advantage to recursion is that some types of algorithms can be more clearly and simply implemented recursively than iteratively. For example, the QuickSort sorting algorithm is quite difficult to implement in an iterative way. Also, some problems, especially AI-related ones, seem to lend themselves to recursive solutions.

When writing recursive methods, you must have a conditional statement, such as an **if**, somewhere to force the method to return without the recursive call being executed. If you don't do this, once you call the method, it will never return. This type of error is very common when working with recursion. Use **WriteLine( )** statements liberally so that you can watch what is going on and abort execution if you see that you have made a mistake.

Understanding static

There will be times when you will want to define a class member that will be used independently of any object of that class. Normally, a class member must be accessed through an object of its class, but it is possible to create a member that can be used by itself, without reference to a specific instance. To create such a member, precede its declaration with the keyword **static**. When a member is declared **static**, it can be accessed before any objects of its class are created and without reference to any object. You can declare both methods and variables to be **static**. The most common example of a **static** member is **Main( )**, which is declared **static** because it must be called by the operating system when your program begins.

Outside the class, to use a **static** member, you must specify the name of its class followed by the dot operator. No object needs to be created. In fact, a **static** member cannot be accessed through an object instance. It must be accessed through its class name. For example, if you want to assign the value 10 to a **static** variable called **count** that is part of a class called **Timer**, use this line:

```
Timer.count = 10;
```

This format is similar to that used to access normal instance variables through an object, except that the class name is used. A **static** method can be called in the same way—by use of the dot operator on the name of the class.

Variables declared as **static** are, essentially, global variables. When objects of its class are declared, no copy of a **static** variable is made. Instead, all instances of the class share the same **static** variable. A **static** variable is initialized when its class is loaded. If no explicit initializer is specified, it is initialized to zero for numeric values, null in the case of object references, or **false** for variables of type **bool**. Thus, a **static** variable always has a value.

The difference between a **static** method and a normal method is that the **static** method can be called through its class name, without any object of that method being created. You have seen an example of this already: the **Sqrt( )** method, which is a **static** method within C#'s **System.Math** class.

Here is an example that creates a **static** variable and a **static** method:

```
// Use static.

using System;

class StaticDemo {
  // a static variable
  public static int val = 100;

  // a static method
  public static int valDiv2() {
    return val/2;
  }
}

class SDemo {
  public static void Main() {

    Console.WriteLine("Initial value of StaticDemo.val is "
                      + StaticDemo.val);

    StaticDemo.val = 8;
    Console.WriteLine("StaticDemo.val is " + StaticDemo.val);
    Console.WriteLine("StaticDemo.valDiv2(): " +
                      StaticDemo.valDiv2());

  }
}
```

The output is shown here:

```
Initial value of StaticDemo.val is 100
StaticDemo.val is 8
StaticDemo.valDiv2(): 4
```

As the output shows, a **static** variable is initialized when the program begins, before any object of its class is created.

There are several restrictions that apply to **static** methods:

1. A **static** method does not have a **this** reference.

2. A **static** method can directly call only other **static** methods. It cannot directly call an instance method of its class. The reason for this is that instance methods operate on specific instances of a class, but a **static** method does not.

3. A **static** method must directly access only **static** data. It cannot directly use an instance variable because it is not operating on an instance of its class.

For example, in the following class, the **static** method **valDivDenom( )** is illegal:

```
class StaticError {
  int denom = 3; // a normal instance variable
  static int val = 1024; // a static variable

  /* Error! Can't directly access a non-static variable
     from within a static method. */
  static int valDivDenom() {
    return val/denom; // won't compile!
  }
}
```

Here, **denom** is a normal instance variable that cannot be accessed within a **static** method. However, the use of **val** is OK since it is a **static** variable.

The same problem occurs when trying to call a non-**static** method from within a **static** method of the same class. For example:

```
using System;

class AnotherStaticError {
  // non-static method.
  void nonStaticMeth() {
    Console.WriteLine("Inside nonStaticMeth().");
  }

  /* Error! Can't directly call a non-static method
     from within a static method. */
  static void staticMeth() {
    nonStaticMeth(); // won't compile
```

```
      }
   }
```

In this case, the attempt to call a non-**static** (that is, instance method) from a **static** method causes a compile-time error.

It is important to understand that a **static** method *can* call instance methods and access instance variables of its class, but it must do so through an object of that class. It is just that it cannot use one without an object qualification. For example, this fragment is perfectly valid:

```
class MyClass {
  // non-static method.
  void nonStaticMeth() {
     Console.WriteLine("Inside nonStaticMeth().");
  }

  /* Can call a non-static method through an
     object reference from within a static method. */
  public static void staticMeth(MyClass ob) {
    ob.nonStaticMeth(); // this is OK
  }
}
```

Because **static** fields are independent of any specific object, they are useful when you need to maintain information that is applicable to an entire class. Here is an example of such a situation. It uses a **static** field to maintain a count of the number of objects that are in existence.

```
// Use a static field to count instances.

using System;

class CountInst {
  static int count = 0;

  // increment count when object is created
  public CountInst() {
    count++;
  }
```

```
  // decrement count when object is destroyed
  ~CountInst() {
    count--;
  }

  public static int getcount() {
    return count;
  }
}

class CountDemo {
  public static void Main() {
    CountInst ob;


    for(int i=0; i < 10; i++) {
      ob = new CountInst();
      Console.WriteLine("Current count: " +
                     CountInst.getcount());
    }


  }
}
```

The output is shown here:

```
Current count: 1
Current count: 2
Current count: 3
Current count: 4
Current count: 5
Current count: 6
Current count: 7
Current count: 8
Current count: 9
Current count: 10
```

Each time that an object of type **CountInst** is created, the **static** field **count** is incremented. Each time an object is recycled, **count** is decremented. Thus, **count** always contains a count of the number of objects currently in existence. This is possible only through the use of a **static** field. There is no way for an instance variable to maintain the count because the count relates to the class as a whole, not to a specific instance.

Here is one more example that uses **static**. Earlier in this chapter you saw how a class factory could be used to create objects. In that example, the class factory was a non-**static** method, which meant that it could be called only through an object reference. This meant that a default object of the class needed to be created so that the factory method could be called. However, a better way to implement a class factory is as a **static** method, which allows the class factory to be called without creating an unnecessary object. Here is the class factory example rewritten to reflect this improvement:

```
// Use a static class factory.

using System;

class MyClass {
  int a, b;

  // Create a class factory for MyClass.
  static public MyClass factory(int i, int j) {
    MyClass t = new MyClass();

    t.a = i;
    t.b = j;

    return t; // return an object
  }

  public void show() {
    Console.WriteLine("a and b: " + a + " " + b);
  }

}

class MakeObjects {
  public static void Main() {
    int i, j;

    // generate objects using the factory
    for(i=0, j=10; i < 10; i++, j--) {
      MyClass ob = MyClass.factory(i, j); // get an object
      ob.show();
    }
```

```
      Console.WriteLine();
   }
 }
```

In this version, **factory( )** is invoked through its class name in this line of code:

```
MyClass ob = MyClass.factory(i, j); // get an object
```

There is no need to create a **MyClass** object prior to using the factory.

Static Constructors

A constructor can also be specified as **static**. A **static** constructor is typically used to initialize attributes that apply to a class rather than an instance. Thus, it is used to initialize aspects of a class before any objects of the class are created. Here is a simple example:

```
// Use a static constructor.

using System;

class Cons {
  public static int alpha;
  public int beta;

  // static constructor
  static Cons() {
    alpha = 99;
    Console.WriteLine("Inside static constructor.");
  }

  // instance constructor
  public Cons() {
    beta = 100;
    Console.WriteLine("Inside instance constructor.");
  }
}

class ConsDemo {
  public static void Main() {
```

```
    Cons ob = new Cons();

    Console.WriteLine("Cons.alpha: " + Cons.alpha);
    Console.WriteLine("ob.beta: " + ob.beta);

  }
}
```

Here is the output:

```
Inside static constructor.
Inside instance constructor.
Cons.alpha: 99
ob.beta: 100
```

Notice that the static constructor is called automatically, and before the instance constructor. This can be generalized. In all cases, the **static** constructor will be executed before any instance constructor. Furthermore, **static** constructors must be private and cannot be called by your program.

Chapter 9

Operator Overloading

C# allows you to define the meaning of an operator relative to a class that you create. This process is called *operator overloading.* By overloading an operator, you expand its usage to your class. The effects of the operator are completely under your control and may differ from class to class. For example, a class that defines a linked list might use the + operator to add an object to the list. A class that implements a stack might use the + to push an object onto the stack. Another class might use the + operator in an entirely different way.

When an operator is overloaded, none of its original meaning is lost. It is simply that a new operation, relative to a specific class, is added. Therefore, overloading the + to handle a linked list, for example, does not cause its meaning relative to integers (that is, addition) to be changed.

A principal advantage of operator overloading is that it allows you to seamlessly integrate a new class type into your programming environment. This *type extensibility* is an important part of the power of an object-oriented language such as C#. Once operators are defined for a class, you can operate on objects of that class using the normal C# expression syntax. You can even use an object in expressions involving other types of data. Operator overloading is one of C#'s most powerful features.

Operator Overloading Fundamentals

Operator overloading is closely related to method overloading. To overload an operator, you use the **operator** keyword to create an *operator method*, which defines the action of the operator relative to its class.

There are two forms of **operator** methods: one for unary operators and one for binary operators. The general form for each is shown here:

```
// General form for overloading a unary operator.
public static ret-type operator op(param-type operand)
{
    // operations
}


// General form for overloading a binary operator.
public static ret-type operator op(param-type1 operand1, param-type1 operand2)
{
    // operations
}
```

Here, the operator that you are overloading, such as + or /, is substituted for *op*. The *ret-type* is the type of value returned by the specified operation. Although it can be of any type you choose, the return value is often of the same type as the class for which the operator is being overloaded. This correlation facilitates the use of the overloaded operator in expressions. For unary operators, the operand is passed in *operand*. For binary operators, the operands are passed in *operand1* and *operand2*.

For unary operators, the operand must be of the same type as the class for which the operator is being defined. For binary operators, at least one of the operands must be of the same type as its class. Thus, you cannot overload any C# operators for objects that you have not created. For example, you can't redefine + for **int** or **string**.

One other point: Operator parameters must not use the **ref** or **out** modifier.

Overloading Binary Operators

To see how operator overloading works, let's start with an example that overloads two binary operators, the + and the –. The following program creates a class called **ThreeD**, which maintains the coordinates of an object in three-dimensional space. The overloaded + adds the individual coordinates of one **ThreeD** object to another. The overloaded – subtracts the coordinates of one object from the other.

```
// An example of operator overloading.

using System;

// A three-dimensional coordinate class.
class ThreeD {
  int x, y, z; // 3-D coordinates

  public ThreeD() { x = y = z = 0; }
  public ThreeD(int i, int j, int k) { x = i; y = j; z = k; }

  // Overload binary +.
  public static ThreeD operator +(ThreeD op1, ThreeD op2)
  {
    ThreeD result = new ThreeD();

    /* This adds together the coordinates of the two points
       and returns the result. */
    result.x = op1.x + op2.x; // These are integer additions
    result.y = op1.y + op2.y; // and the + retains its original
    result.z = op1.z + op2.z; // meaning relative to them.

    return result;
  }

  // Overload binary -.
```

```csharp
    public static ThreeD operator -(ThreeD op1, ThreeD op2)
    {
      ThreeD result = new ThreeD();

      /* Notice the order of the operands. op1 is the left
         operand and op2 is the right. */
      result.x = op1.x - op2.x; // these are integer subtractions
      result.y = op1.y - op2.y;
      result.z = op1.z - op2.z;

      return result;
    }

    // Show X, Y, Z coordinates.
    public void show()
    {
      Console.WriteLine(x + ", " + y + ", " + z);
    }
  }

class ThreeDDemo {
  public static void Main() {
    ThreeD a = new ThreeD(1, 2, 3);
    ThreeD b = new ThreeD(10, 10, 10);
    ThreeD c = new ThreeD();

    Console.Write("Here is a: ");
    a.show();
    Console.WriteLine();
    Console.Write("Here is b: ");
    b.show();
    Console.WriteLine();

    c = a + b; // add a and b together
    Console.Write("Result of a + b: ");
    c.show();
    Console.WriteLine();

    c = a + b + c; // add a, b and c together
    Console.Write("Result of a + b + c: ");
    c.show();
    Console.WriteLine();
```

```
    c = c - a; // subtract a
    Console.Write("Result of c - a: ");
    c.show();
    Console.WriteLine();

    c = c - b; // subtract b
    Console.Write("Result of c - b: ");
    c.show();
    Console.WriteLine();
  }
}
```

This program produces the following output:

```
Here is a: 1, 2, 3

Here is b: 10, 10, 10

Result of a + b: 11, 12, 13

Result of a + b + c: 22, 24, 26

Result of c - a: 21, 22, 23

Result of c - b: 11, 12, 13
```

Let's examine the preceding program carefully, beginning with the overloaded operator **+**. When two objects of type **ThreeD** are operated on by the **+** operator, the magnitudes of their respective coordinates are added together, as shown in **operator+( )**. Notice, however, that this method does not modify the value of either operand. Instead, a new object of type **ThreeD**, which contains the result of the operation, is returned by the method. To understand why the **+** operation does not change the contents of either object, think about the standard arithmetic **+** operation as applied like this: 10+12. The outcome of this operation is 22, but neither 10 nor 12 is changed by it. Although there is no rule that prevents an overloaded operator from altering the value of one of its operands, it is best for the actions of an overloaded operator to be consistent with its usual meaning.

Notice that **operator+( )** returns an object of type **ThreeD**. Although the method could have returned any valid C# type, the fact that it returns a **ThreeD** object allows the **+** operator to be used in compound expressions, such as **a+b+c**. Here, **a+b** generates a result that is of type **ThreeD**. This value can then be added to **c**. Had any other type of value been generated by **a+b**, such an expression would not work.

Here is another important point: when the coordinates are added together inside **operator+( )**, the addition of the individual coordinates results in an integer addition. This is because the individual coordinates, **x**, **y**, and **z**, are integer quantities. The fact that the + operator is overloaded for objects of type **ThreeD** has no effect on the + as it is applied to integer values.

Now, look at **operator–( )**. The – operator works just like the + operator except that the order of the parameters is important. Recall that addition is commutative, but subtraction is not. (That is, A–B is not the same as B–A!) For all binary operators, the first parameter to an operator method will contain the left operand. The second parameter will contain the one on the right. When implementing overloaded versions of the noncommutative operators, you must remember which operand is on the left and which is on the right.

Overloading Unary Operators

The unary operators are overloaded just like the binary operators. The main difference, of course, is that there is only one operand. For example, here is a method that overloads the unary minus for the **ThreeD** class:

```
// Overload unary -.
public static ThreeD operator -(ThreeD op)
{
  ThreeD result = new ThreeD();

  result.x = -op.x;
  result.y = -op.y;
  result.z = -op.z;

  return result;
}
```

Here, a new object is created that contains the negated fields of the operand. This object is then returned. Notice that the operand is unchanged. Again, this is in keeping with the usual meaning of the unary minus. For example, in an expression such as this,

```
a = -b
```

a receives the negation of **b**, but **b** is not changed.

There are, however, two cases in which an operator method will need to change the contents of an operand: ++ and – –. Since the usual meaning of these operators is increment and decrement, an overloaded ++ or – – should usually increment or decrement the operand. Thus, when overloading these two operators, the operand will usually be modified. For example, here is an **operator++( )** method for the **ThreeD** class:

```
// Overload unary ++.
public static ThreeD operator ++(ThreeD op)
{
  // for ++, modify argument
  op.x++;
  op.y++;
  op.z++;

  return op; // operand is returned
}
```

Notice that the object referred to by **op** is modified by this method. Thus, the operand in a **++** operation is incremented. The modified object is also returned. This is necessary to allow the **++** operator to be used in a larger expression.

Here is an expanded version of the previous example program that demonstrates the unary **–** and the **++** operator.

```
// More operator overloading.

using System;

// A three-dimensional coordinate class.
class ThreeD {
  int x, y, z; // 3-D coordinates

  public ThreeD() { x = y = z = 0; }
  public ThreeD(int i, int j, int k) { x = i; y = j; z = k; }

  // Overload binary +.
  public static ThreeD operator +(ThreeD op1, ThreeD op2)
  {
    ThreeD result = new ThreeD();

    /* This adds together the coordinates of the two points
       and returns the result. */
    result.x = op1.x + op2.x;
    result.y = op1.y + op2.y;
    result.z = op1.z + op2.z;

    return result;
  }
```

```csharp
// Overload binary -.
public static ThreeD operator -(ThreeD op1, ThreeD op2)
{
  ThreeD result = new ThreeD();

  /* Notice the order of the operands. op1 is the left
     operand and op2 is the right. */
  result.x = op1.x - op2.x;
  result.y = op1.y - op2.y;
  result.z = op1.z - op2.z;

  return result;
}

// Overload unary -.
public static ThreeD operator -(ThreeD op)
{
  ThreeD result = new ThreeD();

  result.x = -op.x;
  result.y = -op.y;
  result.z = -op.z;

  return result;
}

// Overload unary ++.
public static ThreeD operator ++(ThreeD op)
{
  // for ++, modify argument
  op.x++;
  op.y++;
  op.z++;

  return op;
}

// Show X, Y, Z coordinates.
public void show()
{
  Console.WriteLine(x + ", " + y + ", " + z);
}
```

```csharp
}

class ThreeDDemo {
  public static void Main() {
    ThreeD a = new ThreeD(1, 2, 3);
    ThreeD b = new ThreeD(10, 10, 10);
    ThreeD c = new ThreeD();

    Console.Write("Here is a: ");
    a.show();
    Console.WriteLine();
    Console.Write("Here is b: ");
    b.show();
    Console.WriteLine();

    c = a + b; // add a and b together
    Console.Write("Result of a + b: ");
    c.show();
    Console.WriteLine();

    c = a + b + c; // add a, b and c together
    Console.Write("Result of a + b + c: ");
    c.show();
    Console.WriteLine();

    c = c - a; // subtract a
    Console.Write("Result of c - a: ");
    c.show();
    Console.WriteLine();

    c = c - b; // subtract b
    Console.Write("Result of c - b: ");
    c.show();
    Console.WriteLine();

    c = -a; // assign -a to c
    Console.Write("Result of -a: ");
    c.show();
    Console.WriteLine();

    a++; // increment a
    Console.Write("Result of a++: ");
```

```
    a.show();
  }
}
```

The output from the program is shown here:

```
Here is a: 1, 2, 3

Here is b: 10, 10, 10

Result of a + b: 11, 12, 13

Result of a + b + c: 22, 24, 26

Result of c - a: 21, 22, 23

Result of c - b: 11, 12, 13

Result of -a: -1, -2, -3

Result of a++: 2, 3, 4
```

As you know, the **++** and **– –** have both a prefix and a postfix form. For example, both

```
++a;
```

and

```
a++;
```

are valid uses of the increment operator. However, when overloading the **++** or **– –**, both forms call the same method. Thus, when overloading, there is no way to distinguish between a prefix or postfix form of **++** or **– –**.

Handling Operations on C# Built-in Types

For any given class and operator, an operator method can, itself, be overloaded. One of the most common reasons for this is to allow operations between a class type and other types of data, such as a built-in type. For example, once again consider the **ThreeD** class. To this point, you have seen how to overload the **+** so that it adds the coordinates of one **ThreeD** object to another. However, this is not the only way in which you might want to define addition for **ThreeD**. For example, it might be useful to add an integer value to each coordinate of a **ThreeD** object. Such an operation could be used to translate axes. To perform such an operation, you will need to overload **+** a second time, as shown here:

```
// Overload binary + for object + int.
public static ThreeD operator +(ThreeD op1, int op2)
{
  ThreeD result = new ThreeD();

  result.x = op1.x + op2;
  result.y = op1.y + op2;
  result.z = op1.z + op2;

  return result;
}
```

Notice that the second parameter is of type **int**. Thus, the preceding method allows an integer value to be added to each field of a **ThreeD** object. This is permissible because, as explained earlier, when overloading a binary operator, only one of the operands must be of the same type as the class for which the operator is being overloaded. The other operand can be of any other type.

Here is a version of **ThreeD** that has two overloaded **+** methods:

```
/* Overload addition for object + object, and
   for object + int. */

using System;

// A three-dimensional coordinate class.
class ThreeD {
  int x, y, z; // 3-D coordinates

  public ThreeD() { x = y - z = 0; }
  public ThreeD(int i, int j, int k) { x = i; y = j; z = k; }

  // Overload binary + for object + object.
  public static ThreeD operator +(ThreeD op1, ThreeD op2)
  {
    ThreeD result = new ThreeD();
```

```
    /* This adds together the coordinates of the two points
       and returns the result. */
    result.x = op1.x + op2.x;
    result.y = op1.y + op2.y;
    result.z = op1.z + op2.z;

    return result;
  }

  // Overload binary + for object + int.
  public static ThreeD operator +(ThreeD op1, int op2)
  {
    ThreeD result = new ThreeD();

    result.x = op1.x + op2;
    result.y = op1.y + op2;
    result.z = op1.z + op2;

    return result;
  }

  // Show X, Y, Z coordinates.
  public void show()
  {
    Console.WriteLine(x + ", " + y + ", " + z);
  }
}

class ThreeDDemo {
  public static void Main() {
    ThreeD a = new ThreeD(1, 2, 3);
    ThreeD b = new ThreeD(10, 10, 10);
    ThreeD c = new ThreeD();

    Console.Write("Here is a: ");
    a.show();
    Console.WriteLine();
    Console.Write("Here is b: ");
    b.show();
    Console.WriteLine();

    c = a + b; // object + object
    Console.Write("Result of a + b: ");
```

```
      c.show();
      Console.WriteLine();

      c = b + 10; // object + int
      Console.Write("Result of b + 10: ");
      c.show();
   }
}
```

The output from this program is shown here:

```
Here is a: 1, 2, 3

Here is b: 10, 10, 10

Result of a + b: 11, 12, 13

Result of b + 10: 20, 20, 20
```

As the output confirms, when the + is applied to two objects, their coordinates are added together. When the + is applied to an object and an integer, the coordinates are increased by the integer value.

While the overloading of + just shown certainly adds a useful capability to the **ThreeD** class, it does not quite finish the job. Here is why. The **operator+(ThreeD, int)** method allows statements like this:

ob1 = ob2 + 10;

It does not, unfortunately, allow ones like this:

ob1 = 10 + ob2;

The reason is that the integer argument is the second argument, which is the right-hand operand. The trouble is that the preceding statement puts the integer argument on the left. To allow both forms of statements, you will need to overload the + yet another time. This version must have its first parameter as type **int** and its second parameter as type **ThreeD**. One version of the **operator+( )** method handles *object + integer*, and the other handles *integer + object*. Overloading the + (or any other binary operator) this way allows a built-in type to occur on the left or right side of the operator. Here is a version of **ThreeD** that overloads the + operator as just described:

```
/* Overload the + for object + object,
   object + int, and int + object. */
```

```csharp
using System;

// A three-dimensional coordinate class.
class ThreeD {
  int x, y, z; // 3-D coordinates

  public ThreeD() { x = y = z = 0; }
  public ThreeD(int i, int j, int k) { x = i; y = j; z = k; }

  // Overload binary + for object + object.
  public static ThreeD operator +(ThreeD op1, ThreeD op2)
  {
    ThreeD result = new ThreeD();

    /* This adds together the coordinates of the two points
       and returns the result. */
    result.x = op1.x + op2.x;
    result.y = op1.y + op2.y;
    result.z = op1.z + op2.z;

    return result;
  }

  // Overload binary + for object + int.
  public static ThreeD operator +(ThreeD op1, int op2)
  {
    ThreeD result = new ThreeD();

    result.x = op1.x + op2;
    result.y = op1.y + op2;
    result.z = op1.z + op2;

    return result;
  }

  // Overload binary + for int + object.
  public static ThreeD operator +(int op1, ThreeD op2)
  {
    ThreeD result = new ThreeD();

    result.x = op2.x + op1;
    result.y = op2.y + op1;
```

```
    result.z = op2.z + op1;

    return result;
  }

  // Show X, Y, Z coordinates.
  public void show()
  {
    Console.WriteLine(x + ", " + y + ", " + z);
  }
}

class ThreeDDemo {
  public static void Main() {
    ThreeD a = new ThreeD(1, 2, 3);
    ThreeD b = new ThreeD(10, 10, 10);
    ThreeD c = new ThreeD();

    Console.Write("Here is a: ");
    a.show();
    Console.WriteLine();
    Console.Write("Here is b: ");
    b.show();
    Console.WriteLine();

    c = a + b; // object + object
    Console.Write("Result of a + b: ");
    c.show();
    Console.WriteLine();

    c = b + 10; // object + int
    Console.Write("Result of b + 10: ");
    c.show();
    Console.WriteLine();

    c = 15 + b; // int + object
    Console.Write("Result of 15 + b: ");
    c.show();
  }
}
```

The output from this program is shown here:

```
Here is a: 1, 2, 3

Here is b: 10, 10, 10

Result of a + b: 11, 12, 13

Result of b + 10: 20, 20, 20

Result of 15 + b: 25, 25, 25
```

Overloading the Relational Operators

The relational operators, such as = = or <, can also be overloaded and the process is straightforward. Usually, an overloaded relational operator returns a **true** or **false** value. This is in keeping with the normal usage of these operators and allows the overloaded relational operators to be used in conditional expressions. If you return a different type result, you are greatly restricting the operator's utility.

Here is a version of the **ThreeD** class that overloads the < and > operators:

```
// Overload < and >.

using System;

// A three-dimensional coordinate class.
class ThreeD {
  int x, y, z; // 3-D coordinates

  public ThreeD() { x = y = z = 0; }
  public ThreeD(int i, int j, int k) { x = i; y = j; z = k; }

  // Overload <.
  public static bool operator <(ThreeD op1, ThreeD op2)
  {
    if((op1.x < op2.x) && (op1.y < op2.y) && (op1.z < op2.z))
      return true;
    else
      return false;
  }

  // Overload >.
```

```
  public static bool operator >(ThreeD op1, ThreeD op2)
  {
    if((op1.x > op2.x) && (op1.y > op2.y) && (op1.z > op2.z))
      return true;
    else
      return false;
  }

  // Show X, Y, Z coordinates.
  public void show()
  {
    Console.WriteLine(x + ", " + y + ", " + z);
  }
}

class ThreeDDemo {
  public static void Main() {
    ThreeD a = new ThreeD(5, 6, 7);
    ThreeD b = new ThreeD(10, 10, 10);
    ThreeD c = new ThreeD(1, 2, 3);

    Console.Write("Here is a: ");
    a.show();
    Console.Write("Here is b: ");
    b.show();
    Console.Write("Here is c: ");
    c.show();
    Console.WriteLine();

    if(a > c) Console.WriteLine("a > c is true");
    if(a < c) Console.WriteLine("a < c is true");
    if(a > b) Console.WriteLine("a > b is true");
    if(a < b) Console.WriteLine("a < b is true");
  }
}
```

The output from this program is shown here:

```
Here is a: 5, 6, 7
Here is b: 10, 10, 10
Here is c: 1, 2, 3
```

```
a > c is true
a < b is true
```

An important restriction applies to overloading the relational operators: You must overload them in pairs. For example, if you overload <, you must also overload >, and vice versa. The operator pairs are shown here:

= =	!=
<	>
<=	>=

One other point: If you overload the = = and != operators, you will usually need to override **Object.Equals( )** and **Object.GetHashCode( )**, too. These methods and the technique of overriding are discussed in Chapter 11.

Overloading true and false

The keywords **true** and **false** can also be used as unary operators for the purposes of overloading. Overloaded versions of these operators provide custom determinations of true and false relative to classes that you create. Once **true** and **false** are implemented for a class, you can use objects of that class to control the **if, while, for**, and **do-while** statements, or in a **?** expression. You can even use them to implement special types of logic, such as fuzzy logic.

The **true** and **false** operators must be overloaded as a pair. You cannot overload just one. Both are unary operators and they have this general form:

public static bool operator true(*param-type operand*)
{
   // return true or false
}

public static bool operator false(*param-type operand*)
{
   // return true or false
}

Notice that each returns a **bool** result.

The following example shows how **true** and **false** can be implemented for the **ThreeD** class. Each assumes that a **ThreeD** object is true if at least one coordinate is non-zero. If all three coordinates are zero, then the object is false. The decrement operator is also implemented for the purpose of illustration.

```
// Overload true and false for ThreeD.

using System;

// A three-dimensional coordinate class.
class ThreeD {
  int x, y, z; // 3-D coordinates

  public ThreeD() { x = y = z = 0; }
  public ThreeD(int i, int j, int k) { x = i; y = j; z = k; }

  // Overload true.
  public static bool operator true(ThreeD op) {
    if((op.x != 0) || (op.y != 0) || (op.z != 0))
      return true; // at least one coordinate is non-zero
    else
      return false;
  }

  // Overload false.
  public static bool operator false(ThreeD op) {
    if((op.x == 0) && (op.y == 0) && (op.z == 0))
      return true; // all coordinates are zero
    else
      return false;
  }

  // Overload unary --.
  public static ThreeD operator --(ThreeD op)
  {
    op.x--;
    op.y--;
    op.z--;

    return op;
  }

  // Show X, Y, Z coordinates.
```

```csharp
  public void show()
  {
    Console.WriteLine(x + ", " + y + ", " + z);
  }
}

class TrueFalseDemo {
  public static void Main() {
    ThreeD a = new ThreeD(5, 6, 7);
    ThreeD b = new ThreeD(10, 10, 10);
    ThreeD c = new ThreeD(0, 0, 0);

    Console.Write("Here is a: ");
    a.show();
    Console.Write("Here is b: ");
    b.show();
    Console.Write("Here is c: ");
    c.show();
    Console.WriteLine();

    if(a) Console.WriteLine("a is true.");
    else Console.WriteLine("a is false.");

    if(b) Console.WriteLine("b is true.");
    else Console.WriteLine("b is false.");

    if(c) Console.WriteLine("c is true.");
    else Console.WriteLine("c is false.");

    Console.WriteLine();

    Console.WriteLine("Control a loop using a ThreeD object.");
    do {
      b.show();
      b--;
    } while(b);

  }
}
```

The output is shown here:

```
Here is a: 5, 6, 7
Here is b: 10, 10, 10
Here is c: 0, 0, 0

a is true.
b is true.
c is false.

Control a loop using a ThreeD object.
10, 10, 10
9, 9, 9
8, 8, 8
7, 7, 7
6, 6, 6
5, 5, 5
4, 4, 4
3, 3, 3
2, 2, 2
1, 1, 1
```

Notice how the **ThreeD** objects are used to control **if** statements and a **while** loop. In the case of the **if** statements, the **ThreeD** object is evaluated using **true**. If the result of this operation is true, then the **if** statement succeeds. In the case of the **do-while** loop, each iteration of the loop decrements **b**. The loop repeats as long as **b** evaluates as true (that is, it contains at least one non-zero coordinate). When **b** contains all zero coordinates, it evaluates as false when the **true** operator is applied and the loop stops.

Overloading the Logical Operators

As you know, C# defines the following logical operators: &, |, !, &&, and | |. Of these, only the &, |, and ! can be overloaded. By following certain rules, however, the benefits of the short-circuit && and | | can still be obtained. Each situation is examined here.

A Simple Approach to Overloading the Logical Operators

Let's begin with the simplest situation. If you will not be making use of the short-circuit logical operators, then you can overload & and | as you would intuitively think, with each returning a **bool** result. An overloaded ! will also usually return a **bool** result.

Here is an example that overloads the !, &, and I logical operators for objects of type **ThreeD**. As before, each assumes that a **ThreeD** object is true if at least one coordinate is non-zero. If all three coordinates are zero, then the object is false.

```
// A simple way to overload !, |, and & for ThreeD.

using System;

// A three-dimensional coordinate class.
class ThreeD {
  int x, y, z; // 3-D coordinates

  public ThreeD() { x = y = z = 0; }
  public ThreeD(int i, int j, int k) { x = i; y = j; z = k; }


  // Overload |.
  public static bool operator |(ThreeD op1, ThreeD op2)
  {
    if( ((op1.x != 0) || (op1.y != 0) || (op1.z != 0)) |
        ((op2.x != 0) || (op2.y != 0) || (op2.z != 0)) )
      return true;
    else
      return false;
  }

  // Overload &.
  public static bool operator &(ThreeD op1, ThreeD op2)
  {
    if( ((op1.x != 0) && (op1.y != 0) && (op1.z != 0)) &
        ((op2.x != 0) && (op2.y != 0) && (op2.z != 0)) )
      return true;
    else
      return false;
  }

  // Overload !.
  public static bool operator !(ThreeD op)
  {
    if((op.x != 0) || (op.y != 0) || (op.z != 0))
      return false;
    else return true;
```

```
  }

  // Show X, Y, Z coordinates.
  public void show()
  {
    Console.WriteLine(x + ", " + y + ", " + z);
  }
}

class TrueFalseDemo {
  public static void Main() {
    ThreeD a = new ThreeD(5, 6, 7);
    ThreeD b = new ThreeD(10, 10, 10);
    ThreeD c = new ThreeD(0, 0, 0);

    Console.Write("Here is a: ");
    a.show();
    Console.Write("Here is b: ");
    b.show();
    Console.Write("Here is c: ");
    c.show();
    Console.WriteLine();

    if(!a) Console.WriteLine("a is false.");
    if(!b) Console.WriteLine("b is false.");
    if(!c) Console.WriteLine("c is false.");

    Console.WriteLine();

    if(a & b) Console.WriteLine("a & b is true.");
    else Console.WriteLine("a & b is false.");

    if(a & c) Console.WriteLine("a & c is true.");
    else Console.WriteLine("a & c is false.");

    if(a | b) Console.WriteLine("a | b is true.");
    else Console.WriteLine("a | b is false.");

    if(a | c) Console.WriteLine("a | c is true.");
    else Console.WriteLine("a | c is false.");
  }
}
```

The output from the program is shown here:

```
Here is a: 5, 6, 7
Here is b: 10, 10, 10
Here is c: 0, 0, 0

c is false.

a & b is true.
a & c is false.
a | b is true.
a | c is true.
```

In this approach, the &, |, and ! operator methods each return a **bool** result. This is necessary if the operators are to be used in their normal manner (that is, in places that expect a **bool** result). Recall that for all built-in types, the outcome of a logical operation is a value of type **bool**. Thus, having the overloaded versions of these operators return type **bool** is a rational approach. Unfortunately, this approach works only if you will not be needing the short-circuit operators.

Enabling the Short-Circuit Operators

To enable the use of the && and | | short-circuit operators, you must follow four rules. First, the class must overload & and |. Second, the return type of the overloaded & and | methods must be an object of the class for which the operators are being overloaded. Third, each parameter must be a reference to an object of the class for which the operator is being overloaded. Fourth, the **true** and **false** operators must be overloaded for the class. When these conditions have been met, the short-circuit operators automatically become available for use.

The following program shows how to properly implement the & and | for the **ThreeD** class so that the short-circuit operators && and | | are available.

```
/* A better way to overload !, |, and & for ThreeD.
   This version automatically enables the && and || operators. */

using System;

// A three-dimensional coordinate class.
class ThreeD {
  int x, y, z; // 3-D coordinates

  public ThreeD() { x = y = z = 0; }
```

```
public ThreeD(int i, int j, int k) { x = i; y = j; z = k; }


// Overload | for short-circuit evaluation.
public static ThreeD operator |(ThreeD op1, ThreeD op2)
{
  if( ((op1.x != 0) || (op1.y != 0) || (op1.z != 0)) |
      ((op2.x != 0) || (op2.y != 0) || (op2.z != 0)) )
    return new ThreeD(1, 1, 1);
  else
    return new ThreeD(0, 0, 0);
}

// Overload & for short-circuit evaluation.
public static ThreeD operator &(ThreeD op1, ThreeD op2)
{
  if( ((op1.x != 0) && (op1.y != 0) && (op1.z != 0)) &
      ((op2.x != 0) && (op2.y != 0) && (op2.z != 0)) )
    return new ThreeD(1, 1, 1);
  else
    return new ThreeD(0, 0, 0);
}

// Overload !.
public static bool operator !(ThreeD op)
{
  if(op) return false;
  else return true;
}

// Overload true.
public static bool operator true(ThreeD op) {
  if((op.x != 0) || (op.y != 0) || (op.z != 0))
    return true; // at least one coordinate is non-zero
  else
    return false;
}

// Overload false.
public static bool operator false(ThreeD op) {
  if((op.x == 0) && (op.y == 0) && (op.z == 0))
    return true; // all coordinates are zero
```

```csharp
    else
      return false;
  }

  // Show X, Y, Z coordinates.
  public void show()
  {
    Console.WriteLine(x + ", " + y + ", " + z);
  }
}

class TrueFalseDemo {
  public static void Main() {
    ThreeD a = new ThreeD(5, 6, 7);
    ThreeD b = new ThreeD(10, 10, 10);
    ThreeD c = new ThreeD(0, 0, 0);

    Console.Write("Here is a: ");
    a.show();
    Console.Write("Here is b: ");
    b.show();
    Console.Write("Here is c: ");
    c.show();
    Console.WriteLine();

    if(a) Console.WriteLine("a is true.");
    if(b) Console.WriteLine("b is true.");
    if(c) Console.WriteLine("c is true.");

    if(!a) Console.WriteLine("a is false.");
    if(!b) Console.WriteLine("b is false.");
    if(!c) Console.WriteLine("c is false.");

    Console.WriteLine();

    Console.WriteLine("Use & and |");
    if(a & b) Console.WriteLine("a & b is true.");
    else Console.WriteLine("a & b is false.");

    if(a & c) Console.WriteLine("a & c is true.");
    else Console.WriteLine("a & c is false.");
```

```
      if(a | b) Console.WriteLine("a | b is true.");
      else Console.WriteLine("a | b is false.");

      if(a | c) Console.WriteLine("a | c is true.");
      else Console.WriteLine("a | c is false.");

      Console.WriteLine();

      // now use short-circuit ops
      Console.WriteLine("Use short-circuit && and ||");
      if(a && b) Console.WriteLine("a && b is true.");
      else Console.WriteLine("a && b is false.");

      if(a && c) Console.WriteLine("a && c is true.");
      else Console.WriteLine("a && c is false.");

      if(a || b) Console.WriteLine("a || b is true.");
      else Console.WriteLine("a || b is false.");

      if(a || c) Console.WriteLine("a || c is true.");
      else Console.WriteLine("a || c is false.");
  }
}
```

The output from the program is shown here:

```
Here is a: 5, 6, 7
Here is b: 10, 10, 10
Here is c: 0, 0, 0

a is true.
b is true.
c is false.

Use & and |
a & b is true.
a & c is false.
a | b is true.
a | c is true.

Use short-circuit && and ||
```

```
a && b is true.
a && c is false.
a || b is true.
a || c is true.
```

Let's look closely at how the **&** and **|** are implemented. They are shown here:

```
// Overload | for short-circuit evaluation.
public static ThreeD operator |(ThreeD op1, ThreeD op2)
{
  if( ((op1.x != 0) || (op1.y != 0) || (op1.z != 0)) |
      ((op2.x != 0) || (op2.y != 0) || (op2.z != 0)) )
    return new ThreeD(1, 1, 1);
  else
    return new ThreeD(0, 0, 0);
}


// Overload & for short-circuit evaluation.
public static ThreeD operator &(ThreeD op1, ThreeD op2)
{
  if( ((op1.x != 0) && (op1.y != 0) && (op1.z != 0)) &
      ((op2.x != 0) && (op2.y != 0) && (op2.z != 0)) )
    return new ThreeD(1, 1, 1);
  else
    return new ThreeD(0, 0, 0);
}
```

Notice first that both now return an object of type **ThreeD**. Pay attention to how this object is generated. If the outcome of the operation is true, then a true **ThreeD** object (one in which at least one coordinate is non-zero) is created and returned. If the outcome is false, then a false object is created and returned. Thus, in a statement like this:

```
if(a & b) Console.WriteLine("a & b is true.");
else Console.WriteLine("a & b is false.");
```

the outcome of **a & b** is a **ThreeD** object, which in this case is a true object. Since the operators **true** and **false** are defined, this resulting object is subjected to the **true** operator, and a **bool** result is returned. In this case the result is **true** and the **if** succeeds.

Because the necessary rules have been followed, the short-circuit operators are now available for use on **ThreeD** objects. They work like this. The first operand is tested by using **operator true** (for **||**) or **operator false** (for **&&**). If it can determine the outcome of the operation, then the corresponding **&** or **|** is not evaluated. Otherwise, the corresponding overloaded **&** or **|** is used to determine the result. Thus, using a **&&** or **||** causes the corresponding **&** or **|** to be invoked only when the first operand cannot determine the outcome of the expression. For example, consider this statement from the program:

```
if(a || c) Console.WriteLine("a || c is true.");
```

The **true** operator is first applied to **a**. Since **a** is true in this situation, there is no need to use the **|** operator method. However, if the statement were rewritten like this,

```
if(c || a) Console.WriteLine("c || a is true.");
```

then the **true** operator would first be applied to **c**, which in this case is false. Thus, the **|** operator method would be invoked to determine if **a** is true (which it is in this case).

Although you might at first think that the technique used to enable the short-circuit operators is a bit convoluted, it makes sense if you think about it a bit. By overloading **true** and **false** for a class, you enable the compiler to utilize the short-circuit operators without having to explicitly overload either. Furthermore, you gain the ability to use objects in conditional expressions. In general, unless you need a very narrow implementation of **&** and **|**, you are better off creating a full implementation.

Conversion Operators

In some situations, you will want to use an object of a class in an expression involving other types of data. Sometimes, overloading one or more operators can provide the means of doing this. However, in other cases, what you want is a simple type conversion from the class type to the target type. To handle these cases, C# allows you to create a special type of **operator** method called a *conversion operator*. A conversion operator converts an object of your class into another type. In essence, a conversion operator overloads the cast operator. Conversion operators help fully integrate class types into the C# programming environment by allowing objects of a class to be freely mixed with other data types as long as a conversion to those other types is defined.

There are two forms of conversion operators, implicit and explicit. The general form for each is shown here:

public static operator implicit *target-type*(*source-type v*) { return *value*; }
public static operator explicit *target-type*(*source-type v*) { return *value*; }

Here, *target-type* is the target type that you are converting to, *source-type* is the type you are converting from, and *value* is the value of the class after conversion. The conversion operators return data of type *target-type*, and no other return type specifier is allowed.

If the conversion operator specifies **implicit**, then the conversion is invoked automatically, such as when an object is used in an expression with the target type. When the conversion operator specifies **explicit**, the conversion is invoked when a cast is used. You cannot define both an implicit and explicit conversion operator for the same target and source types.

To illustrate a conversion operator, we will create one for the **ThreeD** class. Suppose you want to convert an object of type **ThreeD** into an integer so it can be used in an integer expression. Further, the conversion will take place by using the product of the three dimensions. To accomplish this, you will use an implicit conversion operator that looks like this:

```
public static implicit operator int(ThreeD op1)
{
  return op1.x * op1.y * op1.z;
}
```

Here is a program that illustrates this conversion operator:

```
// An example that uses an implicit conversion operator.

using System;

// A three-dimensional coordinate class.
class ThreeD {
  int x, y, z; // 3-D coordinates

  public ThreeD() { x = y = z = 0; }
  public ThreeD(int i, int j, int k) { x = i; y = j; z = k; }

  // Overload binary +.
  public static ThreeD operator +(ThreeD op1, ThreeD op2)
  {
    ThreeD result = new ThreeD();

    result.x = op1.x + op2.x;
    result.y = op1.y + op2.y;
    result.z = op1.z + op2.z;

    return result;
  }
```

```
    // An implicit conversion from ThreeD to int.
    public static implicit operator int(ThreeD op1)
    {
      return op1.x * op1.y * op1.z;
    }

    // Show X, Y, Z coordinates.
    public void show()
    {
      Console.WriteLine(x + ", " + y + ", " + z);
    }
}

class ThreeDDemo {
  public static void Main() {
    ThreeD a = new ThreeD(1, 2, 3);
    ThreeD b = new ThreeD(10, 10, 10);
    ThreeD c = new ThreeD();
    int i;

    Console.Write("Here is a: ");
    a.show();
    Console.WriteLine();
    Console.Write("Here is b: ");
    b.show();
    Console.WriteLine();

    c = a + b; // add a and b together
    Console.Write("Result of a + b: ");
    c.show();
    Console.WriteLine();

    i = a; // convert to int
    Console.WriteLine("Result of i = a: " + i);
    Console.WriteLine();

    i = a * 2 - b; // convert to int
    Console.WriteLine("result of a * 2 - b: " + i);
  }
}
```

This program displays the output:

```
Here is a: 1, 2, 3

Here is b: 10, 10, 10

Result of a + b: 11, 12, 13

Result of i = a: 6

result of a * 2 - b: -988
```

As the program illustrates, when a **ThreeD** object is used in an integer expression, such as **i = a**, the conversion is applied to the object. In this specific case, the conversion returns the value 6, which is the product of coordinates stored in **a**. However, when an expression does not require a conversion to **int**, the conversion operator is not called. This is why **c = a+b** does not invoke **operator int( )**.

Remember that you can create different conversion functions to meet different needs. You could define one that converts to **double** or **long**, for example. Each is applied automatically and independently.

An implicit conversion operator is applied automatically when a conversion is required in an expression, when passing an object to a method, in an assignment, and also when an explicit cast to the target type is used. Alternatively, you can create an explicit conversion operator, which is invoked only when an explicit cast is used. An explicit conversion operator is not invoked automatically. For example, here is the previous program reworked to use an explicit conversion to **int**:

```
// Use an explicit conversion.

using System;

// A three-dimensional coordinate class.
class ThreeD {
  int x, y, z; // 3-D coordinates

  public ThreeD() { x = y = z = 0; }
  public ThreeD(int i, int j, int k) { x = i; y = j; z = k; }

  // Overload binary +.
  public static ThreeD operator +(ThreeD op1, ThreeD op2)
  {
    ThreeD result = new ThreeD();
```

```
      result.x = op1.x + op2.x;
      result.y = op1.y + op2.y;
      result.z = op1.z + op2.z;

      return result;
   }

   // This is now explicit.
   public static explicit operator int(ThreeD op1)
   {
      return op1.x * op1.y * op1.z;
   }

   // Show X, Y, Z coordinates.
   public void show()
   {
      Console.WriteLine(x + ", " + y + ", " + z);
   }
}

class ThreeDDemo {
   public static void Main() {
      ThreeD a = new ThreeD(1, 2, 3);
      ThreeD b = new ThreeD(10, 10, 10);
      ThreeD c = new ThreeD();
      int i;

      Console.Write("Here is a: ");
      a.show();
      Console.WriteLine();
      Console.Write("Here is b: ");
      b.show();
      Console.WriteLine();

      c = a + b; // add a and b together
      Console.Write("Result of a + b: ");
      c.show();
      Console.WriteLine();

      i = (int) a; // explicitly convert to int -- cast required
      Console.WriteLine("Result of i = a: " + i);
      Console.WriteLine();
```

```
    i = (int)a * 2 - (int)b; // casts required
    Console.WriteLine("result of a * 2 - b: " + i);

  }
}
```

Because the conversion operator is now marked as explicit, conversion to **int** must be explicitly cast. For example, in this line,

```
i = (int) a; // explicitly convert to int -- cast required
```

if you remove the cast, the program will not compile.

There are a few restrictions to conversion operators:

- Either the target type or the source type of the conversion must be a class that you create. You cannot, for example, redefine the conversion from **double** to **int**.
- You cannot define a conversion to or from **Object**.
- You cannot define both an implicit and an explicit conversion for the same source and target types.
- You cannot define a conversion from a base class to a derived class. (See Chapter 11 for a discussion of base and derived classes.)
- You cannot define a conversion from or to an interface. (See Chapter 12 for a discussion of interfaces.)

In addition to these rules, there are suggestions that you should normally follow when choosing between implicit and explicit conversion operators. Although convenient, implicit conversions should be used only in situations in which the conversion is inherently error-free. To ensure this, implicit conversions should be created only when these two conditions are met: First, no loss of information, such as truncation, overflow, or loss of sign, occurs. Second, the conversion does not cause an exception. If the conversion cannot meet these two requirements, then you should use an explicit conversion.

Operator Overloading Tips and Restrictions

The action of an overloaded operator as applied to the class for which it is defined need not bear any relationship to that operator's default usage, as applied to C#'s built-in types. However, for the purposes of the structure and readability of your code, an overloaded operator should reflect, when possible, the spirit of the operator's original use. For example, the + relative to **ThreeD** is conceptually similar to the + relative to integer types. There would be little benefit in defining the + operator relative to some class in such a way that it acts more the way you would expect the / operator to perform, for instance. The central concept is that while you can give an overloaded operator any meaning you like, for clarity it is best when its new meaning is related to its original meaning.

There are some restrictions to overloading operators. You cannot alter the precedence of any operator. You cannot alter the number of operands required by the operator, although your operator method could choose to ignore an operand. There are several operators that you cannot overload. Perhaps most significantly, you cannot overload any assignment operator, including the compound assignments, such as **+=**. Here are the other operators that cannot be overloaded.

&&	||	[ ]	( )	new	is
sizeof	typeof	?	->	.	=

Although you cannot overload the cast operator **( )** explicitly, you can create conversion operators, as shown earlier, that perform this function.

It may seem like a serious restriction that operators such as **+=** can't be overloaded, but it isn't. In general, if you have defined an operator, then if that operator is used in a compound assignment, your overloaded operator method is invoked. Thus, **+=** automatically uses your version of **operator+( )**. For example, assuming the **ThreeD** class, if you use a sequence like this,

```
ThreeD a = new ThreeD(1, 2, 3);
ThreeD b = new ThreeD(10, 10, 10);

b += a; // add a and b together
```

ThreeD's **operator+( )** is automatically invoked, and **b** will contain the coordinate 11, 12, 13.

One last point: Although you cannot overload the [ ] array indexing operator using an **operator** method, you can create indexers, which are described in the next chapter.

Another Example of Operator Overloading

Throughout this chapter we have been using the **ThreeD** class to demonstrate operator overloading, and in this regard it has served us well. Before concluding this chapter, however, it is useful to work through another example. Although the general principles of operator overloading are the same no matter what class is used, the following example helps show the power of operator overloading—especially where type extensibility is concerned.

This example develops a four-bit integer type and defines several operations for it. As you might know, in the early days of computing, the four-bit quantity was common because it represented half a byte. It is also large enough to hold one hexadecimal digit. Since four bits are half a byte, a four-bit quantity is sometimes referred to as a *nybble*. In the days of front-panel machines in which programmers entered code one nybble at a time, thinking in terms of nybbles was an everyday affair! While not as common now, a four-bit type still makes an interesting addition to the other C# integers. Traditionally, a nybble is an unsigned value.

The following example uses the **Nybble** class to implement a nybble data type. It uses an **int** for its underlying storage, but it restricts the values that can be held to 0 through 15. It defines the following operators:

- Addition of a **Nybble** to a **Nybble**
- Addition of an **int** to a **Nybble**
- Addition of a **Nybble** to an **int**
- Greater than and less than
- The increment operator
- Conversion to **Nybble** from **int**
- Conversion to **int** from **Nybble**

These operations are sufficient to show how a class type can be fully integrated into the C# type system. However, for a complete **Nybble** implementation, you will need to define all of the other operators. You might want to try adding them on your own.

The complete **Nybble** class is shown here along with **NybbleDemo**, which demonstrates its use:

```
// Create a 4-bit type called Nybble.

using System;

// A 4-bit type.
class Nybble {
  int val; // underlying storage

  public Nybble() { val = 0; }

  public Nybble(int i) {
    val = i;
    val = val & 0xF; // retain lower 4 bits
  }
```

```
// Overload binary + for Nybble + Nybble.
public static Nybble operator +(Nybble op1, Nybble op2)
{
  Nybble result = new Nybble();

  result.val = op1.val + op2.val;

  result.val = result.val & 0xF; // retain lower 4 bits

  return result;
}

// Overload binary + for Nybble + int.
public static Nybble operator +(Nybble op1, int op2)
{
  Nybble result = new Nybble();

  result.val = op1.val + op2;

  result.val = result.val & 0xF; // retain lower 4 bits

  return result;
}

// Overload binary + for int + Nybble.
public static Nybble operator +(int op1, Nybble op2)
{
  Nybble result = new Nybble();

  result.val = op1 + op2.val;

  result.val = result.val & 0xF; // retain lower 4 bits

  return result;
}

// Overload ++.
public static Nybble operator ++(Nybble op)
{
  op.val++;

  op.val = op.val & 0xF; // retain lower 4 bits
```

```
    return op;
  }

  // Overload >.
  public static bool operator >(Nybble op1, Nybble op2)
  {
    if(op1.val > op2.val) return true;
    else return false;
  }

  // Overload <.
  public static bool operator <(Nybble op1, Nybble op2)
  {
    if(op1.val < op2.val) return true;
    else return false;
  }

  // Convert a Nybble into an int.
  public static implicit operator int (Nybble op)
  {
    return op.val;
  }

  // Convert an int into a Nybble.
  public static implicit operator Nybble (int op)
  {
    return new Nybble(op);
  }
}

class NybbleDemo {
  public static void Main() {
    Nybble a = new Nybble(1);
    Nybble b = new Nybble(10);
    Nybble c = new Nybble();
    int t;

    Console.WriteLine("a: " + (int) a);
    Console.WriteLine("b: " + (int) b);

    // use a Nybble in an if statement
    if(a < b) Console.WriteLine("a is less than b\n");
```

```
    // Add two Nybbles together
    c = a + b;
    Console.WriteLine("c after c = a + b: " + (int) c);

    // Add an int to a Nybble
    a += 5;
    Console.WriteLine("a after a += 5: " + (int) a);

    Console.WriteLine();

    // use a Nybble in an int expression
    t = a * 2 + 3;
    Console.WriteLine("Result of a * 2 + 3: " + t);

    Console.WriteLine();

    // illustrate int assignment and overflow
    a = 19;
    Console.WriteLine("Result of a = 19: " + (int) a);

    Console.WriteLine();

    // use a Nybble to control a loop
    Console.WriteLine("Control a for loop with a Nybble.");
    for(a = 0; a < 10; a++)
      Console.Write((int) a + " ");

    Console.WriteLine();
  } }
```

The output from the program is shown here:

```
a: 1
b: 10
a is less than b

c after c = a + b: 11
a after a += 5: 6

Result of a * 2 + 3: 15
```

```
Result of a = 19: 3

Control a for loop with a Nybble.
0 1 2 3 4 5 6 7 8 9
```

While most of the operation of **Nybble** should be easy to understand, there is one important point to make: The conversion operators play a large role in the integration of **Nybble** into the C# type system. Because conversions are defined from **Nybble** to **int** and from **int** to **Nybble**, a **Nybble** object can be freely mixed in arithmetic expressions. For example, consider this expression from the program:

```
t = a * 2 + 3;
```

Here, **t** is an **int**, as are 2 and 3, but **a** is a **Nybble**. These two types are compatible in the expression because of the implicit conversion of **Nybble** to **int**. In this case, since the rest of the expression is of type **int**, **a** is converted to **int** by its conversion method.

The conversion from **int** to **Nybble** allows a **Nybble** object to be assigned an **int** value. For example, in the program, the statement

```
a = 19;
```

works like this. The conversion operator from **int** to **Nybble** is executed. This causes a new **Nybble** object to be created that contains the low-order 4 bits of the value 19 (which is 3 because 19 overflows the range of a **Nybble**). This object is then assigned to **a**. Without the conversion operators, such expressions would not be allowed.

The conversion of **Nybble** to **int** is also used by the **for** loop. Without this conversion it would not be possible to write the **for** loop in such a straightforward way.

Chapter 10

Indexers and Properties

his chapter examines two special types of class members that have a close
relationship to each other: indexers and properties. Each of these expands the
power of a class by enhancing its integration into C#'s type system and improving
its resiliency. Indexers provide the mechanism by which an object can be indexed like
an array. Properties offer a streamlined way to manage access to a class' instance data.
They relate to each other because both rely upon another feature of C#: the accessor.

Indexers

As you know, array indexing is performed using the [ ] operator. It is possible to overload
the [ ] operator for classes that you create, but you don't use an **operator** method. Instead,
you create an *indexer*. An indexer allows an object to be indexed like an array. The main
use of indexers is to support the creation of specialized arrays that are subject to one or
more constraints. However, you can use an indexer for any purpose for which an array-
like syntax is beneficial. Indexers can have one or more dimensions. We will begin with
one-dimensional indexers.

Creating One-Dimensional Indexers

A one-dimensional indexer has this general form:

```
element-type this[int index] {
    // The get accessor.
    get {
        // return the value specified by index
    }

    // The set accessor.
    set {
        // set the value specified by index
    }
}
```

Here, *element-type* is the base type of the indexer. Thus, each element accessed by the
indexer will be of type *element-type*. It corresponds to the base type of an array. The
parameter *index* receives the index of the element being accessed. Technically, this
parameter does not have to be of type **int**, but since indexers are typically used to
provide array indexing, an integer type is customary.

Inside the body of the indexer are defined two *accessors* that are called **get** and **set**.
An accessor is similar to a method except that it does not have a return type or parameter
declarations. The accessors are automatically called when the indexer is used, and both
accessors receive *index* as a parameter. If the indexer is on the left side of an assignment

statement, then the **set** accessor is called and the element specified by *index* must be set. Otherwise, the **get** accessor is called and the value associated with *index* must be returned. The **set** method also receives a value called **value**, which contains the value being assigned to the specified index.

One of the benefits of an indexer is that you can control precisely how an array is accessed, heading off improper accesses. Here is an example. In the following program the **FailSoftArray** class implements an array that traps boundary errors, thus preventing runtime exceptions if the array is indexed out-of-bounds. This is accomplished by encapsulating the array as a private member of a class, allowing access to the array only through the indexer. With this approach, any attempt to access the array beyond its boundaries can be prevented, with such an attempt failing gracefully (resulting in a "soft landing" rather than a "crash"). Since **FailSoftArray** uses an indexer, the array can be accessed using the normal array notation.

```
// Use an indexer to create a fail-soft array.

using System;

class FailSoftArray {
  int[] a;      // reference to underlying array

  public int Length; // Length is public

  public bool errflag; // indicates outcome of last operation

  // Construct array given its size.
  public FailSoftArray(int size) {
    a = new int[size];
    Length = size;
  }

  // This is the indexer for FailSoftArray.
  public int this[int index] {
    // This is the get accessor.
    get {
      if(ok(index)) {
        errflag = false;
        return a[index];
      } else {
        errflag = true;
        return 0;
      }
```

```
    }

    // This is the set accessor
    set {
      if(ok(index)) {
        a[index] = value;
        errflag = false;
      }
      else errflag = true;
    }
  }

  // Return true if index is within bounds.
  private bool ok(int index) {
   if(index >= 0 & index < Length) return true;
   return false;
  }
}

// Demonstrate the fail-soft array.
class FSDemo {
  public static void Main() {
    FailSoftArray fs = new FailSoftArray(5);
    int x;

    // show quiet failures
    Console.WriteLine("Fail quietly.");
    for(int i=0; i < (fs.Length * 2); i++)
      fs[i] = i*10;

    for(int i=0; i < (fs.Length * 2); i++) {
      x = fs[i];
      if(x != -1) Console.Write(x + " ");
    }
    Console.WriteLine();

    // now, generate failures
    Console.WriteLine("\nFail with error reports.");
    for(int i=0; i < (fs.Length * 2); i++) {
      fs[i] = i*10;
      if(fs.errflag)
        Console.WriteLine("fs[" + i + "] out-of-bounds");
```

```
    }

    for(int i=0; i < (fs.Length * 2); i++) {
      x = fs[i];
      if(!fs.errflag) Console.Write(x + " ");
      else
        Console.WriteLine("fs[" + i + "] out-of-bounds");
    }
  }
}
```

The output from the program is shown here:

```
Fail quietly.
0 10 20 30 40 0 0 0 0 0

Fail with error reports.
fs[5] out-of-bounds
fs[6] out-of-bounds
fs[7] out-of-bounds
fs[8] out-of-bounds
fs[9] out-of-bounds
0 10 20 30 40 fs[5] out-of-bounds
fs[6] out-of-bounds
fs[7] out-of-bounds
fs[8] out-of-bounds
fs[9] out-of-bounds
```

The indexer prevents the array boundaries from being overrun. Let's look closely at each part of the indexer. It begins with this line:

```
public int this[int index] {
```

This declares an indexer that operates on **int** elements. The index is passed in **index**. The indexer is public, allowing it to be used by code outside of its class.

The **get( )** accessor is shown here:

```
get {
  if(ok(index)) {
    errflag = false;
```

```
      return a[index];
    } else {
      errflag = true;
      return 0;
    }
  }
```

The **get** accessor prevents array boundary errors. If the specified index is within bounds, the element corresponding to the index is returned. If it is out of bounds, no operation takes place and no overrun occurs. In this version of **FailSoftArray**, a variable called **errflag** contains the outcome of each operation. This field can be examined after each operation to assess the success or failure of the operation.

The **set** accessor is shown here. It too prevents a boundary error.

```
set {
  if(ok(index)) {
    a[index] = value;
    errflag = false;
  }
  else errflag = true;
}
```

Here, if **index** is within bounds, the value passed in **value** is assigned to the corresponding element. Otherwise, **errflag** is set to **true**. Recall that in an accessor method, **value** is an automatic parameter that contains the value being assigned. You do not need to (nor can you) declare it.

Indexers do not have to support both **get** and **set**. You can create a read-only indexer by implementing only the **get** accessor. You can create a write-only indexer by implementing only **set**.

Indexers Can Be Overloaded

An indexer can be overloaded. The version executed will be the one that has the closest type-match between its parameter and the argument used as an index. Here is an example that overloads the **FailSoftArray** indexer for indexes of type **double**. The **double** indexer rounds its index to the nearest integer value.

```
// Overload the FailSoftArray indexer.

using System;
```

```
class FailSoftArray {
  int[] a;      // reference to underlying array

  public int Length; // Length is public

  public bool errflag; // indicates outcome of last operation

  // Construct array given its size.
  public FailSoftArray(int size) {
    a = new int[size];
    Length = size;
  }

  // This is the int indexer for FailSoftArray.
  public int this[int index] {
    // This is the get accessor.
    get {
      if(ok(index)) {
        errflag = false;
        return a[index];
      } else {
        errflag = true;
        return 0;
      }
    }

    // This is the set accessor
    set {
      if(ok(index)) {
        a[index] = value;
        errflag = false;
      }
      else errflag = true;
    }
  }

  /* This is another indexer for FailSoftArray.
     This index takes a double argument.  It then
     rounds that argument to the nearest integer
     index. */
  public int this[double idx] {
    // This is the get accessor.
```

```csharp
    get {
      int index;

      // round to nearest int
      if( (idx - (int) idx) < 0.5) index = (int) idx;
      else index = (int) idx + 1;

      if(ok(index)) {
        errflag = false;
        return a[index];
      } else {
        errflag = true;
        return 0;
      }
    }

    // This is the set accessor
    set {
      int index;

      // round to nearest int
      if( (idx - (int) idx) < 0.5) index = (int) idx;
      else index = (int) idx + 1;

      if(ok(index)) {
        a[index] = value;
        errflag = false;
      }
      else errflag = true;
    }
  }

  // Return true if index is within bounds.
  private bool ok(int index) {
   if(index >= 0 & index < Length) return true;
   return false;
  }
}

// Demonstrate the fail-soft array.
class FSDemo {
  public static void Main() {
```

```
    FailSoftArray fs = new FailSoftArray(5);

    // put some values in fs
    for(int i=0; i < fs.Length; i++)
      fs[i] = i;

    // now index with ints and doubles
    Console.WriteLine("fs[1]: " + fs[1]);
    Console.WriteLine("fs[2]: " + fs[2]);

    Console.WriteLine("fs[1.1]: " + fs[1.1]);
    Console.WriteLine("fs[1.6]: " + fs[1.6]);

  }
}
```

This program produces the following output:

```
fs[1]: 1
fs[2]: 2
fs[1.1]: 1
fs[1.6]: 2
```

As the output shows, the **double** indexes are rounded to their nearest integer value. Specifically, 1.1 is rounded to 1, and 1.6 is rounded to 2.

Although overloading an indexer as shown in this program is valid, it is not common. Most often, an indexer is overloaded to enable an object of a class to be used as an index, with the index computed in some special way.

Indexers Do Not Require an Underlying Array

It is important to understand that there is no requirement that an indexer actually operate on an array. It simply must provide functionality that appears "array-like" to the user of the indexer. For example, the following program has an indexer that acts like a read-only array that contains the powers of 2 from 0 to 15. Notice, however, that no actual array exists. Instead, the indexer simply computes the proper value for a given index.

```
// Indexers don't have to operate on actual arrays.

using System;
```

```
class PwrOfTwo {

  /* Access a logical array that contains
     the powers of 2 from 0 to 15. */
  public int this[int index] {
    // Compute and return power of 2.
    get {
      if((index >= 0) && (index < 16)) return pwr(index);
      else return -1;
    }

    // there is no set accessor
  }

  int pwr(int p) {
    int result = 1;

    for(int i=0; i<p; i++)
      result *= 2;

    return result;
  }
}

class UsePwrOfTwo {
  public static void Main() {
    PwrOfTwo pwr = new PwrOfTwo();

    Console.Write("First 8 powers of 2: ");
    for(int i=0; i < 8; i++)
      Console.Write(pwr[i] + " ");
    Console.WriteLine();

    Console.Write("Here are some errors: ");
    Console.Write(pwr[-1] + " " + pwr[17]);

    Console.WriteLine();
  }
}
```

The output from the program is shown here:

```
First 8 powers of 2: 1 2 4 8 16 32 64 128
Here are some errors: -1 -1
```

Notice that the indexer for **PwrOfTwo** includes a **get** accessor, but no **set** accessor. As explained, this means that the indexer is read-only. Thus, a **PwrOfTwo** object can be used on the right side of an assignment statement, but not on the left. For example, attempting to add this statement to the preceding program won't work:

```
pwr[0] = 11; // won't compile
```

This statement will cause a compilation error because there is no **set( )** accessor defined for the indexer.

There are two important restrictions to using indexers. First, because an indexer does not define a storage location, a value produced by an indexer cannot be passed as a **ref** or **out** parameter to a method. Second, an indexer must be an instance member of its class; it cannot be declared **static**.

Multidimensional Indexers

You can create indexers for multidimensional arrays, too. For example, here is a two-dimensional fail-soft array. Pay close attention to the way that the indexer is declared.

```
// A two-dimensional fail-soft array.

using System;

class FailSoftArray2D {
  int[,] a; // reference to underlying 2D array
  int rows, cols; // dimensions
  public int Length; // Length is public

  public bool errflag; // indicates outcome of last operation

  // Construct array given its dimensions.
  public FailSoftArray2D(int r, int c) {
    rows = r;
    cols = c;
    a = new int[rows, cols];
    Length = rows * cols;
  }
```

```csharp
// This is the indexer for FailSoftArray2D.
public int this[int index1, int index2] {
  // This is the get accessor.
  get {
    if(ok(index1, index2)) {
      errflag = false;
      return a[index1, index2];
    } else {
      errflag = true;
      return 0;
    }
  }

  // This is the set accessor.
  set {
    if(ok(index1, index2)) {
      a[index1, index2] = value;
      errflag = false;
    }
    else errflag = true;
  }
}

// Return true if indexes are within bounds.
private bool ok(int index1, int index2) {
  if(index1 >= 0 & index1 < rows &
     index2 >= 0 & index2 < cols)
       return true;

  return false;
  }
}

// Demonstrate a 2D indexer.
class TwoDIndexerDemo {
  public static void Main() {
    FailSoftArray2D fs = new FailSoftArray2D(3, 5);
    int x;

    // show quiet failures
    Console.WriteLine("Fail quietly.");
```

```
    for(int i=0; i < 6; i++)
      fs[i, i] = i*10;

    for(int i=0; i < 6; i++) {
      x = fs[i,i];
      if(x != -1) Console.Write(x + " ");
    }
    Console.WriteLine();

    // now, generate failures
    Console.WriteLine("\nFail with error reports.");
    for(int i=0; i < 6; i++) {
      fs[i,i] = i*10;
      if(fs.errflag)
        Console.WriteLine("fs[" + i + ", " + i + "] out-of-bounds");
    }

    for(int i=0; i < 6; i++) {
      x = fs[i,i];
      if(!fs.errflag) Console.Write(x + " ");
      else
        Console.WriteLine("fs[" + i + ", " + i + "] out-of-bounds");
    }
  }
}
```

The output from this program is shown here:

```
Fail quietly.
0 10 20 0 0 0

Fail with error reports.
fs[3, 3] out-of-bounds
fs[4, 4] out-of-bounds
fs[5, 5] out-of-bounds
0 10 20 fs[3, 3] out-of-bounds
fs[4, 4] out-of-bounds
fs[5, 5] out-of-bounds
```

Properties

Another type of class member is the *property*. A property combines a field with the methods that access it. As some examples earlier in this book have shown, often you will want to create a field that is available to users of an object, but you want to maintain control over the operations allowed on that field. For instance, you might want to limit the range of values that can be assigned to that field. While it is possible to accomplish this goal through the use of a private variable along with methods to access its value, a property offers a better, more streamlined approach.

Properties are similar to indexers. A property consists of a name along with **get** and **set** accessors. The accessors are used to get and set the value of a variable. The key benefit of a property is that its name can be used in expressions and assignments like a normal variable, but in actuality the **get** and **set** accessors are automatically invoked. This is similar to the way that an indexer's **get** and **set** methods are automatically used.

The general form of a property is shown here:

```
type name {
   get {
      // get accessor code
   }

   set {
      // set accessor code
   }
}
```

Here, *type* specifies the type of the property, such as **int**, and *name* is the name of the property. Once the property has been defined, any use of *name* results in a call to its appropriate accessor. The **set** accessor automatically receives a parameter called **value** that contains the value being assigned to the property.

It is important to understand that properties do not define storage locations. Thus, a property manages access to a field. It does not, itself, provide that field. The field must be specified independently of the property.

Here is a simple example that defines a property called **myprop**, which is used to access the field **prop**. In this case, the property allows only positive values to be assigned.

```
// A simple property example.

using System;

class SimpProp {
  int prop; // field being managed by myprop
```

THE C# LANGUAGE

```csharp
    public SimpProp() { prop = 0; }

  /* This is the property that supports access to
     the private instance variable prop.  It
     allows only positive values. */
  public int myprop {
    get {
      return prop;
    }
    set {
      if(value >= 0) prop = value;
    }
  }
}

// Demonstrate a property.
class PropertyDemo {
  public static void Main() {
    SimpProp ob = new SimpProp();

    Console.WriteLine("Original value of ob.myprop: " + ob.myprop);

    ob.myprop = 100; // assign value
    Console.WriteLine("Value of ob.myprop: " + ob.myprop);

    // Can't assign negative value to prop
    Console.WriteLine("Attempting to assign -10 to ob.myprop");
    ob.myprop = -10;
    Console.WriteLine("Value of ob.myprop: " + ob.myprop);
  }
}
```

Output from this program is shown here:

```
Original value of ob.myprop: 0
Value of ob.myprop: 100
Attempting to assign -10 to ob.myprop
Value of ob.myprop: 100
```

Let's examine this program carefully. The program defines one private field, called
prop, and a property called **myprop** that manages access to **prop**. As explained, a property
by itself does not define a storage location. A property simply manages access to a field.

Thus, there is no concept of a property without an underlying field. Furthermore, because **prop** is private, it can be accessed *only* through **myprop**.

The property **myprop** is specified as **public** so that it can be accessed by code outside of its class. This makes sense because it provides access to **prop**, which is private. The **get** accessor simply returns the value of **prop**. The **set** accessor sets the value of **prop** if and only if that value is positive. Thus, the **myprop** property controls what values **prop** can have. This is the essence of why properties are important.

The type of property defined by **myprop** is called a read-write property because it allows its underlying field to be read and written. It is possible, however, to create read-only and write-only properties. To create a read-only property, define only a **get** accessor. To define a write-only property, define only a **set** accessor.

You can use a property to further improve the fail-soft array class. As you know, all arrays have a **Length** property associated with them. Up to now, the **FailSoftArray** class simply used a public integer field called **Length** for this purpose. This is not good practice, though, because it allows **Length** to be set to some value other than the length of the fail-soft array. (For example, a malicious programmer could intentionally corrupt its value.) We can remedy this situation by transforming **Length** into a read-only property, as shown in the following version of **FailSoftArray**:

```
// Add Length property to FailSoftArray.

using System;

class FailSoftArray {
  int[] a; // reference to underlying array
  int len; // length of array -- underlies Length property

  public bool errflag; // indicates outcome of last operation

  // Construct array given its size.
  public FailSoftArray(int size) {
    a = new int[size];
    len = size;
  }

  // Read-only Length property.
  public int Length {
    get {
      return len;
    }
  }
```

```
    // This is the indexer for FailSoftArray.
  public int this[int index] {
    // This is the get accessor.
    get {
      if(ok(index)) {
        errflag = false;
        return a[index];
      } else {
        errflag = true;
        return 0;
      }
    }

    // This is the set accessor
    set {
      if(ok(index)) {
        a[index] = value;
        errflag = false;
      }
      else errflag = true;
    }
  }

  // Return true if index is within bounds.
  private bool ok(int index) {
   if(index >= 0 & index < Length) return true;
   return false;
  }
}

// Demonstrate the improved fail-soft array.
class ImprovedFSDemo {
  public static void Main() {
    FailSoftArray fs = new FailSoftArray(5);
    int x;

    // can read Length
    for(int i=0; i < fs.Length; i++)
      fs[i] = i*10;

    for(int i=0; i < fs.Length; i++) {
      x = fs[i];
```

```
      if(x != -1) Console.Write(x + " ");
    }
    Console.WriteLine();

    // fs.Length = 10; // Error, illegal!
  }
}
```

Length is now a property that uses the private variable **len** for its storage. **Length** defines only a get accessor, which means that it is read-only. Thus, **Length** can be read, but not changed. To prove this to yourself, try removing the comment symbol preceding this line in the program:

```
// fs.Length = 10; // Error, illegal!
```

When you try to compile, you will receive an error message stating that **Length** is read-only.

Although the addition of the **Length** property improves **FailSoftArray**, it is not the only improvement that properties can make. The **errflag** member is also a prime candidate for conversion into a property since access to it should also be limited to read-only. Here is the final improvement of **FailSoftArray**. It creates a property called **Error** that uses the original **errflag** variable as its storage.

```
// Convert errflag into a property.

using System;

class FailSoftArray {
  int[] a; // reference to underlying array
  int len; // length of array

  bool errflag; // now private

  // Construct array given its size.
  public FailSoftArray(int size) {
    a = new int[size];
    len = size;
  }

  // Read-only Length property.
  public int Length {
```

```
    get {
      return len;
    }
  }

  // Read-only Error property.
  public bool Error {
    get {
      return errflag;
    }
  }

  // This is the indexer for FailSoftArray.
  public int this[int index] {
    // This is the get accessor.
    get {
      if(ok(index)) {
        errflag = false;
        return a[index];
      } else {
        errflag = true;
        return 0;
      }
    }

    // This is the set accessor
    set {
      if(ok(index)) {
        a[index] = value;
        errflag = false;
      }
      else errflag = true;
    }
  }

  // Return true if index is within bounds.
  private bool ok(int index) {
   if(index >= 0 & index < Length) return true;
   return false;
  }
}
```

```
// Demonstrate the improved fail-soft array.
class FinalFSDemo {
  public static void Main() {
    FailSoftArray fs = new FailSoftArray(5);

    // use Error property
    for(int i=0; i < fs.Length + 1; i++) {
      fs[i] = i*10;
      if(fs.Error)
        Console.WriteLine("Error with index " + i);
    }

  }
}
```

The creation of the **Error** property has caused two changes to be made to **FailSoftArray**. First, **errflag** has been made private because it is now used as the underlying storage for the **Error** property. Thus, it won't be available directly. Second, the read-only **Error** property has been added. Now, programs that need to detect errors will interrogate **Error**. This is demonstrated in **Main( )**, where a boundary error is intentionally generated, and the **Error** property is used to detect it.

Property Restrictions

Properties have some important restrictions. First, because a property does not define a storage location, it cannot be passed as a **ref** or **out** parameter to a method. Second, you cannot overload a property. (You *can* have two different properties that both access the same variable, but this would be unusual.) Finally, a property should not alter the state of the underlying variable when the **get** accessor is called, although this rule is not enforced by the compiler. A **get** operation should be nonintrusive.

Using Indexers and Properties

Although the preceding examples have demonstrated the basic mechanism of indexers and properties, they haven't displayed their full power. To conclude this chapter, a class called **RangeArray** is developed that uses indexers and properties to create an array type in which the index range of the array is determined by the programmer.

As you know, in C# arrays begin indexing at zero. However, some applications would benefit from an array that allows indexes to begin at any arbitrary point. For example, in some situations it might be more convenient for an array to begin indexing with 1. In another situation it might be beneficial to allow negative indices, such as an array that runs from –5 to 5. The **RangeArray** class developed here allows these and other types of indexing.

Using **RangeArray**, you can write code like this:

```
RangeArray ra = new RangeArray(-5, 10); // array with indexes from -5 to 10

for(int i=-5; i <= 10; i++) ra[i] = i; // index from -5 to 10
```

As you can guess, the first line constructs a **RangeArray** that runs from –5 to 10, inclusive. The first argument specifies the beginning index. The second argument specifies the ending index. Once **ra** has been constructed, it can be indexed from –5 to 10.

The entire **RangeArray** class is shown here, along with **RangeArrayDemo**, which demonstrates the array. As implemented here, **RangeArray** supports arrays of **int**, but you can change the type of data to any other.

```csharp
/* Create a specifiable range array class.
   The RangeArray class allows indexing
   to begin at some value other than zero.
   When you create a RangeArray, you specify
   the beginning and ending index. Negative
   indexes are also  allowed.  For example,
   you can create arrays that index from -5 to 5,
   1 to 10, or 50 to 56.
*/

using System;

class RangeArray {
  // private data
  int[] a; // reference to underlying array
  int lowerBound; // lowest index
  int upperBound; // greatest index

  // data for properties
  int len; // underlying var for Length property
  bool errflag; // underlying var for outcome

  // Construct array given its boundaries.
  public RangeArray(int low, int high) {
    high++;
    if(high <= low) {
      Console.WriteLine("Invalid Indices");
      high = 1; // create a minimal array for safety
```

```
      low = 0;
    }
    a = new int[high - low];
    len = high - low;

    lowerBound = low;
    upperBound = --high;
  }

  // Read-only Length property.
  public int Length {
    get {
      return len;
    }
  }

  // Read-only Error property.
  public bool Error {
    get {
      return errflag;
    }
  }

  // This is the indexer for RangeArray.
  public int this[int index] {
    // This is the get accessor.
    get {
      if(ok(index)) {
        errflag = false;
        return a[index - lowerBound];
      } else {
        errflag = true;
        return 0;
      }
    }

    // This is the set accessor
    set {
      if(ok(index)) {
        a[index - lowerBound] = value;
        errflag = false;
      }
      else errflag = true;
```

```
    }
  }

  // Return true if index is within bounds.
  private bool ok(int index) {
    if(index >= lowerBound & index <= upperBound) return true;
    return false;
  }
}

// Demonstrate the index-range array.
class RangeArrayDemo {
  public static void Main() {
    RangeArray ra = new RangeArray(-5, 5);
    RangeArray ra2 = new RangeArray(1, 10);
    RangeArray ra3 = new RangeArray(-20, -12);

    // Demonstrate ra
    Console.WriteLine("Length of ra: " + ra.Length);

    for(int i = -5; i <= 5; i++)
      ra[i] = i;

    Console.Write("Contents of ra: ");
    for(int i = -5; i <= 5; i++)
      Console.Write(ra[i] + " ");

    Console.WriteLine("\n");

    // Demonstrate ra2
    Console.WriteLine("Length of ra2: " + ra2.Length);

    for(int i = 1; i <= 10; i++)
      ra2[i] = i;

    Console.Write("Contents of ra2: ");
    for(int i = 1; i <= 10; i++)
      Console.Write(ra2[i] + " ");

    Console.WriteLine("\n");

    // Demonstrate ra3
    Console.WriteLine("Length of ra3: " + ra3.Length);
```

```
    for(int i = -20; i <= -12; i++)
      ra3[i] = i;

    Console.Write("Contents of ra3: ");
    for(int i = -20; i <= -12; i++)
      Console.Write(ra3[i] + " ");

    Console.WriteLine("\n");

  }
}
```

The output from the program is shown here:

```
Length of ra: 11
Contents of ra: -5 -4 -3 -2 -1 0 1 2 3 4 5

Length of ra2: 10
Contents of ra2: 1 2 3 4 5 6 7 8 9 10

Length of ra3: 9
Contents of ra3: -20 -19 -18 -17 -16 -15 -14 -13 -12
```

As the output verifies, objects of type **RangeArray** can be indexed in ways other than starting at zero. Let's look more closely at how **RangeArray** is implemented. **RangeArray** begins by defining the following private instance variables:

```
// private data
int[] a; // reference to underlying array
int lowerBound; // lowest index
int upperBound; // greatest index

// data for properties
int len; // underlying var for Length property
bool errflag; // underlying var for outcome
```

The underlying array is referred to by **a**. This array is allocated by the **RangeArray** constructor. The index of the lower bound of the array is stored in **lowerBound**, and the index of the upper bound is stored in **upperBound**. Next, the instances variables that support the **Length** and **Error** properties are declared.

The **RangeArray** constructor is shown here:

```
// Construct array given its boundaries.
public RangeArray(int low, int high) {
  high++;
  if(high <= low) {
    Console.WriteLine("Invalid Indices");
    high = 1; // create a minimal array for safety
    low = 0;
  }
  a = new int[high - low];
  len = high - low;

  lowerBound = low;
  upperBound = --high;
}
```

A **RangeArray** is constructed by passing the lower bound index in **low** and the upper bound index in **high**. The value of **high** is then incremented in order to compute the size of the array because the indices specified are inclusive. Next, a check is made to ensure that the upper index is greater than the lower index. If not, an error is reported and a one-element array is created. Next, storage for the array is allocated and assigned to **a**. Then **len** (which underlies the **Length** property) is set equal to the number of elements in the array. Finally, **lowerBound** and **upperBound** are set.

RangeArray then implements the **Length** and **Error** properties, as shown here:

```
// Read-only Length property.
public int Length {
  get {
    return len;
  }
}

// Read-only Error property.
public bool Error {
  get {
    return errflag;
  }
}
```

These properties are similar to those used by the **FailSoftArray** and work in the same way.

Next, **RangeArray** implements its indexer, as shown here:

```
// This is the indexer for RangeArray.
public int this[int index] {
  // This is the get accessor.
  get {
    if(ok(index)) {
      errflag = false;
      return a[index - lowerBound];
    } else {
      errflag = true;
      return 0;
    }
  }

  // This is the set accessor
  set {
    if(ok(index)) {
      a[index - lowerBound] = value;
      errflag = false;
    }
    else errflag = true;
  }
}
```

This indexer is similar to the one used by **FailSoftArray** with one important exception. Notice the expression that indexes **a**:

```
index - lowerBound
```

This expression transforms the index passed in **index** into a zero-based index suitable for use on **a**. This expression works whether **lowerBound** is positive, negative, or zero. The **ok( )** method is shown here:

```
// Return true if index is within bounds.
private bool ok(int index) {
  if(index >= lowerBound & index <= upperBound) return true;
  return false;
}
```

It is similar to the one used by **FailSoftArray** except that the range is checked by testing it against the values in **lowerBound** and **upperBound**.

RangeArray illustrates just one kind of custom array that you can create through the use of indexers and properties. There are, of course, several others. For example, you can create dynamic arrays, which expand and contract as needed, associative arrays, and sparse arrays. You might want to try creating one of these types of arrays as an exercise.

Chapter 11

Inheritance

I nheritance is one of the three foundational principles of object-oriented programming because it allows the creation of hierarchical classifications. Using inheritance, you can create a general class that defines traits common to a set of related items. This class can then be inherited by other, more specific classes, each adding those things that are unique to it.

In the language of C#, a class that is inherited is called a *base class*. The class that does the inheriting is called a *derived class*. Therefore, a derived class is a specialized version of a base class. It inherits all of the variables, methods, properties, operators, and indexers defined by the base class and adds its own unique elements.

Inheritance Basics

C# supports inheritance by allowing one class to incorporate another class into its declaration. This is done by specifying a base class when a derived class is declared. Let's begin with an example. The following class called **TwoDShape** defines the attributes of a "generic" two-dimensional shape, such as a square, rectangle, triangle, and so on.

```
// A class for two-dimensional objects.
class TwoDShape {
  public double width;
  public double height;

  public void showDim() {
    Console.WriteLine("Width and height are " +
                      width + " and " + height);
  }
}
```

TwoDShape can be used as a base class (that is, as a starting point) for classes that describe specific types of two-dimensional objects. For example, the following program uses **TwoDShape** to derive a class called **Triangle**. Pay close attention to the way that **Triangle** is declared.

```
// A simple class hierarchy.

using System;

// A class for two-dimensional objects.
class TwoDShape {
  public double width;
  public double height;
```

```
    public void showDim() {
      Console.WriteLine("Width and height are " +
                             width + " and " + height);
    }
}

// Triangle is derived from TwoDShape.
class Triangle : TwoDShape {
  public string style; // style of triangle

  // Return area of triangle.
  public double area() {
    return width * height / 2;
  }

  // Display a triangle's style.
  public void showStyle() {
    Console.WriteLine("Triangle is " + style);
  }
}

class Shapes {
  public static void Main() {
    Triangle t1 = new Triangle();
    Triangle t2 = new Triangle();

    t1.width = 4.0;
    t1.height = 4.0;
    t1.style = "isosceles";

    t2.width = 8.0;
    t2.height = 12.0;
    t2.style = "right";

    Console.WriteLine("Info for t1: ");
    t1.showStyle();
    t1.showDim();
    Console.WriteLine("Area is " + t1.area());

    Console.WriteLine();

    Console.WriteLine("Info for t2: ");
    t2.showStyle();
```

```
      t2.showDim();
      Console.WriteLine("Area is " + t2.area());
   }
}
```

The output from this program is shown here:

```
Info for t1:
Triangle is isosceles
Width and height are 4 and 4
Area is 8

Info for t2:
Triangle is right
Width and height are 8 and 12
Area is 48
```

The **Triangle** class creates a specific type of **TwoDShape**, in this case, a triangle. The **Triangle** class includes all of **TwoDShape** and adds the field **style**, the method **area( )**, and the method **showStyle( )**. A description of the type of triangle is stored in **style**, **area( )** computes and returns the area of the triangle, and **showStyle( )** displays the triangle style.

Notice the syntax that **Triangle** uses to inherit **TwoDShape**:

```
class Triangle : TwoDShape {
```

This syntax can be generalized. Whenever one class inherits another, the base class name follows the name of the derived class, separated by a colon. In C#, the syntax for inheriting a class is remarkably simple and easy-to-use.

Because **Triangle** includes all of the members of its base class, **TwoDShape**, it can access **width** and **height** inside **area( )**. Also, inside **Main( )**, objects **t1** and **t2** can refer to **width** and **height** directly, as if they were part of **Triangle**. Figure 11-1 depicts conceptually how **TwoDShape** is incorporated into **Triangle**.

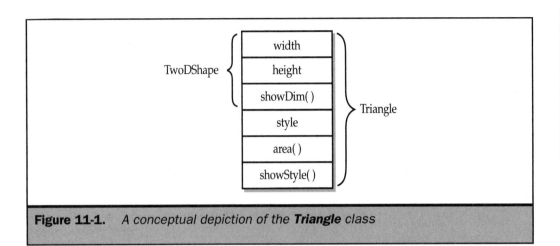

Figure 11-1.   *A conceptual depiction of the **Triangle** class*

Even though **TwoDShape** is a base for **Triangle**, it is also a completely independent, stand-alone class. Being a base class for a derived class does not mean that the base class cannot be used by itself. For example, the following is perfectly valid:

```
TwoDShape shape = new TwoDShape();

shape.width = 10;
shape.height = 20;

shape.showDim();
```

Of course, an object of **TwoDShape** has no knowledge of or access to any classes derived from **TwoDShape**.

The general form of a **class** declaration that inherits a base class is shown here:

class *derived-class-name* : *base-class-name* {
  // body of class
}

You can specify only one base class for any derived class that you create. C# does not support the inheritance of multiple base classes into a single derived class. (This differs from C++, in which you can inherit multiple base classes. Be aware of this when converting C++ code to C#.) You can, however, create a hierarchy of inheritance in which a derived class becomes a base class of another derived class. Of course, no class can be a base class of itself, either directly or indirectly.

A major advantage of inheritance is that once you have created a base class that defines the attributes common to a set of objects, it can be used to create any number of more specific derived classes. Each derived class can precisely tailor its own classification. For example, here is another class derived from **TwoDShape** that encapsulates rectangles:

```
// A derived class of TwoDShape for rectangles.
class Rectangle : TwoDShape {
  // Return true if the rectangle is square.
  public bool isSquare() {
    if(width == height) return true;
    return false;
  }

  // Return area of the rectangle.
  public double area() {
    return width * height;
  }
}
```

The **Rectangle** class includes **TwoDShape** and adds the methods **isSquare( )**, which determines if the rectangle is square, and **area( )**, which computes the area of a rectangle.

Member Access and Inheritance

As you learned in Chapter 8, members of a class are often declared private to prevent their unauthorized use or tampering. Inheriting a class *does not* overrule the private access restriction. Thus, even though a derived class includes all of the members of its base class, it cannot access those members of the base class that are private. For example, if, as shown here, **width** and **height** are made private in **TwoDShape**, then **Triangle** will not be able to access them:

```
// Private members are not inherited.

// This example will not compile.
using System;
```

```
// A class for two-dimensional objects.
class TwoDShape {
  double width;  // now private
  double height; // now private

  public void showDim() {
    Console.WriteLine("Width and height are " +
                        width + " and " + height);
  }
}

// Triangle is derived from TwoDShape.
class Triangle : TwoDShape {
  public string style; // style of triangle

  // Return area of triangle.
  public double area() {
    return width * height / 2; // Error, can't access private member
  }

  // Display a triangle's style.
  public void showStyle() {
    Console.WriteLine("Triangle is " + style);
  }
}
```

The **Triangle** class will not compile because the reference to **width** and **height** inside the **area( )** method causes an access violation. Since **width** and **height** are now private, they are only accessible by other members of their own class. Derived classes have no access to them.

 A private class member will remain private to its class. It is not accessible by any code outside its class, including derived classes.

At first, you might think that it is a serious restriction that derived classes do not have access to the private members of base classes, because it would prevent the use of private members in many situations. However, this is not true, because C# provides various solutions. One is to use **protected** members, which is described in the next section. A second is to use public properties or methods to provide access to private data. As you have seen in the preceding chapters, C# programmers typically grant access to the private members of a class through methods or by making them into properties. Here is a rewrite of the **TwoDShape** classes that makes **width** and **height** into properties:

```
// Use properties to set and get private members.
```

```csharp
using System;

// A class for two-dimensional objects.
class TwoDShape {
  double pri_width;   // now private
  double pri_height;  // now private

  // Properties for width and height.
  public double width {
     get { return pri_width; }
     set { pri_width = value; }
  }

  public double height {
     get { return pri_height; }
     set { pri_height = value; }
  }

  public void showDim() {
    Console.WriteLine("Width and height are " +
                      width + " and " + height);
  }
}

// A derived class of TwoDShape for triangles.
class Triangle : TwoDShape {
  public string style; // style of triangle

  // Return area of triangle.
  public double area() {
    return width * height / 2;
  }

  // Display a triangle's style.
  public void showStyle() {
    Console.WriteLine("Triangle is " + style);
  }
}

class Shapes2 {
  public static void Main() {
    Triangle t1 = new Triangle();
    Triangle t2 = new Triangle();
```

```
      t1.width = 4.0;
      t1.height = 4.0;
      t1.style = "isosceles";

      t2.width = 8.0;
      t2.height = 12.0;
      t2.style = "right";

      Console.WriteLine("Info for t1: ");
      t1.showStyle();
      t1.showDim();
      Console.WriteLine("Area is " + t1.area());

      Console.WriteLine();

      Console.WriteLine("Info for t2: ");
      t2.showStyle();
      t2.showDim();
      Console.WriteLine("Area is " + t2.area());
  }
}
```

When referring to base and derived classes, sometimes the terms *superclass* and *subclass* are used. These terms come from Java programming. What Java calls a superclass, C# calls a base class. What Java calls a subclass, C# calls a derived class. You will commonly hear both sets of terms applied to a class of either language, but this book will continue to use the standard C# terms. C++ also uses the base-class/derived-class terminology.

Using Protected Access

As just explained, a private member of a base class is not accessible by a derived class. This would seem to imply that if you wanted a derived class to have access to some member in the base class, it would need to be public. Of course, making the member public also makes it available to all other code, which may not be desirable. Fortunately, this implication is untrue because C# allows you to create a *protected member.* A protected member is public within a class hierarchy, but private outside that hierarchy.

A protected member is created by using the **protected** access modifier. When a member of a class is declared as **protected**, that member is, with one important exception, private. The exception occurs when a protected member is inherited. In this case, a protected member of the base class becomes a protected member of the derived class and is, therefore, accessible by the derived class. Therefore, by using **protected**, you can create class members that are private to their class but that can still be inherited and accessed by a derived class.

Here is a simple example that uses **protected**:

```
// Demonstrate protected.

using System;

class B {
  protected int i, j; // private to B, but accessible by D

  public void set(int a, int b) {
    i = a;
    j = b;
  }

  public void show() {
    Console.WriteLine(i + " " + j);
  }
}

class D : B {
  int k; // private

  // D can access B's i and j
  public void setk() {
    k = i * j;
  }

  public void showk() {
    Console.WriteLine(k);
  }
}

class ProtectedDemo {
  public static void Main() {
    D ob = new D();

    ob.set(2, 3); // OK, known to D
    ob.show();    // OK, known to D

    ob.setk();  // OK, part of D
    ob.showk(); // OK, part of D
```

```
    }
}
```

In this example, because **B** is inherited by **D** and because **i** and **j** are declared as **protected** in **B**, the **setk( )** method can access them. If **i** and **j** had been declared as private by **B**, then **D** would not have access to them, and the program would not compile.

Like **public** and **private**, **protected** status stays with a member no matter how many layers of inheritance are involved. Therefore, when a derived class is used as a base class for another derived class, any protected member of the initial base class that is inherited by the first derived class is also inherited as protected by a second derived class.

Constructors and Inheritance

In a hierarchy, it is possible for both base classes and derived classes to have their own constructors. This raises an important question: what constructor is responsible for building an object of the derived class? The one in the base class, the one in the derived class, or both? The answer: the constructor for the base class constructs the base class portion of the object, and the constructor for the derived class constructs the derived class part. This makes sense because the base class has no knowledge of or access to any element in a derived class. Thus, their construction must be separate. The preceding examples have relied upon the default constructors created automatically by C#, so this was not an issue. However, in practice, most classes will have constructors. Here you will see how to handle this situation.

When only the derived class defines a constructor, the process is straightforward: simply construct the derived class object. The base class portion of the object is constructed automatically using its default constructor. For example, here is a reworked version of **Triangle** that defines a constructor. It also makes **style** private since it is now set by the constructor.

```
// Add a constructor to Triangle.

using System;

// A class for two dimensional objects.
class TwoDShape {
  double pri_width;  // private
  double pri_height; // private

  // properties for width and height.
  public double width {
```

```
      get { return pri_width; }
      set { pri_width = value; }
  }

  public double height {
      get { return pri_height; }
      set { pri_height = value; }
  }

  public void showDim() {
    Console.WriteLine("Width and height are " +
                      width + " and " + height);
  }
}

// A derived class of TwoDShape for triangles.
class Triangle : TwoDShape {
  string style; // private

  // Constructor
  public Triangle(string s, double w, double h) {
    width = w;   // init the base class
    height = h; // init the base class

    style = s;   // init the derived class
  }

  // Return area of triangle.
  public double area() {
    return width * height / 2;
  }

  // Display a triangle's style.
  public void showStyle() {
    Console.WriteLine("Triangle is " + style);
  }
}

class Shapes3 {
  public static void Main() {
    Triangle t1 = new Triangle("isosceles", 4.0, 4.0);
    Triangle t2 = new Triangle("right", 8.0, 12.0);
```

```
      Console.WriteLine("Info for t1: ");
      t1.showStyle();
      t1.showDim();
      Console.WriteLine("Area is " + t1.area());

      Console.WriteLine();

      Console.WriteLine("Info for t2: ");
      t2.showStyle();
      t2.showDim();
      Console.WriteLine("Area is " + t2.area());
    }
}
```

Here, **Triangle**'s constructor initializes the members of **TwoDShape** that it inherits along with its own **style** field.

When both the base class and the derived class define constructors, the process is a bit more complicated because both the base class and derived class constructors must be executed. In this case you must use another of C#'s keywords: **base**, which has two uses. The first use is to call a base class constructor. The second is to access a member of the base class that has been hidden by a member of a derived class. Here, we will look at its first use.

Calling Base Class Constructors

A derived class can call a constructor defined in its base class by using an expanded form of the derived class' constructor declaration and the **base** keyword. The general form of this expanded declaration is shown here:

derived-constructor(*parameter-list*) : base(*arg-list*) {
   // body of constructor
}

Here, *arg-list* specifies any arguments needed by the constructor in the base class. Notice the placement of the colon.

To see how **base** is used, consider the version **TwoDShape** in the following program. It defines a constructor that initializes the **width** and **height** properties.

```
// Add constructors to TwoDShape.

using System;
```

```csharp
// A class for two-dimensional objects.
class TwoDShape {
  double pri_width;  // private
  double pri_height; // private

  // Constructor for TwoDShape.
  public TwoDShape(double w, double h) {
    width = w;
    height = h;
  }

  // properties for width and height.
  public double width {
     get { return pri_width; }
     set { pri_width = value; }
  }

  public double height {
     get { return pri_height; }
     set { pri_height = value; }
  }

  public void showDim() {
    Console.WriteLine("Width and height are " +
                         width + " and " + height);
  }
}

 // A derived class of TwoDShape for triangles.
class Triangle : TwoDShape {
  string style; // private

  // Call the base class constructor.
  public Triangle(string s, double w, double h) : base(w, h) {
    style = s;
  }

  // Return area of triangle.
  public double area() {
    return width * height / 2;
  }
```

```
    // Display a triangle's style.
  public void showStyle() {
    Console.WriteLine("Triangle is " + style);
  }
}

class Shapes4 {
  public static void Main() {
    Triangle t1 = new Triangle("isosceles", 4.0, 4.0);
    Triangle t2 = new Triangle("right", 8.0, 12.0);

    Console.WriteLine("Info for t1: ");
    t1.showStyle();
    t1.showDim();
    Console.WriteLine("Area is " + t1.area());

    Console.WriteLine();

    Console.WriteLine("Info for t2: ");
    t2.showStyle();
    t2.showDim();
    Console.WriteLine("Area is " + t2.area());
  }
}
```

Here, **Triangle( )** calls **base** with the parameters **w** and **h**. This causes the **TwoDShape( )** constructor to be called, which initializes **width** and **height** using these values. **Triangle** no longer initializes these values itself. It need only initialize the value unique to it: **style**. This leaves **TwoDShape** free to construct its subobject in any manner that it so chooses. Furthermore, **TwoDShape** can add functionality about which existing derived classes have no knowledge, thus preventing existing code from breaking.

Any form of constructor defined by the base class can be called by **base**. The constructor executed will be the one that matches the arguments. For example, here are expanded versions of both **TwoDShape** and **Triangle** that include default constructors and constructors that take one argument.

```
// Add more constructors to TwoDShape.

using System;

class TwoDShape {
```

```
   double pri_width;  // private
   double pri_height; // private

   // Default constructor.
   public TwoDShape() {
     width = height = 0.0;
   }

   // Constructor for TwoDShape.
   public TwoDShape(double w, double h) {
     width = w;
     height = h;
   }

   // Construct object with equal width and height.
   public TwoDShape(double x) {
     width = height = x;
   }

   // Properties for width and height.
   public double width {
      get { return pri_width; }
      set { pri_width = value; }
   }

   public double height {
      get { return pri_height; }
      set { pri_height = value; }
   }

   public void showDim() {
     Console.WriteLine("Width and height are " +
                        width + " and " + height);
   }
}

// A derived class of TwoDShape for triangles.
class Triangle : TwoDShape {
  string style; // private

  /* A default constructor. This automatically invokes
     the default constructor of TwoDShape. */
```

```
  public Triangle() {
    style = "null";
  }

  // Constructor that takes three arguments.
  public Triangle(string s, double w, double h) : base(w, h) {
    style = s;
  }

  // Construct an isosceles triangle.
  public Triangle(double x) : base(x) {
    style = "isosceles";
  }

  // Return area of triangle.
  public double area() {
    return width * height / 2;
  }

  // Display a triangle's style.
  public void showStyle() {
    Console.WriteLine("Triangle is " + style);
  }
}

class Shapes5 {
  public static void Main() {
    Triangle t1 = new Triangle();
    Triangle t2 = new Triangle("right", 8.0, 12.0);
    Triangle t3 = new Triangle(4.0);

    t1 = t2;

    Console.WriteLine("Info for t1: ");
    t1.showStyle();
    t1.showDim();
    Console.WriteLine("Area is " + t1.area());

    Console.WriteLine();

    Console.WriteLine("Info for t2: ");
    t2.showStyle();
```

```
        t2.showDim();
        Console.WriteLine("Area is " + t2.area());

        Console.WriteLine();

        Console.WriteLine("Info for t3: ");
        t3.showStyle();
        t3.showDim();
        Console.WriteLine("Area is " + t3.area());

        Console.WriteLine();
    }
}
```

Here is the output from this version:

```
Info for t1:
Triangle is right
Width and height are 8 and 12
Area is 48

Info for t2:
Triangle is right
Width and height are 8 and 12
Area is 48

Info for t3:
Triangle is isosceles
Width and height are 4 and 4
Area is 8
```

Let's review the key concepts behind **base**. When a derived class specifies a **base** clause, it is calling the constructor of its immediate base class. Thus, **base** always refers to the base class immediately above the calling class. This is true even in a multileveled hierarchy. You pass arguments to the base constructor by specifying them as arguments to **base**. If no **base** clause is present, then the base class' default constructor is called automatically.

Inheritance and Name Hiding

It is possible for a derived class to define a member that has the same name as a member in its base class. When this happens, the member in the base class is hidden within the derived class. While this is not technically an error in C#, the compiler will issue a warning message. This warning alerts you to the fact that a name is being hidden. If your intent is to hide a base class member, then to prevent this warning, the derived class member must be preceded by the **new** keyword. Understand that this use of **new** is separate and distinct from its use when creating an object instance.

Here is an example of name hiding:

```
// An example of inheritance-related name hiding.

using System;

class A {
  public int i = 0;
}

// Create a derived class.
class B : A {
  new int i; // this i hides the i in A

  public B(int b) {
    i = b; // i in B
  }

  public void show() {
    Console.WriteLine("i in derived class: " + i);
  }
}

class NameHiding {
  public static void Main() {
    B ob = new B(2);

    ob.show();
  }
}
```

First, notice the use of **new** when **i** is declared in **B**. In essence, it tells the compiler that you know that a new variable called **i** is being created that hides the **i** in the base class **A**. If you leave **new** out, a warning is generated.

The output produced by this program is shown here:

```
i in derived class: 2
```

Since **B** defines its own instance variable called **i**, it hides the **i** in **A**. Therefore, when **show( )** is invoked on an object of type **B**, the value of **i** as defined by **B** is displayed—not the one defined in **A**.

Using base to Access a Hidden Name

There is a second form of **base** that acts somewhat like **this**, except that it always refers to the base class of the derived class in which it is used. This usage has the following general form:

base.*member*

Here, *member* can be either a method or an instance variable. This form of **base** is most applicable to situations in which a member name in a derived class hides a member by the same name in the base class. Consider this version of the class hierarchy from the preceding example:

```
// Using base to overcome name hiding.

using System;

class A {
  public int i = 0;
}

// Create a derived class.
class B : A {
  new int i; // this i hides the i in A

  public B(int a, int b) {
    base.i = a; // this uncovers the i in A
    i = b; // i in B
  }

  public void show() {
    // this displays the i in A.
    Console.WriteLine("i in base class: " + base.i);

    // this displays the i in B
    Console.WriteLine("i in derived class: " + i);
  }
}

class UncoverName {
  public static void Main() {
    B ob = new B(1, 2);
```

```
      ob.show();
   }
}
```

This program displays the following:

```
i in base class: 1
i in derived class: 2
```

Although the instance variable **i** in **B** hides the **i** in **A**, **base** allows access to the **i** defined in the base class.

Hidden methods can also be called through the use of **base**. Consider this example:

```
// Call a hidden method.

using System;

class A {
  public int i = 0;

  // show() in A
  public void show() {
    Console.WriteLine("i in base class: " + i);
  }
}

// Create a derived class.
class B : A {
  new int i; // this i hides the i in A

  public B(int a, int b) {
    base.i = a; // this uncovers the i in A
    i = b; // i in B
  }

  // This hides show() in A. Notice the use of new.
  new public void show() {
    base.show(); // this calls show() in A

    // this displays the i in B
    Console.WriteLine("i in derived class: " + i);
```

```
   }
}

class UncoverName {
  public static void Main() {
    B ob = new B(1, 2);

    ob.show();
  }
}
```

The output from the program is shown here:

```
i in base class: 1
i in derived class: 2
```

As you can see, **base.show( )** calls the base class version of **show( )**.

One other point: notice that **new** is used in this program to tell the compiler that you know that a new method called **show( )** is being created that hides the **show( )** in **A**.

Creating a Multilevel Hierarchy

Up to this point, we have been using simple class hierarchies consisting of only a base class and a derived class. However, you can build hierarchies that contain as many layers of inheritance as you like. As mentioned, it is perfectly acceptable to use a derived class as a base class of another. For example, given three classes called **A**, **B**, and **C**, **C** can be derived from **B**, which can be derived from **A**. When this type of situation occurs, each derived class inherits all of the traits found in all of its base classes. In this case, **C** inherits all aspects of **B** and **A**.

To see how a multilevel hierarchy can be useful, consider the following program. In it, the derived class **Triangle** is used as a base class to create the derived class called **ColorTriangle**. **ColorTriangle** inherits all of the traits of **Triangle** and **TwoDShape**, and adds a field called **color**, which holds the color of the triangle.

```
// A multilevel hierarchy.

using System;

class TwoDShape {
```

```csharp
    double pri_width;  // private
    double pri_height; // private

    // Default constructor.
    public TwoDShape() {
      width = height = 0.0;
    }

    // Constructor for TwoDShape.
    public TwoDShape(double w, double h) {
      width = w;
      height = h;
    }

    // Construct object with equal width and height.
    public TwoDShape(double x) {
      width = height = x;
    }

    // Properties for width and height.
    public double width {
        get { return pri_width; }
        set { pri_width = value; }
    }

    public double height {
        get { return pri_height; }
        set { pri_height = value; }
    }

    public void showDim() {
      Console.WriteLine("Width and height are " +
                        width + " and " + height);
    }
}

// A derived class of TwoDShape for triangles.
class Triangle : TwoDShape {
  string style; // private

  /* A default constructor. This invokes the default
     constructor of TwoDShape. */
```

```csharp
    public Triangle() {
      style = "null";
    }

    // Constructor
    public Triangle(string s, double w, double h) : base(w, h) {
      style = s;
    }

    // Construct an isosceles triangle.
    public Triangle(double x) : base(x) {
      style = "isosceles";
    }

    // Return area of triangle.
    public double area() {
      return width * height / 2;
    }

    // Display a triangle's style.
    public void showStyle() {
      Console.WriteLine("Triangle is " + style);
    }
}

// Extend Triangle.
class ColorTriangle : Triangle {
  string color;

  public ColorTriangle(string c, string s,
                       double w, double h) : base(s, w, h) {
    color = c;
  }

  // Display the color.
  public void showColor() {
    Console.WriteLine("Color is " + color);
  }
}

class Shapes6 {
  public static void Main() {
    ColorTriangle t1 =
```

```
        new ColorTriangle("Blue", "right", 8.0, 12.0);
    ColorTriangle t2 =
        new ColorTriangle("Red", "isosceles", 2.0, 2.0);

    Console.WriteLine("Info for t1: ");
    t1.showStyle();
    t1.showDim();
    t1.showColor();
    Console.WriteLine("Area is " + t1.area());

    Console.WriteLine();

    Console.WriteLine("Info for t2: ");
    t2.showStyle();
    t2.showDim();
    t2.showColor();
    Console.WriteLine("Area is " + t2.area());
  }
}
```

The output of this program is shown here:

```
Info for t1:
Triangle is right
Width and height are 8 and 12
Color is Blue
Area is 48

Info for t2:
Triangle is isosceles
Width and height are 2 and 2
Color is Red
Area is 2
```

Because of inheritance, **ColorTriangle** can make use of the previously defined classes of **Triangle** and **TwoDShape**, adding only the extra information it needs for its own, specific application. This is part of the value of inheritance; it allows the reuse of code.

This example illustrates one other important point: **base** always refers to the constructor in the closest base class. The **base** in **ColorTriangle** calls the constructor in **Triangle**. The **base** in **Triangle** calls the constructor in **TwoDShape**. In a class hierarchy, if a base class constructor requires parameters, then all derived classes must pass those parameters "up the line." This is true whether or not a derived class needs parameters of its own.

When Are Constructors Called?

In the foregoing discussion of inheritance and class hierarchies, an important question may have occurred to you: When a derived class object is created, whose constructor is executed first, the one in the derived class or the one defined by the base class? For example, given a derived class called **B** and a base class called **A**, is **A**'s constructor called before **B**'s, or vice versa? The answer is that in a class hierarchy, constructors are called in order of derivation, from base class to derived class. Furthermore, this order is the same whether or not **base** is used. If **base** is not used, then the default (parameterless) constructor of each base class will be executed. The following program illustrates the order of constructor execution:

```csharp
// Demonstrate when constructors are called.

using System;

// Create a base class.
class A {
  public A() {
    Console.WriteLine("Constructing A.");
  }
}

// Create a class derived from A.
class B : A {
  public B() {
    Console.WriteLine("Constructing B.");
  }
}

// Create a class derived from B.
class C : B {
  public C() {
    Console.WriteLine("Constructing C.");
  }
}

class OrderOfConstruction {
  public static void Main() {
    C c = new C();
  }
}
```

The output from this program is shown here:

```
Constructing A
Constructing B
Constructing C
```

As you can see, the constructors are called in order of derivation.

If you think about it, it makes sense that constructor functions are executed in order of derivation. Because a base class has no knowledge of any derived class, any initialization it needs to perform is separate from and possibly prerequisite to any initialization performed by the derived class. Therefore, it must be executed first.

Base Class References and Derived Objects

As you know, C# is a strongly typed language. Aside from the standard conversions and automatic promotions that apply to its simple types, type compatibility is strictly enforced. Therefore, a reference variable for one class type cannot normally refer to an object of another class type. For example, consider the following program:

```
// This program will not compile.

class X {
  int a;

  public X(int i) { a = i; }
}

class Y {
  int a;

  public Y(int i) { a = i; }
}

class IncompatibleRef {
  public static void Main() {
    X x = new X(10);
    X x2;
    Y y = new Y(5);

    x2 = x; // OK, both of same type

    x2 = y; // Error, not of same type
  }
}
```

Here, even though class **X** and class **Y** are physically the same, it is not possible to assign a **Y** object to an **X** reference variable, because they have different types. In general, an object reference variable can refer only to objects of its type.

There is, however, an important exception to C#'s strict type enforcement. A reference variable of a base class can be assigned a reference to an object of any class derived from that base class. Here is an example:

```
// A base class reference can refer to a derived class object.

using System;

class X {
  public int a;

  public X(int i) {
    a = i;
  }
}

class Y : X {
  public int b;

  public Y(int i, int j) : base(j) {
    b = i;
  }
}

class BaseRef {
  public static void Main() {
    X x = new X(10);
    X x2;
    Y y = new Y(5, 6);

    x2 = x; // OK, both of same type
    Console.WriteLine("x2.a: " + x2.a);

    x2 = y; // still Ok because Y is derived from X
    Console.WriteLine("x2.a: " + x2.a);

    // X references know only about X members
    x2.a = 19; // OK
//    x2.b = 27; // Error, X doesn't have a b member
  }
}
```

Here, **Y** is now derived from **X**; thus it is permissible for **x2** to be assigned a reference to a **Y** object.

It is important to understand that it is the type of the reference variable—not the type of the object that it refers to—that determines what members can be accessed. That is, when a reference to a derived class object is assigned to a base class reference variable, you will have access only to those parts of the object defined by the base class. This is why **x2** can't access **b** even when it refers to a **Y** object. This makes sense because the base class has no knowledge of what a derived class adds to it. This is why the last line of code in the program is commented out.

Although the preceding discussion may seem a bit esoteric, it has some important practical applications. One is described here. The other is discussed later in this chapter, when virtual methods are covered.

An important place where derived class references are assigned to base class variables is when constructors are called in a class hierarchy. As you know, it is common for a class to define a constructor that takes an object of its class as a parameter. This allows the class to construct a copy of an object. Classes derived from such a class can take advantage of this feature. For example, consider the following versions of **TwoDShape** and **Triangle**. Both add constructors that take an object as a parameter.

```
// Pass a derived class reference to a base class reference.

using System;

class TwoDShape {
  double pri_width;  // private
  double pri_height; // private

  // Default constructor.
  public TwoDShape() {
    width = height = 0.0;
  }

  // Constructor for TwoDShape.
  public TwoDShape(double w, double h) {
    width = w;
    height = h;
  }

  // Construct object with equal width and height.
  public TwoDShape(double x) {
    width = height = x;
  }

  // Construct object from an object.
```

```csharp
  public TwoDShape(TwoDShape ob) {
    width = ob.width;
    height = ob.height;
  }

  // Properties for width and height.
  public double width {
     get { return pri_width; }
     set { pri_width = value; }
  }

  public double height {
     get { return pri_height; }
     set { pri_height = value; }
  }

  public void showDim() {
    Console.WriteLine("Width and height are " +
                       width + " and " + height);
  }
}

// A derived class of TwoDShape for triangles.
class Triangle : TwoDShape {
  string style; // private

  // A default constructor.
  public Triangle() {
    style = "null";
  }

  // Constructor for Triangle.
  public Triangle(string s, double w, double h) : base(w, h) {
    style = s;
  }

  // Construct an isosceles triangle.
  public Triangle(double x) : base(x) {
    style = "isosceles";
  }

  // Construct an object from an object.
```

```
    public Triangle(Triangle ob) : base(ob) {
      style = ob.style;
    }

    // Return area of triangle.
    public double area() {
      return width * height / 2;
    }

    // Display a triangle's style.
    public void showStyle() {
      Console.WriteLine("Triangle is " + style);
    }
  }

class Shapes7 {
  public static void Main() {
    Triangle t1 = new Triangle("right", 8.0, 12.0);

    // make a copy of t1
    Triangle t2 = new Triangle(t1);

    Console.WriteLine("Info for t1: ");
    t1.showStyle();
    t1.showDim();
    Console.WriteLine("Area is " + t1.area());

    Console.WriteLine();

    Console.WriteLine("Info for t2: ");
    t2.showStyle();
    t2.showDim();
    Console.WriteLine("Area is " + t2.area());
  }
}
```

In this program, **t2** is constructed from **t1** and is, thus, identical. The output is shown here:

```
Info for t1:
Triangle is right
```

```
Width and height are 8 and 12
Area is 48

Info for t2:
Triangle is right
Width and height are 8 and 12
Area is 48
```

Pay special attention to this **Triangle** constructor:

```
// Construct an object from an object.
public Triangle(Triangle ob) : base(ob) {
  style = ob.style;
}
```

It receives an object of type **Triangle**, and it passes that object (through **base**) to this **TwoDShape** constructor:

```
// Construct object from an object.
public TwoDShape(TwoDShape ob) {
  width = ob.width;
  height = ob.height;
}
```

The key point is that **TwoDShape( )** is expecting a **TwoDShape** object. However, **Triangle( )** passes it a **Triangle** object. As explained, the reason this works is because a base class reference can refer to a derived class object. Thus, it is perfectly acceptable to pass **TwoDShape( )** a reference to an object of a class derived from **TwoDShape**. Because the **TwoDShape( )** constructor is initializing only those portions of the derived class object that are members of **TwoDShape**, it doesn't matter that the object might also contain other members added by derived classes.

Virtual Methods and Overriding

A *virtual method* is a method that is declared as **virtual** in a base class and redefined in one or more derived classes. Thus, each derived class can have its own version of a virtual method. Virtual methods are interesting because of what happens when one is called through a base class reference. In this situation, C# determines which version of the method to call based upon the *type* of the object *referred to* by the reference—and this determination is made *at runtime*. Thus, when different objects are referred to, different versions of the virtual method are executed. In other words, it is the type of the object being referred to (not the type of the reference) that determines which version of the virtual method will be executed. Therefore, if a base class contains a virtual method and classes are derived from that base class, then when different types of objects are referred to through a base class reference, different versions of the virtual method are executed.

You declare a method as virtual inside a base class by preceding its declaration with the keyword **virtual**. When a virtual method is redefined by a derived class, the **override** modifier is used. Thus, the process of redefining a virtual method inside a derived class is called *method overriding*. When overriding a method, the type signature of the override method must be the same as the virtual method that is being overridden. Also, a virtual method cannot be specified as **static** or **abstract** (discussed later in this chapter).

Method overriding forms the basis for one of C#'s most powerful concepts: *dynamic method dispatch*. Dynamic method dispatch is the mechanism by which a call to an overridden function is resolved at runtime, rather than compile time. Dynamic method dispatch is important because this is how C# implements runtime polymorphism.

Here is an example that illustrates virtual methods and overriding:

```
// Demonstrate a virtual method.

using System;

class Base {
  // Create virtual method in the base class.
  public virtual void who() {
    Console.WriteLine("who() in Base");
  }
}

class Derived1 : Base {
  // Override who() in a derived class.
  public override void who() {
    Console.WriteLine("who() in Derived1");
  }
}

class Derived2 : Base {
  // Override who() again in another derived class.
  public override void who() {
    Console.WriteLine("who() in Derived2");
  }
}
```

```
class OverrideDemo {
  public static void Main() {
    Base baseOb = new Base();
    Derived1 dOb1 = new Derived1();
    Derived2 dOb2 = new Derived2();

    Base baseRef; // a base-class reference

    baseRef = baseOb;
    baseRef.who();

    baseRef = dOb1;
    baseRef.who();

    baseRef = dOb2;
    baseRef.who();
  }
}
```

The output from the program is shown here:

```
who() in Base
who() in Derived1
who() in Derived2
```

This program creates a base class called **Base** and two derived classes, called **Derived1** and **Derived2**. **Base** declares a method called **who( )**, and the derived classes override it. Inside the **Main( )** method, objects of type **Base**, **Derived1**, and **Derived2** are declared. Also, a reference of type **Base**, called **baseRef**, is declared. The program then assigns a reference to each type of object to **baseRef** and uses that reference to call **who( )**. As the output shows, the version of **who( )** executed is determined by the type of object being referred to at the time of the call, not by the class type of **baseRef**.

It is not necessary to override a virtual method. If a derived class does not provide its own version of a virtual method, then the one in the base class is used. For example:

```
/* When a virtual method is not overridden,
   the base class method is used. */

using System;

class Base {
```

```
    // Create virtual method in the base class.
    public virtual void who() {
      Console.WriteLine("who() in Base");
    }
  }

  class Derived1 : Base {
    // Override who() in a derived class.
    public override void who() {
      Console.WriteLine("who() in Derived1");
    }
  }

  class Derived2 : Base {
    // This class does not override who().
  }

  class NoOverrideDemo {
    public static void Main() {
      Base baseOb = new Base();
      Derived1 dOb1 = new Derived1();
      Derived2 dOb2 = new Derived2();

      Base baseRef; // a base-class reference

      baseRef = baseOb;
      baseRef.who();

      baseRef = dOb1;
      baseRef.who();

      baseRef = dOb2;
      baseRef.who(); // calls Base's who()
    }
  }
```

The output from this program is shown here:

```
who() in Base
who() in Derived1
who() in Base
```

Here, **Derived2** does not override **who( )**. Thus, when **who( )** is called on a **derived2** object, the **who( )** in **Base** is executed.

In the case of a multilevel hierarchy, if a derived class does not override a virtual method, then, while moving up the hierarchy, the first override of the method that is encountered is the one executed. For example:

```
/*  In a multilevel hierarchy, the
    first override of a virtual method
    that is found while moving up the
    hierarchy is the one executed. */

using System;

class Base {
  // Create virtual method in the base class.
  public virtual void who() {
    Console.WriteLine("who() in Base");
  }
}

class Derived1 : Base {
  // Override who() in a derived class.
  public override void who() {
    Console.WriteLine("who() in Derived1");
  }
}

class Derived2 : Derived1 {
  // This class also does not override who().
}

class Derived3 : Derived2 {
  // This class does not override who().
}

class NoOverrideDemo2 {
  public static void Main() {
    Derived3 dOb = new Derived3();
    Base baseRef; // a base-class reference

    baseRef = dOb;
    baseRef.who(); // calls Derived1's who()
  }
}
```

The output is shown here:

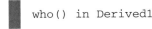
```
who() in Derived1
```

Here, **Derived3** inherits **Derived2**, which inherits **Derived1**, which inherits **Base**. As the output verifies, since **who( )** is not overridden by either **Derived3** or **Derived2**, it is the override of **who( )** in **Derived1** that is executed, since it is the first version of **who( )** that is found.

One other point: Properties can also be modified by the **virtual** keyword and overridden using **override**.

Why Overridden Methods?

Overridden methods allow C# to support runtime polymorphism. Polymorphism is essential to object-oriented programming because it allows a general class to specify methods that will be common to all of its derivatives, while allowing derived classes to define the specific implementation of some or all of those methods. Overridden methods are another way that C# implements the "one interface, multiple methods" aspect of polymorphism.

Part of the key to successfully applying polymorphism is understanding that the base classes and derived classes form a hierarchy that moves from lesser to greater specialization. Used correctly, the base class provides all elements that a derived class can use directly. It also defines those methods that the derived class must implement on its own. This allows the derived class the flexibility to define its own methods, yet still enforces a consistent interface. Thus, by combining inheritance with overridden methods, a base class can define the general form of the methods that will be used by all of its derived classes.

Applying Virtual Methods

To better understand the power of virtual methods, we will apply them to the **TwoDShape** class. In the preceding examples, each class derived from **TwoDShape** defines a method called **area( )**. This suggests that it might be better to make **area( )** a virtual method of the **TwoDShape** class, allowing each derived class to override it, defining how the area is calculated for the type of shape that the class encapsulates. The following program does this. For convenience, it also adds a name property to **TwoDShape**. (This makes it easier to demonstrate the classes.)

```
// Use virtual methods and polymorphism.

using System;

class TwoDShape {
  double pri_width;  // private
```

```
    double pri_height; // private
    string pri_name;   // private

    // A default constructor.
    public TwoDShape() {
      width = height = 0.0;
      name = "null";
    }

    // Parameterized constructor.
    public TwoDShape(double w, double h, string n) {
      width = w;
      height = h;
      name = n;
    }

    // Construct object with equal width and height.
    public TwoDShape(double x, string n) {
      width = height = x;
      name = n;
    }

    // Construct an object from an object.
    public TwoDShape(TwoDShape ob) {
      width = ob.width;
      height = ob.height;
      name = ob.name;
    }

    // Properties for width, height, and name
    public double width {
      get { return pri_width; }
      set { pri_width = value; }
    }

    public double height {
      get { return pri_height; }
      set { pri_height = value; }
    }

    public string name {
      get { return pri_name; }
```

```
    set { pri_name = value; }
  }

  public void showDim() {
    Console.WriteLine("Width and height are " +
                      width + " and " + height);
  }

  public virtual double area() {
    Console.WriteLine("area() must be overridden");
    return 0.0;
  }
}

// A derived class of TwoDShape for triangles.
class Triangle : TwoDShape {
  string style; // private

  // A default constructor.
  public Triangle() {
    style = "null";
  }

  // Constructor for Triangle.
  public Triangle(string s, double w, double h) :
    base(w, h, "triangle") {
      style = s;
  }

  // Construct an isosceles triangle.
  public Triangle(double x) : base(x, "triangle") {
    style = "isosceles";
  }

  // Construct an object from an object.
  public Triangle(Triangle ob) : base(ob) {
    style = ob.style;
  }

  // Override area() for Triangle.
  public override double area() {
    return width * height / 2;
```

```
  }

  // Display a triangle's style.
  public void showStyle() {
    Console.WriteLine("Triangle is " + style);
  }
}

// A derived class of TwoDShape for rectangles.
class Rectangle : TwoDShape {
  // Constructor for Rectangle.
  public Rectangle(double w, double h) :
    base(w, h, "rectangle"){ }

  // Construct a square.
  public Rectangle(double x) :
    base(x, "rectangle") { }

  // Construct an object from an object.
  public Rectangle(Rectangle ob) : base(ob) { }

  // Return true if the rectangle is square.
  public bool isSquare() {
    if(width == height) return true;
    return false;
  }

  // Override area() for Rectangle.
  public override double area() {
    return width * height;
  }
}

class DynShapes {
  public static void Main() {
    TwoDShape[] shapes = new TwoDShape[5];

    shapes[0] = new Triangle("right", 8.0, 12.0);
    shapes[1] = new Rectangle(10);
    shapes[2] = new Rectangle(10, 4);
    shapes[3] = new Triangle(7.0);
    shapes[4] = new TwoDShape(10, 20, "generic");
```

```
    for(int i=0; i < shapes.Length; i++) {
      Console.WriteLine("object is " + shapes[i].name);
      Console.WriteLine("Area is " + shapes[i].area());

      Console.WriteLine();
    }
  }
}
```

The output from the program is shown here:

```
object is triangle
Area is 48

object is rectangle
Area is 100

object is rectangle
Area is 40

object is triangle
Area is 24.5

object is generic
area() must be overridden
Area is 0
```

Let's examine this program closely. First, as explained, **area( )** is declared as **virtual** in the **TwoDShape** class and is overridden by **Triangle** and **Rectangle**. Inside **TwoDShape**, **area( )** is given a placeholder implementation that simply informs the user that this method must be overridden by a derived class. Each override of **area( )** supplies an implementation that is suitable for the type of object encapsulated by the derived class. Thus, if you were to implement a ellipse class, for example, then **area( )** would need to compute the **area( )** of an ellipse.

There is one other important feature in the preceding program. Notice in **Main( )** that **shapes** is declared as an array of **TwoDShape** objects. However, the elements of this array are assigned **Triangle**, **Rectangle**, and **TwoDShape** references. This is valid because a base class reference can refer to a derived class object. The program then cycles through the array, displaying information about each object. Although quite simple, this illustrates the power of both inheritance and method overriding. The type of object stored in a base class reference variable is determined at runtime and acted on accordingly. If an object is derived from **TwoDShape**, then its area can be obtained by calling **area( )**. The interface to this operation is the same no matter what type of shape is being used.

Using Abstract Classes

Sometimes you will want to create a base class that defines only a generalized form that will be shared by all of its derived classes, leaving it to each derived class to fill in the details. Such a class determines the nature of the methods that the derived classes must implement, but does not, itself, provide an implementation of one or more of these methods. One way this situation can occur is when a base class is unable to create a meaningful implementation for a method. This is the case with the version of **TwoDShape** used in the preceding example. The definition of **area( )** is simply a placeholder. It will not compute and display the area of any type of object.

You will see as you create your own class libraries that it is not uncommon for a method to have no meaningful definition in the context of its base class. You can handle this situation two ways. One way, as shown in the previous example, is to simply have it report a warning message. While this approach can be useful in certain situations—such as debugging—usually it is not appropriate. You may have methods that must be overridden by the derived class in order for the derived class to have any meaning. Consider the class **Triangle**. It has no meaning if **area( )** is not defined. In this case, you want some way to ensure that a derived class does, indeed, override all necessary methods. C#'s solution to this problem is the *abstract method*.

An abstract method is created by specifying the **abstract** type modifier. An abstract method contains no body and is, therefore, not implemented by the base class. Thus, a derived class must override it—it cannot simply use the version defined in the base class. As you can probably guess, an abstract method is automatically virtual, and there is no need to use the **virtual** modifier. In fact, it is an error to use **virtual** and **abstract** together.

To declare an abstract method, use this general form:

abstract *type name(parameter-list)*;

As you can see, no method body is present. The **abstract** modifier can be used only on normal methods. It cannot be applied to **static** methods. Properties can also be abstract.

A class that contains one or more abstract methods must also be declared as abstract by preceding its **class** declaration with the **abstract** specifier. Since an abstract class does not define a complete implementation, there can be no objects of an abstract class. Thus, attempting to create an object of an abstract class by using **new** will result in a compile-time error.

When a derived class inherits an abstract class, it must implement all of the abstract methods in the base class. If it doesn't, then the derived class must also be specified as **abstract**. Thus, the **abstract** attribute is inherited until such time that a complete implementation is achieved.

Using an abstract class, you can improve the **TwoDShape** class. Since there is no meaningful concept of area for an undefined two-dimensional figure, the following version of the preceding program declares **area( )** as **abstract** inside **TwoDShape** and **TwoDShape** as **abstract**. This, of course, means that all classes derived from **TwoDShape** must override **area( )**.

```
// Create an abstract class.

using System;

abstract class TwoDShape {
  double pri_width;  // private
  double pri_height; // private
  string pri_name;   // private

  // A default constructor.
  public TwoDShape() {
    width = height = 0.0;
    name = "null";
  }

  // Parameterized constructor.
  public TwoDShape(double w, double h, string n) {
    width = w;
    height = h;
    name = n;
  }

  // Construct object with equal width and height.
  public TwoDShape(double x, string n) {
    width = height = x;
    name = n;
  }

  // Construct an object from an object.
  public TwoDShape(TwoDShape ob) {
    width = ob.width;
    height = ob.height;
    name = ob.name;
  }

  // Properties for width, height, and name
  public double width {
    get { return pri_width; }
    set { pri_width = value; }
  }

  public double height {
    get { return pri_height; }
```

```
      set { pri_height = value; }
   }

   public string name {
      get { return pri_name; }
      set { pri_name = value; }
   }

   public void showDim() {
      Console.WriteLine("Width and height are " +
                         width + " and " + height);
   }

   // Now, area() is abstract.
   public abstract double area();
}

// A derived class of TwoDShape for triangles.
class Triangle : TwoDShape {
   string style; // private

   // A default constructor.
   public Triangle() {
      style = "null";
   }

   // Constructor for Triangle.
   public Triangle(string s, double w, double h) :
      base(w, h, "triangle") {
         style = s;
   }

   // Construct an isosceles triangle.
   public Triangle(double x) : base(x, "triangle") {
      style = "isosceles";
   }

   // Construct an object from an object.
   public Triangle(Triangle ob) : base(ob) {
      style = ob.style;
   }
```

```
    // Override area() for Triangle.
    public override double area() {
      return width * height / 2;
    }

    // Display a triangle's style.
    public void showStyle() {
      Console.WriteLine("Triangle is " + style);
    }
}

// A derived class of TwoDShape for rectangles.
class Rectangle : TwoDShape {
  // Constructor for Rectangle.
  public Rectangle(double w, double h) :
    base(w, h, "rectangle"){ }

  // Construct a square.
  public Rectangle(double x) :
    base(x, "rectangle") { }

  // Construct an object from an object.
  public Rectangle(Rectangle ob) : base(ob) { }

  // Return true if the rectangle is square.
  public bool isSquare() {
    if(width == height) return true;
    return false;
  }

  // Override area() for Rectangle.
  public override double area() {
    return width * height;
  }
}

class AbsShape {
  public static void Main() {
    TwoDShape[] shapes = new TwoDShape[4];

    shapes[0] = new Triangle("right", 8.0, 12.0);
    shapes[1] = new Rectangle(10);
```

```
      shapes[2] = new Rectangle(10, 4);
      shapes[3] = new Triangle(7.0);

      for(int i=0; i < shapes.Length; i++) {
        Console.WriteLine("object is " + shapes[i].name);
        Console.WriteLine("Area is " + shapes[i].area());

        Console.WriteLine();
      }
    }
  }
```

As the program illustrates, all derived classes *must* override **area( )** (or also be declared **abstract**). To prove this to yourself, try creating a derived class that does not override **area( )**. You will receive a compile-time error. Of course, it is still possible to create an object reference of type **TwoDShape**, which the program does. However, it is no longer possible to declare objects of type **TwoDShape**. Because of this, in **Main( )** the **shapes** array has been shortened to 4, and a generic **TwoDShape** object is no longer created.

One other point: Notice that **TwoDShape** still includes the **showDim( )** method and that it is not modified by **abstract**. It is perfectly acceptable—indeed, quite common— for an abstract class to contain concrete methods that a derived class is free to use as-is. Only those methods declared as **abstract** must be overridden by derived classes.

Using sealed to Prevent Inheritance

As powerful and useful as inheritance is, sometimes you will want to prevent it. For example, you might have a class that encapsulates the initialization sequence of some specialized hardware device, such as a medical monitor. In this case, you don't want users of your class to be able to change the way the monitor is initialized, possibly setting the device incorrectly. Whatever the reason, in C# it is easy to prevent a class from being inherited by using the keyword **sealed**.

To prevent a class from being inherited, precede its declaration with **sealed**. As you might expect, it is illegal to declare a class as both **abstract** and **sealed** because an abstract class is incomplete by itself and relies upon its derived classes to provide complete implementations.

Here is an example of a **sealed** class:

```
sealed class A {
  // ...
}

// The following class is illegal.
class B : A { // ERROR! Can't derive class A
  // ...
}
```

As the comments imply, it is illegal for **B** to inherit **A** because **A** is declared as **sealed**.

The object Class

C# defines one special class called **object** that is an implicit base class of all other classes and for all other types (including the value types). In other words, all other types are derived from **object**. This means that a reference variable of type **object** can refer to an object of any other type. Also, since arrays are implemented as classes, a variable of type **object** can also refer to any array. Technically, the C# name **object** is just another name for **System.Object**, which is part of the .NET Framework class library.

The **object** class defines the methods shown in Table 11-1, which means that they are available in every object.

A few of these methods warrant some additional explanation. By default, the **Equals(object)** method determines if the invoking object refers to the same object as the one referred to by the argument. (That is, it determines if the two references are the same.) It returns **true** if the objects are one and the same, and **false** otherwise. You can override this method in classes that you create. Doing so allows you to define what equality means relative to a class. For example, you could define **Equals(object)** so that it compares the contents of two objects for equality. The **Equals(object, object)** method invokes **Equals(object)** to compute its result.

The **GetHashCode( )** method returns a hash code associated with the invoking object. This hash code can be used with any algorithm that employs hashing as a means of accessing stored objects.

As mentioned in Chapter 9, if you overload the = = operator, then you will usually need to override **Equals(object)** and **GetHashCode( )**, because most of the time you will want the = = operator and the **Equals(object)** methods to function the same. When **Equals( )** is overridden, you should also override **GetHashCode( )**, so that the two methods are compatible.

Method	Purpose
public virtual bool Equals(object *ob*)	Determines whether the invoking object is the same as the one referred to by *ob*.
public static bool Equals(object *ob1*, object *ob2*)	Determines whether *ob1* is the same as *ob2*.
protected Finalize( )	Performs shutdown actions prior to garbage collection. In C#, **Finalize( )** is accessed through a destructor.
public virtual int GetHashCode( )	Returns the hash code associated with the invoking object.
public Type GetType( )	Obtains the type of an object at runtime.
protected object MemberwiseClone( )	Makes a "shallow copy" of the object. (The members are copied, but objects referred to by members are not.)
public static bool ReferenceEquals(object *ob1*, object *ob2*)	Determines whether *ob1* and *ob2* refer to the same object.
public virtual string ToString( )	Returns a string that describes the object.

Table 11-1.   *Methods of the* **object** *Class*

The **ToString( )** method returns a string that contains a description of the object on which it is called. Also, this method is automatically called when an object is output using **WriteLine( )**. Many classes override this method. Doing so allows them to tailor a description specifically for the types of objects that they create. For example:

```
// Demonstrate ToString()

using System;

class MyClass {
  static int count = 0;
  int id;

  public MyClass() {
    id = count;
    count++;
  }
```

```
    public override string ToString() {
      return "MyClass object #" + id;
    }
  }

  class Test {
    public static void Main() {
      MyClass ob1 = new MyClass();
      MyClass ob2 = new MyClass();
      MyClass ob3 = new MyClass();

      Console.WriteLine(ob1);
      Console.WriteLine(ob2);
      Console.WriteLine(ob3);

    }
  }
```

The output from the program is shown here:

```
MyClass object #0
MyClass object #1
MyClass object #2
```

Boxing and Unboxing

As explained, all C# types, including the value types, are derived from **object**. Thus, a reference of type **object** can be used to refer to any other type, including value types. When an **object** reference refers to a value type, a process known as *boxing* occurs. Boxing causes the value of a value type to be stored in an object instance. Thus, a value type is "boxed" inside an object. This object can then be used like any other object. In all cases, boxing occurs automatically. You simply assign a value to an **object** reference. C# handles the rest.

Unboxing is the process of retrieving a value from an object. This action is performed using a cast from the **object** reference to the desired value type.

Here is a simple example that illustrates boxing and unboxing:

```
// A simple boxing/unboxing example.

using System;

class BoxingDemo {
  public static void Main() {
```

```
    int x;
    object obj;

    x = 10;
    obj = x; // box x into an object

    int y = (int)obj; // unbox obj into an int
    Console.WriteLine(y);
  }
}
```

This program displays the value 10. Notice that the value in **x** is boxed simply by assigning it to **obj**, which is an **object** reference. The integer value in **obj** is retrieved by casting **obj** to **int**.

Here is another, more interesting example of boxing. In this case, an **int** is passed as an argument to the **sqr( )** method, which uses an **object** parameter.

```
// Boxing also occurs when passing values.

using System;

class BoxingDemo {
  public static void Main() {
    int x;

    x = 10;
    Console.WriteLine("Here is x: " + x);

    // x is automatically boxed when passed to sqr()
    x = BoxingDemo.sqr(x);
    Console.WriteLine("Here is x squared: " + x);
  }

  static int sqr(object o) {
    return (int)o * (int)o;
  }
}
```

The output from the program is shown here:

```
Here is x: 10
Here is x squared: 100
```

Here, the value of **x** is automatically boxed when it is passed to **sqr( )**.

Boxing and unboxing allows C#'s type system to be fully unified. All types derive from **object**. A reference to any type can be assigned to an **object** reference. Boxing/unboxing automatically handles the details for the value types. Furthermore, because all types are derived from **object**, they all have access to **object**'s methods. For example, consider the following rather surprising program:

```
// Boxing makes it possible to call methods on a value!

using System;

class MethOnValue {
  public static void Main() {

    Console.WriteLine(10.ToString());

  }
}
```

This program displays 10. The reason is that the **ToString( )** method returns a string representation of the object on which it is called. In this case, the string representation of 10 is 10!

Is object a Generic Data Type?

Given that **object** is a base class for all other types and that boxing and unboxing of the value types take place automatically, it is possible to use **object** as a generic data type. For example, consider the following program that creates an **object** array and then assigns various other types of data to its elements:

```
// Use object to create a generic array.

using System;

class GenericDemo {
  public static void Main() {
    object[] ga = new object[10];

    // store ints
    for(int i=0; i < 3; i++)
      ga[i] = i;

    // store doubles
```

```
    for(int i=3; i < 6; i++)
      ga[i] = (double) i / 2;


    // store two strings, a bool, and a char
    ga[6] = "Generic Array";
    ga[7] = true;
    ga[8] = 'X';
    ga[9] = "end";

    for(int i = 0; i < ga.Length; i++)
      Console.WriteLine("ga[" + i + "]: " + ga[i] + " ");

  }
}
```

The output is shown here:

```
ga[0]: 0
ga[1]: 1
ga[2]: 2
ga[3]: 1.5
ga[4]: 2
ga[5]: 2.5
ga[6]: Generic Array
ga[7]: True
ga[8]: X
ga[9]: end
```

As this program illustrates, it is possible to use an **object** reference to refer to any type of data. Thus, an **object** array as used by the program can store any type of value. This means that the **object** array is essentially a generic list. Expanding on this concept, it is easy to see how you could construct a stack class, for example, that stored **object** references. This would enable the stack to store any type of data.

Although the generic-type feature of **object** is powerful and can be used quite effectively in some situations, it is a mistake to think that you should use **object** as a way around C#'s otherwise strong type checking. In general, when you need to store an **int**, use an **int** variable; when you need to store a **string**, use a **string** reference; and so on. Reserve **object**'s generic nature for specialized situations.

Chapter 12

Interfaces, Structures, and Enumerations

T his chapter discusses one of C#'s most important features: the interface. An *interface* defines a set of methods that will be implemented by a class. An interface does not, itself, implement any method. Thus, an interface is a purely logical construct that describes functionality without dictating implementation.

Also discussed in this chapter are two more C# data types: structures and enumerations. *Structures* are similar to classes except that they are handled as value types rather than reference types. *Enumerations* are lists of named integer constants. Structures and enumerations contribute to the richness of the C# programming environment.

Interfaces

In object-oriented programming it is sometimes helpful to define what a class must do, but not how it will do it. You have already seen an example of this: the abstract method. An abstract method defines the signature for a method, but provides no implementation. A derived class must provide its own implementation of each abstract method defined by its base class. Thus, an abstract method specifies the *interface* to the method, but not the *implementation.* While abstract classes and methods are useful, it is possible to take this concept a step further. In C#, you can fully separate a class' interface from its implementation by using the keyword **interface**.

Interfaces are syntactically similar to abstract classes. However, in an interface, no method can include a body. That is, an interface provides no implementation whatsoever. It specifies what must be done, but not how. Once an interface is defined, any number of classes can implement it. Also, one class can implement any number of interfaces.

To implement an interface, a class must provide bodies (implementations) for the methods described by the interface. Each class is free to determine the details of its own implementation. Thus, two classes might implement the same interface in different ways, but each class still supports the same set of methods. Therefore, code that has knowledge of the interface can use objects of either class since the interface to those objects is the same. By providing the **interface**, C# allows you to fully utilize the "one interface, multiple methods" aspect of polymorphism.

Interfaces are declared by using the **interface** keyword. Here is a simplified form of an interface declaration:

```
interface name {
  ret-type method-name1(param-list);
  ret-type method-name2(param-list);
  // ...
  ret-type method-nameN(param-list);
}
```

The name of the interface is specified by *name.* Methods are declared using only their return type and signature. They are, essentially, abstract methods. As explained, in an

interface, no method can have an implementation. Thus, each class that includes an **interface** must implement all of the methods. In an interface, methods are implicitly **public**, and no explicit access specifier is allowed.

Here is an example of an **interface**. It specifies the interface to a class that generates a series of numbers.

```
public interface ISeries {
  int getNext(); // return next number in series
  void reset(); // restart
  void setStart(int x); // set starting value
}
```

The name of this interface is **ISeries**. Although the prefix **I** is not necessary, many programmers prefix interfaces with it to differentiate them from classes. **ISeries** is declared **public** so that it can be implemented by any class in any program.

In addition to method signatures, interfaces can declare the signatures for properties, indexers, and events. Events are described in Chapter 15, and we will be concerned with only methods, properties, and indexers here. Interfaces cannot have data members. They cannot define constructors, destructors, or operator methods. Also, no member can be declared as **static**.

Implementing Interfaces

Once an **interface** has been defined, one or more classes can implement that interface. To implement an interface, the name of the interface is specified after the class name in just the same way that a base class is specified. The general form of a class that implements an interface is shown here:

```
class class-name : interface-name {
  // class-body
}
```

The name of the interface being implemented is specified in *interface-name.*

When a class implements an interface, the class must implement the entire interface. It cannot pick and choose which parts to implement, for example.

Classes can implement more than one interface. To implement more than one interface, the interfaces are separated with a comma. A class can inherit a base class and also implement one or more interfaces. In this case, the name of the base class must come first in the comma-separated list.

The methods that implement an interface must be declared **public**. The reason for this is that methods are implicitly public within an interface, so their implementations must also be public. Also, the type signature of the implementing method must match exactly the type signature specified in the **interface** definition.

Here is an example that implements the **ISeries** interface shown earlier. It creates a class called **ByTwos**, which generates a series of numbers, each two greater than the previous one.

```
// Implement ISeries.
class ByTwos : ISeries {
  int start;
  int val;

  public ByTwos() {
    start = 0;
    val = 0;
  }

  public int getNext() {
    val += 2;
    return val;
  }

  public void reset() {
    val = start;
  }

  public void setStart(int x) {
    start = x;
    val = start;
  }
}
```

As you can see, **ByTwos** implements all three methods defined by **ISeries**. As explained, this is necessary since a class cannot create a partial implementation of an interface.

Here is a class that demonstrates **ByTwos**:

```
// Demonstrate the ByTwos interface.

using System;

class SeriesDemo {
  public static void Main() {
    ByTwos ob = new ByTwos();

    for(int i=0; i < 5; i++)
```

```
      Console.WriteLine("Next value is " +
                           ob.getNext());

    Console.WriteLine("\nResetting");
    ob.reset();
    for(int i=0; i < 5; i++)
      Console.WriteLine("Next value is " +
                           ob.getNext());

    Console.WriteLine("\nStarting at 100");
    ob.setStart(100);
    for(int i=0; i < 5; i++)
      Console.WriteLine("Next value is " +
                           ob.getNext());
  }
}
```

To compile **SeriesDemo**, you must include the files that contain **ISeries**, **ByTwos**, and **SeriesDemo** in the compilation. The compiler will automatically compile all three files to create the final executable. For example, if you called these files **ISeries.cs**, **ByTwos.cs**, and **SeriesDemo.cs**, then the following command line will compile the program:

```
>csc SeriesDemo.cs ISeries.cs ByTwos.cs
```

If you are using the Visual Studio IDE, simply add all three files to your C# project. One other point: it is perfectly valid to put all three of these classes in the same file, too. The output from this program is shown here:

```
Next value is 2
Next value is 4
Next value is 6
Next value is 8
Next value is 10

Resetting
Next value is 2
Next value is 4
Next value is 6
Next value is 8
Next value is 10
```

```
Starting at 100
Next value is 102
Next value is 104
Next value is 106
Next value is 108
Next value is 110
```

It is both permissible and common for classes that implement interfaces to define additional members of their own. For example, the following version of **ByTwos** adds the method **getPrevious( )**, which returns the previous value:

```
// Implement ISeries and add getPrevious().
 class ByTwos : ISeries {
   int start;
   int val;
   int prev;

   public ByTwos() {
     start = 0;
     val = 0;
     prev = -2;
   }

   public int getNext() {
     prev = val;
     val += 2;
     return val;
   }

   public void reset() {
     val = start;
     prev = start - 2;
   }

   public void setStart(int x) {
     start = x;
     val = start;
     prev = val - 2;
   }
```

```
    // A method not specified by ISeries.
    public int getPrevious() {
      return prev;
    }
  }
}
```

Notice that the addition of **getPrevious( )** required a change to implementations of the methods defined by **ISeries**. However, since the interface to those methods stays the same, the change is seamless and does not break preexisting code. This is one of the advantages of interfaces.

As explained, any number of classes can implement an **interface**. For example, here is a class called **Primes** that generates a series of prime numbers. Notice that its implementation of **ISeries** is fundamentally different than the one provided by **ByTwos**.

```
// Use ISeries to implement a series of prime numbers.
class Primes : ISeries {
  int start;
  int val;

  public Primes() {
    start = 2;
    val = 2;
  }

  public int getNext() {
    int i, j;
    bool isprime;

    val++;
    for(i = val; i < 1000000; i++) {
      isprime = true;
      for(j = 2; j < (i/j + 1); j++) {
        if((i%j)==0) {
          isprime - false;
          break;
        }
      }
      if(isprime) {
        val = i;
        break;
      }
```

```
    }
    return val;
  }

  public void reset() {
    val = start;
  }

  public void setStart(int x) {
    start = x;
    val = start;
  }
}
```

The key point is that even though **ByTwos** and **Primes** generate completely unrelated series of numbers, both implement **ISeries**. As explained, an interface says nothing about the implementation, so each class is free to implement the interface as it sees fit.

Using Interface References

You might be somewhat surprised to learn that you can declare a reference variable of an interface type. In other words, you can create an interface reference variable. Such a variable can refer to any object that implements its interface. When you call a method on an object through an interface reference, it is the version of the method implemented by the object that is executed. This process is similar to using a base class reference to access a derived class object, as described in Chapter 11.

The following example illustrates the use of an interface reference. It uses the same interface reference variable to call methods on objects of both **ByTwos** and **Primes**.

```
// Demonstrate interface references.

using System;

// Define the interface
public interface ISeries {
  int getNext(); // return next number in series
  void reset(); // restart
  void setStart(int x); // set starting value
}
```

```
// Use ISeries to generate a sequence of even numbers.
class ByTwos : ISeries {
  int start;
  int val;

  public ByTwos() {
    start = 0;
    val = 0;
  }

  public int getNext() {
    val += 2;
    return val;
  }

  public void reset() {
    val = start;
  }

  public void setStart(int x) {
    start = x;
    val = start;
  }
}

// Use ISeries to implement a series of prime numbers.
class Primes : ISeries {
  int start;
  int val;

  public Primes() {
    start = 2;
    val = 2;
  }

  public int getNext() {
    int i, j;
    bool isprime;

    val++;
    for(i = val; i < 1000000; i++) {
      isprime = true;
```

```
        for(j = 2; j < (i/j + 1); j++) {
          if((i%j)==0) {
            isprime = false;
            break;
          }
        }
        if(isprime) {
          val = i;
          break;
        }
      }
      return val;
  }

  public void reset() {
    val = start;
  }

  public void setStart(int x) {
    start = x;
    val = start;
  }
}

class SeriesDemo2 {
  public static void Main() {
    ByTwos twoOb = new ByTwos();
    Primes primeOb = new Primes();
    ISeries ob;

    for(int i=0; i < 5; i++) {
      ob = twoOb;
      Console.WriteLine("Next ByTwos value is " +
                          ob.getNext());
      ob = primeOb;
      Console.WriteLine("Next prime number is " +
                          ob.getNext());
    }
  }
}
```

The output from the program is shown here:

```
Next ByTwos value is 2
Next prime number is 3
Next ByTwos value is 4
Next prime number is 5
Next ByTwos value is 6
Next prime number is 7
Next ByTwos value is 8
Next prime number is 11
Next ByTwos value is 10
Next prime number is 13
```

In **Main( )**, **ob** is declared to be a reference to an **ISeries** interface. This means that it can be used to store references to any object that implements **ISeries**. In this case, it is used to refer to **twoOb** and **primeOb**, which are objects of type **ByTwos** and **Primes**, respectively, which both implement **ISeries**.

One other point: An interface reference variable has knowledge only of the methods declared by its **interface** declaration. Thus, an interface reference cannot be used to access any other variables or methods that might be supported by the object.

Interface Properties

Like methods, properties are specified in an interface without any body. Here is the general form of a property specification:

```
// interface property
type name {
  get;
  set;
}
```

Of course, only **get** or **set** will be present for read-only or write-only properties, respectively.

Here is a rewrite of the **ISeries** interface and the **ByTwos** class that uses a property to obtain and set the next element in the series.

```
// Use a property in an interface.

using System;

public interface ISeries {
  // an interface property
  int next {
```

```csharp
    get; // return the next number in series
    set; // set next number
  }
}

// Implement ISeries.
class ByTwos : ISeries {
  int val;

  public ByTwos() {
    val = 0;
  }

  // get or set value
  public int next {
    get {
      val += 2;
      return val;
    }
    set {
      val = value;
    }
  }
}

// Demonstrate an interface property.
class SeriesDemo3 {
  public static void Main() {
    ByTwos ob = new ByTwos();

    // access series through a property
    for(int i=0; i < 5; i++)
      Console.WriteLine("Next value is " + ob.next);

    Console.WriteLine("\nStarting at 21");
    ob.next = 21;
    for(int i=0; i < 5; i++)
      Console.WriteLine("Next value is " + ob.next);
  }
}
```

The output from this program is shown here:

```
Next value is 2
Next value is 4
Next value is 6
Next value is 8
Next value is 10

Starting at 21
Next value is 23
Next value is 25
Next value is 27
Next value is 29
Next value is 31
```

Interface Indexers

An interface can specify an indexer. An indexer declared in an interface has this general form:

```
// interface indexer
element-type this[int index] {
   get;
   set;
}
```

As before, only **get** or **set** will be present for read-only or write-only indexers, respectively.

Here is another version of **ISeries** that adds a read-only indexer that returns the *i*th element in the series.

```
// Add an indexer in an interface.

using System;

public interface ISeries {
  // an interface property
  int next {
    get; // return the next number in series
    set; // set next number
  }

  // an interface indexer
  int this[int index] {
    get; // return the specified number in series
```

```csharp
  }
}

// Implement ISeries.
class ByTwos : ISeries {
  int val;

  public ByTwos() {
    val = 0;
  }

  // get or set value using a property
  public int next {
    get {
      val += 2;
      return val;
    }
    set {
      val = value;
    }
  }

  // get a value using an index
  public int this[int index] {
    get {
      val = 0;
      for(int i=0; i<index; i++)
        val += 2;
      return val;
    }
  }
}

// Demonstrate an interface indexer.
class SeriesDemo4 {
  public static void Main() {
    ByTwos ob = new ByTwos();

    // access series through a property
    for(int i=0; i < 5; i++)
      Console.WriteLine("Next value is " + ob.next);
```

```
      Console.WriteLine("\nStarting at 21");
      ob.next = 21;
      for(int i=0; i < 5; i++)
        Console.WriteLine("Next value is " +
                          ob.next);

      Console.WriteLine("\nResetting to 0");
      ob.next = 0;

      // access series through an indexer
      for(int i=0; i < 5; i++)
        Console.WriteLine("Next value is " + ob[i]);
  }
}
```

The output from this program is shown here:

```
Next value is 2
Next value is 4
Next value is 6
Next value is 8
Next value is 10

Starting at 21
Next value is 23
Next value is 25
Next value is 27
Next value is 29
Next value is 31

Resetting to 0
Next value is 0
Next value is 2
Next value is 4
Next value is 6
Next value is 8
```

Interfaces Can Be Inherited

One interface can inherit another. The syntax is the same as for inheriting classes.
When a class implements an interface that inherits another interface, it must provide

implementations for all the members defined within the interface inheritance chain.
Following is an example:

```
// One interface can inherit another.

using System;

public interface A {
  void meth1();
  void meth2();
}

// B now includes meth1() and meth2() -- it adds meth3().
public interface B : A {
  void meth3();
}

// This class must implement all of A and B
class MyClass : B {
  public void meth1() {
    Console.WriteLine("Implement meth1().");
  }

  public void meth2() {
    Console.WriteLine("Implement meth2().");
  }

  public void meth3() {
    Console.WriteLine("Implement meth3().");
  }
}

class IFExtend {
  public static void Main() {
    MyClass ob = new MyClass();

    ob.meth1();
    ob.meth2();
    ob.meth3();
  }
}
```

As an experiment you might want to try removing the implementation for **meth1( )** in **MyClass**. This will cause a compile-time error. As stated earlier, any class that implements an interface must implement all methods defined by that interface, including any that are inherited from other interfaces.

Name Hiding with Interface Inheritance

When one interface inherits another, it is possible to declare a member in the derived interface that hides one defined by the base interface. This happens when a member in a derived interface has the same signature as one in the base interface. This will cause a warning message unless you modify the derived interface member with **new**.

Explicit Implementations

When implementing a member of an interface, it is possible to *fully qualify* its name with its interface name. Doing this creates an *explicit interface member implementation,* or *explicit implementation,* for short. For example, given

```
interface IMyIF {
  int myMeth(int x);
}
```

it is legal to implement **IMyIF** as shown here:

```
class MyClass : IMyIF {
  int IMyIF.myMeth(int x) {
    return x / 3;
  }
}
```

As you can see, when the **myMeth( )** member of **IMyIF** is implemented, its complete name, including its interface name, is specified.

You might need to create an explicit implementation of an interface member for two reasons. First, when you implement a method using its fully qualified name, you are providing what amounts to a private implementation that is not exposed to code outside the class. Second, it is possible for a class to implement two interfaces, both of which declare methods by the same name and type signature. Fully qualifying the names removes the ambiguity from this situation. Let's look at an example of each.

Creating a Private Implementation

The following program contains an interface called **IEven**, which defines two methods, **isEven( )** and **isOdd( )**, which determine whether a number is even or odd. **MyClass** then implements **IEven**. When it does so, it implements **isOdd( )** explicitly.

```csharp
// Explicitly implement an interface member.

using System;

interface IEven {
  bool isOdd(int x);
  bool isEven(int x);
}

class MyClass : IEven {
  // explicit implementation
  bool IEven.isOdd(int x) {
    if((x%2) != 0) return true;
    else return false;
  }

  // normal implementation
  public bool isEven(int x) {
    IEven o = this; // reference to invoking object

    return !o.isOdd(x);
  }
}

class Demo {
  public static void Main() {
    MyClass ob = new MyClass();
    bool result;

    result = ob.isEven(4);
    if(result) Console.WriteLine("4 is even.");
    else Console.WriteLine("3 is odd.");

    // result = ob.isOdd(); // Error, not exposed
  }
}
```

Since **isOdd( )** is implemented explicitly, it is not available outside of **MyClass**. This makes its implementation effectively private. Inside **MyClass**, **isOdd( )** can be accessed only through an interface reference. This is why it is invoked through **o** in the implementation for **isEven( )**.

Using Explicit Implementation to Remove Ambiguity

Here is an example in which two interfaces are implemented and both interfaces declare a method called **meth( )**. Explicit implementation is used to eliminate the ambiguity inherent in this situation.

```
// Use explicit implementation to remove ambiguity.

using System;

interface IMyIF_A {
  int meth(int x);
}

interface IMyIF_B {
  int meth(int x);
}

// MyClass implements both interfaces.
class MyClass : IMyIF_A, IMyIF_B {

  // explicitly implement the two meth()s
  int IMyIF_A.meth(int x) {
    return x + x;
  }
  int IMyIF_B.meth(int x) {
    return x * x;
  }

  // call meth() through an interface reference.
  public int methA(int x){
    IMyIF_A a_ob;
    a_ob = this;
    return a_ob.meth(x); // calls IMyIF_A
  }

  public int methB(int x){
```

```
      IMyIF_B b_ob;
      b_ob = this;
      return b_ob.meth(x); // calls IMyIF_B
   }
}

class FQIFNames {
  public static void Main() {
    MyClass ob = new MyClass();

    Console.Write("Calling IMyIF_A.meth(): ");
    Console.WriteLine(ob.methA(3));

    Console.Write("Calling IMyIF_B.meth(): ");
    Console.WriteLine(ob.methB(3));
  }
}
```

The output from this program is shown here:

```
Calling IMyIF_A.meth(): 6
Calling IMyIF_B.meth(): 9
```

Looking at the program, first notice that **meth( )** has the same signature in both **IMyIF_A** and **IMyIF_B**. Thus, when **MyClass** implements both of these interfaces, it must explicitly implement each one separately, fully qualifying its name in the process. Since the only way that an explicitly implemented method can be called is on an interface reference, **methA( )** creates a reference for **IMyIF_A**, and **methB( )** creates a reference for **IMy_IF_B**. The methods then call **meth( )** through these references, thereby removing the ambiguity.

Choosing Between an Interface and an Abstract Class

One of the more challenging parts of C# programming is knowing when to create an interface and when to use an abstract class when you want to describe functionality but not implementation. The general rule is this: When you can fully describe the concept in terms of "what it does" without needing to specify any "how it does it," then you should use an interface. If you need to include some implementation details, then you will need to represent your concept in an abstract class.

The .NET Standard Interfaces

The .NET Framework defines a large number of interfaces that a C# program can use. For example, **System.IComparable** defines the **CompareTo( )** method, which allows objects to be compared when an ordering relationship is required. Interfaces also form an important part of the Collections classes, which provide various types of storage (such as stacks and queues) for groups of objects. For example, **System.Collections.ICollection** defines the functionality common to all collections. **System.Collections.IEnumerator** offers a way to sequence through the elements in a collection. We will be looking at these and other interfaces in Part II.

An Interface Case Study

Before moving on, it will be useful to work through another example that uses an interface. In this section we will create an interface called **ICipher**, which specifies methods that support the encryption of strings. Using an interface for this task makes sense because it is possible to fully separate the "what" of encryption from the "how."

The **ICipher** interface is shown here:

```
// An encryption interface.
public interface ICipher {
  string encode(string str);
  string decode(string str);
}
```

The **ICipher** interface specifies two methods: **encode( )**, which is used to encode a string, and **decode( )**, which is used to decode a string. No other details are specified. This means that implementing classes are free to use any approach to encryption. For example, one class could encode a string based upon a user-specified key. A second could use password protection. A third could use a bit-manipulation cipher, and another could use a simple transposition code. No matter what approach to encryption is used, the interface to encoding and decoding a string is the same. Since there is no need to specify any part of the encryption implementation, an **interface** is the logical choice to represent it.

Here are two classes that implement **ICipher**. The first is **SimpleCipher**, which encodes a string by shifting each character one position higher. For example, A becomes B, B becomes C, and so on. The second is **BitCipher**, which encodes a string by XORing each character with a 16-bit value that acts as a key.

```
/* A simple implementation of ICipher that codes
   a message by shifting each character 1 position
```

```csharp
  higher.   Thus, A becomes B, and so on. */
class SimpleCipher : ICipher {

  // Return an encoded string given plaintext.
  public string encode(string str) {
    string ciphertext = "";

    for(int i=0; i < str.Length; i++)
      ciphertext = ciphertext + (char) (str[i] + 1);

    return ciphertext;
  }


  // Return a decoded string given ciphertext.
  public string decode(string str) {
    string plaintext = "";

    for(int i=0; i < str.Length; i++)
      plaintext = plaintext + (char) (str[i] - 1);

    return plaintext;
  }
}

/* This implementation of ICipher uses bit
   manipulations and key. */
class BitCipher : ICipher {
  ushort key;

  // Specify a key when constructing BitCiphers.
  public BitCipher(ushort k) {
    key = k;
  }

  // Return an encoded string given plaintext.
  public string encode(string str) {
    string ciphertext = "";

    for(int i=0; i < str.Length; i++)
      ciphertext = ciphertext + (char) (str[i] ^ key);

    return ciphertext;
```

```
    }

    // Return a decoded string given ciphertext.
    public string decode(string str) {
      string plaintext = "";

      for(int i=0; i < str.Length; i++)
        plaintext = plaintext + (char) (str[i] ^ key);

      return plaintext;
    }
}
```

As you can see, although **SimpleCipher** and **BitCipher** differ in their implementations, they both implement the **ICipher** interface. The following program demonstrates **SimpleCipher** and **BitCipher**.

```
// Demonstrate ICipher.

using System;

class ICipherDemo {
  public static void Main() {
    ICipher ciphRef;
    BitCipher bit = new BitCipher(27);
    SimpleCipher sc = new SimpleCipher();

    string plain;
    string coded;

    // first, ciphRef refers to the simple cipher
    ciphRef = sc;

    Console.WriteLine("Using simple cipher.");

    plain = "testing";
    coded = ciphRef.encode(plain);
    Console.WriteLine("Cipher text: " + coded);

    plain = ciphRef.decode(coded);
    Console.WriteLine("Plain text: " + plain);
```

```
      // now, let ciphRef refer to the bitwise cipher
      ciphRef = bit;

      Console.WriteLine("\nUsing bitwise cipher.");

      plain = "testing";
      coded = ciphRef.encode(plain);
      Console.WriteLine("Cipher text: " + coded);

      plain = ciphRef.decode(coded);
      Console.WriteLine("Plain text: " + plain);
   }
}
```

The output is shown here:

```
Using simple cipher.
Cipher text: uftujoh
Plain text: testing

Using bitwise cipher.
Cipher text: o~horu|
Plain text: testing
```

One advantage to creating an encryption interface is that any class that implements the interface is accessed in the same way, no matter how the encryption is implemented. For example, consider the following program in which a class called **UnlistedPhone** stores unlisted telephone numbers in an encrypted format. The names and numbers are automatically decoded when needed.

```
// Use ICipher.

using System;

// A class for storing unlisted telephone numbers.
class UnlistedPhone {
   string pri_name;   // supports name property
   string pri_number; // supports number property

   ICipher crypt; // reference to encryption object
```

```
  public UnlistedPhone(string name, string number, ICipher c)
  {
    crypt = c; // store encryption object

    pri_name = crypt.encode(name);
    pri_number = crypt.encode(number);
  }

  public string Name {
    get {
      return crypt.decode(pri_name);
    }
    set {
      pri_name = crypt.encode(value);
    }
  }

  public string Number {
    get {
      return crypt.decode(pri_number);
    }
    set {
      pri_number = crypt.encode(value);
    }
  }
}

// Demonstrate UnlistedPhone
class UnlistedDemo {
  public static void Main() {
    UnlistedPhone phone1 =
        new UnlistedPhone("Tom", "555-3456", new BitCipher(27));
    UnlistedPhone phone2 =
        new UnlistedPhone("Mary", "555-8891", new BitCipher(9));

    Console.WriteLine("Unlisted number for " +
                    phone1.Name + " is " +
                    phone1.Number);

    Console.WriteLine("Unlisted number for " +
                    phone2.Name + " is " +
```

```
                              phone2.Number);
  }
}
```

The output from the program is shown here:

```
Unlisted number for Tom is 555-3456
Unlisted number for Mary is 555-8891
```

Look closely at how **UnlistedPhone** is implemented. Notice that **UnlistedPhone** contains three fields. The first two are the private variables that store the name and telephone number. The third is a reference to an **ICipher** object. When an **UnlistedPhone** object is constructed, it is passed three references. The first two are to the strings holding the name and telephone number. The third is to the encryption object that is used to encode the name and number. A reference to the encryption object is stored in **crypt**. Any type of encryption object is acceptable as long as it implements the **ICipher** interface. In this case, **BitCipher** is used. Thus, **UnlistedPhone** can call the **encode( )** and **decode( )** methods on a **BitCipher** object through the **crypt** reference.

Notice now how the **Name** and **Number** properties work. When a **set** operation occurs, the name or number is automatically encoded by calling **encode( )** on the **crypt** object. When a **get** operation takes place, the name or number is automatically decoded by calling **decode( )**. Neither **Name** nor **Number** has any specific knowledge of the underlying encryption method. They simply access its functionality through its interface.

Since the encryption interface is standardized by **ICipher**, it is possible to change the encryption object without changing any of the inner workings of **UnlistedPhone**'s code. For example, the following program uses **SimpleCipher** rather than **BitCipher** when constructing **UnlistedPhone** objects. The only change that takes place is in the encryption object passed to the constructor for **UnlistedPhone**.

```
// This version uses SimpleCipher.

using System;

class UnlistedDemo {
  public static void Main() {

    // now, use SimpleCipher rather than BitCipher
    UnlistedPhone phone1 =
        new UnlistedPhone("Tom", "555-3456", new SimpleCipher());
```

```
    UnlistedPhone phone2 =
        new UnlistedPhone("Mary", "555-8891", new SimpleCipher());

    Console.WriteLine("Unlisted number for " +
                    phone1.Name + " is " +
                    phone1.Number);

    Console.WriteLine("Unlisted number for " +
                    phone2.Name + " is " +
                    phone2.Number);
    }
}
```

As this program shows, since both **BitCipher** and **SimpleCipher** implement **ICipher**, either can be used to construct **UnlistedPhone** objects.

One last point: The implementation of **UnlistedPhone** also shows the power of accessing objects that implement interfaces through an interface reference. Because the encryption object is referenced through an **ICipher** reference variable, any object that implements the **ICipher** interface can be used. This enables the specific encryption implementation to be changed painlessly and safely without causing any of **UnlistedPhone**'s code to be changed. If **UnlistedPhone** had instead hard-coded a specific type of encryption object, such as **BitCipher**, for the data type of **crypt**, then **UnlistedPhone**'s code would need to be changed if a different encryption scheme is desired.

Structures

As you know, classes are reference types. This means that class objects are accessed through a reference. This differs from the value types, which are accessed directly. However, sometimes it would be useful to be able to access an object directly, in the way that value types are. One reason for this is efficiency. Accessing class objects through a reference adds overhead onto every access. It also consumes space. For very small objects, this extra space might be significant. To address these concerns, C# offers the structure. A *structure* is similar to a class, but is a value type, rather than a reference type.

Structures are declared using the keyword **struct** and are syntactically similar to classes. Here is the general form of a **struct**:

```
struct name : interfaces {
    // member declarations
}
```

The name of the structure is specified by *name.*

Structures cannot inherit other structures or classes, or be used as a base for other structures or classes. (Of course, like all C# types, structures do inherit **object**.) However, a structure can implement one or more interfaces. These are specified after the structure name using a comma-separated list. Like classes, structure members include methods, fields, indexers, properties, operator methods, and events. Structures can also define constructors, but not destructors. However, you cannot define a default (parameterless) constructor for a structure. The reason for this is that a default constructor is automatically defined for all structures, and this default constructor can't be changed. Since structures do not support inheritance, structure members cannot be specified as **abstract**, **virtual**, or **protected**.

A structure object can be created using **new** in the same way as a class object, but it is not required. When **new** is used, the specified constructor is called. When **new** is not used, the object is still created, but it is not initialized. Thus, you will need to perform any initialization manually.

Here is an example that uses a structure to hold information about a book:

```
// Demonstrate a structure.

using System;

// Define a structure.
struct Book {
  public string author;
  public string title;
  public int copyright;

  public Book(string a, string t, int c) {
    author = a;
    title = t;
    copyright = c;
  }
}

// Demonstrate Book structure.
class StructDemo {
  public static void Main() {
    Book book1 = new Book("Herb Schildt",
                    "C# A Beginner's Guide",
                    2001); // explicit constructor

    Book book2 = new Book(); // default constructor
```

```
        Book book3; // no constructor

        Console.WriteLine(book1.title + " by " + book1.author +
                        ", (c) " + book1.copyright);
        Console.WriteLine();

        if(book2.title == null)
          Console.WriteLine("book2.title is null.");
        // now, give book2 some info
        book2.title = "Brave New World";
        book2.author = "Aldous Huxley";
        book2.copyright = 1932;
        Console.Write("book2 now contains: ");
        Console.WriteLine(book2.title + " by " + book2.author +
                        ", (c) " + book2.copyright);

        Console.WriteLine();

//  Console.WriteLine(book3.title); // error, must initialize first
        book3.title = "Red Storm Rising";

        Console.WriteLine(book3.title); // now OK
    }
}
```

The output from this program is shown here:

```
C# A Beginner's Guide by Herb Schildt, (c) 2001

book2.title is null.
book2 now contains: Brave New World by Aldous Huxley, (c) 1932

Red Storm Rising
```

As the program shows, a structure can be initialized either by using **new** to invoke a constructor, or by simply declaring an object. If **new** is used, then the fields of the structure will be initialized, either by the default constructor, which initializes all fields to their default values, or by a user-defined constructor. If **new** is not used, as is the case with **book3**, then the object is not initialized, and its fields must be set prior to using the object.

When you assign one structure to another, a copy of the object is made. This is an important way in which **struct** differs from **class**. As explained earlier in this book, when you assign one class reference to another, you are simply changing the object to which the reference on the left side of the assignment is referring. When you assign one **struct** variable to another, you are making a copy of the object on the right. For example, consider the following program:

```
// Copy a struct.

using System;

// Define a structure.
struct MyStruct {
  public int x;
}

// Demonstrate structure assignment.
class StructAssignment {
  public static void Main() {
    MyStruct a;
    MyStruct b;

    a.x = 10;
    b.x = 20;

    Console.WriteLine("a.x {0}, b.x {1}", a.x, b.x);

    a = b;
    b.x = 30;

    Console.WriteLine("a.x {0}, b.x {1}", a.x, b.x);
  }
}
```

The output is shown here:

```
a.x 10, b.x 20
a.x 20, b.x 30
```

As the output shows, after the assignment

```
a = b;
```

the structure variables **a** and **b** are still separate and distinct. That is, **a** does not refer to or relate to **b** in any way other than containing a copy of **b**'s value. This would not be the case if **a** and **b** were class references. For example, here is the **class** version of the preceding program:

```
// Copy a class.

using System;

// Define a structure.
class MyClass {
  public int x;
}

// Now show a class object assignment.
class ClassAssignment {
  public static void Main() {
    MyClass a = new MyClass();
    MyClass b = new MyClass();

    a.x = 10;
    b.x = 20;

    Console.WriteLine("a.x {0}, b.x {1}", a.x, b.x);

    a = b;
    b.x = 30;

    Console.WriteLine("a.x {0}, b.x {1}", a.x, b.x);
  }
}
```

The output from this version is shown here:

```
a.x 10, b.x 20
a.x 30, b.x 30
```

As you can see, after the assignment of **b** to **a**, both variables refer to same object—the one originally referred to by **b**.

Why Structures?

At this point you might be wondering why C# includes the **struct** since it seems to be a less-capable version of a **class**. The answer lies in efficiency and performance. Because structures are value types, they are operated on directly rather than through a reference. Thus, a **struct** does not require a separate reference variable. This means that less memory is used in some cases. Furthermore, because a **struct** is accessed directly, it does not suffer from the performance loss that is inherent in accessing a class object. Because classes are reference types, all access to class objects is through a reference. This indirection adds overhead to every access. Structures do not incur this overhead. In general, if you need to store a small group of related data but don't need inheritance, or the other benefits that reference types offer, a **struct** can be a more efficient choice.

Here is another example that shows how a structure might be used in practice. It simulates an e-commerce transaction record. Each transaction includes a packet header that contains the packet number and the length of the packet. This is followed by the account number and the amount of the transaction. Because the packet header is a self-contained unit of information, it is organized as a structure. This structure can then be used to create a transaction record, or any other type of information packet.

```
// Structures are good when grouping data.

using System;

// Define a packet structure.
struct PacketHeader {
  public uint packNum; // packet number
  public ushort packLen; // length of packet
}

// Use PacketHeader to create an e-commerce transaction record.
class Transaction {
  static uint transacNum = 0;

  PacketHeader ph;  // incorporate PacketHeader into Transaction
  string accountNum;
  double amount;

  public Transaction(string acc, double val) {
   // create packet header
    ph.packNum = transacNum++;
    ph.packLen = 512;  // arbitrary length
```

```
      accountNum = acc;
      amount = val;
    }

    // Simulate a transaction.
    public void sendTransaction() {
      Console.WriteLine("Packet #:  " + ph.packNum +
                        ", Length: " + ph.packLen +
                        ",\n    Account #: " + accountNum +
                        ", Amount: {0:C}\n", amount);
    }
}

// Demonstrate Packet
class PacketDemo {
  public static void Main() {
    Transaction t = new Transaction("31243", -100.12);
    Transaction t2 = new Transaction("AB4655", 345.25);
    Transaction t3 = new Transaction("8475-09", 9800.00);

    t.sendTransaction();
    t2.sendTransaction();
    t3.sendTransaction();
  }
}
```

The output from the program is shown here:

```
Packet #: 0, Length: 512,
    Account #: 31243, Amount: ($100.12)

Packet #: 1, Length: 512,
    Account #: AB4655, Amount: $345.25

Packet #: 2, Length: 512,
    Account #: 8475-09, Amount: $9,800.00
```

PacketHeader is a good choice for a **struct** because it contains only a small amount of data, and does not use inheritance or even contain methods. As a structure, **PacketHeader** does not incur the additional overhead of a reference, as would a class. Thus, any type of transaction record can use **PacketHeader** without affecting its efficiency.

As a point of interest, C++ also has structures and uses the **struct** keyword. However, C# and C++ structures are not the same. In C++, **struct** defines a class type. Thus, in C++, **struct** and **class** are nearly equivalent. (The difference has to do with the default access of their members, which is private for **class** and public for **struct**.) In C#, a **struct** defines a value type, and a **class** defines a reference type.

Enumerations

An *enumeration* is a set of named integer constants. The keyword **enum** declares an enumerated type. The general form for an enumeration is

enum *name* { *enumeration list* };

Here, the type name of the enumeration is specified by *name*. The *enumeration list* is a comma-separated list of identifiers.

Here is an example. The following code fragment defines an enumeration called **apple** that enumerates various types of apples:

```
enum apple { Jonathan, GoldenDel, RedDel, Winsap,
             Cortland, McIntosh };
```

A key point to understand about an enumeration is that each of the symbols stands for an integer value, with each symbol given a value one greater than the symbol that precedes it. By default, the value of the first enumeration symbol is 0. Thus, **Jonathan** has the value 0, **GoldenDel** has the value 1, and so on.

An enumeration constant can be used anywhere that an integer may be used. However, no implicit conversions are defined between an **enum** type and the built-in integer types, so an explicit cast must be used. Also, a cast must be used when converting between two enumeration types.

The members of an enumeration are accessed through their type name via the dot operator. For example, this

```
Console.WriteLine(apple.RedDel + " has the value " +
                  (int)apple.RedDel);
```

displays this:

```
RedDel has the value 2
```

As the output shows, when an enumerated value is displayed, its name is used. To obtain its integer value, a cast to **int** must be used. (This behavior represents a change from early versions of C# in which an integer representation of an enumerated value, rather than its name, was displayed by default.)

Here is a program that illustrates the **apple** enumeration:

```
// Demonstrate an enumeration.

using System;

class EnumDemo {
  enum apple { Jonathan, GoldenDel, RedDel, Winsap,
               Cortland, McIntosh };

  public static void Main() {
    string[] color = {
      "Red",
      "Yellow",
      "Red",
      "Red",
      "Red",
      "Reddish Green"
    };

    apple i; // declare an enum variable

    // use i to cycle through the enum
    for(i = apple.Jonathan; i <= apple.McIntosh; i++)
      Console.WriteLine(i + " has value of " + (int)i);

    Console.WriteLine();

    // use an enumeration to index an array
    for(i = apple.Jonathan; i <= apple.McIntosh; i++)
      Console.WriteLine("Color of " + i + " is " +
                        color[(int)i]);

  }
}
```

The output from the program is shown here:

```
Jonathan has value of 0
GoldenDel has value of 1
```

```
RedDel has value of 2
Winsap has value of 3
Cortland has value of 4
McIntosh has value of 5

Color of Jonathan is Red
Color of GoldenDel is Yellow
Color of RedDel is Red
Color of Winsap is Red
Color of Cortland is Red
Color of McIntosh is Reddish Green
```

Notice how the **for** loops are controlled by a variable of type **apple**. Since an enumeration is an integer type, an enumeration value can be used anywhere that an integer can. Because the enumerated values in **apple** start at zero, these values can be used to index **color** to obtain the color of the apple. Notice that a cast is required when the enumeration value is used to index the **color** array. As mentioned, there are no implicit conversions defined between integers and enumeration types. An explicit cast is required.

One other point: Since enumerated values are integers, you can use an enumeration type to control a **switch** statement. You will see an example of this shortly.

Initialize an Enumeration

You can specify the value of one or more of the symbols by using an initializer. Do this by following the symbol with an equal sign and an integer value. Symbols that appear after initializers are assigned values greater than the previous initialization value. For example, the following code assigns the value of 10 to **RedDel**:

```
enum apple { Jonathan, GoldenDel, RedDel = 10, Winsap,
             Cortland, McIntosh };
```

Now the values of these symbols are as follows:

Jonathan	0
GoldenDel	1
RedDel	10
Winsap	11
Cortland	12
McIntosh	13

Specifying the Base Type of an Enumeration

By default, enumerations are based on type **int**, but you can create an enumeration of any integer type, except for type **char**. To specify a type other than **int**, put the base type after the enumeration name, separated by a colon. For example, this statement makes **apple** an enumeration based on **byte**:

```
enum apple : byte { Jonathan, GoldenDel, RedDel, Winsap,
                    Cortland, McIntosh };
```

Now **apple.Winsap**, for example, is a **byte** quantity.

Using Enumerations

At first glance you might think that enumerations are an interesting but relatively unimportant part of C#, yet this is not the case. Enumerations are very useful when your program requires the use of one or more specialized symbols. For example, imagine that you are writing a program that controls a conveyor belt in a factory. You might create a method called **conveyor( )** that accepts the following commands as parameters: start, stop, forward, and reverse. Instead of passing **conveyor( )** integers, such as 1 for start, 2 for stop, and so on, which is error-prone, you can create an enumeration that assigns words to these values. Here is an example of this approach:

```
// Simulate a conveyor belt

using System;

class ConveyorControl {
  // enumerate the conveyor commands
  public enum action { start, stop, forward, reverse };

  public void conveyor(action com) {
    switch(com) {
      case action.start:
        Console.WriteLine("Starting conveyor.");
        break;
      case action.stop:
        Console.WriteLine("Stopping conveyor.");
        break;
      case action.forward:
        Console.WriteLine("Moving forward.");
        break;
      case action.reverse:
```

```
          Console.WriteLine("Moving backward.");
          break;
      }
    }
}

class ConveyorDemo {
  public static void Main() {
    ConveyorControl c = new ConveyorControl();

    c.conveyor(ConveyorControl.action.start);
    c.conveyor(ConveyorControl.action.forward);
    c.conveyor(ConveyorControl.action.reverse);
    c.conveyor(ConveyorControl.action.stop);

  }
}
```

The output from the program is shown here:

```
Starting conveyor.
Moving forward.
Moving backward.
Stopping conveyor.
```

Because **conveyor( )** takes an argument of type **action**, only the values defined by **action** can be passed to the method. For example, here an attempt is made to pass the value 22 to **conveyor( )**:

```
c.conveyor(22); // Error!
```

This won't compile because there is no predefined conversion from **int** to **action**. This prevents the passing of invalid commands to **conveyor( )**. Of course, you could use a cast to force a conversion, but this would require a premeditated act, not an accidental misuse. Also, because commands are specified by name rather than by a number, it is less likely that a user of **conveyor( )** will inadvertently pass the wrong value.

There is one other point to note about this example: Notice that an enumeration type is used to control the **switch** statement. As mentioned, because enumerations are considered integer types, they are perfectly valid for use in a **switch**.

Chapter 13

Exception Handling

A n *exception* is an error that occurs at runtime. Using C#'s exception handling subsystem, you can handle runtime errors in a structured and controlled manner. C#'s approach to exception handling is a blend of, and an improvement on, the methods used by C++ and Java. Thus, it will be familiar territory to readers with a background in either of these languages. What makes C#'s exception handling unique, however, is its clean, straightforward implementation.

A principal advantage of exception handling is that it automates much of the error-handling code that previously had to be entered "by hand" into any large program. For example, in a computer language without exception handling, error codes must be returned when a method fails, and these values must be checked manually each time the method is called. This approach is both tedious and error-prone. Exception handling streamlines error-handling by allowing your program to define a block of code, called an *exception handler,* that is executed automatically when an error occurs. It is not necessary to check the success or failure of each specific operation or method call manually. If an error occurs, it will be processed by the exception handler.

Another reason that exception handling is important is that C# defines standard exceptions for common program errors, such as divide-by-zero or index-out-of-range. To respond to these errors, your program must watch for and handle these exceptions.

In the final analysis, to be a successful C# programmer means that you are fully capable of navigating C#'s exception-handling subsystem.

The System.Exception Class

In C#, exceptions are represented by classes. All exception classes must be derived from the built-in exception class **Exception**, which is part of the **System** namespace. Thus, all exceptions are subclasses of **Exception**.

From **Exception** are derived **SystemException** and **ApplicationException**. These support the two general categories of exceptions defined by C#: those generated by the C# runtime system (that is, the Common Language Runtime) and those generated by application programs. Neither **SystemException** nor **ApplicationException** add anything to **Exception**. They simply define the tops of two different exception hierarchies.

C# defines several built-in exceptions that are derived from **SystemException**. For example, when a division-by-zero is attempted, a **DivideByZeroException** exception is generated. As you will see later in this chapter, you can create your own exception classes by deriving them from **ApplicationException**.

Exception Handling Fundamentals

C# exception handling is managed via four keywords: **try**, **catch**, **throw**, and **finally**. They form an interrelated subsystem in which the use of one implies the use of another. Throughout the course of this chapter, each keyword is examined in detail. However, it is useful at the outset to have a general understanding of the role each plays in exception handling. Briefly, here is how they work.

Program statements that you want to monitor for exceptions are contained within a **try** block. If an exception occurs within the **try** block, it is *thrown*. Your code can catch this exception using **catch** and handle it in some rational manner. System-generated exceptions are automatically thrown by the C# runtime system. To manually throw an exception, use the keyword **throw**. Any code that absolutely must be executed upon exiting from a **try** block is put in a **finally** block.

Using try and catch

At the core of exception handling are **try** and **catch**. These keywords work together; you can't have a **try** without a **catch**, or a **catch** without a **try**. Here is the general form of the **try**/**catch** exception-handling blocks:

```
try {
  // block of code to monitor for errors
}
catch (ExcepType1 exOb) {
  // handler for ExcepType1
}
catch (ExcepType2 exOb) {
  // handler for ExcepType2
}
.
.
.
```

Here, *ExcepType* is the type of exception that has occurred. When an exception is thrown, it is caught by its corresponding **catch** statement, which then processes the exception. As the general form shows, there can be more than one **catch** statement associated with a **try**. The type of the exception determines which **catch** statement is executed. That is, if the exception type specified by a **catch** statement matches that of the exception, then that **catch** statement is executed (and all others are bypassed). When an exception is caught, *exOb* will receive its value.

Actually, specifying *exOb* is optional. If the exception handler does not need access to the exception object (as is often the case), there is no need to specify *exOb*. For this reason, many of the examples in this chapter will not specify *exOb*.

Here is an important point: If no exception is thrown, then a **try** block ends normally, and all of its **catch** statements are bypassed. Execution resumes with the first statement following the last **catch**. Thus, **catch** statements are executed only if an exception is thrown.

A Simple Exception Example

Following is a simple example that illustrates how to watch for and catch an exception. As you know, it is an error to attempt to index an array beyond its boundaries. When this occurs, the C# runtime system throws an **IndexOutOfRangeException**, which is a standard exception defined by C#. The following program purposely generates such an exception and then catches it:

```
// Demonstrate exception handling.

using System;

class ExcDemo1 {
  public static void Main() {
    int[] nums = new int[4];

    try {
      Console.WriteLine("Before exception is generated.");

      // Generate an index out-of-bounds exception.
      for(int i=0; i < 10; i++) {
        nums[i] = i;
        Console.WriteLine("nums[{0}]: {1}", i, nums[i]);
      }

      Console.WriteLine("this won't be displayed");
    }
    catch (IndexOutOfRangeException) {
      // catch the exception
      Console.WriteLine("Index out-of-bounds!");
    }
    Console.WriteLine("After catch statement.");
  }
}
```

This program displays the following output:

```
Before exception is generated.
nums[0]: 0
nums[1]: 1
nums[2]: 2
nums[3]: 3
Index out-of-bounds!
After catch statement.
```

Notice that **nums** is an **int** array of four elements. However, the **for** loop tries to index **nums** from 0 to 9, which causes an **IndexOutOfRangeException** to occur when an index value of 4 is tried.

Although quite short, the preceding program illustrates several key points about exception handling. First, the code that you want to monitor for errors is contained within a **try** block. Second, when an exception occurs (in this case, because of the attempt to index **nums** beyond its bounds inside the **for** loop), the exception is thrown out of the **try** block and caught by the **catch** statement. At this point, control passes to the **catch**, and the **try** block is terminated. That is, **catch** is *not* called. Rather, program execution is transferred to it. Thus, the **WriteLine( )** statement following the out-of-bounds index will never execute. After the **catch** statement executes, program control continues with the statements following the **catch**. Thus, it is the job of your exception handler to remedy the problem that caused the exception so that program execution can continue normally.

Notice that no parameter is specified in the **catch** clause. As mentioned, a parameter is needed only when access to the exception object is required. In some cases, the value of the exception object can be used by the exception handler to obtain additional information about the error, but in many cases it is sufficient to simply know that an exception occurred. Thus, it is not unusual for the **catch** parameter to be absent in the exception handler, as is the case in the preceding program.

As explained, if no exception is thrown by a **try** block, no **catch** statements will be executed and program control resumes after the **catch** statement. To confirm this, in the preceding program, change the **for** loop from

```
for(int i=0; i < 10; i++) {
```

to

```
for(int i=0; i < nums.Length; i++) {
```

Now, the loop does not overrun **nums**'s boundary. Thus, no exception is generated, and the **catch** block is not executed.

A Second Exception Example

It is important to understand that all code executed within a **try** block is monitored for exceptions. This includes exceptions that might be generated by a method called from within the **try** block. An exception thrown by a method called from within a **try** block can be caught by that **try** block, assuming, of course, that the method itself did not catch the exception. For example, this is a valid program:

```
/* An exception can be generated by one
   method and caught by another. */

using System;
```

```
class ExcTest {
  // Generate an exception.
  public static void genException() {
    int[] nums = new int[4];

    Console.WriteLine("Before exception is generated.");

    // Generate an index out-of-bounds exception.
    for(int i=0; i < 10; i++) {
      nums[i] = i;
      Console.WriteLine("nums[{0}]: {1}", i, nums[i]);
    }

    Console.WriteLine("this won't be displayed");
  }
}

class ExcDemo2 {
  public static void Main() {

    try {
      ExcTest.genException();
    }
    catch (IndexOutOfRangeException) {
      // catch the exception
      Console.WriteLine("Index out-of-bounds!");
    }
    Console.WriteLine("After catch statement.");
  }
}
```

This program produces the following output, which is the same as that produced by the first version of the program shown earlier:

```
Before exception is generated.
nums[0]: 0
nums[1]: 1
nums[2]: 2
nums[3]: 3
Index out-of-bounds!
After catch statement.
```

Since **genException( )** is called from within a **try** block, the exception that it generates (and does not catch) is caught by the **catch** in **Main( )**. Understand, however, that if **genException( )** had caught the exception, it never would have been passed back to **Main( )**.

The Consequences of an Uncaught Exception

Catching one of C#'s standard exceptions, as the preceding program does, has a side benefit: It prevents abnormal program termination. When an exception is thrown, it must be caught by some piece of code, somewhere. In general, if your program does not catch an exception, it will be caught by the C# runtime system. The trouble is that the runtime system will report an error and terminate the program. For instance, in this example, the index out-of-bounds exception is not caught by the program:

```
// Let the C# runtime system handle the error.

using System;

class NotHandled {
  public static void Main() {
    int[] nums = new int[4];

    Console.WriteLine("Before exception is generated.");

    // Generate an index out-of-bounds exception.
    for(int i=0; i < 10; i++) {
      nums[i] = i;
      Console.WriteLine("nums[{0}]: {1}", i, nums[i]);
    }

  }
}
```

When the array index error occurs, execution is halted and the following error message is displayed:

```
Unhandled Exception: System.IndexOutOfRangeException:
        Index was outside the bounds of the array.
  at NotHandled.Main()
```

While such a message is useful for you while debugging, it would not be something that you would want others to see, to say the least! This is why it is important for your program to handle exceptions itself.

As mentioned earlier, the type of the exception must match the type specified in a **catch** statement. If it doesn't, the exception won't be caught. For example, the following program tries to catch an array boundary error with a **catch** statement for a **DivideByZeroException** (another of C#'s built-in exceptions). When the array boundary is overrun, an **IndexOutOf RangeException** is generated, but it won't be caught by the **catch** statement. This results in abnormal program termination.

```
// This won't work!

using System;

class ExcTypeMismatch {
  public static void Main() {
    int[] nums = new int[4];

    try {
      Console.WriteLine("Before exception is generated.");

      // Generate an index out-of-bounds exception.
      for(int i=0; i < 10; i++) {
        nums[i] = i;
        Console.WriteLine("nums[{0}]: {1}", i, nums[i]);
      }

      Console.WriteLine("this won't be displayed");
    }

    /* Can't catch an array boundary error with a
       DivideByZeroException. */
    catch (DivideByZeroException) {
      // catch the exception
      Console.WriteLine("Index out-of-bounds!");
    }
    Console.WriteLine("After catch statement.");
  }
}
```

The output is shown here:

```
Before exception is generated.
```

```
nums[0]: 0
nums[1]: 1
nums[2]: 2
nums[3]: 3

Unhandled Exception: System.IndexOutOfRangeException:
        Index was outside the bounds of the array.
   at ExcTypeMismatch.Main()
```

As the output demonstrates, a **catch** for **DivideByZeroException** won't catch an **IndexOutOfRangeException**.

Exceptions Let You Handle Errors Gracefully

One of the key benefits of exception handling is that it enables your program to respond to an error and then continue running. For example, consider the following example that divides the elements of one array by the elements of another. If a division-by-zero occurs, a **DivideByZeroException** is generated. In the program, this exception is handled by reporting the error and then continuing with execution. Thus, attempting to divide by zero does not cause an abrupt runtime error resulting in the termination of the program. Instead, it is handled gracefully, allowing program execution to continue.

```
// Handle error gracefully and continue.

using System;

class ExcDemo3 {
  public static void Main() {
    int[] numer = { 4, 8, 16, 32, 64, 128 };
    int[] denom = { 2, 0, 4, 4, 0, 8 };

    for(int i=0; i < numer.Length; i++) {
      try {
        Console.WriteLine(numer[i] + " / " +
                          denom[i] + " is " +
                          numer[i]/denom[i]);
      }
      catch (DivideByZeroException) {
        // catch the exception
        Console.WriteLine("Can't divide by Zero!");
```

```
        }
      }
    }
  }
```

The output from the program is shown here:

```
4 / 2 is 2
Can't divide by Zero!
16 / 4 is 4
32 / 4 is 8
Can't divide by Zero!
128 / 8 is 16
```

This example makes another important point: Once an exception has been handled, it is removed from the system. Therefore, in the program, each pass through the loop enters the **try** block anew—any prior exceptions have been handled. This enables your program to handle repeated errors.

Using Multiple catch Statements

You can associate more than one **catch** statement with a **try**. In fact, it is common to do so. However, each **catch** must catch a different type of exception. For example, the program shown here catches both array boundary and divide-by-zero errors:

```
// Use multiple catch statements.

using System;

class ExcDemo4 {
  public static void Main() {
    // Here, numer is longer than denom.
    int[] numer = { 4, 8, 16, 32, 64, 128, 256, 512 };
    int[] denom = { 2, 0, 4, 4, 0, 8 };

    for(int i=0; i < numer.Length; i++) {
      try {
        Console.WriteLine(numer[i] + " / " +
                          denom[i] + " is " +
                          numer[i]/denom[i]);
```

```
      }
    catch (DivideByZeroException) {
      // catch the exception
      Console.WriteLine("Can't divide by Zero!");
    }
    catch (IndexOutOfRangeException) {
      // catch the exception
      Console.WriteLine("No matching element found.");
    }
  }
 }
}
```

This program produces the following output:

```
4 / 2 is 2
Can't divide by Zero!
16 / 4 is 4
32 / 4 is 8
Can't divide by Zero!
128 / 8 is 16
No matching element found.
No matching element found.
```

As the output confirms, each **catch** statement responds only to its own type of exception.

In general, **catch** expressions are checked in the order in which they occur in a program. Only a matching statement is executed. All other **catch** blocks are ignored.

Catching All Exceptions

Sometimes you will want to catch all exceptions, no matter the type. To do this, use a **catch** statement that specifies no parameter. This creates a "catch all" handler that is useful when you want to ensure that all exceptions are handled by your program. For example, here the only **catch** is the "catch all," and it catches both the **IndexOutOf-RangeException** and the **DivideByZeroException** that is generated by the program:

```
// Use the "catch all" catch statement.

using System;
```

```
class ExcDemo5 {
  public static void Main() {
    // Here, numer is longer than denom.
    int[] numer = { 4, 8, 16, 32, 64, 128, 256, 512 };
    int[] denom = { 2, 0, 4, 4, 0, 8 };

    for(int i=0; i < numer.Length; i++) {
      try {
        Console.WriteLine(numer[i] + " / " +
                          denom[i] + " is " +
                          numer[i]/denom[i]);
      }
      catch {
        Console.WriteLine("Some exception occurred.");
      }
    }
  }
}
```

The output is shown here:

```
4 / 2 is 2
Some exception occurred.
16 / 4 is 4
32 / 4 is 8
Some exception occurred.
128 / 8 is 16
Some exception occurred.
Some exception occurred.
```

There is one point to remember about using a catch all **catch**: It must be the last **catch** clause in the **catch** sequence.

Nesting try Blocks

One **try** block can be nested within another. An exception generated within the inner **try** block that is not caught by a **catch** associated with that **try** is propagated to the outer **try** block. For example, here the **IndexOutOfRangeException** is not caught by the inner **try** block, but by the outer **try**:

```
// Use a nested try block.

using System;

class NestTrys {
  public static void Main() {
    // Here, numer is longer than denom.
    int[] numer = { 4, 8, 16, 32, 64, 128, 256, 512 };
    int[] denom = { 2, 0, 4, 4, 0, 8 };

    try { // outer try
      for(int i=0; i < numer.Length; i++) {
        try { // nested try
          Console.WriteLine(numer[i] + " / " +
                            denom[i] + " is " +
                            numer[i]/denom[i]);
        }
        catch (DivideByZeroException) {
          // catch the exception
          Console.WriteLine("Can't divide by Zero!");
        }
      }
    }
    catch (IndexOutOfRangeException) {
      // catch the exception
      Console.WriteLine("No matching element found.");
      Console.WriteLine("Fatal error -- program terminated.");
    }
  }
}
```

The output from the program is shown here:

```
4 / 2 is 2
Can't divide by Zero!
16 / 4 is 4
32 / 4 is 8
Can't divide by Zero!
128 / 8 is 16
No matching element found.
Fatal error -- program terminated.
```

In this example, an exception that can be handled by the inner **try**—in this case, a divide-by-zero error—allows the program to continue. However, an array boundary error is caught by the outer **try**, which causes the program to terminate.

The preceding program makes an important point that can be generalized. Often, nested **try** blocks are used to allow different categories of errors to be handled in different ways. Some types of errors are catastrophic and cannot be fixed. Some are minor and can be handled immediately. Many programmers use an outer **try** block to catch the most severe errors, allowing inner **try** blocks to handle less serious ones. You can also use an outer **try** block as a "catch all" block for those errors that are not handled by the inner block.

Throwing an Exception

The preceding examples have been catching exceptions generated automatically by C#. However, it is possible to manually throw an exception by using the **throw** statement. Its general form is shown here:

throw *exceptOb*;

The *exceptOb* must be an object of an exception class derived from **Exception**.

Here is an example that illustrates the **throw** statement by manually throwing a **DivideByZeroException**:

```
// Manually throw an exception.

using System;

class ThrowDemo {
  public static void Main() {
    try {
      Console.WriteLine("Before throw.");
      throw new DivideByZeroException();
    }
    catch (DivideByZeroException) {
      // catch the exception
      Console.WriteLine("Exception caught.");
    }
    Console.WriteLine("After try/catch block.");
  }
}
```

The output from the program is shown here:

```
Before throw.
Exception caught.
After try/catch block.
```

Notice how the **DivideByZeroException** was created using **new** in the **throw** statement. Remember that **throw** throws an object. Thus, you must create an object for it to throw—that is, you can't just throw a type. In this case, the default constructor is used to create a **DivideByZeroException** object, but other constructors are available for exceptions.

Most often, exceptions that you throw will be instances of exception classes that you created. As you will see later in this chapter, creating your own exception classes allows you to handle errors in your code as part of your program's overall exception handling strategy.

Rethrowing an Exception

An exception caught by one **catch** statement can be rethrown so that it can be caught by an outer **catch**. The most likely reason for rethrowing an exception is to allow multiple handlers access to the exception. For example, perhaps one exception handler manages one aspect of an exception, and a second handler copes with another aspect. To rethrow an exception, you simply specify **throw**, without specifying an exception. That is, you use this form of **throw**:

```
throw ;
```

Remember that when you rethrow an exception, it will not be recaught by the same **catch** statement. It will propagate to the next **catch** statement.

The following program illustrates rethrowing an exception. In this case, it rethrows an **IndexOutOfRangeException**.

```
// Rethrow an exception.

using System;

class Rethrow {
  public static void genException() {
    // here, numer is longer than denom
    int[] numer = { 4, 8, 16, 32, 64, 128, 256, 512 };
    int[] denom = { 2, 0, 4, 4, 0, 8 };

    for(int i=0; i<numer.Length; i++) {
      try {
        Console.WriteLine(numer[i] + " / " +
```

```
                          denom[i] + " is " +
                          numer[i]/denom[i]);
        }
      catch (DivideByZeroException) {
        // catch the exception
        Console.WriteLine("Can't divide by Zero!");
      }
      catch (IndexOutOfRangeException) {
        // catch the exception
        Console.WriteLine("No matching element found.");
        throw; // rethrow the exception
      }
    }
  }
}

class RethrowDemo {
  public static void Main() {
    try {
      Rethrow.genException();
    }
    catch(IndexOutOfRangeException) {
      // recatch exception
      Console.WriteLine("Fatal error -- " +
                        "program terminated.");
    }
  }
}
```

In this program, divide-by-zero errors are handled locally, by **genException( )**, but
an array boundary error is rethrown. In this case, the **IndexOutOfRangeException** is
handled by **Main( )**.

Using finally

Sometimes you will want to define a block of code that will execute when a **try/catch**
block is left. For example, an exception might cause an error that terminates the current
method, causing its premature return. However, that method may have opened a file
or a network connection that needs to be closed. Such types of circumstances are
common in programming, and C# provides a convenient way to handle them: **finally**.

To specify a block of code to execute when a **try/catch** block is exited, include a **finally** block at the end of a **try**/**catch** sequence. The general form of a **try**/**catch** that includes **finally** is shown here:

```
try {
  // block of code to monitor for errors
}
catch (ExcepType1 exOb) {
  // handler for ExcepType1
}
catch (ExcepType2 exOb) {
  // handler for ExcepType2
}
.
.
.
finally {
  // finally code
}
```

The **finally** block will be executed whenever execution leaves a **try/catch** block, no matter what conditions cause it. That is, whether the **try** block ends normally, or because of an exception, the last code executed is that defined by **finally**. The **finally** block is also executed if any code within the **try** block or any of its **catch** statements returns from the method.

Here is an example of **finally**:

```
// Use finally.

using System;

class UseFinally {
  public static void genException(int what) {
    int t;
    int[] nums = new int[2];

    Console.WriteLine("Receiving " + what);
    try {
      switch(what) {
        case 0:
          t = 10 / what; // generate div-by-zero error
          break;
        case 1:
          nums[4] = 4; // generate array index error.
          break;
        case 2:
```

```
           return; // return from try block
      }
    }
    catch (DivideByZeroException) {
      // catch the exception
      Console.WriteLine("Can't divide by Zero!");
      return; // return from catch
    }
    catch (IndexOutOfRangeException) {
      // catch the exception
      Console.WriteLine("No matching element found.");
    }
    finally {
      Console.WriteLine("Leaving try.");
    }
  }
}

class FinallyDemo {
  public static void Main() {

    for(int i=0; i < 3; i++) {
      UseFinally.genException(i);
      Console.WriteLine();
    }
  }
}
```

Here is the output produced by the program:

```
Receiving 0
Can't divide by Zero!
Leaving try.

Receiving 1
No matching element found.
Leaving try.

Receiving 2
Leaving try.
```

As the output shows, no matter how the **try** block is exited, the **finally** block is executed.

A Closer Look at Exception

Up to this point, we have been catching exceptions, but we haven't been doing anything with the exception object itself. As explained earlier, a **catch** clause allows you to specify an exception type and a parameter. The parameter receives the exception object. Since all exceptions are derived from **Exception**, all exceptions support the members defined by **Exception**. Here we will examine several of its most useful members and constructors, and put the **catch** parameter to good use.

Exception defines several properties. Three of the most interesting are **Message**, **StackTrace**, and **TargetSite**. All are read-only. **Message** contains a string that describes the nature of the error. **StackTrace** contains a string that contains the stack of calls that lead to the exception. **TargetSite** obtains an object that specifies the method that generated the exception.

Exception also defines several methods. The one that you will most often use is **ToString( )**, which returns a string that describes the exception. **ToString( )** is automatically called when an exception is displayed via **WriteLine( )**, for example.

The following program demonstrates these properties and method:

```
// Using Exception members.

using System;

class ExcTest {
  public static void genException() {
    int[] nums = new int[4];

    Console.WriteLine("Before exception is generated.");

    // Generate an index out-of-bounds exception.
      for(int i=0; i < 10; i++) {
        nums[i] = i;
        Console.WriteLine("nums[{0}]: {1}", i, nums[i]);
      }

    Console.WriteLine("this won't be displayed");
  }
}

class UseExcept {
  public static void Main() {

    try {
```

```
        ExcTest.genException();
    }
    catch (IndexOutOfRangeException exc) {
      // catch the exception
      Console.WriteLine("Standard message is: ");
      Console.WriteLine(exc); // calls ToString()
      Console.WriteLine("Stack trace: " + exc.StackTrace);
      Console.WriteLine("Message: " + exc.Message);
      Console.WriteLine("TargetSite: " + exc.TargetSite);
    }
    Console.WriteLine("After catch statement.");
  }
}
```

The output from this program is shown here:

```
Before exception is generated.
nums[0]: 0
nums[1]: 1
nums[2]: 2
nums[3]: 3
Standard message is:
System.IndexOutOfRangeException: Index was outside the bounds of the array.
   at ExcTest.genException()
   at UseExcept.Main()
Stack trace:    at ExcTest.genException()
   at UseExcept.Main()
Message: Index was outside the bounds of the array.
TargetSite: Void genException()
After catch statement.
```

Exception defines four constructors. The two that are most commonly used are shown here:

Exception( )
Exception(string *str*)

The first is the default constructor. The second specifies the **Message** property associated with the exception. When creating your own exception classes, you should implement both of these constructors.

Commonly Used Exceptions

The **System** namespace defines several standard, built-in exceptions. All are derived from **SystemException** since they are generated by the Common Language Runtime when runtime errors occur. Several of the more commonly used standard exceptions defined by C# are shown in Table 13-1.

Most of the exceptions in Table 13-1 are self-explanatory, with the possible exception of **NullReferenceException**. This exception is thrown when there is an attempt to use a null reference as if it referred to an object—for example, if you attempt to call a method on a null reference. A *null reference* is a reference that does not point to any object. One way to create a null reference is to explicitly assign it the value null by using the keyword

Exception	Meaning
ArrayTypeMismatchException	Type of value being stored is incompatible with the type of the array.
DivideByZeroException	Division by zero attempted.
IndexOutOfRangeException	Array index is out of bounds.
InvalidCastException	A runtime cast is invalid.
OutOfMemoryException	A call to **new** fails because insufficient free memory exists.
OverflowException	An arithmetic overflow occurred.
NullReferenceException	An attempt was made to operate on a null reference—that is, a reference that does not refer to an object.
StackOverflowException	The stack was overrun.

Table 13-1. *Commonly Used Exceptions Defined Within the **System** Namespace*

null. Null references can also occur in other ways that are less obvious. Here is a program that demonstrates the **NullReferenceException**:

```
// Use the NullReferenceException.

using System;

class X {
  int x;
  public X(int a) {
    x = a;
  }

  public int add(X o) {
    return x + o.x;
  }
}

// Demonstrate NullReferenceException.
class NREDemo {
  public static void Main() {
    X p = new X(10);
    X q = null; // q is explicitly assigned null
    int val;

    try {
      val = p.add(q); // this will lead to an exception
    } catch (NullReferenceException) {
      Console.WriteLine("NullReferenceException!");
      Console.WriteLine("fixing...\n");

      // now, fix it
      q = new X(9);
      val = p.add(q);
    }

    Console.WriteLine("val is {0}", val);

  }
}
```

The output from the program is shown here:

```
NullReferenceException!
fixing...

val is 19
```

The program creates a class called **X** that defines a member called **x**, and the **add( )** method, which adds the invoking object's **x** to the **x** in the object passed as a parameter. In **Main( )**, two **X** objects are created. The first, **p**, is initialized. The second, **q**, is not. Instead, it is explicitly assigned **null**. Then **p.meth( )** is called with **q** as an argument. Since **q** does not refer to any object, a **NullReferenceException** is generated when the attempt is made to obtain the value of **q.x**.

An interesting exception is **StackOverflowException**, which is thrown when the system stack is overrun. One situation in which this can happen is when a recursive method runs wild. A program that makes extensive use of recursion may want to watch for this exception, taking appropriate action if it occurs. Be careful, however. Since the system stack is exhausted when this exception is thrown, often the best action is to simply start returning from the recursive calls.

Deriving Exception Classes

Although C#'s built-in exceptions handle most common errors, C#'s exception handling mechanism is not limited to these errors. In fact, part of the power of C#'s approach to exceptions is its ability to handle exceptions that you create. You can use custom exceptions to handle errors in your own code. Creating an exception is easy. Just define a class derived from **Exception**. As a general rule, exceptions defined by you should be derived from **ApplicationException** since this is the hierarchy reserved for application-related exceptions. Your derived classes don't need to actually implement anything—it is their existence in the type system that allows you to use them as exceptions.

The exception classes that you create will automatically have the properties and methods defined by **Exception** available to them. Of course, you can override one or more of these members in exception classes that you create.

Here is an example that makes use of a custom exception type. At the end of Chapter 10 an array class called **RangeArray** was developed. As you may recall, **RangeArray** supports single-dimension **int** arrays in which the starting and ending index is specified by the user. For example, an array that ranges from –5 to 27 is perfectly legal for a **RangeArray**. In Chapter 10, if an index was out of range, a special error variable defined by **RangeArray** was set. This meant that the error variable had to be checked after each operation by the code that used **RangeArray**. Of course, such an approach is error-prone and clumsy. A far better design is to have **RangeArray** throw a custom exception when a range error occurs. This is precisely what the following version of **RangeArray** does:

```csharp
// Use a custom Exception for RangeArray errors.

using System;

// Create a RangeArray exception.
class RangeArrayException : ApplicationException {
  // Implement the standard constructors
  public RangeArrayException() : base() { }
  public RangeArrayException(string str) : base(str) { }

  // Override ToString for RangeArrayException.
  public override string ToString() {
    return Message;
  }
}

// An improved version of RangeArray.
class RangeArray {
  // private data
  int[] a; // reference to underlying array
  int lowerBound; // lowest index
  int upperBound; // greatest index

  int len; // underlying var for Length property

  // Construct array given its size.
  public RangeArray(int low, int high) {
    high++;
    if(high <= low) {
      throw new RangeArrayException("Low index not less than high.");
    }
    a = new int[high - low];
    len = high - low;

    lowerBound = low;
    upperBound = --high;
  }
```

```
  // Read-only Length property.
  public int Length {
    get {
      return len;
    }
  }

  // This is the indexer for RangeArray.
  public int this[int index] {
    // This is the get accessor.
    get {
      if(ok(index)) {
        return a[index - lowerBound];
      } else {
        throw new RangeArrayException("Range Error.");
      }
    }

    // This is the set accessor.
    set {
      if(ok(index)) {
        a[index - lowerBound] = value;
      }
      else throw new RangeArrayException("Range Error.");
    }
  }

  // Return true if index is within bounds.
  private bool ok(int index) {
    if(index >= lowerBound & index <= upperBound) return true;
    return false;
  }
}

// Demonstrate the index range array.
class RangeArrayDemo {
  public static void Main() {
    try {
      RangeArray ra = new RangeArray(-5, 5);
      RangeArray ra2 = new RangeArray(1, 10);

      // Demonstrate ra
```

```
      Console.WriteLine("Length of ra: " + ra.Length);

    for(int i = -5; i <= 5; i++)
      ra[i] = i;

    Console.Write("Contents of ra: ");
    for(int i = -5; i <= 5; i++)
      Console.Write(ra[i] + " ");

    Console.WriteLine("\n");

    // Demonstrate ra2
    Console.WriteLine("Length of ra2: " + ra2.Length);

    for(int i = 1; i <= 10; i++)
      ra2[i] = i;

    Console.Write("Contents of ra2: ");
    for(int i = 1; i <= 10; i++)
      Console.Write(ra2[i] + " ");

    Console.WriteLine("\n");

  } catch (RangeArrayException exc) {
      Console.WriteLine(exc);
  }

  // Now, demonstrate some errors.
  Console.WriteLine("Now generate some range errors.");

  // Use an invalid constructor.
  try {
    RangeArray ra3 = new RangeArray(100, -10); // Error

  } catch (RangeArrayException exc) {
      Console.WriteLine(exc);
  }

  // Use an invalid index.
  try {
    RangeArray ra3 = new RangeArray(-2, 2);
```

```
      for(int i = -2; i <= 2; i++)
        ra3[i] = i;

      Console.Write("Contents of ra3: ");
      for(int i = -2; i <= 10; i++) // generate range error
        Console.Write(ra3[i] + " ");

    } catch (RangeArrayException exc) {
      Console.WriteLine(exc);
    }
  }
}
```

The output from the program is shown here:

```
Length of ra: 11
Contents of ra: -5 -4 -3 -2 -1 0 1 2 3 4 5

Length of ra2: 10
Contents of ra2: 1 2 3 4 5 6 7 8 9 10

Now generate some range errors.
Low index not less than high.
Contents of ra3: -2 -1 0 1 2 Range Error.
```

When a range error occurs, **RangeArray** throws an object of type **RangeArrayException**. This class is derived from **ApplicationException**. As explained, an exception class that you create should normally be derived from **ApplicationException**. Notice that a range error can occur during construction of a **RangeArray**. To catch these exceptions implies that **RangeArray** objects must be constructed from within a **try** block, as the program illustrates. By using an exception to report errors, **RangeArray** now acts like one of C#'s built-in types and can be fully integrated into a program's exception handling mechanism.

Before moving on, you might want to experiment with this program a bit. For example, try commenting-out the override of **ToString( )** and observe the results. Also, try creating an exception using the default constructor, and observe what C# generates as its default message.

Catching Derived Class Exceptions

You need to be careful how you order **catch** statements when trying to catch exception types that involve base and derived classes, because a **catch** clause for a base class will also match any of its derived classes. For example, since the base class of all exceptions is **Exception**, catching **Exception** catches all possible exceptions. Of course, using **catch** without an argument provides a cleaner way to catch all exceptions, as described earlier. However, the issue of catching derived class exceptions is very important in other contexts, especially when you create exceptions of your own.

If you want to catch exceptions of both a base class type and a derived class type, put the derived class first in the **catch** sequence. If you don't, then the base class **catch** will also catch all derived classes. This rule is self-enforcing because putting the base class first causes unreachable code to be created, since the derived class **catch** clause can never execute. In C#, an unreachable **catch** clause is an error.

The following program creates two exception classes called **ExceptA** and **ExceptB**. **ExceptA** is derived from **ApplicationException**. **ExceptB** is derived from **ExceptA**. The program then throws an exception of each type.

```
// Derived exceptions must appear before base class exceptions.

using System;

// Create an exception.
class ExceptA : ApplicationException {
  public ExceptA() : base() { }
  public ExceptA(string str) : base(str) { }

  public override string ToString() {
    return Message;
  }
}

// Create an exception derived from ExceptA
class ExceptB : ExceptA {
  public ExceptB() : base() { }
  public ExceptB(string str) : base(str) { }

  public override string ToString() {
    return Message;
  }
}
```

```
class OrderMatters {
  public static void Main() {
    for(int x = 0; x < 3; x++) {
      try {
        if(x==0) throw new ExceptA("Caught an ExceptA exception");
        else if(x==1) throw new ExceptB("Caught an ExceptB exception");
        else throw new Exception();
      }
      catch (ExceptB exc) {
        // catch the exception
        Console.WriteLine(exc);
      }
      catch (ExceptA exc) {
        // catch the exception
        Console.WriteLine(exc);
      }
      catch (Exception exc) {
        Console.WriteLine(exc);
      }
    }
  }
}
```

The output from the program is shown here:

```
Caught an ExceptA exception
Caught an ExceptB exception
System.Exception: Exception of type System.Exception was thrown.
   at OrderMatters.Main()
```

Notice the order of the **catch** statements. This is the only order in which they can occur. Since **ExceptB** is derived from **ExceptA**, the **catch** statement for **ExceptB** must be before the one for **ExceptA**. Similarly, the **catch** for **Exception** (which is the base class for all exceptions) must appear last. To prove this point for yourself, try rearranging the **catch** statements. Doing so will result in a compile-time error.

One good use of a base-class **catch** clause is to catch an entire category of exceptions. For example, imagine that you are creating a set of exceptions for some device. If you derive all of the exceptions from a common base class, then applications that don't need to know precisely what problem occurred could simply catch the base class exception, avoiding the unnecessary duplication of code.

Using checked and unchecked

A special feature in C# relates to the generation of overflow exceptions in arithmetic computations. As you know, it is possible for some types of arithmetic computations to produce a result that exceeds the range of the data type involved in the computation. When this occurs, the result is said to *overflow*. For example, consider the following sequence:

```
byte a, b, result;
a = 127;
b = 127;

result = (byte)(a * b);
```

Here, the product of **a** and **b** exceeds the range of a **byte** value. Thus, the result overflows the type of the result.

C# allows you to specify whether your code will raise an exception when overflow occurs by using the keywords **checked** and **unchecked**. To specify that an expression be checked for overflow, use **checked**. To specify that overflow be ignored, use **unchecked**. In this case, the result is truncated to fit into the target type of the expression.

The **checked** keyword has these two general forms. One checks a specific expression and is called the *operator form* of **checked**. The other checks a block of statements.

checked (*expr*)

checked {
    // statements to be checked
}

Here, *expr* is the expression being checked. If a checked expression overflows, an **OverflowException** is thrown.

The **unchecked** keyword has these two general forms. One is the operator form, which ignores overflow for a specific expression. The other ignores overflow for a block of statements.

unchecked (*expr*)

unchecked {
    // statements for which overflow is ignored
}

Here, *expr* is the expression that is not being checked for overflow. If an unchecked expression overflows, then truncation will occur.

Here is a program that demonstrates both **checked** and **unchecked**:

```
// Using checked and unchecked.

using System;

class CheckedDemo {
  public static void Main() {
    byte a, b;
    byte result;

    a = 127;
    b = 127;

    try {
      result = unchecked((byte)(a * b));
      Console.WriteLine("Unchecked result: " + result);

      result = checked((byte)(a * b)); // this causes exception
      Console.WriteLine("Checked result: " + result);
    }
    catch (OverflowException exc) {
      // catch the exception
      Console.WriteLine(exc);
    }
  }
}
```

The output from the program is shown here:

```
Unchecked result: 1
System.OverflowException: Arithmetic operation resulted in an overflow.
   at CheckedDemo.Main()
```

As is evident, the unchecked expression resulted in a truncation. The checked expression caused an exception.

The preceding program demonstrated the use of **checked** and **unchecked** for a single expression. The following program shows how to check and uncheck a block of statements.

```
// Using checked and unchecked with statement blocks.
```

```
using System;

class CheckedBlocks {
  public static void Main() {
    byte a, b;
    byte result;

    a = 127;
    b = 127;

    try {
      unchecked {
        a = 127;
        b = 127;
        result = unchecked((byte)(a * b));
        Console.WriteLine("Unchecked result: " + result);

        a = 125;
        b = 5;
        result = unchecked((byte)(a * b));
        Console.WriteLine("Unchecked result: " + result);
      }

      checked {
        a = 2;
        b = 7;
        result = checked((byte)(a * b)); // this is OK
        Console.WriteLine("Checked result: " + result);

        a = 127;
        b = 127;
        result = checked((byte)(a * b)); // this causes exception
        Console.WriteLine("Checked result: " + result);
      }
    }
    catch (OverflowException exc) {
      // catch the exception
      Console.WriteLine(exc);
    }
  }
}
```

The output from the program is shown here:

```
Unchecked result: 1
Unchecked result: 113
Checked result: 14
System.OverflowException: Arithmetic operation resulted in an overflow.
   at CheckedBlocks.Main()
```

As you can see, the unchecked block results in the overflow being truncated. When overflow occurred in the checked block, an exception was raised.

One reason that you may need to used **checked** or **unchecked** is that the checked/unchecked status of overflow is determined by the setting of a compiler option and the execution environment, itself. Thus, for some types of programs, it is best to explicitly specify the overflow check status.

Chapter 14

Using I/O

The earlier chapters of this book have used parts of the C# I/O system, such as **Console.WriteLine( )**, but they haven't provided much formal explanation. Because the C# I/O system is built upon a hierarchy of classes, it was not possible to present its theory and details without first discussing classes, inheritance, and exceptions. Now it is time to examine C#'s approach to I/O in detail. Because C# uses the I/O system and classes defined by the .NET Framework, a discussion of I/O under C# is also a discussion of the .NET I/O system in general.

This chapter examines C#'s approach to both console I/O and file I/O. Be forewarned that C#'s I/O system is quite large. This chapter describes the most important and commonly used features.

C#'s I/O Is Built Upon Streams

C# programs perform I/O through streams. A *stream* is an abstraction that either produces or consumes information. A stream is linked to a physical device by the C# I/O system. All streams behave in the same manner, even if the actual physical devices they are linked to differ. Thus, the I/O classes and methods can be applied to many types of devices. For example, the same methods that you use to write to the console can also be used to write to a disk file.

Byte Streams and Character Streams

At the lowest level, all C# I/O systems operate on bytes. This makes sense because many devices are byte oriented when it comes to I/O operations. Frequently, though, we humans prefer to communicate using characters. Recall that in C#, **char** is a 16-bit type and **byte** is an 8-bit type. If you are using the ASCII character set, it is easy to convert between **char** and **byte**; just ignore the high-order byte of the **char** value. But this won't work for the rest of the Unicode characters, which need both bytes. Thus, byte streams are not perfectly suited to handling character-based I/O. To solve this problem, C# defines several classes that convert a byte stream into a character stream, handling the translation of **byte**-to-**char** and **char**-to-**byte** for you automatically.

The Predefined Streams

Three predefined streams, which are exposed through the properties called **Console.In**, **Console.Out**, and **Console.Error**, are available to all programs that use the **System** namespace. **Console.Out** refers to the standard output stream. By default, this is the console. When you call **Console.WriteLine( )**, for example, it automatically sends information to **Console.Out**. **Console.In** refers to standard input, which is by default the keyboard. **Console.Error** refers to the standard error stream, which is also the console by default. However, these streams can be redirected to any compatible I/O device. The standard streams are character streams. Thus, these streams read and write characters.

The Stream Classes

C# defines both byte stream and character stream classes. However, the character stream classes are really just wrappers that convert an underlying byte stream into a character stream, handling any conversion automatically. Thus, the character streams, while logically separate, are built upon byte streams.

All stream classes are defined within the **System.IO** namespace. To use these classes, you will usually include the following statement near the top of your program:

```
using System.IO;
```

The reason that you don't have to specify **System.IO** for console input and output is that the **Console** class is defined in the **System** namespace.

The Stream Class

At the core of C#'s streams is **System.IO.Stream**. **Stream** represents a byte stream and is a base class for all other stream classes. It is also abstract, which means that you cannot instantiate a **Stream** object. **Stream** defines a set of standard stream operations. Table 14-1 shows several commonly used methods defined by **Stream**.

Method	Description
void Close( )	Closes the stream.
void Flush( )	Writes the contents of the stream to the physical device.
int ReadByte( )	Returns an integer representation of the next available byte of input. Returns –1 when the end of the file is encountered.
int Read(byte[ ] *buf*, int *offset*, int *numBytes*)	Attempts to read up to *numBytes* bytes into *buf* starting at *buf*[*offset*], returning the number of bytes successfully read.
long Seek(long *offset*, SeekOrigin *origin*)	Sets the current position in the stream to the specified *offset* from the specified *origin*.
void WriteByte(byte *b*)	Writes a single byte to an output stream.
void Write(byte[ ] *buf*, int *offset*, int *numBytes*)	Writes a subrange of *numBytes* bytes from the array *buf*, beginning at *buf*[*offset*].

Table 14-1.   *Some of the Methods Defined by **Stream***

In general, if an I/O error occurs, the methods shown in Table 14-1 will throw an **IOException**. If an invalid operation is attempted, such as attempting to write to a stream that is read-only, a **NotSupportedException** is thrown.

Notice that **Stream** defines methods that read and write data. However, not all streams will support both of these operations, because it is possible to open read-only or write-only streams. Also, not all streams will support position requests via **Seek( )**. To determine the capabilities of a stream, you will use one or more of **Stream**'s properties. They are shown in Table 14-2. Also shown are the **Length** and **Position** properties, which contain the length of the stream and its current position.

The Byte Stream Classes

From **Stream** are derived the three concrete byte stream classes shown here:

Stream Class	Description
BufferedStream	Wraps a byte stream and adds buffering. Buffering provides a performance enhancement in many cases.
FileStream	A byte stream designed for file I/O.
MemoryStream	A byte stream that uses memory for storage.

It is also possible for you to derive your own stream classes. However, for the vast majority of applications, the built-in streams will be sufficient.

Method	Description
bool CanRead	This property is true if the stream can be read. This property is read-only.
bool CanSeek	This property is true if the stream supports position requests. This property is read-only.
bool CanWrite	This property is true if the stream can be written. This property is read-only.
long Length	This property contains the length of the stream. This property is read-only.
long Position	This property represents the current position of the stream. This property is read/write.

Table 14-2.   *The Properties Defined by **Stream***

The Character Stream Wrapper Classes

To create a character stream, wrap a byte stream inside one of C#'s character stream wrappers. At the top of the character stream hierarchy are the abstract classes **TextReader** and **TextWriter**. **TextReader** handles input and **TextWriter** handles output. The methods defined by these two abstract classes are available to all of their subclasses. Thus, they form a minimal set of I/O functions that all character streams will have.

Table 14-3 shows the input methods in **TextReader**. In general, these methods can throw an **IOException** on error. (Some can throw other types of exceptions, too.) Of particular interest is the **ReadLine( )** method, which reads an entire line of text, returning it as a **string**. This method is useful when reading input that contains embedded spaces.

Method	Description
void Close( )	Closes the input source.
int Peek( )	Obtains the next character from the input stream, but does not remove that character. Returns –1 if no character is available.
int Read( )	Returns an integer representation of the next available character from the invoking input stream. Returns –1 when the end of the stream is encountered.
int Read(char[ ] *buf*, int *offset*, int *numChars*)	Attempts to read up to *numChars* characters into *buf* starting at *buf[offset]*, returning the number of characters successfully read.
int ReadBlock(char[ ] *buf*, int *offset*, int *numChars*)	Attempts to read up to *numChars* characters into *buf* starting at *buf[offset]*, returning the number of characters successfully read.
string ReadLine( )	Reads the next line of text and returns it as a string. Null is returned if an attempt is made to read at end-of-file.
string ReadToEnd( )	Reads all of the remaining characters in a stream and returns them as a string.

Table 14-3. *The Input Methods Defined by **TextReader***

TextWriter defines versions of **Write( )** and **WriteLine( )** that output all of the built-in types. For example, here are just a few of their overloaded versions:

Method	Description
void Write(int *val*)	Write an **int**.
void Write(double *val*)	Write a **double**.
void Write(bool *val*)	Write a **bool**.
void WriteLine(string *val*)	Write a **string** followed by a newline.
void WriteLine(uint *val*)	Write a **uint** followed by a newline.
void WriteLine(char *val*)	Write a character followed by a newline.

In addition to **Write( )** and **WriteLine( )**, **TextWriter** also defines the **Close( )** and **Flush( )** methods shown here:

```
virtual void Close( )
virtual void Flush( )
```

Flush( ) causes any data remaining in the output buffer to be written to the physical medium. **Close( )** closes the stream.

The **TextReader** and **TextWriter** classes are implemented by several character-based stream classes, including those shown in the following table. Thus, these streams provide the methods and properties specified by **TextReader** and **TextWriter**.

Stream Class	Description
StreamReader	Read characters from a byte stream. This class wraps a byte input stream.
StreamWriter	Write characters to a byte stream. This class wraps a byte output stream.
StringReader	Read characters from a string.
StringWriter	Write characters to a string.

Binary Streams

In addition to byte streams and character streams, C# defines two binary stream classes that can be used to read and write binary data directly. These streams are called **BinaryReader** and **BinaryWriter**. We will look closely at these later in this chapter when binary file I/O is discussed.

Now that you understand the general layout of the C# I/O system, the rest of this chapter will examine its various pieces in detail, beginning with console I/O.

Console I/O

Console I/O is accomplished through the standard streams **Console.In**, **Console.Out**, and **Console.Error**. You have been using console I/O since Chapter 2, so you already are familiar with it. As you will see, it has some additional capabilities.

Before we begin, it is important here to emphasize a point made earlier in this book: Most real applications of C# will not be text-based, console programs. Rather, they will be graphically oriented programs or components that rely upon a windowed interface for interaction with the user. Thus, the portion of C#'s I/O system that relates to console input and output is not widely used. Although text-based programs are excellent as teaching examples, for short utility programs, and some types of components, they are not suitable for most real-world applications.

Reading Console Input

Console.In is an instance of **TextReader**, and you can use the methods and properties defined by **TextReader** to access it. However, you will usually use the methods provided by **Console**, which automatically read from **Console.In**. **Console** defines two input methods: **Read( )** and **ReadLine( )**.

To read a single character, use the **Read( )** method:

static int Read( )

Read( ) returns the next character read from the console. It waits until the user presses a key and then returns the result. The character is returned as an **int**, which must be cast to **char**. **Read( )** returns –1 on error. This method will throw an **IOException** on failure. By default, console input is line-buffered, so you must press ENTER before any character that you type will be sent to your program.

Here is a program that reads a character from the keyboard using **Read( )**:

```
// Read a character from the keyboard.

using System;

class KbIn {
  public static void Main() {
    char ch;

    Console.Write("Press a key followed by ENTER: ");

    ch = (char) Console.Read(); // get a char

    Console.WriteLine("Your key is: " + ch);
  }
}
```

Here is a sample run:

```
Press a key followed by ENTER: t
Your key is: t
```

The fact that **Read( )** is line-buffered is a source of annoyance at times. When you press ENTER, a carriage-return, line-feed sequence is entered into the input stream. Furthermore, these characters are left pending in the input buffer until you read them. Thus, for some applications, you may need to remove them (by reading them) before the next input operation.

To read a string of characters, use the **ReadLine( )** method. It is shown here:

static string ReadLine( )

ReadLine( ) reads characters until you press ENTER and returns them in a **string** object. This method will throw an **IOException** on failure.

Here is a program that demonstrates reading a string from **Console.In** by using **ReadLine( )**:

```
// Input from the console using ReadLine().

using System;

class ReadString {
  public static void Main() {
    string str;

    Console.WriteLine("Enter some characters.");
    str = Console.ReadLine();
    Console.WriteLine("You entered: " + str);
  }
}
```

Here is a sample run:

```
Enter some characters.
This is a test.
You entered: This is a test.
```

Although the **Console** methods are the easiest way to read from **Console.In**, you can call methods on the underlying **TextReader**. For example, here is the preceding program rewritten to use the methods defined by **TextReader**:

```
// Read a string from the keyboard, using Console.In directly.

using System;

class ReadChars2 {
  public static void Main() {
    string str;

    Console.WriteLine("Enter some characters.");

    str = Console.In.ReadLine();

    Console.WriteLine("You entered: " + str);
  }
}
```

Notice how **ReadLine( )** is now invoked directly on **Console.In**. The key point here is that if you need access to the methods defined by the **TextReader** that underlies **Console.In**, you will invoke those methods as shown in this example.

Writing Console Output

Console.Out and **Console.Error** are objects of type **TextWriter**. Console output is most easily accomplished with **Write( )** and **WriteLine( )**, with which you are already familiar. Versions of these methods exist that output for each of the built-in types. **Console** defines its own versions of **Write( )** and **WriteLine( )** so that they can be called directly on **Console**, as you have been doing throughout this book. However, you can invoke these (and other) methods on the **TextWriter** that underlies **Console.Out** and **Console.Error** if you choose.

Here is a program that demonstrates writing to **Console.Out** and **Console.Error**:

```
// Write to Console.Out and Console.Error.

using System;

class ErrOut {
  public static void Main() {
    int a=10, b=0;
    int result;

    Console.Out.WriteLine("This will generate an exception.");
    try {
```

```
      result = a / b; // generate an exception
    } catch(DivideByZeroException exc) {
      Console.Error.WriteLine(exc.Message);
    }
  }
}
```

The output from the program is shown here:

```
This will generate an exception.
Attempted to divide by zero.
```

Sometimes newcomers to programming are confused about when to use **Console .Error**. Since both **Console.Out** and **Console.Error** default to writing their output to the console, why are there two different streams? The answer lies in the fact that the standard streams can be redirected to other devices. For example, **Console.Error** can be redirected to write to a disk file, rather than the screen. Thus, it is possible to direct error output to a log file, for example, without affecting console output. Conversely, if console output is redirected and error output is not, then error messages will appear on the console, where they can be seen. We will examine redirection later, after file I/O has been described.

FileStream and Byte-Oriented File I/O

C# provides classes that allow you to read and write files. Of course, disk files are the most common type of files. At the operating system level, all files are byte oriented. As you would expect, C# has methods to read and write bytes from and to a file. Thus, reading and writing files using byte streams is very common. C# also allows you to wrap a byte-oriented file stream within a character-based object. Character-based file operations are useful when text is being stored. Character streams are discussed later in this chapter. Byte-oriented I/O is described here.

To create a byte-oriented stream attached to a file, you will use the **FileStream** class. **FileStream** is derived from **Stream** and contains all of **Stream**'s functionality.

Remember, the stream classes, including **FileStream**, are defined in **System.IO**. Thus, you will usually include

```
using System.IO;
```

near the top of any program that uses them.

Opening and Closing a File

To create a byte stream linked to a file, create a **FileStream** object. **FileStream** defines several constructors. Perhaps its most commonly used one is shown here:

> FileStream(string *filename*, FileMode *mode*)

Here, *filename* specifies the name of the file to open, which can include a full path specification. The *mode* parameter specifies how the file will be opened. It must be one of the values defined by the **FileMode** enumeration. These values are shown in Table 14-4. This constructor opens a file for read/write access.

If a failure occurs when attempting to open the file, an exception will be thrown. If the file cannot be opened because it does not exist, **FileNotFoundException** will be thrown. If the file cannot be opened because of an I/O error, **IOException** will be thrown. Other possible exceptions are **ArgumentNullException** (the filename is null), **ArgumentException** (the mode parameter is invalid), **SecurityException** (user does not have access rights), and **DirectoryNotFoundException** (specified directory is invalid).

Value	Description
FileMode.Append	Output is appended to the end of file.
FileMode.Create	Creates a new output file. Any preexisting file by the same name will be destroyed.
FileMode.CreateNew	Creates a new output file. The file must not already exist.
FileMode.Open	Opens a preexisting file.
FileMode.OpenOrCreate	Opens a file if it exists, or creates the file if it does not already exist.
FileMode.Truncate	Opens a preexisting file, but reduces its length to zero.

Table 14-4.   *The **FileMode** Values*

The following shows one way to open the file **test.dat** for input:

```
FileStream fin;

try {
  fin = new FileStream("test.dat", FileMode.Open);
}
catch(FileNotFoundException exc) {
  Console.WriteLine(exc.Message);
  return;
}
catch {
  Console.WriteLine("Cannot open file.");
  return;
}
```

Here, the first **catch** clause catches the file-not-found error. The second **catch**, which is a "catch all" clause, handles the other possible file errors. You could also check for each error individually, reporting more specifically the problem that occurred. For the sake of simplicity, the examples in this book will catch only **FileNotFoundException** or **IOException** but your real-world code may need to handle the other possible exceptions, depending upon the circumstances.

As mentioned, the **FileStream** constructor just described opens a file that has read/write access. If you want to restrict access to just reading or just writing, use this constructor instead:

FileStream(string *filename*, FileMode *mode*, FileAccess *how*)

As before, *filename* specifies the name of the file to open, and *mode* specifies how the file will be opened. The value passed in *how* determines how the file can be accessed. It must be one of the values defined by the **FileAccess** enumeration, which are shown here:

FileAccess.Read   FileAccess.Write   FileAccess.ReadWrite

For example, this opens a read-only file:

```
FileStream fin = new FileStream("test.dat", FileMode.Open, FileAccess.Read);
```

When you are done with a file, you should close it by calling **Close( )**. Its general form is shown here:

void Close( )

Closing a file releases the system resources allocated to the file, allowing them to be used by another file. **Close( )** can throw an **IOException**.

Reading Bytes from a FileStream

FileStream defines two methods that read bytes from a file: **ReadByte( )** and **Read( )**. To read a single byte from a file, use **ReadByte( )**, whose general form is shown here:

> int ReadByte( )

Each time it is called, it reads a single byte from the file and returns it as an integer value. It returns –1 when the end of the file is encountered. Possible exceptions include **NotSupportedExeption** (the stream is not opened for input) and **ObjectDisposedException** (the stream is closed).

To read a block of bytes, use **Read( )**, which has this general form:

> int Read(byte[ ] *buf*, int *offset*, int *numBytes*)

Read( ) attempts to read up to *numBytes* bytes into *buf* starting at *buf*[*offset*]. It returns the number of bytes successfully read. An **IOException** is thrown if an I/O error occurs. Several other types of exceptions are possible, including **NotSupportedException**, which is thrown if reading is not supported by the stream.

The following program uses **ReadByte( )** to input and display the contents of a text file, the name of which is specified as a command-line argument. Note the **try/catch** blocks that handle the two errors that might occur when this program is first executed: the specified file not being found or the user forgetting to include the name of the file. You can use this same approach any time you use command-line arguments.

```
/* Display a text file.

   To use this program, specify the name
   of the file that you want to see.
   For example, to see a file called TEST.CS,
   use the following command line.

   ShowFile TEST.CS
*/

using System;
using System.IO;

class ShowFile {
  public static void Main(string[] args) {
    int i;
```

```
         FileStream fin;

         try {
           fin = new FileStream(args[0], FileMode.Open);
         } catch(FileNotFoundException exc) {
           Console.WriteLine(exc.Message);
           return;
         } catch(IndexOutOfRangeException exc) {
           Console.WriteLine(exc.Message + "\nUsage: ShowFile File");
           return;
         }

         // read bytes until EOF is encountered
         do {
           try {
             i = fin.ReadByte();
           } catch(Exception exc) {
             Console.WriteLine(exc.Message);
             return;
           }
           if(i != -1) Console.Write((char) i);
         } while(i != -1);

         fin.Close();
       }
     }
```

Writing to a File

To write a byte to a file, use the **WriteByte( )** method. Its simplest form is shown here:

   void WriteByte(byte *val*)

This method writes the byte specified by *val* to the file. If an error occurs during writing, an **IOException** is thrown. If the underlying stream is not opened for output, a **NotSupportedException** is thrown.

You can write an array of bytes to a file by calling **Write( )**. It is shown here:

   void Write(byte[ ] *buf*, int *offset*, int *numBytes*)

Write( ) writes *numBytes* bytes from the array *buf*, beginning at *buf*[*offset*], to the file. If an error occurs during writing, an **IOException** is thrown. If the underlying stream is not opened for output, a **NotSupportedException** is thrown. Other exceptions are also possible.

As you may know, when file output is performed, often that output is not immediately written to the actual physical device. Instead, output is buffered by the operating system until a sizable chunk of data can be written all at once. This improves the efficiency of the system. For example, disk files are organized by sectors, which might be anywhere from 128 bytes long, on up. Output is usually buffered until an entire sector can be written all at once. However, if you want to cause data to be written to the physical device whether the buffer is full or not, you can call **Flush( )**, shown here:

void Flush( )

An **IOException** is thrown on failure.

Once you are done with an output file, you must remember to close it using **Close( )**. Doing so ensures that any output remaining in a disk buffer is actually written to the disk. Thus, there is no reason to call **Flush( )** before closing a file.

Here is a simple example that writes to a file:

```
// Write to a file.

using System;
using System.IO;

class WriteToFile {
  public static void Main(string[] args) {
    FileStream fout;

    // open output file
    try {
      fout = new FileStream("test.txt", FileMode.Create);
    } catch(IOException exc) {
      Console.WriteLine(exc.Message + "\nError Opening Output File");
      return;
    }

    // Write the alphabet to the file.
    try {
      for(char c = 'A'; c <= 'Z'; c++)
        fout.WriteByte((byte) c);
    } catch(IOException exc) {
      Console.WriteLine(exc.Message + "File Error");
```

```
   }

     fout.Close();
   }
}
```

The program first opens a file called **test.txt** for output. It then writes the uppercase alphabet to the file. Finally, it closes the file. Notice how possible errors are handled by the **try/catch** blocks. After this program executes, **test.txt** will contain the following output:

```
ABCDEFGHIJKLMNOPQRSTUVWXYZ
```

Using FileStream to Copy a File

One advantage to the byte-oriented I/O used by **FileStream** is that you can use it on all types of files—not just those that contain text. For example, the following program copies any type of file, including executable files. The names of the source and destination files are specified on the command line.

```
/* Copy a file.

   To use this program, specify the name
   of the source file and the destination file.
   For example, to copy a file called FIRST.DAT
   to a file called SECOND.DAT, use the following
   command line.

   CopyFile FIRST.DAT SECOND.DAT
*/

using System;
using System.IO;

class CopyFile {
  public static void Main(string[] args) {
    int i;
    FileStream fin;
    FileStream fout;

    try {
      // open input file
```

```
    try {
      fin = new FileStream(args[0], FileMode.Open);
    } catch(FileNotFoundException exc) {
      Console.WriteLine(exc.Message + "\nInput File Not Found");
      return;
    }

    // open output file
    try {
      fout = new FileStream(args[1], FileMode.Create);
    } catch(IOException exc) {
      Console.WriteLine(exc.Message + "\nError Opening Output File");
      return;
    }
  } catch(IndexOutOfRangeException exc) {
    Console.WriteLine(exc.Message + "\nUsage: CopyFile From To");
    return;
  }

  // Copy File
  try {
    do {
      i = fin.ReadByte();
      if(i != -1) fout.WriteByte((byte)i);
    } while(i != -1);
  } catch(IOException exc) {
    Console.WriteLine(exc.Message + "File Error");
  }

  fin.Close();
  fout.Close();
  }
}
```

Character-Based File I/O

Although byte-oriented file handling is quite common, C# also supplies character-based streams. The advantage to the character streams is that they operate directly on Unicode characters. Thus, if you want to store Unicode text, the character streams are certainly your best option. In general, to perform character-based file operations, you will wrap a

FileStream inside either a **StreamReader** or a **StreamWriter**. These classes automatically convert a byte stream into a character stream, and vice versa.

Remember that at the operating system level, a file consists of a set of bytes. Using a **StreamReader** or **StreamWriter** does not alter this fact.

StreamWriter is derived from **TextWriter**. **StreamReader** is derived from **TextReader**. Thus, **StreamWriter** and **StreamReader** have access to the methods and properties defined by their base classes.

Using StreamWriter

To create a character-based output stream, wrap a **Stream** object (such as a **FileStream**) inside a **StreamWriter**. **StreamWriter** defines several constructors. One of its most popular is shown here:

StreamWriter(Stream *stream*)

Here, *stream* is the name of an open stream. This constructor throws an **ArgumentException** if *stream* is not opened for output and an **ArgumentNullException** if *stream* is null. Once created, a **StreamWriter** automatically handles the conversion of characters to bytes.

Here is a simple key-to-disk utility that reads lines of text entered at the keyboard and writes them to a file called **test.txt**. Text is read until the user enters the word "stop". It uses a **FileStream** wrapped in a **StreamWriter** to output to the file.

```
/* A simple key-to-disk utility that
   demonstrates a StreamWriter. */

using System;
using System.IO;

class KtoD {
  public static void Main() {
    string str;
    FileStream fout;

    try {
      fout = new FileStream("test.txt", FileMode.Create);
    }
    catch(IOException exc) {
      Console.WriteLine(exc.Message + "Cannot open file.");
      return ;
    }
    StreamWriter fstr_out = new StreamWriter(fout);
```

```
      Console.WriteLine("Enter text ('stop' to quit).");
      do {
        Console.Write(": ");
        str = Console.ReadLine();

        if(str != "stop") {
          str = str + "\r\n"; // add newline
          try {
            fstr_out.Write(str);
          } catch(IOException exc) {
            Console.WriteLine(exc.Message + "File Error");
            return ;
          }
        }
      } while(str != "stop");

      fstr_out.Close();
    }
  }
```

In some cases, it might be more convenient to open a file directly using **StreamWriter**. To do so, use one of these constructors:

StreamWriter(string *filename*)
StreamWriter(string *filename*, bool *appendFlag*)

Here, *filename* specifies the name of the file to open, which can include a full path specifier. In the second form, if *appendFlag* is true, then output is appended to the end of an existing file. Otherwise, output overwrites the specified file. In both cases, if the file does not exist, it is created. Also, both throw an **IOException** if an I/O error occurs. Other exceptions are also possible.

Here is the key-to-disk program rewritten so that it uses **StreamWriter** to open the output file:

```
// Open a file using StreamWriter.

using System;
using System.IO;

class KtoD {
  public static void Main() {
    string str;
```

```
StreamWriter fstr_out;

// Open the file directly using StreamWriter.
try {
  fstr_out = new StreamWriter("test.txt");
}
catch(IOException exc) {
  Console.WriteLine(exc.Message + "Cannot open file.");
  return ;
}

Console.WriteLine("Enter text ('stop' to quit).");
do {
  Console.Write(": ");
  str = Console.ReadLine();

  if(str != "stop") {
    str = str + "\r\n"; // add newline
    try {
      fstr_out.Write(str);
    } catch(IOException exc) {
      Console.WriteLine(exc.Message + "File Error");
      return ;
    }
  }
} while(str != "stop");

fstr_out.Close();
  }
}
```

Using a StreamReader

To create a character-based input stream, wrap a byte stream inside a **StreamReader**.
StreamReader defines several constructors. A frequently used constructor is shown here:

> StreamReader(Stream *stream*)

Here, *stream* is the name of an open stream. This constructor throws an
ArgumentNullException if *stream* is null. It throws **ArgumentException** if *stream*
is not opened for input. Once created, a **StreamReader** will automatically handle
the conversion of bytes to characters.

The following program creates a simple disk-to-screen utility that reads a text file called **test.txt** and displays its contents on the screen. Thus, it is the complement of the key-to-disk utility shown in the previous section:

```
/* A simple disk-to-screen utility that
   demonstrates a FileReader. */

using System;
using System.IO;

class DtoS {
  public static void Main() {
    FileStream fin;
    string s;

    try {
      fin = new FileStream("test.txt", FileMode.Open);
    }
    catch(FileNotFoundException exc) {
      Console.WriteLine(exc.Message + "Cannot open file.");
      return ;
    }

    StreamReader fstr_in = new StreamReader(fin);

    // Read the file line-by-line.
    while((s = fstr_in.ReadLine()) != null) {
      Console.WriteLine(s);
    }

    fstr_in.Close();
  }
}
```

Notice how the end of the file is determined. When the reference returned by **ReadLine( )** is null, the end of the file has been reached.

As with **StreamWriter**, in some cases you might find it easier to open a file directly using **StreamReader**. To do so, use this constructor:

StreamReader(string *filename*)

Here, *filename* specifies the name of the file to open, which can include a full path specifier. The file must exist. If it doesn't, a **FileNotFoundException** is thrown. If *filename* is null, then an **ArgumentNullException** is thrown. If *filename* is an empty string, **ArgumentException** is thrown.

Redirecting the Standard Streams

As mentioned earlier, the standard streams, such as **Console.In**, can be redirected. By far, the most common redirection is to a file. When a standard stream is redirected, input and/or output is automatically directed to the new stream, bypassing the default devices. By redirecting the standard streams, your program can read commands from a disk file, create log files, or even read input from a network connection.

Redirection of the standard streams can be accomplished in two ways. First, when you execute a program on the command line, you can use the < and > operators to redirect **Console.In** and/or **Console.Out**, respectively. For example, given this program:

```
using System;

class Test {
  public static void Main() {
    Console.WriteLine("This is a test.");
  }
}
```

executing the program like this,

Test > log

will cause the line "This is a test." to be written to a file called **log**. Input can be redirected in the same way. The thing to remember when input is redirected is that you must make sure that what you specify as an input source contains sufficient input to satisfy the demands of the program. If it doesn't, the program will hang.

The < and > command-line redirection operators are not part of C# but are provided by the operating system. Thus, if your environment supports I/O redirection (as is the case with Windows), you can redirect standard input and standard output without making any changes to your program. However, there is a second way that you can redirect the standard streams that is under program control. To do so, you will use the **SetIn( )**, **SetOut( )**, and **SetError( )** methods shown here, which are members of **Console**:

static void SetIn(TextReader *input*)
static void SetOut(TextWriter *output*)
static void SetError(TextWriter *output*)

Thus, to redirect input, call **SetIn( )**, specifying the desired stream. You can use any input stream as long as it is derived from **TextReader**. To redirect output to a file, specify a **FileStream** that is wrapped in a **StreamWriter**. The following program shows an example:

```
// Redirect Console.Out.

using System;
using System.IO;

class Redirect {
  public static void Main() {
    StreamWriter log_out;

    try {
      log_out = new StreamWriter("logfile.txt");
    }
    catch(IOException exc) {
      Console.WriteLine(exc.Message + "Cannot open file.");
      return ;
    }

    // Direct standard output to the log file.
    Console.SetOut(log_out);
    Console.WriteLine("This is the start of the log file.");

    for(int i=0; i<10; i++) Console.WriteLine(i);

    Console.WriteLine("This is the end of the log file.");
    log_out.Close();
  }
}
```

When you run this program, you won't see any of the output on the screen, but the file **logfile.txt** will contain the following:

```
This is the start of the log file.
0
1
2
3
4
5
6
```

```
7
8
9
This is the end of the log file.
```

On your own, you might want to experiment with redirecting the other built-in streams.

Reading and Writing Binary Data

So far, we have just been reading and writing bytes or characters, but it is possible—indeed, common—to read and write other types of data. For example, you might want to create a file that contains **int**s, **double**s, or **short**s. To read and write binary values of the C# built-in types, you will use **BinaryReader** and **BinaryWriter**. It is important to understand that this data is read and written using its internal, binary format, not its human-readable text form.

BinaryWriter

A **BinaryWriter** is a wrapper around a byte stream that manages the writing of binary data. Its most commonly used constructor is shown here:

BinaryWriter(Stream *outputStream*)

Here, *outputStream* is the stream to which data is written. To write output to a file, you can use the object created by **FileStream** for this parameter. If *outputStream* is null, then an **ArgumentNullException** is thrown. If *outputStream* has not been opened for writing, **ArgumentException** is thrown.

BinaryWriter defines methods that can write all of C#'s built-in types. Several are shown in Table 14-5. Notice that a **string** is written using its internal format, which includes a length specifier. **BinaryWriter** also defines the standard **Close( )** and **Flush( )** methods, which work as described earlier.

Method	Description
void Write(sbyte *val*)	Writes a signed byte.
void Write(byte *val*)	Writes an unsigned byte.
void Write(byte[ ] *buf*)	Writes an array of bytes.
void Write(short *val*)	Writes a short integer.
void Write(ushort *val*)	Writes an unsigned short integer.
void Write(int *val*)	Writes an integer.
void Write(uint *val*)	Writes an unsigned integer.
void Write(long *val*)	Writes a long integer.
void Write(ulong *val*)	Writes an unsigned long integer.
void Write(float *val*)	Writes a **float**.
void Write(double *val*)	Writes a **double**.
void Write(char *val*)	Writes a character.
void Write(char[ ] *buf*)	Writes an array of characters.
void Write(string *val*)	Writes a **string** using its internal representation, which includes a length specifier.

Table 14-5.   *Commonly Used Output Methods Defined by **BinaryWriter***

BinaryReader

A **BinaryReader** is a wrapper around a byte stream that handles the reading of binary data. Its most commonly used constructor is shown here:

BinaryReader(Stream *inputStream*)

Here, *inputStream* is the stream from which data is read. To read from a file, you can use the object created by **FileStream** for this parameter. If *inputStream* is null, then an **ArgumentNullException** is thrown. If *inputStream* has not been opened for reading, **ArgumentException** is thrown.

BinaryReader provides methods for reading all of C#'s simple types. The most commonly used are shown in Table 14-6. Notice that **ReadString( )** reads a string that is stored using its internal format, which includes a length specifier. All methods throw an **EndOfStreamException** when the end of the stream has been encountered. They throw an **IOException** if an error occurs. **BinaryReader** also defines three versions of **Read( )**, which are shown here:

Method	Description
int Read( )	Returns an integer representation of the next available character from the invoking input stream. Returns –1 when the end of the file is encountered.
int Read(byte[ ] *buf*, int *offset*, int *num*)	Attempts to read up to *num* bytes into *buf* starting at *buf[offset]*, returning the number of bytes successfully read.
int Read(char[ ] *buf*, int *offset*, int *num*)	Attempts to read up to *num* characters into *buf* starting at *buf[offset]*, returning the number of characters successfully read.

These methods will throw an **IOException** on failure.

Also defined is the standard **Close( )** method.

Method	Description
bool ReadBoolean( )	Reads a **bool**.
byte ReadByte( )	Reads a **byte**.
sbyte ReadSByte( )	Reads an **sbyte**.
byte[ ] ReadBytes(int *num*)	Reads *num* bytes and returns them as an array.
char ReadChar( )	Reads a **char**.
char[ ] ReadChars(int *num*)	Reads *num* characters and returns them as an array.
double ReadDouble( )	Reads a **double**.

Table 14-6. *Commonly Used Input methods Defined By* **BinaryReader**

Method	Description
float ReadSingle( )	Reads a **float**.
short ReadInt16( )	Reads a **short**.
int ReadInt32( )	Reads an **int**.
long ReadInt64( )	Reads a **long**.
ushort ReadUInt16( )	Reads a **ushort**.
uint ReadUInt32( )	Reads a **uint**.
ulong ReadUInt64( )	Reads a **ulong**.
string ReadString( )	Reads a **string** that is represented in its internal, binary format, which includes a length specifier. This method should only be used to read a string that has been written using a **BinaryWriter**.

Table 14-6. *Commonly Used Input Methods Defined By **BinaryReader*** (continued)

Demonstrating Binary I/O

Here is a program that demonstrates **BinaryReader** and **BinaryWriter**. It writes and then reads back various types of data to and from a file.

```
// Write and then read back binary data.

using System;
using System.IO;

class RWData {
  public static void Main() {
    BinaryWriter dataOut;
    BinaryReader dataIn;

    int i = 10;
    double d = 1023.56;
    bool b = true;

    try {
      dataOut = new
```

```
                 BinaryWriter(new FileStream("testdata", FileMode.Create));
    }
    catch(IOException exc) {
      Console.WriteLine(exc.Message + "\nCannot open file.");
      return;
    }

    try {
      Console.WriteLine("Writing " + i);
      dataOut.Write(i);

      Console.WriteLine("Writing " + d);
      dataOut.Write(d);

      Console.WriteLine("Writing " + b);
      dataOut.Write(b);

      Console.WriteLine("Writing " + 12.2 * 7.4);
      dataOut.Write(12.2 * 7.4);

    }
    catch(IOException exc) {
      Console.WriteLine(exc.Message + "\nWrite error.");
    }

    dataOut.Close();

    Console.WriteLine();

    // Now, read them back.
    try {
      dataIn = new
          BinaryReader(new FileStream("testdata", FileMode.Open));
    }
    catch(FileNotFoundException exc) {
      Console.WriteLine(exc.Message + "\nCannot open file.");
      return;
    }

    try {
      i = dataIn.ReadInt32();
      Console.WriteLine("Reading " + i);
```

```
      d = dataIn.ReadDouble();
      Console.WriteLine("Reading " + d);

      b = dataIn.ReadBoolean();
      Console.WriteLine("Reading " + b);

      d = dataIn.ReadDouble();
      Console.WriteLine("Reading " + d);
    }
    catch(IOException exc) {
      Console.WriteLine(exc.Message + "Read error.");
    }

    dataIn.Close();
  }
}
```

The output from the program is shown here:

```
Writing 10
Writing 1023.56
Writing True
Writing 90.28

Reading 10
Reading 1023.56
Reading True
Reading 90.28
```

If you examine the **testdata** file produced by this program, you will find that it contains binary data, not human-readable text.

Here is a more practical example that shows how powerful binary I/O is. The following program implements a very simple inventory program. For each item in the inventory, the program stores the item's name, the number on hand, and its cost. Next, the program prompts the user for the name of an item. It then searches the database. If the item is found, the inventory information is displayed.

```
/* Use BinaryReader and BinaryWriter to implement
   a simple inventory program. */
```

```csharp
using System;
using System.IO;

class Inventory {
  public static void Main() {
    BinaryWriter dataOut;
    BinaryReader dataIn;

    string item; // name of item
    int onhand;   // number on hand
    double cost; // cost

    try {
      dataOut = new
        BinaryWriter(new FileStream("inventory.dat",
                                    FileMode.Create));
    }
    catch(IOException exc) {
      Console.WriteLine(exc.Message + "\nCannot open file.");
      return;
    }

    // Write some inventory data to the file.
    try {
      dataOut.Write("Hammers");
      dataOut.Write(10);
      dataOut.Write(3.95);

      dataOut.Write("Screwdrivers");
      dataOut.Write(18);
      dataOut.Write(1.50);

      dataOut.Write("Pliers");
      dataOut.Write(5);
      dataOut.Write(4.95);

      dataOut.Write("Saws");
      dataOut.Write(8);
      dataOut.Write(8.95);
    }
    catch(IOException exc) {
      Console.WriteLine(exc.Message + "\nWrite error.");
```

```csharp
    }

    dataOut.Close();

    Console.WriteLine();

    // Now, open inventory file for reading.
    try {
      dataIn = new
          BinaryReader(new FileStream("inventory.dat",
                      FileMode.Open));
    }
    catch(FileNotFoundException exc) {
      Console.WriteLine(exc.Message + "\nCannot open file.");
      return;
    }

    // Lookup item entered by user.
    Console.Write("Enter item to lookup: ");
    string what = Console.ReadLine();
    Console.WriteLine();

    try {
      for(;;) {
        // Read an inventory entry.
        item = dataIn.ReadString();
        onhand = dataIn.ReadInt32();
        cost = dataIn.ReadDouble();

        /* See if the item matches the one requested.
           If so, display information */
        if(item.CompareTo(what) == 0) {
          Console.WriteLine(onhand + " " + item + " on hand. " +
                            "Cost: {0:C} each", cost);
          Console.WriteLine("Total value of {0}· {1:C}." ,
                            item, cost * onhand);
          break;
        }
      }
    }
    catch(EndOfStreamException) {
      Console.WriteLine("Item not found.");
```

```
    }
    catch(IOException exc) {
      Console.WriteLine(exc.Message + "Read error.");
    }

    dataIn.Close();
  }
}
```

Here is a sample run:

```
Enter item to lookup: Screwdrivers

18 Screwdrivers on hand. Cost: $1.50 each
Total value of Screwdrivers: $27.00.
```

In the program, notice how inventory information is stored in its binary format. Thus, the number of items on hand and the cost are stored using their binary format rather than their human-readable text-based equivalents. This makes it possible to perform computations on the numeric data without having to convert it from its human-readable form.

There is one other point of interest in the inventory program. Notice how the end of the file is detected. Since the binary input methods throw an **EndOfStreamException** when the end of the stream is reached, the program simply reads the file until either it finds the desired item or this exception is generated. Thus, no special mechanism is needed to detect the end of the file.

Random Access Files

Up to this point, we have been using *sequential files,* which are files that are accessed in a strictly linear fashion, one byte after another. However, C# also allows you to access the contents of a file in random order. To do this, you will use the **Seek( )** method defined by **FileStream**. This method allows you to set the file position indicator (also called the file pointer) to any point within a file.

The method **Seek( )** is shown here:

long Seek(long *newPos*, SeekOrigin *origin*)

Here, *newPos* specifies the new position, in bytes, of the file pointer from the location specified by *origin*. The origin will be one of these values, which are defined by the **SeekOrigin** enumeration:

Value	Meaning
SeekOrigin.Begin	Seek from the beginning of the file.
SeekOrigin.Current	Seek from the current location.
SeekOrigin.End	Seek from the end of the file.

After a call to **Seek( )**, the next read or write operation will occur at the new file position. If an error occurs while seeking, an **IOException** is thrown. If the underlying stream does not support position requests, a **NotSupportedException** is thrown.

Here is an example that demonstrates random access I/O. It writes the uppercase alphabet to a file and then reads it back in non-sequential order.

```
// Demonstrate random access.

using System;
using System.IO;

class RandomAccessDemo {
  public static void Main() {
    FileStream f;
    char ch;

    try {
      f = new FileStream("random.dat", FileMode.Create);
    }
    catch(IOException exc) {
      Console.WriteLine(exc.Message);
      return ;
    }

    // Write the alphabet.
    for(int i=0; i < 26; i++) {
      try {
        f.WriteByte((byte)('A'+i));
      }
      catch(IOException exc) {
        Console.WriteLine(exc.Message);
        return ;
      }
    }
  }
```

```
    try {
      // Now, read back specific values
      f.Seek(0, SeekOrigin.Begin); // seek to first byte
      ch = (char) f.ReadByte();
      Console.WriteLine("First value is " + ch);

      f.Seek(1, SeekOrigin.Begin); // seek to second byte
      ch = (char) f.ReadByte();
      Console.WriteLine("Second value is " + ch);

      f.Seek(4, SeekOrigin.Begin); // seek to 5th byte
      ch = (char) f.ReadByte();
      Console.WriteLine("Fifth value is " + ch);

      Console.WriteLine();

      // Now, read every other value.
      Console.WriteLine("Here is every other value: ");
      for(int i=0; i < 26; i += 2) {
        f.Seek(i, SeekOrigin.Begin); // seek to ith byte
        ch = (char) f.ReadByte();
        Console.Write(ch + " ");
      }
    }
    catch(IOException exc) {
      Console.WriteLine(exc.Message);
    }

    Console.WriteLine();
    f.Close();
  }
}
```

The output from the program is shown here:

```
First value is A
Second value is B
Fifth value is E

Here is every other value:
A C E G I K M O Q S U W Y
```

Using MemoryStream

Sometimes it is useful to read input from or to write output to an array, rather than
directly from or to a device. To do this, you will use **MemoryStream**. **MemoryStream**
is an implementation of **Stream** that uses an array of bytes for input and/or output.
Here is one of the constructors that it defines:

MemoryStream(byte[ ] *buf*)

Here, *buf* is an array of bytes that will be used for the source and/or target of I/O
requests. The stream created by this constructor can be written and read, and supports
Seek( ). You must remember to make *buf* large enough to hold whatever output you
will be directing to it.

Here is a program that demonstrates the use of **MemoryStream**:

```
// Demonstrate MemoryStream.

using System;
using System.IO;

class MemStrDemo {
  public static void Main() {
    byte[] storage = new byte[255];

    // Create a memory-based stream.
    MemoryStream memstrm = new MemoryStream(storage);

    // Wrap memstrm in a reader and a writer.
    StreamWriter memwtr = new StreamWriter(memstrm);
    StreamReader memrdr = new StreamReader(memstrm);

    // Write to storage, through memwtr.
    for(int i=0; i < 10; i++)
      memwtr.WriteLine("byte [" + i + "]: " + i);

    // put a period at the end
    memwtr.Write('.');

    memwtr.Flush();

    Console.WriteLine("Reading from storage directly: ");

    // Display contents of storage directly.
    foreach(char ch in storage) {
```

THE C# LANGUAGE

```
      if (ch == '.') break;
      Console.Write(ch);
    }

    Console.WriteLine("\nReading through memrdr: ");

    // Read from memstrm using the stream reader.
    memstrm.Seek(0, SeekOrigin.Begin); // reset file pointer

    string str = memrdr.ReadLine();
    while(str != null) {
      str = memrdr.ReadLine();
      if(str.CompareTo(".") == 0) break;
      Console.WriteLine(str);
    }
  }
}
```

The output from the program is shown here:

```
Reading from storage directly:
byte [0]: 0
byte [1]: 1
byte [2]: 2
byte [3]: 3
byte [4]: 4
byte [5]: 5
byte [6]: 6
byte [7]: 7
byte [8]: 8
byte [9]: 9

Reading through memrdr:
byte [1]: 1
byte [2]: 2
byte [3]: 3
byte [4]: 4
byte [5]: 5
byte [6]: 6
byte [7]: 7
byte [8]: 8
byte [9]: 9
```

In the program, an array of bytes called **storage** is created. This array is then used as the underlying storage for a **MemoryStream** called **memstrm**. From **memstrm** are created a **StreamReader** called **memrdr** and a **StreamWriter** called **memwtr**. Using **memwtr**, output is written to the memory-based stream. Notice that after the output has been written, **flush( )** is called on **memwtr**. This is necessary to ensure that the contents of **memwtr**'s buffer are actually written to the underlying array. Next, the contents of the underlying byte array are displayed manually, using a **foreach** loop. Then, using **Seek( )**, the file pointer is reset to the start of the stream, and the memory stream is read using **memrdr**.

Memory-based streams are quite useful in programming. For example, you can construct complicated output in advance, storing it in the array until it is needed. This technique is especially useful when programming for a GUI environment, such as Windows. You can also redirect a standard stream to read from an array. This might be useful for feeding test information into a program, for example.

Using StringReader and StringWriter

For some applications it might be easier to use a **string** rather than a **byte** array for the underlying storage when performing memory-based I/O operations. When this is the case, use **StringReader** and **StringWriter**. **StringReader** inherits **TextReader**, and **StringWriter** inherits **TextWriter**. Thus, these streams have access to methods defined by those two classes. For example, you can call **ReadLine( )** on a **StringReader**, and **WriteLine( )** on a **StringWriter**.

The constructor for **StringReader** is shown here:

StringReader(string *str*)

Here, *str* is the string that will be read from.
StringWriter defines several constructors. The one that we will use here is this:

StringWriter( )

This constructor creates a writer that will put its output into a string. This string is automatically created by **StringWriter**. You can obtain the contents of this string by calling **ToString( )**.

Here is an example that uses **StringReader** and **StringWriter**:

```
// Demonstrate StringReader and StringWriter

using System;
using System.IO;

class StrRdrDemo {
```

```
public static void Main() {
  // Create a StringWriter
  StringWriter strwtr = new StringWriter();

  // Write to StringWriter.
  for(int i=0; i < 10; i++)
    strwtr.WriteLine("This is i: " + i);

  // Create a StringReader

  StringReader strrdr = new StringReader(strwtr.ToString());

  // Now, read from StringReader.
  string str = strrdr.ReadLine();
  while(str != null) {
    str = strrdr.ReadLine();
    Console.WriteLine(str);
  }

  }
}
```

The output is shown here:

```
This is i: 1
This is i: 2
This is i: 3
This is i: 4
This is i: 5
This is i: 6
This is i: 7
This is i: 8
This is i: 9
```

The program first creates a **StringWriter** called **strwtr** and outputs to it using **WriteLine( )**. Next, it creates a **StringReader** using the string contained in **strwtr**. This string is obtained by calling **ToString( )** on **strwtr**. Finally, the contents of this string are read using **ReadLine( )**.

Converting Numeric Strings to Their Internal Representation

Before leaving the topic of I/O, we will examine a technique that is useful when reading numeric strings. As you know, C#'s **WriteLine( )** method provides a convenient way to output various types of data to the console, including numeric values of the built-in types, such as **int** and **double**. Thus, **WriteLine( )** automatically converts numeric values into their human-readable form. However, C# does not provide the reverse: an input method that reads and converts strings representing numeric values into their internal, binary format. For example, there is no input method that reads a string such as "100" and automatically converts it into its corresponding binary value that can be stored in an **int** variable. To accomplish this task, you will need to use a method that is defined for all of the built-in numeric types: **Parse( )**.

Before we begin, it is necessary to state an important fact: all of C#'s built-in types, such as **int** and **double**, are actually just *aliases* (that is, other names) for structures defined by the .NET Framework. In fact, Microsoft explicitly states that the C# type and .NET structure type are indistinguishable. One is just another name for the other. Because C#'s value types are supported by structures, the value types have members defined for them.

For the numeric types, the .NET structure names and their C# keyword equivalents are shown here:

.NET Structure Name	C# Name
Decimal	decimal
Double	double
Single	float
Int16	short
Int32	int
Int64	long
UInt16	ushort
UInt32	uint
UInt64	ulong
Byte	byte
Sbyte	sbyte

The structures are defined inside the **System** namespace. Thus, the fully qualified name for **Int32** is **System.Int32**. These structures offer a wide array of methods that help fully integrate the value types into C#'s object hierarchy. As a side benefit, the numeric structures also define static methods that convert a numeric string into its corresponding binary equivalent. These conversion methods are shown here. Each returns a binary value that corresponds to the string.

Structure	Conversion Method
Decimal	static decimal Parse(string *str*)
Double	static double Parse(string *str*)
Single	static float Parse(string *str*)
Int64	static long Parse(string *str*)
Int32	static int Parse(string *str*)
Int16	static short Parse(string *str*)
UInt64	static ulong Parse(string *str*)
UInt32	static uint Parse(string *str*)
UInt16	static ushort Parse(string *str*)
Byte	static byte Parse(string *str*)
SByte	static sbyte Parse(string *str*)

The **Parse( )** methods will throw a **FormatException** if *str* does not contain a valid number as defined by the invoking type. **ArgumentNullException** is thrown if *str* is null, and **OverflowException** is thrown if the value in *str* exceeds the invoking type.

The parsing methods give you an easy way to convert a numeric value, read as a string from the keyboard or a text file, into its proper internal format. For example, the following program averages a list of numbers entered by the user. It first asks the user for the number of values to be averaged. It then reads that number using **ReadLine( )** and uses **Int32.Parse( )** to convert the string into an integer. Next, it inputs the values, using **Double.Parse( )** to convert the strings into their **double** equivalents.

```
// This program averages a list of numbers entered by the user.

using System;
using System.IO;

class AvgNums {
  public static void Main() {
```

```
    string str;
    int n;
    double sum = 0.0;
    double avg, t;

    Console.Write("How many numbers will you enter: ");
    str = Console.ReadLine();
    try {
      n = Int32.Parse(str);
    }
    catch(FormatException exc) {
      Console.WriteLine(exc.Message);
      n = 0;
    }
    catch(OverflowException exc) {
      Console.WriteLine(exc.Message);
      n = 0;
    }

    Console.WriteLine("Enter " + n + " values.");
    for(int i=0; i < n ; i++)  {
      Console.Write(": ");
      str = Console.ReadLine();
      try {
        t = Double.Parse(str);
      } catch(FormatException exc) {
        Console.WriteLine(exc.Message);
        t = 0.0;
      }
      catch(OverflowException exc) {
        Console.WriteLine(exc.Message);
        t = 0;
      }
      sum += t;
    }
    avg = sum / n;
    Console.WriteLine("Average is " + avg);
  }
}
```

Here is a sample run:

```
How many numbers will you enter: 5
Enter 5 values.
: 1.1
: 2.2
: 3.3
: 4.4
: 5.5
Average is 3.3
```

One last point: You must use the right parsing method for the type of value you are trying to convert. For example, trying to use **Int32.Parse( )** on a string that contains a floating-point value will not produce the desired result.

The
Complete
Reference

Chapter 15

Delegates and Events

This chapter examines two innovative C# features: delegates and events. A *delegate* provides a way to encapsulate a method. An *event* is a notification that some action has occurred. Delegates and events are related because an event is built upon a delegate. Both expand the set of programming tasks to which C# can be applied.

Delegates

Let's begin by defining the term *delegate*. In straightforward language, a delegate is an object that can refer to a method. Thus, when you create a delegate, you are creating an object that can hold a reference to a method. Furthermore, the method can be called through this reference. Thus, a delegate can invoke the method to which it refers.

The idea of a reference to a method may seem strange at first because usually we think of references referring to objects, but in reality there is little difference. As explained earlier in this book, a reference is essentially a memory address. Thus, a reference to an object is, essentially, the address of the object. Even though a method is not an object, it too has a physical location in memory, and the address of its entry point is the address called when the method is invoked. This address can be assigned to a delegate. Once a delegate refers to a method, the method can be called through that delegate.

Note   *If you are familiar with C/C++, then it will help to know that a delegate in C# is similar to a function pointer in C/C++.*

It is important to understand that the same delegate can be used to call different methods during the runtime of a program by simply changing the method to which the delegate refers. Thus, the method that will be invoked by a delegate is not determined at compile time, but rather at runtime. This is the principal advantage of a delegate.

A delegate is declared using the keyword **delegate**. The general form of a delegate declaration is shown here:

delegate *ret-type name(parameter-list)*;

Here, *ret-type* is the type of value returned by the methods that the delegate will be calling. The name of the delegate is specified by *name*. The parameters required by the methods called through the delegate are specified in the *parameter-list*. A delegate can call only methods whose return type and parameter list (that is, its signature) match those specified by the delegate's declaration.

A delegate can invoke either an instance method associated with an object or a **static** method associated with a class. All that matters is that the return type and signature of the method agree with that of the delegate.

To see delegates in action, let's begin with the simple example shown here:

```
// A simple delegate example.

using System;

// Declare a delegate.
delegate string strMod(string str);

class DelegateTest {
  // Replaces spaces with hyphens.
  static string replaceSpaces(string a) {
    Console.WriteLine("Replaces spaces with hyphens.");
    return a.Replace(' ', '-');
  }

  // Remove spaces.
  static string removeSpaces(string a) {
    string temp = "";
    int i;

    Console.WriteLine("Removing spaces.");
    for(i=0; i < a.Length; i++)
      if(a[i] != ' ') temp += a[i];

    return temp;
  }

  // Reverse a string.
  static string reverse(string a) {
    string temp = "";
    int i, j;

    Console.WriteLine("Reversing string.");
    for(j=0, i=a.Length-1; i >= 0; i--, j++)
      temp += a[i];

    return temp;
  }

  public static void Main() {
    // Construct a delegate.
    strMod strOp = new strMod(replaceSpaces);
```

```
        string str;

        // Call methods through the delegate.
        str = strOp("This is a test.");
        Console.WriteLine("Resulting string: " + str);
        Console.WriteLine();

        strOp = new strMod(removeSpaces);
        str = strOp("This is a test.");
        Console.WriteLine("Resulting string: " + str);
        Console.WriteLine();

        strOp = new strMod(reverse);
        str = strOp("This is a test.");
        Console.WriteLine("Resulting string: " + str);
    }
}
```

The output from the program is shown here:

```
Replaces spaces with hyphens.
Resulting string: This-is-a-test.

Removing spaces.
Resulting string: Thisisatest.

Reversing string.
Resulting string: .tset a si sihT
```

Let's examine this program closely. The program declares a delegate called **strMod** that takes one **string** parameter and returns a **string**. In **DelegateTest**, three **static** methods are declared, each with a matching signature. These methods perform some type of string modification. Notice that **replaceSpaces( )** uses one of **string**'s methods, called **Replace( )**, to replace spaces with hyphens.

In **Main( )**, a **strMod** reference called **strOp** is created and assigned a reference to **replaceSpaces( )**. Pay close attention to this line:

```
strMod strOp = new strMod(replaceSpaces);
```

Notice how the method **replaceSpaces( )** is passed as a parameter. Only its name is used; no parameters are specified. This can be generalized. When instantiating a delegate, you specify only the name of the method to which you want the delegate to refer. Also, the method's declaration must match that of the delegate's declaration. If it doesn't, a compile-time error will result.

Next, **replaceSpaces( )** is called through the delegate instance **strOp**, as shown here:

```
str = strOp("This is a test.");
```

Because **strOp** refers to **replaceSpaces( )**, it is **replaceSpaces( )** that is invoked.

Next, **strOp** is assigned a reference to **removeSpaces( )**, and then **strOp** is called again. This time, **removeSpaces( )** is invoked.

Finally, **strOp** is assigned a reference to **reverse( )** and **strOp** is called. This results in **reverse( )** being called.

The key point of the example is that the invocation of **strOp** results in a call to the method referred to by **strOp** at the time at which the invocation occurred. Thus, the method to call is resolved at runtime, not compile time.

Although the preceding example used **static** methods, a delegate can also refer to instance methods. It must do so, however, through an object reference. For example, here is a rewrite of the previous example, which encapsulates the string operations inside a class called **StringOps**:

```
// Delegates can refer to instance methods, too.

using System;

// Declare a delegate.
delegate string strMod(string str);

class StringOps {
  // Replaces spaces with hyphens.
  public string replaceSpaces(string a) {
    Console.WriteLine("Replaces spaces with hyphens.");
    return a.Replace(' ', '-');
  }

  // Remove spaces.
  public string removeSpaces(string a) {
    string temp = "";
    int i;

    Console.WriteLine("Removing spaces.");
    for(i=0; i < a.Length; i++)
      if(a[i] != ' ') temp += a[i];
```

```
      return temp;
  }

  // Reverse a string.
  public string reverse(string a) {
    string temp = "";
    int i, j;

    Console.WriteLine("Reversing string.");
    for(j=0, i=a.Length-1; i >= 0; i--, j++)
      temp += a[i];

    return temp;
  }
}

class DelegateTest {
  public static void Main() {
    StringOps so = new StringOps(); // create an instance of StringOps

    // Construct a delegate.
    strMod strOp = new strMod(so.replaceSpaces);
    string str;

    // Call methods through delegates.
    str = strOp("This is a test.");
    Console.WriteLine("Resulting string: " + str);
    Console.WriteLine();

    strOp = new strMod(so.removeSpaces);
    str = strOp("This is a test.");
    Console.WriteLine("Resulting string: " + str);
    Console.WriteLine();

    strOp = new strMod(so.reverse);
    str = strOp("This is a test.");
    Console.WriteLine("Resulting string: " + str);
  }
}
```

This program produces the same output as the first, but in this case, the delegate refers to methods on an instance of **StringOps**.

Multicasting

One of the most exciting features of a delegate is its support for *multicasting*. In simple terms, multicasting is the ability to create an *invocation list,* or chain, of methods that will be automatically called when a delegate is invoked. Such a chain is very easy to create. Simply instantiate a delegate, and then use the += operator to add methods to the chain. To remove a method, use – =. (You can also use the +, –, and = operators separately to add and subtract delegates, but += and – = are more common.) The only restriction is that the delegate being multicast must have a **void** return type.

Here is an example of multicasting. It reworks the preceding examples by changing the string manipulation method's return type to **void** and using a **ref** parameter to return the altered string to the caller.

```
// Demonstrate multicasting.

using System;

// Declare a delegate.
delegate void strMod(ref string str);

class StringOps {
  // Replaces spaces with hyphens.
  static void replaceSpaces(ref string a) {
    Console.WriteLine("Replaces spaces with hyphens.");
    a = a.Replace(' ', '-');
  }

  // Remove spaces.
  static void removeSpaces(ref string a) {
    string temp = "";
    int i;

    Console.WriteLine("Removing spaces.");
    for(i=0; i < a.Length; i++)
      if(a[i] != ' ') temp += a[i];

    a = temp;
  }

  // Reverse a string.
  static void reverse(ref string a) {
    string temp = "";
```

```
    int i, j;

    Console.WriteLine("Reversing string.");
    for(j=0, i=a.Length-1; i >= 0; i--, j++)
      temp += a[i];

    a = temp;
  }

public static void Main() {
  // Construct delegates.
  strMod strOp;
  strMod replaceSp = new strMod(replaceSpaces);
  strMod removeSp = new strMod(removeSpaces);
  strMod reverseStr = new strMod(reverse);
  string str = "This is a test";

  // Set up multicast.
  strOp = replaceSp;
  strOp += reverseStr;

  // Call multicast.
  strOp(ref str);
  Console.WriteLine("Resulting string: " + str);
  Console.WriteLine();

  // Remove replace and add remove.
  strOp -= replaceSp;
  strOp += removeSp;

  str = "This is a test."; // reset string

  // Call multicast.
  strOp(ref str);
  Console.WriteLine("Resulting string: " + str);
  Console.WriteLine();
  }
}
```

Here is the output:

```
Replaces spaces with hyphens.
Reversing string.
Resulting string: tset-a-si-sihT

Reversing string.
Removing spaces.
Resulting string: .tsetasisihT
```

In **Main( )**, four delegate instances are created. One, **strOp**, is null. The other three refer to specific string modification methods. Next, a multicast is created that calls **removeSpaces( )** and **reverse( )**. This is accomplished via the following lines:

```
strOp = replaceSp;
strOp += reverseStr;
```

First, **strOp** is assigned a reference to **replaceSp**. Next, using **+=**, **reverseStr** is added. When **strOp** is invoked, both methods are invoked, replacing spaces with hyphens, and reversing the string, as the output illustrates.

Next, **replaceSp** is removed from the chain, using this line:

```
strOp -= replaceSp;
```

and **removeSp** is added using this line:

```
strOp += removeSp;
```

Then, **StrOp** is again invoked. This time, spaces are removed and the string is reversed.

Delegate chains are a powerful mechanism because they allow you to define a set of methods that can be executed as a unit. This can increase the structure of some types of code. Also, as you will soon see, delegate chains have a special value to events.

System.Delegate

All delegates are classes that are implicitly derived from **System.Delegate**. You don't normally need to use its members directly, and this book makes no explicit use of **System.Delegate**. However, its members may be useful in certain specialized situations.

Why Delegates

Although the preceding examples show the "how" behind delegates, they don't really illustrate the "why." In general, delegates are useful for two main reasons. First, as the next section will show, delegates support events. Second, delegates give your program a way to execute a method at runtime without having to know precisely what that method is at compile time. This ability is quite useful when you want to create a framework that allows components to be plugged in. For example, imagine a drawing program (a bit like the standard Windows Paint accessory). Using a delegate, you could allow the user to plug in special color filters or image analyzers. Furthermore, the user could create a sequence of these filters or analyzers. Such a scheme would be easily handled using a delegate.

Events

Built upon the foundation of delegates is another important C# feature: the *event*. An event is, essentially, an automatic notification that some action has occurred. Events work like this: An object that has an interest in an event registers an event handler for that event. When the event occurs, all registered handlers are called. Event handlers are represented by delegates.

Events are members of a class and are declared using the **event** keyword. Its most commonly used form is shown here:

event *event-delegate object*;

Here, *event-delegate* is the name of the delegate used to support the event, and *object* is the name of the specific event object being created.

Let's begin with a very simple example:

```
// A very simple event demonstration.

using System;

// Declare a delegate for an event.
delegate void MyEventHandler();

// Declare an event class.
class MyEvent {
  public event MyEventHandler SomeEvent;

  // This is called to fire the event.
  public void OnSomeEvent() {
    if(SomeEvent != null)
      SomeEvent();
  }
}

class EventDemo {
```

```
  // An event handler.
  static void handler() {
    Console.WriteLine("Event occurred");
  }

  public static void Main() {
    MyEvent evt = new MyEvent();

    // Add handler() to the event list.
    evt.SomeEvent += new MyEventHandler(handler);

    // Fire the event.
    evt.OnSomeEvent();
  }
}
```

This program displays the following output:

```
Event occurred
```

Although simple, this program contains all the elements essential to proper event handling. Let's look at it carefully.

The program begins by declaring a delegate for the event handler, as shown here:

```
delegate void MyEventHandler();
```

All events are activated through a delegate. Thus, the event delegate defines the signature for the event. In this case, there are no parameters, but event parameters are allowed. Because events are commonly multicast, an event should return **void**.

Next, an event class, called **MyEvent**, is created. Inside the class, an event object called **SomeEvent** is declared, using this line:

```
public event MyEventHandler SomeEvent;
```

Notice the syntax. This is the way that all types of events are declared.

Also declared inside **MyEvent** is the method **OnSomeEvent( )**, which is the method that a program will call to signal (or "fire") an event. (That is, this is the method called when the event occurs.) It calls an event handler through the **SomeEvent** delegate, as shown here:

```
if(SomeEvent != null)
  SomeEvent();
```

THE C# LANGUAGE

Notice that a handler is called if and only if **SomeEvent** is not **null**. Since other parts of your program must register an interest in an event in order to receive event notifications, it is possible that **OnSomeEvent( )** could be called before any event handler has been registered. To prevent calling a **null** object, the event delegate must be tested to ensure that it is not **null**.

Inside **EventDemo**, an event handler called **handler( )** is created. In this example, the event handler simply displays a message, but other handlers could perform more meaningful actions. In **Main( )**, a **MyEvent** object is created, and **handler( )** is registered as a handler for this event, as shown here:

```
MyEvent evt = new MyEvent();

// Add handler() to the event list.
evt.SomeEvent += new MyEventHandler(handler);
```

Notice that the handler is added using the += operator. Events support only += and – =. In this case, **handler( )** is a **static** method, but event handlers can also be instance methods. Finally, the event is fired as shown here:

```
// Fire the event.
evt.OnSomeEvent();
```

Calling **OnSomeEvent( )** causes all registered event handlers to be called. In this case, there is only one registered handler, but there could be more, as the next section explains.

A Multicast Event Example

Like delegates, events can be multicast. This enables multiple objects to respond to an event notification. Here is an event multicast example:

```
// An event multicast demonstration.

using System;

// Declare a delegate for an event.
delegate void MyEventHandler();

// Declare an event class.
class MyEvent {
  public event MyEventHandler SomeEvent;

    // This is called to fire the event.
```

```csharp
    public void OnSomeEvent() {
      if(SomeEvent != null)
        SomeEvent();
    }
}

class X {
  public void Xhandler() {
    Console.WriteLine("Event received by X object");
  }
}

class Y {
  public void Yhandler() {
    Console.WriteLine("Event received by Y object");
  }
}

class EventDemo {
  static void handler() {
    Console.WriteLine("Event received by EventDemo");
  }

  public static void Main() {
    MyEvent evt = new MyEvent();
    X xOb = new X();
    Y yOb = new Y();

    // Add handlers to the event list.
    evt.SomeEvent += new MyEventHandler(handler);
    evt.SomeEvent += new MyEventHandler(xOb.Xhandler);
    evt.SomeEvent += new MyEventHandler(yOb.Yhandler);

    // Fire the event.
    evt.OnSomeEvent();
    Console.WriteLine();

    // Remove a handler.
    evt.SomeEvent -= new MyEventHandler(xOb.Xhandler);
    evt.OnSomeEvent();
  }
}
```

The output from the program is shown here:

```
Event received by EventDemo
Event received by X object
Event received by Y object

Event received by EventDemo
Event received by Y object
```

This example creates two additional classes, called **X** and **Y**, which also define event handlers compatible with **MyEventHandler**. Thus, these handlers can become part of the event chain. Notice that the handlers in **X** and **Y** are not **static**. This means that objects of each must be created, and the handler linked to each object instance must be added to the event chain. The differences between instance and **static** handlers is examined in the next section.

Instance Methods vs. static Methods as Event Handlers

Although both instance methods and **static** methods can be used as event handlers, they do differ in one important way. When a **static** method is used as a handler, an event notification applies to the class (and implicitly to all objects of the class). When an instance method is used as an event handler, events are sent to specific object instances. Thus, each object of a class that wants to receive an event notification must register individually. In practice, most event handlers are instance methods, but, of course, this is subject to the specific application. Let's look at an example of each.

The following program creates a class called **X** that defines an instance method as an event handler. This means that each **X** object must register individually to receive events. To demonstrate this fact, the program multicasts an event to three objects of type **X**.

```
/* Individual objects receive notifications when instance
   event handlers are used. */

using System;

// Declare a delegate for an event.
delegate void MyEventHandler();

// Declare an event class.
class MyEvent {
  public event MyEventHandler SomeEvent;

  // This is called to fire the event.
```

```
  public void OnSomeEvent() {
    if(SomeEvent != null)
      SomeEvent();
  }
}

class X {
  int id;

  public X(int x) { id = x; }

  // This is an instance method that will be used as an event handler.
  public void Xhandler() {
    Console.WriteLine("Event received by object " + id);
  }
}

class EventDemo {
  public static void Main() {
    MyEvent evt = new MyEvent();
    X o1 = new X(1);
    X o2 = new X(2);
    X o3 = new X(3);

    evt.SomeEvent += new MyEventHandler(o1.Xhandler);
    evt.SomeEvent += new MyEventHandler(o2.Xhandler);
    evt.SomeEvent += new MyEventHandler(o3.Xhandler);

    // Fire the event.
    evt.OnSomeEvent();
  }
}
```

The output from this program is shown here:

```
Event received by object 1
Event received by object 2
Event received by object 3
```

As the output shows, each object registers its interest in an event separately, and each receives a separate notification.

Alternatively, when a **static** method is used as an event handler, events are handled independently of any object, as the following program shows:

```
/* A class receives the notification when
   a static method is used as an event handler. */

using System;

// Declare a delegate for an event.
delegate void MyEventHandler();

// Declare an event class.
class MyEvent {
  public event MyEventHandler SomeEvent;

  // This is called to fire the event.
  public void OnSomeEvent() {
    if(SomeEvent != null)
      SomeEvent();
  }
}

class X {

  /* This is a static method that will be used as
     an event handler. */
  public static void Xhandler() {
    Console.WriteLine("Event received by class.");
  }
}

class EventDemo {
  public static void Main() {
    MyEvent evt = new MyEvent();

    evt.SomeEvent += new MyEventHandler(X.Xhandler);

    // Fire the event.
    evt.OnSomeEvent();
  }
}
```

The output from this program is shown here:

```
Event received by class.
```

In the program, notice that no object of type **X** is ever created. However, since **handler( )** is a **static** method of **X**, it can be attached to **SomeEvent** and executed when **OnSomeEvent( )** is called.

Using Event Accessors

There are two forms of the **event** statement. The form used in the preceding examples created events that automatically manage the event handler invocation list, including the adding and subtracting of event handlers to and from the list. Thus, you did not need to implement any of the list management functionality yourself. Because they manage the details for you, these types of events are by far the most commonly used. It is possible, however, to provide the event handler list operations yourself, perhaps to implement some type of specialized event storage mechanism.

To take control of the event handler list, you will use the second form of the **event** statement, which allows the use of *event accessors*. The accessors give you control over how the event handler list is implemented. This form is shown here:

```
event event-delegate event-name {
    add {
      // code to add an event to the chain
    }

    remove {
      // code to remove an event from the chain
    }
}
```

This form includes the two event accessors **add** and **remove**. The **add** accessor is called when an event handler is added to the event chain, by using +=. The **remove** accessor is called when an event handler is removed from the chain, by using – =.

When **add** or **remove** is called, it receives the handler to add or remove as a parameter. As with other types of accessors, this parameter is called **value**. By implementing **add** and **remove**, you can define a custom event-handler storage scheme. For example, you could use an array, a stack, or a queue to store the handlers.

Here is an example that uses the accessor form of **event**. It uses an array to hold the event handlers. Because the array is only three elements long, only three event handlers can be held in the chain at any one time.

```csharp
// Create a custom means of managing the event invocation list.

using System;

// Declare a delegate for an event.
delegate void MyEventHandler();

// Declare an event class that holds up to 3 events.
class MyEvent {
  MyEventHandler[] evnt = new MyEventHandler[3];

  public event MyEventHandler SomeEvent {
    // Add an event to the list.
    add {
      int i;

      for(i=0; i < 3; i++)
        if(evnt[i] == null) {
          evnt[i] = value;
          break;
        }
      if (i == 3) Console.WriteLine("Event list full.");
    }

    // Remove an event from the list.
    remove {
      int i;

      for(i=0; i < 3; i++)
        if(evnt[i] == value) {
          evnt[i] = null;
          break;
        }
      if (i == 3) Console.WriteLine("Event handler not found.");
    }
  }

  // This is called to fire the events.
```

```
    public void OnSomeEvent() {
      for(int i=0; i < 3; i++)
        if(evnt[i] != null) evnt[i]();
    }

}

// Create some classes that use MyEventHandler.
class W {
  public void Whandler() {
    Console.WriteLine("Event received by W object");
  }
}

class X {
  public void Xhandler() {
    Console.WriteLine("Event received by X object");
  }
}

class Y {
  public void Yhandler() {
    Console.WriteLine("Event received by Y object");
  }
}

class Z {
  public void Zhandler() {
    Console.WriteLine("Event received by Z object");
  }
}

class EventDemo {
  public static void Main() {
    MyEvent evt = new MyEvent();
    W wOb = new W();
    X xOb = new X();
    Y yOb = new Y();
    Z zOb = new Z();

    // Add handlers to the event list.
    Console.WriteLine("Adding events.");
```

```
evt.SomeEvent += new MyEventHandler(wOb.Whandler);
evt.SomeEvent += new MyEventHandler(xOb.Xhandler);
evt.SomeEvent += new MyEventHandler(yOb.Yhandler);

// Can't store this one -- full.
evt.SomeEvent += new MyEventHandler(zOb.Zhandler);
Console.WriteLine();

// Fire the events.
evt.OnSomeEvent();
Console.WriteLine();

// Remove a handler.
Console.WriteLine("Remove xOb.Xhandler.");
evt.SomeEvent -= new MyEventHandler(xOb.Xhandler);
evt.OnSomeEvent();

Console.WriteLine();

// Try to remove it again.
Console.WriteLine("Try to remove xOb.Xhandler again.");
evt.SomeEvent -= new MyEventHandler(xOb.Xhandler);
evt.OnSomeEvent();

Console.WriteLine();

// Now, add Zhandler.
Console.WriteLine("Add zOb.Zhandler.");
evt.SomeEvent += new MyEventHandler(zOb.Zhandler);
evt.OnSomeEvent();

  }
}
```

The output from the program is shown here:

```
Adding events.
Event list full.

Event received by W object
Event received by X object
```

```
Event received by Y object

Remove xOb.Xhandler.
Event received by W object
Event received by Y object

Try to remove xOb.Xhandler again.
Event handler not found.
Event received by W object
Event received by Y object

Add zOb.Zhandler.
Event received by W object
Event received by Z object
Event received by Y object
```

Let's examine this program closely. First, an event handler delegate called
MyEventHandler is defined. Next, **MyEvent** begins by defining a three-element
array of event handlers called **evnt**, as shown here:

```
MyEventHandler[] evnt = new MyEventHandler[3];
```

This array will be used to store the event handlers that are added to the event chain.
The elements in **evnt** are initialized to **null** by default.

Next is the accessor-based **event** statement, shown here:

```
public event MyEventHandler SomeEvent {
  // Add an event to the list.
  add {
    int i;

    for(i=0; i < 3; i++)
      if(evnt[i] == null) {
        evnt[i] = value;
        break;
      }
    if (i == 3) Console.WriteLine("Event list full.");
  }

  // Remove an event from the list.
  remove {
```

```
    int i;

    for(i=0; i < 3; i++)
      if(evnt[i] == value) {
        evnt[i] = null;
        break;
      }
    if (i == 3) Console.WriteLine("Event handler not found.");
  }
}
```

When an event handler is added, **add** is called and a reference to the handler (contained in **value**) is put into the first unused element of **evnt**. If no element is free, then an error is reported. Since **evnt** is only three elements long, only three event handlers can be stored. When an event handler is removed, **remove** is called and the **evnt** array is searched for the reference to the handler passed in **value**. If it is found, its element in the array is assigned **null**, thus removing the handler from the list.

When an event is fired, **OnSomeEvent( )** is called. It cycles through the **evnt** array, calling each event handler in turn.

As the preceding example shows, it is relatively easy to implement a custom event-handler storage mechanism if one is needed. For most applications, though, the default storage provided by the non-accessor form of **event** is better. The accessor-based form of **event** can be useful in certain specialized situations, however. For example, if you have a program in which event handlers need to be executed in order of their priority and not in the order in which they are added to the chain, then you could use a priority queue to store the handlers.

Miscellaneous Event Features

Events can be specified in interfaces. Implementing classes must supply the event. Events can be specified as **abstract**. A derived class must implement the event. Accessor-based events cannot, however, be **abstract**. An event can be specified as **sealed**. An event can be virtual, which means that it can be overridden in a derived class.

.NET Event Guidelines

C# allows you to write any type of event that you desire. However, for component compatibility with the .NET Framework, you will need to follow the guidelines that Microsoft has established for this purpose. At the core of these guidelines is the requirement that event handlers have two parameters. The first is a reference to the object that generated the event. The second is a parameter of type **EventArgs** that contains any other information required by the handler. Thus, .NET-compatible event handlers will have this general form:

```
void handler(object source, EventArgs arg) {
  // ...
}
```

Typically, the *source* parameter is passed **this** by the calling code. The **EventArgs** parameter contains additional information and can be ignored if it is not needed.

The **EventArgs** class itself does not contain fields that you use to pass additional data to a handler. Instead, **EventArgs** is used as a base class from which you will derive a class that contains the necessary fields. However, since many handlers do not require extra data, **EventArgs** does include the **static** field **Empty**, which specifies an object that contains no data.

Here is an example that creates a .NET-compatible event:

```
// A .NET-compatible event.

using System;

// Derive a class from EventArgs.
class MyEventArgs : EventArgs {
  public int eventnum;
}

// Declare a delegate for an event.
delegate void MyEventHandler(object source, MyEventArgs arg);

// Declare an event class.
class MyEvent {
  static int count = 0;

  public event MyEventHandler SomeEvent;

  // This fires SomeEvent.
  public void OnSomeEvent() {
    MyEventArgs arg = new MyEventArgs();

    if(SomeEvent != null) {
      arg.eventnum = count++;
      SomeEvent(this, arg);
    }
  }
```

```
  }

  class X {
    public void handler(object source, MyEventArgs arg) {
      Console.WriteLine("Event " + arg.eventnum +
                        " received by an X object.");
      Console.WriteLine("Source is " + source);
      Console.WriteLine();
    }
  }

  class Y {
    public void handler(object source, MyEventArgs arg) {
      Console.WriteLine("Event " + arg.eventnum +
                        " received by a Y object.");
      Console.WriteLine("Source is " + source);
      Console.WriteLine();
    }
  }


  class EventDemo {
    public static void Main() {
      X ob1 = new X();
      Y ob2 = new Y();
      MyEvent evt = new MyEvent();

      // Add handler() to the event list.
      evt.SomeEvent += new MyEventHandler(ob1.handler);
      evt.SomeEvent += new MyEventHandler(ob2.handler);

      // Fire the event.
      evt.OnSomeEvent();
      evt.OnSomeEvent();
    }
  }
```

Here is the output:

```
Event 0 received by an X object.
Source is MyEvent
```

```
Event 0 received by a Y object.
Source is MyEvent

Event 1 received by an X object.
Source is MyEvent

Event 1 received by a Y object.
Source is MyEvent
```

In this example, **MyEventArgs** is derived from **EventArgs**. **MyEventArgs** adds just one field of its own: **eventnum**. The event handler delegate **MyEventHandler** now takes the two parameters required by the .NET Framework. As explained, the first is an object reference to the generator of the event. The second is a reference to **EventArgs** or a class derived from **EventArgs**. In this case, it is a reference to an object of type **MyEventArgs**.

Using EventHandler

For many events, the **EventArgs** parameter is unused. To help facilitate the creation of code in these situations, the .NET Framework includes a built-in delegate type called **EventHandler**, which can be used to declare event handlers in which no extra information is needed. Here is an example that uses **EventHandler**:

```
// Use the built-in EventHandler delegate.

using System;

// Declare an event class.
class MyEvent {
  public event EventHandler SomeEvent; // uses EventHandler delegate

  // This is called to fire SomeEvent.
  public void OnSomeEvent() {
    if(SomeEvent != null)
      SomeEvent(this, EventArgs.Empty);
  }
}

class EventDemo {
  static void handler(object source, EventArgs arg) {
    Console.WriteLine("Event occurred");
    Console.WriteLine("Source is " + source);
```

```
  }

  public static void Main() {
    MyEvent evt = new MyEvent();

    // Add handler() to the event list.
    evt.SomeEvent += new EventHandler(handler);

    // Fire the event.
    evt.OnSomeEvent();
  }
}
```

In this case, the **EventArgs** parameter is unused and is passed the placeholder object **EventArgs.Empty**. The output is shown here:

```
Event occurred
Source is MyEvent
```

Applying Events: A Case Study

Events are frequently used in message-based environments, such as Windows. In such an environment, a program simply waits until it receives a message, and then it takes the appropriate action. Such an architecture is well suited for C#-style event handling because it is possible to create event handlers for various messages and simply to invoke a handler when a message is received. For example, the left-button mouse click message could be tied to an event. When a left-button click is received, all registered handlers are notified.

Although developing a Windows program that demonstrates this approach is beyond the scope of this chapter, it is possible to give an idea of how such an approach would work. The following program creates an event handler that processes keystrokes. The event is called **KeyPress**, and each time a key is pressed, the event is fired by calling **OnKeyPress( )**.

```
// A keypress event example.

using System;

// Derive a custom EventArgs class that holds the key.
class KeyEventArgs : EventArgs {
```

```
    public char ch;
}

// Declare a delegate for an event.
delegate void KeyHandler(object source, KeyEventArgs arg);

// Declare a key-press event class.
class KeyEvent {
  public event KeyHandler KeyPress;

  // This is called when a key is pressed.
  public void OnKeyPress(char key) {
    KeyEventArgs k = new KeyEventArgs();

    if(KeyPress != null) {
      k.ch = key;
      KeyPress(this, k);
    }
  }
}

// A class that receives key-press notifications.
class ProcessKey {
  public void keyhandler(object source, KeyEventArgs arg) {
    Console.WriteLine("Received keystroke: " + arg.ch);
  }
}

// Another class that receives key-press notifications.
class CountKeys {
  public int count = 0;

  public void keyhandler(object source, KeyEventArgs arg) {
    count++;
  }
}

// Demonstrate KeyEvent.
class KeyEventDemo {
  public static void Main() {
    KeyEvent kevt = new KeyEvent();
    ProcessKey pk = new ProcessKey();
```

```
    CountKeys ck = new CountKeys();
    char ch;

    kevt.KeyPress += new KeyHandler(pk.keyhandler);
    kevt.KeyPress += new KeyHandler(ck.keyhandler);

    Console.WriteLine("Enter some characters. " +
                      "Enter a period to stop.");
    do {
      ch = (char) Console.Read();
      kevt.OnKeyPress(ch);
    } while(ch != '.');
    Console.WriteLine(ck.count + " keys pressed.");
  }
}
```

Here is a sample run:

```
Enter some characters. Enter a period to stop.
test.
Received keystroke: t
Received keystroke: e
Received keystroke: s
Received keystroke: t
Received keystroke: .
5 keys pressed.
```

The program begins by deriving a class called **KeyEventArgs**, which is used to pass a keystroke to an event handler. Next, a delegate called **KeyHandler** defines the event handler for keystroke events. The class **KeyEvent** encapsulates the key-press event.

The program creates two classes that handle keystrokes: **ProcessKey** and **CountKeys**. The **ProcessKey** class includes a handler called **keyhandler( )** that displays the keystrokes. **CountKeys** keeps an ongoing count of the number of key presses. In **Main( )**, a **KeyEvent** object is created. Next, objects of **ProcessKey** and **CountKeys** are created, and references to their **keyhandler( )** methods are added to the **kevt.KeyPress** invocation list. Then a loop is started that calls **kevt.OnKeyPress( )** when a key is pressed. This causes the registered event handlers to be notified.

Chapter 16

Namespaces, the Preprocessor, and Assemblies

This chapter discusses three C# features that give you greater control over the organization and accessibility of a program. These are namespaces, the preprocessor, and assemblies.

Namespaces

The namespace was mentioned briefly in Chapter 2 because it is a concept fundamental to C#. In fact, every C# program makes use of a namespace in one way or another. We didn't need to examine namespaces in detail before now because C# automatically provides a default namespace for your program. Thus, the programs in earlier chapters simply used the default namespace. In the real world, however, many programs will need to create their own namespaces or interact with other namespaces. Here, they are examined in detail.

A *namespace* defines a declarative region that provides a way to keep one set of names separate from another. In essence, names declared in one namespace will not conflict with the same names declared in another. The namespace used by the .NET Framework library (which is the C# library) is **System**. This is why you have included

```
using System;
```

near the top of every program. As you saw in Chapter 14, the I/O classes are defined within a namespace subordinate to **System** called **System.IO**. There are many other namespaces subordinate to **System** that hold other parts of the C# library.

Namespaces are important because there has been an explosion of variable, method, property, and class names over the past few years. These include library routines, third-party code, and your own code. Without namespaces, all of these names would compete for slots in the global namespace and conflicts would arise. For example, if your program defined a class called **Finder**, it could conflict with another class called **Finder** supplied by a third-party library that your program uses. Fortunately, namespaces prevent this type of problem, because a namespace localizes the visibility of names declared within it.

Declaring a Namespace

A namespace is declared using the **namespace** keyword. The general form of **namespace** is shown here:

```
namespace name {
  // members
}
```

Here, *name* is the name of the namespace. Anything defined within a **namespace** is within the scope of that **namespace**. Thus, **namespace** defines a scope. Within a namespace you can declare classes, structures, delegates, enumerations, interfaces, or another namespace.

Here is an example of a **namespace** that creates a namespace called **Counter**. It localizes the name used to implement a simple countdown counter class called **CountDown**.

```
// Declare a namespace for counters.

namespace Counter {
  // A simple countdown counter.
  class CountDown {
    int val;

    public CountDown(int n) {
      val = n;
    }

    public void reset(int n) {
      val = n;
    }

    public int count() {
      if(val > 0) return val--;
      else return 0;
    }
  }
}
```

Here, the class **CountDown** is declared within the scope defined by the **Counter** namespace.

Here is a program that demonstrates the use of the **Counter** namespace:

```
// Demonstrate a namespace.

using System;

// Declare a namespace for counters.
namespace Counter {
  // A simple countdown counter.
  class CountDown {
    int val;

    public CountDown(int n) { val = n; }

    public void reset(int n) {
```

```
        val = n;
      }

    public int count() {
      if(val > 0) return val--;
      else return 0;
    }
  }
}

class NSDemo {
  public static void Main() {
    Counter.CountDown cd1 = new Counter.CountDown(10);
    int i;

    do {
      i = cd1.count();
      Console.Write(i + " ");
    } while(i > 0);
    Console.WriteLine();

    Counter.CountDown cd2 = new Counter.CountDown(20);

    do {
      i = cd2.count();
      Console.Write(i + " ");
    } while(i > 0);
    Console.WriteLine();

    cd2.reset(4);
    do {
      i = cd2.count();
      Console.Write(i + " ");
    } while(i > 0);
    Console.WriteLine();
  }
}
```

The output from the program is shown here:

```
10 9 8 7 6 5 4 3 2 1 0
20 19 18 17 16 15 14 13 12 11 10 9 8 7 6 5 4 3 2 1 0
4 3 2 1 0
```

There are some important aspects of this program that warrant close examination. First, since **CountDown** is declared within the **Counter** namespace, when an object is created, **CountDown** must be qualified with **Counter**, as shown here:

```
Counter.CountDown cd1 = new Counter.CountDown(10);
```

However, once an object of type **Counter** has been created, it is not necessary to further qualify it or any of its members with the namespace. Thus, **cd1.count( )** can be called directly without namespace qualification, as this line shows:

```
i = cd1.count();
```

Namespaces Prevent Name Conflicts

The key point about a namespace is that names declared within it won't conflict with similar names declared outside of it. For example, in the following program, another class called **CountDown** is created, but this one is in a namespace called **Counter2**:

```
// Namespaces prevent name conflicts.

using System;

// Declare a namespace for counters.
namespace Counter {
  // A simple countdown counter.
  class CountDown {
    int val;

    public CountDown(int n) {
      val = n;
    }

    public void reset(int n) {
      val = n;
    }

    public int count() {
      if(val > 0) return val--;
      else return 0;
    }
  }
}
```

```
// Declare another namespace.
namespace Counter2 {
  /* This CountDown is in the default namespace and
     does not conflict with the one in Counter. */
  class CountDown {
    public void count() {
      Console.WriteLine("This is count() in the " +
                           "Counter2 namespace.");
    }
  }
}

class NSDemo {
  public static void Main() {
    // This is CountDown in the Counter namespace.
    Counter.CountDown cd1 = new Counter.CountDown(10);

    // This is CountDown in the default namespace.
    Counter2.CountDown cd2 = new Counter2.CountDown();

    int i;

    do {
      i = cd1.count();
      Console.Write(i + " ");
    } while(i > 0);
    Console.WriteLine();

    cd2.count();
  }
}
```

The output is shown here:

```
10 9 8 7 6 5 4 3 2 1 0
This is count() in the Counter2 namespace.
```

As the output confirms, the **CountDown** class inside **Counter** is separate from the **CountDown** class in the **Counter2** namespace, and no name conflicts arise. Although this example is quite simple, it is easy to see how putting classes that you write in a namespace helps prevent name conflicts between your code and code written by others.

using

As explained in Chapter 2, if your program includes frequent references to the members of a namespace, having to specify the namespace each time you need to refer to one quickly becomes tedious. The **using** directive alleviates this problem. Throughout this book you have been using **using** to bring the C# **System** namespace into view, so you are already familiar with it. As you would expect, **using** can also be used to bring namespaces that you create into view.

There are two forms of the **using** directive. The first is shown here:

using *name*;

Here, *name* specifies the name of the namespace you want to access. This is the form of **using** that you have already seen. All of the members defined within the specified namespace are brought into view (that is, they become part of the current namespace) and can be used without qualification. A **using** directive must be specified at the top of each file, prior to any other declarations.

The following program reworks the counter example from the previous section to show how you can employ **using** to bring a namespace that you create into view:

```
// Demonstrate a namespace.

using System;

// Bring Counter into view.
using Counter;

// Declare a namespace for counters.
namespace Counter {
  // A simple countdown counter.
  class CountDown {
    int val;

    public CountDown(int n) {
      val = n;
    }

    public void reset(int n) {
      val = n;
    }

    public int count() {
      if(val > 0) return val--;
```

```
      else return 0;
    }
  }
}

class NSDemo {
  public static void Main() {
    // now, CountDown can be used directly.
    CountDown cd1 = new CountDown(10);
    int i;

    do {
      i = cd1.count();
      Console.Write(i + " ");
    } while(i > 0);
    Console.WriteLine();

    CountDown cd2 = new CountDown(20);

    do {
      i = cd2.count();
      Console.Write(i + " ");
    } while(i > 0);
    Console.WriteLine();

    cd2.reset(4);
    do {
      i = cd2.count();
      Console.Write(i + " ");
    } while(i > 0);
    Console.WriteLine();
  }
}
```

The program illustrates one other important point: using one namespace does not override another. When you bring a namespace into view, it simply adds its names to whatever other namespaces are currently in effect. Thus, both **System** and **Counter** have been brought into view.

A Second Form of using

The **using** directive has a second form, which is shown here:

using *alias* = *name*;

Here, *alias* becomes another name for the class or namespace specified by *name*. The counting program is reworked once again so that an alias for **Counter.CountDown** called **Count** is created.

```csharp
// Demonstrate a using alias.

using System;

// Create an alias for Counter.CountDown.
using Count = Counter.CountDown;

// Declare a namespace for counters.
namespace Counter {
  // A simple countdown counter.
  class CountDown {
    int val;

    public CountDown(int n) {
      val = n;
    }

    public void reset(int n) {
      val = n;
    }

    public int count() {
      if(val > 0) return val--;
      else return 0;
    }
  }
}

class NSDemo {
  public static void Main() {
    // Here, Count is used as a name for Counter.CountDown.
    Count cd1 = new Count(10);
    int i;

    do {
      i = cd1.count();
      Console.Write(i + " ");
    } while(i > 0);
    Console.WriteLine();
```

```
    Count cd2 = new Count(20);

    do {
      i = cd2.count();
      Console.Write(i + " ");
    } while(i > 0);
    Console.WriteLine();

    cd2.reset(4);
    do {
      i = cd2.count();
      Console.Write(i + " ");
    } while(i > 0);
    Console.WriteLine();
  }
}
```

Once **Count** has been specified as another name for **Counter.CountDown**, it can be used to declare objects without any further namespace qualification. For example, in the program, this line

```
    Count cd1 = new Count(10);
```

creates a **CountDown** object.

Namespaces Are Additive

There can be more than one namespace declaration of the same name. This allows a namespace to be split over several files or even separated within the same file. For example, the following program defines two **Counter** namespaces. One contains the **CountDown** class. The other contains the **CountUp** class. When compiled, the contents of both **Counter** namespaces are added together.

```
// Namespaces are additive.

using System;

// Bring Counter into view.
using Counter;

// Here is one Counter namespace.
```

```
namespace Counter {
  // A simple countdown counter.
  class CountDown {
    int val;

    public CountDown(int n) {
      val = n;
    }

    public void reset(int n) {
      val = n;
    }

    public int count() {
      if(val > 0) return val--;
      else return 0;
    }
  }
}

// Here is another Counter namespace.
namespace Counter {
  // A simple count-up counter.
  class CountUp {
    int val;
    int target;

    public int Target {
      get{
        return target;
      }
    }

    public CountUp(int n) {
      target = n;
      val = 0;
    }

    public void reset(int n) {
      target = n;
      val = 0;
    }
```

```
      public int count() {
        if(val < target) return val++;
        else return target;
      }
    }
  }

class NSDemo {
  public static void Main() {
    CountDown cd = new CountDown(10);
    CountUp cu = new CountUp(8);
    int i;

    do {
      i = cd.count();
      Console.Write(i + " ");
    } while(i > 0);
    Console.WriteLine();

    do {
      i = cu.count();
      Console.Write(i + " ");
    } while(i < cu.Target);

  }
}
```

This program produces the following output:

```
10 9 8 7 6 5 4 3 2 1 0
0 1 2 3 4 5 6 7 8
```

Notice one other thing: The statement

```
using Counter;
```

brings into view the entire contents of the **Counter** namespace. Thus, both **CountDown** and **CountUp** can be referred to directly, without namespace qualification. It doesn't matter that the **Counter** namespace was split into two parts.

Namespaces Can Be Nested

One namespace can be nested within another. Consider this program:

```
// Namespaces can be nested.

using System;

namespace NS1 {
  class ClassA {
    public ClassA() {
      Console.WriteLine("constructing ClassA");
    }
  }
  namespace NS2 { // a nested namespace
    class ClassB {
      public ClassB() {
        Console.WriteLine("constructing ClassB");
      }
    }
  }
}

class NestedNSDemo {
  public static void Main() {
    NS1.ClassA a= new NS1.ClassA();

 // NS2.ClassB b = new NS2.ClassB(); // Error!!! NS2 is not in view

    NS1.NS2.ClassB b = new NS1.NS2.ClassB(); // this is right
  }
}
```

This program produces the following output:

```
constructing ClassA
constructing ClassB
```

In the program, the namespace **NS2** is nested within **NS1**. Thus, to refer to **ClassB**, you must qualify it with both the **NS1** and **NS2** namespaces. **NS2** by itself is insufficient. As shown, the namespace names are separated by a period.

You can specify a nested namespace using a single **namespace** statement by separating each namespace with a period. For example, this

```
namespace OuterNS {
  namespace InnerNS {
    // ...
  }
}
```

can also be specified like this:

```
namespace OuterNS.InnerNS {
  // ...
}
```

The Default Namespace

If you don't declare a namespace for your program, then the default namespace is used. This is why you have not needed to use **namespace** for the programs in the preceding chapters. While the default namespace is convenient for the short, sample programs found in this book, most real-world code will be contained within a namespace. The main reason for encapsulating your code within a namespace is that it prevents name conflicts. Namespaces are another tool that you have to help you organize programs and make them viable in today's complex, networked environment.

The Preprocessor

C# defines several *preprocessor directives*, which affect the way that your program's source file is interpreted by the compiler. These directives affect the text of the source file in which they occur, prior to the translation of the program into object code. The preprocessing directives are largely a holdover from C++. In fact, the C# preprocessor is very similar to the one defined by C++. The term *preprocessor directive* comes from the fact that these instructions were traditionally handled by a separate compilation phase called the *preprocessor*. Today's modern compiler technology no longer requires a separate preprocessing stage to handle the directives, but the name has stuck.

C# defines the following preprocessor directives:

#define	#elif	#else	#endif
#endregion	#error	#if	#line
#region	#undef	#warning	

All preprocessor directives begin with a **#** sign. In addition, each preprocessor directive must be on its own line.

Frankly, given C#'s modern, object-oriented architecture, there is not as much need for the preprocessor directives as there is in older languages. Nevertheless, they can be of value from time to time, especially for conditional compilation. Each directive is examined in turn.

#define

The **#define** directive defines a character sequence called a *symbol*. The existence or nonexistence of a symbol can be determined by **#if** or **#elif** and is used to control compilation. Here is the general form for **#define**:

> #define *symbol*

Notice that there is no semicolon in this statement. There may be any number of spaces between the **#define** and the symbol, but once the symbol begins, it is terminated only by a newline. For example, to define the symbol **EXPERIMENTAL**, use this directive:

```
#define EXPERIMENTAL
```

Note   *In C/C++ you can use **#define** to perform textual substitutions, such as defining a name for a value, and to create function-like macros. C# does not support these uses of **#define**. In C#, **#define** is used only to define a symbol.*

#if and #endif

The **#if** and **#endif** directives enable conditional compilation of a sequence of code based upon whether an expression involving one or more symbols evaluates to true. A symbol is true if it has been defined. It is false otherwise. Thus, if a symbol has been defined by a **#define** directive, it will evaluate as true.

The general form of **#if** is

> #if *symbol-expression*
>   *statement sequence*
> #endif

If the expression following **#if** is true, the code that is between it and **#endif** is compiled. Otherwise, the intervening code is skipped. The **#endif** directive marks the end of an **#if** block.

A symbol expression can be as simple as just the name of a symbol. You can also use these operators in a symbol expression: **!, = =, !=, &&,** and **| |**. Parentheses are also allowed.

Here is an example that uses **#if**, **#endif**, and **#define**:

```
// Demonstrate #if, #endif, and #define.

#define EXPERIMENTAL

using System;

class Test {
  public static void Main() {

    #if EXPERIMENTAL
      Console.WriteLine("Compiled for experimental version.");
    #endif

    Console.WriteLine("This is in all versions.");
  }
}
```

This program displays the following:

```
Compiled for experimental version.
This is in all versions.
```

The program defines the symbol **EXPERIMENTAL**. Thus, when the **#if** is encountered, the symbol expression evaluates to true, and the first **WriteLine( )** statement is compiled. If you remove the definition of **EXPERIMENTAL** and recompile the program, the first **WriteLine( )** statement will not be compiled, because the **#if** will evaluate to false. In all cases, the second **WriteLine( )** statement is compiled because it is not part of the **#if** block.

As explained, you can use a symbol expression in an **#if**. For example:

```
// Use a symbol expression.

#define EXPERIMENTAL
#define TRIAL

using System;

class Test {
  public static void Main() {

    #if EXPERIMENTAL
```

```
      Console.WriteLine("Compiled for experimental version.");
    #endif

    #if EXPERIMENTAL && TRIAL
       Console.Error.WriteLine("Testing experimental trial version.");
    #endif

    Console.WriteLine("This is in all versions.");
  }
}
```

The output from this program is shown here:

```
Compiled for experimental version.
Testing experimental trial version.
This is in all versions.
```

In this example, two symbols are defined, **EXPERIMENTAL** and **TRIAL**. The second **WriteLine( )** statement is compiled only if both are defined.

#else and #elif

The **#else** directive works much like the **else** that is part of the C# language: It establishes an alternative if **#if** fails. The previous example can be expanded as shown here:

```
// Demonstrate #else.

#define EXPERIMENTAL

using System;

class Test {
  public static void Main() {

    #if EXPERIMENTAL
      Console.WriteLine("Compiled for experimental version.");
    #else
      Console.WriteLine("Compiled for release.");
    #endif

    #if EXPERIMENTAL && TRIAL
```

```
    Console.Error.WriteLine("Testing experimental trial version.");
#else
    Console.Error.WriteLine("Not experimental trial version.");
#endif

    Console.WriteLine("This is in all versions.");
  }
}
```

The output is shown here:

```
Compiled for experimental version.
Not experimental trial version.
This is in all versions.
```

Since **TRIAL** is no longer defined, the **#else** portion of the second conditional code sequence is used.

Notice that **#else** marks both the end of the **#if** block and the beginning of the **#else** block. This is necessary because there can be only one **#endif** associated with any **#if**.

The **#elif** directive means "else if" and establishes an if-else-if chain for multiple compilation options. **#elif** is followed by a symbol expression. If the expression is true, that block of code is compiled, and no other **#elif** expressions are tested. Otherwise, the next block in the series is checked. The general form for **#elif** is

#if *symbol-expression*
   statement sequence
#elif *symbol-expression*
   statement sequence
#elif *symbol-expression*
   statement sequence
#elif *symbol-expression*
   statement sequence
#elif *symbol-expression*

   .
   .
   .

#endif

For example:

```
// Demonstrate #elif.

#define RELEASE
```

```
using System;

class Test {
  public static void Main() {

    #if EXPERIMENTAL
      Console.WriteLine("Compiled for experimental version.");
    #elif RELEASE
      Console.WriteLine("Compiled for release.");
    #else
      Console.WriteLine("Compiled for internal testing.");
    #endif

    #if TRIAL && !RELEASE
        Console.WriteLine("Trial version.");
    #endif

    Console.WriteLine("This is in all versions.");
  }
}
```

The output is shown here:

```
Compiled for release.
This is in all versions.
```

#undef

The **#undef** directive removes a previously defined definition of the symbol that follows it. That is, it "undefines" a symbol. The general form for **#undef** is

#undef *symbol*

Here's an example:

```
#define SMALL

#if SMALL
  // ...
#undef SMALL
// at this point SMALL is undefined.
```

After the **#undef** directive, **SMALL** is no longer defined.

#undef is used principally to allow symbols to be localized to only those sections of code that need them.

#error

The **#error** directive forces the compiler to stop compilation. It is used for debugging. The general form of the **#error** directive is

#error *error-message*

When the **#error** directive is encountered, the error message is displayed. For example, when the compiler encounters this line,

```
#error This is a test error!
```

compilation stops and the error message "This is a test error!" is displayed.

#warning

The **#warning** directive is similar to **#error**, except that a warning rather than an error is produced. Thus, compilation is not stopped. The general form of the **#warning** directive is

#warning *warning-message*

#line

The **#line** directive sets the line number and filename for the file that contains the **#line** directive. The number and the name are used when errors or warnings are output during compilation. The general form for **#line** is

#line *number "filename"*

where *number* is any positive integer and becomes the new line number, and the optional *filename* is any valid file identifier, which becomes the new filename. **#line** is primarily used for debugging and special applications.

To return the line numbering to its original condition, specify **default**, as shown here:

```
#line default
```

#region and #endregion

The **#region** and **#endregion** directives let you define a region that will be expanded or collapsed when using outlining in the Visual Studio IDE. The general form is shown here:

```
#region region-name
   // code sequence
#endregion
```

Here, *region-name* is the name of the region.

Assemblies and the internal Access Modifier

An integral part of C# programming is the assembly. An *assembly* is a file (or files) that contains all deployment and version information for a program. Assemblies are fundamental to the .NET environment. To quote Microsoft, "Assemblies are the building blocks of the .NET Framework." Assemblies are the mechanisms that support safe component interaction, interlanguage operability, and versioning. An assembly also defines a scope.

An assembly is composed of four sections. The first is the assembly *manifest*. The manifest contains information about the assembly itself. This data includes such things as the name of the assembly, its version number, type mapping information, and cultural settings. The second section is *type metadata*, which is information about the data types used by the program. Amongst other benefits, type metadata aids in cross-language interoperability. The third part of an assembly is the *program code*, which is stored in Microsoft Intermediate Language (MSIL) format. The fourth constituent of an assembly is the resources used by the program.

Fortunately, when using C#, assemblies are produced automatically, with little or no extra effort on your part. The reason for this is that the **exe** file created when you compile a C# program is actually an assembly that contains your program's executable code as well as other types of information. Thus, when you compile a C# program, an assembly is automatically produced.

There are many other features and topics that relate to assemblies, but a discussion of these is outside the scope of this book. (Assemblies are an integral part of .NET development, but are not technically a feature of the C# language.) However, there is one part of C# that relates directly to the assembly: the **internal** access modifier, and it is examined next.

The internal Access Modifier

In addition to the access modifiers **public**, **private**, and **protected**, which you have been using throughout this book, C# also defines **internal**. The **internal** modifier declares that a member is known throughout all files in an assembly, but unknown outside that assembly. Thus, in simplified terms, a member marked as **internal** is known throughout a program, but not elsewhere. The **internal** access modifier is particularly useful when creating software components.

The **internal** modifier can be applied to classes and to members of classes, and to structures and members of structures. The **internal** modifier can also be applied to interface and enumeration declarations.

You can use **protected** in conjunction with **internal** to produce the **protected internal** access modifier pair. The **protected internal** access level can be given only to class members. A member declared with **protected internal** access is accessible within its own assembly or to derived types.

Here is an example that uses **internal**:

```
// Use internal.

using System;

class InternalTest {
  internal int x;
}

class InternalDemo {
  public static void Main() {
    InternalTest ob = new InternalTest();

    ob.x = 10; // can access -- in same file

    Console.WriteLine("Here is ob.x: " + ob.x);

  }
}
```

Inside **InternalTest**, the field x is declared **internal**. This means that it is accessible within the program, as its use in **InternalDemo** shows, but unavailable outside the program.

Chapter 17

Runtime Type ID, Reflection, and Attributes

T his chapter discusses three interrelated and powerful C# features: runtime type identification, reflection, and attributes. *Runtime type ID* is the mechanism that lets you identify a type during the execution of a program. *Reflection* is the feature that enables you to obtain information about a type. Using this information, you can construct and use objects at runtime. This feature is very powerful because it lets a program add functionality dynamically, during execution. An *attribute* describes a characteristic of some element of a C# program. For example, you can specify attributes for classes, methods, and fields, among others. Attributes can be interrogated at runtime, and the attribute information obtained. Attributes use both runtime type identification and reflection.

Runtime Type Identification

Runtime type identification (RTTI) allows the type of an object to be determined during program execution. RTTI is useful for many reasons. For example, you can discover precisely what type of object is being referred to by a base-class reference. Another use of RTTI is to test in advance whether a cast will succeed, preventing an invalid cast exception. Runtime type identification is also a key component of reflection.

C# includes three keywords that support runtime type identification: **is**, **as**, and **typeof**. Each is examined in turn.

Testing a Type with is

You can determine whether an object is of a certain type by using the **is** operator. Its general form is shown here:

expr is *type*

Here, *expr* is an expression whose type is being tested against *type*. If the type of *expr* is the same as, or compatible with, *type*, then the outcome of this operation is true. Otherwise, it is false. Thus, if the outcome is true, *expr* can be cast to *type*.

Here is an example that uses **is**:

```
// Demonstrate is.

using System;

class A {}
class B : A {}

class UseIs {
  public static void Main() {
    A a = new A();
```

```
    B b = new B();

    if(a is A) Console.WriteLine("a is an A");
    if(b is A)
      Console.WriteLine("b is an A because it is derived from A");
    if(a is B)
      Console.WriteLine("This won't display -- a not derived from B");

    if(b is B) Console.WriteLine("B is a B");
    if(a is object) Console.WriteLine("a is an Object");
  }
}
```

The output is shown here:

```
a is an A
b is an A because it is derived from A
B is a B
a is an Object
```

Most of the **is** expressions are self-explanatory, but two may need a little discussion. First, notice this statement:

```
if(b is A)
  Console.WriteLine("b is an A because it is derived from A");
```

The **if** succeeds because **b** is a reference of type **B**, which is derived from type **A**. Thus, **b** is compatible with **A**. However, the reverse is not true. When this line is executed,

```
if(a is B)
  Console.WriteLine("This won't display -- a not derived from B");
```

the **if** does not succeed, because **a** is of type **A**, which is not derived from **B**. Thus, they are not compatible.

Using as

Sometimes you will want to try a cast at runtime but not raise an exception if the cast fails. To do this, use the **as** operator, which has this general form:

expr as *type*

Here, *expr* is the expression being cast to *type*. If the cast succeeds, then a reference to *type* is returned. Otherwise, a null reference is returned.

The **as** operator offers a streamlined alternative to **is** in some cases. For example, consider the following program that uses **is** to prevent an invalid cast from occurring:

```
// Use is to avoid an invalid cast.

using System;

class A {}
class B : A {}

class CheckCast {
  public static void Main() {
    A a = new A();
    B b = new B();

    // Check to see if a can be cast to B.
    if(a is B)   // if so, do the cast
      b = (B) a;
    else // if not, skip the cast
      b = null;

    if(b==null)
      Console.WriteLine("Cast b = (B) a is NOT allowed.");
    else
      Console.WriteLine("Cast b = (B) a is allowed");
  }
}
```

This program displays the following output:

```
Cast b = (B) a is NOT allowed.
```

As the output shows, since **a** is not a **B**, the cast of **a** to **B** is invalid and is prevented by the **if** statement. However, this approach requires two steps. First, the validity of the cast must be confirmed. Second, the cast must be made. These steps can be combined into one through the use of **as**, as the following program shows:

```
// Demonstrate as.

using System;
```

```
class A {}
class B : A {}

class CheckCast {
  public static void Main() {
    A a = new A();
    B b = new B();

    b = a as B; // cast, if possible

    if(b==null)
      Console.WriteLine("Cast b = (B) a is NOT allowed.");
    else
      Console.WriteLine("Cast b = (B) a is allowed");
  }
}
```

Here is the output, which is the same as before:

```
Cast b = (B) a is NOT allowed.
```

In this version, the **as** statement checks the validity of the cast and then, if valid, performs the cast, all in one statement.

Using typeof

Although useful in their own ways, the **as** and **is** operators simply test the compatibility of two types. Often, you will need to obtain information about a type. To do this, C# supplies the **typeof** operator. It retrieves a **System.Type** object for a given type. Using this object, you can determine the type's characteristics.

The **typeof** operator has this general form:

typeof(*type*)

Here, *type* is the type being obtained. The **Type** object returned encapsulates the information associated with *type*.

Once you have obtained a **Type** object for a given type, you can obtain information about it through the use of various properties, fields, and methods defined by **Type**. **Type** is a large class with many members, and a discussion is deferred until the following section, where reflection is examined. However, to briefly demonstrate **Type**, the following program uses three of its properties: **FullName**, **IsClass**, and **IsAbstract**. To obtain the full name of the type, use **FullName**. **IsClass** returns true if the type is a class. **IsAbstract** returns true if a class is abstract.

```
// Demonstrate typeof.

using System;
using System.IO;

class UseTypeof {
  public static void Main() {
    Type t = typeof(StreamReader);

    Console.WriteLine(t.FullName);

    if(t.IsClass) Console.WriteLine("Is a class.");
    if(t.IsAbstract) Console.WriteLine("Is abstract.");
    else Console.WriteLine("Is concrete.");

  }
}
```

This program outputs the following:

```
System.IO.StreamReader
Is a class.
Is concrete.
```

This program obtains a **Type** object that describes **StreamReader**. It then displays the full name and determines if it is a class and if it is abstract.

Reflection

As mentioned at the start of this chapter, *reflection* is the feature of C# that enables you to obtain information about a type. The term *reflection* comes from the way the process works: A **Type** object mirrors the underlying type that it represents. To obtain information, you ask the **Type** object questions, and it returns (reflects) the information associated with the type back to you. Reflection is a powerful mechanism because it allows you to learn and use the capabilities of types that are known only at runtime.

Many of the classes that support reflection are part of the .NET Reflection API, which is in the **System.Reflection** namespace. Thus, you will normally include the following in programs that use reflection:

```
using System.Reflection;
```

The Reflection Core: System.Type

System.Type is at the core of the reflection subsystem because it encapsulates a type. It contains many properties and methods that you will use to obtain information about a type at runtime. **Type** is derived from an abstract class called **System.Reflection.MemberInfo**. **MemberInfo** defines the following abstract, read-only properties:

Type DeclaringType	The type of the class or interface in which the member is declared.
MemberTypes MemberType	The type of the member.
string Name	The name of the type.
Type ReflectedType	The type of the object being reflected.

Notice that the type of **MemberType** is **MemberTypes**. **MemberTypes** is an enumeration that defines values that indicate the various member types. Among others, these include

```
MemberTypes.Constructor
MemberTypes.Method
MemberTypes.Field
MemberTypes.Event
MemberTypes.Property
```

Thus, the type of a member can be determined by checking **MemberType**. For example, if **MemberType** equals **MemberTypes.Method**, then that member is a method.

    MemberInfo includes two abstract methods: **GetCustomAttributes( )** and **IsDefined( )**. These both relate to attributes.

    To the methods and properties defined by **MemberInfo**, **Type** adds a great many of its own. For example, here are several commonly used methods defined by **Type**:

Method	Purpose
ConstructorInfo[ ] GetConstructors( )	Obtains a list of the constructors for the specified type.
EventInfo[ ] GetEvents( )	Obtains a list of events for the specified type.
FieldInfo[ ] GetFields( )	Obtains a list of the fields for the specified type.
MemberInfo[ ] GetMembers( )	Obtains a list of the members for the specified type.
MethodInfo[ ] GetMethods( )	Obtains a list of methods for the specified type.
PropertyInfo[ ] GetProperties( )	Obtains a list of properties for the specified type.

Here are several commonly used, read-only properties defined by **Type**:

Property	Purpose
Assembly Assembly	Obtains the assembly for the specified type.
TypeAttributes Attributes	Obtains the attributes for the specified type.
Type BaseType	Obtains the immediate base type for the specified type.
string FullName	Obtains the complete name of the specified type.
bool IsAbstract	Is true if the specified type is abstract.
bool isArray	Is true if the specified type is an array.
bool IsClass	Is true if the specified type is a class.
bool IsEnum	Is true if the specified type is an enumeration.
string Namespace	Obtains the namespace for the specified type.

Using Reflection

Using **Type**'s methods and properties, it is possible to obtain detailed information about a type at runtime. This is an extremely powerful feature, because once you have obtained information about a type, you can invoke its constructors, call its methods, and use its properties. Thus, reflection enables you to use code that was not available at compile time.

The Reflection API is quite large, and it is not possible to cover the entire topic here. (Complete coverage of Reflection could easily fill an entire book!) However, because the Reflection API is logically designed, once you understand how to use a part of it, the rest just falls into place. With this thought in mind, the following sections demonstrate four key reflection techniques: obtaining information about methods, invoking methods, constructing objects, and loading types from assemblies.

Obtaining Information About Methods

Once you have a **Type** object, you can obtain a list of methods supported by the type by using **GetMethods( )**. One form is shown here:

MethodInfo[ ] GetMethods( )

It returns an array of **MethodInfo** objects that describe the methods supported by the invoking type. **MethodInfo** is in the **System.Reflection** namespace.

MethodInfo is derived from the abstract class **MethodBase**, which inherits **MemberInfo**. Thus, the properties and methods defined by all three of these classes are available for your use. For example, to obtain the name of a method, use the **Name**

property. Two members that are of particular interest at this time are **ReturnType** and **GetParameters( )**.

The return type of a method is found in the **ReturnType** property, which is an object of **Type**.

The method **GetParameters( )** returns a list of the parameters associated with a method. It has this general form:

ParameterInfo[ ] GetParameters( )

The parameter information is held in a **ParameterInfo** object. **ParameterInfo** defines a large number of properties and methods that describe the parameter. Two properties that are of particular value are **Name**, which is a string that contains the name of the parameter, and **ParameterType**, which describes the parameter's type. The parameter's type is encapsulated within a **Type** object.

Here is a program that uses reflection to obtain the methods supported by a class called **MyClass**. For each method, it displays the return type and name of the method, and the name and type of any parameters that each method may have.

```
// Analyze methods using reflection.

using System;
using System.Reflection;

class MyClass {
  int x;
  int y;

  public MyClass(int i, int j) {
    x = i;
    y = j;
  }

  public int sum() {
    return x+y;
  }

  public bool isBetween(int i) {
    if(x < i && i < y) return true;
    else return false;
  }

  public void set(int a, int b) {
    x = a;
```

```csharp
      y = b;
    }

    public void set(double a, double b) {
      x = (int) a;
      y = (int) b;
    }

    public void show() {
      Console.WriteLine(" x: {0}, y: {1}", x, y);
    }
  }

  class ReflectDemo {
    public static void Main() {
      Type t = typeof(MyClass); // get a Type object representing MyClass

      Console.WriteLine("Analyzing methods in " + t.Name);
      Console.WriteLine();

      Console.WriteLine("Methods supported: ");

      MethodInfo[] mi = t.GetMethods();

      // Display methods supported by MyClass.
      foreach(MethodInfo m in mi) {
        // Display return type and name.
        Console.Write("   " + m.ReturnType.Name +
                      " " + m.Name + "(");

        // Display parameters.
        ParameterInfo[] pi = m.GetParameters();

        for(int i=0; i < pi.Length; i++) {
          Console.Write(pi[i].ParameterType.Name +
                      " " + pi[i].Name);
          if(i+1 < pi.Length) Console.Write(", ");
        }

        Console.WriteLine(")");
```

```
        Console.WriteLine();
      }
    }
}
```

The output is shown here:

```
Analyzing methods in MyClass

Methods supported:
    Int32 GetHashCode()

    Boolean Equals(Object obj)

    String ToString()

    Int32 sum()

    Boolean isBetween(Int32 i)

    Void set(Int32 a, Int32 b)

    Void set(Double a, Double b)

    Void show()

    Type GetType()
```

Notice that in addition to the methods defined by **MyClass**, the methods defined by **object** are also displayed. This is because all types in C# inherit **object**. Also notice that the .NET structure names are used for the type names. Observe that **set( )** is displayed twice. This is because **set( )** is overloaded. One version takes **int** arguments. The other takes **double** arguments.

Let's look at this program closely. First, notice that **MyClass** defines a public constructor and a number of public methods, including the overloaded **set( )** method.

Inside **Main( )**, a **Type** object representing **MyClass** is obtained using this line of code:

```
Type t = typeof(MyClass); // get a Type object representing MyClass
```

Using **t** and the Reflection API, the program then displays information about the methods supported by **MyClass**. First, a list of the methods is obtained by the following statement:

```
MethodInfo[] mi = t.GetMethods();
```

Next, a **foreach** loop is established that cycles through **mi**. With each pass, the return type, name, and parameters for each method are displayed by the following code:

```
// Display return type and name.
Console.Write("    " + m.ReturnType.Name +
                " " + m.Name + "(");

// Display parameters.
ParameterInfo[] pi = m.GetParameters();

for(int i=0; i < pi.Length; i++) {
  Console.Write(pi[i].ParameterType.Name +
                " " + pi[i].Name);
  if(i+1 < pi.Length) Console.Write(", ");
}
```

In this sequence, the parameters associated with each method are obtained by calling **GetParameters( )** and stored in the **pi** array. Then a **for** loop cycles through the **pi** array, displaying the type and name of each parameter. The key point is that this information is obtained dynamically at runtime without relying on prior knowledge of **MyClass**.

A Second Form of GetMethods( )

A second form of **GetMethods( )** lets you specify various flags that filter the methods that are retrieved. It has this general form:

MethodInfo[ ] GetMethods(BindingFlags *flags*)

This version obtains only those methods that match the criteria that you specify. **BindingFlags** is an enumeration. Several of its most commonly used values are shown here:

Value	Meaning
DeclaredOnly	Retrieves only those methods defined by the specified class. Inherited methods are not included.
Instance	Retrieves instance methods.
NonPublic	Retrieves nonpublic methods.

Value	Meaning
Public	Retrieves public methods.
Static	Retrieves **static** methods.

You can OR together two or more flags. In fact, minimally you must include either **Instance** or **Static** with **Public** or **NonPublic**. Failure to do so will result in no methods being retrieved.

One of the main uses of the **BindingFlags** form of **GetMethods( )** is to obtain a list of the methods defined by a class without also retrieving the inherited methods. This is especially useful for preventing the methods defined by **object** from being obtained. For example, try substituting this call to **GetMethods( )** into the preceding program:

```
// Now, only methods declared by MyClass are obtained.
MethodInfo[] mi = t.GetMethods(BindingFlags.DeclaredOnly |
                               BindingFlags.Instance |
                               BindingFlags.Public) ;
```

After making this change, the program produces the following output:

```
Analyzing methods in MyClass

Methods supported:
   Int32 sum()

   Boolean isBetween(Int32 i)

   Void set(Int32 a, Int32 b)

   Void set(Double a, Double b)

   Void show()
```

As you can see, only those methods explicitly defined by **MyClass** are displayed.

Calling Methods Using Reflection

Once you know what methods a type supports, you can call one or more of them. To do this, you will use the **Invoke( )** method that is contained in **MethodInfo**. It is shown here:

object Invoke(object *ob*, object[ ] *args*)

Here, *ob* is a reference to the object on which the method is invoked. For **static** methods, *ob* must be **null**. Any arguments that need to be passed to the method are specified in the array *args*. If no arguments are needed, *args* must be **null**. Also, *args* must contain exactly the same number of elements as there are arguments. Therefore, if two arguments are needed, then *args* must be two elements long. It can't, for example, be three or four elements long.

To call a method, simply call **Invoke( )** on an instance of **MethodInfo** that was obtained by calling **GetMethods( )**. The following program demonstrates the procedure:

```csharp
// Invoke methods using reflection.

using System;
using System.Reflection;

class MyClass {
  int x;
  int y;

  public MyClass(int i, int j) {
    x = i;
    y = j;
  }

  public int sum() {
    return x+y;
  }

  public bool isBetween(int i) {
    if((x < i) && (i < y)) return true;
    else return false;
  }

  public void set(int a, int b) {
    Console.Write("Inside set(int, int). ");
    x = a;
    y = b;
    show();
  }

  // Overload set.
  public void set(double a, double b) {
    Console.Write("Inside set(double, double). ");
```

```
    x = (int) a;
    y = (int) b;
    show();
  }

  public void show() {
    Console.WriteLine("Values are x: {0}, y: {1}", x, y);
  }
}

class InvokeMethDemo {
  public static void Main() {
    Type t = typeof(MyClass);
    MyClass reflectOb = new MyClass(10, 20);
    int val;

    Console.WriteLine("Invoking methods in " + t.Name);
    Console.WriteLine();
    MethodInfo[] mi = t.GetMethods();

    // Invoke each method.
    foreach(MethodInfo m in mi) {
      // Get the parameters.
      ParameterInfo[] pi = m.GetParameters();

      if(m.Name.CompareTo("set")==0 &&
         pi[0].ParameterType == typeof(int)) {
        object[] args = new object[2];
        args[0] = 9;
        args[1] = 18;
        m.Invoke(reflectOb, args);
      }
      else if(m.Name.CompareTo("set")==0 &&
         pi[0].ParameterType == typeof(double)) {
        object[] args = new object[2];
        args[0] = 1.12;
        args[1] = 23.4;
        m.Invoke(reflectOb, args);
      }
      else if(m.Name.CompareTo("sum")==0) {
        val = (int) m.Invoke(reflectOb, null);
        Console.WriteLine("sum is " + val);
```

```
        }
      else if(m.Name.CompareTo("isBetween")==0) {
        object[] args = new object[1];
        args[0] = 14;
        if((bool) m.Invoke(reflectOb, args))
          Console.WriteLine("14 is between x and y");
      }
      else if(m.Name.CompareTo("show")==0) {
        m.Invoke(reflectOb, null);
      }
    }
  }
}
```

The output is shown here:

```
Invoking methods in MyClass

sum is 30
14 is between x and y
Inside set(int, int). Values are x: 9, y: 18
Inside set(double, double). Values are x: 1, y: 23
Values are x: 1, y: 23
```

Look closely at how the methods are invoked. First, a list of methods is obtained. Then, inside the **foreach** loop, parameter information is retrieved. Next, using a series of if/else statements, each method is executed with the proper type and number of arguments. Pay special attention to the way that the overloaded **set( )** method is executed by the following code:

```
if(m.Name.CompareTo("set")==0 &&
   pi[0].ParameterType == typeof(int)) {
  object[] args = new object[2];
  args[0] = 9;
  args[1] = 18;
  m.Invoke(reflectOb, args);
}
else if(m.Name.CompareTo("set")==0 &&
  pi[0].ParameterType == typeof(double)) {
  object[] args = new object[2];
  args[0] = 1.12;
  args[1] = 23.4;
  m.Invoke(reflectOb, args);
}
```

If the name of the method is **set**, then the type of the first parameter is tested to determine which version of the method was found. If it was **set(int, int)**, then **int** arguments are loaded into **args** and **set( )** is called. Otherwise, **double** arguments are used.

Obtaining a Type's Constructors

In the previous example, there is no advantage to using reflection to invoke methods on **MyClass** since an object of type **MyClass** was explicitly created. It would be easier to just call its methods normally. However, the power of reflection starts to become apparent when an object is created dynamically at runtime. To do this, you will need to first obtain a list of the constructors. Then you will create an instance of the type by invoking one of the constructors. This mechanism allows you to instantiate any type of object at runtime without naming it in a declaration statement.

To obtain the constructors for a type, call **GetConstructors( )** on a **Type** object. One commonly used form is shown here:

ConstructorInfo[ ] GetConstructors( )

It returns an array of **ConstructorInfo** objects that describe the constructors.

ConstructorInfo is derived from the abstract class **MethodBase**, which inherits **MemberInfo**. It also defines several members of its own. The one we are interested in is **GetParameters( )**, which returns a list of the parameters associated with a constructor. It works just like **GetParameters( )** defined by **MethodInfo**, described earlier.

Once an appropriate constructor has been found, an object is created by calling the **Invoke( )** method defined by **ConstructorInfo**. It is shown here:

object Invoke(object[ ] *args*)

Any arguments that need to be passed to the method are specified in the array *args*. If no arguments are needed, *args* must be **null**. Also, *args* must contain exactly the same number of elements as there are arguments. **Invoke( )** returns a reference to the object.

The following program uses reflection to create an instance of **MyClass**:

```
// Create an object using reflection.

using System;
using System.Reflection;

class MyClass {
  int x;
  int y;

  public MyClass(int i) {
    Console.WriteLine("Constructing MyClass(int, int). ");
    x = y = i;
```

```
    }

    public MyClass(int i, int j) {
      Console.WriteLine("Constructing MyClass(int, int). ");
      x = i;
      y = j;
      show();
    }

    public int sum() {
      return x+y;
    }

    public bool isBetween(int i) {
      if((x < i) && (i < y)) return true;
      else return false;
    }

    public void set(int a, int b) {
      Console.Write("Inside set(int, int). ");
      x = a;
      y = b;
      show();
    }

    // Overload set.
    public void set(double a, double b) {
      Console.Write("Inside set(double, double). ");
      x = (int) a;
      y = (int) b;
      show();
    }

    public void show() {
      Console.WriteLine("Values are x: {0}, y: {1}", x, y);
    }

}

class InvokeConsDemo {
  public static void Main() {
    Type t = typeof(MyClass);
```

```
int val;

// Get constructor info.
ConstructorInfo[] ci = t.GetConstructors();

Console.WriteLine("Available constructors: ");
foreach(ConstructorInfo c in ci) {
  // Display return type and name.
  Console.Write("    " + t.Name + "(");

  // Display parameters.
  ParameterInfo[] pi = c.GetParameters();

  for(int i=0; i < pi.Length; i++) {
    Console.Write(pi[i].ParameterType.Name +
                  " " + pi[i].Name);
    if(i+1 < pi.Length) Console.Write(", ");
  }

  Console.WriteLine(")");
}
Console.WriteLine();

// Find matching constructor.
int x;

for(x=0; x < ci.Length; x++) {
  ParameterInfo[] pi =  ci[x].GetParameters();
  if(pi.Length == 2) break;
}

if(x == ci.Length) {
  Console.WriteLine("No matching constructor found.");
  return;
}
else
  Console.WriteLine("Two-parameter constructor found.\n");

// Construct the object.
object[] consargs = new object[2];
consargs[0] = 10;
consargs[1] = 20;
```

```
object reflectOb = ci[x].Invoke(consargs);

Console.WriteLine("\nInvoking methods on reflectOb.");
Console.WriteLine();
MethodInfo[] mi = t.GetMethods();

// Invoke each method.
foreach(MethodInfo m in mi) {
  // Get the parameters.
  ParameterInfo[] pi = m.GetParameters();

  if(m.Name.CompareTo("set")==0 &&
     pi[0].ParameterType == typeof(int)) {
    // This is set(int, int).
    object[] args = new object[2];
    args[0] = 9;
    args[1] = 18;
    m.Invoke(reflectOb, args);
  }
  else if(m.Name.CompareTo("set")==0 &&
          pi[0].ParameterType == typeof(double)) {
    // This is set(double, double).
    object[] args = new object[2];
    args[0] = 1.12;
    args[1] = 23.4;
    m.Invoke(reflectOb, args);
  }
  else if(m.Name.CompareTo("sum")==0) {
    val = (int) m.Invoke(reflectOb, null);
    Console.WriteLine("sum is " + val);
  }
  else if(m.Name.CompareTo("isBetween")==0) {
    object[] args = new object[1];
    args[0] = 14;
    if((bool) m.Invoke(reflectOb, args))
      Console.WriteLine("14 is between x and y");
  }
  else if(m.Name.CompareTo("show")==0) {
    m.Invoke(reflectOb, null);
  }
}
}
}
}
```

The output is shown here:

```
Available constructors:
   MyClass(Int32 i)
   MyClass(Int32 i, Int32 j)

Two-parameter constructor found.

Constructing MyClass(int, int).
Values are x: 10, y: 20

Invoking methods on reflectOb.

sum is 30
14 is between x and y
Inside set(int, int). Values are x: 9, y: 18
Inside set(double, double). Values are x: 1, y: 23
Values are x: 1, y: 23
```

Let's look at how reflection is used to construct a **MyClass** object. First, a list of the public constructors is obtained using the following statement:

```
ConstructorInfo[] ci = t.GetConstructors();
```

Next, for the sake of illustration, the constructors are displayed. Then the list is searched for a constructor that takes two arguments, using this code:

```
for(x=0; x < ci.Length; x++) {
  ParameterInfo[] pi =  ci[x].GetParameters();
  if(pi.Length == 2) break;
}
```

If the constructor is found (as it will be in this case), an object is instantiated by the following sequence:

```
// Construct the object.
object[] consargs = new object[2];
consargs[0] = 10;
consargs[1] = 20;
object reflectOb = ci[x].Invoke(consargs);
```

After the call to **Invoke( )**, **reflectOb** will refer to an object of type **MyClass**.

One important point needs to be made. In this example, for the sake of simplicity, it was assumed that the only two-argument constructor was one that took two **int** arguments. In a real-world application, this would have to be verified by checking the parameter type of each argument.

Obtaining Types from Assemblies

In the preceding example, everything about **MyClass** has been discovered using reflection except for one item: the type **MyClass**, itself. That is, although the preceding examples dynamically determined information about **MyClass**, they still relied upon the fact that the type name **MyClass** was known in advance and used in a **typeof** statement to obtain a **Type** object upon which all of the reflection methods either directly or indirectly operated. Although this might be useful in a number of circumstances, the full power of reflection is found when the types available to a program are determined dynamically by analyzing the contents of other assemblies.

As you know from Chapter 16, an assembly carries with it type information about the classes, structures, and so on, that it contains. The Reflection API allows you to load an assembly, discover information about it, and create instances of any of its publicly available types. Using this mechanism, a program can search its environment, utilizing functionality that might be available without having to explicitly define that functionality at compile time. This is an extremely potent, and exciting, concept. For example, you can imagine a program that acts as a "type browser," displaying the types available on a system. Another application could be a design tool that lets you visually "wire together" a program that is composed of the various types supported by the system. Since all information about a type is discoverable, there is no inherent limitation to ways reflection can be applied.

To obtain information about an assembly, you will first create an **Assembly** object. The **Assembly** class does not define a public constructor. Instead, an **Assembly** object is obtained by calling one of its methods. The one that we will use is **LoadFrom( )**. The form we will use is shown here:

static Assembly LoadFrom(string *filename*)

Here, *filename* specifies the name of the assembly.

Once you have obtained an **Assembly** object, you can discover the types that it defines by calling **GetTypes( )** on it. Here is its general form:

Type[ ] GetTypes( )

It returns an array of the types contained in the assembly.

To demonstrate the discovery of types in an assembly, you will need two files. The first will contain a set of classes that will be discovered by the second. To begin, create a file called **MyClasses.cs** that contains the following:

```
// A file that contains three classes.  Call this file MyClasses.cs.

using System;

class MyClass {
  int x;
  int y;

  public MyClass(int i) {
    Console.WriteLine("Constructing MyClass(int). ");
    x = y = i;
    show();
  }

  public MyClass(int i, int j) {
    Console.WriteLine("Constructing MyClass(int, int). ");
    x = i;
    y = j;
    show();
  }

  public int sum() {
    return x+y;
  }

  public bool isBetween(int i) {
    if((x < i) && (i < y)) return true;
    else return false;
  }

  public void set(int a, int b) {
    Console.Write("Inside set(int, int). ");
    x = a;
    y = b;
    show();
  }

  // Overload set.
  public void set(double a, double b) {
    Console.Write("Inside set(double, double). ");
    x = (int) a;
    y = (int) b;
    show();
```

```
    }

  public void show() {
    Console.WriteLine("Values are x: {0}, y: {1}", x, y);
  }

}

class AnotherClass {
  string remark;

  public AnotherClass(string str) {
    remark = str;
  }

  public void show() {
    Console.WriteLine(remark);
  }
}

class Demo {
  public static void Main() {
    Console.WriteLine("This is a placeholder.");
  }
}
```

This file contains **MyClass**, which we have been using in the previous examples. It also adds a second class called **AnotherClass** and a third class called **Demo**. Thus, the assembly produced by this program will contain three classes. Next, compile this file so that the file **MyClasses.exe** is produced. This is the assembly that will be interrogated.

The program that will discover information about **MyClasses.exe** is shown here. Enter it at this time.

```
/* Locate an assembly, determine types, and create
   an object using reflection. */

using System;
using System.Reflection;

class ReflectAssemblyDemo {
  public static void Main() {
```

```
int val;

// Load the MyClasses.exe assembly.
Assembly asm = Assembly.LoadFrom("MyClasses.exe");

// Discover what types MyClasses.exe contains.
Type[] alltypes = asm.GetTypes();
foreach(Type temp in alltypes)
  Console.WriteLine("Found: " + temp.Name);

Console.WriteLine();

// Use the first type, which is MyClass in this case.
Type t = alltypes[0]; // use first class found
Console.WriteLine("Using: " + t.Name);

// Obtain constructor info.
ConstructorInfo[] ci = t.GetConstructors();

Console.WriteLine("Available constructors: ");
foreach(ConstructorInfo c in ci) {
  // Display return type and name.
  Console.Write("   " + t.Name + "(");

  // Display parameters.
  ParameterInfo[] pi = c.GetParameters();

  for(int i=0; i < pi.Length; i++) {
    Console.Write(pi[i].ParameterType.Name +
                  " " + pi[i].Name);
    if(i+1 < pi.Length) Console.Write(", ");
  }

  Console.WriteLine(")");
}
Console.WriteLine();

// Find matching constructor.
int x;

for(x=0; x < ci.Length; x++) {
  ParameterInfo[] pi =  ci[x].GetParameters();
```

```
    if(pi.Length == 2) break;
}

if(x == ci.Length) {
  Console.WriteLine("No matching constructor found.");
  return;
}
else
  Console.WriteLine("Two-parameter constructor found.\n");

// Construct the object.
object[] consargs = new object[2];
consargs[0] = 10;
consargs[1] = 20;
object reflectOb = ci[x].Invoke(consargs);

Console.WriteLine("\nInvoking methods on reflectOb.");
Console.WriteLine();
MethodInfo[] mi = t.GetMethods();

// Invoke each method.
foreach(MethodInfo m in mi) {
  // Get the parameters.
  ParameterInfo[] pi = m.GetParameters();

  if(m.Name.CompareTo("set")==0 &&
     pi[0].ParameterType == typeof(int)) {
    // This is set(int, int).
    object[] args = new object[2];
    args[0] = 9;
    args[1] = 18;
    m.Invoke(reflectOb, args);
  }
  else if(m.Name.CompareTo("set")==0 &&
     pi[0].ParameterType == typeof(double)) {
    // This is set(double, double).
    object[] args = new object[2];
    args[0] = 1.12;
    args[1] = 23.4;
    m.Invoke(reflectOb, args);
  }
  else if(m.Name.CompareTo("sum")==0) {
```

```
      val = (int) m.Invoke(reflectOb, null);
      Console.WriteLine("sum is " + val);
    }
    else if(m.Name.CompareTo("isBetween")==0) {
      object[] args = new object[1];
      args[0] = 14;
      if((bool) m.Invoke(reflectOb, args))
        Console.WriteLine("14 is between x and y");
    }
    else if(m.Name.CompareTo("show")==0) {
      m.Invoke(reflectOb, null);
    }
  }
}

}
}
```

The output from the program is shown here:

```
Found: MyClass
Found: AnotherClass
Found: Demo

Using: MyClass
Available constructors:
   MyClass(Int32 i)
   MyClass(Int32 i, Int32 j)

Two-parameter constructor found.

Constructing MyClass(int, int).
Values are x: 10, y: 20

Invoking methods on reflectOb.

sum is 30
14 is between x and y
Inside set(int, int). Values are x: 9, y: 18
Inside set(double, double). Values are x: 1, y: 23
Values are x: 1, y: 23
```

As the output shows, all three classes contained within **MyClasses.exe** were found. The first one, which in this case was **MyClass**, was then used to instantiate an object and execute methods. All of this was accomplished without prior knowledge of the contents of **MyClasses.exe** being required.

The types in **MyClasses.exe** are discovered using this sequence of code, which is near the start of **Main( )**:

```
// Load the MyClasses.exe assembly.
Assembly asm = Assembly.LoadFrom("MyClasses.exe");

// Discover what types MyClasses.exe contains.
Type[] alltypes = asm.GetTypes();
foreach(Type temp in alltypes)
  Console.WriteLine("Found: " + temp.Name);
```

You can use such a sequence whenever you need to dynamically load and interrogate an assembly.

On a related point, an assembly need not be an **exe** file. Assemblies can also be contained in dynamic link library (DLL) files that use the **dll** extension. For example, if you were to compile **MyClasses.cs** using this command line,

```
csc /t:library MyClasses.cs
```

then the output file would be **MyClasses.dll**. One advantage to putting code into a DLL is that no **Main( )** method is required. All **exe** files require an entry point, such as **Main( )**. This is why the **Demo** class contained a placeholder **Main( )** method. Entry points are not required by DLLs. If you try making **MyClass** into a DLL, you will need to change the call to **LoadFrom( )** as shown here:

```
Assembly asm = Assembly.LoadFrom("MyClasses.dll");
```

Fully Automating Type Discovery

Before we leave the topic of reflection, one last example will be instructive. Even though the preceding program was able to fully use **MyClass** without explicitly specifying **MyClass** in the program, it still relied upon prior knowledge of the contents of **MyClass**. For example, it knew the names of its methods, such as **set** and **sum**. However, using reflection it is possible to utilize a type about which you have no prior knowledge. To do this, you must discover all information necessary to construct an object and to generate method calls. Such an approach would be useful to a visual design tool, for example, because it could utilize the types available on the system.

To see how the full dynamic discovery of a type can be accomplished, consider the following example, which loads the **MyClasses.exe** assembly, constructs a **MyClass** object, and then calls all of the methods declared by **MyClass**, all without assuming any prior knowledge:

```
// Utilize MyClass without assuming any prior knowledge.

using System;
using System.Reflection;

class ReflectAssemblyDemo {
  public static void Main() {
    int val;
    Assembly asm = Assembly.LoadFrom("MyClasses.exe");

    Type[] alltypes = asm.GetTypes();

    Type t = alltypes[0]; // use first class found

    Console.WriteLine("Using: " + t.Name);

    ConstructorInfo[] ci = t.GetConstructors();

    // Use first constructor found.
    ParameterInfo[] cpi = ci[0].GetParameters();
    object reflectOb;

    if(cpi.Length > 0) {
      object[] consargs = new object[cpi.Length];

      // initialize args
      for(int n=0; n < cpi.Length; n++)
        consargs[n] = 10 + n * 20;

      // construct the object
      reflectOb = ci[0].Invoke(consargs);
    } else
      reflectOb = ci[0].Invoke(null);


    Console.WriteLine("\nInvoking methods on reflectOb.");
    Console.WriteLine();
```

```csharp
    // Ignore inherited methods.
    MethodInfo[] mi = t.GetMethods(BindingFlags.DeclaredOnly |
                                   BindingFlags.Instance |
                                   BindingFlags.Public) ;

    // Invoke each method.
    foreach(MethodInfo m in mi) {
      Console.WriteLine("Calling {0} ", m.Name);

      // Get the parameters.
      ParameterInfo[] pi = m.GetParameters();

      // Execute methods.
      switch(pi.Length) {
        case 0: // no args
          if(m.ReturnType == typeof(int)) {
            val = (int) m.Invoke(reflectOb, null);
            Console.WriteLine("Result is " + val);
          }
          else if(m.ReturnType == typeof(void)) {
            m.Invoke(reflectOb, null);
          }
          break;
        case 1: // one arg
          if(pi[0].ParameterType == typeof(int)) {
            object[] args = new object[1];
            args[0] = 14;
            if((bool) m.Invoke(reflectOb, args))
              Console.WriteLine("14 is between x and y");
            else
              Console.WriteLine("14 is not between x and y");
          }
          break;
        case 2: // two args
          if((pi[0].ParameterType == typeof(int)) &&
             (pi[1].ParameterType == typeof(int))) {
            object[] args = new object[2];
            args[0] = 9;
            args[1] = 18;
            m.Invoke(reflectOb, args);
          }
          else if((pi[0].ParameterType == typeof(double)) &&
```

```
                (pi[1].ParameterType == typeof(double))) {
            object[] args = new object[2];
            args[0] = 1.12;
            args[1] = 23.4;
            m.Invoke(reflectOb, args);
          }
          break;
      }
      Console.WriteLine();
    }

  }
}
```

Here is the output produced by the program:

```
Using: MyClass
Constructing MyClass(int).
Values are x: 10, y: 10

Invoking methods on reflectOb.

Calling sum
Result is 20

Calling isBetween
14 is not between x and y

Calling set
Inside set(int, int). Values are x: 9, y: 18

Calling set
Inside set(double, double). Values are x: 1, y: 23

Calling show
Values are x: 1, y: 23
```

The operation of the program is straightforward, but a couple of points are worth mentioning. First, notice that only the methods explicitly declared by **MyClass** are obtained and used. This is accomplished by using the **BindingFlags** form of **GetMethods( )**. The reason for this is to prevent calling the methods inherited from **object**. Second, notice how the number of parameters and return type of each method are obtained dynamically. A **switch** statement determines the number of parameters. Within each **case**, the parameter type(s) and return type are checked. A method call is then constructed based on this information.

Attributes

C# allows you to add declarative information to a program in the form of an *attribute*. An attribute defines additional information that is associated with a class, structure, method, and so on. For example, you might define an attribute that determines the type of button that a class will display. Attributes are specified between square brackets, preceding the item to which they apply. Thus, an attribute is not a member of a class. Rather, an attribute specifies supplemental information that is attached to an item.

Attribute Basics

An attribute is supported by a class that inherits **System.Attribute**. Thus, all attribute classes must be subclasses of **Attribute**. Although **Attribute** defines substantial functionality, this functionality is not always needed when working with attributes. By convention, attribute classes use the suffix **Attribute**. For example, **ErrorAttribute** would be a name for an attribute class that described an error.

When an attribute class is declared, it is preceded by an attribute called **AttributeUsage**. This built-in attribute specifies the types of items to which the attribute can be applied.

Creating an Attribute

In an attribute class, you will define the members that support the attribute. Often attribute classes are quite simple, containing just a small number of fields or properties. For example, an attribute might define a remark that describes the item to which the attribute is being attached. Such an attribute might look like this:

```
[AttributeUsage(AttributeTargets.All)]
public class RemarkAttribute : Attribute {
  string pri_remark; // underlies remark property

  public RemarkAttribute(string comment) {
    pri_remark = comment;
  }

  public string remark {
    get {
```

```
      return pri_remark;
    }
  }
}
```

Let's look at this class, line-by-line.

The name of this attribute is **RemarkAttribute**. Its declaration is preceded by the **AttributeUsage** attribute, which specifies that **RemarkAttribute** can be applied to all types of items. Using **AttributeUsage**, it is possible to narrow the list of items to which an attribute can be attached, and we will examine its capabilities later in this chapter.

Next, **RemarkAttribute** is declared and it inherits **Attribute**. Inside **RemarkAttribute** there is one private field, **pri_remark**, which supports one public, read-only property: **remark**. This property holds the description that will be associated with the attribute. There is one public constructor that takes a string argument and assigns it to **remark**.

At this point, no other steps are needed, and **RemarkAttribute** is ready for use.

Attaching an Attribute

Once you have defined an attribute class, you can attach the attribute to an item. An attribute precedes the item to which it is attached and is specified by enclosing its constructor inside square brackets. For example, here is how **RemarkAttribute** can be associated with a class:

```
[RemarkAttribute("This class uses an attribute.")]
class UseAttrib {
  // ...
}
```

This constructs a **RemarkAttribute** that contains the comment "This class uses an attribute." This attribute is then associated with **UseAttrib**.

When attaching an attribute, it is not actually necessary to specify the **Attribute** suffix. For example, the preceding class could be declared this way:

```
[Remark("This class uses an attribute.")]
class UseAttrib {
  // ...
}
```

Here, only the name **Remark** is used. Although the short form is correct, it is usually safer to use the full name when attaching attributes, because it avoids possible confusion and ambiguity.

Obtaining an Object's Attributes

Once an attribute has been attached to an item, other parts of the program can retrieve the attribute. To retrieve an attribute, you will usually use one of two methods. The first is **GetCustomAttributes( )**, which is defined by **MemberInfo** and inherited by **Type**. It retrieves a list of all attributes attached to an item and has this general form:

object[ ] GetCustomAttributes(bool *searchBases*)

If *searchBases* is true, then the attributes of all base classes through the inheritance chain will be included. Otherwise, only those attributes defined by the specified type will be found.

The second method is **GetCustomAttribute( )**, which is defined by **Attribute**. One of its forms is shown here:

static Attribute GetCustomAttribute(MemberInfo *mi*, Type *attribtype*)

Here, *mi* is a **MemberInfo** object that describes the item for which an attribute is being obtained. The attribute desired is specified by *attribtype*. You will use this method when you know the name of the attribute you want to obtain, which is often the case. For example, to obtain a reference to the **RemarkAttribute**, you can use this sequence:

```
// Retrieve the RemarkAttribute.
Type tRemAtt = typeof(RemarkAttribute);
RemarkAttribute ra = (RemarkAttribute)
    Attribute.GetCustomAttribute(t, tRemAtt);
```

Once you have a reference to an attribute, you can access its members. Thus, information associated with an attribute is available to a program that uses an element to which an attribute is attached. For example, the following statement displays the **remark** field:

```
Console.WriteLine(ra.remark);
```

The following program puts together all of the pieces and demonstrates the use of **RemarkAttribute**:

```
// A simple attribute example.

using System;
using System.Reflection;

[AttributeUsage(AttributeTargets.All)]
```

```csharp
public class RemarkAttribute : Attribute {
  string pri_remark; // underlies remark property

  public RemarkAttribute(string comment) {
    pri_remark = comment;
  }

  public string remark {
    get {
      return pri_remark;
    }
  }
}

[RemarkAttribute("This class uses an attribute.")]
class UseAttrib {
  // ...
}

class AttribDemo {
  public static void Main() {
    Type t = typeof(UseAttrib);

    Console.Write("Attributes in " + t.Name + ": ");

    object[] attribs = t.GetCustomAttributes(false);
    foreach(object o in attribs) {
      Console.WriteLine(o);
    }

    Console.Write("Remark: ");

    // Retrieve the RemarkAttribute.
    Type tRemAtt = typeof(RemarkAttribute);
    RemarkAttribute ra = (RemarkAttribute)
          Attribute.GetCustomAttribute(t, tRemAtt);

    Console.WriteLine(ra.remark);
  }
}
```

The output from the program is shown here:

```
Attributes in UseAttrib: RemarkAttribute
Remark: This class uses an attribute.
```

Positional vs. Named Parameters

In the preceding example, **RemarkAttribute** was initialized by passing the description string to the constructor, using the normal constructor syntax. In this case, the **comment** parameter to **RemarkAttribute( )** is called a *positional parameter*. This term relates to the fact that the argument is linked to the parameter by its position. This is the way that all methods and constructors work in C#. However, for an attribute, you can also create *named parameters*, which can be assigned initial values by using their names.

A named parameter is supported by either a public field or property, which must not be read-only. Any such field or property is automatically able to be used as a named parameter. A named parameter is given a value by an assignment statement that is located within the attribute's constructor when the attribute is specified for some item. Here is the general form of an attribute specification that includes named parameters:

[*attrib*(*positional-param-list*, *named-param1* = *value*, *named-param2* = *value*, ...)]

The positional parameters (if they exist) come first. Next, each named parameter is assigned a value. The order of the named parameters is not important. Named parameters do not need to be given a value. In this case, their default values will be used.

To understand how to use a named parameter, it is best to work through an example. Here is a version of **RemarkAttribute** that adds a field called **supplement**, which can be used to hold a supplemental remark:

```
[AttributeUsage(AttributeTargets.All)]
public class RemarkAttribute : Attribute {
  string pri_remark; // underlies remark property

  public string supplement; // this is a named parameter

  public RemarkAttribute(string comment) {
    pri_remark = comment;
    supplement = "None";
  }

  public string remark {
    get {
      return pri_remark;
    }
  }
}
```

As you can see, **supplement** is initialized to the string "None" by the constructor. There is no way of using the constructor to assign it a different initial value. However, **supplement** can be used as a named parameter, as shown here:

```
[RemarkAttribute("This class uses an attribute.",
        supplement = "This is additional info.")]
class UseAttrib {
  // ...
}
```

Pay close attention to the way **RemarkAttribute**'s constructor is called. First, the positional argument is specified as it was before. Next is a comma, followed by the named parameter, **supplement**, which is assigned a value. Finally, the closing **)** ends the call to the constructor. Thus, the named parameter is initialized within the call to the constructor. This syntax can be generalized. Positional parameters must be specified in the order in which they appear. Named parameters are specified by assigning values to their names.

Here is a program that demonstrates the **supplement** field:

```
// Use a named attribute parameter.

using System;
using System.Reflection;

[AttributeUsage(AttributeTargets.All)]
public class RemarkAttribute : Attribute {
  string pri_remark; // underlies remark property

  public string supplement; // this is a named parameter

  public RemarkAttribute(string comment) {
    pri_remark = comment;
    supplement = "None";
  }

  public string remark {
    get {
      return pri_remark;
    }
  }
}
```

```
[RemarkAttribute("This class uses an attribute.",
                 supplement = "This is additional info.")]
class UseAttrib {
  // ...
}

class NamedParamDemo {
  public static void Main() {
    Type t = typeof(UseAttrib);

    Console.Write("Attributes in " + t.Name + ": ");

    object[] attribs = t.GetCustomAttributes(false);
    foreach(object o in attribs) {
      Console.WriteLine(o);
    }

    // Retrieve the RemarkAttribute.
    Type tRemAtt = typeof(RemarkAttribute);
    RemarkAttribute ra = (RemarkAttribute)
          Attribute.GetCustomAttribute(t, tRemAtt);

    Console.Write("Remark: ");
    Console.WriteLine(ra.remark);

    Console.Write("Supplement: ");
    Console.WriteLine(ra.supplement);
  }
}
```

The output from the program is shown here:

```
Attributes in UseAttrib: RemarkAttribute
Remark: This class uses an attribute.
Supplement: This is additional info.
```

As explained, a property can also be used as a named parameter. For example, here an **int** property called **priority** is added to **RemarkAttribute**:

```
// Use a property as a named attribute parameter.

using System;
```

```
using System.Reflection;

[AttributeUsage(AttributeTargets.All)]
public class RemarkAttribute : Attribute {
  string pri_remark; // underlies remark property

  int pri_priority; // underlies priority property

  public string supplement; // this is a named parameter

  public RemarkAttribute(string comment) {
    pri_remark = comment;
    supplement = "None";
  }

  public string remark {
    get {
      return pri_remark;
    }
  }

  // Use a property as a named parameter.
  public int priority {
    get {
      return pri_priority;
    }
    set {
      pri_priority = value;
    }
  }
}

[RemarkAttribute("This class uses an attribute.",
                 supplement = "This is additional info.",
                 priority = 10)]
class UseAttrib {
  // ...
}

class NamedParamDemo {
  public static void Main() {
    Type t = typeof(UseAttrib);
```

```
    Console.Write("Attributes in " + t.Name + ": ");

    object[] attribs = t.GetCustomAttributes(false);
    foreach(object o in attribs) {
      Console.WriteLine(o);
    }

    // Retrieve the RemarkAttribute.
    Type tRemAtt = typeof(RemarkAttribute);
    RemarkAttribute ra = (RemarkAttribute)
          Attribute.GetCustomAttribute(t, tRemAtt);

    Console.Write("Remark: ");
    Console.WriteLine(ra.remark);

    Console.Write("Supplement: ");
    Console.WriteLine(ra.supplement);

    Console.WriteLine("Priority: " + ra.priority);
  }
}
```

The output is shown here:

```
Attributes in UseAttrib: RemarkAttribute
Remark: This class uses an attribute.
Supplement: This is additional info.
Priority: 10
```

There is one point of interest in the program. Notice the attribute specified before **UseAttrib** that is shown here:

```
[RemarkAttribute("This class uses an attribute.",
             supplement = "This is additional info.",
             priority = 10)]
```

The named attributes **supplement** and **priority** are *not* in any special order. These two assignments can be reversed without any change to the attribute.

Using the Built-in Attributes

C# defines three built-in attributes: **AttributeUsage**, **Conditional**, and **Obsolete**. They are examined here.

AttributeUsage

As mentioned earlier, the **AttributeUsage** attribute specifies the types of items to which an attribute can be applied. **AttributeUsage** is another name for the **System.AttributeUsageAttribute** class. **AttributeUsage** has the following constructor:

> AttributeUsage(AttributeTargets *item*)

Here, *item* specifies the item or items upon which the attribute can be used. **AttributeTargets** is an enumeration that defines the following values:

All	Assembly	Class	Constructor
Delegate	Enum	Event	Field
Interface	Method	Module	Parameter
Property	ReturnValue	Struct	

Two or more of these values can be ORed together. For example, to specify an attribute that can be applied only to fields and properties, use

```
AttributeTargets.Field | AttributeTargets.Property
```

AttributeUsage supports two named parameters. The first is **AllowMultiple**, which is a **bool** value. If this value is true, then the attribute can be applied more than one time to a single item. The second is **Inherited**, which is also a **bool** value. If this value is true, then the attribute is inherited by derived classes. Otherwise, it is not inherited. The default setting for both **AllowMultiple** and **Inherited** is false.

The Conditional Attribute

Conditional is perhaps C#'s most interesting built-in attribute. It allows you to create *conditional methods*. A conditional method is invoked only when a specific symbol has been defined via **#define**. Otherwise, the method is bypassed. Thus, a conditional method offers an alternative to conditional compilation using **#if**.

Conditional is another name for **System.Diagnostics.ConditionalAttribute**. To use the **Conditional** attribute, you must include the **System.Diagnostics** namespace.

Let's begin with an example:

```csharp
// Demonstrate the Conditional attribute.

#define TRIAL

using System;
using System.Diagnostics;

class Test {

  [Conditional("TRIAL")]
  void trial() {
    Console.WriteLine("Trial version, not for distribution.");
  }

  [Conditional("RELEASE")]
  void release() {
    Console.WriteLine("Final release version.");
  }

  public static void Main() {
    Test t = new Test();

    t.trial(); // call only if TRIAL is defined
    t.release(); // called only if RELEASE is defined
  }
}
```

The output from this program is shown here:

```
Trial version, not for distribution.
```

Let's look closely at this program to understand why this output is produced. First, notice that the program defines the symbol **TRIAL**. Next, notice how the methods **trial( )** and **release( )** are coded. They are both preceded with the **Conditional** attribute, which has this general form:

[Conditional "*symbol*"]

Where *symbol* is the symbol that determines whether the method will be executed. This attribute can be used only on methods. If the symbol is defined, then when the method is called, it will be executed. If the symbol is not defined, then the method is not executed.

Inside **Main( )**, both **trial( )** and **release( )** are called. However, only **TRIAL** is defined. Thus, **trial( )** is executed. The call to **release( )** is ignored. If you define **RELEASE**, then **release( )** will also be called. If you remove the definition for **TRIAL**, then **trial( )** will not be called.

Conditional methods have a few restrictions. They must return **void**. They must be members of a class, not an interface. They cannot be preceded with the **override** keyword.

The Obsolete Attribute

The **Obsolete** attribute, which is short for **System.ObsoleteAttribute**, lets you mark a program element as obsolete. It has this general form:

[Obsolete("*message*")]

Here, *message* is displayed when that program element is compiled. Here is a short example:

```
// Demonstrate the Obsolete attribute.

using System;

class Test {

  [Obsolete("Use myMeth2, instead.")]
  static int myMeth(int a, int b) {
    return a / b;
  }

  // Improved version of myMeth.
  static int myMeth2(int a, int b) {
    return b == 0 ? 0 : a /b;
  }

  public static void Main() {
   // warning displayed for this
    Console.WriteLine("4 / 3 is " + Test.myMeth(4, 3));

   // no warning here
    Console.WriteLine("4 / 3 is " + Test.myMeth2(4, 3));
  }
}
```

When the call to **myMeth( )** is encountered in **Main( )** when this program is compiled, a warning will be generated that tells the user to use **myMeth2( )** instead.

A second form of **Obsolete** is shown here:

[Obsolete("*message*", *error*)]

Here, *error* is a Boolean value. If it is true, then use of the obsolete item generates a compilation error rather than a warning. The difference is, of course, that a program containing an error cannot be compiled into an executable program.

The Complete Reference

C#

Chapter 18

Unsafe Code, Pointers, and Miscellaneous Topics

589

This chapter covers a feature of C# whose name usually takes programmers by surprise: unsafe code. Unsafe code often involves the use of pointers. Together, unsafe code and pointers enable C# to be used to create applications that you might normally associate with C++: high-performance, systems code. Moreover, the inclusion of unsafe code and pointers gives C# capabilities that are lacking in Java.

This chapter concludes by discussing the few keywords that have not been covered by the preceding chapters.

Unsafe Code

C# allows you to write what is called "unsafe" code. While this statement might seem shocking, it really isn't. Unsafe code is not code that is poorly written; it is code that does not execute under the full management of the Common Language Runtime (CLR). As explained in Chapter 1, C# is normally used to create managed code. It is possible, however, to write code that does not execute under the full control of the CLR. This unmanaged code is not subject to the same controls and constraints as managed code, so it is called "unsafe" because it is not possible to verify that it won't perform some type of harmful action. Thus, the term *unsafe* does not mean that the code is inherently flawed. It just means that it is possible for the code to perform actions that are not subject to the supervision of the managed context.

Given that unsafe code might cause problems, you might ask why anyone would want to create such code. The answer is that managed code prevents the use of *pointers*. If you are familiar with C or C++, then you know that pointers are variables that hold the addresses of other objects. Thus, pointers are a bit like references in C#. The main difference is that a pointer can point anywhere in memory; a reference always points to an object of its type. Since a pointer can point anywhere in memory, it is possible to misuse a pointer. It is also easy to introduce a coding error when using pointers. This is why C# does not support pointers when creating managed code. Pointers are, however, both useful and necessary for some types of programming (such as system-level utilities), and C# does allow you to create and use pointers. All pointer operations must be marked as unsafe, since they execute outside the managed context.

The declaration and use of pointers in C# parallels that of C/C++—if you know how to use pointers in C/C++, then you can use them in C#. But remember, the point of C# is the creation of managed code. Its ability to support unmanaged code allows it to be applied to a special class of problems. It is not for normal C# programming. In fact, to compile unmanaged code, you must use the **/unsafe** compiler option.

Since pointers are at the core of unsafe code, we will begin there.

Pointer Basics

Pointers are variables that hold the addresses of other variables. For example, if **x** contains the address of **y**, then **x** is said to "point to" **y**. Once a pointer points to a variable, the value of that variable can be obtained or changed through the pointer. Operations through pointers are often referred to as *indirection.*

Declaring a Pointer

Pointer variables must be declared as such. The general form of a pointer variable declaration is

type* var-name;

Here, *type* is the pointer's base type, which must be a nonreference type. Thus, you cannot declare a pointer to a class object. A pointer's base type is also referred to as its *referent type.* Notice the placement of the *. It follows the type name. *var-name* is the name of the pointer variable.

Here is an example. To declare **ip** to be a pointer to an **int**, use this declaration:

```
int* ip;
```

For a **float** pointer, use

```
float* fp;
```

In general, in a declaration statement, following a type name with an * creates a pointer type.

The type of data that a pointer will point to is determined by its base type. Thus, in the preceding examples, **ip** can be used to point to an **int**, and **fp** can be used to point to a **float**. Understand, however, that there is nothing that actually prevents a pointer from pointing elsewhere. This is why pointers are potentially unsafe.

If you come from a C/C++ background, then you need to be aware of an important difference between the way C# and C/C++ declare pointers. When you declare a pointer type in C/C++, the * is not distributive over a list of variables in a declaration. Thus, in C/C++, this statement

```
int* p, q;
```

declares an **int** pointer called **p** and an **int** called **q**. It is equivalent to the following two declarations:

```
int* p;
int q;
```

However, in C#, the * *is* distributive and the declaration

```
int* p, q;
```

creates two pointer variables. Thus, in C# it is the same as these two declarations:

```
int* p;
int* q;
```

This is an important difference to keep in mind when porting C/C++ code to C#.

The * and & Pointer Operators

Two operators are used with pointers: * and &. The & is a unary operator that returns the memory address of its operand. (Recall that a unary operator requires only one operand.) For example,

```
int* ip;
int num = 10;

ip = &num;
```

puts into **ip** the memory address of the variable **num**. This address is the location of the variable in the computer's internal memory. It has *nothing* to do with the *value* of **num**. Thus, **ip** *does not* contain the value 10 (**num**'s initial value). It contains the address at which **num** is stored. The operation of & can be remembered as returning "the address of" the variable it precedes. Therefore, the preceding assignment statement could be verbalized as "**ip** receives the address of **num**."

The second operator is *, and it is the complement of &. It is a unary operator that refers to the value of the variable located at the address specified by its operand. That is, it refers to the value of the variable pointed to by a pointer. Continuing with the same example, if **ip** contains the memory address of the variable **num**, then

```
int val = *ip;
```

will place into **val** the value 10, which is the value of **num**, which is pointed to by **ip**. The operation of * can be remembered as "at address." In this case, then, the statement could be read as "**val** receives the value at address **ip**."

The * can also be used on the left side of an assignment statement. In this usage, it sets the value pointed to by the pointer. For example:

```
*ip = 100;
```

This statement assigns 100 to the variable pointed to by **ip**, which is **num** in this case. Thus, this statement can be read as "at address **ip**, put the value 100."

Using unsafe

Any code that uses pointers must be marked as unsafe by using the **unsafe** keyword. You can mark an individual statement or an entire method **unsafe**. For example, here is a program that uses pointers inside **Main( )**, which is marked unsafe:

```
// Demonstrate pointers and unsafe.

using System;

class UnsafeCode {
  // mark Main as unsafe
  unsafe public static void Main() {
    int count = 99;
    int* p; // create an int pointer

    p = &count; // put address of count into p

    Console.WriteLine("Initial value of count is " + *p);

    *p = 10; // assign 10 to count via p

    Console.WriteLine("New value of count is " + *p);
  }
}
```

The output of this program is shown here:

```
Initial value of count is 99
New value of count is 10
```

Using fixed

The **fixed** modifier is often used when working with pointers. It prevents a managed variable from being moved by the garbage collector. This is needed when a pointer refers to a field in a class object, for example. Since the pointer has no knowledge of the actions of the garbage collector, if the object is moved, the pointer will point to the wrong object. Here is the general form of **fixed**:

```
fixed (type* p = &var) {
  // use fixed object
}
```

Here, *p* is a pointer that is being assigned the address of a variable. The object will remain at its current memory location until the block of code has executed. You can also use a single statement for the target of a **fixed** statement. The **fixed** keyword can be used only in an unsafe context. You can declare more than one fixed pointer at a time using a comma-separated list.

Here is an example of **fixed**:

```
// Demonstrate fixed.

using System;

class Test {
  public int num;
  public Test(int i) { num = i; }
}

class FixedCode {
  // mark Main as unsafe
  unsafe public static void Main() {
    Test o = new Test(19);

    fixed (int* p = &o.num) { // use fixed to put address of o.num into p

      Console.WriteLine("Initial value of o.num is " + *p);

      *p = 10; // assign to count via p

      Console.WriteLine("New value of o.num is " + *p);
    }
  }
}
```

The output from this program is shown here:

```
Initial value of o.num is 19
New value of o.num is 10
```

Here, **fixed** prevents **o** from being moved. Because **p** points to **o.num**, if **o** were moved, then **p** would point to an invalid location.

Accessing Structure Members Through a Pointer

A pointer can point to an object of a structure type as long as the structure does not contain reference types. When you access a member of a structure through a pointer, you must use the arrow operator, which is –>, rather than the dot (.) operator. For example, given this structure,

```
struct MyStruct {
  public int x;
  public int y;
  public int sum() { return x + y; }
}
```

here is how you would access its members through a pointer:

```
MyStruct o = new MyStruct();
MyStruct* p; // declare a pointer

p = &o;
p->x = 10;
p->y = 20;

Console.WriteLine("Sum is " + p->sum());
```

Pointer Arithmetic

There are only four arithmetic operators that can be used on pointers: ++, – –, +, and –. To understand what occurs in pointer arithmetic, we will begin with an example. Let **p1** be an **int** pointer with a current value of 2,000 (that is, it contains the address 2,000). After this expression,

```
p1++;
```

the contents of **p1** will be 2,004, not 2,001! The reason is that each time **p1** is incremented, it will point to the *next* **int**. Since **int** in C# is 4 bytes long, incrementing **p1** increases its value by 4. The reverse is true of decrements. Each decrement decreases **p1**'s value by 4. For example,

```
p1--;
```

will cause **p1** to have the value 1,996, assuming that it previously was 2,000.

Generalizing from the preceding example, each time that a pointer is incremented, it will point to the memory location of the next element of its base type. Each time it is decremented, it will point to the location of the previous element of its base type.

Pointer arithmetic is not limited to only increment and decrement operations. You can also add or subtract integers to or from pointers. The expression

```
p1 = p1 + 9;
```

makes **p1** point to the ninth element of **p1**'s base type, beyond the one it is currently pointing to.

Although you cannot add pointers, you can subtract one pointer from another (provided they are both of the same base type). The remainder will be the number of elements of the base type that separate the two pointers.

Other than addition and subtraction of a pointer and an integer, or the subtraction of two pointers, no other arithmetic operations can be performed on pointers. For example, you cannot add or subtract **float** or **double** values to or from pointers.

To see the effects of pointer arithmetic, execute the next short program. It prints the actual physical addresses to which an integer pointer (**ip**) and a floating-point pointer (**fp**) are pointing. Observe how each changes, relative to its base type, each time the loop is repeated.

```csharp
// Demonstrate the effects of pointer arithmethic.

using System;

class PtrArithDemo {
  unsafe public static void Main() {
    int x;
    int i;
    double d;

    int* ip = &i;
    double* fp = &d;

    Console.WriteLine("int      double\n");

    for(x=0; x < 10; x++) {
      Console.WriteLine((uint) (ip) + " " +
                        (uint) (fp));
      ip++;
      fp++;
    }
  }
}
```

Sample output is shown here. Your output may differ, but the intervals will be the same.

```
int      double

1243464 1243468
1243468 1243476
1243472 1243484
1243476 1243492
1243480 1243500
1243484 1243508
1243488 1243516
1243492 1243524
1243496 1243532
1243500 1243540
```

As the output shows, pointer arithmetic is performed relative to the base type of the pointer. Since an **int** is 4 bytes and a **double** is 8 bytes, the addresses change in multiples of these values.

Pointer Comparisons

Pointers can be compared using the relational operators, such as = =, <, and >. However, for the outcome of a pointer comparison to be meaningful, usually the two pointers must have some relationship to each other. For example, if **p1** and **p2** are pointers that point to two separate and unrelated variables, then any comparison between **p1** and **p2** is generally meaningless. However, if **p1** and **p2** point to variables that are related to each other, such as elements of the same array, then **p1** and **p2** can be meaningfully compared.

Here is an example that uses pointer comparison to find the middle element of an array:

```
// Demonstrate pointer comparison.

using System;

class PtrCompDemo {
  unsafe public static void Main() {

    int[] nums = new int[11];
    int x;
```

```
    // find the middle
    fixed (int* start = &nums[0]) {
      fixed(int* end = &nums[nums.Length-1]) {
        for(x=0; start+x <= end-x; x++) ;
      }
    }
    Console.WriteLine("Middle element is " + x);
  }
}
```

Here is the output:

```
Middle element is 6
```

This program finds the middle element by initially setting **start** to the first element of the array and **end** to the last element of the array. Then, using pointer arithmetic, the **start** pointer is increased and the **end** pointer is decreased until **start** is less than or equal to **end**.

One other point: The pointers **start** and **end** must be created within a **fixed** statement because they point to elements of an array, which is a reference type. Recall that in C#, arrays are implemented as objects and might be moved by the garbage collector.

Pointers and Arrays

In C#, pointers and arrays are related. For example, the name of an array without any index generates a pointer to the start of the array. Consider the following program:

```
/* An array name without an index yields a pointer to the
   start of the array. */

using System;

class PtrArray {
  unsafe public static void Main() {
    int[] nums = new int[10];

    fixed(int* p = &nums[0], p2 = nums) {
      if(p == p2)
        Console.WriteLine("p and p2 point to same address.");
    }
  }
}
```

The output is shown here:

```
p and p2 point to same address.
```

As the output shows, the expression

```
&nums[0]
```

is the same as

```
nums
```

Since the second form is shorter, most programmers use it when a pointer to the start of an array is needed.

Indexing a Pointer

When a pointer refers to an array, the pointer can be indexed as if it were an array. This syntax provides an alternative to pointer arithmetic that can be more convenient in some situations. Here is an example:

```
// Index a pointer as if it were an array.

using System;

class PtrIndexDemo {
  unsafe public static void Main() {
    int[] nums = new int[10];

    // index pointer
    Console.WriteLine("Index pointer like array.");
    fixed (int* p = nums) {
      for(int i=0; i < 10; i++)
        p[i] = i; // index pointer like array

      for(int i=0; i < 10; i++)
        Console.WriteLine("p[{0}]: {1} ", i, p[i]);
    }

    // use pointer arithmetic
    Console.WriteLine("\nUse pointer arithmetic.");
    fixed (int* p = nums) {
```

```
      for(int i=0; i < 10; i++)
        *(p+i) = i; // use pointer arithmetic

      for(int i=0; i < 10; i++)
        Console.WriteLine("*(p+{0}): {1} ", i, *(p+i));
    }
  }
}
```

The output is shown here:

```
Index pointer like array.
p[0]: 0
p[1]: 1
p[2]: 2
p[3]: 3
p[4]: 4
p[5]: 5
p[6]: 6
p[7]: 7
p[8]: 8
p[9]: 9

Use pointer arithmetic.
*(p+0): 0
*(p+1): 1
*(p+2): 2
*(p+3): 3
*(p+4): 4
*(p+5): 5
*(p+6): 6
*(p+7): 7
*(p+8): 8
*(p+9): 9
```

As the program illustrates, a pointer expression with this general form

*(ptr + i)

can be rewritten using array-indexing syntax like this:

ptr[i]

There are two important points to understand about indexing a pointer: First, no boundary checking is applied. Thus, it is possible to access an element beyond the end of the array to which the pointer refers. Second, a pointer does not have a **Length** property. So, using the pointer, there is no way of knowing how long the array is.

Pointers and Strings

Although strings are implemented as objects in C#, it is possible to access the characters in a string through a pointer. To do so, you will assign a pointer to the start of the string to a **char*** pointer using a **fixed** statement like this:

fixed(char* *p = str*) { // ...

After the **fixed** statement executes, **p** will point to the start of the array of characters that make up the string. This array is *null-terminated*, which means that it ends with a 0. You can use this fact to test for the end of the array. Null-terminated character arrays are the way that strings are implemented in C/C++. Thus, obtaining a **char*** pointer to a **string** allows you to operate on strings in much the same way that you do in C/C++.

Here is a program that demonstrates accessing a string through a **char*** pointer:

```
// Use fixed to get a pointer to the start of a string.

using System;

class FixedString {
  unsafe public static void Main() {
    string str = "this is a test";

    // Point p to start of str.
    fixed(char* p = str) {

      // Display the contents of str via p.
      for(int i=0; p[i] != 0; i++)
        Console.Write(p[i]);
    }

    Console.WriteLine();

  }
}
```

The output is shown here:

```
this is a test
```

Multiple Indirection

You can have a pointer point to another pointer that points to the target value. This situation is called *multiple indirection,* or *pointers to pointers.* Pointers to pointers can be confusing. Figure 18-1 helps clarify the concept of multiple indirection. As you can see, the value of a normal pointer is the address of the variable that contains the value desired. In the case of a pointer to a pointer, the first pointer contains the address of the second pointer, which points to the variable that contains the value desired.

Multiple indirection can be carried on to whatever extent desired, but more than a pointer to a pointer is rarely needed. In fact, excessive indirection is difficult to follow and prone to conceptual errors.

A variable that is a pointer to a pointer must be declared as such. You do this by placing an additional * after the type name. For example, the following declaration tells the compiler that **q** is a pointer to a pointer of type **int**:

```
int** q;
```

You should understand that **q** is not a pointer to an integer, but rather a pointer to an **int** pointer.

To access the target value indirectly pointed to by a pointer to a pointer, you must apply the * operator twice, as in this example:

```
using System;

class MultipleIndirect {
  unsafe public static void Main() {
    int x;     // holds an int value
    int* p;   // holds an int pointer
    int** q; // holds a pointer to an int pointer

    x = 10;
    p = &x; // put address of x into p
    q = &p; // put address of p into q

    Console.WriteLine(**q); // display the value of x
  }
}
```

The output is the value of **x**, which is 10. In the program, **p** is declared as a pointer to an **int** and **q** as a pointer to an **int** pointer.

One last point: Do not confuse multiple indirection with high-level data structures, such as linked lists, that use pointers. These are two fundamentally different concepts.

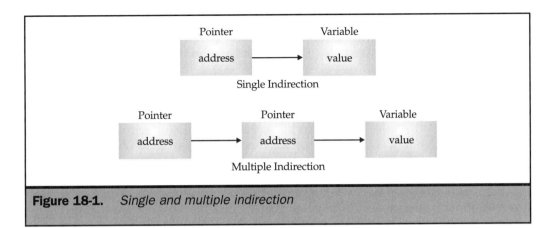

Figure 18-1.   *Single and multiple indirection*

Arrays of Pointers

Pointers can be arrayed like any other data type. The declaration for an **int** pointer array of size 3 is

```
int * [] ptrs = new int * [3];
```

To assign the address of an **int** variable called **var** to the third element of the pointer array, write

```
ptrs[2] = &var;
```

To find the value of **var**, write

```
*ptrs[2]
```

Miscellaneous Keywords

To conclude Part I, the few remaining keywords defined by C# that have not been described elsewhere are briefly discussed.

sizeof

Occasionally you might find it useful to know the size, in bytes, of one of C#'s value types. To obtain this information, use the **sizeof** operator. It has this general form:

sizeof(*type*)

THE C# LANGUAGE

Here, *type* is the type whose size is being obtained. The **sizeof** operator can be used only in an unsafe context. Thus, it is intended primarily for special-case situations, especially when working with a blend of managed and unmanaged code.

lock

The **lock** keyword is used when working with *multiple threads*. In C#, a program can contain two or more *threads of execution*. When this is the case, pieces of the program are multitasked. Thus, pieces of the program execute independently, and conceptually speaking, simultaneously. This raises the prospect of a special type of problem: What if two threads try to use a resource that can be used by only one thread at a time? To solve this problem, you can create a *critical code section* that will be executed by one and only one thread at a time. This is accomplished by **lock**. Its general form is shown here:

```
lock(obj) {
  // critical section
}
```

Here, *obj* is an object that seeks to obtain the lock. If one thread has already entered the critical section, then a second thread will wait until the first thread executes. When the lock is granted, the critical section can be executed. (See Chapter 21 for additional details.)

readonly

You can create a read-only field in a class by declaring it as **readonly**. A **readonly** field can be initialized, but not changed after that. Thus, **readonly** fields are a good way to create constants , such as array dimensions, that are used throughout a program. Both static and nonstatic **readonly** fields are allowed.

Here is an example that creates a **readonly** field:

```
// Demonstrate readonly.

using System;

class MyClass {
  public static readonly int SIZE = 10;
}

class DemoReadOnly {
  public static void Main() {
    int[]nums = new int[MyClass.SIZE];

    for(int i=0; i<MyClass.SIZE; i++)
      nums[i] = i;
```

```
    foreach(int i in nums)
      Console.Write(i + " ");

    // MyClass.SIZE = 100; // Error!!! can't change
  }
}
```

Here, **MyClass.SIZE** is initialized to 10. After that, it can be used, but not changed. To prove this, try removing the comments from before the last line and then compiling the program. As you will see, an error will result.

stackalloc

You can allocate memory from the stack by using **stackalloc**. It can be used only when initializing local variables and has this general form:

type *p* = stackalloc *type*[*size*]

Here, *p* is a pointer that receives the address of the memory that is large enough to hold *size* number of objects of *type*. **stackalloc** must be used in an unsafe context.

Normally, memory for objects is allocated from the *heap,* which is a region of free memory. Allocating memory from the stack is the exception. Variables allocated on the stack are not garbage-collected. Rather, they exist only while the block in which they are declared is executing. When the block is left, the memory is freed. One advantage to using **stackalloc** is that you don't need to worry about the memory being moved about by the garbage collector.

Here is an example that uses **stackalloc**:

```
// Demonstrate stackalloc.

using System;

class UseStackAlloc {
  unsafe public static void Main() {
    int* ptrs = stackalloc int[3];

    ptrs[0] = 1;
    ptrs[1] = 2;
    ptrs[2] = 3;

    for(int i=0; i < 3; i++)
      Console.WriteLine(ptrs[i]);
  }
}
```

The output is shown here:

```
1
2
3
```

The using Statement

In addition to the **using** *directive* discussed earlier, **using** has a second form that is called the **using** *statement*. It has these general forms:

using (*obj*) {
  // use *obj*
}

using (*type obj = initializer*) {
  // use *obj*
}

Here, *obj* is an object that is being used inside the **using** block. In the first form, the object is declared outside the **using** statement. In the second form, the object is declared within the **using** statement. When the block concludes, the **Dispose( )** method (defined by the **System.IDisposable** interface) will be called on *obj*. The **using** statement applies only to objects that implement the **System.IDisposable** interface.

Here is an example of each form of the **using** statement:

```
// Demonstrate using statement.

using System;
using System.IO;

class UsingDemo {
  public static void Main() {
    StreamReader sr = new StreamReader("test.txt");

    // Use object inside using statement.
    using(sr) {
      Console.WriteLine(sr.ReadLine());
      sr.Close();
    }
```

```
    // Create StreamReader inside the using statement.
    using(StreamReader sr2 = new StreamReader("test.txt")) {
      Console.WriteLine(sr2.ReadLine());
      sr2.Close();
    }
  }
}
```

The class **StreamReader** implements the **IDisposable** interface (through its base class **TextReader**). Thus, it can be used in a **using** statement. (See Chapter 24 for a discussion of **IDisposable**.)

const and volatile

The **const** modifier is used to declare fields or local variables that cannot be changed. These variables must be given initial values when they are declared. Thus, a **const** variable is essentially a constant. For example,

```
const int i = 10;
```

creates a **const** variable called **i** that has the value 10.

The **volatile** modifier tells the compiler that a field's value may be changed in ways not explicitly specified by the program. For example, a field that holds the current system time might be updated automatically by the operating system. In this situation, the contents of the field are altered without any explicit assignment statement. The reason the external alteration of a field may be important is that the C# compiler is permitted to optimize certain expressions automatically, on the assumption that the content of a field is unchanged if it does not occur on the left side of an assignment statement. However, if factors outside the immediate code, such as a second thread of execution, change the value of the field, this assumption is wrong. By using **volatile**, you are telling the compiler that it must obtain the value of this field each time it is accessed.

The
Complete
Reference

Part II

Exploring the C# Library

Part II explores the C# library. As explained in Part I, the class library used by C# is the .NET Framework library. Thus, the material in this section applies not only to C# but to the .NET Framework as a whole.

The C# library is organized into namespaces. To use a portion of the library, you will normally import its namespace by including a **using** directive. Of course, you can also fully qualify the name of the item with its namespace name, but most often it is simply easier to import the entire namespace.

The C# library is large, and it is beyond the scope of this book to examine each part of it. (A complete description would easily fill an entire book!) Instead, Part II examines the core elements of the library, many of which are contained in the **System** namespace. Also discussed are the collection classes, multithreading, and networking.

The I/O classes are discussed in Chapter 14.

Chapter 19

Exploring the System Namespace

This chapter explores the **System** namespace. **System** is the top-level namespace of the C# library. It directly contains those classes, structures, interfaces, delegates, and enumerations that are most commonly used by a C# program or that are deemed otherwise integral to the .NET Framework. Thus, **System** defines the core of the C# library.

System also contains many nested namespaces that support specific subsystems, such as **System.Net**. Several of these subsystems are described later in this book. This chapter is concerned only with the members of **System**, itself.

The Members of System

In addition to a large number of exception classes, **System** contains the following classes:

Activator	AppDomain	AppDomainSetup
Array	AssemblyLoadEventArgs	Attribute
AttributeUsageAttribute	BitConverter	Buffer
CharEnumerator	CLSCompliantAttribute	Console
ContextBoundObject	ContextStaticAttribute	Convert
DBNull	Delegate	Enum
Environment	EventArgs	Exception
FlagsAttribute	GC	LoaderOptimizationAttribute
LocalDataStoreSlot	MarshalByRefObject	Math
MTAThreadAttribute	MulticastDelegate	NonSerializedAttribute
Object	ObsoleteAttribute	OperatingSystem
ParamArrayAttribute	Random	ResolveEventArgs
SerializableAttribute	STAThreadAttribute	String
ThreadStaticAttribute	TimeZone	Type
UnhandledExceptionEventArgs	Uri	UriBuilder
ValueType	Version	WeakReference

System defines the following structures:

ArgIterator	Boolean	Byte
Char	DateTime	Decimal
Double	Guid	Int16
Int32	Int64	IntPtr
RuntimeArgumentHandle	RuntimeFieldHandle	RuntimeMethodHandle
RuntimeTypeHandle	SByte	Single
TimeSpan	TypedReference	UInt16
UInt32	UInt64	UIntPtr
Void		

System defines the following interfaces:

IAppDomainSetup	IAsyncResult	ICloneable
IComparable	IConvertible	ICustomFormatter
IDisposable	IFormatProvider	IFormattable
IServiceProvider		

System defines the following delegates:

AssemblyLoadEventHandler	AsyncCallback	CrossAppDomainDelegate
EventHandler	ResolveEventHandler	UnhandledExceptionEventHandler

System defines these enumerations:

AttributeTargets	DayOfWeek	Environment.SpecialFolder
LoaderOptimization	PlatformID	TypeCode
UriHostNameType	UriPartial	

As the preceding tables show, **System** is quite large. It is not possible to examine all of its constituents in detail in a single chapter. Furthermore, some of the members of **System** apply to the .NET Framework, in general, but are not typically used by the C# programmer. Also, several of **System**'s classes, such as **Type**, **Exception**, and **Attribute**, have been discussed in Part I or elsewhere in this book. Finally, because **System.String**, which defines the C# **string** type, is such a large and important topic, it is covered in Chapter 20 along with formatting. For these reasons, this chapter explores only those members that are most commonly used by C# programmers and that are not covered elsewhere.

The Math Class

Math defines several standard mathematical operations, such as square root, sine, cosine, and logarithms. The methods defined by **Math** are shown in Table 19-1. All angles are in radians. Notice that all of the methods defined by **Math** are **static**. Thus, there is no need to construct a **Math** object, and no public **Math** constructors are provided.

Math also defines these two fields:

    public const double E
    public const double PI

E is the value of the natural logarithm base, commonly referred to as *e*. **PI** is the value of pi.

The **Math** class is **sealed**, which means that it cannot be inherited.

Method	Meaning
public static double Abs(double *v*)	Returns the absolute value of *v*.
public static float Abs(float *v*)	Returns the absolute value of *v*.
public static decimal Abs(decimal *v*)	Returns the absolute value of *v*.
public static int Abs(int *v*)	Returns the absolute value of *v*.
public static short Abs(short *v*)	Returns the absolute value of *v*.
public static long Abs(long *v*)	Returns the absolute value of *v*.
public static sbyte Abs(sbyte *v*)	Returns the absolute value of *v*.
public static double Acos(double *v*)	Returns the arc cosine of *v*. The value of *v* must be between –1 and 1.
public static double Asin(double *v*)	Returns the arc sine of *v*. The value of *v* must be between –1 and 1.
public static double Atan(double *v*)	Returns the arc tangent of *v*.
public static double Atan2(double *y*, double *x*)	Returns the arc tangent of y/x.
public static double Ceiling(double *v*)	Returns the smallest integer (represented as a floating-point value) not less than *v*. For example, given 1.02, **Ceiling( )** returns 2.0. Given –1.02, **Ceiling( )** returns –1.
public static double Cos(double *v*)	Returns the cosine of *v*.
public static double Cosh(double *v*)	Returns the hyperbolic cosine of *v*.
public static double Exp(double *v*)	Returns the natural logarithm base *e* raised to the *v* power.
public static double Floor(double *v*)	Returns the largest integer (represented as a floating-point value) not greater than *v*. For example, given 1.02, **Floor( )** returns 1.0. Given –1.02, **Floor( )** returns –2.
public static double IEEERemainder(double *dividend*, double *divisor*)	Returns the remainder of *dividend* / *divisor*.
public static double Log(double *v*)	Returns the natural logarithm for *v*.
public static double Log(double *v*, double *base*)	Returns the logarithm for *v* using base *base*.

Table 19-1.   *The Methods Defined by* **Math**

THE C# CLASS LIBRARY

Method	Meaning
public static double Log10(double *v*)	Returns the base 10 logarithm for *v*.
public static double Max(double *v1*, double *v2*)	Returns the greater of *v1* and *v2*.
public static float Max(float *v1*, float *v2*)	Returns the greater of *v1* and *v2*.
public static decimal Max(decimal *v1*, decimal *v2*)	Returns the greater of *v1* and *v2*.
public static int Max(int *v1*, int *v2*)	Returns the greater of *v1* and *v2*.
public static short Max(short *v1*, short *v2*)	Returns the greater of *v1* and *v2*.
public static long Max(long *v1*, long *v2*)	Returns the greater of *v1* and *v2*.
public static uint Max(uint *v1*, uint *v2*)	Returns the greater of *v1* and *v2*.
public static ushort Max(ushort *v1*, ushort *v2*)	Returns the greater of *v1* and *v2*.
public static ulong Max(ulong *v1*, ulong *v2*)	Returns the greater of *v1* and *v2*.
public static byte Max(byte *v1*, byte *v2*)	Returns the greater of *v1* and *v2*.
public static sbyte Max(sbyte *v1*, sbyte *v2*)	Returns the greater of *v1* and *v2*.
public static double Min(double *v1*, double *v2*)	Returns the lesser of *v1* and *v2*.
public static float Min(float *v1*, float *v2*)	Returns the lesser of *v1* and *v2*.
public static decimal Min(decimal *v1*, decimal *v2*)	Returns the lesser of *v1* and *v2*.
public static int Min(int *v1*, int *v2*)	Returns the lesser of *v1* and *v2*.
public static short Min(short *v1*, short *v2*)	Returns the lesser of *v1* and *v2*.
public static long Min(long *v1*, long *v2*)	Returns the lesser of *v1* and *v2*.
public static uint Min(uint *v1*, uint *v2*)	Returns the lesser of *v1* and *v2*.
public static ushort Min(ushort *v1*, ushort *v2*)	Returns the lesser of *v1* and *v2*.
public static ulong Min(ulong *v1*, ulong *v2*)	Returns the lesser of *v1* and *v2*.
public static byte Min(byte *v1*, byte *v2*)	Returns the lesser of *v1* and *v2*.
public static sbyte Min(sbyte *v1*, sbyte *v2*)	Returns the lesser of *v1* and *v2*.
public static double Pow(double *base*, double *exp*)	Returns *base* raised to the *exp* power($base^{exp}$).

Table 19-1. *The Methods Defined by* **Math** (continued)

Method	Meaning
public static double Round(double *v*)	Returns *v* rounded to the nearest whole number.
public static decimal Round(decimal *v*)	Returns *v* rounded to the nearest whole number.
public static double Round(double *v*, int *frac*)	Returns *v* rounded to the number of fractional digits specified by *frac*.
public static decimal Round(decimal *v*, int *frac*)	Returns *v* rounded to the number of fractional digits specified by *frac*.
public static int Sign(double *v*)	Returns –1 if *v* is less than zero, 0 if *v* is zero, and 1 if *v* is greater than zero.
public static int Sign(float *v*)	Returns –1 if *v* is less than zero, 0 if *v* is zero, and 1 if *v* is greater than zero.
public static int Sign(decimal *v*)	Returns –1 if *v* is less than zero, 0 if *v* is zero, and 1 if *v* is greater than zero.
public static int Sign(int *v*)	Returns –1 if *v* is less than zero, 0 if *v* is zero, and 1 if *v* is greater than zero.
public static int Sign(short *v*)	Returns –1 if *v* is less than zero, 0 if *v* is zero, and 1 if *v* is greater than zero.
public static int Sign(long *v*)	Returns –1 if *v* is less than zero, 0 if *v* is zero, and 1 if *v* is greater than zero.
public static int Sign(sbyte *v*)	Returns –1 if *v* is less than zero, 0 if *v* is zero, and 1 if *v* is greater than zero.
public static double Sin(double *v*)	Returns the sine of *v*.
public static double Sinh(double *v*)	Returns the hyperbolic sine of *v*.
public static double Sqrt(double *v*)	Returns the square root of *v*.
public static double Tan(double *v*)	Returns the tangent of *v*.
public static double Tanh(double *v*)	Returns the hyperbolic tangent of *v*.

Table 19-1. *The Methods Defined by* **Math** (continued)

Here is an example that uses **Sqrt( )** to help implement the Pythagorean theorem. It computes the length of the hypotenuse given the lengths of the two opposing sides of a right triangle.

```
// Implement the Pythagorean Theorem.

using System;
```

```
class Pythagorean {
  public static void Main() {
    double s1;
    double s2;
    double hypot;
    string str;

    Console.WriteLine("Enter length of first side: ");
    str = Console.ReadLine();
    s1 = Double.Parse(str);

    Console.WriteLine("Enter length of second side: ");
    str = Console.ReadLine();
    s2 = Double.Parse(str);

    hypot = Math.Sqrt(s1*s1 + s2*s2);

    Console.WriteLine("Hypotenuse is " + hypot);
  }
}
```

Here is a sample run:

```
Enter length of first side: 3
Enter length of second side: 4
Hypotenuse is 5
```

Next is an example that uses the **Pow( )** method to compute the initial investment required to achieve a desired future value given the annual rate of return and the number of years. The formula to compute the initial investment is shown here:

$$\text{InitialInvestment} = \text{FutureValue} / (1 + \text{InterestRate})^{\text{Years}}$$

Because **Pow( )** requires **double** arguments, the interest rate and the number of years are held in a **double** value. The future value and initial investment use the **decimal** type.

```
/* Compute the initial investment needed to attain
   a known future value given annual rate of return
   and the time period in years. */

using System;
```

```csharp
class InitialInvestment {
  public static void Main() {
    decimal InitInvest; // initial investment
    decimal FutVal;     // future value

    double NumYears;    // number of years
    double IntRate;     // annual rate of return as a decimal

    string str;

    Console.Write("Enter future value: ");
    str = Console.ReadLine();
    try {
      FutVal = Decimal.Parse(str);
    } catch(FormatException exc) {
      Console.WriteLine(exc.Message);
      return;
    }

    Console.Write("Enter interest rate (such as 0.085): ");
    str = Console.ReadLine();
    try {
      IntRate = Double.Parse(str);
    } catch(FormatException exc) {
      Console.WriteLine(exc.Message);
      return;
    }

    Console.Write("Enter number of years: ");
    str = Console.ReadLine();
    try {
      NumYears = Double.Parse(str);
    } catch(FormatException exc) {
      Console.WriteLine(exc.Message);
      return;
    }

    InitInvest = FutVal / (decimal) Math.Pow(IntRate+1.0, NumYears);


    Console.WriteLine("Initial investment required: {0:C}",
                      InitInvest);
  }
}
```

Here is a sample run:

```
Enter future value: 10000
Enter interest rate (such as 0.085): 0.07
Enter number of years: 10
Initial investment required: $5,083.49
```

The Value-Type Structures

The value-type structures were introduced in Chapter 14 when they were used to convert strings holding human-readable numeric values into their equivalent binary values. Here they are examined in detail.

The value-type structures underlie the C# value types. By using the members defined by these structures, you can perform operations relating to the value types. The .NET structure names and their C# keyword equivalents are shown here:

.NET Structure Name	C# Name
Boolean	bool
Char	char
Decimal	decimal
Double	double
Single	float
Int16	short
Int32	int
Int64	long
UInt16	ushort
UInt32	uint
UInt64	ulong
Byte	byte
SByte	sbyte

The following sections examine each of these structures.

Note   *Some methods defined by the value-type structures take a parameter of type* **IFormatProvider** *or* **NumberStyles**. **IFormatProvider** *is briefly described later in this chapter.* **NumberStyles** *is an enumeration found in the* **System.Globalization** *namespace. The topic of formatting is discussed in Chapter 20.*

The Integer Structures

The integer structures are

Byte	SByte	Int16	UInt16
Int32	UInt32	Int64	UInt64

Each of these structures contains the same methods. They are shown in Table 19-2. The only difference from structure to structure is the return type of **Parse( )**. For each structure, **Parse( )** returns a value of the type represented by the structure. For example, for **Int32**, **Parse( )** returns an **int** value. For **UInt16**, **Parse( )** returns a **ushort** value. For an example that demonstrates **Parse( )**, see Chapter 14.

In addition to the methods shown in Table 19-2, the integer structures also define the following **const** fields:

MaxValue
MinValue

For each structure, these fields contain the largest and smallest value that that type of integer can hold.

All of the integer structures implement the following interfaces: **IComparable**, **IConvertible**, and **IFormattable**.

Method	Meaning
public int CompareTo(object *v*)	Compares the numerical value of the invoking object with that of *v*. Returns zero if the values are equal. Returns a negative value if the invoking object has a lower value. Returns a positive value if the invoking object has a greater value.
public override bool Equals(object *v*)	Returns **true** if the value of the invoking object equals the value of *v*.
public override int GetHashCode( )	Returns the hash code for the invoking object.

Table 19-2. *Methods Supported by the Integer Structures*

Method	Meaning
public TypeCode GetTypeCode( )	Returns the **TypeCode** enumeration value for the equivalent value type. For example, for **Int32**, the type code is **TypeCode.Int32**.
public static *retType* Parse(string *str*)	Returns the binary equivalent of the numeric string in *str*. If the string does not represent a numeric value as defined by the structure type, an exception is thrown.
public static *retType* Parse(string *str*, IFormatProvider *fmtpvdr*)	Returns the binary equivalent of the numeric string in *str* using the culture-specific information provided by *fmtpvdr*. If the string does not represent a numeric value as defined by the structure type, an exception is thrown.
public static *retType* Parse(string *str*, NumberStyles *styles*)	Returns the binary equivalent of the numeric string in *str* using the style information provided by *styles*. If the string does not represent a numeric value as defined by the structure type, an exception is thrown.
public static *retType* Parse(string *str*, NumberStyles *styles*, IFormatProvider *fmtpvdr*)	Returns the binary equivalent of the numeric string in *str* using the style information provided by *styles* and the culture-specific format information provided by *fmtpvdr*. If the string does not represent a numeric value as defined by the structure type, an exception is thrown.
public override string ToString( )	Returns the string representation of the value of the invoking object.
public string ToString(string *format*)	Returns the string representation of the value of the invoking object as specified by the format string passed in *format*.

Table 19-2. *Methods Supported by the Integer Structures* (continued)

Method	Meaning
public string ToString(IFormatProvider *fmtpvdr*)	Returns the string representation of the value of the invoking object using the culture-specific information specified in *fmtpvdr*.
public string ToString(string *format*, IFormatProvider *fmtpvdr*)	Returns the string representation of the value of the invoking object using the culture-specific information specified in *fmtpvdr* and the format specified by *format*.

Table 19-2. *Methods Supported by the Integer Structures* (continued)

The Floating-Point Structures

There are two floating-point structures: **Double** and **Single**. **Single** represents **float**. Its methods are shown in Table 19-3, and its fields are shown in Table 19-4. **Double** represents **double**. Its methods are shown in Table 19-5, and its fields are shown in Table 19-6. As is the case with the integer structures, you can specify culture-specific information and format information in a call to **Parse( )** or **ToString( )**.

The floating-point structures implement the following interfaces: **IComparable**, **IConvertible**, and **IFormattable**.

Method	Meaning
public int CompareTo(object *v*)	Compares the numerical value of the invoking object with that of *v*. Returns zero if the values are equal. Returns a negative value if the invoking object has a lower value. Returns a positive value if the invoking object has a greater value.
public override bool Equals(object *v*)	Returns **true** if the value of the invoking object equals the value of *v*.

Table 19-3. *The Methods Supported by* **Single**

Method	Meaning
public override int GetHashCode( )	Returns the hash code for the invoking object.
public TypeCode GetTypeCode( )	Returns the **TypeCode** enumeration value for **Single**, which is **TypeCode.Single**.
public static bool IsInfinity(float *v*)	Returns **true** if *v* represents infinity (either positive or negative). Otherwise, returns **false**.
public static bool IsNaN(float *v*)	Returns **true** if *v* is not a number. Otherwise, returns **false**.
public static bool IsPositiveInfinity(float *v*)	Returns **true** if *v* represents positive infinity. Otherwise, returns **false**.
public static bool IsNegativeInfinity(float *v*)	Returns **true** if *v* represents negative infinity. Otherwise, returns **false**.
public static float Parse(string *str*)	Returns the binary equivalent of the numeric string in *str*. If the string does not represent a **float** value, an exception is thrown.
public static float Parse(string *str*, IFormatProvider *fmtpvdr*)	Returns the binary equivalent of the numeric string in *str* using the culture-specific information provided by *fmtpvdr*. If the string does not represent a **float** value, an exception is thrown.
public static float Parse(string *str*, NumberStyles *styles*)	Returns the binary equivalent of the numeric string in *str* using the style information provided by *styles*. If the string does not represent a **float** value, an exception is thrown.
public static float Parse(string *str*, NumberStyles *styles*, IFormatProvider *fmtpvdr*)	Returns the binary equivalent of the numeric string in *str* using the style information provided by *styles* and the culture-specific format information provided by *fmtpvdr*. If the string does not represent a **float** value, an exception is thrown.

Table 19-3.   *The Methods Supported by **Single*** (continued)

Method	Meaning
public override string ToString( )	Returns the string representation of the value of the invoking object.
public string ToString(string *format*)	Returns the string representation of the value of the invoking object as specified by the format string passed in *format*.
public string ToString(IFormatProvider *fmtpvdr*)	Returns the string representation of the value of the invoking object using the culture-specific information specified in *fmtpvdr*.
public string ToString(string *format*, IFormatProvider *fmtpvdr*)	Returns the string representation of the value of the invoking object using the culture-specific information specified in *fmtpvdr* and the format specified by *format*.

Table 19-3. *The Methods Supported by* **Single** (continued)

Field	Meaning
public const float Epsilon	The smallest non-zero positive value.
public const float MaxValue	The largest value that a **float** can hold.
public const float MinValue	The smallest value that a **float** can hold.
public const float NaN	A value that is not a number.
public const float NegativeInfinity	A value representing negative infinity.
public const float PositiveInfinity	A value representing positive infinity.

Table 19-4. *The Fields Supported by* **Single**

Method	Meaning
public int CompareTo(object *v*)	Compares the numerical value of the invoking object with that of *v*. Returns zero if the values are equal. Returns a negative value if the invoking object has a lower value. Returns a positive value if the invoking object has a greater value.
public override bool Equals(object *v*)	Returns **true** if the value of the invoking object equals the value of *v*.
public override int GetHashCode( )	Returns the hash code for the invoking object.
public TypeCode GetTypeCode( )	Returns the **TypeCode** enumeration value for **Double**, which is **TypeCode.Double**.
public static bool IsInfinity(double *v*)	Returns **true** if *v* represents infinity (either positive or negative). Otherwise, returns **false**.
public static bool IsNaN(double *v*)	Returns **true** if *v* is not a number. Otherwise, returns **false**.
public static bool IsPositiveInfinity(double *v*)	Returns **true** if *v* represents positive infinity. Otherwise, returns **false**.
public static bool IsNegativeInfinity(double *v*)	Returns **true** if *v* represents negative infinity. Otherwise, returns **false**.
public static double Parse(string *str*)	Returns the binary equivalent of the numeric string in *str*. If the string does not represent a **double** value, an exception is thrown.
public static double Parse(string *str*, IFormatProvider *fmtpvdr*)	Returns the binary equivalent of the numeric string in *str* using the culture-specific information provided by *fmtpvdr*. If the string does not represent a **double** value, an exception is thrown.
public static double Parse(string *str*, NumberStyles *styles*)	Returns the binary equivalent of the numeric string in *str* using the style information provided by *styles*. If the string does not represent a **double** value, an exception is thrown.

Table 19-5. *The Methods Supported by **Double***

Method	Meaning

public static double
   Parse(string *str*,
       NumberStyles *styles*,
       IFormatProvider *fmtpvdr*)
	Returns the binary equivalent of the numeric string in *str* using the style information provided by *styles* and the culture-specific format information provided by *fmtpvdr*. If the string does not represent a **double** value, an exception is thrown.

public override string ToString( )	Returns the string representation of the value of the invoking object.
public string ToString(string *format*)	Returns the string representation of the value of the invoking object as specified by the format string passed in *format*.
public string ToString(IFormatProvider *fmtpvdr*)	Returns the string representation of the value of the invoking object using the culture-specific information specified in *fmtpvdr*.

public string
   ToString(string *format*,
       IFormatProvider *fmtpvdr*)
	Returns the string representation of the value of the invoking object using the culture-specific information specified in *fmtpvdr* and the format specified by *format*.

Table 19-5.   *The Methods Supported by* **Double** *(continued)*

Field	Meaning
public const double Epsilon	The smallest non-zero positive value.
public const double MaxValue	The largest value that a **double** can hold.
public const double MinValue	The smallest value that a **double** can hold.
public const double NaN	A value that is not a number.
public const double NegativeInfinity	A value representing negative infinity.
public const double PositiveInfinity	A value representing positive infinity.

Table 19-6.   *Fields Supported by* **Double**

Decimal

The **Decimal** structure is a bit more complicated than its integer and floating-point relatives. It contains many constructors, fields, methods, and operators that help integrate **decimal** with the other numeric types supported by C#. For example, several of the methods provide conversions between **decimal** and the other numeric types.

Decimal offers eight public constructors. The following six are the most commonly used:

```
public Decimal(int v)
public Decimal(uint v)
public Decimal(long v)
public Decimal(ulong v)
public Decimal(float v)
public Decimal(double v)
```

Each constructs a **Decimal** from the specified value.

You can also construct a **Decimal** by specifying its constituent parts using this constructor:

```
public Decimal(int low, int middle, int high, bool signFlag, byte scaleFactor)
```

A **decimal** value consists of three parts. The first is a 96-bit integer, the second is a sign flag, and the third is a scaling factor. The 96-bit integer is passed in 32-bit chunks through *low, middle,* and *high.* The sign is passed through *signFlag,* which is **false** for a positive number and **true** for a negative number. The scaling factor is passed in *scaleFactor,* which must be a value between 0 and 28. This factor specifies the power of 10 (that is, $10^{scaleFactor}$) by which the number is divided, thus yielding its fractional component.

Instead of passing each component separately, you can specify the constituents of a **Decimal** in an array of integers, using this constructor:

```
public Decimal(int[ ] parts)
```

The first three **int**s in *parts* contain the 96-bit integer value. In *parts*[3], bit 31 contains the sign flag (zero for positive, 1 for negative), and bits 16 through 23 contain the scale factor.

Decimal implements the following interfaces: **IComparable, IConvertible,** and **IFormattable**.

Here is an example that constructs a **decimal** value by hand:

```
// Manually create a decimal number.

using System;
```

```
class CreateDec {
  public static void Main() {
    decimal d = new decimal(12345, 0, 0, false, 2);

    Console.WriteLine(d);
  }
}
```

The output is shown here:

```
123.45
```

In this example, the value of the 96-bit integer is 12345. Its sign is positive, and it has two decimal fractions.

The methods defined by **Decimal** are shown in Table 19-7. The fields defined by **Decimal** are shown in Table 19-8. **Decimal** also defines a large number of operators and conversions that allow **decimal** values to be used in expressions with other numeric types. The rules governing the use of **decimal** in expressions and assignments are described in Chapter 3.

Method	Meaning
public static decimal Add(decimal *v1*, decimal *v2*)	Returns *v1* + *v2*.
public static int CompareTo(decimal *v1*, decimal *v2*)	Compares the numerical value of *v1* with that of *v2*. Returns zero if the values are equal. Returns a negative value if *v1* is less than *v2*. Returns a positive value if *v1* is greater than *v2*.
public int CompareTo(object *v*)	Compares the numerical value of the invoking object with that of *v*. Returns zero if the values are equal. Returns a negative value if the invoking object has a lower value. Returns a positive value if the invoking object has a greater value.
public static decimal Divide(decimal *v1*, decimal *v2*)	Returns *v1* / *v2*.
public override bool Equals(object *v*)	Returns **true** if the value of the invoking object equals the value of *v*.

Table 19-7. *The Methods Defined by **Decimal***

Method	Meaning
public static bool Equals(decimal *v1*, decimal *v2*)	Returns **true** if *v1* equals *v2*.
public static decimal Floor(decimal *v*)	Returns the largest integer (represented as a decimal value) not greater than *v*. For example, given 1.02, **Floor( )** returns 1.0. Given –1.02, **Floor( )** returns –2.
public static decimal FromOACurrency(long *v*)	Converts the OLE Automation value in *v* into its **decimal** equivalent and returns the result.
public static int[ ] GetBits(decimal *v*)	Returns the binary representation of *v* and returns it in an array of **ints**. The organization of this array is as described in the text.
public override int GetHashCode( )	Returns the hash code for the invoking object.
public TypeCode GetTypeCode( )	Returns the **TypeCode** enumeration value for **Decimal**, which is **TypeCode.Decimal**.
public static decimal Multiply(decimal *v1*, decimal *v2*)	Returns *v1* * *v2*.
public static decimal Negate(decimal *v*)	Returns –*v*.
public static decimal Parse(string *str*)	Returns the binary equivalent of the numeric string in *str*. If the string does not represent a **decimal** value, an exception is thrown.
public static decimal Parse(string *str*, IFormatProvider *fmtpvdr*)	Returns the binary equivalent of the numeric string in *str* using the culture-specific information provided by *fmtpvdr*. If the string does not represent a **decimal** value, an exception is thrown.
public static decimal Parse(string *str*, NumberStyles *styles*)	Returns the binary equivalent of the numeric string in *str*, using the style information provided by *styles*. If the string does not represent a **decimal** value, an exception is thrown.

Table 19-7.   *The Methods Defined by **Decimal** (continued)*

Method	Meaning

public static decimal
    Parse(string *str*,
        NumberStyles *styles*,
        IFormatProvider *fmtpvdr*)
	Returns the binary equivalent of the numeric string in *str* using the style information provided by *styles* and the culture-specific format information provided by *fmtpvdr*. If the string does not represent a **decimal** value, an exception is thrown.

public static decimal Remainder(decimal *v1*, decimal *v2*)	Returns the remainder of the integer division *v1* / *v2*.
public static decimal Round(decimal *v*, int *decPlaces*)	Returns the value of *v* rounded to the number of decimal places specified by *decPlaces*, which must be between 0 and 28.
public static decimal Subtract(decimal *v1*, decimal *v2*)	Returns *v1* – *v2*.
public static byte ToByte(decimal *v*)	Returns the **byte** equivalent of *v*. Any fractional component is truncated. An **OverflowException** occurs if *v* is not within the range of a **byte**.
public static double ToDouble(decimal *v*)	Returns the **double** equivalent of *v*. A loss of precision may occur because **double** has fewer significant digits than does **decimal**.
public static short ToInt16(decimal *v*)	Returns the **short** equivalent of *v*. Any fractional component is truncated. An **OverflowException** occurs if *v* is not within the range of a **short**.
public static int ToInt32(decimal *v*)	Returns the **int** equivalent of *v*. Any fractional component is truncated. An **OverflowException** occurs if *v* is not within the range of an **int**.
public static long ToInt64(decimal *v*)	Returns the **long** equivalent of *v*. Any fractional component is truncated. An **OverflowException** occurs if *v* is not within the range of a **long**.
public static long ToOACurrency(decimal *v*)	Converts *v* into the equivalent OLE Automation value and returns the result.

Table 19-7.   *The Methods Defined by **Decimal*** (continued)

Method	Meaning
public static sbyte ToSByte(decimal *v*)	Returns the **sbyte** equivalent of *v*. Any fractional component is truncated. An **OverflowException** occurs if *v* is not within the range of an **sbyte**.
public static float ToSingle(decimal *v*)	Returns the **float** equivalent of *v*. A loss of precision may occur because **float** has fewer significant digits than does **decimal**.
public override string ToString( )	Returns the string representation of the value of the invoking object.
public string ToString(string *format*)	Returns the string representation of the value of the invoking object as specified by the format string passed in *format*.
public string ToString(IFormatProvider *fmtpvdr*)	Returns the string representation of the value of the invoking object using the culture-specific information specified in *fmtpvdr*.
public string ToString(string *format*, IFormatProvider *fmtpvdr*)	Returns the string representation of the value of the invoking object using the culture-specific information specified in *fmtpvdr* and the format specified by *format*.
public static ushort ToUInt16(decimal *v*)	Returns the **ushort** equivalent of *v*. Any fractional component is truncated. An **OverflowException** occurs if *v* is not within the range of a **ushort**.
public static uint ToUInt32(decimal *v*)	Returns the **uint** equivalent of *v*. Any fractional component is truncated. An **OverflowException** occurs if *v* is not within the range of a **uint**.
public static ulong ToUInt64(decimal *v*)	Returns the **ulong** equivalent of *v*. Any fractional component is truncated. An **OverflowException** occurs if *v* is not within the range of a **ulong**.
public static decimal Truncate(decimal *v*)	Returns the whole-number portion of *v*. Thus, it truncates any fractional digits.

Table 19-7.   *The Methods Defined by **Decimal** (continued)*

Field	Meaning
public static readonly decimal MaxValue	The largest value that a **decimal** can hold.
public static readonly decimal MinusOne	The **decimal** representation of –1.
public static readonly decimal MinValue	The smallest value that a **decimal** can hold.
public static readonly decimal One	The decimal representation of 1.
public static readonly decimal Zero	The decimal representation of 0.

Table 19-8. *Fields Supported by Decimal*

Char

The value-type structure that is perhaps the most useful on a day-to-day basis is **Char**, because it supplies a large number of methods that allow you to process and categorize characters. For example, you can convert a lowercase character to uppercase by calling **ToUpper( )**. You can determine if a character is a digit by calling **IsDigit( )**.

The methods defined by **Char** are shown in Table 19-9. **Char** defines the following fields:

    public const char MaxValue
    public const char MinValue

These represent the largest and smallest values that a **char** variable can hold.

Char implements the following interfaces: **IComparable** and **IConvertible**.

Method	Meaning
public int CompareTo(object *v*)	Compares the character in the invoking object with that of *v*. Returns zero if the characters are equal. Returns a negative value if the invoking object has a lower value. Returns a positive value if the invoking object has a greater value.

Table 19-9. *Methods Defined by Char*

Method	Meaning
public override bool Equals(object *v*)	Returns **true** if the value of the invoking object equals the value of *v*.
public override int GetHashCode( )	Returns the hash code for the invoking object.
public static double GetNumericValue(char *ch*)	Returns the numeric value of *ch* if *ch* is a digit. Otherwise, returns –1.
public static double GetNumericValue(string *str*, int *idx*)	Returns the numeric value of *str*[*idx*] if that character is a digit. Otherwise, returns –1.
public TypeCode GetTypeCode( )	Returns the **TypeCode** enumeration value for **Char**, which is **TypeCode.Char**.
public static UnicodeCategory GetUnicodeCategory(char *ch*)	Returns the **UnicodeCategory** enumeration value for *ch*. **UnicodeCategory** is an enumeration defined by **System.Globalization** that categorizes Unicode characters.
public static UnicodeCategory GetUnicodeCategory(string *str*, int *idx*)	Returns the **UnicodeCategory** enumeration value for *str*[*idx*]. **UnicodeCategory** is an enumeration defined by **System.Globalization** that categorizes Unicode characters.
public static bool IsControl(char *ch*)	Returns **true** if *ch* is a control character. Otherwise, returns **false**.
public static bool IsControl(string *str*, int *idx*)	Returns **true** if *str*[*idx*] is a control character. Otherwise, returns **false**.
public static bool IsDigit(char *ch*)	Returns **true** if *ch* is a digit. Otherwise, returns **false**.
public static bool IsDigit(string *str*, int *idx*)	Returns **true** if *str*[*idx*] is a digit. Otherwise, returns **false**.
public static bool IsLetter(char *ch*)	Returns **true** if *ch* is a letter of the alphabet. Otherwise, returns **false**.
public static bool IsLetter(string *str*, int *idx*)	Returns **true** if *str*[*idx*] is a letter of the alphabet. Otherwise, returns **false**.
public static bool IsLetterOrDigit(char *ch*)	Returns **true** if *ch* is either a letter of the alphabet or a digit. Otherwise, returns **false**.

Table 19-9. *Methods Defined by **Char*** (continued)

Method	Meaning
public static bool IsLetterOrDigit(string *str*, int *idx*)	Returns **true** if *str*[*idx*] is either a letter of the alphabet or a digit. Otherwise, returns **false**.
public static bool IsLower(char *ch*)	Returns **true** if *ch* is a lowercase letter of the alphabet. Otherwise, returns **false**.
public static bool IsLower(string *str*, int *idx*)	Returns **true** if *str*[*idx*] is a lowercase of the alphabet. Otherwise, returns **false**.
public static bool IsNumber(char *ch*)	Returns **true** if *ch* is a hexadecimal digit, which is 0 through 9 or A through F. Otherwise, returns **false**.
public static bool IsNumber(string *str*, int *idx*)	Returns **true** if *str*[*idx*] is a hexadecimal digit, which is 0 through 9 or A through F. Otherwise, returns **false**.
public static bool IsPunctuation(char *ch*)	Returns **true** if *ch* is a punctuation character. Otherwise, returns **false**.
public static bool IsPunctuation(string *str*, int *idx*)	Returns **true** if *str*[*idx*] is a punctuation character. Otherwise, returns **false**.
public static bool IsSeparator(char *ch*)	Returns **true** if *ch* is a separator character, such as a space. Otherwise, returns **false**.
public static bool IsSeparator(string *str*, int *idx*)	Returns **true** if *str*[*idx*] is a separator character, such as a space. Otherwise, returns **false**.
public static bool IsSurrogate(char *ch*)	Returns **true** if *ch* is a Unicode surrogate character. Otherwise, returns **false**.
public static bool IsSurrogate(string *str*, int *idx*)	Returns **true** if *str*[*idx*] is a Unicode surrogate character. Otherwise, returns **false**.
public static bool IsSymbol(char *ch*)	Returns **true** if *ch* is a symbolic character, such as the currency symbol. Otherwise, returns **false**.
public static bool IsSymbol(string *str*, int *idx*)	Returns **true** if *str*[*idx*] is a symbolic character, such as the currency symbol. Otherwise, returns **false**.
public static bool IsUpper(char *ch*)	Returns **true** if *ch* is an uppercase letter. Otherwise, returns **false**.

Table 19-9. *Methods Defined by* **Char** (continued)

Method	Meaning
public static bool IsUpper(string *str*, int *idx*)	Returns **true** if *str[idx]* is an uppercase letter. Otherwise, returns **false**.
public static bool IsWhiteSpace(char *ch*)	Returns **true** if *ch* is a whitespace character, such as a space or tab. Otherwise, returns **false**.
public static bool IsWhiteSpace(string *str*, int *idx*)	Returns **true** if *str[idx]* is a whitespace character, such as a space or tab. Otherwise, returns **false**.
public static char Parse(string *str*)	Returns the **char** equivalent of the character in *str*. If *str* contains more than one character, a **FormatException** is thrown.
public static char ToLower(char *ch*)	Returns the lowercase equivalent of *ch* if *ch* is an uppercase letter. Otherwise, *ch* is returned unchanged.
public static char ToLower(char *ch*, CultureInfo *c*)	Returns the lowercase equivalent of *ch* if *ch* is an uppercase letter. Otherwise, *ch* is returned unchanged. The conversion is handled in accordance with the specified cultural information. **CultureInfo** is a class defined in **System.Globalization**.
public static char ToUpper(char *ch*)	Returns the uppercase equivalent of *ch* if *ch* is a lowercase letter. Otherwise, *ch* is returned unchanged.
public static char ToUpper(char *ch*, CultureInfo *c*)	Returns the uppercase equivalent of *ch* if *ch* is a lowercase letter. Otherwise, *ch* is returned unchanged. The conversion is handled in accordance with the specified cultural information. **CultureInfo** is a class defined in **System.Globalization**.
public override string ToString( )	Returns the string representation of the value of the invoking **Char**.
public static string ToString(char *ch*)	Returns the string representation of *ch*.
public string ToString(IFormatProvider *fmtpvdr*)	Returns the string representation of the invoking **Char** using the specified culture information.

Table 19-9.   *Methods Defined by* ***Char*** *(continued)*

Here is a program that demonstrates several of the methods defined by **Char**:

```csharp
// Demonstrate several Char methods.

using System;

class CharDemo {
  public static void Main() {
    string str = "This is a test. $23";
    int i;

    for(i=0; i < str.Length; i++) {
      Console.Write(str[i] + " is");
      if(Char.IsDigit(str[i]))
        Console.Write(" digit");
      if(Char.IsLetter(str[i]))
        Console.Write(" letter");
      if(Char.IsLower(str[i]))
        Console.Write(" lowercase");
      if(Char.IsUpper(str[i]))
        Console.Write(" uppercase");
      if(Char.IsSymbol(str[i]))
        Console.Write(" symbol");
      if(Char.IsSeparator(str[i]))
        Console.Write(" separator");
      if(Char.IsWhiteSpace(str[i]))
        Console.Write(" whitespace");
      if(Char.IsPunctuation(str[i]))
        Console.Write(" punctuation");

      Console.WriteLine();
    }

    Console.WriteLine("Original: " + str);

    // Convert to upper case.
    string newstr = "";
    for(i=0; i < str.Length; i++)
      newstr += Char.ToUpper(str[i]);

    Console.WriteLine("Uppercased: " + newstr);

  }
}
```

The output is shown here:

```
T is letter uppercase
h is letter lowercase
i is letter lowercase
s is letter lowercase
  is separator whitespace
i is letter lowercase
s is letter lowercase
  is separator whitespace
a is letter lowercase
  is separator whitespace
t is letter lowercase
e is letter lowercase
s is letter lowercase
t is letter lowercase
. is punctuation
  is separator whitespace
$ is symbol
2 is digit
3 is digit
Original: This is a test. $23
Uppercased: THIS IS A TEST. $23
```

The Boolean Structure

The **Boolean** structure supports the **bool** data type. The methods defined by **Boolean** are shown in Table 19-10. It defines these fields:

> public static readonly string FalseString
> public static readonly string TrueString

These contain the human-readable forms of **true** and **false**. For example, if you output **FalseString** using a call to **WriteLine( )**, the string "False" is displayed.

Boolean implements the following interfaces: **IComparable** and **IConvertible**.

Method	Meaning
public int CompareTo(object *v*)	Compares the value of the invoking object with that of *v*. Returns zero if the values are equal. Returns a negative value if the invoking object is **false** and *v* is **true**. Returns a positive value if the invoking object is **true** and *v* is **false**.

Table 19-10. *Methods Defined by **Boolean***

Method	Meaning
public override bool Equals(object *v*)	Returns **true** if the value of the invoking object equals the value of *v*.
public override int GetHashCode( )	Returns the hash code for the invoking object.
public TypeCode GetTypeCode( )	Returns the **TypeCode** enumeration value for **Boolean**, which is **TypeCode.Boolean**.
public static bool Parse(string *str*)	Returns the **bool** equivalent of the string in *str*. If the string is neither "True" nor "False", an exception is thrown. However, case differences are ignored.
public override string ToString( )	Returns the string representation of the value of the invoking object.
string ToString(IFormatProvider *fmtpvdr*)	Returns the string representation of the value of the invoking object using the culture-specific information specified in *fmtpvdr*.

Table 19-10.   *Methods Defined by **Boolean*** (continued)

The Array Class

One very useful class in **System** is **Array**. **Array** is a base class for all arrays in C#. Thus, its methods can be applied to arrays of any of the built-in types or to arrays of types that you create. **Array** defines the properties shown in Table 19-11. It defines the methods shown in Table 19-12.

   Array implements the following interfaces: **ICloneable**, **ICollection**, **IEnumerable**, and **IList**. **ICollection**, **IEnumerable**, and **IList** are defined in the **System.Collections** namespace and are described in Chapter 22.

   Several methods use a parameter of type **IComparer**. This interface is defined in **System.Collections**. It defines a method called **Compare( )**, which compares the values of two objects. It is shown here:

   int Compare(object *v1*, object *v2*)

It returns greater than zero if *v1* is greater than *v2*, less than zero if *v1* is less than *v2*, and zero if the two values are equal.

   The next few sections demonstrate several commonly used array operations.

Sorting and Searching Arrays

One of the most commonly used array operations is sorting. Because of this, **Array** supports a rich complement of sorting methods. Using **Sort( )**, you can sort an entire array, a range within an array, or a pair of arrays that contain corresponding key/value pairs. Once an array has been sorted, you can efficiently search it using **BinarySearch( )**. Here is a program that demonstrates the **Sort( )** and **BinarySearch( )** methods by sorting an array of **int**s:

```
// Sort an array and search for a value.

using System;

class SortDemo {
  public static void Main() {
    int[] nums = { 5, 4, 6, 3, 14, 9, 8, 17, 1, 24, -1, 0 };

    // Display original order.
    Console.Write("Original order: ");
    foreach(int i in nums)
      Console.Write(i + " ");
    Console.WriteLine();

    // Sort the array.
    Array.Sort(nums);

    // Display sorted order.
    Console.Write("Sorted order:    ");
    foreach(int i in nums)
      Console.Write(i + " ");
    Console.WriteLine();


    // Search for 14.
    int idx = Array.BinarySearch(nums, 14);

    Console.WriteLine("Index of 14 is " + idx);
  }
}
```

The output is shown here:

```
Original order: 5 4 6 3 14 9 8 17 1 24 -1 0
Sorted order:    -1 0 1 3 4 5 6 8 9 14 17 24
Index of 14 is 9
```

THE C# CLASS LIBRARY

In the preceding example, the array had a base type of **int**, which is a value type. All methods defined by **Array** are automatically available to all of the built-in value types. However, this may not be the case for arrays of object references. To sort or search an array of object references, the class type of those objects must implement the **IComparable** interface. If the class does not implement **IComparable**, a runtime exception will occur when attempting to sort or search the array. Fortunately, **IComparable** is easy to implement, because it consists of just this one method:

int CompareTo(object *v*)

This method compares the invoking object against the value in *v*. It returns greater than zero if the invoking object is greater than *v*, zero if the two objects are equal, and less than zero if the invoking object is less than *v*. Here is an example that illustrates sorting and searching an array of user-defined class objects:

```
// Sort and search an array of objects.

using System;

class MyClass : IComparable {
  public int i;

  public MyClass(int x) { i = x; }

  // Implement IComparable.
  public int CompareTo(object v) {
    return i - ((MyClass)v).i;
  }
}

class SortDemo {
  public static void Main() {
    MyClass[] nums = new MyClass[5];

    nums[0] = new MyClass(5);
    nums[1] = new MyClass(2);
    nums[2] = new MyClass(3);
    nums[3] = new MyClass(4);
    nums[4] = new MyClass(1);

    // Display original order.
    Console.Write("Original order: ");
    foreach(MyClass o in nums)
      Console.Write(o.i + " ");
    Console.WriteLine();
```

```
    // Sort the array.
    Array.Sort(nums);

    // Display sorted order.
    Console.Write("Sorted order:    ");
    foreach(MyClass o in nums)
      Console.Write(o.i + " ");
    Console.WriteLine();

    // Search for MyClass(2).
    MyClass x = new MyClass(2);
    int idx = Array.BinarySearch(nums, x);

    Console.WriteLine("Index of MyClass(2) is " + idx);
  }
}
```

The output is shown here:

```
Original order: 5 2 3 4 1
Sorted order:    1 2 3 4 5
Index of MyClass(2) is 1
```

Reversing an Array

Sometimes it is useful to reverse the contents of an array. For example, you might
want to change an array that has been sorted into ascending order into one sorted in
descending order. Reversing an array is easy: simply call **Reverse( )**. Using **Reverse( )**,
you can reverse all or part of an array. The following program demonstrates the process:

```
// Reverse an array.

using System;

class ReverseDemo {
  public static void Main() {
    int[] nums = { 1, 2, 3, 4, 5 };

    // Display original order.
    Console.Write("Original order: ");
    foreach(int i in nums)
      Console.Write(i + " ");
    Console.WriteLine();
```

THE C# CLASS LIBRARY

```
    // Reverse the entire array.
    Array.Reverse(nums);

    // Display reversed order.
    Console.Write("Reversed order: ");
    foreach(int i in nums)
      Console.Write(i + " ");
    Console.WriteLine();

    // Reverse a range.
    Array.Reverse(nums, 1, 3);

    // Display reversed order.
    Console.Write("Range reversed: ");
    foreach(int i in nums)
      Console.Write(i + " ");
    Console.WriteLine();
  }
}
```

The output is shown here:

```
Original order: 1 2 3 4 5
Reversed order: 5 4 3 2 1
Range reversed: 5 2 3 4 1
```

Copying an Array

Copying all or part of one array to another is another common array operation. To copy an array, use **Copy( )**. **Copy( )** can put elements at the start of the destination array or into the middle, depending upon which version of **Copy( )** you use. **Copy( )** is demonstrated by the following program:

```
// Copy an array.

using System;

class CopyDemo {
  public static void Main() {
    int[] source = { 1, 2, 3, 4, 5 };
```

```
      int[] target = { 11, 12, 13, 14, 15 };
      int[] source2 = { -1, -2, -3, -4, -5 };

      // Display source.
      Console.Write("source: ");
      foreach(int i in source)
        Console.Write(i + " ");
      Console.WriteLine();

      // Display original target.
      Console.Write("Original contents of target: ");
      foreach(int i in target)
        Console.Write(i + " ");
      Console.WriteLine();

      // Copy the entire array.
      Array.Copy(source, target, source.Length);

      // Display copy.
      Console.Write("target after copy:  ");
      foreach(int i in target)
        Console.Write(i + " ");
      Console.WriteLine();

      // Copy into middle of target.
      Array.Copy(source2, 2, target, 3, 2);

      // Display copy.
      Console.Write("target after copy:  ");
      foreach(int i in target)
        Console.Write(i + " ");
      Console.WriteLine();
  }
}
```

The output is shown here:

```
source: 1 2 3 4 5
Original contents of target: 11 12 13 14 15
target after copy:  1 2 3 4 5
target after copy:  1 2 3 -3 -4
```

Property	Meaning
public virtual bool IsFixedSize { get; }	A read-only property that is **true** if the array is of fixed size and **false** if the array is dynamic.
public virtual bool IsReadOnly { get; }	A read-only property that is **true** if the **Array** object is read-only and **false** if it is not.
public virtual bool IsSynchronized { get; }	A read-only property that is **true** if the array is safe for use in a multithreaded environment and **false** if it is not.
public int Length { get; }	A read-only property that contains the number of elements in the array.
public int Rank { get; }	A read-only property that contains the number of dimensions in the array.
public virtual object SyncRoot { get; }	A read-only property that contains the object that must be used to synchronize access to the array.

Table 19-11. *Properties Defined by Array*

Method	Meaning
public static int BinarySearch(Array *a*, object *v*)	Searches the array specified by *a* for the value specified by *v*. Returns the index of the first match. If *v* is not found, returns a negative value. The array must be sorted and one-dimensional.
public static int BinarySearch(Array *a*, object *v*, IComparer *comp*)	Searches the array specified by *a* for the value specified by *v*, using the comparison method specified by *comp*. Returns the index of the first match. If *v* is not found, returns a negative value. The array must be sorted and one-dimensional.

Table 19-12. *Methods Defined by Array*

Method	Meaning

public static int
    BinarySearch(Array *a*, int *start*,
            int *count*, object *v*)
	Searches a portion of the array specified by *a* for the value specified by *v*. The search begins at the index specified by *start* and is restricted to *count* elements. Returns the index of the first match. If *v* is not found, returns a negative value. The array must be sorted and one-dimensional.

public static int
    BinarySearch(Array *a*, int *start*,
            int *count*, object *v*,
            IComparer *comp*)
	Searches a portion of the array specified by *a* for the value specified by *v*, using the comparison method specified by *comp*. The search begins at the index specified by *start* and is restricted to *count* elements. Returns the index of the first match. If *v* is not found, returns a negative value. The array must be sorted and one-dimensional.

public static void Clear(Array *a*, int *start*, int *count*)	Sets the specified elements of *a* to zero. The elements to be zeroed begin at the index specified by *start* and run for *count* elements.
public virtual object Clone( )	Returns a copy of the invoking array. The copy refers to the same elements as does the original. This is called a "shallow copy." Thus, changes to the elements affect both arrays since they both use the same elements.

public static void Copy(Array *source*,
             Array *dest*,
            int *count*)
	Beginning at the start of each array, copies *count* elements from *source* to *dest*. When both arrays are of the same reference type, then **Copy( )** makes a "shallow copy," which means that both arrays will refer to the same elements.

public static void Copy(Array *source*,
             int *srcStart*,
            Array *dest*,
            int *destStart*,
            int *count*)
	Copies *count* elements from *source*[*srcStart*] to *dest*[*destStart*]. When both arrays are of the same reference type, then **Copy( )** makes a "shallow copy," which means that both arrays will refer to the same elements.

Table 19-12.   *Methods Defined by **Array** (continued)*

Method	Meaning
public virtual void CopyTo(Array *dest*, int *start*)	Copies the elements of the invoking array to *dest*, beginning at *dest*[*start*].
public static Array CreateInstance(Type *t*, int *size*)	Returns a reference to a one-dimensional array that contains *size* elements of type *t*.
public static Array CreateInstance(Type *t*, int *size1*, int *size2*)	Returns a reference to a *size1*-by-*size2* two-dimensional array. Each element is of type *t*.
public static Array CreateInstance(Type *t*, int *size1*, int *size2*, int *size3*)	Returns a reference to a *size1*-by-*size2*-by-*size3* three-dimensional array. Each element is of type *t*.
public static Array CreateInstance(Type *t*, int[ ] *sizes*)	Returns a reference to a multi-dimensional array that has the dimensions specified in *sizes*. Each element is of type *t*.
public static Array CreateInstance(Type *t*, int[ ] *sizes*, int[ ] *startIndexes*)	Returns a reference to a multi-dimensional array that has the dimensions specified in *sizes*. Each element is of type *t*. The starting index of each dimension is specified in *startIndexes*. Thus, it is possible to create arrays that begin at some index other than zero.
public override bool Equals(object *v*)	Returns **true** if the value of the invoking object equals the value of *v*.
public virtual IEnumerator GetEnumerator( )	Returns an enumerator object for the array. An enumerator enables you to cycle through an array. Enumerators are described in Chapter 22 (Collections).
public int GetLength(int *dim*)	Returns the length of the specified dimension. The dimension is zero-based; thus, to get the length of the first dimension, pass 0. To obtain the length of the second dimension, pass 1.

Table 19-12. *Methods Defined by* **Array** *(continued)*

Method	Meaning
public int GetLowerBound(int *dim*)	Returns the first index of the specified dimension, which is usually zero. The parameter *dim* is zero-based; thus, to get the start index of the first dimension, pass 0. To obtain the start index of the second dimension, pass 1.
public override int GetHashCode( )	Returns the hash code for the invoking object.
public TypeCode GetTypeCode( )	Returns the **TypeCode** enumeration value for **Array**, which is **TypeCode.Array**.
public int GetUpperBound(int *dim*)	Returns the last index of the specified dimension. The parameter *dim* is zero-based; thus, to get the last index of the first dimension, pass 0. To obtain the last index of the second dimension, pass 1.
public object GetValue(int *idx*)	Returns the value of the element at index *idx* within the invoking array. The array must be one-dimensional.
public object GetValue(int *idx1*, int *idx2*)	Returns the value of the element at [*idx1*, *idx2*] within the invoking array. The array must be two-dimensional.
public object GetValue(int *idx1*, int *idx2*, int *idx3*)	Returns the value of the element at [*idx1*, *idx2*, *idx3*] within the invoking array. The array must be three-dimensional.
public object GetValue(int[ ] *idxs*)	Returns the value of the element at the specified indices within the invoking array. The array must have as many dimensions as *idxs* has elements.
public static int IndexOf(Array *a*, object *v*)	Returns the index of the first element within the one-dimensional array *a* that has the value specified by *v*. Returns –1 if the value is not found. (If the array has a lower bound other than 0, then the failure value is the lower bound –1.)

Table 19-12.   *Methods Defined by **Array*** (continued)

Method	Meaning
public static int IndexOf(Array *a*, object *v*, int *start*)	Returns the index of the first element within the one-dimensional array *a* that has the value specified by *v*. The search begins at *a*[*start*]. Returns –1 if the value is not found. (If the array has a lower bound other than 0, then the failure value is the lower bound –1.)
public static int IndexOf(Array *a*, object *v*, int *start*, int *count*)	Returns the index of the first element within the one-dimensional array *a* that has the value specified by *v*. The search begins at *a*[*start*] and runs for *count* elements. Returns –1 if the value is not found within the specified range. (If the array has a lower bound other than 0, then the failure value is the lower bound –1.)
public void Initialize( )	Initializes each element in the invoking array by calling the element's default constructor. This method can be used only on arrays of value types.
public static int LastIndexOf(Array *a*, object *v*)	Returns the index of the last element within the one-dimensional array *a* that has the value specified by *v*. Returns –1 if the value is not found. (If the array has a lower bound other than 0, then the failure value is the lower bound –1.)
public static int LastIndexOf(Array *a*, object *v*, int *start*)	Returns the index of the last element within a range of the one-dimensional array *a* that has the value specified by *v*. The search proceeds in reverse order, beginning at *a*[*start*] and stopping at *a*[0]. Returns –1 if the value is not found. (If the array has a lower bound other than 0, then the failure value is the lower bound –1.)

Table 19-12. *Methods Defined by* **Array** *(continued)*

Method	Meaning
public static int LastIndexOf(Array *a*, object *v*, int *start*, int *count*)	Returns the index of the last element within a range of the one-dimensional array *a* that has the value specified by *v*. The search proceeds in reverse order, beginning at *a*[*start*] and running for *count* elements. Returns –1 if the value is not found within the specified range. (If the array has a lower bound other than 0, then the failure value is the lower bound –1.)
public static void Reverse(Array *a*)	Reverses the elements in *a*.
public static void Reverse(Array *a*, int *start*, int *count*)	Reverses a range of elements in *a*. The range reversed begins at *a*[*start*] and runs for *count* elements.
public void SetValue(object *v*, int *idx*)	Sets the value of the element at index *idx* within the invoking array to *v*. The array must be one-dimensional.
public void SetValue(object *v*, int *idx1*, int *idx2*)	Sets the value of the element at indices [*idx1*, *idx2*] within the invoking array to *v*. The array must be two-dimensional.
public void SetValue(object *v*, int *idx1*, int *idx2*, int *idx3*)	Sets the value of the element at indices [*idx1*, *idx2*, *idx3*] within the invoking array to *v*. The array must be three-dimensional.
public void SetValue(object *v*, int[ ] *idxs*)	Sets the value of the element at the specified indices within the invoking array to *v*. The array must have as many dimensions as *idxs* has elements.
public static void Sort(Array *a*)	Sorts *a* into ascending order. The array must be one-dimensional.
public static void Sort(Array *a*, IComparer *comp*)	Sorts *a* into ascending order using the comparison method specified by *comp*. The array must be one-dimensional.

Table 19-12. *Methods Defined by **Array** (continued)*

Method	Meaning
public static void Sort(Array *k*, Array *v*)	Sorts a pair of one-dimensional arrays into ascending order. The *k* array contains the sort keys. The *v* array contains the values linked to those keys. Thus, the two arrays contain key/value pairs. After the sort, both arrays are in ascending key order.
public static void Sort(Array *k*, Array *v*, IComparer *comp*)	Sorts a pair of one-dimensional arrays into ascending order using the comparison method specified by *comp*. The *k* array contains the sort keys. The *v* array contains the values linked to those keys. Thus, the two arrays contain key/value pairs. After the sort, both are in ascending key order.
public static void Sort(Array *a*, int *start*, int *count*)	Sorts a range of *a* into ascending order. The range begins at *a[start]* and runs for *count* elements. The array must be one-dimensional.
public static void Sort(Array *a*, int *start*, int *count*, IComparer *comp*)	Sorts a range of *a* into ascending order using the comparison method specified by *comp*. The range begins at *a[start]* and runs for *count* elements. The array must be one-dimensional.
public static void Sort(Array *k*, Array *v*, int *start*, int *count*)	Sorts a range within a pair of one-dimensional arrays into ascending order. Within both arrays, the range to sort begins at the index passed in *start* and runs for *count* elements. The *k* array contains the sort keys. The *v* array contains the values linked to those keys. Thus, the two arrays contain key/value pairs. After the sort, both ranges are in ascending-key order.

Table 19-12.   *Methods Defined by **Array** (continued)*

Method	Meaning
public static void Sort(Array *k*, Array *v*, int *start*, int *count*, IComparer *comp*)	Sorts a range within a pair of one-dimensional arrays into ascending order using the comparison method specified by *comp*. Within both arrays, the range to sort begins at the index passed in *start* and runs for *count* elements. The *k* array contains the sort keys. The *v* array contains the values linked to those keys. Thus, the two arrays contain key/value pairs. After the sort, both ranges are in ascending-key order.

Table 19-12.   *Methods Defined by* **Array** *(continued)*

BitConverter

In programming we often need to convert a built-in data type into an array of bytes. For example, some hardware device might require an integer value, but that value must be sent one byte at a time. The reverse situation also frequently occurs. Sometimes data will be received as an ordered sequence of bytes that needs to be converted into one of the built-in types. For example, a device might output integers, sent as a stream of bytes. Whatever your conversion needs, C# provides the **BitConverter** class to solve them.

BitConverter contains the methods shown in Table 19-13. It defines the following field:

    public static readonly bool IsLittleEndian

This field is **true** if the current environment stores a word with the least significant byte first and the most significant byte second. This is called "little-endian" format. **IsLittleEndian** is **false** if the current environment stores a word with the most significant byte first and the least significant byte second. This is called "big-endian" format. Intel Pentium–based machines use little-endian format.

BitConverter is **sealed**, which means that it cannot be inherited.

Method	Meaning
public static long DoubleToInt64Bits(double *v*)	Converts *v* into a **long** integer and returns the result.
public static byte[ ] GetBytes(bool *v*)	Converts *v* into a 1-byte array and returns the result.
public static byte[ ] GetBytes(char *v*)	Converts *v* into a 2-byte array and returns the result.
public static byte[ ] GetBytes(double *v*)	Converts *v* into an 8-byte array and returns the result.
public static byte[ ] GetBytes(float *v*)	Converts *v* into a 4-byte array and returns the result.
public static byte[ ] GetBytes(int *v*)	Converts *v* into a 4-byte array and returns the result.
public static byte[ ] GetBytes(long *v*)	Converts *v* into an 8-byte array and returns the result.
public static byte[ ] GetBytes(short *v*)	Converts *v* into a 2-byte array and returns the result.
public static byte[ ] GetBytes(uint *v*)	Converts *v* into a 4-byte array and returns the result.
public static byte[ ] GetBytes(ulong *v*)	Converts *v* into an 8-byte array and returns the result.
public static byte[ ] GetBytes(ushort *v*)	Converts *v* into a 2-byte array and returns the result.
public static double Int64BitsToDouble(long *v*)	Converts *v* into a **double** floating-point value and returns the result.
public static bool ToBoolean(byte[ ] *a*, int *idx*)	Converts the byte at *a*[*idx*] into its **bool** equivalent and returns the result. A non-zero value is converted to **true**; zero is converted to **false**.
public static char ToChar(byte[ ] *a*, int *start*)	Converts two bytes starting at *a*[*start*] into its **char** equivalent and returns the result.
public static double ToDouble(byte[ ] *a*, int *start*)	Converts eight bytes starting at *a*[*start*] into its **double** equivalent and returns the result.
public static short ToInt16(byte[ ] *a*, int *start*)	Converts two bytes starting at *a*[*start*] into its **short** equivalent and returns the result.

Table 19-13.   *Methods Defined by* **BitConverter**

Method	Meaning
public static int ToInt32(byte[ ] *a*, int *start*)	Converts four bytes starting at *a*[*start*] into its **int** equivalent and returns the result.
public static long ToInt64(byte[ ] *a*, int *start*)	Converts eight bytes starting at *a*[*start*] into its **long** equivalent and returns the result.
public static float ToSingle(byte[ ] *a*, int *start*)	Converts four bytes starting at *a*[*start*] into its **float** equivalent and returns the result.
public static string ToString(byte[ ] *a*)	Converts the bytes in *a* into a string. The string contains the hexadecimal values associated with the bytes, separated by hyphens.
public static string ToString(byte[ ] *a*, int *start*)	Converts the bytes in *a*, beginning at *a*[*start*], into a string. The string contains the hexadecimal values associated with the bytes, separated by hyphens.
public static string ToString(byte[ ] *a*, int *start*, int *count*)	Converts the bytes in *a*, beginning at *a*[*start*] and running for *count* bytes, into a string. The string contains the hexadecimal values associated with the bytes, separated by hyphens.
public static ushort ToUInt16(byte[ ] *a*, int *start*)	Converts two bytes starting at *a*[*start*] into its **ushort** equivalent and returns the result.
public static uint ToUInt32(byte[ ] *a*, int *start*)	Converts four bytes starting at *a*[*start*] into its **uint** equivalent and returns the result.
public static ulong ToUInt64(byte[ ] *a*, int *start*)	Converts eight bytes starting at *a*[*start*] into its **ulong** equivalent and returns the result.

Table 19-13. *Methods Defined by **BitConverter** (continued)*

Generating Random Numbers with Random

To generate a sequence of pseudorandom numbers, you will use the **Random** class. Sequences of random numbers are useful in a variety of situations, including simulations and modeling. The starting point of the sequence is determined by a *seed* value, which can be automatically provided by **Random** or explicitly specified.

Random defines these two constructors:

```
public Random( )
public Random(int seed)
```

The first version creates a **Random** object that uses the system time to compute the seed value. The second uses the value of *seed* as the seed value.

Random defines the methods shown in Table 19-14.

Method	Meaning
public virtual int Next( )	Returns the next random integer, which will be between 0 and **Int32.MaxValue**–1, inclusive.
public virtual int Next(int *upperBound*)	Returns the next random integer that is between 0 and *upperBound*–1, inclusive.
public virtual int Next(int *lowerBound*, int *upperBound*)	Returns the next random integer that is between *lowerBound* and *upperBound*–1, inclusive.
public virtual void NextBytes(byte[ ] *buf*)	Fills *buf* with a sequence of random integers. Each byte in the array will be between 0 and **Byte.MaxValue**–1, inclusive.
public virtual double NextDouble( )	Returns the next random value from the sequence represented as a floating-point number that is greater than or equal to 0.0 and less than 1.0.
protected virtual double Sample( )	Returns the next random value from the sequence represented as a floating-point number that is greater than or equal to 0.0 and less than 1.0. To create a skewed or specialized distribution, override this method in a derived class.

Table 19-14.   *Methods Defined by* **Random**

Here is a program that demonstrates **Random** by creating a pair of computerized dice:

```
// An automated pair of dice.

using System;

class RandDice {
  public static void Main() {
    Random ran = new Random();

    Console.Write(ran.Next(1, 7) + " ");
    Console.WriteLine(ran.Next(1, 7));
  }
}
```

Here are three sample runs:

```
5 2
4 4
1 6
```

The program works by first creating a **Random** object. Then it requests the two random values, each between 1 and 6.

Memory Management and the GC Class

The **GC** class encapsulates the C# garbage-collection facility. The methods defined by **GC** are shown in Table 19-15. It defines the read-only property shown here:

public static int MaxGeneration { get; }

MaxGeneration contains the generation number of the oldest piece of allocated memory. Each time an allocation occurs (such as through the use of **new**), the allocated memory is given a generation number of zero. The generation numbers of older allocated units are increased. Thus, **MaxGeneration** indicates the number of the oldest unit of allocated memory. Generation numbers help improve the efficiency of the garbage collector.

For most applications, you will not use any of the capabilities of **GC**. However, in specialized cases, they can be very useful. For example, you might want to use **Collect( )** to force garbage collection to occur at a time of your choosing. Normally, garbage collection occurs at times unspecified by your program. Since garbage collection takes time, you might not want it to occur during some time-critical task, or you might want to take advantage of idle time to perform garbage collection and other types of "housekeeping" chores.

GC is **sealed**, which means that it cannot be inherited.

Method	Meaning
public static void Collect( )	Initiates garbage collection.
public static void Collect(int *MaxGen*)	Initiates garbage collection for memory with generation numbers of 0 through *MaxGen*.
public static int GetGeneration(object *o*)	Returns the generation number for the memory referred to by *o*.
public static int GetGeneration(WeakReference *o*)	Returns the generation number for the memory referred to by the weak reference specified by *o*. A weak reference does not prevent the object from being garbage-collected.
public static long GetTotalMemory(bool *collect*)	Returns the total number of bytes currently allocated. If *collect* is **true**, garbage collection occurs first.
public static void KeepAlive(object *o*)	Creates a reference to *o*, thus preventing it from being garbage collected.
public static void ReRegisterForFinalize(object *o*)	Causes the finalizer (i.e., the destructor) for *o* to be called. This method undoes the effects of **SuppressFinalize( )**.
public static void SuppressFinalize(object *o*)	Prevents the finalizer (i.e., the destructor) for *o* from being called.
public static void WaitForPendingFinalizers( )	Halts execution of the invoking thread of execution until all pending finalizers (i.e., destructors) have been called.

Table 19-15. *Methods Defined by* **GC**

Object

Object is the class that underlies the C# **object** type. The members of **Object** were discussed in Chapter 11, but because of its central role in C#, its methods are repeated in Table 19-16 for your convenience. **Object** defines one constructor, which is shown here:

Object( )

It constructs an empty object.

Method	Purpose
public virtual bool Equals(object *ob*)	Returns **true** if the invoking object is the same as the one referred to by *object*. Returns **false** otherwise.
public static bool Equals(object *ob1*, object *ob2*)	Returns **true** if *ob1* is the same as *ob2*. Returns **false** otherwise.
protected Finalize( )	Performs shutdown actions prior to garbage collection. In C#, **Finalize( )** is accessed through a destructor.
public virtual int GetHashCode( )	Returns the hash code associated with the invoking object.
public Type GetType( )	Obtains the type of an object at runtime.
protected object MemberwiseClone( )	Makes a "shallow copy" of the object. This is one in which the members are copied, but objects referred to by members are not.
public static bool ReferenceEquals(object *ob1*, object *ob2*)	Returns **true** if *ob1* and *ob2* refer to the same object. Returns **false** otherwise.
public virtual string ToString( )	Returns a string that describes the object.

Table 19-16. *Methods Defined by* **Object**

The IComparable Interface

Many classes will need to implement the **IComparable** interface because it enables one object to be compared to another by various methods defined by the C# library. **IComparable** is easy to implement because it consists of just this one method:

int CompareTo(object *v*)

This method compares the invoking object against the value in *v*. It returns greater than zero if the invoking object is greater than *v*, zero if the two objects are equal, and less than zero if the invoking object is less than *v*.

The IConvertible Interface

The **IConvertible** interface is implemented by all of the value-type structures. It specifies various type conversions. Normally, classes that you create will not need to implement this interface.

The ICloneable Interface

By implementing the **ICloneable** interface, you enable a copy of an object to be made. **ICloneable** defines only one method, **Clone( )**, which is shown here:

object Clone( )

This method makes a copy of the invoking object. How you implement **Clone( )** determines how the copy is made. In general, there are two types of copies: deep and shallow. When a deep copy is made, the copy and original are completely independent. Thus, if the original object contained a reference to another object *O*, then a copy of *O* will also be made. In a shallow copy, members are copied, but objects referred to by members are not. If an object refers to some other object *O*, then after a shallow copy, both the copy and the original will refer to the same *O*, and any changes to *O* affect both the copy and the original. Usually, you will implement **Clone( )** so that it performs a deep copy. Shallow copies can be made by using **MemberwiseClone( )**, which is defined by **Object**.

Here is an example that illustrates **ICloneable**. It creates a class called **Test** that contains a reference to a class called **X**. **Test** uses **Clone( )** to create a deep copy.

```
// Demonstrate ICloneable.

using System;

class X {
  public int a;
```

```
    public X(int x) { a = x; }
}

class Test : ICloneable {
  public X o;
  public int b;

  public Test(int x, int y) {
    o = new X(x);
    b = y;
  }

  public void show(string name) {
    Console.Write(name + " values are ");
    Console.WriteLine("o.a: {0}, b: {1}", o.a, b);
  }

  // Make a deep copy of the invoking object.
  public object Clone() {
    Test temp = new Test(o.a, b);
    return temp;
  }

}

class CloneDemo {
  public static void Main() {
    Test ob1 = new Test(10, 20);

    ob1.show("ob1");

    Console.WriteLine("Make ob2 a clone of ob1.");
    Test ob2 = (Test) ob1.Clone();

    ob2.show("ob2");

    Console.WriteLine("Changing ob1.o.a to 99 and ob1.b to 88.");
    ob1.o.a = 99;
    ob1.b = 88;

    ob1.show("ob1");
    ob2.show("ob2");
  }
}
```

The output is shown here:

```
ob1 values are o.a: 10, b: 20
Make ob2 a clone of ob1.
ob2 values are o.a: 10, b: 20
Changing ob1.o.a to 99 and ob1.b to 88.
ob1 values are o.a: 99, b: 88
ob2 values are o.a: 10, b: 20
```

As the output shows, **ob2** is a clone of **ob1**, but **ob1** and **ob2** are completely separate objects. Changing one does not affect the other. This is accomplished by allocating a new **X** object for the copy and giving it the same value as the **X** object in the original.

To implement a shallow copy, simply have **Clone( )** call **MemberwiseClone( )** defined by **Object**. For example, try changing **Clone( )** in the preceding program as shown here:

```
// Make a shallow copy of the invoking object.
public object Clone() {
  Test temp = (Test) MemberwiseClone();
  return temp;
}
```

After making this change, the output of the program will look like this:

```
ob1 values are o.a: 10, b: 20
Make ob2 a clone of ob1.
ob2 values are o.a: 10, b: 20
Changing ob1.o.a to 99 and ob1.b to 88.
ob1 values are o.a: 99, b: 88
ob2 values are o.a: 99, b: 20
```

Notice that **o** in **ob1** and **o** in **ob2** both refer to the same **X** object. Changing one affects both. Of course, the **int** field **b** in each is still separate because the value types are not accessed via references.

IFormatProvider and IFormattable

The **IFormatProvider** interface defines one method called **GetFormat( )**, which returns an object that controls the formatting of data into a human-readable string. The general form of **GetFormat( )** is shown here:

object GetFormat(Type *fmt*)

Here, *fmt* specifies the format object to obtain. Formatting is described in Chapter 20.

The **IFormattable** interface supports the formatting of human-readable output. **IFormattable** defines this method:

string ToString(string *fmt*, IFormatProvider *fmtpvdr*)

Here, *fmt* specifies formatting instructions and *fmtpvdr* specifies the format provider. Formatting is described in detail in Chapter 20.

The Complete Reference

Chapter 20

Strings and Formatting

This chapter examines the **String** class. As all programmers know, string handling is a part of almost any program. For this reason, the **String** class defines an extensive set of methods, properties, and fields that give you detailed control of the construction and manipulation of strings. Closely related to string handling is the formatting of data into its human-readable form. Using the formatting subsystem, you can format the C# numeric types, date and time, and enumerations.

Strings in C#

An overview of C#'s string handling was presented in Chapter 7, and that discussion is not repeated here. However, it is worthwhile to review how strings are implemented in C# before examining the **String** class.

In all computer languages, a *string* is a sequence of characters, but precisely how such a sequence is implemented varies from language to language. In some computer languages, such as C++, strings are arrays of characters, but this is not the case with C#. Instead, C# strings are objects of the built-in **string** data type. Thus, **string** is a reference type. Moreover, **string** is C#'s name for **System.String**, the standard .NET string type. Thus, a C# string has access to all of the methods, properties, fields, and operators defined by **String**.

Once a string has been created, the character sequence that comprises a string cannot be altered. This restriction allows C# to implement strings more efficiently. Although this restriction probably sounds like a serious drawback, it isn't. When you need a string that is a variation on one that already exists, simply create a new string that contains the desired changes, and discard the original string if it is no longer needed. Since unused string objects are automatically garbage-collected, you don't need to worry about what happens to the discarded strings. It must be made clear, however, that **string** reference variables may, of course, change the object to which they refer. It is just that the character sequence of a specific **string** object cannot be changed after it is created.

To create a string that can be changed, C# offers a class called **StringBuilder**, which is in the **System.Text** namespace. For most purposes, however, you will want to use **string**, not **StringBuilder**.

The String Class

String is defined in the **System** namespace. It implements the **IComparable**, **ICloneable**, **IConvertible**, and **IEnumerable** interfaces. **String** is a sealed class, which means that it cannot be inherited. **String** provides string-handling functionality for C#. It underlies C#'s built-in **string** type and is part of the .NET Framework. The next few sections examine **String** in detail.

The String Constructors

The **String** class defines several constructors that allow you to construct a string in a variety of ways. To create a string from a character array, use one of these constructors:

public String(char[ ] *chrs*)
public String(char[ ] *chrs*, int *start*, int *count*)

The first form constructs a string that contains the characters in *chrs*. The second form uses *count* characters from *chrs*, beginning at the index specified by *start*.

You can create a string that contains a specific character repeated a number of times using this constructor:

public String(char *ch*, int *count*)

Here, *ch* specifies the character that will be repeated *count* times.

You can construct a string given a pointer to a character array using one of these constructors:

unsafe public String(char* *chrs*)
unsafe public String(char* *chrs*, int *start*, int *count*)

The first form constructs a string that contains the characters pointed to by *chrs*. It is assumed that *chrs* points to a null-terminated array, which is used in its entirety. The second form uses *count* characters from the array pointed to by *chrs*, beginning at the index specified by *start*.

You can construct a string given a pointer to an array of bytes using one of these constructors:

unsafe public String(sbyte* *chrs*)
unsafe public String(sbyte* *chrs*, int *start*, int *count*)
unsafe public String(sbyte* *chrs*, int *start*, int *count*, Encoding *en*)

The first form constructs a string that contains the bytes pointed to by *chrs*. It is assumed that *chrs* points to a null-terminated array, which is used in its entirety. The second form uses *count* characters from the array pointed to by *chrs*, beginning at the index specified by *start*. The third form lets you specify how the bytes are encoded. The default encoding is **ASCIIEncoding**. The **Encoding** class is in the **System.Text** namespace.

A string literal automatically creates a string object. For this reason, a **string** object is often initialized by assigning it a string literal, as shown here:

```
string str = "a new string";
```

The String Field, Indexer, and Property

The **String** class defines one field, shown here:

public static readonly string Empty

Empty specifies an empty string, which is a string that contains no characters. This differs from a null **String** reference, which simply refers to no object.

There is one read-only indexer defined for **String**, which is shown here:

public char this[int idx] { get; }

This indexer allows you to obtain the character at a specified index. Like arrays, the indexing for strings begins at zero. Since **String** objects are immutable, it makes sense that **String** supports a read-only indexer.

There is one read-only property:

public int Length { get; }

Length returns the number of characters in the string.

The String Operators

The **String** class overloads two operators: = = and !=. To test two strings for equality, use the = = operator. Normally, when the = = operator is applied to object references, it determines if both references refer to the same object. This differs for objects of type **String**. When the = = is applied to two **String** references, the contents of the strings, themselves, are compared for equality. The same is true for the != operator: When comparing **String** objects, the contents of the strings are compared. However, the other relational operators, such as < or >=, compare the references, just like they do for other types of objects. To determine if one string is greater than or less than another, use the **Compare( )** method defined by **String**.

The String Methods

The **String** class defines a large number of methods. Furthermore, many of the methods have two or more overloaded forms. For this reason it is neither practical nor useful to list them all. Instead, several of the more commonly used methods will be presented, along with examples that illustrate their use.

Comparing Strings

Perhaps the most frequently used string-handling operation is the comparison of one string to another. Because of its importance, **String** provides a wide array of comparison methods. These are shown in Table 20-1. The **Compare( )** method is the most versatile. It can compare two strings in their entirety or in parts. It can use case-sensitive comparisons or ignore case. In general, string comparisons use dictionary order to determine whether one string is greater than, equal to, or less than another. You can also specify cultural information that governs the comparison.

The following program demonstrates several versions of **Compare( )**:

```
// Compare strings.

using System;

class CompareDemo {
  public static void Main() {
    string str1 = "one";
    string str2 = "one";
    string str3 = "ONE";
    string str4 = "two";
    string str5 = "one, too";


    if(String.Compare(str1, str2) == 0)
      Console.WriteLine(str1 + " and " + str2 +
                        " are equal.");
    else
      Console.WriteLine(str1 + " and " + str2 +
                        " are not equal.");


    if(String.Compare(str1, str3) == 0)
      Console.WriteLine(str1 + " and " + str3 +
                        " are equal.");
    else
      Console.WriteLine(str1 + " and " + str3 +
                        " are not equal.");

    if(String.Compare(str1, str3, true) == 0)
      Console.WriteLine(str1 + " and " + str3 +
                        " are equal ignoring case.");
    else
      Console.WriteLine(str1 + " and " + str3 +
```

```
                               " are not equal ignoring case.");

      if(String.Compare(str1, str5) == 0)
        Console.WriteLine(str1 + " and " + str5 +
                          " are equal.");
      else
        Console.WriteLine(str1 + " and " + str5 +
                          " are not equal.");

      if(String.Compare(str1, 0, str5, 0, 3) == 0)
        Console.WriteLine("First part of " + str1 + " and " +
                          str5 + " are equal.");
      else
        Console.WriteLine("First part of " + str1 + " and " +
                          str5 + " are not equal.");

      int result = String.Compare(str1, str4);
      if(result < 0)
        Console.WriteLine(str1 + " is less than " + str4);
      else if(result > 0)
        Console.WriteLine(str1 + " is greater than " + str4);
      else
        Console.WriteLine(str1 + " equals " + str4);
  }
}
```

The output is shown here:

```
one and one are equal.
one and ONE are not equal.
one and ONE are equal ignoring case.
one and one, too are not equal.
First part of one and one, too are equal.
one is less than two
```

Method	Description
public static int Compare(string *str1*, string *str2*)	Compares the string referred to by *str1* with *str2*. Returns greater than zero if *str1* is greater than *str2*, less than zero if *str1* is less than *str2*, and zero if *str1* and *str2* are equal.

public static int
    Compare(string *str1*, string *str2*,
            bool *ignoreCase*)
	Compares the string referred to by *str1* with *str2*. Returns greater than zero if *str1* is greater than *str2*, less than zero if *str1* is less than *str2*, and zero if *str1* and *str2* are equal. If *ignoreCase* is **true**, the comparison ignores case differences. Otherwise, case differences matter.

public static int
    Compare(string *str1*, string *str2*,
            bool *ignoreCase*,
            CultureInfo *ci*)
	Compares the string referred to by *str1* with *str2* using the cultural information passed in *ci*. Returns greater than zero if *str1* is greater than *str2*, less than zero if *str1* is less than *str2*, and zero if *str1* and *str2* are equal. If *ignoreCase* is **true**, the comparison ignores case differences. Otherwise, case differences matter. The **CultureInfo** class is defined in the **System.Globalization** namespace.

public static int
    Compare(string *str1*, int *start1*,
            string *str2*, int *start2*,
            int *count*)
	Compares portions of the strings referred to by *str1* and *str2*. The comparison begins at *str1*[*start1*] and *str2*[*start2*] and runs for *count* characters. Returns greater than zero if *str1* is greater than *str2*, less than zero if *str1* is less than *str2*, and zero if *str1* and *str2* are equal.

public static int
    Compare(string *str1*, int *start1*,
            string *str2*, int *start2*,
            int *count*,
            bool *ignoreCase*)
	Compares portions of the strings referred to by *str1* and *str2*. The comparison begins at *str1*[*start1*] and *str2*[*start2*] and runs for *count* characters. Returns greater than zero if *str1* is greater than *str2*, less than zero if *str1* is less than *str2*, and zero if *str1* and *str2* are equal. If *ignoreCase* is **true**, the comparison ignores case differences. Otherwise, case differences matter.

Table 20-1.   *The **String** Comparison Methods*

Method	Description

public static int
  Compare(string *str1*, int *start1*,
    string *str2*, int *start2*,
    int *count*,
    bool *ignoreCase*,
    CultureInfo *ci*)
	Compares portions of the strings referred to by *str1* and *str2* using the cultural information passed in *ci*. The comparison begins at *str1*[*start1*] and *str2*[*start2*] and runs for *count* characters. Returns greater than zero if *str1* is greater than *str2*, less than zero if *str1* is less than *str2*, and zero if *str1* and *str2* are equal. If *ignoreCase* is **true**, the comparison ignores case differences. Otherwise, case differences matter. The **CultureInfo** class is defined in the **System.Globalization** namespace.

public static int CompareOrdinal(string *str1*, string *str2*)	Compares the string referred to by *str1* with *str2* independently of culture, region, or language. Returns greater than zero if *str1* is greater than *str2*, less than zero if *str1* is less than *str2*, and zero if *str1* and *str2* are equal.

public static int
  CompareOrdinal(string *str1*, int *start1*,
    string *str2*, int *start2*,
    int *count*)
	Compares portions of the strings referred to by *str1* and *str2* independently of culture, region, or language. The comparison begins at *str1*[*start1*] and *str2*[*start2*] and runs for *count* characters. Returns greater than zero if *str1* is greater than *str2*, less than zero if *str1* is less than *str2*, and zero if *str1* and *str2* are equal.

public int CompareTo(object *str*)	Compares the invoking string with *str*. Returns greater than zero if the invoking string is greater than *str*, less than zero if the invoking string is less than *str*, and zero if the two are equal.
public int CompareTo(string *str*)	Compares the invoking string with *str*. Returns greater than zero if the invoking string is greater than *str*, less than zero if the invoking string is less than *str*, and zero if the two are equal.

Table 20-1. *The **String** Comparison Methods* (continued)

Concatenating Strings

There are two ways to concatenate (join together) two or more strings. First, you can use the + operator, as demonstrated in Chapter 7. Second, you can use one of the various concatenation methods defined by **String**. Although using + is the easiest approach in many cases, the concatenation methods give you some additional options.

The method that performs concatenation is called **Concat( )**, and its simplest form is shown here:

public static string Concat(string *str1*, string *str2*)

This method returns a string that contains *str2* concatenated to the end of *str1*. Another form of **Concat( )**, shown here, concatenates three strings:

public static string Concat(string *str1*, string *str2*, string *str3*)

In this version, a string that contains the concatenation of *str1*, *str2*, and *str3* is returned. Frankly, it is easier to use the + operator to perform these operations rather than the **Concat( )** method.

A more useful version of **Concat( )**, shown next, concatenates an arbitrary number of strings:

public static string Concat(params string[ ] *strs*)

Here, *strs* refers to a variable number of arguments that are concatenated, and the result is returned. The following program demonstrates this version of **Concat( )**:

```
// Demonstrate Concat().

using System;

class ConcatDemo {
  public static void Main() {

    string result = String.Concat("This ", "is ", "a ",
                                  "test ", "of ", "the ",
                                  "String ", "class.");

    Console.WriteLine("result: " + result);

  }
}
```

The output is shown here:

```
result: This is a test of the String class.
```

Some versions of the **Concat( )** method take **object** references, rather than **string** references. These obtain the string representation of the objects with which they are called and return a string containing the concatenation of those strings. These versions of **Concat( )** are shown here:

public static string Concat(object *v1*, object *v2*)
public static string Concat(object *v1*, object *v2*, object *v3*)
public static string Concat(params object[ ] *v*)

The first returns a string that contains the string representation of *v2* concatenated to the end of the string representation of *v1*. The second returns a string that contains the concatenation of the string representations of *v1*, *v2*, and *v3*. The third returns a string that contains the concatenation of the string representations of the arguments passed in *v*. To see how useful these methods can be, consider the following program:

```
// Demonstrate Concat().

using System;

class ConcatDemo {
  public static void Main() {

    string result = String.Concat("hi ", 10, " ",
                                  20.0, " ",
                                  false, " ",
                                  23.45M);

    Console.WriteLine("result: " + result);
  }
}
```

The output is shown here:

```
result: hi 10 20 False 23.45
```

In this example, **Concat( )** concatenates the string representations of various types of data. For each argument, the **ToString( )** method associated with that argument is called to obtain a string representation. Thus, for the value 10, **Int32.ToString( )** is invoked. **Concat( )** then concatenates those strings and returns the result. This form of

Concat( ) is very convenient because it prevents you from having to manually obtain string representations prior to concatenation.

Searching a String

String offers two sets of methods that allow you to search a string. You can search for either a substring or a character. You can also search for the first or last occurrence of either. To search for the first occurrence of a character or substring, use the **IndexOf( )** method. Here are two of its forms:

```
public int IndexOf(char ch)
public int IndexOf(String str)
```

The first form returns the index of the first occurrence of the character *ch* within the invoking string. The second form returns the first occurrence of the string *str*. Both return –1 if the item is not found.

To search for the last occurrence of a character or substring, use the **LastIndexOf( )** method. Here are two of its forms:

```
public int LastIndexOf(char ch)
public int LastIndexOf(string str)
```

The first form returns the index of the last occurrence of the character *ch* within the invoking string. The second form returns the index of the last occurrence of the string *str*. Both return –1 if the item is not found.

String offers two interesting supplemental search methods: **IndexOfAny( )** and **LastIndexOfAny( )**. These search for the first or last character that matches any of a set of characters. Here are their simplest forms:

```
public int IndexOfAny(char[ ] a)
public int LastIndexOfAny(char[ ] a)
```

IndexOfAny( ) returns the index of the first occurrence of any character in *a* that is found within the invoking string. **LastIndexOfAny( )** returns the index of the last occurrence of any character in *a* that is found within the invoking string. Both return –1 if no match is found.

When working with strings, it is often useful to know if a string begins with or ends with a given substring. To accomplish these tasks, use the **StartsWith( )** and **EndsWith( )** methods, shown here:

```
public bool StartsWith(string str)
public bool EndsWith(string str)
```

StartsWith( ) returns **true** if the invoking string begins with the string passed in *str*. **EndsWith( )** returns **true** if the invoking string ends with the string passed in *str*. Both return **false** on failure.

Here is a program that demonstrates several of the string search methods:

```csharp
// Search strings.

using System;

class StringSearchDemo {
  public static void Main() {
    string str = "C# has powerful string handling.";
    int idx;

    Console.WriteLine("str: " + str);

    idx = str.IndexOf('h');
    Console.WriteLine("Index of first 'h': " + idx);

    idx = str.LastIndexOf('h');
    Console.WriteLine("Index of last 'h': " + idx);

    idx = str.IndexOf("ing");
    Console.WriteLine("Index of first \"ing\": " + idx);

    idx = str.LastIndexOf("ing");
    Console.WriteLine("Index of last \"ing\": " + idx);

    char[] chrs = { 'a', 'b', 'c' };
    idx = str.IndexOfAny(chrs);
    Console.WriteLine("Index of first 'a', 'b', or 'c': " + idx);

    if(str.StartsWith("C# has"))
      Console.WriteLine("str begins with \"C# has\"");

    if(str.EndsWith("ling."))
      Console.WriteLine("str ends with \"ling.\"");
  }
}
```

The output from the program is shown here:

```
str: C# has powerful string handling.
Index of first 'h': 3
Index of last 'h': 23
Index of first "ing": 19
```

```
Index of last "ing": 28
Index of first 'a', 'b', or 'c': 4
str begins with "C# has"
str ends with "ling."
```

Several of the search methods have additional forms that allow you to begin a search at a specified index or to specify a range to search within. All versions of the **String** search methods are shown in Table 20-2.

Method	Description
public bool EndsWith(string *str*)	Returns **true** if the invoking string ends with the string passed in *str*. Otherwise, **false** is returned.
public int IndexOf(char *ch*)	Returns the index of the first occurrence of *ch* within the invoking string. Returns –1 if *ch* is not found.
public int IndexOf(string *str*)	Returns the index of the first occurrence of *str* within the invoking string. Returns –1 if *str* is not found.
public int IndexOf(char *ch*, int *start*)	Returns the index of the first occurrence of *ch* within the invoking string. Searching begins at the index specified by *start*. Returns –1 if *ch* is not found.
public int IndexOf(string *str*, int *start*)	Returns the index of the first occurrence of *str* within the invoking string. Searching begins at the index specified by *start*. Returns –1 if *str* is not found.
public int IndexOf(char *ch*, int *start*, int *count*)	Returns the index of the first occurrence of *ch* within the invoking string. Searching begins at the index specified by *start* and runs for *count* elements. Returns –1 if *ch* is not found.
public int IndexOf(string *str*, int *start*, int *count*)	Returns the index of the first occurrence of *str* within the invoking string. Searching begins at the index specified by *start* and runs for *count* elements. Returns –1 if *str* is not found.

Table 20-2. *The Search Methods Offered by* **String**

Method	Description
public int IndexOfAny(char[ ] *a*)	Returns the index of the first occurrence of any character in *a* that is found within the invoking string. Returns –1 if no match is found.
public int IndexOfAny(char[ ] *a*, int *start*)	Returns the index of the first occurrence of any character in *a* that is found within the invoking string. Searching begins at the index specified by *start*. Returns –1 if no match is found.
public int IndexOfAny(char[ ] *a*, int *start*, int *count*)	Returns the index of the first occurrence of any character in *a* that is found within the invoking string. Searching begins at the index specified by *start* and runs for *count* elements. Returns –1 if no match is found.
public int LastIndexOf(char *ch*)	Returns the index of the last occurrence of *ch* within the invoking string. Returns –1 if *ch* is not found.
public int LastIndexOf(string *str*)	Returns the index of the last occurrence of *str* within the invoking string. Returns –1 if *str* is not found.
public int LastIndexOf(char *ch*, int *start*)	Returns the index of the last occurrence of *ch* within a range of the invoking string. The search proceeds in reverse order, beginning at the index specified by *start* and stopping at zero. Returns –1 if the *ch* is not found.
public int LastIndexOf(string *str*, int *start*)	Returns the index of the last occurrence of *str* within a range of the invoking string. The search proceeds in reverse order, beginning at the index specified by *start* and stopping at zero. Returns –1 if *str* is not found.
public int LastIndexOf(char *ch*, int *start*, int *count*)	Returns the index of the last occurrence of *ch* within the invoking string. The search proceeds in reverse order, beginning at the index specified by *start* and running for *count* elements. Returns –1 if *ch* is not found.

Table 20-2. *The Search Methods Offered by* **String** *(continued)*

Method	Description
public int LastIndexOf(string *str*, int *start*, int *count*)	Returns the index of the last occurrence of *str* within the invoking string. The search proceeds in reverse order, beginning at the index specified by *start* and running for *count* elements. Returns –1 if *str* is not found.
public int LastIndexOfAny(char[ ] *a*)	Returns the index of the last occurrence of any character in *a* that is found within the invoking string. Returns –1 if no match is found.
public int LastIndexOfAny(char[ ] *a*, int *start*)	Returns the index of the last occurrence of any character in *a* that is found within the invoking string. The search proceeds in reverse order, beginning at the index specified by *start* and stopping at zero. Returns –1 if no match is found.
public int LastIndexOfAny(char[ ] *a*, int *start*, int *count*)	Returns the index of the last occurrence of any character in *a* that is found within the invoking string. The search proceeds in reverse order, beginning at the index specified by *start* and running for *count* elements. Returns –1 if no match is found.
public bool StartsWith(string *str*)	Returns **true** if the invoking string begins with the string passed in *str*. Otherwise, **false** is returned.

Table 20-2. *The Search Methods Offered by* **String** (continued)

Splitting and Joining Strings

Two fundamental string-handling operations are split and join. A *split* decomposes a string into its constituent parts. A *join* constructs a string from a set of parts. To split a string, **String** defines **Split( )**. To join a set of strings, **String** provides **Join( )**.

The general forms for **Split( )** are shown here:

```
public string[ ] split(params char[ ] seps)
public string[ ] split(params char[ ] seps, int count)
```

The first form splits the invoking string into pieces and returns an array containing the substrings. The characters that delimit each substring are passed in *seps*. If *seps* is null, then whitespace is used as the separator. In the second form, no more than *count* substrings will be returned.

The two forms of the **Join( )** method are shown here:

public static string Join(string *sep*, string[ ] *strs*)
public static string Join(string *sep*, string[ ] *strs*, int *start*, int *count*)

The first form returns a string that contains the concatenation of the strings in *strs*. The second form returns a string that contains the concatenation of *count* strings in *strs*, beginning at *strs[start]*. For both versions, each string is separated from the next by the string specified by *sep*.

The following program demonstrates **Split( )** and **Join( )**:

```
// Split and join strings.

using System;

class SplitAndJoinDemo {
  public static void Main() {
    string str = "One if by land, two if by sea.";
    char[] seps = {' ', '.', ',' };

    // Split the string into parts.
    string[] parts = str.Split(seps);
    Console.WriteLine("Pieces from split: ");
    for(int i=0; i < parts.Length; i++)
      Console.WriteLine(parts[i]);

    // Now, join the parts.
    string whole = String.Join(" | ", parts);
    Console.WriteLine("Result of join: ");
    Console.WriteLine(whole);
  }
}
```

Here is the output:

```
Pieces from split:
One
if
```

```
by
land

two
if
by
sea

Result of join:
One | if | by | land |   | two | if | by | sea |
```

Splitting a string is an important string-manipulation procedure, because it is often used to obtain the individual *tokens* that comprise the string. For example, a database program might use **Split( )** to decompose a query such as "show me all balances greater than 100" into its individual parts, such as "show" and "100". In the process, the separators are removed. Thus, "show" (without any leading or trailing spaces) is obtained, not " show ". The following program illustrates this concept. It tokenizes strings containing binary mathematical operations, such as 10 + 5. It then performs the operation and displays the result.

```
// Tokenize strings.

using System;

class TokenizeDemo {
  public static void Main() {
    string[] input = {
                       "100 + 19",
                       "100 / 3.3",
                       "-3 * 9",
                       "100 - 87"
                     };
    char[] seps = {' '};

    for(int i=0; i < input.Length; i++) {
      // split string into parts
      string[] parts = input[i].Split(seps);
      Console.Write("Command: ");
      for(int j=0; j < parts.Length; j++)
        Console.Write(parts[j] + " ");
```

```
      Console.Write(", Result: ");
      double n = Double.Parse(parts[0]);
      double n2 = Double.Parse(parts[2]);

      switch(parts[1]) {
        case "+":
          Console.WriteLine(n + n2);
          break;
        case "-":
          Console.WriteLine(n - n2);
          break;
        case "*":
          Console.WriteLine(n * n2);
          break;
        case "/":
          Console.WriteLine(n / n2);
          break;
      }
    }
  }
}
```

Here is the output:

```
Command: 100 + 19 , Result: 119
Command: 100 / 3.3 , Result: 30.3030303030303
Command: -3 * 9 , Result: -27
Command: 100 - 87 , Result: 13
```

Padding and Trimming Strings

Sometimes you will want to remove leading and trailing spaces from a string. This type of operation, called *trimming,* is often needed by command processors. For example, a database might recognize the word "print". However, a user might enter this command with one or more leading or trailing spaces. Any such spaces must be removed before the string can be recognized by the database. Conversely, sometimes you will want to pad a string with spaces so that it meets some minimal length. For example, if you are preparing formatted output, you might need to ensure that each line is of a certain length in order to maintain an alignment. Fortunately, C# includes methods that make these types of operations easy.

To trim a string, use one of these **Trim( )** methods:

public string Trim( )
public string Trim(params char[ ] *chrs*)

The first form removes leading and trailing whitespace from the invoking string. The second form removes leading and trailing occurrences of the characters specified by *chrs*. In both cases the resulting string is returned.

You can pad a string by adding characters to either the left or the right side of the string. To pad a string on the left, use one of the methods shown here:

public string PadLeft(int *len*)
public string PadLeft(int *len*, char *ch*)

The first form adds spaces on the left as needed to the invoking string so that its total length equals *len*. The second form adds the characters specified by *ch* as needed to the invoking string so that its total length equals *len*. In both cases, the resulting string is returned.

To pad a string to the right, use one of these methods:

public string PadRight(int *len*)
public string PadRight(int *len*, char *ch*)

The first form adds spaces on the right as needed to the invoking string so that its total length equals *len*. The second form adds the characters specified by *ch* as needed to the invoking string so that its total length equals *len*. In both cases, the resulting string is returned.

The following program demonstrates trimming and padding:

```
// Trimming and padding.

using System;

class TrimPadDemo {
  public static void Main() {
    string str = "test";

    Console.WriteLine("Original string: " + str);

    // Pad on left with spaces.
    str = str.PadLeft(10);
    Console.WriteLine("|" + str + "|");
```

```
        // Pad on right with spaces.
        str = str.PadRight(20);
        Console.WriteLine("|" + str + "|");

        // Trim spaces.
        str = str.Trim();
        Console.WriteLine("|" + str + "|");

        // Pad on left with #s.
        str = str.PadLeft(10, '#');
        Console.WriteLine("|" + str + "|");

        // Pad on right with #s.
        str = str.PadRight(20, '#');
        Console.WriteLine("|" + str + "|");

        // Trim #s.
        str = str.Trim('#');
        Console.WriteLine("|" + str + "|");
    }
}
```

The output is shown here:

```
Original string: test
|        test|
|        test           |
|test|
|######test|
|######test#########|
|test|
```

Inserting, Removing, and Replacing

You can insert a string into another using the **Insert( )** method, shown here:

public string Insert(int *start*, string *str*)

Here, *str* is inserted into the invoking string at the index specified by *start*. The resulting string is returned.

You can remove a portion of a string using **Remove( )**, shown next:

public string Remove(int *start*, int *count*)

The number of characters to remove is specified by *count*. The index at which the removal begins is specified by *start*. The result is returned.

You can replace a portion of a string by using **Replace( )**. It has these forms:

public string Replace(char *ch1*, char *ch2*)
public string Replace(string *str1*, string *str2*)

The first form replaces all occurrences of *ch1* in the invoking string with *ch2*. The second form replaces all occurrences of *str1* in the invoking string with *str2*. In both cases, the resulting string is returned.

Here is an example that demonstrates **Insert( )**, **Remove( )**, and **Replace( )**:

```
// Inserting, replacing, and removing.

using System;

class InsRepRevDemo {
  public static void Main() {
    string str = "This test";

    Console.WriteLine("Original string: " + str);

    // Insert
    str = str.Insert(5, "is a ");
    Console.WriteLine(str);

    // Replace string
    str = str.Replace("is", "was");
    Console.WriteLine(str);

    // Replace characters
    str = str.Replace('a', 'X');
    Console.WriteLine(str);

    // Remove
    str = str.Remove(4, 5);
    Console.WriteLine(str);
  }
}
```

The output is shown here:

```
Original string: This test
This is a test
```

THE C# CLASS LIBRARY

```
Thwas was a test
ThwXs wXs X test
ThwX X test
```

Changing Case

String offers two convenient methods that enable you to change the case of letters within a string. These are called **ToUpper( )** and **ToLower( )**, and they are shown here:

>   public string ToLower( )
>   public string ToUpper( )

ToLower( ) lowercases all letters within the invoking string. **ToUpper( )** uppercases all letters within the invoking string. The resulting string is returned. There are also versions of these methods that allow you to specify cultural settings.

Using the Substring( ) Method

You can obtain a portion of a string by using the **Substring( )** method. It has these two forms:

>   public string Substring(int *idx*)
>   public string Substring(int *idx*, int *count*)

In the first form, the substring begins at the index specified by *idx* and runs to the end of the invoking string. In the second form, the substring begins at *idx* and runs for *count* characters. In each case the substring is returned.

The following program demonstrates the **Substring( )** method:

```
// Use Substring().

using System;

class SubstringDemo {
  public static void Main() {
    string str = "ABCDEFGHIJKLMNOPQRSTUVWXYZ";

    Console.WriteLine("str: " + str);

    Console.Write("str.Substring(15): ");
    string substr = str.Substring(15);
    Console.WriteLine(substr);
```

```
    Console.Write("str.Substring(0, 15): ");
    substr = str.Substring(0, 15);
    Console.WriteLine(substr);
  }
}
```

The following output is produced:

```
str: ABCDEFGHIJKLMNOPQRSTUVWXYZ
str.Substring(15): PQRSTUVWXYZ
str.Substring(0, 15): ABCDEFGHIJKLMNO
```

Formatting

When a human-readable form of a built-in type, such as **int** or **double**, is needed, a string representation must be created. Although C# automatically supplies a default format for this representation, it is also possible to specify a format of your own choosing. For example, as you saw in Part I, it is possible to output numeric data using a dollars and cents format. A number of methods format data, including **Console.WriteLine( )**, **String.Format( )**, and the **ToString( )** method defined for the numeric structure types. The same approach to formatting is used by all three; once you have learned to format data for one, you can apply it to the others.

Formatting Overview

Formatting is governed by two components: *format specifiers* and *format providers*. The form that the string representation of a value will take is controlled through the use of a format specifier. Thus, it is the format specifier that dictates how the human-readable form of the data will look. For example, to output a numeric value using scientific notation, you will use the E format specifier.

In many cases, the precise format of a value will be affected by the culture and language in which the program is running. For example, in the United States, money is represented in dollars. In Europe, money is represented in euros. To handle the cultural and language differences, C# uses format providers. A format provider defines the way that a format specifier will be interpreted. A format provider is created by implementing the **IFormatProvider** interface. Format providers are predefined for the built-in numeric types and many other types in the .NET Framework. In general, you can format data without having to worry about specifying a format provider, and format providers are not examined further in this book.

To format data, you include a format specifier in a call to a method that supports formatting. The use of format specifiers was introduced in Chapter 3, but is worthwhile reviewing here. The discussion that follows uses **WriteLine( )**, but the same basic approach applies to other methods that support formatting.

To format data using **WriteLine( )**, use the version of **WriteLine( )** shown here:

WriteLine("*format string*", *arg0, arg1, ... , argN*);

In this version, the arguments to **WriteLine( )** are separated by commas and not **+** signs. The *format string* contains two items: regular, printing characters that are displayed as-is, and format commands.

Format commands take this general form:

{*argnum, width: fmt*}

Here, *argnum* specifies the number of the argument (starting from zero) to display. The minimum width of the field is specified by *width,* and the format specifier is represented by *fmt*. Both *width* and *fmt* are optional. Thus, in its simplest form, a format command simply indicates which argument to display. For example, {0} indicates *arg0*, {1} specifies *arg1*, and so on.

During execution, when a format command is encountered in the format string, the corresponding argument, as specified by *argnum,* is substituted and displayed. Thus, it is the position of a format specification within the format string that determines where its matching data will be displayed.

If *fmt* is present, then the data is displayed using the specified format. Otherwise, the default format is used. If *width* is present, then output is padded with spaces to ensure that the minimum field width is attained. If *width* is positive, output is right-justified. If *width* is negative, output is left-justified.

The remainder of this chapter examines formatting and format specifiers in detail.

The Numeric Format Specifiers

Several format specifiers are defined for numeric data. They are shown in Table 20-3. Each format specifier can include an optional precision specifier. For example, to specify that a value be represented as a fixed-point value with two decimal places, use F2.

As explained, the precise effect of certain format specifiers depends upon the cultural settings. For example, the currency specifier, C, automatically displays a value in the monetary format of the selected culture. For most users, the default cultural information matches their locale and language. Thus, the same format specifier can be used without concern about the cultural context in which the program is executed.

Here is a program that demonstrates several of the numeric format specifiers:

```
// Demonstrate various format specifiers.
```

```
using System;

class FormatDemo {
  public static void Main() {
    double v = 17688.65849;
    double v2 = 0.15;
    int x = 21;

    Console.WriteLine("{0:F2}", v);

    Console.WriteLine("{0:N5}", v);

    Console.WriteLine("{0:e}", v);

    Console.WriteLine("{0:r}", v);

    Console.WriteLine("{0:p}", v2);

    Console.WriteLine("{0:X}", x);

    Console.WriteLine("{0:D12}", x);

    Console.WriteLine("{0:C}", 189.99);
  }
}
```

The output is shown here:

```
17688.66
17,688.65849
1.768866e+004
17688.65849
15.00 %
15
000000000021
$189.99
```

Notice the effect of the precision specifier in several of the formats.

Specifier	Format	Meaning of Precision Specifier
C	Currency (that is, a monetary value).	Specifies the number of decimal places.
c	Same as C.	
D	Whole number numeric data. (Use with integers only.)	Minimum number of digits. Leading zeros will be used to pad the result, if necessary.
d	Same as D.	
E	Scientific notation (uses uppercase E).	Specifies the number of decimal places. The default is six.
e	Scientific notation (uses lowercase e).	Specifies the number of decimal places. The default is six.
F	Fixed-point notation.	Specifies the number of decimal places.
f	Same as F.	
G	Use either E or F format, whichever is shorter.	See E and F.
g	Use either e or f format, whichever is shorter.	See e and f.
N	Fixed-point notation, with comma separators.	Specifies the number of decimal places.
n	Same as N.	
P	Percentage	Specifies the number of decimal places.
p	Same as P.	
R or r	Numeric value that can be parsed, using **Parse( )**, back into its equivalent internal form. (This is called the "round-trip" format.)	Not used.
X	Hexadecimal (uses uppercase letters *A* through *F*).	Minimum number of digits. Leading zeros will be used to pad the result, if necessary.

Table 20-3. *The Format Specifiers*

Specifier	Format	Meaning of Precision Specifier
x	Hexadecimal (uses lowercase letters *a* through *f*).	Minimum number of digits. Leading zeros will be used to pad the result if necessary.

Table 20-3. *The Format Specifiers* (continued)

Using String.Format( ) and ToString( ) to Format Data

Although embedding format commands into **WriteLine( )** is a convenient way to format output, sometimes you will want to create a string that contains the formatted data, but not immediately display that string. Doing so lets you format data in advance, allowing you to output it later, to the device of your choosing. This is especially useful in a GUI environment, such as Windows, in which console-based I/O is rarely used.

In general, there are two ways to obtain the formatted string representation of a value. One way is to use **String.Format( )**. The other is to pass a format specifier to the **ToString( )** method of the built-in numeric types. Each approach is examined here.

Using String.Format( ) to Format Values

You can obtain a formatted value by calling one of the **Format( )** methods defined by **String**. They are shown in Table 20-4. **Format( )** works much like **WriteLine( )**, except that it returns a formatted string rather than outputting it to the console.

Method	Description
public static string Format(string *str*, object *v*)	Formats *v* according to the first format command in *str*. Returns a copy of *str* in which formatted data has been substituted for the format command.

Table 20-4. *The **Format( )** Methods*

Method	Description
public static string Format(string *str*, object *v1*, object *v2*)	Formats *v1* according to the first format command in *str*, and *v2* according to the second format command in *str*. Returns a copy of *str* in which formatted data has been substituted for the format commands.
public static string Format(string *str*, object *v1*, object *v2*, object *v3*)	Formats *v1*, *v2*, and *v3* according to the corresponding format commands in *str*. Returns a copy of *str* in which formatted data has been substituted for the format commands.
public static string Format(string *str*, params object[ ] *v*)	Formats the values passed in *v* according to the format commands in *str*. Returns a copy of *str* in which formatted data has been substituted for each format command.
public static string Format(IFormatProvider *fmtprvdr*, string *str*, params object[ ] *v*)	Formats the values passed in *v* according to the format commands in *str* using the format provider specified by *fmtprvdr*. Returns a copy of *str* in which formatted data has been substituted for each format command.

Table 20-4. *The Format( ) Methods* (continued)

Here is the previous format demonstration program rewritten to use **String.Format( )**. It produces the same output as the earlier version.

```
// Use String.Format() to format a value.

using System;

class FormatDemo {
  public static void Main() {
    double v = 17688.65849;
```

```
      double v2 = 0.15;
      int x = 21;

      string str = String.Format("{0:F2}", v);
      Console.WriteLine(str);

      str = String.Format("{0:N5}", v);
      Console.WriteLine(str);

      str = String.Format("{0:e}", v);
      Console.WriteLine(str);

      str = String.Format("{0:r}", v);
      Console.WriteLine(str);

      str = String.Format("{0:p}", v2);
      Console.WriteLine(str);

      str = String.Format("{0:X}", x);
      Console.WriteLine(str);

      str = String.Format("{0:D12}", x);
      Console.WriteLine(str);

      str = String.Format("{0:C}", 189.99);
      Console.WriteLine(str);
   }
}
```

Like **WriteLine( )**, **String.Format( )** lets you embed regular text along with format specifiers, and you can use more than one format specifier and value. For example, consider this program, which displays the running sum and product of the numbers 1 through 10:

```
// A closer look at Format().

using System;

class FormatDemo2 {
  public static void Main() {
    int i;
```

```
    int sum = 0;
    int prod = 1;
    string str;

    /* Display the running sum and product
       for the numbers 1 through 10. */
    for(i=1; i <= 10; i++) {
      sum += i;
      prod *= i;
      str = String.Format("Sum:{0,3:D}  Product:{1,8:D}",
                           sum, prod);
      Console.WriteLine(str);
    }
  }
}
```

The output is shown here:

```
Sum:  1  Product:        1
Sum:  3  Product:        2
Sum:  6  Product:        6
Sum: 10  Product:       24
Sum: 15  Product:      120
Sum: 21  Product:      720
Sum: 28  Product:     5040
Sum: 36  Product:    40320
Sum: 45  Product:   362880
Sum: 55  Product:  3628800
```

In the program, pay close attention to this statement:

```
str = String.Format("Sum:{0,3:D}  Product:{1,8:D}",
                     sum, prod);
```

This call to **Format( )** contains two format specifiers, one for **sum** and one for **prod**. Notice that the argument numbers are specified just as they are when using **WriteLine( )**. Also, notice that regular text, such as "Sum:" is included. This text is passed through and becomes part of the output string.

Using ToString( ) to Format Data

For all of the built-in numeric structure types, such as **Int32** or **Double**, you can use **ToString( )** to obtain a formatted string representation of the value. To do so, you will use this version of **ToString( )**:

public string ToString(string *fmt*)

It returns the string representation of the invoking object as specified by the format specifier passed in *fmt*. For example, the following program creates a monetary representation of the value 188.99 through the use of the C format specifier:

```
string str = 189.99.ToString("C");
```

Notice how the format specifier is passed directly to **ToString( )**. Unlike embedded format commands used by **WriteLine( )** or **Format( )**, which supply an argument-number and field-width component, **ToString( )** requires only the format specifier, itself.

Here is a rewrite of the previous format program that uses **ToString( )** to obtain formatted strings. It produces the same output as the earlier versions.

```
// Use ToString() to format values.

using System;

class ToStringDemo {
  public static void Main() {
    double v = 17688.65849;
    double v2 = 0.15;
    int x = 21;

    string str = v.ToString("F2");
    Console.WriteLine(str);

    str = v.ToString("N5");
    Console.WriteLine(str);

    str = v.ToString("e");
    Console.WriteLine(str);
```

```
        str = v.ToString("r");
        Console.WriteLine(str);

        str = v2.ToString("p");
        Console.WriteLine(str);

        str = x.ToString("X");
        Console.WriteLine(str);

        str = x.ToString("D12");
        Console.WriteLine(str);

        str = 189.99.ToString("C");
        Console.WriteLine(str);
    }
}
```

Creating a Custom Numeric Format

Although the predefined numeric format specifiers are quite useful, C# gives you the ability to define your own, custom format using a feature sometimes called *picture format*. The term *picture format* comes from the fact that you create a custom format by specifying an example (that is, picture) of how you want the output to look. This approach was mentioned briefly in Part I. Here it is examined in detail.

The Custom Format Placeholder Characters

When you create a custom format, you specify that format by creating an example (or picture) of what you want the data to look like. To do this, you use the characters shown in Table 20-5 as placeholders. Each is examined in turn.

The period specifies where the decimal point will be located.

The # placeholder specifies a digit position. The # can occur on the left or right side of the decimal point, or by itself. When one or more #s occur on the right side of the decimal point, they specify the number of decimal digits to display. The value is rounded if necessary. When the # occurs to the left of the decimal point, it specifies the digit positions for the whole-number part of the value. Leading zeros will be added if necessary. If the whole-number portion of the value has more digits than there are #s, the entire whole-number portion will be displayed. In no cases will the whole-number portion of a value be truncated. If there is no decimal point, then the # causes the value to be rounded to its integer value. A zero value that is not significant, such as a trailing zero, will not be displayed. This causes a somewhat odd quirk, however, because a format such as ##.## displays nothing at all if the value being formatted is zero. To output a zero value, use the 0 placeholder described next.

The 0 placeholder causes a leading or trailing 0 to be added to ensure that a minimum number of digits will be present. It can be used on both the right and left side of the decimal point. For example,

```
Console.WriteLine("{0:00##.#00}", 21.3);
```

displays this output:

```
0021.300
```

Values containing more digits will be displayed in full on the left side of the decimal point and rounded on the right side.

You can insert commas into large numbers by specifying a pattern that embeds a comma within a sequence of #s. For example, this:

```
Console.WriteLine("{0:#,###.#}", 3421.3);
```

displays

```
3,421.3.
```

It is not necessary to specify each comma for each position. Specifying one comma causes it to be inserted into the value every third digit from the left. For example,

```
Console.WriteLine("{0:#,###.#}", 8763421.3);
```

produces this output:

```
8,763,421.3.
```

Commas have a second meaning. When they occur on the immediate left of the decimal point, they act as a scaling factor. Each comma causes the value to be divided by 1,000. For example,

```
Console.WriteLine("Value in thousands: {0:#,###,.#}", 8763421.3);
```

produces this output:

```
Value in thousands: 8,763.4
```

As the output shows, the value is scaled in terms of thousands.

In addition to the placeholders, a custom format specifier can contain other characters. Any other characters are simply passed through, appearing in the formatted string exactly as they appear in the format specifier. For example, this **WriteLine( )** statement:

```
Console.WriteLine("Fuel efficiency is {0:##.# mpg}", 21.3);
```

produces this output:

```
Fuel efficiency is 21.3 mpg
```

You can also use the escape sequences, such as \t or \n, if necessary.

The E and e placeholders cause a value to be displayed in scientific notation. At least one 0, but possibly more, must follow the E or e. The 0's indicate the number of decimal digits that will be displayed. The decimal component will be rounded to fit the format. Using an uppercase E causes an uppercase E to be displayed; using a lowercase e causes a lowercase e to be displayed. To ensure that a sign character precedes the exponent, use the $E+$ or $e+$ forms. To display a sign character for negative values only, use E, e, $E-$, or $e-$.

The ";" is a separator that enables you to specify different formats for positive, negative, and zero values. Here is the general form of a custom format specifier that uses the ";":

positive-fmt;negative-fmt;zero-fmt

Here is an example:

```
Console.WriteLine("{0:#.##;(#.##);0.00}", num);
```

If **num** is positive, the value is displayed with two decimal places. If **num** is negative, the value is displayed with two decimal places and is between a set of parentheses. If **num** is zero, the string 0.00 is displayed. When using the separators, you don't need to supply all parts. If you just want to specify how positive and negative values will look, omit the zero format. To use the default for negative values, omit the negative format. In this case, the positive format and the zero format will be separated by two semicolons.

The following program demonstrates just a few of the many possible custom formats that you can create:

```csharp
// Using custom formats.

using System;

class PictureFormatDemo {
  public static void Main() {
    double num = 64354.2345;

    Console.WriteLine("Default format: " + num);

    // Display with 2 decimal places.
    Console.WriteLine("Value with two decimal places: " +
                      "{0:#.##}", num);

    // Display with commas and 2 decimal places.
    Console.WriteLine("Add commas: {0:#,###.##}", num);

    // Display using scientific notation.
    Console.WriteLine("Use scientific notation: " +
                      "{0:#.###e+00}", num);

    // Scale the value by 1000.
    Console.WriteLine("Value in 1,000s: " +
                      "{0:#0,}", num);

    /* Display positive, negative, and zero
       values differently. */
    Console.WriteLine("Display positive, negative, " +
                      "and zero values differently.");
    Console.WriteLine("{0:#.#;(#.##);0.00}", num);
    num = -num;
    Console.WriteLine("{0:#.##;(#.##);0.00}", num);
    num = 0.0;
    Console.WriteLine("{0:#.##;(#.##);0.00}", num);

    // Display a percentage.
```

```
    num = 0.17;
    Console.WriteLine("Display a percentage: {0:#%}", num);
  }
}
```

The output is shown here:

```
Default format: 64354.2345
Value with two decimal places: 64354.23
Add commas: 64,354.23
Use scientific notation: 6.435e+04
Value in 1,000s: 64
Display positive, negative, and zero values differently.
64354.2
(64354.23)
0.00
Display a percentage: 17%
```

Placeholder	Meaning
#	Digit.
.	Decimal point.
,	Thousands separator.
%	Percentage.
0	Pads with leading and trailing zeros.
;	Separates sections that describe the format for positive, negative, and zero values.
E0 E+0 E-0 e0 e+0 e-0	Scientific notation.

Table 20-5. *Custom Format Placeholder Characters*

Formatting Date and Time

In addition to formatting numeric values, another data type to which formatting is often applied is **DateTime**. As explained in Chapter 19, **DateTime** represents date and time. Date and time values can be displayed a variety of ways. Here are just a few examples:

02/25/2002
Monday, February 25, 2002
12:59:00
12:59:00 PM

Also, the date and time representations can vary from country to country. For these reasons, C# provides an extensive formatting subsystem for time and date values.

Date and time formatting is handled through format specifiers. The format specifiers for date and time are shown in Table 20-6. Because the specific date and time representation may vary from country to country and by language, the precise representation generated will be influenced by the cultural settings of the computer.

Specifier	Format
D	Date in long form.
d	Date in short form.
T	Time in long form.
t	Time in short form.
F	Date and time in long form.
f	Date and time in short form.
G	Date in short form, time in long form.
g	Date in short form, time in short form.
M	Month and day.
m	Same as M.

Table 20-6. *The Date and Time Format Specifiers*

Specifier	Format
R	Date and time in standard, GMT form.
r	Same as R.
s	A sortable form of date and time.
U	Long form, universal sortable form of date and time; time is displayed as UTC.
u	Short form, universal sortable form of date and time.
Y	Month and year.
y	Same as Y.

Table 20-6.   *The Date and Time Format Specifiers* (continued)

Here is a program that demonstrates the date and time format specifiers:

```
// Format time and date information.

using System;

class TimeAndDateFormatDemo {
  public static void Main() {
    DateTime dt = DateTime.Now; // obtain current time

    Console.WriteLine("d format: {0:d}", dt);
    Console.WriteLine("D format: {0:D}", dt);

    Console.WriteLine("t format: {0:t}", dt);
    Console.WriteLine("T format: {0:T}", dt);

    Console.WriteLine("f format: {0:f}", dt);
    Console.WriteLine("F format: {0:F}", dt);

    Console.WriteLine("g format: {0:g}", dt);
    Console.WriteLine("G format: {0:G}", dt);
```

```
Console.WriteLine("m format: {0:m}", dt);
Console.WriteLine("M format: {0:M}", dt);

Console.WriteLine("r format: {0:r}", dt);
Console.WriteLine("R format: {0:R}", dt);

Console.WriteLine("s format: {0:s}", dt);

Console.WriteLine("u format: {0:u}", dt);
Console.WriteLine("U format: {0:U}", dt);

Console.WriteLine("y format: {0:y}", dt);
Console.WriteLine("Y format: {0:Y}", dt);
    }
}
```

Sample output is shown here:

```
d format: 2/28/2002
D format: Thursday, February 28, 2002
t format: 9:32 AM
T format: 9:32:34 AM
f format: Thursday, February 28, 2002 9:32 AM
F format: Thursday, February 28, 2002 9:32:34 AM
g format: 2/28/2002 9:32 AM
G format: 2/28/2002 9:32:34 AM
m format: February 28
M format: February 28
r format: Thu, 28 Feb 2002 09:32:34 GMT
R format: Thu, 28 Feb 2002 09:32:34 GMT
s format: 2002-02-28T09:32:34
u format: 2002-02-28 09:32:34Z
U format: Thursday, February 28, 2002 3:32:34 PM
y format: February, 2002
Y format: February, 2002
```

The next program creates a very simple clock. The time is updated once every second. At the top of each hour, the computer's bell is sounded. It uses the **ToString( )** method of **DateTime** to obtain the formatted time prior to outputting it. If the top of the hour has been reached, then the alert character (\a) is appended to the formatted time, thus ringing the bell.

```
// A simple clock.

using System;

class SimpleClock {
  public static void Main() {
    string t;
    int seconds;

    DateTime dt = DateTime.Now;
    seconds = dt.Second;

    for(;;) {
      dt = DateTime.Now;

      // update time if seconds change
      if(seconds != dt.Second) {
        seconds = dt.Second;

        t = dt.ToString("T");

        if(dt.Minute==0 && dt.Second==0)
          t = t + "\a"; // ring bell at top of hour

        Console.WriteLine(t);
      }
    }
  }
}
```

Creating a Custom Date and Time Format

Although the standard date and time format specifiers will apply to the vast majority of situations, you can create your own, custom formats. The process is similar to creating custom formats for the numeric types, as described earlier. In essence, you simply create an example (picture) of what you want the date and time information to look like. To create a custom date and time format, you will use one or more of the placeholders shown in Table 20-7.

If you examine Table 20-7, you will see that the placeholders *d*, *f*, *g*, *m*, *M*, *s*, and *t* are the same as the date and time format specifiers shown in Table 20-6. In general, if one of these characters is used by itself, it is interpreted as a format specifier. Otherwise, it is assumed to be a placeholder. If you want use one of these characters by itself but have it interpreted as a placeholder, then precede the character with a %.

The following program demonstrates several custom time and date formats:

```
// Format time and date information.

using System;

class CustomTimeAndDateFormatsDemo {
  public static void Main() {
    DateTime dt = DateTime.Now;

    Console.WriteLine("Time is {0:hh:mm tt}", dt);
    Console.WriteLine("24 hour time is {0:hh:mm}", dt);
    Console.WriteLine("Date is {0:ddd MMM dd, yyyy}", dt);

    Console.WriteLine("Era: {0:gg}", dt);

    Console.WriteLine("Time with seconds: " +
                      "{0:HH:mm:ss tt}", dt);

    Console.WriteLine("Use m for day of month: {0:m}", dt);
    Console.WriteLine("use m for minutes: {0:%m}", dt);
  }
}
```

The output is shown here:

```
Time is 01:49 PM
24 hour time is 01:49
Date is Thu Feb 28, 2002
Era: A.D.
Time with seconds: 13:49:28 PM
Use m for day of month: February 28
use m for minutes: 49
```

Placeholder	Replaced By
d	Day of month as a number between 1 and 31.
dd	Day of month as a number between 1 and 31. A leading zero prefixes the values 1 through 9.
ddd	Abbreviated weekday name.
dddd	Full weekday name.
f, ff, fff, ffff, fffff, ffffff, fffffff	Fractional seconds, with the number of decimal places specified by the number of fs.
g	Era.
h	Hour as a number between 1 and 12.
hh	Hour as a number between 1 and 12. A leading zero prefixes the values 1 through 9.
H	Hour as a number between 0 and 23.
HH	Hour as a number between 0 and 23. A leading zero prefixes the values 0 through 9.
m	Minutes.
mm	Minutes. A leading zero prefixes the values 0 through 9.
M	Month as a number between 1 and 12.
MM	Month as a number between 1 and 12. A leading zero prefixes the values 1 through 9.
MMM	Abbreviated month name.
MMMM	Full month name.
s	Seconds.
ss	Seconds. A leading zero prefixes the values 0 through 9.
t	A or P, indicating A.M. or P.M.
tt	A.M. or P.M.
y	Year as two digits, unless only one digit is needed.
yy	Year as two digits. A leading zero prefixes the values 0 through 9.

Table 20-7.   *The Custom Date and Time Placeholder Characters*

Placeholder	Replaced By
yyyy	Year using four digits.
z	Time zone offset in hours.
zz	Time zone offset in hours. A leading zero prefixes the values 0 through 9.
zzz	Time zone offset in hours and minutes.
:	Separator for time components.
/	Separator for date components.
%fmt	The standard format associated with fmt.

Table 20-7.   *The Custom Date and Time Placeholder Characters* (continued)

Formatting Enumerations

C# allows you to format the values defined by an enumeration. In general, enumeration values can be displayed using their name or their value. The enumeration format specifiers are shown in Table 20-8. Pay special attention to the G and F formats. Enumerations that will be used to represent bit-fields can be preceded by the **Flags** attribute. Typically, bit-fields hold values that represent individual bits and are arranged in powers of two. If the **Flags** attribute is present, then the G specifier will display the names of all of the values that comprise the value, assuming the value is valid. The F specifier will display the names of all of the values that comprise the value if the value can be constructed by ORing together two or more fields defined by the enumeration.

The following program demonstrates the enumeration specifiers:

```
// Format an enumeration.

using System;

class EnumFmtDemo {
  enum Direction { North, South, East, West }
  [Flags] enum Status { Ready=0x1, OffLine=0x2,
                        Waiting=0x4, TransmitOK=0x8,
                        RecieveOK=0x10, OnLine=0x20 }
```

```
public static void Main() {
  Direction d = Direction.West;

  Console.WriteLine("{0:G}", d);
  Console.WriteLine("{0:F}", d);
  Console.WriteLine("{0:D}", d);
  Console.WriteLine("{0:X}", d);

  Status s = Status.Ready | Status.TransmitOK;

  Console.WriteLine("{0:G}", s);
  Console.WriteLine("{0:F}", s);
  Console.WriteLine("{0:D}", s);
  Console.WriteLine("{0:X}", s);
  }
}
```

The output is shown here:

```
West
West
3
00000003
Ready, TransmitOK
Ready, TransmitOK
9
00000009
```

Specifier	Meaning
G	Displays the name of the value. If the enumeration is preceded by the **Flags** attribute, then all names that are part of the value will be displayed (assuming a valid value).
g	Same as G.
F	Displays the name of the value. However, if the value can be created by ORing together two or more values defined by the enumeration, then the names of each part of the value will be displayed. This applies whether or not the **Flags** attribute has been specified.
f	Same as F.
D	Displays the value as a decimal integer.
d	Same as D.
X	Displays the value as a hexadecimal integer. Leading zeros will be added to ensure that at least eight digits are shown.
x	Same as X.

Table 20-8.   *The Enumeration Format Specifiers*

Chapter 21

Multithreaded Programming

lthough C# contains many innovative features, one of its most exciting is its built-in support for *multithreaded programming.* A multithreaded program contains two or more parts that can run concurrently. Each part of such a program is called a *thread,* and each thread defines a separate path of execution. Thus, multithreading is a specialized form of multitasking.

Multithreaded programming relies on a combination of features defined by the C# language and by classes in the .NET Framework. Because support for multithreading is built into C#, many of the problems associated with multithreading in other languages are minimized or eliminated.

Multithreading Fundamentals

There are two distinct types of multitasking: process-based and thread-based. It is important to understand the difference between the two. A *process* is, in essence, a program that is executing. Thus, *process-based multitasking* is the feature that allows your computer to run two or more programs concurrently. For example, it is process-based multitasking that allows you to run a word processor at the same time you are using a spreadsheet or browsing the Internet. In process-based multitasking, a program is the smallest unit of code that can be dispatched by the scheduler.

A *thread* is a dispatchable unit of executable code. The name comes from the concept of a "thread of execution." In a *thread-based* multitasking environment, all processes have at least one thread, but they can have more. This means that a single program can perform two or more tasks at once. For instance, a text editor can be formatting text at the same time that it is printing, as long as these two actions are being performed by two separate threads.

The differences between process-based and thread-based multitasking can be summarized like this: Process-based multitasking handles the concurrent execution of programs. Thread-based multitasking deals with the concurrent execution of pieces of the same program.

The principal advantage of multithreading is that it enables you to write very efficient programs because it lets you utilize the idle time that is present in most programs. As you probably know, most I/O devices, whether they be network ports, disk drives, or the keyboard, are much slower than the CPU. Thus, a program will often spend a majority of its execution time waiting to send or receive information to or from a device. By using multithreading, your program can execute another task during this idle time. For example, while one part of your program is sending a file over the Internet, another part can be reading keyboard input, and still another can be buffering the next block of data to send.

A thread can be in one of several states. It can be *running.* It can be *ready to run* as soon as it gets CPU time. A running thread can be *suspended,* which is a temporary halt to its execution. It can later be *resumed.* A thread can be *blocked* when waiting for a resource. A thread can be *terminated,* in which case its execution ends and cannot be resumed.

The .NET Framework defines two types of threads: *foreground* and *background*. By default, when you create a thread, it is a foreground thread, but you can change it to a background thread. The only difference between foreground and background threads is that a background thread will be automatically terminated when all foreground threads in its process have stopped.

Along with thread-based multitasking comes the need for a special type of feature called *synchronization*, which allows the execution of threads to be coordinated in certain well-defined ways. C# has a complete subsystem devoted to synchronization, and its key features are also described here.

All processes have at least one thread of execution, which is usually called the *main thread* because it is the one that is executed when your program begins. Thus, the main thread is the thread that all of the preceding example programs in the book have been using. From the main thread you can create other threads.

C# and the .NET Framework support both process-based and thread-based multitasking. Thus, using C#, you can create and manage both processes and threads. However, little programming effort is required to start a new process, because each process is largely separate from the next. Rather, it is C#'s support for multithreading that is important. Because support for multithreading is built in, C# makes it easier to construct high-performance, multithreaded programs than do other languages, such as C++ (which contains no built-in support for multithreading).

The classes that support multithreaded programming are defined in the **System.Threading** namespace. Thus, you will usually include this statement at the start of any multithreaded program:

```
using System.Threading;
```

The Thread Class

C#'s multithreading system is built upon the **Thread** class, which encapsulates a thread of execution. The **Thread** class is **sealed**, which means that it cannot be inherited. **Thread** defines several methods and properties that help manage threads. Throughout this chapter, several of its most commonly used members will be examined.

Creating a Thread

To create a thread, you instantiate an object of type **Thread**. **Thread** defines the following constructor:

public Thread(ThreadStart *entryPoint*)

Here, *entryPoint* is the name of the method that will be called to begin execution of the thread. **ThreadStart** is a delegate defined by the .NET Framework as shown here:

public delegate void ThreadStart( )

Thus, your entry point method must have a **void** return type and take no arguments.

Once created, the new thread will not start running until you call its **Start( )** method, which is defined by **Thread**. The **Start( )** method is shown here:

public void Start( )

Once started, the thread will run until the method specified by *entryPoint* returns. Thus, when *entryPoint* returns, the thread automatically stops. If you try to call **Start( )** on a thread that has already been started, a **ThreadStateException** will be thrown.

Remember that **Thread** is defined in the **System.Threading** namespace.

Here is an example that creates a new thread and starts it running:

```
// Create a thread of execution.

using System;
using System.Threading;

class MyThread {
  public int count;
  string thrdName;

  public MyThread(string name) {
    count = 0;
    thrdName = name;
  }

  // Entry point of thread.
  public void run() {
    Console.WriteLine(thrdName + " starting.");

    do {
      Thread.Sleep(500);
      Console.WriteLine("In " + thrdName +
                        ", count is " + count);
      count++;
    } while(count < 10);

    Console.WriteLine(thrdName + " terminating.");
  }
}

class MultiThread {
  public static void Main() {
```

```
    Console.WriteLine("Main thread starting.");

    // First, construct a MyThread object.
    MyThread mt = new MyThread("Child #1");

    // Next, construct a thread from that object.
    Thread newThrd = new Thread(new ThreadStart(mt.run));

    // Finally, start execution of the thread.
    newThrd.Start();

    do {
      Console.Write(".");
      Thread.Sleep(100);
    } while (mt.count != 10);

    Console.WriteLine("Main thread ending.");
  }
}
```

Let's look closely at this program. **MyThread** defines a class that will be used to create a second thread of execution. Inside its **run( )** method, a loop is established that counts from 0 to 9. Notice the call to **Sleep( )**, which is a **static** method defined by **Thread**. The **Sleep( )** method causes the thread from which it is called to suspend execution for the specified period of milliseconds. The form used by the program is shown here:

public static void Sleep(int *milliseconds*)

The number of milliseconds to suspend is specified in *milliseconds*. If *milliseconds* is zero, the calling thread is suspended only to allow a waiting thread to execute.

Inside **Main( )**, a new **Thread** object is created by the following sequence of statements:

```
// First, construct a MyThread object.
MyThread mt = new MyThread("Child #1");

// Next, construct a thread from that object.
Thread newThrd = new Thread(new ThreadStart(mt.run));

// Finally, start execution of the thread.
newThrd.Start();
```

As the comments suggest, first an object of **MyThread** is created. This object is then used to construct a **Thread** object by passing the **mt.run( )** method as the entry point. Finally, execution of the new thread is started by calling **Start( )**. This causes the child thread's **run( )** method to begin. After calling **Start( )**, execution of the main thread returns to **Main( )**, and it enters **Main( )**'s **do** loop. Both threads continue running, sharing the CPU, until their loops finish. The output produced by this program is as follows:

```
Main thread starting.
Child #1 starting.
......In Child #1, count is 0
.....In Child #1, count is 1
.....In Child #1, count is 2
.....In Child #1, count is 3
.....In Child #1, count is 4
.....In Child #1, count is 5
.....In Child #1, count is 6
.....In Child #1, count is 7
.....In Child #1, count is 8
.....In Child #1, count is 9
Child #1 terminating.
Main thread ending.
```

Often in a multithreaded program, you will want the main thread to be the last thread to finish running. Technically, a program continues to run until all of its foreground threads have finished. Thus, having the main thread finish last is not a requirement. It is, however, good practice to follow because it clearly defines your program's endpoint. The preceding program ensures that the main thread will finish last, because the **do** loop stops when **count** equals 10. Since **count** will equal 10 only after **newThrd** has terminated, the main thread finishes last. Later in this chapter, you will see better ways for one thread to wait until another finishes.

Some Simple Improvements

While the preceding program is perfectly valid, some easy improvements will make it more efficient. First, it is possible to have a thread begin execution as soon as it is created. In the case of **MyThread**, this is done by instantiating a **Thread** object inside **MyThread**'s constructor. Second, there is no need for **MyThread** to store the name of the thread since **Thread** defines a property called **Name** that can be used for this purpose. **Name** is defined like this:

public string Name { get; set; }

Since **Name** is a read-write property, you can use it to set the name of a thread or to retrieve the thread's name.

Here is a version of the preceding program that makes these two improvements:

```
// An alternate way to start a thread.

using System;
using System.Threading;

class MyThread {
  public int count;
  public Thread thrd;

  public MyThread(string name) {
    count = 0;
    thrd = new Thread(new ThreadStart(this.run));
    thrd.Name = name; // set the name of the thread
    thrd.Start(); // start the thread
  }

  // Entry point of thread.
  void run() {
    Console.WriteLine(thrd.Name + " starting.");

    do {
      Thread.Sleep(500);
      Console.WriteLine("In " + thrd.Name +
                        ", count is " + count);
      count++;
    } while(count < 10);

    Console.WriteLine(thrd.Name + " terminating.");
  }
}

class MultiThreadImproved {
  public static void Main() {
    Console.WriteLine("Main thread starting.");

    // First, construct a MyThread object.
    MyThread mt = new MyThread("Child #1");
```

```
      do {
        Console.Write(".");
        Thread.Sleep(100);
      } while (mt.count != 10);

      Console.WriteLine("Main thread ending.");
    }
  }
```

This version produces the same output as before. Notice that the thread object is stored in **thrd** inside **MyThread**.

Creating Multiple Threads

The preceding examples have created only one child thread. However, your program can spawn as many threads as it needs. For example, the following program creates three child threads:

```
// Create multiple threads of execution.

using System;
using System.Threading;

class MyThread {
  public int count;
  public Thread thrd;

  public MyThread(string name) {
    count = 0;
    thrd = new Thread(new ThreadStart(this.run));
    thrd.Name = name;
    thrd.Start();
  }

  // Entry point of thread.
  void run() {
    Console.WriteLine(thrd.Name + " starting.");

    do {
      Thread.Sleep(500);
      Console.WriteLine("In " + thrd.Name +
```

```
                              ", count is " + count);
      count++;
    } while(count < 10);

    Console.WriteLine(thrd.Name + " terminating.");
  }
}

class MoreThreads {
  public static void Main() {
    Console.WriteLine("Main thread starting.");

    // Construct three threads.
    MyThread mt1 = new MyThread("Child #1");
    MyThread mt2 = new MyThread("Child #2");
    MyThread mt3 = new MyThread("Child #3");

    do {
      Console.Write(".");
      Thread.Sleep(100);
    } while (mt1.count < 10 ||
             mt2.count < 10 ||
             mt3.count < 10);

    Console.WriteLine("Main thread ending.");
  }
}
```

Sample output from this program is shown next:

```
Main thread starting.
.Child #1 starting.
Child #2 starting.
Child #3 starting.
....In Child #1, count is 0
In Child #2, count is 0
In Child #3, count is 0
.....In Child #1, count is 1
In Child #2, count is 1
In Child #3, count is 1
.....In Child #1, count is 2
```

```
In Child #2, count is 2
In Child #3, count is 2
.....In Child #1, count is 3
In Child #2, count is 3
In Child #3, count is 3
.....In Child #1, count is 4
In Child #2, count is 4
In Child #3, count is 4
.....In Child #1, count is 5
In Child #2, count is 5
In Child #3, count is 5
.....In Child #1, count is 6
In Child #2, count is 6
In Child #3, count is 6
.....In Child #1, count is 7
In Child #2, count is 7
In Child #3, count is 7
.....In Child #1, count is 8
In Child #2, count is 8
In Child #3, count is 8
.....In Child #1, count is 9
Child #1 terminating.
In Child #2, count is 9
Child #2 terminating.
In Child #3, count is 9
Child #3 terminating.
Main thread ending.
```

As you can see, once started, all three child threads share the CPU. Because
of differences between system configurations, operating systems, and other
environmental factors, when you run the program, the output that you see may
differ slightly from that shown here.

Determining When a Thread Ends

Often it is useful to know when a thread has ended. In the preceding examples,
this was accomplished by watching the **count** variable—hardly a satisfactory or
generalizable solution. Fortunately, **Thread** provides two means by which you can
determine whether a thread has ended. First, you can interrogate the read-only
IsAlive property for the thread. It is defined like this:

   public bool IsAlive { get; }

IsAlive returns **true** if the thread upon which it is called is still running. It returns **false** otherwise. To try **IsAlive**, substitute this version of **MoreThreads** for the one shown in the preceding program:

```
// Use IsAlive to wait for threads to end.
class MoreThreads {
  public static void Main() {
    Console.WriteLine("Main thread starting.");

    // Construct three threads.
    MyThread mt1 = new MyThread("Child #1");
    MyThread mt2 = new MyThread("Child #2");
    MyThread mt3 = new MyThread("Child #3");

    do {
      Console.Write(".");
      Thread.Sleep(100);
    } while (mt1.thrd.IsAlive &&
             mt2.thrd.IsAlive &&
             mt3.thrd.IsAlive);

    Console.WriteLine("Main thread ending.");
  }
}
```

This version produces the same output as before. The only difference is that it uses **IsAlive** to wait for the child threads to terminate.

Another way to wait for a thread to finish is to call **Join( )**. Its simplest form is shown here:

public void Join( )

Join( ) waits until the thread on which it is called terminates. Its name comes from the concept of the calling thread waiting until the specified thread *joins* it. A **ThreadStateException** will be thrown if the thread has not been started. Additional forms of **Join( )** allow you to specify a maximum amount of time that you want to wait for the specified thread to terminate.

Here is a program that uses **Join( )** to ensure that the main thread is the last to stop:

```
// Use Join().

using System;
```

```
using System.Threading;

class MyThread {
  public int count;
  public Thread thrd;

  public MyThread(string name) {
    count = 0;
    thrd = new Thread(new ThreadStart(this.run));
    thrd.Name = name;
    thrd.Start();
  }

  // Entry point of thread.
  void run() {
    Console.WriteLine(thrd.Name + " starting.");

    do {
      Thread.Sleep(500);
      Console.WriteLine("In " + thrd.Name +
                        ", count is " + count);
      count++;
    } while(count < 10);

    Console.WriteLine(thrd.Name + " terminating.");
  }
}

// Use Join() to wait for threads to end.
class JoinThreads {
  public static void Main() {
    Console.WriteLine("Main thread starting.");

    // Construct three threads.
    MyThread mt1 = new MyThread("Child #1");
    MyThread mt2 = new MyThread("Child #2");
    MyThread mt3 = new MyThread("Child #3");

    mt1.thrd.Join();
    Console.WriteLine("Child #1 joined.");

    mt2.thrd.Join();
```

```
    Console.WriteLine("Child #2 joined.");

    mt3.thrd.Join();
    Console.WriteLine("Child #3 joined.");

    Console.WriteLine("Main thread ending.");
  }
}
```

Sample output from this program is shown here. Remember that when you try the program, your output may vary slightly.

```
Main thread starting.
Child #1 starting.
Child #2 starting.
Child #3 starting.
In Child #1, count is 0
In Child #2, count is 0
In Child #3, count is 0
In Child #1, count is 1
In Child #2, count is 1
In Child #3, count is 1
In Child #1, count is 2
In Child #2, count is 2
In Child #3, count is 2
In Child #1, count is 3
In Child #2, count is 3
In Child #3, count is 3
In Child #1, count is 4
In Child #2, count is 4
In Child #3, count is 4
In Child #1, count is 5
In Child #2, count is 5
In Child #3, count is 5
In Child #1, count is 6
In Child #2, count is 6
In Child #3, count is 6
In Child #1, count is 7
In Child #2, count is 7
In Child #3, count is 7
In Child #1, count is 8
```

```
In Child #2, count is 8
In Child #3, count is 8
In Child #1, count is 9
Child #1 terminating.
In Child #2, count is 9
Child #2 terminating.
In Child #3, count is 9
Child #3 terminating.
Child #1 joined.
Child #2 joined.
Child #3 joined.
Main thread ending.
```

As you can see, after the calls to **Join( )** return, the threads have stopped executing.

The IsBackground Property

As mentioned earlier, the .NET Framework defines two types of threads: foreground and background. The only difference between the two is that a process won't end until all of its foreground threads have ended, but background threads are terminated automatically after all foreground threads have stopped. By default, a thread is created as a foreground thread. It can be changed to a background thread by using the **IsBackground** property defined by **Thread** as shown here:

   public bool IsBackground { get; set; }

To set a thread to background, simply assign **IsBackground** a **true** value. A value of **false** indicates a foreground thread.

Thread Priorities

Each thread has a priority setting associated with it. A thread's priority determines, in part, how much CPU time a thread receives. In general, low-priority threads receive little CPU time. High-priority threads receive a lot. As you might expect, how much CPU time a thread receives profoundly affects its execution characteristics and its interaction with other threads currently executing in the system.

It is important to understand that factors other than a thread's priority can also affect how much CPU time a thread receives. For example, if a high-priority thread is waiting on some resource, perhaps for keyboard input, it will be blocked, and a lower-priority thread will run. Thus, in this situation a low-priority thread may gain greater access to the CPU than the high-priority thread over a specific period.

When a child thread is started, its receives a default priority setting. You can change a thread's priority through the **Priority** property, which is a member of **Thread**. This is its general form:

public ThreadPriority Priority{ get; set; }

ThreadPriority is an enumeration that defines the following five priority settings:

ThreadPriority.Highest
ThreadPriority.AboveNormal
ThreadPriority.Normal
ThreadPriority.BelowNormal
ThreadPriority.Lowest

The default priority setting for a thread is **ThreadPriority.Normal**.

To understand how priorities affect thread execution, we will use an example that executes two threads, one having a higher priority than the other. The threads are created as instances of the **MyThread** class. The **run( )** method contains a loop that counts the number of iterations. The loop stops when either the count reaches 1,000,000,000 or the static variable **stop** is **true**. Initially, **stop** is set to **false**. The first thread to count to 1,000,000,000 sets **stop** to **true**. This causes the second thread to terminate with its next timeslice. Each time through the loop, the string in **currentName** is checked against the name of the executing thread. If they don't match, it means that a task-switch occurred. Each time a task-switch happens, the name of the new thread is displayed and **currentName** is given the name of the new thread. This allows you to watch how often each thread has access to the CPU. After both threads stop, the number of iterations for each loop is displayed.

```
// Demonstrate thread priorities.

using System;
using System.Threading;

class MyThread {
  public int count;
  public Thread thrd;

  static bool stop = false;
  static string currentName;

  /* Construct a new thread. Notice that this
     constructor does not actually start the
     threads running. */
```

```csharp
  public MyThread(string name) {
    count = 0;
    thrd = new Thread(new ThreadStart(this.run));
    thrd.Name = name;
    currentName = name;
  }

  // Begin execution of new thread.
  void run() {
    Console.WriteLine(thrd.Name + " starting.");
    do {
      count++;

      if(currentName != thrd.Name) {
        currentName = thrd.Name;
        Console.WriteLine("In " + currentName);
      }

    } while(stop == false && count < 1000000000);
    stop = true;

    Console.WriteLine(thrd.Name + " terminating.");
  }
}

class PriorityDemo {
  public static void Main() {
    MyThread mt1 = new MyThread("High Priority");
    MyThread mt2 = new MyThread("Low Priority");

    // Set the priorities.
    mt1.thrd.Priority = ThreadPriority.AboveNormal;
    mt2.thrd.Priority = ThreadPriority.BelowNormal;

    // Start the threads.
    mt1.thrd.Start();
    mt2.thrd.Start();

    mt1.thrd.Join();
    mt2.thrd.Join();
```

```
    Console.WriteLine();
    Console.WriteLine(mt1.thrd.Name + " thread counted to " +
                   mt1.count);
    Console.WriteLine(mt2.thrd.Name + " thread counted to " +
                   mt2.count);
  }
}
```

Here is the output produced when the program was run on a 1-GHz Pentium-based computer under Windows 2000:

```
High Priority starting.
In High Priority
Low Priority starting.
In Low Priority
In High Priority
In Low Priority
In High Priority
In Low Priority
In High Priority
In Low Priority
In High Priority
In Low Priority
In High Priority
In Low Priority
In High Priority
High Priority terminating.
Low Priority terminating.

High Priority thread counted to 1,000,000,000
Low Priority thread counted to 25,600,064
```

In this run, the high-priority thread got approximately 98 percent of the CPU time. Of course, the precise output you see may vary, depending upon the speed of your CPU and the number of other tasks running in the system. Which version of Windows you are running can even have an effect.

Because multithreaded code can behave differently in different environments, you should never base your code on the execution characteristics of a single environment. For example, in the preceding example, it would be a mistake to assume that the low-priority thread will always execute at least a small amount of time before the high-priority thread finishes. In a different environment, the high-priority thread might complete before the low-priority thread has executed even once, for example.

Synchronization

When using multiple threads, it is sometimes necessary for a program to coordinate the activities of two or more of the threads. The process by which this is achieved is called *synchronization*. The most common reason for using synchronization is when two or more threads need access to a shared resource that can be used by only one thread at a time. For example, when one thread is writing to a file, a second thread must be prevented from doing so at the same time. Another situation in which synchronization is needed is when one thread is waiting for an event that is caused by another thread. In this case, there must be some means by which the first thread is held in a suspended state until the event has occurred. Then the waiting thread must resume execution.

Key to synchronization is the concept of a *lock*, which controls access to a block of code within an object. When an object is locked by one thread, no other thread can gain access to the locked block of code. When the thread releases the lock, the object is available for use by another thread.

The lock feature is built into the C# language. Thus, all objects can be synchronized. Synchronization is supported by the keyword **lock**. Since synchronization was designed into C# from the start, it is much easier to use than you might first expect. In fact, for many programs, the synchronization of objects is almost transparent.

The general form of **lock** is shown here:

```
lock(object) {
    // statements to be synchronized
}
```

Here, *object* is a reference to the object being synchronized. If you want to synchronize only a single statement, the curly braces are not needed. A **lock** statement ensures that the section of code protected by the lock for the given object can be used only by the thread that obtains the lock. All other threads are blocked until the lock is removed. The lock is released when the block is exited.

The following program demonstrates synchronization by controlling access to a method called **sumIt( )**, which sums the elements of an integer array:

```
// Use lock to synchronize access to an object.

using System;
using System.Threading;

class SumArray {
  int sum;

  public int sumIt(int[] nums) {
    lock(this) { // lock the entire method
```

```
      sum = 0; // reset sum

      for(int i=0; i < nums.Length; i++) {
        sum += nums[i];
        Console.WriteLine("Running total for " +
                Thread.CurrentThread.Name +
                " is " + sum);
        Thread.Sleep(10); // allow task-switch
      }
      return sum;
    }
  }
}

class MyThread {
  public Thread thrd;
  int[] a;
  int answer;

  /* Create one SumArray object for all
     instances of MyThread. */
  static SumArray sa = new SumArray();

  // Construct a new thread.
  public MyThread(string name, int[] nums) {
    a = nums;
    thrd = new Thread(new ThreadStart(this.run));
    thrd.Name = name;
    thrd.Start(); // start the thread
  }

  // Begin execution of new thread.
  void run() {
    Console.WriteLine(thrd.Name + " starting.");

    answer = sa.sumIt(a);

    Console.WriteLine("Sum for " + thrd.Name +
                      " is " + answer);

    Console.WriteLine(thrd.Name + " terminating.");
  }
```

```
  }

class Sync {
  public static void Main() {
    int[] a = {1, 2, 3, 4, 5};

    MyThread mt1 = new MyThread("Child #1", a);
    MyThread mt2 = new MyThread("Child #2", a);

    mt1.thrd.Join();
    mt2.thrd.Join();
  }
}
```

The output from the program is shown here:

```
Child #1 starting.
Running total for Child #1 is 1
Child #2 starting.
Running total for Child #1 is 3
Running total for Child #1 is 6
Running total for Child #1 is 10
Running total for Child #1 is 15
Running total for Child #2 is 1
Sum for Child #1 is 15
Child #1 terminating.
Running total for Child #2 is 3
Running total for Child #2 is 6
Running total for Child #2 is 10
Running total for Child #2 is 15
Sum for Child #2 is 15
Child #2 terminating.
```

As the output shows, both threads compute the proper sum of 15.

Let's examine this program in detail. The program creates three classes. The first is **SumArray**. It defines the method **sumIt( )**, which sums an integer array. The second class is **MyThread**, which uses a **static** object called **sa** that is of type **SumArray**. Thus, only one object of **SumArray** is shared by all objects of type **MyThread**. This object is used to obtain the sum of an integer array. Notice that **SumArray** stores the running total in a field called **sum**. Thus, if two threads use **sumIt( )** concurrently, both will be attempting to use **sum** to hold the running total. Since this will cause errors, access to **sumIt( )** must be synchronized. Finally, the class **Sync** creates two threads and has them compute the sum of an integer array.

Inside **sumIt( )**, the **lock** statement prevents simultaneous use of the method by different threads. Notice that **lock** uses **this** as the object being synchronized. This is the way **lock** is normally called when the invoking object is being locked. **Sleep( )** is called to purposely allow a task-switch to occur, if one can—but it can't in this case. Because the code within **sumIt( )** is locked, it can be used by only one thread at a time. Thus, when the second child thread begins execution, it does not enter **sumIt( )** until after the first child thread is done with it. This ensures that the correct result is produced.

To understand the effects of **lock** fully, try removing it from the body of **sumIt( )**. After doing this, **sumIt( )** is no longer synchronized, and any number of threads can use it concurrently on the same object. The problem with this is that the running total is stored in **sum**, which will be changed by each thread that calls **sumIt( )**. Thus, when two threads call **sumIt( )** at the same time on the same object, incorrect results are produced because **sum** reflects the summation of both threads, mixed together. For example, here is sample output from the program after **lock** has been removed from **sumIt( )**:

```
Child #1 starting.
Running total for Child #1 is 1
Child #2 starting.
Running total for Child #2 is 1
Running total for Child #1 is 3
Running total for Child #2 is 5
Running total for Child #1 is 8
Running total for Child #2 is 11
Running total for Child #1 is 15
Running total for Child #2 is 19
Running total for Child #1 is 24
Running total for Child #2 is 29
Sum for Child #1 is 29
Child #1 terminating.
Sum for Child #2 is 29
Child #2 terminating.
```

As the output shows, both child threads are using **sumIt( )** at the same time on the same object, and the value of **sum** is corrupted.

The effects of **lock** are summarized here:

1. For any given object, once a lock has been placed on a section of code, the object is locked and no other thread can acquire the lock.

2. Other threads trying to acquire the lock on the same object will enter a wait state until the code is unlocked.

3. When a thread leaves the locked block, the object is unlocked.

THE C# CLASS LIBRARY

One other thing to understand about **lock** is that it should be used only on objects that are either **private** or **internal**. If this is not the case, then some thread external to your program could obtain a lock and not release it.

An Alternative Approach

Although locking a method's code, as shown in the previous example, is an easy and effective means of achieving synchronization, it will not work in all cases. For example, you might want to synchronize access to a method of a class you did not create, which is itself not synchronized. This can occur if you want to use a class that was written by a third party and for which you do not have access to the source code. Thus, it is not possible for you to add a **lock** statement to the appropriate method within the class. How can access to an object of this class be synchronized? Fortunately, the solution to this problem is simple: lock access to the object from code outside the object by specifying the object in a **lock** statement. For example, here is alternative implementation of the preceding program. Notice that the code within **sumIt( )** is no longer locked. Instead, calls to **sumIt( )** are locked within **MyThread**.

```
// Another way to use lock to synchronize access to an object.

using System;
using System.Threading;

class SumArray {
  int sum;

  public int sumIt(int[] nums) {
    sum = 0; // reset sum

    for(int i=0; i < nums.Length; i++) {
      sum += nums[i];
      Console.WriteLine("Running total for " +
            Thread.CurrentThread.Name +
            " is " + sum);
      Thread.Sleep(10); // allow task-switch
    }
    return sum;
  }
}

class MyThread {
```

```
    public Thread thrd;
    int[] a;
    int answer;

    /* Create one SumArray object for all
       instances of MyThread. */
    static SumArray sa = new SumArray();

    // Construct a new thread.
    public MyThread(string name, int[] nums) {
      a = nums;
      thrd = new Thread(new ThreadStart(this.run));
      thrd.Name = name;
      thrd.Start(); // start the thread
    }

    // Begin execution of new thread.
    void run() {
      Console.WriteLine(thrd.Name + " starting.");

      // Lock calls to sumIt().
      lock(sa) answer = sa.sumIt(a);

      Console.WriteLine("Sum for " + thrd.Name +
                        " is " + answer);

      Console.WriteLine(thrd.Name + " terminating.");
    }
}

class Sync {
  public static void Main() {
    int[] a = {1, 2, 3, 4, 5};

    MyThread mt1 = new MyThread("Child #1", a);
    MyThread mt2 = new MyThread("Child #2", a);

    mt1.thrd.Join();
    mt2.thrd.Join();
  }
}
```

Here, the call to **sa.sumIt( )** is locked, rather than the code inside **sumIt( )**, itself. The code that accomplishes this is shown here:

```
// Lock calls to sumIt().
lock(sa) answer = sa.sumIt(a);
```

The program produces the same correct results as the original approach.

Locking a Static Method

Since **lock** works with an object, you might at first think that you can't lock code within a **static** method since there is no object to lock on. However, this is wrong. To lock a **static** method, use the following form of **lock**:

```
lock(typeof(class)) {
    // locked block
}
```

Here, *class* is the name of the class that contains the **static** method.

The Monitor Class and lock

The C# keyword **lock** is actually just shorthand for using the synchronization features defined by the **Monitor** class, which is defined in the **System.Threading** namespace. **Monitor** defines several methods that control or manage synchronization. For example, to obtain a lock on an object, call **Enter( )**. To release a lock, call **Exit( )**. These methods are shown here:

> public static void Enter(object *syncOb*)
> public static void Exit(object *syncOb*)

Here, *syncOb* is the object being synchronized. If the object is not available when **Enter( )** is called, the calling thread will wait until it becomes available. Microsoft states that a **lock** block is "precisely equivalent" to calling **Enter( )** and then **Exit( )**. Since **lock** is built into C#, it is the preferred method of obtaining a lock on an object when programming in C#.

One useful method in **Monitor** is **TryEnter( )**. One of its forms is shown here:

> public static bool TryEnter(object *syncOb*)

It returns **true** if the calling thread obtains a lock on *syncOb* and **false** if it doesn't. In no case does the calling thread wait. You could use this method to implement an alternative if the desired object is unavailable.

Monitor also defines these three methods: **Wait( )**, **Pulse( )**, and **PulseAll( )**. They are described in the next section.

Thread Communication Using Wait( ), Pulse( ), and PulseAll( )

Consider the following situation. A thread called *T* is executing inside a **lock** block and needs access to a resource, called *R*, that is temporarily unavailable. What should *T* do? If *T* enters some form of polling loop that waits for *R*, then *T* ties up the object, blocking other threads' access to it. This is a less than optimal solution because it partially defeats the advantages of programming for a multithreaded environment. A better solution is to have *T* temporarily relinquish control of the object, allowing another thread to run. When *R* becomes available, *T* can be notified and resume execution. Such an approach relies upon some form of interthread communication in which one thread can notify another that it is blocked, and be notified when it can resume execution. C# supports interthread communication with the **Wait( )**, **Pulse( )**, and **PulseAll( )** methods.

The **Wait( )**, **Pulse( )**, and **PulseAll( )** methods are defined by the **Monitor** class. These methods can be called only from within a locked block of code. Here is how they are used. When a thread is temporarily blocked from running, it calls **Wait( )**. This causes the thread to go to sleep and the lock for that object to be released, allowing another thread to use the object. At a later point, the sleeping thread is awakened when some other thread enters the same lock and calls **Pulse( )** or **PulseAll( )**. A call to **Pulse( )** resumes the first thread in the queue of threads waiting for the lock. A call to **PulseAll( )** signals the release of the lock to all waiting threads.

Here are two commonly used forms of **Wait( )**:

public static bool Wait(object *waitOb*)
public static bool Wait(object *waitOb*, int *milliseconds*)

The first form waits until notified. The second form waits until notified or until the specified period of milliseconds has expired. For both, *waitOb* specifies the object upon which to wait.

Here are the general forms for **Pulse( )** and **PulseAll( )**:

public static void Pulse(object *waitOb*)
public static void PulseAll(object *waitOb*)

Here, *waitOb* is the object being released.

A **SynchronizationLockException** will be thrown if **Wait( )**, **Pulse( )**, or **PulseAll( )** is called from code that is not within a **lock** block.

An Example that Uses Wait( ) and Pulse( )

To understand the need for and the application of **Wait( )** and **Pulse( )**, we will create a program that simulates the ticking of a clock by displaying the words "Tick" and "Tock" on the screen. To accomplish this, we will create a class called **TickTock** that contains two methods: **tick( )** and **tock( )**. The **tick( )** method displays the word "Tick" and **tock( )** displays "Tock". To run the clock, two threads are created, one that calls **tick( )** and one that calls **tock( )**. The goal is to make the two threads execute in a way that the output from the program displays a consistent "Tick Tock"—that is, a repeated pattern of one "Tick" followed by one "Tock".

```
// Use Wait() and Pulse() to create a ticking clock.

using System;
using System.Threading;

class TickTock {

  public void tick(bool running) {
    lock(this) {
      if(!running) { // stop the clock
        Monitor.Pulse(this); // notify any waiting threads
        return;
      }

      Console.Write("Tick ");
      Monitor.Pulse(this); // let tock() run

      Monitor.Wait(this); // wait for tock() to complete
    }
  }

  public void tock(bool running) {
    lock(this) {
      if(!running) { // stop the clock
        Monitor.Pulse(this); // notify any waiting threads
        return;
      }

      Console.WriteLine("Tock");
      Monitor.Pulse(this); // let tick() run

      Monitor.Wait(this); // wait for tick to complete
    }
  }
}

class MyThread {
```

```
  public Thread thrd;
  TickTock ttOb;

  // Construct a new thread.
  public MyThread(string name, TickTock tt) {
    thrd = new Thread(new ThreadStart(this.run));
    ttOb = tt;
    thrd.Name = name;
    thrd.Start();
  }

  // Begin execution of new thread.
  void run() {
    if(thrd.Name == "Tick") {
      for(int i=0; i<5; i++) ttOb.tick(true);
      ttOb.tick(false);
    }
    else {
      for(int i=0; i<5; i++) ttOb.tock(true);
      ttOb.tock(false);
    }
  }
}

class TickingClock {
  public static void Main() {
    TickTock tt = new TickTock();
    MyThread mt1 = new MyThread("Tick", tt);
    MyThread mt2 = new MyThread("Tock", tt);

    mt1.thrd.Join();
    mt2.thrd.Join();
    Console.WriteLine("Clock Stopped");
  }
}
```

Here is the output produced by the program:

```
Tick Tock
Tick Tock
Tick Tock
```

```
Tick Tock
Tick Tock
Clock Stopped
```

Let's take a close look at this program. In **Main( )**, a **TickTock** object called **tt** is created, and this object is used to start two threads of execution. Inside the **run( )** method of **MyThread**, if the name of the thread is "Tick", calls to **tick( )** are made. If the name of the thread is "Tock", the **tock( )** method is called. Five calls that pass **true** as an argument are made to each method. The clock runs as long as **true** is passed. A final call that passes **false** to each method stops the clock.

The most important part of the program is found in the **tick( )** and **tock( )** methods. We will begin with the **tick( )** method, which, for convenience, is shown here:

```
public void tick(bool running) {
  lock(this) {
    if(!running) { // stop the clock
      Monitor.Pulse(this); // notify any waiting threads
      return;
    }

    Console.Write("Tick ");
    Monitor.Pulse(this); // let tock() run

    Monitor.Wait(this); // wait for tock() to complete
  }
}
```

First, notice that the code in **tick( )** is contained within a **lock** block. Recall, **Wait( )** and **Pulse( )** can be used only inside synchronized blocks. The method begins by checking the value of the **running** parameter. This parameter is used to provide a clean shutdown of the clock. If it is **false**, then the clock has been stopped. If this is the case, a call to **Pulse( )** is made to enable any waiting thread to run. We will return to this point in a moment. Assuming that the clock is running when **tick( )** executes, the word "Tick" is displayed, and then a call to **Pulse( )** takes place followed by a call to **Wait( )**. The call to **Pulse( )** allows a thread waiting on the same object to run. The call to **Wait( )** causes **tick( )** to suspend until another thread calls **Pulse( )**. Thus, when **tick( )** is called, it displays one "Tick", lets another thread run, and then suspends.

The **tock( )** method is an exact copy of **tick( )**, except that it displays "Tock". Thus, when entered, it displays "Tock", calls **Pulse( )**, and then waits. When viewed as a pair, a call to **tick( )** can be followed only by a call to **tock( )**, which can be followed only by a call to **tick( )**, and so on. Therefore, the two methods are mutually synchronized.

The reason for the call to **Pulse( )** when the clock is stopped is to allow a final call to **Wait( )** to succeed. Remember, both **tick( )** and **tock( )** execute a call to **Wait( )** after displaying their message. The problem is that when the clock is stopped, one of the methods will still be waiting. Thus, a final call to **Pulse( )** is required in order for the waiting method to run. As an experiment, try removing this call to **Pulse( )** and watch what happens. As you will see, the program will "hang" and you will need to press CTRL-C to exit. The reason for this is that when the final call to **tock( )** calls **Wait( )**, there is no corresponding call to **Pulse( )** that lets **tock( )** conclude. Thus, **tock( )** just sits there, waiting forever.

Before moving on, if you have any doubt that the calls to **Wait( )** and **Pulse( )** are actually needed to make the "clock" run right, substitute this version of **TickTock** into the preceding program. It has all calls to **Wait( )** and **Pulse( )** removed.

```
// A non-functional version of TickTock.
class TickTock {

  public void tick(bool running) {
    lock(this) {
      if(!running) { // stop the clock
        return;
      }

      Console.Write("Tick ");
    }
  }

  public void tock(bool running) {
    lock(this) {
      if(!running) { // stop the clock
        return;
      }

      Console.WriteLine("Tock");
    }
  }
}
```

After the substitution, the output produced by the program will look like this:

```
Tick Tick Tick Tick Tick Tock
Tock
Tock
```

```
Tock
Tock
Clock Stopped
```

Clearly, the **tick( )** and **tock( )** methods are no longer synchronized!

Deadlock

When developing multithreaded programs, you must be careful to avoid deadlock. *Deadlock* is, as the name implies, a situation in which one thread is waiting for another thread to do something, but that other thread is waiting on the first. Thus, both threads are suspended, waiting for each other, and neither executes. This situation is analogous to two overly polite people both insisting that the other step through a door first!

Avoiding deadlock seems easy, but it's not. For example, deadlock can occur in roundabout ways. Consider the **TickTock** class. As explained, if a final **Pulse( )** is not executed by **tick( )** or **tock( )**, then one or the other will be waiting indefinitely and the program is deadlocked. Often the cause of the deadlock is not readily understood just by looking at the source code to the program, because concurrently executing threads can interact in complex ways at runtime. To avoid deadlock, careful programming and thorough testing are required. In general, if a multithreaded program occasionally "hangs," deadlock is the likely cause.

Using MethodImplAttribute

It is possible to synchronize an entire method by using the **MethodImplAttribute** attribute. This approach can be used as an alternative to the **lock** statement in cases in which the entire contents of a method are to be locked. **MethodImplAttribute** is defined within the **System.Runtime.CompilerServices** namespace. The constructor that applies to synchronization is shown here:

   public MethodImplAttribute(MethodImplOptions *opt*)

Here, *opt* specifies the implementation attribute. To synchronize a method, specify **MethodImplOptions.Synchronized**. This attribute causes the entire method to be locked.

Here is a rewrite of the **TickTock** class that uses **MethodImplAttribute** to provide synchronization:

```
// Use MethodImplAttribute to synchronize a method.

using System;
```

```
using System.Threading;
using System.Runtime.CompilerServices;

class TickTock {

  /* The following attribute synchronizes the entire
     tick() method. */
  [MethodImplAttribute(MethodImplOptions.Synchronized)]
  public void tick(bool running) {
    if(!running) { // stop the clock
      Monitor.Pulse(this); // notify any waiting threads
      return;
    }

    Console.Write("Tick ");
    Monitor.Pulse(this); // let tock() run

    Monitor.Wait(this); // wait for tock() to complete
  }


  /* The following attribute synchronizes the entire
     tock() method. */
  [MethodImplAttribute(MethodImplOptions.Synchronized)]
  public void tock(bool running) {
    if(!running) { // stop the clock
      Monitor.Pulse(this); // notify any waiting threads
      return;
    }

    Console.WriteLine("Tock");
    Monitor.Pulse(this); // let tick() run

    Monitor.Wait(this); // wait for tick to complete
  }

}

class MyThread {
  public Thread thrd;
  TickTock ttOb;

  // Construct a new thread.
```

```
    public MyThread(string name, TickTock tt) {
      thrd = new Thread(new ThreadStart(this.run));
      ttOb = tt;
      thrd.Name = name;
      thrd.Start();
    }

    // Begin execution of new thread.
    void run() {
      if(thrd.Name == "Tick") {
        for(int i=0; i<5; i++) ttOb.tick(true);
        ttOb.tick(false);
      }
      else {
        for(int i=0; i<5; i++) ttOb.tock(true);
        ttOb.tock(false);
      }
    }
}

class TickingClock {
  public static void Main() {
    TickTock tt = new TickTock();
    MyThread mt1 = new MyThread("Tick", tt);
    MyThread mt2 = new MyThread("Tock", tt);

    mt1.thrd.Join();
    mt2.thrd.Join();
    Console.WriteLine("Clock Stopped");
  }
}
```

The proper Tick Tock output is the same as before.

When locking an entire method, the choice of using **lock** or **MethodImplAttribute** is yours. Both produce the same results. Since **lock** is a keyword built into C#, that is the approach that the examples in this book will use.

Suspending, Resuming, and Stopping Threads

It is sometimes useful to suspend execution of a thread. For example, a thread might be used to display the time of day. If the user does not desire a clock, its thread can be suspended. Later, when the clock is desired, its thread can be resumed. Whatever the case, it is a simple matter to suspend and resume a thread. Sometimes you will want to stop a thread. Stopping a thread differs from suspending a thread in that a stopped thread is removed from the system and cannot be restarted.

To suspend a thread, use **Thread.Suspend( )**. To resume a suspended thread, use **Thread.Resume( )**. Their general forms are shown here:

```
public void Suspend( )
public void Resume( )
```

Both of these can throw a **ThreadStateException** if the calling thread is not in the proper state. For example, attempting to resume a thread that is not suspended results in an exception.

To stop a thread, use **Thread.Abort( )**. Its simplest form is shown here:

```
public void Abort( )
```

Abort( ) causes a **ThreadAbortException** to be thrown to the thread on which **Abort( )** is called. This exception causes the thread to terminate. This exception can also be caught by your code (but is automatically rethrown in order to stop the thread). **Abort( )** may not always be able to stop a thread immediately, so if it is important that a thread be stopped before your program continues, you will need to follow a call to **Abort( )** with a call to **Join( )**. Also, in rare cases, it is possible that **Abort( )** won't be able to stop a thread. One way this could happen is if a **finally** block goes into an infinite loop.

The following example shows how to suspend, resume, and stop a thread:

```csharp
// Suspending, resuming, and stopping a thread.

using System;
using System.Threading;

class MyThread {
  public Thread thrd;

  public MyThread(string name) {
    thrd = new Thread(new ThreadStart(this.run));
    thrd.Name = name;
    thrd.Start();
  }

  // This is the entry point for thread.
  void run() {
    Console.WriteLine(thrd.Name + " starting.");

    for(int i = 1; i <= 1000; i++) {
```

```
        Console.Write(i + " ");
        if((i%10)==0) {
          Console.WriteLine();
          Thread.Sleep(250);
        }
    }
    Console.WriteLine(thrd.Name + " exiting.");
  }
}

class SuspendResumeStop {
  public static void Main() {
    MyThread mt1 = new MyThread("My Thread");

    Thread.Sleep(1000); // let child thread start executing

    mt1.thrd.Suspend();
    Console.WriteLine("Suspending thread.");
    Thread.Sleep(1000);

    mt1.thrd.Resume();
    Console.WriteLine("Resuming thread.");
    Thread.Sleep(1000);

    mt1.thrd.Suspend();
    Console.WriteLine("Suspending thread.");
    Thread.Sleep(1000);

    mt1.thrd.Resume();
    Console.WriteLine("Resuming thread.");
    Thread.Sleep(1000);

    Console.WriteLine("Stopping thread.");
    mt1.thrd.Abort();

    mt1.thrd.Join(); // wait for thread to terminate

    Console.WriteLine("Main thread terminating.");
  }
}
```

The output from this program is shown here:

```
My Thread starting.
1 2 3 4 5 6 7 8 9 10
11 12 13 14 15 16 17 18 19 20
21 22 23 24 25 26 27 28 29 30
31 32 33 34 35 36 37 38 39 40
Suspending thread.
41 42 43 44 45 46 47 48 49 50
Resuming thread.
51 52 53 54 55 56 57 58 59 60
61 62 63 64 65 66 67 68 69 70
71 72 73 74 75 76 77 78 79 80
81 82 83 84 85 86 87 88 89 90
Suspending thread.
91 92 93 94 95 96 97 98 99 100
Resuming thread.
101 102 103 104 105 106 107 108 109 110
111 112 113 114 115 116 117 118 119 120
121 122 123 124 125 126 127 128 129 130
131 132 133 134 135 136 137 138 139 140
Stopping thread.
Main thread terminating.
```

An Abort( ) Alternative

You might find a second form of **Abort( )** useful in some cases. Its general form is shown here:

public void Abort(object *info*)

Here, *info* contains any information that you want to pass to the thread when it is being stopped. This information is accessible through the **ExceptionState** property of **ThreadAbortException**. You might use this to pass a termination code to a thread. The following program demonstrates this form of **Abort( )**:

```
// Using Abort(object).

using System;
using System.Threading;
```

```csharp
class MyThread {
  public Thread thrd;

  public MyThread(string name) {
    thrd = new Thread(new ThreadStart(this.run));
    thrd.Name = name;
    thrd.Start();
  }

  // This is the entry point for thread.
  void run() {
    try {
      Console.WriteLine(thrd.Name + " starting.");

      for(int i = 1; i <= 1000; i++) {
        Console.Write(i + " ");
        if((i%10)==0) {
          Console.WriteLine();
          Thread.Sleep(250);
        }
      }
      Console.WriteLine(thrd.Name + " exiting normally.");
    } catch(ThreadAbortException exc) {
      Console.WriteLine("Thread aborting, code is " +
                         exc.ExceptionState);
    }
  }
}

class UseAltAbort {
  public static void Main() {
    MyThread mt1 = new MyThread("My Thread");

    Thread.Sleep(1000); // let child thread start executing

    Console.WriteLine("Stopping thread.");
    mt1.thrd.Abort(100);

    mt1.thrd.Join(); // wait for thread to terminate

    Console.WriteLine("Main thread terminating.");
  }
}
```

The output is shown here:

```
My Thread starting.
1 2 3 4 5 6 7 8 9 10
11 12 13 14 15 16 17 18 19 20
21 22 23 24 25 26 27 28 29 30
31 32 33 34 35 36 37 38 39 40
Stopping thread.
Thread aborting, code is 100
Main thread terminating.
```

As the output shows, the value 100 is passed to **Abort( )**. This value is then accessed through the **ExceptionState** property of the **ThreadAbortException** caught by the thread when it is terminated.

Canceling Abort( )

A thread can override a request to abort. To do so, the thread must catch the **ThreadAbortException** and then call **ResetAbort( )**. This prevents the exception from being automatically rethrown when the thread's exception handler ends. **ResetAbort( )** is declared like this:

public static void ResetAbort( )

A call to **ResetAbort( )** can fail if the thread does not have the proper security setting to cancel the abort.

The following program demonstrates **ResetAbort( )**:

```
// Using ResetAbort().

using System;
using System.Threading;

class MyThread {
  public Thread thrd;

  public MyThread(string name) {
    thrd = new Thread(new ThreadStart(this.run));
    thrd.Name = name;
    thrd.Start();
  }

  // This is the entry point for thread.
```

```
    void run() {
      Console.WriteLine(thrd.Name + " starting.");

      for(int i = 1; i <= 1000; i++) {
        try {
          Console.Write(i + " ");
          if((i%10)==0) {
            Console.WriteLine();
            Thread.Sleep(250);
          }
        } catch(ThreadAbortException exc) {
          if((int)exc.ExceptionState == 0) {
            Console.WriteLine("Abort Cancelled! Code is " +
                              exc.ExceptionState);
            Thread.ResetAbort();
          }
          else
            Console.WriteLine("Thread aborting, code is " +
                              exc.ExceptionState);
        }
      }
      Console.WriteLine(thrd.Name + " exiting normally.");
    }
}

class ResetAbort {
  public static void Main() {
    MyThread mt1 = new MyThread("My Thread");

    Thread.Sleep(1000); // let child thread start executing

    Console.WriteLine("Stopping thread.");
    mt1.thrd.Abort(0); // this won't stop the thread

    Thread.Sleep(1000); // let child execute a bit longer

    Console.WriteLine("Stopping thread.");
    mt1.thrd.Abort(100); // this will stop the thread

    mt1.thrd.Join(); // wait for thread to terminate

    Console.WriteLine("Main thread terminating.");
```

```
   }
}
```

The output is shown here:

```
My Thread starting.
1 2 3 4 5 6 7 8 9 10
11 12 13 14 15 16 17 18 19 20
21 22 23 24 25 26 27 28 29 30
31 32 33 34 35 36 37 38 39 40
Stopping thread.
Abort Cancelled! Code is 0
41 42 43 44 45 46 47 48 49 50
51 52 53 54 55 56 57 58 59 60
61 62 63 64 65 66 67 68 69 70
71 72 73 74 75 76 77 78 79 80
Stopping thread.
Thread aborting, code is 100
Main thread terminating.
```

In this example, if **Abort( )** is called with an argument that equals zero, then the abort request is cancelled by the thread by calling **ResetAbort( )**, and the thread's execution continues. Any other value causes the thread to stop.

Determining a Thread's State

The state of a thread can be obtained from the **ThreadState** property provided by **Thread**. It is shown here:

public ThreadState ThreadState{ get; }

The state of the thread is returned as a value defined by the **ThreadState** enumeration. It defines the following values:

ThreadState.Aborted	ThreadState.AbortRequested
ThreadState.Background	ThreadState.Running
ThreadState.Stopped	ThreadState.StopRequested
ThreadState.Suspended	ThreadState.SuspendRequested
ThreadState.Unstarted	ThreadState.WaitSleepJoin

All but one of these values is self-explanatory. The one that needs some explanation is **ThreadState.WaitSleepJoin**. A thread enters this state when it is waiting because of a call to **Wait( )**, **Sleep( )**, or **Join( )**.

Using the Main Thread

As mentioned at the start of this chapter, all C# programs have at least one thread of execution, called the *main thread*, which is given to the program automatically when it begins running. The main thread can be handled just like all other threads.

To access the main thread, you must obtain a **Thread** object that refers it. You do this through the **CurrentThread** property, which is a member of **Thread**. Its general form is shown here:

```
public static Thread CurrentThread{ get; }
```

This method returns a reference to the thread in which it is called. Therefore, if you use **CurrentThread** while execution is inside the main thread, you will obtain a reference to the main thread. Once you have this reference, you can control the main thread just like any other thread.

The following program obtains a reference to the main thread, and then gets and sets the main thread's name and priority:

```csharp
// Control the main thread.

using System;
using System.Threading;

class UseMain {
  public static void Main() {
    Thread thrd;

    // Get the main thread.
    thrd = Thread.CurrentThread;

    // Display main thread's name.
    if(thrd.Name == null)
      Console.WriteLine("Main thread has no name.");
    else
      Console.WriteLine("Main thread is called: " +
                        thrd.Name);

    // Display main thread's priority.
```

```
      Console.WriteLine("Priority: " +
                           thrd.Priority);

      Console.WriteLine();

      // Set the name and priority.
      Console.WriteLine("Setting name and priority.\n");
      thrd.Name = "Main Thread";
      thrd.Priority = ThreadPriority.AboveNormal;

      Console.WriteLine("Main thread is now called: " +
                           thrd.Name);

      Console.WriteLine("Priority is now: " +
                           thrd.Priority);
  }
}
```

The output from the program is shown here:

```
Main thread has no name.
Priority: Normal

Setting name and priority.

Main thread is now called: Main Thread
Priority is now: AboveNormal
```

One word of caution: You need to be careful about what operations you perform on the main thread. For example, if you add this call to **Join( )** to the end of **Main( )**,

```
      thrd.Join();
```

the program will never terminate because it will be waiting for the main thread to end!

Multithreading Tips

The key to effectively utilizing multithreading is to think concurrently rather than serially. For example, when you have two subsystems within a program that can execute concurrently, make them into individual threads. A word of caution is in order, however. If you create too many threads, you can actually degrade the performance of your program rather than enhance it. Remember, there is some overhead associated with context switching. If you create too many threads, more CPU time will be spent changing contexts than in executing your program!

Starting a Separate Task

Although thread-based multitasking is what you will use most often when programming in C#, it is possible to utilize process-based multitasking where appropriate. When using process-based multitasking, instead of starting another thread within the same program, one program starts the execution of another program. In C#, you do this by using the **Process** class. **Process** is defined within the **System.Diagnostics** namespace. To conclude this chapter, a brief look at starting and managing another process is offered.

The easiest way to start another process is to use the **Start( )** method defined by **Process**. Here is one of its simplest forms:

public static Process Start(string *name*)

Here, *name* specifies the name of an executable file that will be executed, or a file that is associated with an executable.

When a process that you create ends, call **Close( )** to free the memory associated with that process. It is shown here:

public void Close( )

You can terminate a process in two ways. If the process is a Windows GUI application, then to terminate the process, call **CloseMainWindow( )**, shown here:

public bool CloseMainWindow( )

This method sends a message to the process, instructing it to stop. It returns **true** if the message was received. It returns **false** if the application was not a GUI program, or does not have a main window. Furthermore, **CloseMainWindow( )** is only a request to shut down. If the application ignores the request, then the application will not be terminated.

To positively terminate a process, call **Kill( )**, shown here:

public void Kill( )

Use **Kill( )** carefully. It causes an uncontrolled termination of the process. Any unsaved data associated with the process will most likely be lost.

You can wait for a process to end by calling **WaitForExit( )**. Its two forms are shown here:

public void WaitForExit( )
public bool WaitForExit(int *milliseconds*)

The first form waits until the process terminates. The second waits for only the specified number of milliseconds. The second form returns **true** if the process has terminated and **false** if it is still running.

The following program demonstrates how to create, wait for, and close a process. It starts the standard Windows utility program **WordPad.exe**. It then waits for WordPad to end.

```
// Starting a new process.

using System;
using System.Diagnostics;

class StartProcess {
  public static void Main() {
    Process newProc = Process.Start("wordpad.exe");

    Console.WriteLine("New process started.");

    newProc.WaitForExit();

    newProc.Close(); // free resources

    Console.WriteLine("New process ended.");
  }
}
```

When you run this program, WordPad will start up, and you will see the message "New process started." The program will then wait until you close WordPad. Once WordPad has been terminated, the final message "New process ended." is displayed.

Chapter 22

Working with Collections

In C#, a *collection* is a group of objects. The **System.Collections** namespace contains a large number of interfaces and classes that define and implement various types of collections. Collections simplify many programming tasks because they offer off-the-shelf solutions to several common, but sometimes tedious-to-develop, data structures. For example, there are built-in collections that support stacks, queues, and hash tables. Collections are a state-of-the-art technology that merits close attention by all C# programmers.

Collections Overview

The principal benefit of collections is that they standardize the way groups of objects are handled by your programs. All collections are designed around a set of cleanly defined interfaces. Several built-in implementations of these interfaces, such as **ArrayList**, **Hashtable**, **Stack**, and **Queue**, are provided, which you can use as-is. You can also implement your own collection, but you will seldom need to.

The .NET Framework supports three general types of collections: general purpose, specialized, and bit based. The general-purpose collections implement several fundamental data structures, including a dynamic array, stack, and queue. They also include *dictionaries*, in which you can store key/value pairs. The general-purpose collections operate on data of type **object**. Thus, they can be used to store any type of data.

The special-purpose collections operate on a specific type of data or operate in a unique way. For example, there are specialized collections for strings. There are also specialized collections that use a singly linked list.

Bit-based collection classes store groups of bits. The bit-based collections support a different set of operations than do the other types of collections. For example, the main bit-based collection is **BitArray**, which supports bitwise operations, such as AND and XOR.

Fundamental to all collections is the concept of an *enumerator*, which is supported by the **IEnumerator** and **IEnumerable** interfaces. An enumerator provides a standardized way of accessing the elements within a collection, one at a time. Thus, it *enumerates* the contents of a collection. Because each collection must implement **IEnumerable**, the elements of any collection class can be accessed through the methods defined by **IEnumerator**. Therefore, with only small changes, the code that cycles through one type of collection can be used to cycle through another. As a point of interest, the **foreach** loop uses the enumerator to cycle through the contents of a collection.

One last thing: If you are familiar with C++, then you will find it helpful to know that C# collection classes are similar in spirit to the Standard Template Library (STL) classes defined by C++. What C++ calls a container, C# calls a collection. The same is true of Java. If you are familiar with Java's Collections Framework, then you will have no trouble learning to use C# collections.

The Collection Interfaces

System.Collections defines a number of interfaces. It is necessary to begin with the collection interfaces because they determine the functionality common to all of the collection classes. The interfaces that underpin collections are summarized in Table 22-1. The following sections examine each interface in detail.

The ICollection Interface

The **ICollection** interface is the foundation upon which all collections are built. It declares the core methods and properties that all collections will have. It also inherits the **IEnumerable** interface. An understanding of **ICollection** is necessary for a clear understanding of how the collections framework operates.

ICollection defines the following properties:

Property	Meaning
int Count { get; }	The number of items currently held in the collection.
bool IsSynchronized { get; }	Is **true** if the collection is synchronized and **false** if it is not. By default, collections are not synchronized. It is possible, though, to obtain a synchronized version of most collections.
object SyncRoot { get; }	An object upon which the collection can be synchronized.

Count is the most often used property because it contains the number of elements currently held in a collection. If **Count** is zero, then the collection is empty.

ICollection defines the following method:

  void CopyTo(Array *target*, int *startIdx*)

CopyTo( ) copies the contents of a collection to the array specified by *target,* beginning at the index specified by *startIdx.* Thus, **CopyTo( )** provides a pathway from a collection to a standard C# array.

Since **ICollection** inherits **IEnumerable**, it also includes the sole method defined by **IEnumerable**: **GetEnumerator( )**, which is shown here:

  IEnumerator GetEnumerator( )

It returns the enumerator for the collection.

Interface	Description
ICollection	Defines the elements that all collections must have.
IEnumerable	Defines the **GetEnumerator( )** method, which supplies the enumerator for a collection class.
IEnumerator	Provides methods that enable the contents of a collection to be obtained one at a time.
IList	Defines a collection that can be accessed via an indexer.
IDictionary	Defines a collection that consists of key/value pairs.
IDictionaryEnumerator	Defines the enumerator for a collection that implements **IDictionary**.
IComparer	Defines the **Compare( )** method that performs a comparison on objects stored in a collection.
IHashCodeProvider	Defines a hash function.

Table 22-1. *The Collection Interfaces*

The IList Interface

The **IList** interface inherits **ICollection** and declares the behavior of a collection that allows elements to be accessed via a zero-based index. In addition to the methods defined by **ICollection**, **IList** defines several of its own. These are summarized in Table 22-2. Several of these methods imply the modification of a collection. If the collection is read-only or of fixed size, then these methods will throw a **NotSupportedException**.

Method	Description
int Add(object *obj*)	Adds *obj* into the invoking collection. Returns the index at which the object is stored.
void Clear( )	Deletes all elements from the invoking collection.
bool Contains(object *obj*)	Returns **true** if the invoking collection contains the object passed in *obj* and **false** otherwise.

Table 22-2. *The Methods Defined by **IList***

Method	Description
int IndexOf(object *obj*)	Returns the index of *obj* if *obj* is contained within the invoking collection. If *obj* is not found, –1 is returned.
void Insert(int *idx*, object *obj*)	Inserts *obj* at the index specified by *idx*. Elements at and below *idx* are moved down to make room for *obj*.
void Remove(object *obj*)	Removes the first occurrence of *obj* from the invoking collection. Elements at and below the removed element are moved up to close the gap.
void RemoveAt(int *idx*)	Removes the object at the index specified by *idx* from the invoking collection. Elements at and below *idx* are moved up to close the gap.

Table 22-2. *The Methods Defined by* **IList** (continued)

Objects are added to an **IList** collection by calling **Add( )**. Notice that **Add( )** takes an argument of type **object**. Since **object** is a base class for all types, any type of object can be stored in a collection. This includes the value types, because boxing and unboxing will automatically take place.

You can remove an element using **Remove( )** or **RemoveAt( )**. **Remove( )** removes the specified object. **RemoveAt( )** removes the object at a specified index. To empty the collection, call **Clear( )**.

You can determine whether a collection contains a specific object by calling **Contains( )**. You can obtain the index of an object by calling **IndexOf( )**. You can insert an element at a specific index by calling **Insert( )**.

IList defines the following properties:

```
bool IsFixedSize { get; }
bool IsReadOnly { get; }
```

If the collection is of fixed size, **IsFixedSize** is **true**. This means that elements cannot be inserted or removed. If the collection is read-only, then **IsReadOnly** is **true**. This means the contents of the collection cannot be changed.

IList defines the following indexer:

```
object this[int idx] { get; set; }
```

You will use this indexer to get or set the value of an element. However, you cannot use it to add a new element to the collection. To add an element to a list, call **Add( )**. Once it is added, you can access the element through the indexer.

The IDictionary Interface

The **IDictionary** interface defines the behavior of a collection that maps unique keys to values. A key is an object that you use to retrieve a value at a later date. Thus, a collection that implements **IDictionary** stores key/value pairs. Once the pair is stored, you can retrieve it by using its key. **IDictionary** inherits **ICollection**. The methods declared by **IDictionary** are summarized in Table 22-3. Several methods throw a **NotSupportedException** if an attempt is made to specify a null key.

To add a key/value pair to an **IDictionary** collection, use **Add( )**. Notice that the key and its value are specified separately. To remove an element, specify the key of the object in a call to **Remove( )**. To empty the collection, call **Clear( )**.

You can determine whether a collection contains a specific object by calling **Contains( )** with the key of the desired item. **GetEnumerator( )** obtains an enumerator compatible with an **IDictionary** collection. This enumerator operates on key/value pairs.

IDictionary defines the following properties:

Property	Description
bool IsFixedSize { get; }	Is **true** if the dictionary is of fixed size.
bool IsReadOnly { get; }	Is **true** if the dictionary is read-only.
ICollection Keys { get; }	Obtains a collection of the keys.
ICollection Values { get; }	Obtains a collection of the values.

Method	Description
void Add(object *k*, object *v*)	Adds the key/value pair specified by *k* and *v* to the invoking collection. *k* must not be null. An **ArgumentException** is thrown if *k* is already stored in the collection.
void Clear( )	Removes all key/value pairs from the invoking collection.
bool Contains(object *k*)	Returns **true** if the invoking collection contains *k* as a key. Otherwise, returns **false**.

Table 22-3. *The Methods Defined by IDictionary*

Method	Description
IDictionaryEnumerator GetEnumerator( )	Returns the enumerator for the invoking collection.
void Remove(object *k*)	Removes the entry whose key equals *k*.

Table 22-3.   *The Methods Defined by **IDictionary** (continued)*

Notice that the keys and values contained within the collection are available as separate lists through the **Keys** and **Values** properties.

IDictionary defines the following indexer:

    object this[object *key*] { get; set; }

You can use this indexer to get or set the value of an element. You can also use it to add a new element to the collection. Notice that the "index" is not actually an index, but rather the key of the item.

IEnumerable, IEnumerator, and IDictionaryEnumerator

IEnumerable is the interface that a class must implement if it is to support enumerators. As explained, all of the collection classes implement **IEnumerable** because it is inherited by **ICollection**. The sole method defined by **IEnumerable** is **GetEnumerator( )**, which is shown here:

    IEnumerator GetEnumerator( )

It returns the enumerator for the collection. Also, implementing **IEnumerable** allows the contents of a collection to be obtained by a **foreach** loop.

IEnumerator is the interface that defines the functionality of an enumerator. Using its methods, you can cycle through the contents of a collection. For collections that store key/value pairs (dictionaries), **GetEnumerator( )** returns an object of type **IDictionaryEnumerator**, rather than **IEnumerator**. **IDictionaryEnumerator** inherits **IEnumerator** and adds functionality to facilitate the enumeration of dictionaries.

The methods defined by **IEnumerator** and the techniques needed to use it are described later in this chapter.

IComparer

The **IComparer** interface defines a method called **Compare( )**, which defines the way two objects are compared. It is shown here:

    int Compare(object *v1*, object *v2*)

It must return greater than zero if *v1* is greater than *v2*, less than zero if *v1* is less than *v2*, and zero if the two values are the same. This interface can be used to specify how the elements of the collection should be sorted.

IHashCodeProvider

IHashCodeProvider is the interface to implement when you want to specify a custom version of **GetHashCode( )**. Recall that all objects inherit **Object.GetHashCode( )**, which is the hash code method that is used by default. By implementing **IHashCodeProvider**, you can specify an alternative method. Normally, there is no reason to implement **IHashCodeProvider**.

The DictionaryEntry Structure

System.Collections defines one structure type called **DictionaryEntry**. Collections that hold key/value pairs store those pairs in a **DictionaryEntry** object. This structure defines the following two properties:

```
public object Key { get; set; }
public object Value { get; set; }
```

These properties are used to access the key or value associated with an entry. You can construct a **DictionaryEntry** object by using the following constructor:

```
public DictionaryEntry(object k, object v)
```

Here, *k* is the key and *v* is the value.

The General-Purpose Collection Classes

Now that you are familiar with the collection interfaces, we can examine the standard classes that implement them. As explained, the collection classes are divided into three main subdivisions: general purpose, bit based, and special purpose. The *general-purpose* classes can be used to store objects of any type. The *bit-based* collections store bits. The *special-purpose* collections offer strongly typed (designed to operate on a specific type of data) or otherwise specialized implementations. This section examines the general-purpose collection classes. The bit-based and specialized collection classes are discussed later in this chapter.

The general-purpose collection classes are summarized here:

Class	Description
ArrayList	A dynamic array. This is an array that can grow as needed.
Hashtable	A hash table for key/value pairs.

Class	Description
Queue	A first-in, first-out list.
SortedList	A sorted list of key/value pairs.
Stack	A first-in, last-out list.

The following sections examine these collection classes and illustrate their use.

ArrayList

The **ArrayList** class supports dynamic arrays, which can grow or shrink as needed. In C#, standard arrays are of a fixed length, which cannot be changed during program execution. This means that you must know in advance how many elements an array will hold. But sometimes you may not know until runtime precisely how large an array you will need. To handle this situation, use **ArrayList**. An **ArrayList** is a variable-length array of object references that can dynamically increase or decrease in size. An **ArrayList** is created with an initial size. When this size is exceeded, the collection is automatically enlarged. When objects are removed, the array can be shrunk. **ArrayList** is perhaps the most important collection, and we will examine it in depth here.

ArrayList implements **ICollection**, **IList**, **IEnumerable**, and **ICloneable**. **ArrayList** has the constructors shown here:

```
public ArrayList( )
public ArrayList(ICollection c)
public ArrayList(int capacity)
```

The first constructor builds an empty **ArrayList** with an initial capacity of 16. The second constructor builds an **ArrayList** that is initialized with the elements and capacity of the collection specified by *c*. The third constructor builds an array list that has the specified initial *capacity*. The capacity is the size of the underlying array that is used to store the elements. The capacity grows automatically as elements are added to an **ArrayList**. Each time the list must be enlarged, its capacity is doubled.

In addition to the methods defined by the interfaces that it implements, **ArrayList** defines several methods of its own. Some of the more commonly used ones are shown in Table 22-4. An **ArrayList** can be sorted by calling **Sort( )**. Once sorted, it can be efficiently searched by **BinarySearch( )**. The contents of an **ArrayList** can be reversed by calling **Reverse( )**.

ArrayList supports several methods that operate on a range of elements within a collection. You can insert another collection into an **ArrayList** by calling **InsertRange( )**. You can remove a range by calling **RemoveRange( )**. You can overwrite a range within an **ArrayList** with the elements of another collection by calling **SetRange( )**. You can also sort or search a range rather than the entire collection.

THE C# CLASS LIBRARY

By default, an **ArrayList** is not synchronized. To obtain a synchronized wrapper around a collection, call **Synchronized( )**.

Method	Description
public virtual void AddRange(ICollection *c*)	Adds the elements in *c* to the end of the invoking **ArrayList**.
public virtual int BinarySearch(object *v*)	Searches the invoking collection for the value passed in *v*. The index of the matching element is returned. If the value is not found, a negative value is returned. The invoking list must be sorted.
public virtual int BinarySearch(object *v*, IComparer *comp*)	Searches the invoking collection for the value passed in *v* using the comparison object specified by *comp*. The index of the matching element is returned. If the value is not found, a negative value is returned. The invoking list must be sorted.
public virtual int BinarySearch(int *startIdx*, int *count*, object *v*, IComparer *comp*)	Searches the invoking collection for the value passed in *v* using the comparison object specified by *comp*. The search begins at *startIdx* and runs for *count* elements. The index of the matching element is returned. If the value is not found, a negative value is returned. The invoking list must be sorted.
public virtual void CopyTo(Array *ar*, int *startIdx*)	Copies the contents of the invoking collection, beginning at *startIdx*, to the array specified by *ar*, which must be a one-dimensional array compatible with the type of the elements in the collection.
public virtual void CopyTo(int *srcIdx*, Array *ar*, int *destIdx*, int *count*)	Copies a portion of the invoking collection, beginning at *srcIdx* and running for *count* elements, to the array specified by *ar*, beginning at *destIdx*. *ar* must be a one-dimensional array compatible with the type of the elements in the collection.

Table 22-4. *Several Commonly Used Methods Defined by **ArrayList***

Method	Description
public virtual ArrayList GetRange(int *idx*, int *count*)	Returns a portion of the invoking **ArrayList**. The range returned begins at *idx* and runs for *count* elements. The returned object refers to the same elements as the invoking object.
public static ArrayList FixedSize(ArrayList *ar*)	Wraps *ar* in a fixed-size **ArrayList** and returns the result.
public virtual void InsertRange(int *startIdx*, ICollection *c*)	Inserts the elements of *c* into the invoking collection, starting at the index specified by *startIdx*.
public virtual int LastIndexOf(object *v*)	Returns the index of the last occurrence of *v* in the invoking collection. Returns –1 if *v* is not found.
public static ArrayList ReadOnly(ArrayList *ar*)	Wraps *ar* in a read-only **ArrayList** and returns the result.
public virtual void RemoveRange(int *idx*, int *count*)	Removes *count* elements from the invoking collection, beginning at *idx*.
public virtual void Reverse( )	Reverses the contents of the invoking collection.
public virtual void Reverse(int *startIdx*, int *count*)	Reverses *count* elements of the invoking collection, beginning at *startIdx*.
public virtual void SetRange(int *startIdx*, ICollection *c*)	Replaces elements within the invoking collection, beginning at *startIdx*, within those specified by *c*.
public virtual void Sort( )	Sorts the collection into ascending order.
public virtual void Sort(IComparer *comp*)	Sorts the collection using the specified comparison object. If *comp* is null, the default comparison for each object is used.
public virtual void Sort(int *startIdx*, int *endIdx*, IComparer *comp*)	Sorts a portion of the collection using the specified comparison object. The sort begins at *startIdx* and ends at *endIdx*. If *comp* is null, the default comparison for each object is used.

Table 22-4. *Several Commonly Used Methods Defined by **ArrayList** (continued)*

THE C# CLASS LIBRARY

Method	Description
public static ArrayList Synchronized(ArrayList *list*)	Returns a synchronized version of the invoking **ArrayList**.
public virtual object[ ] ToArray( )	Returns an array that contains copies of the elements of the invoking object.
public virtual Array ToArray(Type *type*)	Returns an array that contains copies of the elements of the invoking object. The type of the elements in the array are specified by *type*.
public virtual void TrimToSize( )	Sets **Capacity** to **Count**.

Table 22-4. *Several Commonly Used Methods Defined by **ArrayList*** (continued)

In addition to those properties defined by the interfaces that it implements, **ArrayList** adds **Capacity**, shown here:

public virtual int Capacity { get; set; }

Capacity gets or sets the capacity of the invoking **ArrayList**. The capacity is the number of elements that can be held before the **ArrayList** must be enlarged. As mentioned, an **ArrayList** grows automatically, so it is not necessary to set the capacity manually. However, for efficiency reasons, you might want to set the capacity when you know in advance how many elements the list will contain. This prevents the overhead associated with the allocation of more memory.

Conversely, if you want to reduce the size of the array that underlies an **ArrayList**, you can set **Capacity** to a smaller value. However, this value must not be smaller than **Count**. Recall that **Count** is a property defined by **ICollection** that holds the number of objects currently stored in a collection. Attempting to set **Capacity** to a value less than **Count** causes an **ArgumentOutOfRangeException** to be generated. To obtain an **ArrayList** that is precisely as large as the number of items that it is currently holding, set **Capacity** equal to **Count**. You can also call **TrimToSize( )**.

The following program demonstrates **ArrayList**. It creates an **ArrayList** and then adds characters to it. The list is then displayed. Some of the elements are removed, and the list is displayed again. Next, more elements are added, forcing the capacity of the list to be increased. Finally, the contents of elements are changed.

```
// Demonstrate ArrayList.

using System;
```

```
using System.Collections;

class ArrayListDemo {
  public static void Main() {
    // create an array list
    ArrayList al = new ArrayList();

    Console.WriteLine("Initial capacity: " +
                       al.Capacity);
    Console.WriteLine("Initial number of elements: " +
                       al.Count);

    Console.WriteLine();

    Console.WriteLine("Adding 6 elements");
    // Add elements to the array list
    al.Add('C');
    al.Add('A');
    al.Add('E');
    al.Add('B');
    al.Add('D');
    al.Add('F');

    Console.WriteLine("Current capacity: " +
                       al.Capacity);
    Console.WriteLine("Number of elements: " +
                       al.Count);

    // Display the array list using array indexing.
    Console.Write("Current contents: ");
    for(int i=0; i < al.Count; i++)
      Console.Write(al[i] + " ");
    Console.WriteLine("\n");

    Console.WriteLine("Removing 2 elements");
    // Remove elements from the array list.
    al.Remove('F');
    al.Remove('A');

    Console.WriteLine("Current capacity: " +
                       al.Capacity);
    Console.WriteLine("Number of elements: " +
```

```
                              al.Count);

    // Use foreach loop to display the list.
    Console.Write("Contents: ");
    foreach(char c in al)
      Console.Write(c + " ");
    Console.WriteLine("\n");

    Console.WriteLine("Adding 20 more elements");
    // Add enough elements to force al to grow.
    for(int i=0; i < 20; i++)
      al.Add((char)('a' + i));
    Console.WriteLine("Current capacity: " +
                      al.Capacity);
    Console.WriteLine("Number of elements after adding 20: " +
                      al.Count);
    Console.Write("Contents: ");
    foreach(char c in al)
      Console.Write(c + " ");
    Console.WriteLine("\n");

    // Change contents using array indexing.
    Console.WriteLine("Change first three elements");
    al[0] = 'X';
    al[1] = 'Y';
    al[2] = 'Z';
    Console.Write("Contents: ");
    foreach(char c in al)
      Console.Write(c + " ");
    Console.WriteLine();
  }
}
```

The output from this program is shown here:

```
Initial capacity: 16
Initial number of elements: 0

Adding 6 elements
Current capacity: 16
Number of elements: 6
```

```
Current contents: C A E B D F

Removing 2 elements
Current capacity: 16
Number of elements: 4
Contents: C E B D

Adding 20 more elements
Current capacity: 32
Number of elements after adding 20: 24
Contents: C E B D a b c d e f g h i j k l m n o p q r s t

Change first three elements
Contents: X Y Z D a b c d e f g h i j k l m n o p q r s t
```

Notice that the collection starts out empty, with an initial capacity of 16. The capacity is increased as needed. Each time it is increased, the capacity is doubled.

Sorting and Searching an ArrayList

An **ArrayList** can be sorted by **Sort( )**. Once sorted, it can be efficiently searched by **BinarySearch( )**. The following program demonstrates these methods:

```csharp
// Sort and search an ArrayList.

using System;
using System.Collections;

class SortSearchDemo {
  public static void Main() {
    // create an array list
    ArrayList al = new ArrayList();

    // Add elements to the array list
    al.Add(55);
    al.Add(43);
    al.Add(-4);
    al.Add(88);
    al.Add(3);
    al.Add(19);

    Console.Write("Original contents: ");
```

```
      foreach(int i in al)
        Console.Write(i + " ");
      Console.WriteLine("\n");

      // Sort
      al.Sort();

      // Use foreach loop to display the list.
      Console.Write("Contents after sorting: ");
      foreach(int i in al)
        Console.Write(i + " ");
      Console.WriteLine("\n");

      Console.WriteLine("Index of 43 is " +
                        al.BinarySearch(43));
    }
}
```

The output is shown here:

```
Original contents: 55 43 -4 88 3 19

Contents after sorting: -4 3 19 43 55 88

Index of 43 is 3
```

Although an **ArrayList** can store objects of any type within the same list, when sorting or searching a list, it is necessary for those objects to be comparable. For example, the preceding program would have generated an exception if the list had included a string. (It is possible to create custom comparison methods that would allow the comparison of strings and integers, however. Custom comparators are discussed later in this chapter.)

Obtaining an Array from an ArrayList

When working with **ArrayList**, you will sometimes want to obtain an actual array that contains the contents of the list. You can do this by calling **ToArray( )**. There are several reasons why you might want to convert a collection into an array. Here are two. You may want to obtain faster processing times for certain operations, or you might need to pass an array to a method that is not overloaded to accept a collection. Whatever the reason, converting an **ArrayList** to an array is a trivial matter, as the following program shows:

```
// Convert an ArrayList into an array.

using System;
using System.Collections;

class ArrayListToArray {
  public static void Main() {
    ArrayList al = new ArrayList();

    // Add elements to the array list.
    al.Add(1);
    al.Add(2);
    al.Add(3);
    al.Add(4);

    Console.Write("Contents: ");
    foreach(int i in al)
      Console.Write(i + " ");
    Console.WriteLine();

    // Get the array.
    int[] ia = (int[]) al.ToArray(typeof(int));
    int sum = 0;

    // sum the array
    for(int i=0; i<ia.Length; i++)
      sum += ia[i];

    Console.WriteLine("Sum is: " + sum);
  }
}
```

The output from the program is shown here:

```
Contents: 1 2 3 4
Sum is: 10
```

The program begins by creating a collection of integers. Next, **ToArray( )** is called with the type specified as **int**. This causes an array of integers to be created. Since the return type of **ToArray( )** is **Array**, the contents of the array must still be cast to **int[ ]**. Finally, the values are summed.

Hashtable

Hashtable creates a collection that uses a hash table for storage. As most readers will know, a *hash table* stores information using a mechanism called *hashing*. In hashing, the informational content of a key is used to determine a unique value, called its *hash code*. The hash code is then used as the index at which the data associated with the key is stored in the table. The transformation of the key into its hash code is performed automatically—you never see the hash code, itself. The advantage of hashing is that it allows the execution time of lookup, retrieve, and set operations to remain constant, even for large sets. **Hashtable** implements the **IDictionary**, **ICollection**, **IEnumerable**, **ISerializable**, **IDeserializationCallback**, and **ICloneable** interfaces.

Hashtable defines many constructors, including these frequently used ones:

```
public Hashtable( )
public Hashtable(IDictionary c)
public Hashtable(int capacity)
public Hashtable(int capacity, float fillRatio)
```

The first form constructs a default **Hashtable**. The second form initializes the **Hashtable** by using the elements of *c*. The third form initializes the capacity of the **Hashtable** to *capacity*. The fourth form initializes both the capacity and fill ratio. The fill ratio (also called the *load factor*) must be between 0.1 and 1.0, and it determines how full the hash table can be before it is resized upward. Specifically, when the number of elements is greater than the capacity of the table multiplied by its fill ratio, the table is expanded. For constructors that do not take a fill ratio, 1.0 is used.

In addition to the methods defined by the interfaces that it implements, **Hashtable** also defines several methods of its own. Some commonly used ones are shown in Table 22-5. To determine if a **Hashtable** contains a key, call **ContainsKey( )**. To see if a specific value is stored, call **ContainsValue( )**. To enumerate the contents of a **Hashtable**, obtain an **IDictionaryEnumerator** by calling **GetEnumerator( )**. Recall that **IDictionaryEnumerator** is used to enumerate the contents of a collection that stores key/value pairs.

Method	Description
public virtual bool ContainsKey(object *k*)	Returns **true** if *k* is a key in the invoking **Hashtable**. Returns **false** otherwise.
public virtual bool ContainsValue(object *v*)	Returns **true** if *v* is a value in the invoking **Hashtable**. Returns **false** otherwise.

Table 22-5.   *Several Commonly Used Methods Defined by **Hashtable***

Method	Description
public virtual IDictionaryEnumerator GetEnumerator( )	Returns an **IDictionaryEnumerator** for the invoking **Hashtable**.
public static Hashtable Synchronized(Hashtable *ht*)	Returns a synchronized version of the **Hashtable** passed in *ht*.

Table 22-5. *Several Commonly Used Methods Defined by **Hashtable*** (continued)

In addition to those properties defined by the interfaces implemented by **Hashtable**, it adds two public properties of its own. You can obtain a collection of a **Hashtable**'s keys or values by using the properties shown here:

```
public virtual ICollection Keys { get; }
public virtual ICollection Values { get; }
```

Because **Hashtable** does not maintain an ordered collection, there is no specific order to the collection of keys or values obtained. **Hashtable** also defines two protected properties called **Hcp** and **Comparer**, which are available to inheriting classes.

Hashtable stores key/value pairs in the form of a **DictionaryEntry** structure, but most of the time you won't be aware of it directly because the properties and methods work with keys and values individually. For example, when you add an element to a **Hashtable**, you call **Add( )**, which takes two arguments: the key and the value.

It is important to note that **Hashtable** does not guarantee the order of its elements. This is because the process of hashing does not usually lend itself to the creation of sorted tables.

Here is an example that demonstrates **Hashtable**:

```
// Demonstrate Hashtable.

using System;
using System.Collections;

class HashtableDemo {
  public static void Main() {
    // Create a hash table.
    Hashtable ht = new Hashtable();
```

```
      // Add elements to the table
      ht.Add("house", "Dwelling");
      ht.Add("car", "Means of transport");
      ht.Add("book", "Collection of printed words");
      ht.Add("apple", "Edible fruit");

      // Can also add by using the indexer.
      ht["tractor"] = "Farm implement";

      // Get a collection of the keys.
      ICollection c = ht.Keys;

      // Use the keys to obtain the values.
      foreach(string str in c)
        Console.WriteLine(str + ": " + ht[str]);
    }
}
```

The output from this program is shown here:

```
tractor: Farm implement
book: Collection of printed words
apple: Edible fruit
car: Means of transport
house: Dwelling
```

As the output shows, the key/value pairs are not stored in sorted order. Notice how the contents of the hash table **ht** were obtained and displayed. First, a collection of the keys was retrieved by using the **Keys** property. Each key was then used to index **ht**, yielding the value associated with each key. Remember, the indexer defined by **IDictionary** and implemented by **Hashtable** uses a key as the index.

SortedList

SortedList creates a collection that stores key/value pairs in sorted order, based on the value of the keys. **SortedList** implements the **IDictionary, ICollection, IEnumerable**, and **ICloneable** interfaces.

SortedList has several constructors, including those shown here:

public SortedList( )
public SortedList(IDictionary *c*)

public SortedList(int *capacity*)
public SortedList(IComparer *comp*)

The first constructor builds an empty collection with an initial capacity of 16. The second constructor builds a **SortedList** that is initialized with the elements and capacity of *c*. The third constructor builds an empty **SortedList** that has the initial capacity specified by *capacity*. The capacity is the size of the underlying array that is used to store the elements. The fourth form lets you specify a comparison method that will be used to compare the objects contained in the list. This form creates an empty collection with an initial capacity of 16.

The capacity of a **SortedList** grows automatically as needed when elements are added to an array list. When the current capacity is exceeded, the capacity is doubled. The advantage of specifying a capacity when creating a **SortedList** is that that you can prevent or minimize the overhead associated with resizing the collection. Of course, it makes sense to specify an initial capacity only if you have some idea of how many elements will be stored.

In addition to the methods defined by the interfaces that it implements, **SortedList** also defines several methods of its own. Some of the most commonly used ones are shown in Table 22-6. To determine if a **SortedList** contains a key, call **ContainsKey( )**. To see if a specific value is stored, call **ContainsValue( )**. To enumerate the contents of a **Hashtable**, obtain an **IDictionaryEnumerator** by calling **GetEnumerator( )**. Recall that **IDictionaryEnumerator** is used to enumerate the contents of a collection that stores key/value pairs. You can obtain a synchronized wrapper around a **SortedList** by calling **Synchronized( )**.

There are various ways to set or obtain a value or key. To obtain the value associated with a specific index, call **GetByIndex( )**. To set a value given its index, call **SetByIndex( )**. You can retrieve the key associated with a specific index by calling **GetKey( )**. To obtain a

Method	Description
public virtual bool ContainsKey(object *k*)	Returns **true** if *k* is a key in the invoking **SortedList**. Returns **false** otherwise.
public virtual bool ContainsValue(object *v*)	Returns **true** if *v* is a value in the invoking **SortedList**. Returns **false** otherwise.
public virtual object GetByIndex(int *idx*)	Returns the value at the index specified by *idx*.

Table 22-6.   *Several Commonly Used Methods Defined by **SortedList***

Method	Description
public virtual IDictionaryEnumerator GetEnumerator( )	Returns an **IDictionaryEnumerator** for the invoking **SortedList**.
public virtual object GetKey(int *idx*)	Returns the value of the key at the index specified by *idx*.
public virtual IList GetKeyList( )	Returns an **IList** collection of the keys in the invoking **SortedList**.
public virtual IList GetValueList( )	Returns an **IList** collection of the values in the invoking **SortedList**.
public virtual int IndexOfKey(object *k*)	Returns the index of the key specified by *k*. Returns –1 if the key is not in the list.
public virtual int IndexOfValue(object *v*)	Returns the index of the first occurrence of the value specified by *v*. Returns –1 if the value is not in the list.
public virtual void SetByIndex(int *idx*, object *v*)	Sets the value at the index specified by *idx* to the value passed in *v*.
public static SortedList Synchronized(SortedList *sl*)	Returns a synchronized version of the **SortedList** passed in *sl*.
public virtual void TrimToSize( )	Sets **Capacity** to **Count**.

Table 22-6. *Several Commonly Used Methods Defined by **SortedList*** (continued)

list of all the keys, use **GetKeyList( )**. To get a list of all the values, use **GetValueList( )**. You can obtain the index of a key by calling **IndexOfKey( )** and the index of value by calling **IndexOfValue( )**. Of course, **SortedList** also supports the indexer defined by **IDictionary** that lets you set or obtain a value given its key.

In addition to those properties defined by the interfaces that it implements, **SortedList** adds two of its own. You can obtain a read-only collection of a **SortedList**'s keys or values by using the properties shown here:

```
public virtual ICollection Keys { get; }
public virtual ICollection Values { get; }
```

The order of the keys and values reflects that of the **SortedList**.

Like **Hashtable**, a **SortedList** stores key/value pairs in the form of a **DictionaryEntry** structure, but you will usually access the keys and values individually using the methods and properties defined by **SortedList**.

The following program demonstrates **SortedList**. It reworks and expands the **Hashtable** demonstration program from the previous section, substituting **SortedList**. When you examine the output, you will see that the **SortedList** version is sorted by key.

```
// Demonstrate a SortedList.

using System;
using System.Collections;

class SLDemo {
  public static void Main() {
    // Create a sorted SortedList.
    SortedList sl = new SortedList();

    // Add elements to the table
    sl.Add("house", "Dwelling");
    sl.Add("car", "Means of transport");
    sl.Add("book", "Collection of printed words");
    sl.Add("apple", "Edible fruit");

    // Can also add by using the indexer.
    sl["tractor"] = "Farm implement";

    // Get a collection of the keys.
    ICollection c = sl.Keys;

    // Use the keys to obtain the values.
    Console.WriteLine("Contents of list via indexer.");
    foreach(string str in c)
      Console.WriteLine(str + ": " + sl[str]);

    Console.WriteLine();

    // Display list using integer indexes.
    Console.WriteLine("Contents by integer indexes.");
    for(int i=0; i<sl.Count; i++)
      Console.WriteLine(sl.GetByIndex(i));

    Console.WriteLine();
```

```
      // Show integer indexes of entries.
      Console.WriteLine("Integer indexes of entries.");
      foreach(string str in c)
        Console.WriteLine(str + ": " + sl.IndexOfKey(str));
   }
}
```

The output is shown here:

```
Contents of list via indexer.
apple: Edible fruit
book: Collection of printed words
car: Means of transport
house: Dwelling
tractor: Farm implement

Contents by integer indexes.
Edible fruit
Collection of printed words
Means of transport
Dwelling
Farm implement

Integer indexes of entries.
apple: 0
book: 1
car: 2
house: 3
tractor: 4
```

Stack

As most readers know, a stack is a first-in, last-out list. To visualize a stack, imagine a stack of plates on a table. The first plate put down is the last one to be picked up. The stack is one of the most important data structures in computing. It is frequently used in system software, compilers, and AI-based backtracking routines, to name just a few.

The collection class that supports a stack is called **Stack**. It implements the **ICollection**, **IEnumerable**, and **ICloneable** interfaces. **Stack** is a dynamic collection that grows as needed to accommodate the elements it must store. Each time the capacity must be increased, the capacity is doubled.

Stack defines the following constructors:

public Stack( )
public Stack(int *capacity*)
public Stack(ICollection *c*)

The first form creates an empty stack with an initial capacity of 10. The second form creates an empty stack with the initial capacity specified by *capacity*. The third form creates a stack that contains the elements and capacity of the collection specified by *c*.

In addition to the methods defined by the interfaces that it implements, **Stack** defines the methods shown in Table 22-7. In general, here is how you use **Stack**. To put an object on the top of the stack, call **Push( )**. To remove and return the top element, call **Pop( )**. An **InvalidOperationException** is thrown if you call **Pop( )** when the invoking stack is empty. You can use **Peek( )** to return, but not remove, the top object.

THE C# CLASS LIBRARY

Method	Description
public virtual bool Contains(object *v*)	Returns **true** if *v* is on the invoking stack. If *v* is not found, **false** is returned.
public virtual void Clear( )	Sets **Count** to zero, which effectively clears the stack.
public virtual object Peek( )	Returns the element on the top of the stack, but does not remove it.
public virtual object Pop( )	Returns the element on the top of the stack, removing it in the process.
public virtual void Push(object *v*)	Pushes *v* onto the stack.
public static Stack Synchronized(Stack *stk*)	Returns a synchronized version of the **Stack** passed in *stk*.
public virtual object[ ] ToArray( )	Returns an array that contains copies of the elements of the invoking stack.

Table 22-7.   *The Methods Defined by* ***Stack***

Here is an example that creates a stack, pushes several **Integer** objects onto it, and then pops them off again.

```csharp
// Demonstrate the Stack class.

using System;
using System.Collections;

class StackDemo {
  static void showPush(Stack st, int a) {
    st.Push(a);
    Console.WriteLine("Push(" + a + ")");

    Console.Write("stack: ");
    foreach(int i in st)
      Console.Write(i + " ");

    Console.WriteLine();
  }

  static void showPop(Stack st) {
    Console.Write("Pop -> ");
    int a = (int) st.Pop();
    Console.WriteLine(a);

    Console.Write("stack: ");
    foreach(int i in st)
      Console.Write(i + " ");

    Console.WriteLine();
  }

  public static void Main() {
    Stack st = new Stack();

    foreach(int i in st)
      Console.Write(i + " ");

    Console.WriteLine();

    showPush(st, 22);
    showPush(st, 65);
```

```
      showPush(st, 91);
      showPop(st);
      showPop(st);
      showPop(st);

      try {
        showPop(st);
      } catch (InvalidOperationException) {
        Console.WriteLine("Stack empty.");
      }
    }
}
```

Here's the output produced by the program. Notice how the exception handler for **InvalidOperationException** manages a stack underflow.

```
Push(22)
stack: 22
Push(65)
stack: 65 22
Push(91)
stack: 91 65 22
Pop -> 91
stack: 65 22
Pop -> 65
stack: 22
Pop -> 22
stack:
Pop -> Stack empty.
```

Queue

Another familiar data structure is the queue, which is a first-in, first-out list. That is, the first item put in a queue is the first item retrieved. Queues are common in real life. For example, lines at a bank or fast-food restaurant are queues. In programming, queues are used to hold such things as the currently executing processes in the system, a list of pending database transactions, or data packets received over the Internet. They are also often used in simulations.

The collection class that supports a queue is called **Queue**. It implements the **ICollection**, **IEnumerable**, and **ICloneable** interfaces. **Queue** is a dynamic collection that grows as needed to accommodate the elements it must store. When more room is needed, the size of the queue is increased by a growth factor, which by default is 2.0.

Queue defines the following constructors:

public Queue( )
public Queue (int *capacity*)
public Queue (int *capacity*, float *growFact*)
public Queue (ICollection *c*)

The first form creates an empty queue with an initial capacity of 32 and uses the default growth factor of 2.0. The second form creates an empty queue with the initial capacity specified by *capacity* and a growth factor of 2.0. The third form allows you to specify a growth factor in *growFact*. The fourth form creates a queue that contains the elements and capacity of the collection specified by *c*. In this form, the default growth factor of 2.0 is used.

In addition to the methods defined by the interfaces that it implements, **Queue** defines the methods shown in Table 22-8. In general, here is how you use **Queue**. To put an object in the queue, call **Enqueue( )**. To remove and return the object at the front of the queue, call **Dequeue( )**. An **InvalidOperationException** is thrown if you call

Method	Description
public virtual bool Contains(object *v*)	Returns **true** if *v* is in the invoking queue. If *v* is not found, **false** is returned.
public virtual void Clear( )	Sets **Count** to zero, which effectively clears the queue.
public virtual object Dequeue( )	Returns the object at the front of the invoking queue. The object is removed in the process.
public virtual void Enqueue(object *v*)	Adds *v* to the end of the queue.
public virtual object Peek( )	Returns the object at the front of the invoking queue, but does not remove it.
public static Queue Synchronized(Queue *q*)	Returns a synchronized version of *q*.
public virtual object[ ] ToArray( )	Returns an array that contains copies of the elements of the invoking queue.
public virtual void TrimToSize( )	Sets **Capacity** to **Count**.

Table 22-8. *The Methods Defined by* **Queue**

Dequeue( ) when the invoking queue is empty. You can use **Peek( )** to return, but not remove, the next object.

Here is an example that demonstrates **Queue**:

```
// Demonstrate the Queue class.

using System;
using System.Collections;

class QueueDemo {
  static void showEnq(Queue q, int a) {
    q.Enqueue(a);
    Console.WriteLine("Enqueue(" + a + ")");

    Console.Write("queue: ");
    foreach(int i in q)
      Console.Write(i + " ");

    Console.WriteLine();
  }

  static void showDeq(Queue q) {
    Console.Write("Dequeue -> ");
    int a = (int) q.Dequeue();
    Console.WriteLine(a);

    Console.Write("queue: ");
    foreach(int i in q)
      Console.Write(i + " ");

    Console.WriteLine();
  }

  public static void Main() {
    Queue q = new Queue();

    foreach(int i in q)
      Console.Write(i + " ");

    Console.WriteLine();

    showEnq(q, 22);
```

```
      showEnq(q, 65);
      showEnq(q, 91);
      showDeq(q);
      showDeq(q);
      showDeq(q);

      try {
        showDeq(q);
      } catch (InvalidOperationException) {
        Console.WriteLine("Queue empty.");
      }
    }
  }
}
```

The output is shown here:

```
Enqueue(22)
queue: 22
Enqueue(65)
queue: 22 65
Enqueue(91)
queue: 22 65 91
Dequeue -> 22
queue: 65 91
Dequeue -> 65
queue: 91
Dequeue -> 91
queue:
Dequeue -> Queue empty.
```

Storing Bits with BitArray

The **BitArray** class supports a collection of bits. Because it stores bits rather than objects, **BitArray** has capabilities different from those of the other collections. However, it still supports the basic collection underpinning by implementing **ICollection** and **IEnumerable**. It also implements **ICloneable**.

BitArray defines several constructors. You can construct a **BitArray** from an array of Boolean values using this constructor:

public BitArray(bool[ ] *bits*)

In this case, each element of *bits* becomes a bit in the collection. Thus, each bit in the collection corresponds to an element of *bits*. Furthermore, the ordering of the elements of *bits* and the bits in the collection are the same.

You can create a **BitArray** from an array of bytes using this constructor:

public BitArray(byte[ ] *bits*)

Here, the bit pattern in *bits* becomes the bits in the collection, with *bits*[0] specifying the first 8 bits, *bits*[1] specifying the second 8 bits, and so on. In similar fashion, you can construct a **BitArray** from an array of **int**s using this constructor:

public BitArray(int[ ] *bits*)

In this case, *bits*[0] specifies the first 32 bits, *bits*[1] specifies the second 32 bits, and so on.

You can create a **BitArray** of a specific size using this constructor:

public BitArray(int *size*)

Here, *size* specifies the number of bits. The bits in the collection are initialized to **false**. To specify a size and initial value of the bits, use the following constructor:

public BitArray(int *size*, bool *v*)

In this case, all bits in the collection will be set to the value passed in *v*.

Finally, you can create a new **BitArray** from an existing one by using this constructor:

public BitArray(BitArray *bits*)

The new object will contain the same collection of bits as *bits*, but the two collections will otherwise be separate.

BitArrays can be indexed. Each index specifies an individual bit, with an index of zero indicating the low-order bit.

In addition to the methods specified by the interfaces that it implements, **BitArray** defines the methods shown in Table 22-9. Notice that **BitArray** does not supply a **Synchronized( )** method. Thus, a synchronized wrapper is not available, and the **IsSynchronized** property is always **false**. However, you can control access to a **BitArray** by synchronizing on the object provided by **SyncRoot**.

To the properties specified by the interfaces that it implements, **BitArray** adds **Length**, which is shown here:

public int Length { get; set; }

Length sets or obtains the number of bits in the collection. Thus, **Length** gives the same value as does the standard **Count** property, which is defined for all collections. However, **Count** is read-only, but **Length** is not. Thus, **Length** can be used to change the size of a

Method	Description
public BitArray And(BitArray *ba*)	ANDs the bits of the invoking object with those specified by *ba* and returns a **BitArray** that contains the result.
public bool Get(int *idx*)	Returns the value of the bit at the index specified by *idx*.
public BitArray Not( )	Performs a bitwise, logical NOT on the invoking collection and returns a **BitArray** that contains the result.
public BitArray Or(BitArray *ba*)	ORs the bits of the invoking object with those specified by *ba* and returns a **BitArray** that contains the result.
public void Set(int *idx*, bool *v*)	Sets the bit at the index specified by *idx* to *v*.
public void SetAll(bool *v*)	Sets all bits to *v*.
public BitArray Xor(BitArray *ba*)	XORs the bits of the invoking object with those specified by *ba* and returns a **BitArray** that contains the result.

Table 22-9.   *The Methods Defined by* **BitArray**

BitArray. If you shorten a **BitArray**, bits are truncated from the high-order end. If you lengthen a **BitArray**, false bits are added to the high-order end.

BitArray defines the following indexer:

object this[int *idx*] { get; set; }

You can use this indexer to get or set the value of an element.

Here is an example that demonstrates **BitArray**:

```
// Demonstrate BitArray.

using System;
using System.Collections;

class BADemo {
  public static void showbits(string rem,
```

```
                          BitArray bits) {
    Console.WriteLine(rem);
    for(int i=0; i < bits.Count; i++)
      Console.Write("{0, -6} ", bits[i]);
    Console.WriteLine("\n");
  }

  public static void Main() {
    BitArray ba = new BitArray(8);
    byte[] b = { 67 };
    BitArray ba2 = new BitArray(b);

    showbits("Original contents of ba:", ba);

    ba = ba.Not();

    showbits("Contents of ba after Not:", ba);

    showbits("Contents of ba2:", ba2);

    BitArray ba3 = ba.Xor(ba2);

    showbits("Result of ba XOR ba2:", ba3);
  }
}
```

The output is shown here:

```
Original contents of ba:
False  False  False  False  False  False  False  False

Contents of ba after Not:
True   True   True   True   True   True   True   True

Contents of ba2:
True   True   False  False  False  False  True   False

Result of ba XOR ba2:
False  False  True   True   True   True   False  True
```

THE C# CLASS LIBRARY

The Specialized Collections

The .NET Framework provides some specialized collections that are optimized to work on a specific type of data, or in a specific way. These collection classes are defined inside the **System.Collections.Specialized** namespace. They are synopsized in the following table:

Specialized Collection	Description
CollectionsUtil	A collection that ignores case differences in strings.
HybridDictionary	A collection that uses a **ListDictionary** to store key/value pairs when there are few elements in the collection. When the collection grows beyond a certain size, a **Hashtable** is automatically used to store the elements.
ListDictionary	A collection that stores key/value pairs in a linked list. It is recommended only for small collections.
NameValueCollection	A sorted collection of key/value pairs in which both the key and value are of type **string**.
StringCollection	A collection optimized for storing strings.
StringDictionary	A hash table of key/value pairs in which both the key and the value are of type **string**.

System.Collections also defines three abstract base classes, **CollectionBase**, **ReadOnlyCollectionBase**, and **DictionaryBase**, which can be inherited and used as a starting point for developing custom specialized collections.

Accessing a Collection via an Enumerator

Often you will want to cycle through the elements in a collection. For example, you might want to display each element. One way to do this is to use a **foreach** loop, as the preceding examples have done. Another way is to use an enumerator. An enumerator is an object that implements the **IEnumerator** interface.

IEnumerator defines one property called **Current**, which is shown here:

object Current { get; }

Current obtains the current element being enumerated. Since **Current** is a read-only property, an enumerator can only be used to retrieve, but not modify, the objects in a collection.

IEnumerator defines two methods. The first is **MoveNext( )**:

bool MoveNext( )

Each call to **MoveNext( )** moves the current position of the enumerator to the next element in the collection. It returns **true** if the next element is available, or **false**, if the **end** of the collection has been reached. Prior to the first call to **MoveNext( )**, the value of **Current** is undefined.

You can reset the enumerator to the start of the collection by calling **Reset( )**, shown here:

void Reset( )

After calling **Reset( )**, enumeration begins at the start of the collection, and you must call **MoveNext( )** to obtain the first element.

Using an Enumerator

Before you can access a collection through an enumerator, you must obtain one. Each of the collection classes provides a **GetEnumerator( )** method that returns an enumerator to the start of the collection. Using this enumerator, you can access each element in the collection, one element at a time. In general, to use an enumerator to cycle through the contents of a collection, follow these steps:

1. Obtain an enumerator to the start of the collection by calling the collection's **GetEnumerator( )** method.
2. Set up a loop that makes a call to **MoveNext( )**. Have the loop iterate as long as **MoveNext( )** returns **true**.
3. Within the loop, obtain each element through **Current**.

Here is an example that implements these steps. It uses an **ArrayList**, but the general principles apply to any type of collection.

```
// Demonstrate an enumerator.

using System;
using System.Collections;

class EnumeratorDemo {
  public static void Main() {
    ArrayList list = new ArrayList(1);

    for(int i=0; i < 10; i++)
```

```
      list.Add(i);

    // Use enumerator to access list.
    IEnumerator etr = list.GetEnumerator();
    while(etr.MoveNext())
      Console.Write(etr.Current + " ");

    Console.WriteLine();

    // Re-enumerate the list.
    etr.Reset();
    while(etr.MoveNext())
      Console.Write(etr.Current + " ");

    Console.WriteLine();
  }
}
```

The output is shown here:

```
0 1 2 3 4 5 6 7 8 9
0 1 2 3 4 5 6 7 8 9
```

In general, when you need to cycle through a collection, a **foreach** loop is more convenient to use than an enumerator. However, an enumerator gives you a little extra control by allowing you to reset the enumerator at will.

Using the IDictionaryEnumerator

A collection class that implements **IDictionary** stores key/value pairs. To iterate the elements of such a collection, you will use an **IDictionaryEnumerator** instead of an **IEnumerator**. The **IDictionaryEnumerator** inherits **IEnumerator** and adds three properties. The first is

DictionaryEntry Entry { get; }

Entry obtains the next key/value pair from the enumerator in the form of a **DictionaryEntry** structure. Recall that **DictionaryEntry** defines two properties, called **Key** and **Value**, which can be used to access the key or value contained within the entry. The other two properties defined by **IDictionaryEnumerator** are shown here:

object Key { get; }
object Value { get; }

These allow you to access the key or value directly.

An **IDictionaryEnumerator** is used just like a regular enumerator, except that you will obtain the current value through the **Entry**, **Key**, or **Value** properties rather than **Current**. Thus, after obtaining an **IDictionaryEnumerator**, you must call **MoveNext( )** to obtain the first element. Continue to call **MoveNext( )** to obtain the rest of the elements in the collection. **MoveNext( )** returns **false** when there are no more elements.

Here is an example that enumerates the elements in a **Hashtable** through an **IDictionaryEnumerator**:

```
// Demonstrate IDictionaryEnumerator.

using System;
using System.Collections;

class IDicEnumDemo {
  public static void Main() {
    // Create a hash table.
    Hashtable ht = new Hashtable();

    // Add elements to the table
    ht.Add("Tom", "555-3456");
    ht.Add("Mary", "555-9876");
    ht.Add("Todd", "555-3452");
    ht.Add("Ken", "555-7756");

    // Demonstrate enumerator
    IDictionaryEnumerator etr = ht.GetEnumerator();
    Console.WriteLine("Display info using through Entry.");
    while(etr.MoveNext())
     Console.WriteLine(etr.Entry.Key + ": " +
                       etr.Entry.Value);

    Console.WriteLine();

    Console.WriteLine("Display info using Key and Value directly.");
    etr.Reset();
    while(etr.MoveNext())
     Console.WriteLine(etr.Key + ": " +
                       etr.Value);

  }
}
```

The output is shown here:

```
Display info using through Entry.
Tom: 555-3456
Todd: 555-3452
Ken: 555-7756
Mary: 555-9876

Display info using Key and Value directly.
Tom: 555-3456
Todd: 555-3452
Ken: 555-7756
Mary: 555-9876
```

Storing User-Defined Classes in Collections

For the sake of simplicity, the foregoing examples have stored built-in types, such as **int**, **string**, or **char**, in a collection. Of course, collections are not limited to the storage of built-in objects. Quite the contrary. The power of collections is that they can store any type of object, including objects of classes that you create. For example, consider the following example that uses an **ArrayList** to store inventory information that is encapsulated by the **Inventory** class:

```csharp
// A simple inventory example.

using System;
using System.Collections;

class Inventory {
  string name;
  double cost;
  int onhand;

  public Inventory(string n, double c, int h) {
    name = n;
    cost = c;
    onhand = h;
  }

  public override string ToString() {
    return
      String.Format("{0,-10}Cost: {1,6:C}  On hand: {2}",
```

THE C# CLASS LIBRARY

```
                        name, cost, onhand);
    }
}

class InventoryList {
  public static void Main() {
    ArrayList inv = new ArrayList();

    // Add elements to the list
    inv.Add(new Inventory("Pliers", 5.95, 3));
    inv.Add(new Inventory("Wrenches", 8.29, 2));
    inv.Add(new Inventory("Hammers", 3.50, 4));
    inv.Add(new Inventory("Drills", 19.88, 8));

    Console.WriteLine("Inventory list:");
    foreach(Inventory i in inv) {
      Console.WriteLine("    " + i);
    }
  }
}
```

The output from the program is shown here:

```
Inventory list:
Pliers     Cost:  $5.95  On hand: 3
   Wrenches  Cost:  $8.29  On hand: 2
   Hammers   Cost:  $3.50  On hand: 4
   Drills    Cost: $19.88  On hand: 8
```

In the program, notice that no special actions were required to store objects of type **Inventory** in a collection. Because all types inherit **object**, any type of object can be stored in any general-purpose collection.

There is one other thing to notice about the preceding program: it is quite short. When you consider that it sets up a dynamic array that can store, retrieve, and process inventory information in less than 40 lines of code, the power of collections begins to become apparent. As most readers will know, if all of this functionality had to be coded by hand, the program would have been several times longer. Collections offer off-the-shelf solutions to a wide variety of programming problems. You should use them whenever the situation warrants.

There is one limitation to the preceding program that may not be immediately apparent: the collection can't be sorted. The reason for this is that **ArrayList** has no way to know how to compare two **Inventory** objects. There are two ways to remedy this situation. First, **Inventory** can implement the **IComparable** interface. This interface defines how two objects of a class are compared. Second, an **IComparer** object can be specified when comparisons are required. The following sections illustrate both approaches.

Implementing IComparable

If you want to sort an **ArrayList** of user-defined objects (or if you want to store those objects in a **SortedList**), then the collection must know how to compare those objects. One way to do this is for the object being stored to implement the **IComparable** interface. **IComparable** defines only one method: **CompareTo( )**, which determines how comparisons are performed. The general form of **CompareTo( )** is shown here:

    int CompareTo(object *obj*)

CompareTo( ) compares the invoking object to *obj*. To sort in ascending order, your implementation must return zero if the objects are equal, a positive value if the invoking object is greater than *obj*, and a negative value if the invoking object is less than *obj*. You can sort in descending order by reversing the outcome of the comparison. The method can throw an **ArgumentException** if the type of *obj* is not compatible for comparison with the invoking object.

Here is an example that shows how to implement **IComparable**. It adds **IComparable** to the **Inventory** class developed in the preceding section. By implementing **IComparable**, it allows a collection of **Inventory** objects to be sorted.

```
// Implement IComparable.

using System;
using System.Collections;

class Inventory : IComparable {
  string name;
  double cost;
  int onhand;

  public Inventory(string n, double c, int h) {
    name = n;
    cost = c;
    onhand = h;
  }

  public override string ToString() {
    return
```

```
          String.Format("{0,-10}Cost: {1,6:C}  On hand: {2}",
                       name, cost, onhand);
  }

  // Implement the IComparable interface.
  public int CompareTo(object obj) {
    Inventory b;
    b = (Inventory) obj;
    return name.CompareTo(b.name);
  }
}

class IComparableDemo {
  public static void Main() {
    ArrayList inv = new ArrayList();

    // Add elements to the list
    inv.Add(new Inventory("Pliers", 5.95, 3));
    inv.Add(new Inventory("Wrenches", 8.29, 2));
    inv.Add(new Inventory("Hammers", 3.50, 4));
    inv.Add(new Inventory("Drills", 19.88, 8));

    Console.WriteLine("Inventory list before sorting:");
    foreach(Inventory i in inv) {
      Console.WriteLine("    " + i);
    }
    Console.WriteLine();

    // Sort the list.
    inv.Sort();

    Console.WriteLine("Inventory list after sorting:");
    foreach(Inventory i in inv) {
      Console.WriteLine("    " + i);
    }
  }
}
```

Here is the output. Notice that after the call to **Sort( )**, the inventory is sorted by name.

```
Inventory list before sorting:
    Pliers    Cost: $5.95  On hand: 3
```

```
Wrenches  Cost:    $8.29  On hand: 2
Hammers   Cost:    $3.50  On hand: 4
Drills    Cost:   $19.88  On hand: 8

Inventory list after sorting:
  Drills    Cost:   $19.88  On hand: 8
  Hammers   Cost:    $3.50  On hand: 4
  Pliers    Cost:    $5.95  On hand: 3
  Wrenches  Cost:    $8.29  On hand: 2
```

Specifying an IComparer

Although implementing **IComparable** for classes that you create is the easiest way to allow objects of those classes to be sorted by a collection, you can approach the problem a different way by using **IComparer**. To use **IComparer**, first create a class that implements **IComparer**, and then specify an object of that class when comparisons are required. **IComparer** defines only one method, **Compare( )**, which is shown here:

int Compare(object *obj1*, object *obj2*)

Compare( ) compares *obj1* to *obj2*. To sort in ascending order, your implementation must return zero if the objects are equal, a positive value if *obj1* is greater than *obj2*, and a negative value if *obj1* is less than *obj2*. You can sort in descending order by reversing the outcome of the comparison. The method can throw an **ArgumentException** if the type of *obj* is not compatible for comparison with the invoking object.

An **IComparer** can be specified when constructing a **SortedList**, when calling **ArrayList.Sort(IComparer)**, and at various other places throughout the collection classes. The main advantage of using **IComparer** is that you can sort objects of classes that do not implement **IComparable**.

The following program reworks the inventory program so that it uses an **IComparer** to sort the inventory list. It first creates a class called **CompInv** that implements **IComparer** and compares two **Inventory** objects. An object of this class is then used in a call to **Sort( )** to sort the inventory list.

```
// Use IComparer.

using System;
using System.Collections;

// Create an IComparer for Inventory objects.
class CompInv : IComparer {
  // Implement the IComparable interface.
```

```
  public int Compare(object obj1, object obj2) {
    Inventory a, b;
    a = (Inventory) obj1;
    b = (Inventory) obj2;
    return a.name.CompareTo(b.name);
  }
}

class Inventory {
  public string name;
  double cost;
  int onhand;

  public Inventory(string n, double c, int h) {
    name = n;
    cost = c;
    onhand = h;
  }

  public override string ToString() {
    return
      String.Format("{0,-10}Cost: {1,6:C}  On hand: {2}",
                    name, cost, onhand);
  }
}

class MailList {
  public static void Main() {
    CompInv comp = new CompInv();
    ArrayList inv = new ArrayList();

    // Add elements to the list
    inv.Add(new Inventory("Pliers", 5.95, 3));
    inv.Add(new Inventory("Wrenches", 8.29, 2));
    inv.Add(new Inventory("Hammers", 3.50, 4));
    inv.Add(new Inventory("Drills", 19.88, 8));

    Console.WriteLine("Inventory list before sorting:");
    foreach(Inventory i in inv) {
      Console.WriteLine("   " + i);
    }
    Console.WriteLine();
```

```
// Sort the list using an IComparer.
inv.Sort(comp);

Console.WriteLine("Inventory list after sorting:");
foreach(Inventory i in inv) {
  Console.WriteLine("    " + i);
}
    }
}
```

The output is the same as the previous version of the program.

Collection Summary

Collections give you, the programmer, a powerful set of well-engineered solutions to some of programming's most common tasks. Think of using a collection the next time you need to store and retrieve information. Collections need not be reserved for only the "large jobs," such as corporate databases, mailing lists, or inventory systems. They are also effective when applied to smaller jobs. For example, a **SortedList** would make an excellent collection to hold a list of appointments for the day. The types of problems that will benefit from a collections-based solution are limited only by your imagination.

Chapter 23

Networking Through the Internet

C# is a language designed for the modern computing environment, of which the Internet is an important part. A main design criteria for C# was, therefore, to include those features necessary for using the Internet. Although previous languages, such as C and C++, could be used to access the Internet, download files, and obtain resources, the process was not as streamlined as most programmers would like. C# remedies that situation. Using standard features of C# and the .NET Library, it is finally easy to "Internet-enable" your applications.

Support for networking is contained in two namespaces. The first is **System.Net**. It defines a large number of high-level, easy-to-use classes that support the various types of operations common to the Internet. The second is **System.Net.Sockets**. This namespace supports *sockets*, which offer low-level control over networking. For most applications, the classes provided by **System.Net** are a better choice because of the convenience they offer, and it is the namespace we will be using in this chapter.

Note *Support for server-side, ASP.NET-based network applications is found in the* *System.Web namespace.*

The System.Net Members

System.Net is a large namespace that contains many members. Although we won't examine them all here, it is worthwhile to list them so that you have an idea of what is available for your use. The classes defined by **System.Net** are shown here:

AuthenticationManager	Authorization	Cookie
CookieCollection	CookieContainer	CookieException
CredentialCache	Dns	DnsPermission
DnsPermissionAttribute	EndPoint	EndpointPermission
FileWebRequest	FileWebResponse	GlobalProxySelection
HttpVersion	HttpWebRequest	HttpWebResponse
IPAddress	IPEndPoint	IPHostEntry
NetworkCredential	ProtocolViolationException	ServicePoint
ServicePointManager	SocketAddress	SocketPermission
SocketPermissionAttribute	WebClient	WebException
WebHeaderCollection	WebPermission	WebPermissionAttribute
WebProxy	WebRequest	WebResponse

System.Net defines the following interfaces:

IAuthenticationModule	ICertificatePolicy	ICredentials
IWebProxy	IWebRequestCreate	

It defines four enumerations:

HttpStatusCode	NetworkAccess
TransportType	WebExceptionStatus

Finally, **System.Net** defines one delegate: **HttpContinueDelegate**.

Although **System.Net** defines many members, only a few are needed to accomplish most Internet programming tasks. At the core of networking are the abstract classes **WebRequest** and **WebResponse**. These classes are inherited by classes that support a specific network protocol. (A *protocol* defines the rules used to send information over a network.) For example, the derived classes that support the standard HTTP protocol are **HttpWebRequest** and **HttpWebResponse**.

Even though **WebRequest** and **WebResponse** are easy to use, for some tasks, you can employ an even simpler approach based on **WebClient**. For example, if you only need to upload or download a file, then **WebClient** is often the best way to accomplish it.

Uniform Resource Identifiers

Fundamental to Internet programming is the Uniform Resource Identifier (URI). A *URI* describes the location of some resource on the network. A URI is also commonly called a *URL*, which is short for Uniform Resource Locator. Because Microsoft uses the term *URI* when describing the members of **System.Net**, this book will do so, too. You are no doubt familiar with URIs because you use one every time you enter an address into your Internet browser.

A URI has the following general form:

Protocol://ServerID/FilePath?Query

Protocol specifies the protocol being used, such as HTTP. *ServerID* identifies the specific server, such as Osborne.com or Weather.com. *FilePath* specifies the path to a specific file. If *FilePath* is not specified, the default page at the specified *ServerID* is obtained. Finally, *Query* specifies information that will be sent to the server. *Query* is optional. In C#, URIs are encapsulated by the **Uri** class, which is examined later in this chapter.

Internet Access Fundamentals

The classes contained in **System.Net** support a request/response model of Internet interaction. In this approach, your program, which is the client, requests information from the server and then waits for the response. For example, your program might send to the server the URI of some web site. The response that you will receive is the hypertext associated with that URI. This request/response approach is both convenient and simple to use, because most of the details are handled for you.

The hierarchy of classes topped by **WebRequest** and **WebResponse** implement what Microsoft calls *pluggable protocols*. As most readers know, there are several different types of network communication protocols. The most common for Internet use is HTTP (HyperText Transfer Protocol). Another is FTP (File Transfer Protocol). When a URI is constructed, the prefix of the URI specifies the protocol. For example, HTTP://MyWebSite.com uses the prefix *HTTP*, which specifies HyperText Transfer Protocol.

As mentioned earlier, **WebRequest** and **WebResponse** are abstract classes that define the general request/response operations that are common to all protocols. From them are derived concrete classes that implement specific protocols. Derived classes register themselves, using the static method **RegisterPrefix( )**, which is defined by **WebRequest**. When you create a **WebRequest** object, the protocol specified by the URI's prefix will automatically be used, if it is available. The advantage of this "pluggable" approach is that most of your code remains the same no matter what type of protocol you are using.

The .NET runtime automatically defines the HTTP protocol. Thus, if you specify a URI that uses the HTTP prefix, you will automatically receive the HTTP-compatible class that supports it. The classes that support HTTP are **HttpWebRequest** and **HttpWebResponse**. These classes inherit **WebRequest** and **WebResponse**, and add several members of their own, which apply to the HTTP protocol.

System.Net supports both synchronous and asynchronous communication. For many Internet applications, synchronous transactions are the best choice because they are easy to use. With synchronous communications, your program sends a request and then waits until the response is received. For some types of high-performance applications, asynchronous communication is better. Using the asynchronous approach, your program can continue processing while waiting for information to be transferred. However, asynchronous communications are more difficult to implement. Furthermore, not all programs benefit from an asynchronous approach. For example, often when information is needed from the Internet, there is nothing to do until the information is received. In cases like this, the potential gains from the asynchronous approach are not realized. Because synchronous Internet access is both easier to use and more universally applicable, it is the only type examined in this chapter.

Since **WebRequest** and **WebResponse** are at the heart of **System.Net**, they will be examined next.

WebRequest

The **WebRequest** class manages a network request. It is abstract because it does not implement a specific protocol. It does, however, define those methods and properties common to all requests. The methods defined by **WebRequest** that support synchronous communications are shown in Table 23-1. The properties defined by **WebRequest** are shown in Table 23-2. The default values for the properties are determined by derived classes. **WebRequest** defines no public constructors.

Method	Description
public static WebRequest Create(string *uri*);	Creates a **WebRequest** object for the URI specified by the string passed by *uri*. The object returned will implement the protocol specified by the prefix of the URI. Thus, the object will be of a class that inherits **WebRequest**. A **NotSupportedException** is thrown if the requested protocol is not available. A **UriFormatException** is thrown if the URI format is invalid.
public static WebRequest Create(Uri *uri*);	Creates a **WebRequest** object for the URI specified by *uri*. The object returned will implement the protocol specified by the prefix of the URI. Thus, the object will be of a class that inherits **WebRequest**. A **NotSupportedException** is thrown if the requested protocol is not available.
public virtual Stream GetRequestStream( )	Returns an output stream associated with the previously requested URI.
public virtual WebResponse GetResponse( )	Sends the previously created request and waits for a response. When a response is received, it is returned as a **WebReponse** object. Your program will use this object to obtain information from the specified URI. A **WebException** is thrown if an error occurs while obtaining the response.

Table 23-1. *The Methods Defined by **WebRequest** that Support Synchronous Communications*

Property	Description
public virtual string ConnectionGroupName { get; set; }	Obtains or sets the connection group name. Connection groups are a way of creating a set of requests. They are not needed for simple Internet transactions.
public virtual long ContentLength { get; set; }	Obtains or sets the length of the content.
public virtual string ContentType { get; set; }	Obtains or sets the description of the content.
public virtual ICredentials Credentials { get; set; }	Obtains or sets credentials. Credentials are needed for those sites that require user authentication.
public virtual WebHeaderCollection Headers{ get; set; }	Obtains or sets a collection of the headers.
public virtual string Method { get; set; }	Obtains or sets the protocol.
public virtual bool PreAuthenticate { get; set; }	If **true**, authentication information is included when the request is sent. If **false**, authentication information is provided only when requested by the URI.
public virtual IWebProxy Proxy { get; set; }	Obtains or sets the proxy server. This applies only to environments in which a proxy server is used.
public virtual Uri RequestUri { get; }	Obtains the URI of the request.
public virtual int Timeout { get; set; }	Obtains or sets the number of milliseconds that a request will wait for a response. To wait forever, use **Timeout.Infinite**.

Table 23-2. *The Properties Defined by* **WebRequest**

To send a request to a URI, you must first create an object of a class derived from **WebRequest** that implements the desired protocol. This is done by calling **Create( )**, which is a **static** method defined by **WebRequest**. **Create( )** returns an object of a class that inherits **WebRequest** and implements a specific protocol.

Method	Description
public virtual void Close( )	Closes the response. It also closes the response stream returned by **GetResponseStream( )**.
public virtual Stream GetResponse Stream( )	Returns an input stream connected to the requested URI. Using this stream, data can be read from the URI.

Table 23-3.   *The Methods Defined by* **WebResponse**

WebResponse

WebResponse encapsulates a response that is obtained as the result of a request. **WebResponse** is an abstract class. Inheriting classes create specific, concrete versions of it that support a protocol. A **WebResponse** object is normally obtained by calling the **GetResponse( )** method defined by **WebRequest**. This object will be an instance of a concrete class derived from **WebReponse** that implements a specific protocol. The methods defined by **WebResponse** are shown in Table 23-3 above. The properties defined by **WebResponse** are shown in Table 23-4. The values of these properties are set based on each individual response. **WebResponse** defines no public constructors.

Property	Description
public virtual long ContentLength { get; set; }	Obtains or sets the length of the content being received. This will be –1 if the content length is not available.
public virtual string ContentType { get; set; }	Obtains a description of the content.
public virtual WebHeaderCollection Headers{ get; }	Obtains a collection of the headers associated with the URI.
public virtual Uri ReponseUri { get; }	Obtains the URI that generated the response. This may differ from the one requested if the response was redirected to another URI.

Table 23-4.   *The Properties Defined by* **WebResponse**

HttpWebRequest and HttpWebResponse

The classes **HttpWebRequest** and **HttpWebResponse** inherit the **WebRequest** and **WebResponse** classes and implement the HTTP protocol. In the process, both add several properties that give you detailed information about an HTTP transaction. Some of these properties are used later in this chapter. However, for simple Internet operations, you will not often need to use these extra capabilities.

A Simple First Example

Internet access centers around **WebRequest** and **WebResponse**. Before we examine the process in detail, it will be useful to see an example that illustrates the request/response approach to Internet access. After you see these classes in action, it is easier to understand why they are organized as they are.

The following program performs a simple, yet very common, Internet operation. It obtains the hypertext contained at a specific URI. In this case, the content of Osborne.com, the web site for the Osborne division of McGraw-Hill (the publisher of this book) is obtained, but you can substitute another web site, as long as it is publicly accessible. The program displays the hypertext on the screen in chunks of 400 characters, so you can see what is being received before it scrolls off the screen.

```
// Access the Internet.

using System;
using System.Net;
using System.IO;

class NetDemo {
  public static void Main() {
    int ch;

    // First, create a WebRequest to a URI.
    HttpWebRequest req = (HttpWebRequest)
         WebRequest.Create("http://www.osborne.com");

    // Next, send that request and return the response.
    HttpWebResponse resp = (HttpWebResponse)
         req.GetResponse();

    // From the response, obtain an input stream.
    Stream istrm = resp.GetResponseStream();

    /* Now, read and display the html present at
       the specified URI.  So you can see what is
```

```
                   being displayed, the data is shown
                   400 characters at a time.  After each 400
                   characters are displayed, you must press
                   ENTER to get the next 400. */

    for(int i=1; ; i++) {
      ch =  istrm.ReadByte();
      if(ch == -1) break;
      Console.Write((char) ch);
      if((i%400)==0) {
        Console.Write("\nPress a key.");
        Console.Read();
      }
    }

    // Close the Response. This also closes istrm.
    resp.Close();
  }
}
```

The first part of the output is shown here. (Of course, the precise content will
change over time.)

```
<!DOCTYPE HTML PUBLIC "-//W3C//DTD HTML 4.0 Transitional//EN">

<HTML>
<HEAD>
<TITLE>Find all the right computer books and learning tools at Osborne
McGraw-Hill</TITLE>
<META NAME="Title" CONTENT="Find all the right computer books and learning
tools at Osborne McGraw-Hill">
<META NAME="Keywords" CONTENT="osborne, mcgraw-hill, mcgraw hill, it books,
computer books, database books, programming
Press a key.
books, networking books, certification books, computing books, computer
application books, hardware books, information technology books, operating
systems, web development, oracle press, communications, complete reference,
how to do everything, yellow pages, book publisher, certification study
guide, reference book, security, network security, ebusiness, e-business,
a+, network+, i-net+, cisco ce
Press a key.
  .
  .
  .
```

This is part of the hypertext associated with the Osborne.com web site. Since the program simply displays the content character-by-character, it is not formatted as it would be by a browser. It is displayed in its raw form.

Let's examine this program line-by-line. First, notice that the **System.Net** namespace is used. As explained, this is the namespace that contains the networking classes. Also notice that **System.IO** is included. This namespace is needed because the information from the web site is read using a **Stream** object.

The program begins by creating a **WebRequest** object that contains the desired URI. Notice that the **Create( )** method, rather than a constructor, is used for this purpose. **Create( )** is a **static** member of **WebRequest**. Even though **WebRequest** is an abstract class, it is still possible to call a **static** method of that class. **Create( )** returns a **WebRequest** object that has the proper protocol "plugged in," based on the protocol prefix of the URI. In this case, the protocol is HTTP. Thus, **Create( )** returns an **HttpWebRequest( )** object. Of course, its return value must still be cast to **HttpWebRequest** when it is assigned to the **HttpWebRequest** reference called **req**. At this point, the request has been created, but not yet sent to the specified URI.

To send the request, the program calls **GetResponse( )** on the **WebRequest** object. After the request has been sent, **GetResponse( )** waits for a response. Once a response has been received, **GetResponse( )** returns a **WebResponse** object that encapsulates the response. This object is assigned to **resp**. Since, in this case, the response uses the HTTP protocol, the result is cast to **HttpWebResponse**. Among other things, the response contains a stream that can be used to read data from the URI.

Next, an input stream is obtained by calling **GetResponseStream( )** on **resp**. This is a standard **Stream** object, having all of the attributes and features of any other input stream. A reference to the stream is assigned to **istrm**. Using **istrm**, the data at the specified URI can be read in the same way that a file is read.

Next, the program reads the data from Osborne.com and displays it on the screen. Since there is a lot of information, the display pauses every 400 characters and waits for you to press ENTER. This way the first part of the information won't simply scroll off the screen. Notice that the characters are read using **ReadByte( )**. Recall that this method returns the next character from the input stream as an **int**, which must be cast to **char**. It returns –1 when the end of the stream has been reached.

Finally, the response is closed by calling **Close( )** on **resp**. Closing the response stream automatically closes the input stream, too. It is important to close the response between each request. If you don't, it is possible to exhaust the network resources and prevent the next connection.

Before leaving this example, one other important point needs to be made: It was not actually necessary to use an **HttpWebRequest** or **HttpWebResponse** object to display the hypertext from the Osborne.com web site. Because the preceding program did not use any HTTP-specific features, the standard methods defined by **WebRequest** and **WebResponse** were sufficient to handle this task. Thus, the calls to **Create( )** and **GetResponse( )** could have been written like this:

```
// First, create a WebRequest to a URI.
WebRequest req =  WebRequest.Create("http://www.osborne.com");

// Next, send that request and return the response.
WebResponse resp =  req.GetResponse();
```

Microsoft suggests that in cases in which you don't need to employ a cast to a specific type of protocol implementation, it is better to use **WebRequest** and **WebResponse** because it allows protocols to be changed with no impact on your code. However, since all of the examples in this chapter will be using HTTP, and a few will be using HTTP-specific features, the programs will use **HttpWebRequest** and **HttpWebResponse**.

Handling Network Errors

Although the program in the preceding section is correct, it is not resilient. Even the simplest network error will cause it to end abruptly. Although this isn't a problem for the example programs shown in this chapter, it is something that must be avoided in real-world applications. To fully handle all network exceptions that the program might generate, you must monitor calls to **Create( )**, **GetResponse( )**, and **GetResponseStream( )**. Each type of potential error is described next.

Exceptions Generated by Create( )

The **Create( )** method defined by **WebRequest** can generate three exceptions. If the protocol specified by the URI prefix is not supported, then **NotSupportedException** is thrown. If the URI format is invalid, **UriFormatException** is thrown. It can also throw an **ArgumentNullException** if it is called with a null reference, but this is not an error generated by networking.

Exceptions Generated by GetReponse( )

If an error occurs when obtaining a response by calling **GetResponse( )**, a **WebException** is thrown. In addition to the members defined for all exceptions, **WebException** adds two properties that relate to network errors: **Response** and **Status**.

You can obtain a reference to the **WebResponse** object inside an exception handler through the **Response** property. This is the object that would have been returned by **GetReponse( )** if an exception had not occurred. It is defined like this:

public WebResponse Response { get; }

When an error occurs, you can use the **Status** property of **WebException** to find out what went wrong. It is defined like this:

public WebExceptionStatus {get; }

WebExceptionStatus is an enumeration that contains the following values:

ConnectFailure	ConnectionClosed	KeepAliveFailure
NameResolutionFailure	Pending	PipelineFailure
ProtocolError	ProxyNameResolutionFailure	ReceiveFailure
RequestCanceled	SecureChannelFailure	SendFailure
ServerProtocolViolation	Success	Timeout
TrustFailure		

Once the cause of the error has been determined, your program can take appropriate action.

Exceptions Generated by GetResponseStream( )

The **GetResponseStream( )** method of **GetResponse** can throw a **ProtocolViolationException**, which in general means that some error occurred relative to the specified protocol. As it relates to **GetResponseStream( )**, it means that no valid response stream is available. Also, an **IOException** could occur while reading the stream.

Using Exception Handling

The following program adds handlers for all possible network exceptions to the example shown earlier:

```
// Handle network exceptions.

using System;
using System.Net;
using System.IO;
```

```
class NetExcDemo {
  public static void Main() {
    int ch;

    try {

      // First, create a WebRequest to a URI.
      HttpWebRequest req = (HttpWebRequest)
            WebRequest.Create("http://www.osborne.com");

      // Next, send that request and return the response.
      HttpWebResponse resp = (HttpWebResponse)
            req.GetResponse();

      // From the response, obtain an input stream.
      Stream istrm = resp.GetResponseStream();

      /* Now, read and display the html present at
         the specified URI.  So you can see what is
         being displayed, the data is shown
         400 characters at a time.  After each 400
         characters are displayed, you must press
         ENTER to get the next 400. */

      for(int i=1; ; i++) {
        ch =  istrm.ReadByte();
        if(ch == -1) break;
        Console.Write((char) ch);
        if((i%400)==0) {
          Console.Write("\nPress a key.");
          Console.Read();
        }
      }


      // Close the Response. This also closes istrm.
      resp.Close();

    } catch(WebException exc) {
      Console.WriteLine("Network Error: " + exc.Message +
                        "\nStatus code: " + exc.Status);
    } catch(ProtocolViolationException exc) {
      Console.WriteLine("Protocol Error: " + exc.Message);
```

```
      } catch(UriFormatException exc) {
        Console.WriteLine("URI Format Error: " + exc.Message);
      } catch(NotSupportedException exc) {
        Console.WriteLine("Unknown Protocol: " + exc.Message);
      } catch(IOException exc) {
        Console.WriteLine("I/O Error: " + exc.Message);
      }
    }
  }
}
```

Now the exceptions that the networking methods might generate have been caught. For example, if you change the call to **Create( )** as shown here,

```
WebRequest.Create("http://www.osborne.com/moonrocket");
```

and then recompile and run the program, you will see this output:

```
Network Error: The remote server returned an error: (404) Not Found.
Status code: ProtocolError
```

Since the Osborne.com web site does not have a directory called "moonrocket," this URI is not found, as the output confirms.

To keep the examples short and uncluttered, most of the programs in this chapter will not contain full exception handling. However, your real-world applications should.

The URI Class

In Table 23-1 you will notice that **WebRequest.Create( )** has two different versions. One accepts the URI as a string. This is the version used by the preceding programs. The other takes the URI as an instance of the **Uri** class. The **Uri** class encapsulates a URI. Using **Uri**, you can construct a URI that can be passed to **Create( )**. You can also dissect a **Uri**, obtaining its parts. Although you don't need to use **Uri** for many simple Internet operations, you may find it valuable in more sophisticated situations.

Uri defines several constructors. Two commonly used ones are shown here:

public Uri(string *uri*)
public Uri(string *base*, string *rel*)

The first form constructs a **Uri** given a URI in string form. The second constructs a **Uri** by adding a relative URI specified by *rel* to an absolute base URI specified by *base*. An absolute URI defines a complete URI. A relative URI defines only the path.

Uri defines many fields, properties, and methods that help you manage URIs or that give you access to the various parts of a URI. Of particular interest are the properties shown here:

Property	Description
public string Host { get; }	Obtains the name of the server.
public string LocalPath { get; }	Obtains the file path.
public string PathAndQuery { get; }	Obtains the file path and query string.
public int Port { get; }	Obtains the port number for the specified protocol. For HTTP, the port is 80.
public string Query { get; }	Obtains the query string.
public string Scheme { get; }	Obtains the protocol.

These properties are useful for breaking a URI into its constituent parts. The following program demonstrates their use:

```
// Use Uri.

using System;
using System.Net;

class UriDemo {
  public static void Main() {

    Uri sample = new Uri("http://MySite.com/somefile.txt?SomeQuery");

    Console.WriteLine("Host: " + sample.Host);
    Console.WriteLine("Port: " + sample.Port);
    Console.WriteLine("Scheme: " + sample.Scheme);
    Console.WriteLine("Local Path: " + sample.LocalPath);
    Console.WriteLine("Query: " + sample.Query);
    Console.WriteLine("Path and query: " + sample.PathAndQuery);

  }
}
```

The output is shown here:

```
Host: mysite.com
Port: 80
Scheme: http
Local Path: /somefile.txt
Query: ?SomeQuery
Path and query: /somefile.txt?SomeQuery
```

Accessing Additional HTTP Response Information

When using **HttpWebResponse**, you have access to information other than the content of the specified resource. This information includes such things as the time the URI was last modified and the name of the server, and is available through various properties associated with the response. These properties, which include the four defined by **WebResponse**, are shown in Table 23-5. The following sections illustrate how to use representative samples.

Property	Description
public string CharacterSet { get; }	Obtains the name of the character set being used.
public string ContentEncoding { get; }	Obtains the name of the encoding scheme.
public long ContentLength { get; }	Obtains the length of the content being received. This will be –1 if the content length is not available.
public string ContentType { get; }	Obtains a description of the content.
public CookieCollection Cookies { get; set; }	Obtains or sets a list of the cookies attached to the response.
public WebHeaderCollection Headers{ get; }	Obtains a collection of the headers attached to the response.

Table 23-5.   *The Properties Defined by **HttpWebResponse***

Property	Description
public DateTime LastModified { get; }	Obtains the time at which the URI was last changed.
public string Method { get; }	Obtains a string that specifies the response method.
public Version ProtocolVersion { get; }	Obtains a **Version** object that describes the version of HTTP used in the transaction.
public Uri ReponseUri { get; }	Obtains the URI that generated the response. This may differ from the one requested if the response was redirected to another URI.
public string Server { get; }	Obtains a string that represents the name of the server.
public HttpStatusCode StatusCode { get; }	Obtains an **HttpStatusCode** object that describes the status of the transaction.
public string StatusDescription { get; }	Obtains a string that represents the status of the transaction in a human-readable form.

Table 23-5.   *The Properties Defined by **HttpWebResponse*** (continued)

Accessing the Header

You can access the header information associated with an HTTP response through the **Headers** property defined by **HttpWebResponse**. It is shown here:

    public WebHeaderCollection Headers{ get; }

An HTTP header consists of pairs of names and values represented as strings. Each name/value pair is stored in a **WebHeaderCollection**. This specialized collection stores key/value pairs and can be used like any other collection. (See Chapter 22.) A **string** array of the names can be obtained from the **AllKeys** property. You can obtain the value associated with a name by using the indexer. The indexer is overloaded to accept either a numeric index or the name.

The following program displays all of the headers associated with Osborne.com:

```
// Examine the headers.

using System;
using System.Net;

class HeaderDemo {
  public static void Main() {

    // Create a WebRequest to a URI.
    HttpWebRequest req = (HttpWebRequest)
          WebRequest.Create("http://www.osborne.com");

    // Send that request and return the response.
    HttpWebResponse resp = (HttpWebResponse)
          req.GetResponse();

    // Obtain a list of the names.
    string[] names = resp.Headers.AllKeys;

    // Display the header name/value pairs.
    Console.WriteLine("{0,-20}{1}\n", "Name", "Value");
    foreach(string n in names)
      Console.WriteLine("{0,-20}{1}", n, resp.Headers[n]);

    // Close the Response.
    resp.Close();
  }
}
```

Here is the output that was produced. (Remember, the header information at Osborne.com is subject to change, so you might see something a bit different.)

```
Name                Value

Date                Mon, 14 Jan 2002 17:45:50 GMT
Server              Apache/1.3.9 (Unix) PHP/3.0.14
Keep-Alive          timeout=30, max=500
Connection          Keep-Alive
Transfer-Encoding   chunked
Content-Type        text/html
```

Accessing Cookies

You can gain access to the cookies associated with an HTTP response through the **Cookies** property defined by **HttpWebResponse**. Cookies contain information that is stored by a browser. They consist of name/value pairs, and they facilitate certain types of Web access. **Cookies** is defined like this:

    public CookieCollection Cookies { get; set; }

CookieCollection implements **ICollection** and **IEnumerable**, and can be used like any other collection. (See Chapter 22.) It has an indexer that allows a cookie to be obtained by specifying its index or its name.

   CookieCollection stores objects of type **Cookie**. **Cookie** defines several properties that give you access to the various pieces of information associated with a cookie. The two that we will use here are **Name** and **Value**, which are defined like this:

    public string Name { get; set; }
    public string Value { get; set; }

The name of the cookie is contained in **Name**, and its value is found in **Value**.

   To obtain a list of the cookies associated with a response, you must supply a cookie container in the request. For this purpose, **HttpWebRequest** defines the property **CookieContainer**, shown here:

    public CookieContainer CookieContainer { get; set; }

CookieContainer provides various fields, properties, and methods that let you store cookies. However, for many applications you won't need to work with **CookieContainer** directly. Instead, you will use the **CookieCollection** obtained from the response. The **CookieContainer** simply provides the underlying storage mechanism for the cookies.

   The following program displays the names and values of the cookies associated with the URI specified on the command line. Remember, not all web sites use cookies, so you might have to try a few until you find one that does.

```
/* Examine Cookies.

   To see what cookies a Web Site uses,
   specify its name on the command line.
   For example, if you call this program
   Cookie, then

     Cookie http://MSN.COM

   displays the cookies associated with MSN.COM.
*/

using System;
```

```
using System.Net;

class CookieDemo {
  public static void Main(string[] args) {

    if(args.Length != 1) {
      Console.WriteLine("Usage: CookieDemo <uri>");
      return ;
    }

    // Create a WebRequest to the specified URI.
    HttpWebRequest req = (HttpWebRequest)
          WebRequest.Create(args[0]);

    // Get an empty cookie container.
    req.CookieContainer = new CookieContainer();

    // Send the request and return the response.
    HttpWebResponse resp = (HttpWebResponse)
          req.GetResponse();

    // Display the cookies.
    Console.WriteLine("Number of cookies: " +
                        resp.Cookies.Count);
    Console.WriteLine("{0,-20}{1}", "Name", "Value");

    for(int i=0; i < resp.Cookies.Count; i++)
      Console.WriteLine("{0, -20}{1}",
                          resp.Cookies[i].Name,
                          resp.Cookies[i].Value);

    // Close the Response.
    resp.Close();
  }
}
```

Using the LastModified Property

Sometimes you will want to know when a URI was last updated. This is easy to find out when using **HttpWebResponse**, because it defines the **LastModified** property. It is shown here:

    public DateTime LastModified { get; }

LastModified obtains the time that the content of the URI was last modified.

The following program displays the time and date at which the Microsoft.com web site was last updated:

```
// Use LastModified.

using System;
using System.Net;

class HeaderDemo {
  public static void Main() {

    HttpWebRequest req = (HttpWebRequest)
           WebRequest.Create("http://www.Microsoft.com");

    HttpWebResponse resp = (HttpWebResponse)
           req.GetResponse();

    Console.WriteLine("Last modified: " + resp.LastModified);

    resp.Close();
  }
}
```

MiniCrawler: A Case Study

To show how easy **WebRequest** and **WebReponse** make Internet programming, a skeletal web crawler called MiniCrawler is developed. A web crawler is a program that simply moves from link to link to link. Search engines use web crawlers to catalog content. MiniCrawler is very simple. It starts at the URI that you specify and then reads the content at that address, looking for a link. If a link is found, it then asks if you want to go to that link, search for another link on the existing page, or quit.

MiniCrawler has several limitations. First, only absolute links that are specified using the **href=** hypertext command are found. Relative links are not used. Second, there is no way to go back to an earlier link. Third, it displays only the links and no surrounding contents. Despite these limitations, the skeleton is fully functional, and you will have no trouble enhancing MiniCrawler to perform any operation you desire. In fact, adding features to MiniCrawler is a good way to learn more about the networking classes and networking in general.

Here is the entire code for MiniCrawler:

```
// MiniCrawler: A skeletal Web crawler.

using System;
```

```
using System.Net;
using System.IO;

class MiniCrawler {

  // Find a link in a content string.
  static string FindLink(string htmlstr,
                          ref int startloc) {
    int i;
    int start, end;
    string uri = null;
    string lowcasestr = htmlstr.ToLower();

    i = lowcasestr.IndexOf("href=\"http", startloc);
    if(i != -1) {
      start = htmlstr.IndexOf('"', i) + 1;
      end = htmlstr.IndexOf('"', start);
      uri = htmlstr.Substring(start, end-start);
      startloc = end;
    }

    return uri;
  }

  public static void Main(string[] args) {
    string link = null;
    string str;
    string answer;

    int curloc; // holds current location in response

    if(args.Length != 1) {
      Console.WriteLine("Usage: MiniCrawler <uri>");
      return ;
    }

    string uristr = args[0]; // holds current URI

    try {

      do {
        Console.WriteLine("Linking to " + uristr);

        // Create a WebRequest to the specified URI.
```

```
HttpWebRequest req = (HttpWebRequest)
      WebRequest.Create(uristr);

uristr = null; // disallow further use of this URI

// Send that request and return the response.
HttpWebResponse resp = (HttpWebResponse)
      req.GetResponse();

// From the response, obtain an input stream.
Stream istrm = resp.GetResponseStream();

// Wrap the input stream in a StreamReader.
StreamReader rdr = new StreamReader(istrm);

// Read in the entire page.
str = rdr.ReadToEnd();

curloc = 0;

do {
  // Find the next URI to link to.
  link = FindLink(str, ref curloc);

  if(link != null) {
    Console.WriteLine("Link found: " + link);

    Console.Write("Link, More, Quit?");
    answer = Console.ReadLine();

    if(string.Compare(answer, "L", true) == 0) {
      uristr = string.Copy(link);
      break;
    } else if(string.Compare(answer, "Q", true) == 0) {
      break;
    } else if(string.Compare(answer, "M", true) == 0) {
      Console.WriteLine("Searching for another link.");
    }
  } else {
    Console.WriteLine("No link found.");
    break;
  }
```

```
    } while(link.Length > 0);

    // Close the Response.
    resp.Close();
  } while(uristr != null);

} catch(WebException exc) {
  Console.WriteLine("Network Error: " + exc.Message +
                    "\nStatus code: " + exc.Status);
} catch(ProtocolViolationException exc) {
  Console.WriteLine("Protocol Error: " + exc.Message);
} catch(UriFormatException exc) {
  Console.WriteLine("URI Format Error: " + exc.Message);
} catch(NotSupportedException exc) {
  Console.WriteLine("Unknown Protocol: " + exc.Message);
} catch(IOException exc) {
  Console.WriteLine("I/O Error: " + exc.Message);
}

Console.WriteLine("Terminating MiniCrawler.");
  }
}
```

Here is part of a sample session:

```
C:>MiniCrawler http://osborne.com
Linking to http://osborne.com
Link found: http://www.osborne.com/aboutus/aboutus.shtml
Link, More, Quit? M
Searching for another link.
Link found: http://www.osborne.com/downloads/downloads.shtml
Link, More, Quit? L
Linking to http://www.osborne.com/downloads/downloads.shtml
 .
 .
 .
```

Let's take a close look at how MiniCrawler works. The URI at which MiniCrawler begins is specified on the command line. In **Main( )**, this URI is stored in the string called **uristr**. A request is created to this URI and then **uristr** is set to null, which indicates that this URI has already been used. Next, the request is sent and the response is obtained. The content is then read by wrapping the stream returned by **Get.ResponseStream( )** inside a **StreamReader**, and then calling **ReadToEnd( )**, which returns the entire contents of the stream as a string.

Using the content, the program then searches for a link. It does this by calling **FindLink( )**, which is a **static** method also defined by **MiniCrawler**. **FindLink( )** is called with the content string and the starting location at which to begin searching. The parameters that receive these values are **htmlstr** and **startloc**, respectively. Notice that **startloc** is a **ref** parameter. **FindLink( )** first creates a lowercase copy of the content string and then looks for a substring that matches **href="http**, which indicates a link. If a match is found, the URI is copied to **uri**, and the value of **startloc** is updated to the end of the link. Because **startloc** is a **ref** parameter, this causes its corresponding argument to be updated in **Main( )**, enabling the next search to begin where the previous one left off. Finally, **uri** is returned. Since **uri** was initialized to null, if no match is found, a null reference is returned, which indicates failure.

Back in **Main( )**, if the link returned by **FindLink( )** is not null, the link is displayed, and the user is asked what to do. The user can go to that link by pressing L, search the existing content for another link by pressing M, or quit the program by pressing Q. If the user presses L, the link is followed and the content of the link is obtained. The new content is then searched for a link. This process continues until all potential links are exhausted.

You might find it interesting to increase the power of MiniCrawler. For example, try completely automating the crawler by having it go to each link that it finds without user interaction. That is, starting at an initial page, have it go to the first link it finds. Then, in the new page, have it go to the first link, and so on. Once a dead-end is reached, have it backtrack one level, find the next link, and then resume linking. To accomplish this scheme, you will need to use a stack to hold the URIs and the current location of the search within a URI. One way to do this is to use a **Stack** collection. As an extra challenge, try creating tree-like output that displays the links.

Using WebClient

Before concluding this chapter, a brief discussion of **WebClient** is warranted. As mentioned near the start of this chapter, if your application only needs to upload or download data to or from the Internet, then you can use **WebClient** instead of **WebRequest** and **WebResponse**. The advantage to **WebClient** is that it handles many of the details for you.

WebClient defines one constructor, shown here:

public WebClient( )

It defines the properties shown in Table 23-6 and the methods shown in Table 23-7. All methods throw a **UriFormatException** if the specified URI is invalid, and a **WebException** if an error occurs during transmission.

THE C# CLASS LIBRARY

Property	Description
public string BaseAddress { get; set; }	Obtains or sets the base address of the desired URI. By default, this property is null. If this property is set, then addresses specified by the **WebClient** methods will be relative to the base address.
public ICredentials Credentials { get; set; }	Obtains or sets authentication information. This property is null by default.
public WebHeaderCollection Headers{ get; set; }	Obtains or sets the collection of the request headers.
public NameValueCollection QueryString { get; set; }	Obtains or sets a query string consisting of name/value pairs that can be attached to a request. The query string is separated from the URI by a **?**. If more than one name/value pair exist, then an @ separates each pair.
public WebHeaderCollection ResponseHeaders{ get; }	Obtains a collection of the response headers.

Table 23-6.   *The Properties Defined by* **WebClient**

Method	Description
public byte[ ] DownloadData(string *uri*)	Downloads the information at the URI specified by *uri* and returns the result in an array of bytes.
public void DownloadFile(string *uri*, string *fname*)	Downloads the information at the URI specified by *uri* and stores the result in the file specified by *fname*.
public Stream OpenRead(string *uri*)	Returns an input stream from which the information at the URI specified by *uri* can be read. This stream must be closed after reading is completed.

Table 23-7.   *The Methods Defined by* **WebClient**

Method	Description
public Stream OpenWrite(string *uri*)	Returns an output stream to which information can be written to the URI specified by *uri*. This stream must be closed after writing is completed.
public Stream OpenWrite(string *uri*, string *how*)	Returns an output stream to which information can be written to the URI specified by *uri*. This stream must be closed after writing is completed. The string passed in *how* specifies how the information will be written.
public byte[ ] UploadData(string *uri*, byte[ ] *info*)	Writes the information specified by *info* to the URI specified by *uri*. The response is returned.
public byte[ ] UploadData(string *uri*, string *how*, byte[ ] *info*)	Writes the information specified by *info* to the URI specified by *uri*. The response is returned. The string passed in *how* specifies how the information will be written.
public byte[ ] UploadFile(string *uri*, string *fname*)	Writes the information in the file specified by *fname* to the URI specified by *uri*. The response is returned.
public byte[ ] UploadFile(string *uri*, string *how*, string *fname*)	Writes the information in the file specified by *fname* to the URI specified by *uri*. The response is returned. The string passed in *how* specifies how the information will be written.
public byte[ ] UploadValues(string *uri*, NameValueCollection *vals*)	Writes the values in the collection specified by *vals* to the URI specified by *uri*. The response is returned.
public byte[ ] UploadValues(string *uri*, string *how*, NameValueCollection *vals*)	Writes the values in the collection specified by *vals* to the URI specified by *uri*. The response is returned. The string passed in *how* specifies how the information will be written.

Table 23-7.   *The Methods Defined by **WebClient** (continued)*

The following program demonstrates how to use **WebClient** to download data into a file:

```
// Use WebClient to download information into a file.

using System;
using System.Net;
using System.IO;

class WebClientDemo {
  public static void Main() {
    WebClient user = new WebClient();
    string uri = "http://www.osborne.com";
    string fname = "data.txt";

    try {
      Console.WriteLine("Downloading data from " +
                          uri + " to " + fname);
      user.DownloadFile(uri, fname);
    } catch (WebException exc) {
      Console.WriteLine(exc);
    } catch (UriFormatException exc) {
      Console.WriteLine(exc);
    }

    Console.WriteLine("Download complete.");
  }
}
```

This program downloads the information at Osborne.com and puts it into a file called **data.txt**. Notice how few lines of code are involved, especially considering that both possible exceptions are handled. By changing the string specified by **uri**, you can download information from any URI.

Although **WebRequest** and **WebResponse** give you greater control and access to more information, **WebClient** is all that many applications will need. It is particularly useful when the only thing that an application needs to do is download information from the Web. For example, you might use **WebClient** to allow an application to obtain documentation updates.

The Complete Reference

Part III

Applying C#

Part III illustrates three applications of C#. The first is the building and managing of components. Because many of the features of C# were designed expressly to facilitate their creation, components are an important part of C# programming. The second application uses C# to create a Windows program using the classes defined by **System.Windows.Forms**. Finally, the book concludes by applying C# to a "pure code" example: a recursive-descent parser that evaluates algebraic expressions.

Chapter 24

Building Components

Although C# can be used to write nearly any type of application, one of its most important is the component. Component-based programming is so integral to C# that it is sometimes referred to as a *component-oriented language*. Because C# and the .NET Framework were designed with components in mind, the component programming model is substantially simplified and streamlined over older approaches. For example, if the term *component* makes you think of *COM components* and all the trouble they can be, don't worry. C#-based components are much easier to write.

What Is a Component?

Let's begin by defining what is meant by the term *component*. Here is a general definition: A component is an independent, reusable unit of binary functionality. This definition describes four key characteristics of a component. Each is examined, in turn.

A component is independent. This means that each component is self-contained (that is, *encapsulated*). Thus, a component provides all the functionality it needs. Furthermore, its inner workings are not exposed to the outside; the precise implementation of the component can change without affecting the code that uses the component.

A component is reusable, which means that a component can be used by any other program that requires its functionality. A program that uses a component is called a *client*. Thus, a component can be used by any number of clients.

A component is a single unit of functionality. This is a key concept. As viewed from the client, a component performs a specific function, or a set of functions. The functionality provided by a component can be used by an application, but a component, by itself, is not a stand-alone program.

Finally, a component's reusability is provided in a binary form. This is fundamental. Although any number of clients can use a component, they do so without access to the component's source code. The functionality of a component is exposed to clients through its public members. Thus, a component controls what functionality is available to clients and what functionality it keeps private.

The Component Model

Although the definition just given does accurately describe a software component, another issue fundamentally affects a component: the model it implements. For a client to use a component, both the client and the component must use the same set of rules. The set of rules that define the form and nature of a component is called the *component model*. It is the component model that defines how a component and a client interact.

The component model is important because reusable, binary functionality can be created in any number of ways. There are different ways to pass parameters and to return values, for example. Also, there are different ways to handle the allocation and release of memory or system resources. For clients to be able to use components freely, both must follow the rules defined by the component model. In essence, the component model defines the contract between the client and the component by which both agree to abide.

As a point of interest, prior to C# and the .NET Framework, most components were *COM components*. COM, which standards for Component Object Model, was designed for the traditional Windows environment and C++. As such, it did not receive the benefits of the modern memory management that C# and the .NET Framework provide. As a result, the COM contract was rather difficult to implement and error-prone. Fortunately, C# and the .NET Framework have eliminated nearly all of these troubles. So if you have had bad experiences with COM in the past, you will be pleasantly surprised by the ease with which components are created in C#.

What Is a C# Component?

Because of the way C# works, any class fulfills the general definition of a component. For instance, once compiled, a class can be used in its binary form by any number of other applications. Does this mean that any class is a component? The answer is no. For a class to become a component, it must follow the component model defined by the .NET Framework. Fortunately, this is extremely easy to do: It simply implements the **System.ComponentModel.IComponent** interface. By implementing **IComponent**, a component satisfies the set of rules necessary to be a component compatible with the .NET Framework.

Although implementing **IComponent** is not difficult, in many situations a better alternative exists: A class can inherit **System.ComponentModel.Component**. The **Component** class provides a default implementation of **IComponent**. It also supplies other useful component-related features. Most components will inherit **Component** rather than implement **IComponent** themselves, because much of the clerical work has been done for you. Thus, in C#, creating a component requires no "heavy lifting" on your part.

Containers and Sites

Two other constructs are closely related to C# components: *containers* and *sites*. A container is a grouping of components. Containers simplify programs that use multiple components. A site helps link containers and components. Both of these constructs are examined in detail later.

C# VS COM Components

C# components are much easier to implement and use than are components based on COM. Those familiar with COM know that when using a COM component, you need to perform *reference counting* to ensure that a component stays in memory. In this scheme, each time a reference is added to a component, your code must make a call to **AddRef( )**. Each time a reference is removed, your code must call **Release( )**. The trouble is that this approach is error-prone. Fortunately, reference counting is not required by C# components. Since C# uses garbage collection, a component automatically stays in memory until there are no more references to it.

Because **IComponent** and **Component** are at the core of component programming, we will examine them next.

IComponent

IComponent defines the contract that components must follow. **IComponent** specifies only one property and one event. The property is **Site** and is shown here:

    ISite Site { get; set; }

Site obtains or sets the site of the component. A site identifies the component. This property is null if the component is not stored in a container.

The event defined by **IComponent** is **Disposed**, and is shown here:

    event EventHandler Disposed

A client that needs to receive a notification when a component is destroyed registers an event handler through the **Disposed** event.

IComponent also inherits **System.IDisposable**, which defines the method **Dispose( )**, as shown here:

    void Dispose( )

This method frees any resources used by the object.

Component

Although you can implement **IComponent** to create a component, it is much easier to inherit **Component** because it provides a default implementation of **IComponent**. This approach will be used in the examples in this chapter. By inheriting **Component**, your class automatically fulfills the rules necessary to make a .NET-compatible component.

The **Component** class defines only the default constructor. Normally, you won't construct a **Component** object directly, since the main use of **Component** is as a base class for components that you create.

Component defines two public properties. The first is **Container**, shown here:

    public IContainer Container { get; }

Container obtains the container that holds the invoking component. Null is returned if the component is not contained. **Container** is set by the container, and not by the component.

The second property is **Site**, which is defined by **IComponent**. It is implemented as a virtual property by **Component**, as shown here:

    public virtual ISite Site {get; set; }

It obtains or sets the **ISite** object linked to the component. **Site** is null if the component is not held in a container. **Site** is set by the container and not by the component.

Component defines two public methods. The first is an override of **ToString( )**. The second is the **Dispose( )** method. It has two forms. The first is shown here:

    public void Dispose( )

It frees any resources used by the invoking component. This method implements the **Dispose( )** method specified by the **IDisposable** interface. To release a component and its resources, the client will call this version of **Dispose( )**.

The second form of **Dispose( )** is shown next:

    protected virtual public void Dispose(bool *how*)

If *how* is **true**, this version frees both managed and unmanaged resources used by the invoking component. If *how* is **false**, it frees only unmanaged resources. Because this version of **Dispose( )** is protected, it cannot be called by client code. Instead, it is called by the first version of **Dispose( )**. In other words, calling the first version of **Dispose( )** generates a call to **Dispose(bool)**.

In general, your component will override **Dispose(bool)** when it holds resources that need to be freed when the component is no longer needed. If your component does not hold any resources, then the default implementation of **Dispose(bool)** supplied by **Component** is sufficient.

Component inherits the class **MarshalByRefObject**, which is used when a component is instantiated outside its local application environment, such as when a component is created in another process or on a different computer connected via a network. In order for data, such as method arguments and return values, to be exchanged, a mechanism must be in place that defines how the data is sent. By default, information is marshalled by value, but by inheriting **MarshalByRefObject**, data is marshalled by reference. Thus, a C# component marshals data by reference.

A Simple Component

At this point it will be useful to work through a simple example before presenting any more theory. The following program creates a component called **CipherComp** that implements a very simple encryption strategy. A character is encoded by adding 1 to it. It is decoded by subtracting 1. To encrypt a string, call **Encode( )**, passing the plaintext as an argument. To decipher an encrypted string, call **Decode( )**, this time passing the ciphertext as an argument. In both cases, the translated string is returned.

```
// A simple Cipher component.  Call this file CipherLib.cs.

using System.ComponentModel;
```

```
namespace CipherLib { // put component in its own namespace

  // Notice that CipherComp inherits Component.
  public class CipherComp : Component {

    // Encode a string.
    public string Encode(string msg) {
      string temp = "";

      for(int i=0; i < msg.Length; i++)
        temp += (char) (msg[i] + 1);

      return temp;
    }

    // Decode a string.
    public string Decode(string msg) {
      string temp = "";

      for(int i=0; i < msg.Length; i++)
        temp += (char) (msg[i] - 1);


      return temp;
    }
  }
}
```

Let's examine this code closely. First, as the comment at the top of the file suggests, to follow along with the example, call the file **CipherLib.cs**. This makes it easier to use the component if you are using the Visual Studio IDE. Next, notice that **System.ComponentModel** is included. As explained, this is the namespace that supports component programming.

The **CipherComp** class is enclosed within a namespace called **CipherLib**. Putting a component within its own namespace prevents the global namespace from becoming cluttered and is a good practice to follow. It is not technically necessary, though.

The **CipherComp** class inherits **Component**. This means that **CipherComp** fulfills the contract necessary to be a .NET-compatible component. Since **CipherComp** is very simple, it does not need to perform any component-related functions on its own. **Component** handles all the clerical details.

Next, notice that **CipherComp** does not allocate any resources. Specifically, it does not hold any references to any other objects. It simply defines two methods called **Encode( )** and **Decode( )**. Because **CipherComp** does not hold any resources, it does not need to implement **Dispose(bool)**. Of course, both **Encode( )** and **Decode( )** return string references, but these references are owned by the calling code and not by the **CipherComp** object.

Compiling CipherLib

A component must be compiled into a **dll** rather than an **exe** file. If you are using the Visual Studio IDE, you will want to create a Class Library project for **CipherLib**. When using the command line compiler, you will specify the **/t:library** option. For example, to compile **CipherLib**, you can use this command line:

```
csc /t:library CipherLib.cs
```

This creates a file called **CipherLib.dll**, which contains the **CipherComp** component.

A Client that Uses CipherComp

After you have created a component, it is ready for use. For example, the following program is a client of **CipherComp**, which it uses to encode and decode a string.

```
// A client that uses CipherComp.

using System;
using CipherLib; // import CipherComp's namespace

class CipherCompClient {
  public static void Main() {
    CipherComp cc = new CipherComp();

    string text = "This is a test";

    string ciphertext = cc.Encode(text);
    Console.WriteLine(ciphertext);

    string plaintext = cc.Decode(ciphertext);
    Console.WriteLine(plaintext);

    cc.Dispose(); // free resources
  }
}
```

Notice that the client includes the **CipherLib** namespace. This brings the **CipherComp** component into view. Of course, it would have been possible to fully qualify each reference to **CipherComp**, but including its namespace is easier. Next, **CipherComp** is used like any other class.

Notice the call to **Dispose( )** at the end of the program. As explained, by calling **Dispose( )**, the client causes the component to free any resources that it might be holding. Although components use the same garbage collection mechanism used by any other type of C# object, garbage collection is performed only sporadically. By calling **Dispose( )**, you cause the component to release its resources immediately. This can be important in certain situations, such as when a component holds a limited resource, such as a network connection. Because **CipherComp** does not hold any resources of its own, the call to **Dispose( )** is not actually needed in this example. However, because **Dispose( )** is part of the component contract, it is a good idea for you to get into the habit of calling it when you are done using a component.

To compile the client program, you must tell the compiler to reference **CipherLib.dll**. To do this, use the **/r** option. For example, the following command line compiles the client program:

```
csc /r:CipherLib.dll client.cs
```

If you are using the Visual Studio IDE, you will need to add **CipherLib.dll** as a reference to the client.

When you run the program, you will see the following output:

```
Uijt!jt!b!uftu
This is a test
```

Overriding Dispose( )

The version of the **CipherComp** component just shown does not hold any system resource, nor does it create and hold any objects. For these reasons, it was not necessary to override **Dispose(bool)**. However, if your component does hold resources, then you will usually need to override **Dispose(bool)** so that the resources can be freed in a deterministic fashion. Fortunately, this is easy to do.

Before we begin, it is important to understand why a component will usually need to free its own resources, rather than relying on the normal C# garbage collection mechanism. As explained earlier in this book, as far as your program is concerned, garbage collection is a non-deterministic occurrence. It happens as needed (or when otherwise deemed appropriate by the garbage collector) and not just because objects are available to recycle. Thus, if a component holds a resource, such as an open file, which needs to be released in order for it to be used by another program, there must be some way to deterministically release this resource when a client is done using the component. Simply removing all references to the component does not solve the problem because the component will still be holding a reference to the needed resource until the next time garbage is collected. The solution is for the component to implement **Dispose(bool)**.

When overriding **Dispose(bool)**, you must follow a few rules:

1. When **Dispose(bool)** is called with a **true** argument, your version must release all resources, both managed and unmanaged, associated with the component. When it is called with a **false** argument, your version must release only the unmanaged resources, if any.

2. **Dispose(bool)** must be able to be called repeatedly, without harm.

3. **Dispose(bool)** must call the base class implementation of **Dispose(bool)**.

4. The destructor for your component should simply call **Dispose(false)**.

To satisfy rule 2, your component will need to keep track of when it has been disposed. This is usually done by maintaining a private field that indicates the disposed status.

Here is a skeletal component that implements **Dispose(bool)**:

```
// A skeletal implementation of a component that uses Dispose(bool).
class MyComp : Component {
  bool isDisposed; // true if component is disposed

  public MyComp {
    isDisposed = false;
    // ...
  }

  ~MyComp() {
    Dispose(false);
  }

  protected override void Dispose(bool dispAll) {
    if(!isDisposed) {
      if(dispAll) {
        // release managed resources here
        isDisposed = true; // set component to disposed
      }
      // release unmanaged resources here
      base.Dispose(dispAll);
    }
  }
}
```

When you call **Dispose( )** on an instance of a component, **Dispose(bool)** is automatically called to clean up any resources owned by the component.

Demonstrating Dispose(bool)

To illustrate **Dispose(bool)**, we will enhance **CipherComp** so that it keeps a log of all encryption operations. To do this, it writes the result of each call to **Encode( )** or **Decode( )** to a file. This additional functionality is transparent to the user of **CipherComp**. It relies on **Dispose(bool)** to close the file when the component is no longer needed. Calls to **WriteLine( )** are included to show when and how **Dispose(bool)** gets called.

```
// An enhanced cipher component that maintains a log file.

using System;
using System.ComponentModel;
using System.IO;

namespace CipherLib {

  // An Cipher component that maintains a log file.
  public class CipherComp : Component {
    static int useID = 0;
    int id; // instance id
    bool isDisposed; // true if component is disposed.
    FileStream log;

    // Constructor
    public CipherComp() {
      isDisposed = false; // component not disposed
      try {
        log = new FileStream("CipherLog" + useID, FileMode.Create);
        id = useID;
        useID++;
      } catch (FileNotFoundException exc) {
        Console.WriteLine(exc);
        log = null;
      }
    }

    // Destructor
    ~CipherComp() {
```

```
      Console.WriteLine("Destructor for component "
                      + id);
      Dispose(false);
  }

  // Encode the file. Return and store result.
  public string Encode(string msg) {

    string temp = "";

    for(int i=0;i < msg.Length; i++)
      temp += (char) (msg[i] + 1);

    // Store in log file.
    for(int i=0; i < temp.Length; i++)
      log.WriteByte((byte) temp[i]);

    return temp;
  }

  // Decode the message. Return and store result.
  public string Decode(string msg) {

    string temp = "";

    for(int i=0; i < msg.Length; i++)
      temp += (char) (msg[i] - 1);

    // Store in log file.
    for(int i=0; i < temp.Length; i++)
      log.WriteByte((byte) temp[i]);

    return temp;
  }

  protected override void Dispose(bool dispAll) {
    Console.WriteLine("Dispose(" + dispAll +
                    ") for component " + id);

    if(!isDisposed) {
      if(dispAll) {
        Console.WriteLine("Closing file for " +
                        "component " + id);
```

```
            log.Close(); // close encoded file
            isDisposed = true;
        }
        // no unmanaged resources to release
        base.Dispose(dispAll);
    }
  }
 }
}
```

Let's examine this version of **CipherComp** closely. It begins with these fields:

```
static int useID = 0;
int id; // instance id
bool isDisposed; // true if component is disposed.
FileStream log;
```

The first field is a static **int** that will be used to identify each instance of **CipherComp**. The value in **useID** will be incorporated into the log file name so that each instance of **CipherComp** writes to its own log file. The **id** field holds the ID of the component, which is the value of **useID** at the time the component was created. The **isDisposed** field indicates whether the component has been disposed. The fourth field is **log** and it is a **FileStream** reference that will refer to the log file.

Next is **CipherComp's** constructor, shown here:

```
public CipherComp() {
isDisposed = false; // component not disposed
  try {
    log = new FileStream("CipherLog" + useID, FileMode.Create);
    id = useID;
    useID++;
  } catch (FileNotFoundException exc) {
    Console.WriteLine(exc);
    log = null;
  }
}
```

In the constructor, **isDisposed** is initialized to **false**, which indicates that this **CipherComp** object is usable. Next, the log file is opened. Notice that the file name is a concatenation of "CipherLog" and the string representation of **useID**. Next, the value of **useID** is assigned to **id** and then **useID** is incremented. Thus, each instance of **CipherComp** uses a separate log file, and each component has a unique ID. An important point here is that creating a **CipherComp** object now opens a file, which is a system resource that must be released when the component is no longer needed. However, the client has no direct ability to release the file. In fact, the client does not even know that a file has been opened. Thus, closing the file must be handled by **Dispose(bool)**.

Encode( ) encodes its string argument and returns the result. It also writes that result to the log file. Since **log** remains open, repeated calls to **Encode( )** add output to the file. For example, using **Encode( )** to encrypt three different strings results in a log file that contains all three encoded strings. **Decode( )** works in the same way, except that it deciphers its argument.

Now, let's look closely at **Dispose(bool)**, which is overridden by **CipherComp**. It is shown here for your convenience:

```
protected override void Dispose(bool dispAll) {
  Console.WriteLine("Dispose(" + dispAll +
                    ") for component " + id);

  if(!isDisposed) {
    if(dispAll) {
      Console.WriteLine("Closing file for " +
                        "component " + id);
      log.Close(); // close encoded file
      isDisposed = true;
    }
    // no unmanaged resources to release
    base.Dispose(dispAll);
  }
}
```

Notice that **Dispose(bool)** is **protected**. This method is not to be called from client code. Rather, it is called by the publicly accessible **Dispose( )** method, which is implemented by **Component**. Inside **Dispose(bool)**, the value of **isDisposed** is checked. If the object has already been disposed, no action is taken. If it is **false**, the parameter **dispAll** is checked. If it is **true**, the log file is closed and **isDisposed** is set to **true**. Recall that, by convention, when **dispAll** is **true**, all resources are to be freed. When it is **false**, only the unmanaged resources (of which there are none in this case) are to be freed. Finally, **Dispose(bool)** as implemented by the base class (in this case **Component**) is called. This ensures that any resources used by the base class are released. The calls to **WriteLine( )** are included only for the sake of illustration. A real-world **Dispose(bool)** method would not include them.

Now look at the destructor for **CipherComp**, shown here:

```
~CipherComp() {
Console.WriteLine("Destructor for component "
                    + id);
   Dispose(false);
}
```

The destructor simply calls **Dispose(bool)** with a **false** argument. The reason for
this is easy to understand. If the destructor for the component is being executed, the
component is being recycled by the garbage collection. In this case, all managed
resources will be automatically freed. The only thing that the destructor must do is
release any unmanaged resources. The call to **WriteLine( )** is made only for the sake
of illustration and would not occur in a real program.

Because the changes to **CipherComp** do not affect its public interface, it can be
used just as before. For example, here is a client program that encodes and decodes
two strings:

```
// Another client that uses CipherComp.

using System;
using CipherLib; // import CipherComp's namespace

class CipherCompClient {
  public static void Main() {
    CipherComp cc = new CipherComp();

    string text = "Testing";

    string ciphertext = cc.Encode(text);
    Console.WriteLine(ciphertext);

    string plaintext = cc.Decode(ciphertext);
    Console.WriteLine(plaintext);

    text = "Components are powerful.";

    ciphertext = cc.Encode(text);
    Console.WriteLine(ciphertext);
```

```
    plaintext = cc.Decode(ciphertext);
    Console.WriteLine(plaintext);

    cc.Dispose(); // free resources
  }
}
```

The output from the program is shown here:

```
Uftujoh
Testing
Dpnqpofout!bsf!qpxfsgvm/
Components are powerful.
Dispose(True) for component 0
Closing file for component 0
```

After the program runs, a log file called **CipherLog0** will contain the following:

```
UftujohTestingDpnqpofout!bsf!qpxfsgvm/Components are powerful.
```

This is the concatenation of the two strings that were encoded and decoded.

In the output, notice that **Dispose(bool)** is called with a **true** argument. This happens because the program calls **Dispose( )** on the **CipherComp** object. As explained earlier, **Dispose( )** then calls **Dispose(bool)** with a **true** argument, indicating that all resources are to be released. As an experiment, comment out the call to **Dispose( )** in the client program, and then compile and run it. You will now see this output:

```
Uftujoh
Testing
Dpnqpofout!bsf!qpxfsgvm/
Components are powerful.
Destructor for component 0
Dispose(False) for component 0
Dispose(False) for component 0
```

Because no call to **Dispose( )** was made, the **CipherComp** component is not explicitly disposed. It is, of course, destroyed when the program ends. Thus, as the output shows, its destructor is called, which in turn calls **Dispose(bool)** with a **false** argument. The second call to **Dispose(bool)** occurs because of the call to the base-class version of

Dispose( ) inside **CipherComp's Dispose(bool)** method. This causes **Dispose(bool)** to be called a second time. This is unnecessary in this case, but because **Dispose( )** can't know how it was called, it is unavoidable but harmless.

The same basic approach to implementing **Dispose(bool)** can be used by any component that you create.

Preventing a Disposed Component from Being Used

Although **CipherComp** as just shown does properly dispose of itself, it still has one problem that must be addressed by any real-world component: It does not prevent a client from attempting to use a disposed component. For example, nothing stops a client from disposing of a **CipherComp** component and then attempting to call **Encode( )** on it. Fortunately, this is easy to remedy: The component must simply check the **isDisposed** field each time the component is used. For example, here are better ways to write **Encode( )** and **Decode( )**:

```
// Encode the file. Return and store result.
public string Encode(string msg) {

  // Prevent use of a disposed component.
  if(isDisposed) {
    Console.WriteLine("Error: Component disposed.");
    return null;
  }

  string temp = "";

  for(int i=0;i < msg.Length; i++)
    temp += (char) (msg[i] + 1);

  // Store in log file.
  for(int i=0; i < temp.Length; i++)
    log.WriteByte((byte) temp[i]);

  return temp;
}

// Decode the message. Return and store result.
public string Decode(string msg) {
```

```
// Prevent use of a disposed component.
if(isDisposed) {
  Console.WriteLine("Error: Component disposed.");
  return null;
}

string temp = "";

for(int i=0; i < msg.Length; i++)
  temp += (char) (msg[i] - 1);

// Store in log file.
for(int i=0; i < temp.Length; i++)
  log.WriteByte((byte) temp[i]);

return temp;
}
```

In both methods, if **isDisposed** is true, an error message is displayed, and no other action is taken. Of course, in a real-world component, your code will normally throw an exception if an attempt is made to use a disposed object.

Employing the using Statement

As explained in Chapter 18, the **using** statement can be used to release an object automatically, rather than calling **Dispose( )** explicitly. Recall that it has these general forms:

using (*obj*) {
  // use *obj*
}

using (*type obj = initializer*) {
  // use *obj*
}

Here, *obj* is an object that is being used inside the **using** block. In the first form, the object is declared outside the **using** statement. In the second form, the object is declared within the **using** statement. When the block concludes, the **Dispose( )** method is automatically called. The **using** statement applies only to objects that implement the **System.IDisposable** interface (which, of course, all components do).

Here is a client for **CipherComp** that employs **using** rather than calling **Dispose( )** directly:

```
// Employ the using statement.

using System;
using CipherLib; // import CipherComp's namespace

class CipherCompClient {
  public static void Main() {

    // cc will be disposed when this block ends.
    using(CipherComp cc = new CipherComp()) {

      string text = "The using statement.";

      string ciphertext = cc.Encode(text);
      Console.WriteLine(ciphertext);

      string plaintext = cc.Decode(ciphertext);
      Console.WriteLine(plaintext);
    }

  }
}
```

The output from the program is shown here:

```
Uif!vtjoh!tubufnfou/
The using statement.
Dispose(True) for component 0
Closing file for component 0
```

As the output shows, **Dispose( )** was called automatically when the **using** block ended. Whether you use **using** or explicitly call **Dispose( )** is up to you, but **using** does streamline your code.

Containers

When working with components, you may find it useful to store them in a container. As explained earlier, a container defines a group of components. Its main advantage is that it allows a group of components to be managed collectively. For example, you can dispose of all of the components in a container by calling **Dispose( )** on the container. In general, containers make working with multiple components much easier.

To create a container, you will create an object of the **Container** class, which is defined in the **System.ComponentModel** namespace. It has this constructor:

   public Container( )

This creates an empty container.

Once you have created a **Container** object, you add components to it by calling **Add( )**. It has the two forms shown here:

   public virtual void Add(IComponent *comp*)
   public virtual void Add(IComponent *comp*, string *compName*)

The first form adds *comp* to the container. The second form adds *comp* to the container and gives it the name specified by *compName*. The name must be unique, and case differences are ignored. An **ArgumentException** is thrown if you attempt to use a name that is already in the container. This name is obtainable through the **Site** property of the component.

To remove a component from a container, use **Remove( )**, as shown here:

   public virtual void Remove(IComponent *comp*)

This method is assumed to succeed because it either removes *comp*, or *comp* was not in the container in the first place. In either case, *comp* is not in the container after the call to **Remove( )**.

Container implements **Dispose( )**. When **Dispose( )** is called on a container, all components stored in the container will have their **Dispose( )** methods called. Thus, you can dispose of all the components in a container with a single call to **Dispose( )**.

Container defines one property called **Components**, which is defined like this:

   public virtual ComponentCollection Components { get; }

This property obtains a collection of the components that are stored in the invoking container.

Recall that **Component** defines properties called **Container** and **Site**, which will be included in all derived components. When a component is stored in a container, the object's **Container** and **Site** properties are automatically set. The **Container** property refers to the container in which the component is stored. **Site** refers to information about the component, including its name, the name of its container, and whether it is in design mode. The **Site** property returns an **ISite** reference. This interface defines the following properties:

Property	Description
IComponent Component { get; }	Obtains a reference to the component.
IContainer Container { get; }	Obtains a reference to the container.
bool DesignMode { get; }	True if the component is being used by a design tool.
string Name { get; set; }	Obtains or sets the name of the component.

You can use these properties to obtain information about the runtime container or component at runtime.

Demonstrating a Container

The following program uses a container to store two **CipherComp** components. The first is added to the container without specifying a name. The second is given the name "Second Component". Next, operations occur on both components. Then the name of the second component is displayed via its **Site** property. Finally, **Dispose( )** is called on the container, releasing both components. (A **using** statement could have been employed here, but for the sake of illustration, **Dispose( )** is called explicitly.)

```
// Demonstrate a component container.

using System;
using System.ComponentModel;
using CipherLib; // import CipherComp's namespace

class UseContainer {
  public static void Main(string[] args) {
    string str = "Using containers.";
    Container cont = new Container();

    CipherComp cc = new CipherComp();
    CipherComp cc2 = new CipherComp();

    cont.Add(cc);
    cont.Add(cc2, "Second Component");
```

```
      Console.WriteLine("First message: " +  str);
      str = cc.Encode(str);
      Console.WriteLine("First message encoded: " +
                    str);

      str = cc.Decode(str);
      Console.WriteLine("First message decoded: " +
                    str);

      str = "one, two, three";
      Console.WriteLine("Second message: " +  str);

      str = cc2.Encode(str);
      Console.WriteLine("Second message encoded: " +
                    str);

      str = cc2.Decode(str);
      Console.WriteLine("Second message decoded: " +
                    str);

      Console.WriteLine("\ncc2's name: " + cc2.Site.Name);

      Console.WriteLine();

      // Release both components.
      cont.Dispose();
    }
}
```

The output from the program is shown here:

```
First message: Using containers.
First message encoded: Vtjoh!dpoubjofst/
First message decoded: Using containers.
Second message: one, two, three
Second message encoded: pof-!uxp-!uisff
Second message decoded: one, two, three

cc2's name: Second Component
```

```
Dispose(True) for component 1
Closing file for component 1
Dispose(True) for component 0
Closing file for component 0
```

As you can see, by calling **Dispose( )** on the container, all components stored in that container are disposed. This is a major benefit when working with many components or component instances.

Are Components the Future of Programming?

Organizing an application around a set of components is a powerful way to approach the job of programming, because components enable you to handle greater complexity. Increasing program complexity has long been known to be the single greatest challenge faced by programmers. Beginners learn early in their programming careers that the longer the program, the longer the debugging time. As program size grows, so usually does its complexity, and there is a limit to the amount of complexity we, as humans, can manage. From a purely combinatorial standpoint, the more individual lines of code there are, the greater the chance for side effects and unwanted interactions. As most programmers today know, programs are growing exceedingly complex.

Software components help us manage complexity through "divide and conquer." By compartmentalizing units of functionality into independent components, the programmer can reduce the apparent complexity of a program. Using a component-oriented approach, a program is organized as a set of well-defined building blocks (components) that can be used without concern over their implementation details. The net effect of this approach is that complexity is reduced. Taken to its logical conclusion, the bulk of an application could be constructed of nothing but components "wired together," with one component feeding into another. Such an approach might be called *component-oriented programming*.

Given the power of components, and the ease with which they can be created using C#, are components the future of programming? The answer for many programmers is an unqualified "Yes!"

Chapter 25

Creating Form-Based Windows Applications

M ost of the programs shown in this book are console applications. Console applications are good for demonstrating the elements of the C# language and are appropriate for some types of utility programs, such as file filters. Of course, most modern applications are designed for the Windows graphics user interface (GUI) environment, and this book would seem incomplete without demonstrating how to use C# to create a Windows application.

In the past, creating Windows applications was a challenging endeavor. It was not uncommon for a newcomer to spend several weeks just learning the basic elements of a Windows application. Fortunately, C# and the .NET Framework have changed all that. The .NET library contains an entire subsystem that supports Windows Forms, which greatly simplifies the creation of a Windows program. Using C# and the **System.Windows.Forms** library, Windows applications are much easier to create, and the entire development process has been significantly streamlined.

Windows programming is a *very* large topic, with entire series of books devoted to it. It is, obviously, not possible to describe all aspects of it in a single chapter. Instead, this chapter provides a "jump-start" to form-based Windows programming. It explains how to create a window, create a menu, implement a button, and respond to a message. Once you have worked through this chapter, you will easily be able to advance to other aspects of forms-based Windows programming.

A Brief History of Windows Programming

To appreciate the benefits that C# and the .NET Framework bring to Windows programming, it is necessary for you to understand a bit of its history. When Windows was first created, programs interacted directly with the Windows API (Application Programming Interface), which is an extensive set of methods defined by Windows that programs call to access the various functions provided by Windows. API-based programs are very long and complicated. For example, even a skeletal API-based program requires about 50 lines of code. API-based programs that perform any useful function have *at least* several hundred lines of code, and real applications have thousands of lines of code. Thus, in the early days, Windows programs were difficult to write and maintain.

In response to this problem, class libraries were created that encapsulated the functionality of the API. The most important of these is MFC (Microsoft Foundation Classes). Many readers of this book will be familiar with MFC. MFC is written in C++, and MFC-based programs are also written in C++. Because MFC brought object-oriented benefits, the process of creating a Windows program was simplified. However, MFC programs were still fairly complicated affairs, involving separate header files, code files, and resource files. Furthermore, MFC was only a "thin wrapper" around the API, so many Windows-based activities still required a significant number of explicit program statements.

C# and the .NET Framework's Forms library offer a fully object-oriented way to approach Windows programming. Instead of providing just a wrapper around the API, the Forms library defines a streamlined, integrated, logically consistent way of managing the development of a Windows application. This level of integration is made possible by the unique features of the C# language, such as delegates and events. Furthermore, because of C#'s use of garbage collection, the especially troubling problem of "memory leaks" has been nearly eliminated.

If you have already programmed for Windows using either the API or MFC, you will find C#'s approach remarkably refreshing. For the first time since Windows was created, it is nearly as easy to create a Windows application as it is to create a console application.

Two Ways to Write a Form-Based Windows Application

Before we begin, an important point needs to be made. Visual Studio includes a sophisticated set of design tools that automate much of the process of creating a Windows application. Using these tools, you can visually construct and position the various controls and menus used by your application. Visual Studio will also "rough in" the classes and methods that are needed for each feature. Frankly, the Visual Studio design tools are a good choice for creating most real-world Windows applications. However, there is no requirement that you use those tools. You can also create a Windows program by using a text editor and then compiling it, just like you can for console- based applications.

Because this book is about C#, not Visual Studio, and because the Windows programs contained in this chapter are quite short, all programs will be shown in a form in which they can be entered using a text editor. However, the general structure, design, and organization of the programs is the same as that created by the design tools. Thus, the material in this chapter applies to either approach.

How Windows Interacts with the User

The first thing that you must learn about Windows programming is how the user and Windows interact, because this defines the architecture that all Windows programs share. This interaction is fundamentally different than the console-based programs shown in the other parts of this book. When you write a console program, it is your program that initiates interaction with the operating system. For example, it is the program that requests such things as input and output by calling **Read( )** or **WriteLine( )**. Thus, programs written in the "traditional way" call the operating system. The operating system does not call your program. However, in a large measure, Windows works in the opposite way. It is Windows that calls your program. The process works like this: A program waits until it is sent a *message* by Windows. Once a message is received, your program is expected to take an appropriate action. Your program may call a method defined by Windows when responding to a message, but it is still Windows that initiates the activity. More than anything else, it is the message-based interaction with Windows that dictates the general form of all Windows programs.

There are many different types of messages that Windows may send to your program. For example, each time the mouse is clicked on a window belonging to your program, a mouse-clicked message will be sent. Another type of message is sent when a button is pressed or when a menu item is selected. Keep one fact firmly in mind: As far as your program is concerned, messages arrive randomly. This is why Windows programs resemble interrupt-driven programs. You can't know what message will be next.

Windows Forms

At the core of a C# Windows program is the *form*. A form encapsulates the basic functionality necessary to create a window, display it on the screen, and receive messages. A form can represent any type of window, including the main window of the application, a child window, or even a dialog box.

When a form is first created, it is empty. To add functionality, you add menus and controls, such as pushbuttons, lists, and check boxes. Thus, you can think of a form as a container for other Windows objects.

When a message is sent to the window, it is translated into an event. Therefore, to handle a Windows message, you will simply register an event handler for that message with the form. Then, whenever that message is received, your event handler is automatically called.

The Form Class

A form is created by instantiating an object of the **Form** class, or of any class derived from **Form**. **Form** contains significant functionality of its own, and it inherits additional functionality. Two of its most important base classes are **System.ComponentModel. Component**, which was discussed in Chapter 24, and **System.Windows.Forms.Control**. The **Control** class defines features common to all Windows controls. Since **Form** inherits **Control**, it too is a control. This fact allows forms to be used to create controls. Several of the members of **Form** and **Control** are used in the examples that follow.

A Skeletal Form-Based Windows Program

We will begin by creating a minimal form-based Windows application. This application simply creates and displays a window. It contains no other features. However, this skeleton does show the steps necessary to construct a fully-functional window. This framework is the starting point upon which most types of Windows applications will be built. The skeletal form-based Windows program is shown here:

```
// A form-based Windows Skeleton.

using System;
using System.Windows.Forms;

// WinSkel is derived from Form.
class WinSkel : Form {

  public WinSkel() {
    // Give the window a name.
    Text = "A Windows Skeleton";
  }

  // Main is used only to start the application.
  [STAThread]
  public static void Main() {
    WinSkel skel = new WinSkel(); // create a form

    // Start the window running.
    Application.Run(skel);
  }
}
```

The window created by this program is shown in Figure 25-1.

Let's examine this program, line-by-line. First, notice that both **System** and **System.Windows.Forms** are included. **System** is needed because of the **STAThread** attribute that precedes **Main( )**. **System.Windows.Forms** supports the Windows Forms subsystem, as just explained.

Next, a class called **WinSkel** is created. It inherits **Form**. Thus, **WinSkel** defines a specific type of form. In this case, it is a minimal form.

Inside the **WinSkel** constructor is the following line of code:

```
Text = "A Windows Skeleton";
```

Text is the property that sets the title of the window. Thus, this assignment causes the title bar in the window to contain **A Windows Skeleton**. **Text** is defined like this.

public virtual string Text { get; set; }

Text is inherited from **Control**.

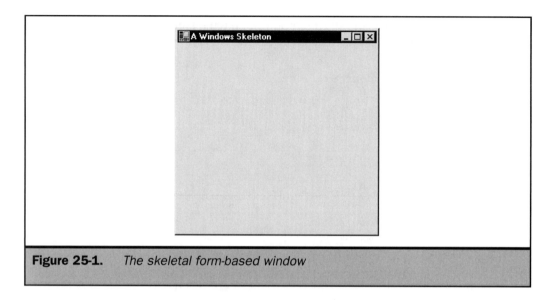

Figure 25-1. *The skeletal form-based window*

Next is the **Main( )** method, which is declared much like the **Main( )** methods found throughout the rest of this book. It is the method at which program execution begins. Notice, however, that it is preceded by the **STAThread** property. Microsoft states that the **Main( )** method of a Windows program should have this property. It sets the threading model for the program to a *single-threaded apartment* (STA). (A discussion of threading models and apartments are beyond the scope of this chapter, but briefly, a Windows application can use one of two different threading models: single-threaded apartment or multi-threaded apartment.)

Inside **Main( )**, a **WinSkel** object is created. This object is then passed to the **Run( )** method defined by the **Application** class, as shown here:

```
Application.Run(skel);
```

This starts the window running. The **Application** class is defined within **System.Windows.Forms**, and it encapsulates aspects common to all Windows applications. The **Run( )** method used by the skeleton is shown here.

```
public static void Run(Form ob)
```

It takes a reference to a form as a parameter. Since **WinSkel** inherits **Form**, an object of type **WinSkel** can be passed to **Run( )**.

When the program is run, it creates the window shown in Figure 25-1. The window has the default size, which is 300 pixels wide and 300 pixels tall. The window is fully functional. It can be resized, moved, minimized, maximized, and closed. Thus, the basic features needed by nearly all windows were achieved by writing only a few lines of form-based code. In contrast, the same program written using the C language and directly calling the Windows API would have required approximately five times as many lines of code!

The preceding skeleton defines the outline that most form-based Windows applications will take. In general, to create a form, you create a class that inherits **Form**. Initialize the form to meet your needs, create an object of your derived class, and then call **Application.Run( )** on that object.

Compiling the Windows Skeleton

You can compile a Windows program using either the command-line compiler or Visual Studio. For the very short programs shown in this chapter, the command-line compiler is the easiest way; but for real applications, you will probably want to use the IDE. (Also, as explained at the start of this chapter, you will probably want to use the design tools provided by Visual Studio.) Each way is shown here.

Compiling from the Command Line

Assuming that you call the skeleton **WinSkel.cs**, then to compile the skeleton from the comand line, use this command:

```
csc /t:winexe WinSkel.cs
```

The **/t:winexe** switch tells the compiler to create a Windows application rather than a console program. To run the program, simply enter **WinSkel** at the command line.

Compiling from the IDE

To compile the program using the Visual Studio IDE, first create a new Windows Application project. Do this by selecting File | New | Project. Then select Windows Application in the New Project dialog box. Call the project **WinSkel**. This project will have a file called **Form1.cs** associated with it. Delete that file. Next, right-click on the

WinSkel project name and select Add, and then select Add New Item. You will see the dialog box shown here:

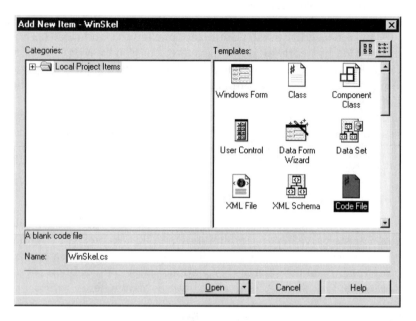

Select C# Code File, and name the file **WinSkel.cs**. Now, enter the skeleton code exactly as shown, and then build the solution. To run the project, select Debug I Start Without Debugging.

Adding a Button

In general, the functionality of a window is expressed by two types of items: controls and menus. It is through these items that a user interacts with your program. Menus are described later in this chapter. Here you will see how to add a control to a window.

Windows defines many different types of controls, including pushbuttons, check boxes, radio buttons, and list boxes, to name just a few. Although each type of control is different, they all work in more or the less the same way. Here, we will add a pushbutton to a window, but the same basic procedure can be used to add other types of controls.

Button Basics

A pushbutton is encapsulated by the **Button** class. It inherits the abstract class **ButtonBase**. Because it is a control, it inherits the **Control** class. **Button** defines only one constructor, which is shown here:

public Button( )

This creates a button that has a default size and location within the window. It contains no description. Before a button can be used, it will need to be given a description by assigning a string to its **Text** property.

To specify the location of the button within the window, you must assign the coordinates of its upper-left corner to the **Location** property. The **Location** property is inherited from **Control** and defined like this:

public Point Location { get; set; }

The coordinates are contained within a **Point** structure, which is defined in the **System.Drawing** namespace. It includes these two properties:

public int X { get; set; }
public int Y { get; set; }

Thus, to create a button that contains the description "Press Here" and is positioned at location 100, 200, you use the following sequence:

```
Button MyButton = new Button();
MyButton.Text = "Press Here";
MyButton.Location = new Point(100, 200);
```

Adding a Button to a Form

After you have created a button, you must add it to a form. You do this by calling the **Add( )** method on the collection of controls linked to that form. This collection is available through the **Controls** property, which is inherited from the **Control** class. The **Add( )** method is defined like this:

public virtual void Add(Control *cntl*)

Here, *cntl* is the control being added. Once a control has been added to a form, it will be displayed when the form is displayed.

A Simple Button Example

The following program adds a button to the skeleton shown earlier. At this time, the button does not do anything, but it is present in the form and can be clicked.

```
// Add a Button.

using System;
using System.Windows.Forms;
using System.Drawing;
```

```
class ButtonForm : Form {
  Button MyButton = new Button();

  public ButtonForm() {
    Text = "Using a Button";

    MyButton = new Button();
    MyButton.Text = "Press Here";
    MyButton.Location = new Point(100, 200);

    Controls.Add(MyButton);
  }

  [STAThread]
  public static void Main() {
    ButtonForm skel = new ButtonForm();

    Application.Run(skel);
  }
}
```

This program creates a class called **ButtonForm**, which is derived from **Form**. It contains a **Button** field called **MyButton**. Inside the constructor, the button is created, initialized, and added to the form. When run, the program displays the window shown in Figure 25-2. You can click the button, but nothing will happen. To make the button do something, you must add a message handler, as described in the next section.

Handling Messages

In order for a program to respond to a button press (or any other type of control interaction), it must handle the message that the button generates. In general, when a user interacts with a control, those interactions are passed to your program as messages. In a forms-based C# program, these messages are processed by event handlers. Therefore, to receive messages, your program adds its own event handler onto the list of handlers called when a message is generated. For button-press messages, this means adding your handler to the **Click** event.

The **Click** event is defined by **Button**. (**Click** is inherited from **Control**.) It has this general form:

   public Event EventHandler Click;

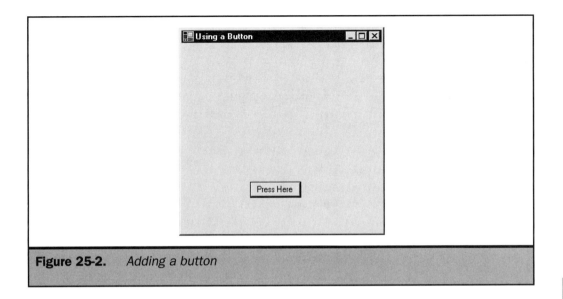

Figure 25-2. *Adding a button*

The **EventHandler** delegate is defined as shown here:

public delegate void EventHandler(object *who*, EventArgs *args*)

The object that generated the event is passed in *who*. Any information associated with that event is passed in *args*. For many events, *args* will be an object of a class derived from **EventArgs**. Since a button click does not require any additional information, we don't need to worry about event arguments when handling the button.

The following program adds button-response code to the preceding program. Each time the button is clicked, the location of the button is changed.

```
// Handle button messages.

using System;
using System.Windows.Forms;
using System.Drawing;

class ButtonForm : Form {
  Button MyButton = new Button();

  public ButtonForm() {
    Text = "Respond to a Button";

    MyButton = new Button();
```

```
    MyButton.Text = "Press Here";
    MyButton.Location = new Point(100, 200);

    // Add button event handler to list.
    MyButton.Click += new EventHandler(MyButtonClick);

    Controls.Add(MyButton);
  }

  [STAThread]
  public static void Main() {
    ButtonForm skel = new ButtonForm();

    Application.Run(skel);
  }

  // Handler for MyButton.
  protected void MyButtonClick(object who, EventArgs e) {

    if(MyButton.Top == 200)
      MyButton.Location = new Point(10, 10);
    else
      MyButton.Location = new Point(100, 200);
  }
}
```

Let's look closely at the event handling code in this program. The event handler for the button click is shown here:

```
// Handler for MyButton.
protected void MyButtonClick(object who, EventArgs e) {

  if(MyButton.Top == 200)
    MyButton.Location = new Point(10, 10);
  else
    MyButton.Location = new Point(100, 200);
}
```

MyButtonClick( ) uses the same signature used by the **EventHandler** delegate shown earlier, which means that it can be added to the **Click** event chain. Notice that it is modified with **protected**. This is not technically necessary, but it is a good idea because event handlers are not intended to be called except in response to events.

Inside the handler, the location of the top of the button is determined from the **Top** property. All controls define the following properties, which specify the coordinates of the upper left and lower right corners.

```
public int Top { get; set; }
public int Bottom { get; }
public int Left { get; set; }
public int Right { get; }
```

Notice that the location of the control can be changed by setting **Top** and **Left**, but not by setting **Bottom** and **Right** because they are read-only. (To change the size of a control, you can use the **Width** and **Height** properties.)

When the button click event is received, if the top of the control is at its original location of 200, the location is changed to 10, 10. Otherwise, it is returned to its original location of 100, 200. Therefore, each time you click the button, the location of the button changes.

Before **MyButtonClick( )** can receive messages, it must be added to the event handler chain linked to the button's **Click** event. This is done inside the **ButtonForm** constructor, using this statement:

```
MyButton.Click += new EventHandler(MyButtonClick);
```

After this is done, each time the button is clicked, **MyButtonClick( )** is called.

An Alternative Implementation

As a point of interest, **MyButtonClick( )** could have been written in a slightly different way. Recall that the *who* parameter of an event handler receives a reference to the object that generated the call. In the case of a button click event, this is the button that was clicked. Thus, **MyButtonClick( )** could have been written like this:

```
// An Alternative button handler.
protected void MyButtonClick(object who, EventArgs e) {
  Button b = (Button) who;

  if(b.Top == 200)
    b.Location = new Point(10, 10);
  else
    b.Location = new Point(100, 200);
}
```

In this version, **who** is cast to **Button**, and this reference (rather than the **MyButton** field) is used to access the button object. Although there is no advantage to this approach in this case, it is easy to imagine situations in which it would be quite valuable. For example, such an approach allows a button event handler to be written independently of any specific button.

Using a Message Box

One of the most useful built-in features of Windows is the *message box*. A message box is a predefined window that lets you display a message. You can also obtain simple responses from the user, such as Yes, No, or OK. In a form-based program, a message box is supported by the **MessageBox** class. You don't create an object of that class, however. Instead, to display a message box, call the **static** method **Show( )**, which is defined by **MessageBox**.

The **Show( )** method has several forms. The one we will be using is shown here:

public static DialogResult Show(string *msg*, string *caption*,
MessageBoxButtons *mbb*)

The string passed through *msg* is displayed in the body of the box. The caption of the message box window is passed in *caption*. The buttons that will be displayed are specified by *mbb*. The user's response is returned.

MessageBoxButtons is an enumeration that defines the following values:

AbortRetryIgnore	OK	OKCancel
RetryCancel	YesNo	YesNoCancel

Each of these values describes the buttons that will be included in a message box. For example, if *mbb* contains **YesNo**, then the Yes and No buttons are included in the message box.

The value returned by **Show( )** indicates which button was pressed. It will be one of these values:

Abort	Cancel	Ignore	No
None	OK	Retry	Yes

Your program can examine the return value to determine the course of action that the user desires. For example, if the message box prompts the user before overwriting a file, your program can prevent the overwrite if the user clicks Cancel, and it can allow the overwrite if the user clicks OK.

The following program adds a stop button and a message box to the preceding example. In the stop button handler, a message box is displayed that asks if the user wants to stop the program. If the user clicks Yes, the program is stopped. If the user clicks No, the program continues running.

```
// Add a stop button.

using System;
using System.Windows.Forms;
using System.Drawing;

class ButtonForm : Form {
  Button MyButton;
  Button StopButton;

  public ButtonForm() {
    Text = "Adding a Stop Button";

    // Create the buttons.
    MyButton = new Button();
    MyButton.Text = "Press Here";
    MyButton.Location = new Point(100, 200);

    StopButton = new Button();
    StopButton.Text = "Stop";
    StopButton.Location = new Point(100, 100);

    // Add the button event handlers to the window.
    MyButton.Click += new EventHandler(MyButtonClick);
    Controls.Add(MyButton);
    StopButton.Click += new EventHandler(StopButtonClick);
    Controls.Add(StopButton);
  }

  [STAThread]
  public static void Main() {
    ButtonForm skel = new ButtonForm();

    Application.Run(skel);
  }

  // Handler for MyButton.
  protected void MyButtonClick(object who, EventArgs e) {
```

```
    if(MyButton.Top == 200)
      MyButton.Location = new Point(10, 10);
    else
      MyButton.Location = new Point(100, 200);
  }


  // Handler for StopButton.
  protected void StopButtonClick(object who, EventArgs e) {

    // If users answers Yes, terminate the program.
    DialogResult result = MessageBox.Show("Stop Program?",
                          "Terminate",
                          MessageBoxButtons.YesNo);

    if(result == DialogResult.Yes) Application.Exit();
  }
}
```

Let's look closely at how the message box is used. Inside the **ButtonForm** constructor, a second button is added. This button contains the text "Stop", and its event handler is linked to **StopButtonClick( )**.

Inside **StopButtonClick( )**, the message box is displayed by the following statement:

```
// If user answers Yes, terminate the program.
DialogResult result = MessageBox.Show("Stop Program?",
                      "Terminate",
                      MessageBoxButtons.YesNo);
```

Here, the message inside the box is "Stop Program?", the caption is "Terminate," and the buttons to be displayed are Yes and No. When **Show( )** returns, the user's response is assigned to **result**. That response is then examined by the following code to determine the course of action:

```
if(result == DialogResult.Yes) Application.Exit();
```

If the user clicks the Yes button, the program is stopped by calling **Application.Exit( )**, which causes the immediate termination of the program. Otherwise, no action is taken and the program continues running.

Sample output is shown in Figure 25-3.

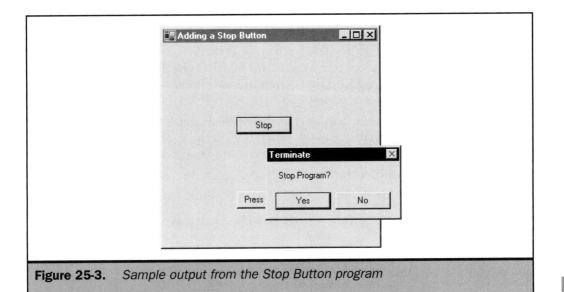

Figure 25-3. *Sample output from the Stop Button program*

Adding a Menu

The main window of nearly all Windows applications includes a menu across the top. This is called the *main menu*. The main menu typically contains top-level categories, such as File, Edit, and Tools. From the main menu descend *drop down menus*, which contain the actual selections associated with the categories. When a menu item is selected, a message is generated. Therefore, to process a menu selection, your program will assign an event handler to each menu item.

A main menu is constructed from a combination of two classes. The first is **MainMenu**, which encapsulates the overall structure of the menu. The second is **MenuItem**, which encapsulates an individual selection. A menu selection can either represent a final action, such as Close, or activate another drop-down menu. Both **MainMenu** and **MenuItem** inherit the **Menu** class. Because menus are such a bedrock resource in Windows programming, many options are available and the topic of menus is quite large. Fortunately, it is easy to create a standard main menu.

When a menu item is selected, a **Click** event is generated. **Click** is defined by **MenuItem**. Therefore, to handle a menu selection, your program will add its handler to the **Click** event list for that item.

Each form has a **Menu** property, which is defined like this:

public MainMenu Menu { get; set; }

By default, no menu is assigned to this property. To display a main menu, this property must be set to the menu that you create.

Creating a main menu is straightforward, but it does involve several steps.

1. Create a **MainMenu** object.

2. To the **MainMenu** object, add **MenuItem**s that describe the top-level categories. These menu items are added to the **MenuItems** collection associated with the main menu.

3. To each top-level **MenuItem**, add the list of **MenuItem**s that defines the drop-down menu associated with that top-level entry. These menu items are added to the **MenuItems** collection associated with each top-level menu.

4. Add the event handlers for each selection.

5. Assign the **MainMenu** object to the **Menu** property associated with the form.

The following sequence shows how to create a File menu that contains three selections: Open, Close, and Exit.

```
// Create a main menu object.
MainMenu MyMenu = new MainMenu();

// Add a top-level menu item to the menu.
MenuItem m1 = new MenuItem("File");
MyMenu.MenuItems.Add(m1);

// Create File submenu
MenuItem subm1 = new MenuItem("Open");
m1.MenuItems.Add(subm1);

MenuItem subm2 = new MenuItem("Close");
m1.MenuItems.Add(subm2);

MenuItem subm3 = new MenuItem("Exit");
m1.MenuItems.Add(subm3);
```

Let's examine this sequence carefully. It begins by creating a **MainMenu** object called **MyMenu**. This object will be at the top of the menu structure. Next, a menu item called **m1** is created. This is the File heading. It is added directly to **MyMenu** and is a top-level selection. Next, the drop-down menu associated with File is created. Notice that these menu items are added to the File menu item, **m1**. When one **MenuItem** is added to another, the added item becomes part of the drop-down menu associated with the item to which it is added. Thus, after the items **subm1** through **subm3** have been added to **m1**, selecting File will cause a drop-down menu containing Open, Close, and Exit to be displayed.

Once the menu has been constructed, the event handlers associated with each entry must be assigned. As explained, a user making a selection generates a **Click** event. Thus, the following sequence assigns the handlers for **subm1** through **subm3**.

```
// Add event handlers for the menu items.
subm1.Click += new EventHandler(MMOpenClick);
subm2.Click += new EventHandler(MMCloseClick);
subm3.Click += new EventHandler(MMExitClick);
```

Therefore, if the user selects Exit, **MMExitClick( )** is executed.

Finally, the **MainMenu** object must be assigned to the **Menu** property of the form, as shown here:

```
Menu = MyMenu;
```

After this assignment takes place, the menu will be displayed when the window is created, and selections will be sent to the proper handler.

The following program puts together all the pieces and demonstrates how to create a main menu and handle menu selections.

```
// Add a Main Menu.

using System;
using System.Windows.Forms;

class MenuForm : Form {
  MainMenu MyMenu;

  public MenuForm() {
    Text = "Adding a Main Menu";

    // Create a main menu object.
    MyMenu  = new MainMenu();

    // Add top-level menu items to the menu.
    MenuItem m1 = new MenuItem("File");
    MyMenu.MenuItems.Add(m1);

    MenuItem m2 = new MenuItem("Tools");
    MyMenu.MenuItems.Add(m2);

    // Create File submenu
    MenuItem subm1 = new MenuItem("Open");
    m1.MenuItems.Add(subm1);

    MenuItem subm2 = new MenuItem("Close");
```

```csharp
    m1.MenuItems.Add(subm2);

    MenuItem subm3 = new MenuItem("Exit");
    m1.MenuItems.Add(subm3);

    // Create Tools submenu
    MenuItem subm4 = new MenuItem("Coordinates");
    m2.MenuItems.Add(subm4);

    MenuItem subm5 = new MenuItem("Change Size");
    m2.MenuItems.Add(subm5);

    MenuItem subm6 = new MenuItem("Restore");
    m2.MenuItems.Add(subm6);


    // Add event handlers for the menu items.
    subm1.Click += new EventHandler(MMOpenClick);
    subm2.Click += new EventHandler(MMCloseClick);
    subm3.Click += new EventHandler(MMExitClick);
    subm4.Click += new EventHandler(MMCoordClick);
    subm5.Click += new EventHandler(MMChangeClick);
    subm6.Click += new EventHandler(MMRestoreClick);

    // Assign the menu to the form.
    Menu = MyMenu;
  }

  [STAThread]
  public static void Main() {
    MenuForm skel = new MenuForm();

    Application.Run(skel);
  }

  // Handler for main menu Coordinates selection.
  protected void MMCoordClick(object who, EventArgs e) {
    // Create a string that contains the coordinates.
    string size =
      String.Format("{0}: {1}, {2}\n{3}: {4}, {5} ",
                    "Top, Left", Top, Left,
                    "Bottom, Right", Bottom, Right);
```

```
    // Display a message box.
    MessageBox.Show(size, "Window Coordinates",
                    MessageBoxButtons.OK);
  }

  // Handler for main menu Change selection.
  protected void MMChangeClick(object who, EventArgs e) {
    Width = Height = 200;
  }

  // Handler for main menu Restore selection.
  protected void MMRestoreClick(object who, EventArgs e) {
    Width = Height = 300;
  }

  // Handler for main menu Open selection.
  protected void MMOpenClick(object who, EventArgs e) {

    MessageBox.Show("Inactive", "Inactive",
                    MessageBoxButtons.OK);
  }

  // Handler for main menu Close selection.
  protected void MMCloseClick(object who, EventArgs e) {

    MessageBox.Show("Inactive", "Inactive",
                    MessageBoxButtons.OK);
  }

  // Handler for main menu Exit selection.
  protected void MMExitClick(object who, EventArgs e) {

    DialogResult result = MessageBox.Show("Stop Program?",
                          "Terminate",
                           MessageBoxButtons.YesNo);

    if(result == DialogResult.Yes) Application.Exit();
  }
}
```

Sample output is shown in Figure 25-4.

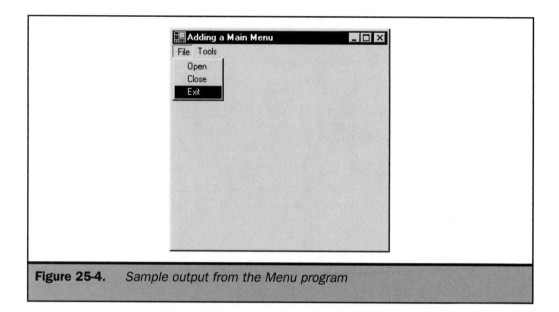

Figure 25-4. *Sample output from the Menu program*

This program defines two drop-down menus. The first is accessed via the File menu. It contains the Open, Close, and Exit selections. The menu handlers for Open and Close are simply placeholders that perform no function other than displaying a message box to that effect. The Close handler asks if you want to stop the program. If you answer Yes, the program is terminated.

The Tools menu has these selections: Coordinates, Change Size, and Restore. Selecting Coordinates causes the coordinates of the upper left and lower right corners of the window to be displayed in a message box. Try moving the window and then displaying its coordinates. Each time the window is moved to a new location, its coordinates change.

Choosing Change Size causes the window to be reduced in size so that its width and height are both 200 pixels long. This is done through the **Width** and **Height** properties, shown here:

```
public int Width { get; set; }
public int Height { get; set; }
```

By default, a form-based window is 300 by 300. Selecting Restore returns the window to its default size.

What Next?

As stated at the outset, Windows programming is a very large topic. This is true no matter how you approach it, although forms certainly streamline the process. Windows is a feature-rich environment that places significant demands on the programmer. If you are new to Windows programming, you can expect to spend a few weeks learning about its various subsystems. One place to start is by studying the controls defined within **System.Windows.Forms**. You will also need to learn how to handle several common Windows messages, such as those that request the redrawing of a window. Another important subsystem is found in **Windows.Drawing**, which defines various classes that control how output is displayed in the window. **Windows.Drawing** encapsulates the functionality that is provided by the Windows GDI (Graphics Device Interface). Try writing many short programs, observing the precise behavior and appearance associated with each new option or technique.

Chapter 26

A Recursive-Descent
Expression Parser

How do you write a program that will take as input a string containing a numeric expression, such as (10 – 5) * 3, and compute the proper answer? If there is still a "high priesthood" among programmers, it must be those few who know how to do this. Many otherwise accomplished programmers are mystified by the way a high-level language converts algebraic expressions into instructions that a computer can execute. This procedure is called *expression parsing*, and it is the backbone of all language compilers and interpreters, spreadsheets, and anything else that needs to convert numeric expressions into a form that the computer can use.

Although mysterious to the uninitiated, expression parsing is a well-defined task for which there is a rather elegant solution. This is because expression parsing works according to the strict rules of algebra. This chapter develops what is commonly referred to as a *recursive-descent parser* and all the necessary support routines that enable you to evaluate numeric expressions. Once you have mastered the operation of the parser, you can easily enhance and modify it to suit your needs.

Aside from being a useful piece of code in itself, the parser developed here also serves a second purpose: It illustrates the power and range of the C# language. A parser is a "pure code" application. It doesn't interface to the network, use a GUI, or make use of limited system resources. It is the type of code that in the past one would normally write in C++. The fact that a parser can be easily created using C# proves that C# is up to any programming task.

Expressions

Because an expression parser evaluates an algebraic expression, it is important that you understand the constituent parts of an expression. Although expressions can be made up of all types of information, this chapter deals only with numeric expressions. For our purposes, numeric expressions are composed of the following items:

- Numbers
- The operators +, –, /, *, ^, %, =
- Parentheses
- Variables

Here, the caret operator (^) indicates exponentiation (not the XOR as it does in C#) and the equal sign (=) is the assignment operator. These items can be combined in expressions according to the rules of algebra. Here are some examples:

10 – 8
(100 – 5) * 14 / 6
a + b – c
10 ^ 5
a = 10 – b

Assume this precedence for each operator:

highest	+ – (unary)
	^
	* / %
	+ –
lowest	=

Operators of equal precedence evaluate from left to right.

The parser developed in this chapter will be subject to a few constraints. First, all variables are single letters (in other words, 26 variables, **A** through **Z**, are available). The variables are not case sensitive (**a** and **A** are treated as the same variable). Second, all numeric values are assumed to be **double**, although you could easily modify the parser to handle other types of values. Finally, to keep the logic clear and easy to understand, only rudimentary error checking is included.

Parsing Expressions: The Problem

If you haven't thought much about the problem of expression parsing, you might assume that it is a simple task, but it isn't. To better understand the problem, try to evaluate this sample expression:

10 – 2 * 3

You know that this expression is equal to the value 4. Although you could easily create a program that would compute that *specific* expression, the question is how to create a program that gives the correct answer for any *arbitrary* expression. At first you might think of a routine something like this:

```
a = get first operand
while(operands present) {
    op = get operator
    b = get second operand
    a = a op b
}
```

This routine gets the first operand, the operator, and the second operand to perform the first operation; then it gets the next operator and operand to perform the next operation; and so on. However, if you use this basic approach, the expression 10 – 2 * 3 evaluates to 24 (that is, 8 * 3) instead of 4, because this procedure neglects the precedence of the operators. You cannot just evaluate the operands and operators in order from left to right because the rules of algebra dictate that multiplication must be done before subtraction. Some beginners think that this problem can be easily overcome, and sometimes, in very restricted cases, it can. But the problem only gets worse when you add parentheses, exponentiation, variables, unary operators, and the like.

Although there are a number of ways to write a routine that evaluates expressions, the one developed here is the approach most easily written by a person. It is called a *recursive-descent parser*, and in the course of this chapter you will see how it got its name. (Some of the other methods used to write parsers employ complex tables that must be generated by another computer program. These are sometimes called *table-driven parsers*.)

Parsing an Expression

There are a number of ways to parse and evaluate an expression. For a recursive-descent parser, think of expressions as *recursive data structures*—that is, expressions that are defined in terms of themselves. If, for the moment, we assume that expressions can use only +, –, *, /, and parentheses, all expressions can be defined by the following rules:

    expression -> term [+ term] [– term]
    term -> factor [* factor] [/ factor]
    factor -> variable, number, or (expression)

The square brackets designate an optional element, and the -> means produces. In fact, these rules are usually called the *production rules* of the expression. Therefore, for the definition of *term* you could say: "Term produces factor times factor or factor divided by factor." Notice that the precedence of the operators is implicit in the way an expression is defined.

The expression

    10 + 5 * B

has two terms: 10, and 5 * B. The second term contains two factors: 5 and B. These factors consist of one number and one variable.

On the other hand, the expression

    14 * (7 – C)

has two factors: 14 and (7 – C). The factors consist of one number and one parenthesized expression. The parenthesized expression contains two terms: one number and one variable.

This process forms the basis for a recursive-descent parser, which is a set of mutually recursive methods that work in a chainlike fashion and implement the production rules. At each appropriate step, the parser performs the specified operations in the algebraically correct sequence. To see how the production rules are used to parse an expression, let's work through an example using the following expression:

9/3 – (100 + 56)

Here is the sequence that you will follow.

1. Get the first term, 9/3.
2. Get each factor and divide the integers. The resulting value is 3.
3. Get the second term, (100 + 56). At this point, start recursively analyzing the second subexpression.
4. Get each term and add. The resulting value is 156.
5. Return from the recursive call and subtract 156 from 3. The answer is –153.

If you are a little confused at this point, don't feel bad. This is a fairly complex concept that takes some getting used to. There are two basic things to remember about this recursive view of expressions. First, the precedence of the operators is implicit in the way the production rules are defined. Second, this method of parsing and evaluating expressions is very similar to the way humans evaluate mathematical expressions.

The remainder of this chapter develops two parsers. The first will parse and evaluate floating-point expressions of type **double**, which consist only of literal values. This parser illustrates the basics of the recursive-descent method of parsing. The second adds the ability to use variables.

Dissecting an Expression

To evaluate an expression, a parser needs to be fed the individual components of that expression. For example, the expression

A * B – (W + 10)

contains these individual parts: **A**, *****, **B**, **–**, **(**, **W**, **+**, **10**, and **)**. In the language of parsing, each component of an expression is called a *token*, and each token represents an indivisible unit of the expression. Since *tokenizing* an expression is fundamental to parsing, let's look at it before examining the parser itself.

To render an expression into tokens, you need a method that sequentially returns each token in the expression individually, moving from start to finish. The method must also be able to skip over spaces and detect the end of the expression. In the parser developed here, the method that performs this task is called **GetToken( )**.

Both parsers in this chapter are encapsulated within the **Parser** class. Although this class is described in detail later, the first part of it needs to be shown here so that the workings of **GetToken( )** can be explained. **Parser** begins by defining the enumerations and fields shown here:

```
class Parser {
  // Enumerate token types.
  enum Types { NONE, DELIMITER, VARIABLE, NUMBER };
  // Enumerate error types.
  enum Errors { SYNTAX, UNBALPARENS, NOEXP, DIVBYZERO };

  string exp;    // refers to expression string
  int expIdx;    // current index into the expression
  string token;  // holds current token
  Types tokType; // holds token's type
```

Parser begins by defining two enumerations. The first is **Types**. When parsing an expression, a token typically has a type associated with it. For the parsers developed in this chapter, only three types are needed: variable, number, and delimiter. These are represented by the values **VARIABLE**, **NUMBER**, and **DELIMITER** defined by the **Types** enumeration. The **DELIMITER** category is used for both operators and parentheses. The **NONE** type is just a placeholder value for an undefined token. The **Errors** enumeration represents various parsing errors.

A reference to the string that holds the expression being parsed is stored in **exp**. Thus, **exp** will refer to a string such as "10+4". The index of the next token within that string is held in **expIdx**, which is initially zero. The token that is obtained is stored in **token**, and its type is stored in **tokType**.

The **GetToken( )** method that is used by the parser is shown here. Each time it is called, it obtains the next token from an expression in the string referred to by **exp**, beginning at **expIdx**. In other words, each time **GetToken( )** is called, it obtains the next token at **exp[expIdx]**. It puts this token into the **token** field. It puts the type of the token into **tokType**. **GetToken( )** uses the **IsDelim( )** method, which is also shown here.

```
// Obtain the next token.
void GetToken()
{
  tokType = Types.NONE;
  token = "";

  if(expIdx == exp.Length) return; // at end of expression

  // skip over white space
  while(expIdx < exp.Length &&
        Char.IsWhiteSpace(exp[expIdx])) ++expIdx;
```

```
  // trailing whitespace ends expression
  if(expIdx == exp.Length) return;

  if(IsDelim(exp[expIdx])) { // is operator
    token += exp[expIdx];
    expIdx++;
    tokType = Types.DELIMITER;
  }
  else if(Char.IsLetter(exp[expIdx])) { // is variable
    while(!IsDelim(exp[expIdx])) {
      token += exp[expIdx];
      expIdx++;
      if(expIdx >= exp.Length) break;
    }
    tokType = Types.VARIABLE;
  }
  else if(Char.IsDigit(exp[expIdx])) { // is number
    while(!IsDelim(exp[expIdx])) {
      token += exp[expIdx];
      expIdx++;
      if(expIdx >= exp.Length) break;
    }
    tokType = Types.NUMBER;
  }
}

// Return true if c is a delimiter.
bool IsDelim(char c)
{
  if((" +-/*%^=()".IndexOf(c) != -1))
    return true;
  return false;
}
```

Look closely at **GetToken( )**. After the first few initializations, **GetToken( )** checks to determine whether the end of the expression has been reached by seeing if **expIdx** is equal to **exp.Length**. Since **expIdx** is an index into the expression being analyzed, if it equals the length of the expression string, the expression has been fully parsed.

If there are still more tokens to retrieve from the expression, **GetToken( )** first skips over any leading spaces. Once the spaces have been skipped, **exp[expIdx]** contains either a digit, a variable, an operator, or, if trailing spaces end the expression, a space. If the next character is an operator, it is returned as a string in **token**, and **DELIMITER** is stored in **tokType**. If the next character is a letter instead, it is assumed to be one of the variables. It is returned as a string in **token** and **tokType** is assigned the value **VARIABLE**. If the next character is a digit, the entire number is read and stored in its string form in **token** and its type is **NUMBER**. Finally, if the next character is none of the preceding, **token** will contain a null string.

To keep the code in **GetToken( )** clear, a certain amount of error checking has been omitted and some assumptions have been made. For example, any unrecognized character can end an expression as long as it is preceded by a space. Also, in this version, variables can be of any length, but only the first letter is significant. You can add more error checking and other details as your specific application dictates.

To better understand how **GetToken( )** works, consider this expression:

A + 100 – (B * C) / 2

When tokenizing this expression, **GetToken( )** obtains the following tokens and types:

Token	Token type
A	VARIABLE
+	DELIMITER
100	NUMBER
–	DELIMITER
(	DELIMITER
B	VARIABLE
*	DELIMITER
C	VARIABLE
)	DELIMITER
/	DELIMITER
2	NUMBER

Remember that **token** always holds a string, even if it contains just a single character.

A Simple Expression Parser

Here is the first version of the parser. It can evaluate expressions that consist solely of literals, operators, and parentheses. Although **GetToken( )** can process variables, the parser does nothing with them. Once you understand how this simplified parser works, we will add the ability to handle variables.

```
/*
   This module contains the recursive descent
   parser that does not use variables.
*/

using System;

// Exception class for parser errors.
class ParserException : ApplicationException {
  public ParserException(string str) : base(str) { }

  public override string ToString() {
    return Message;
  }
}

class Parser {
  // Enumerate token types.
  enum Types { NONE, DELIMITER, VARIABLE, NUMBER };
  // Enumerate error types.
  enum Errors { SYNTAX, UNBALPARENS, NOEXP, DIVBYZERO };

  string exp;     // refers to expression string
  int expIdx;     // current index into the expression
  string token;   // holds current token
  Types tokType;  // holds token's type

  // Parser entry point.
  public double Evaluate(string expstr)
  {
    double result;

    exp = expstr;
    expIdx = 0;

    try {
      GetToken();
      if(token == "") {
        SyntaxErr(Errors.NOEXP); // no expression present
        return 0.0;
      }

      EvalExp2(out result);
```

```
      if(token != "") // last token must be null
        SyntaxErr(Errors.SYNTAX);

      return result;
    } catch (ParserException exc) {
      // Add other error handling here, as desired.
      Console.WriteLine(exc);
      return 0.0;
    }
}

// Add or subtract two terms.
void EvalExp2(out double result)
{
  string op;
  double partialResult;

  EvalExp3(out result);
  while((op = token) == "+" || op == "-") {
    GetToken();
    EvalExp3(out partialResult);
    switch(op) {
      case "-":
        result = result - partialResult;
        break;
      case "+":
        result = result + partialResult;
        break;
    }
  }
}

// Multiply or divide two factors.
void EvalExp3(out double result)
{
  string op;
  double partialResult = 0.0;

  EvalExp4(out result);
  while((op = token) == "*" ||
        op == "/" || op == "%") {
    GetToken();
```

```csharp
      EvalExp4(out partialResult);
      switch(op) {
        case "*":
          result = result * partialResult;
          break;
        case "/":
          if(partialResult == 0.0)
            SyntaxErr(Errors.DIVBYZERO);
          result = result / partialResult;
          break;
        case "%":
          if(partialResult == 0.0)
            SyntaxErr(Errors.DIVBYZERO);
          result = (int) result % (int) partialResult;
          break;
      }
    }
}

// Process an exponent.
void EvalExp4(out double result)
{
  double partialResult, ex;
  int t;

  EvalExp5(out result);
  if(token == "^") {
    GetToken();
    EvalExp4(out partialResult);
    ex = result;
    if(partialResult == 0.0) {
      result = 1.0;
      return;
    }
    for(t=(int)partialResult-1; t > 0; t--)
      result = result * (double)ex;
  }
}

// Evaluate a unary + or -.
void EvalExp5(out double result)
{
```

```
    string  op;

  op = "";
  if((tokType == Types.DELIMITER) &&
      token == "+" || token == "-") {
    op = token;
    GetToken();
  }
  EvalExp6(out result);
  if(op == "-") result = -result;
}

// Process a parenthesized expression.
void EvalExp6(out double result)
{
  if((token == "(")) {
    GetToken();
    EvalExp2(out result);
    if(token != ")")
      SyntaxErr(Errors.UNBALPARENS);
    GetToken();
  }
  else Atom(out result);
}

// Get the value of a number.
void Atom(out double result)
{
  switch(tokType) {
    case Types.NUMBER:
      try {
        result = Double.Parse(token);
      } catch (FormatException) {
        result = 0.0;
        SyntaxErr(Errors.SYNTAX);
      }
      GetToken();
      return;
    default:
      result = 0.0;
      SyntaxErr(Errors.SYNTAX);
      break;
```

```
    }
}

// Handle a syntax error.
void SyntaxErr(Errors error)
{
  string[] err = {
    "Syntax Error",
    "Unbalanced Parentheses",
    "No Expression Present",
    "Division by Zero"
  };

  throw new ParserException(err[(int)error]);
}

// Obtain the next token.
void GetToken()
{
  tokType = Types.NONE;
  token = "";

  if(expIdx == exp.Length) return; // at end of expression

  // skip over white space
  while(expIdx < exp.Length &&
        Char.IsWhiteSpace(exp[expIdx])) ++expIdx;

  // trailing whitespace ends expression
  if(expIdx == exp.Length) return;

  if(IsDelim(exp[expIdx])) { // is operator
    token += exp[expIdx];
    expIdx++;
    tokType = Types.DELIMITER;
  }
  else if(Char.IsLetter(exp[expIdx])) { // is variable
    while(!IsDelim(exp[expIdx])) {
      token += exp[expIdx];
      expIdx++;
      if(expIdx >= exp.Length) break;
    }
```

```
          tokType = Types.VARIABLE;
       }
     else if(Char.IsDigit(exp[expIdx])) { // is number
         while(!IsDelim(exp[expIdx])) {
           token += exp[expIdx];
           expIdx++;
           if(expIdx >= exp.Length) break;
         }
         tokType = Types.NUMBER;
       }
     }
   }

   // Return true if c is a delimiter.
   bool IsDelim(char c)
   {
     if((" +-/*%^=()".IndexOf(c) != -1))
       return true;
     return false;
   }

}
```

The parser as it is shown can handle the following operators: +, –, *, /, and %. In addition, it can handle integer exponentiation (^) and the unary minus. The parser can also deal with parentheses correctly.

To use the parser, first create an object of type **Parser**. Then, call **Evaluate( )**, passing the expression string that you want evaluated as an argument. **Evaluate( )** returns the result. The following example demonstrates the parser:

```
// Demonstrate the parser.

using System;

class ParserDemo {
  public static void Main()
  {
    string expr;
    Parser p = new Parser();

    Console.WriteLine("Enter an empty expression to stop.");
```

```
    for(;;) {
      Console.Write("Enter expression: ");
      expr = Console.ReadLine();
      if(expr == "") break;
      Console.WriteLine("Result: " + p.Evaluate(expr));
    }
  }
}
```

Here is a sample run:

```
Enter an empty expression to stop.
Enter expression: 10-2*3
Result: 4

Enter expression: (10-2)*3
Result: 24

Enter expression: 10/3.5
Result: 2.85714285714286
```

Understanding the Parser

Let's now take a detailed look at **Parser**. As mentioned earlier when **GetToken( )** was
discussed, **Parser** contains four private fields. The string containing the expression to
be evaluated is referred to by **exp**. This field is set each time **Evaluate( )** is called. It is
important to remember that the parser evaluates expressions that are contained in
standard C# strings. For example, the following strings contain expressions that the
parser can evaluate:

"10 – 5"
"2 * 3.3 / (3.1416 * 3.3)"

The current index into **exp** is stored in **expIdx**. When parsing begins execution, **expIdx**
is set to zero. **expIdx** is incremented as the parser moves through the expression. The
token field holds the current token, and **tokType** contains the token type.

  The entry point to the parser is through **Evaluate( )**, which must be called with a
string containing the expression to be analyzed. The methods **EvalExp2( )** through
EvalExp6( ) along with **Atom( )** form the recursive-descent parser. They implement an
enhanced set of the expression production rules discussed earlier. The comments at the
top of each method describes what function they perform. In the next version of the
parser, a method called **EvalExp1( )** will also be added.

SyntaxErr( ) handles syntax errors in the expression. The methods **GetToken( )** and **IsDelim( )** dissect the expression into its component parts, as described earlier. The parser uses **GetToken( )** to obtain tokens from the expression, starting at the beginning of the expression and working to the end. Based on the type of token obtained, different actions are taken.

To understand exactly how the parser evaluates an expression, work through the following expression:

10 – 3 * 2

When **Evaluate( )**, the entry point into the parser, is called, it gets the first token. If the token is a null string, the message **No Expression Present** is displayed and **Evaluate( )** returns 0.0. However, in this case, the token contains the number **10**. Next, **EvalExp2( )** is called. **EvalExp2( )** then calls **EvalExp3( )**, and **EvalExp3( )** calls **EvalExp4( )**, which in turn calls **EvalExp5( )**. Then **EvalExp5( )** determines if the token is a unary plus or minus; in this case, it is not, so **EvalExp6( )** is called. At this point **EvalExp6( )** either recursively calls **EvalExp2( )** (in the case of a parenthesized expression) or **Atom( )** to find the value of a number. Since the token is not a left parenthesis, **Atom( )** is executed and **result** is assigned the value 10. Next, another token is retrieved, and the methods begin to return up the chain. Since the token is now the operator **–**, the methods return up to **EvalExp2( )**.

What happens next is very important. Because the token is **–**, it is saved in **op**. The parser then gets the next token, which is **3**, and the descent down the chain begins again. As before, **Atom( )** is entered. The value 3 is returned in **result** and the token * is read. This causes a return back up the chain to **EvalExp3( )**, where the final token **2** is read. At this point, the first arithmetic operation occurs—the multiplication of **2** and **3**. The result is returned to **EvalExp2( )** and the subtraction is performed. The subtraction yields the answer 4. Although the process may at first seem complicated, you can work through some other examples to verify that this method functions correctly every time.

If an error occurs while parsing, the **SyntaxErr( )** method is called. This method throws a **ParserException** that describes the error. **ParserException** is a custom exception defined at the top of the parser file.

This parser would be suitable for use by a simple desktop calculator, as illustrated by the previous program. Before it could be used in a computer language, a database, or a sophisticated calculator, however, it would need the ability to handle variables. This is the subject of the next section.

Adding Variables to the Parser

All programming languages, many calculators, and spreadsheets use variables to store values for later use. Before the parser can be used for such applications, it needs to be expanded to include variables. To accomplish this, you need to add several things to the parser. First, of course, are the variables themselves. As stated earlier, we will use the letters **A** through **Z** for variables. The variables are stored in an array inside the **Parser** class. Each variable uses one array location in a 26-element array of **double**s. Therefore, add the following field to the **Parser** class:

```
double[] vars = new double[26];
```

You will also need to add the following **Parser** constructor, which initializes the variables:

```
public Parser() {
  // Initialize the variables to zero.
  for(int i=0; i < vars.Length; i++)
    vars[i] = 0.0;
}
```

The variables are initialized to 0.0 as a courtesy to the user.

You will also need a method to look up the value of a given variable. Because the variables are named **A** through **Z**, they can easily be used to index the array **vars** by subtracting the ASCII value for **A** from the variable name. The method **FindVar( )**, shown here, accomplishes this:

```
// Return the value of a variable.
double FindVar(string vname)
{
  if(!Char.IsLetter(vname[0])){
    SyntaxErr(Errors.SYNTAX);
    return 0.0;
  }
  return vars[Char.ToUpper(vname[0])-'A'];
}
```

As this method is written, it will actually accept long variable names, such s **A12** or **test**, but only the first letter is significant. You can change this feature to fit your needs.

You must also modify the **Atom( )** method to handle both numbers and variables. The new version is shown here:

```
// Get the value of a number or variable.
void Atom(out double result)
{
  switch(tokType) {
    case Types.NUMBER:
      try {
```

```
      result = Double.Parse(token);
    } catch (FormatException) {
      result = 0.0;
      SyntaxErr(Errors.SYNTAX);
    }
    GetToken();
    return;
  case Types.VARIABLE:
    result = FindVar(token);
    GetToken();
    return;
  default:
    result = 0.0;
    SyntaxErr(Errors.SYNTAX);
    break;
  }
}
```

Technically, these additions are all that is needed for the parser to use variables correctly; however, there is no way for these variables to be assigned a value. To enable a variable to be given a value, the parser needs to be able to handle the assignment operator, which is =. To implement assignment, we will add another method, **EvalExp1( )**, to the **Parser** class. This method will now begin the recursive-descent chain. This means that it, not **EvalExp2( )**, must be called by **Evaluate( )** to begin parsing the expression. **EvalExp1( )** is shown here:

```
// Process an assignment.
void EvalExp1(out double result)
{
  int varIdx;
  Types ttokType;
  string temptoken;

  if(tokType == Types.VARIABLE) {
    // save old token
    temptoken = String.Copy(token);
    ttokType = tokType;

    // Compute the index of the variable.
    varIdx = Char.ToUpper(token[0]) - 'A';
```

```
      GetToken();
      if(token != "=") {
        PutBack(); // return current token
        // restore old token -- not an assignment
        token = String.Copy(temptoken);
        tokType = ttokType;
      }
      else {
        GetToken(); // get next part of exp
        EvalExp2(out result);
        vars[varIdx] = result;
        return;
      }
    }

    EvalExp2(out result);
  }
```

EvalExp1( ) needs to look ahead to determine whether an assignment is actually being made. This is because a variable name always precedes an assignment, but a variable name alone does not guarantee that an assignment expression follows. That is, the parser will accept A = 100 as an assignment, but is also smart enough to know that A/10 is not an assignment. To accomplish this, **EvalExp1( )** reads the next token from the input stream. If it is not an equal sign, the token is returned to the input stream for later use by calling **PutBack( )**, shown here:

```
// Return a token to the input stream.
void PutBack()
{
  for(int i=0; i < token.Length; i++) expIdx--;
}
```

After making all the necessary changes, the parser will now look like this:

```
/*
   This module contains the recursive descent
   parser that recognizes variables.
*/

using System;
```

```csharp
// Exception class for parser errors.
class ParserException : ApplicationException {
  public ParserException(string str) : base(str) { }

  public override string ToString() {
    return Message;
  }
}

class Parser {
  // Enumerate token types.
  enum Types { NONE, DELIMITER, VARIABLE, NUMBER };
  // Enumerate error types.
  enum Errors { SYNTAX, UNBALPARENS, NOEXP, DIVBYZERO };

  string exp;     // refers to expression string
  int expIdx;     // current index into the expression
  string token;   // holds current token
  Types tokType;  // holds token's type

  // Array for variables.
  double[] vars = new double[26];

  public Parser() {
    // Initialize the variables to zero.
    for(int i=0; i < vars.Length; i++)
      vars[i] = 0.0;
  }

  // Parser entry point.
  public double Evaluate(string expstr)
  {
    double result;

    exp = expstr;
    expIdx = 0;

    try {
      GetToken();
      if(token == "") {
        SyntaxErr(Errors.NOEXP); // no expression present
        return 0.0;
```

```
    }

    EvalExp1(out result); // now, call EvalExp1() to start

    if(token != "") // last token must be null
      SyntaxErr(Errors.SYNTAX);

    return result;
  } catch (ParserException exc) {
    // Add other error handling here, as desired.
    Console.WriteLine(exc);
    return 0.0;
  }
}

// Process an assignment.
void EvalExp1(out double result)
{
  int varIdx;
  Types ttokType;
  string temptoken;

  if(tokType == Types.VARIABLE) {
    // save old token
    temptoken = String.Copy(token);
    ttokType = tokType;

    // Compute the index of the variable.
    varIdx = Char.ToUpper(token[0]) - 'A';

    GetToken();
    if(token != "=") {
      PutBack(); // return current token
      // restore old token -- not an assignment
      token = String.Copy(temptoken);
      tokType = ttokType;
    }
    else {
      GetToken(); // get next part of exp
      EvalExp2(out result);
      vars[varIdx] = result;
      return;
```

```
      }
    }

    EvalExp2(out result);
  }

  // Add or subtract two terms.
  void EvalExp2(out double result)
  {
    string op;
    double partialResult;

    EvalExp3(out result);
    while((op = token) == "+" || op == "-") {
      GetToken();
      EvalExp3(out partialResult);
      switch(op) {
        case "-":
          result = result - partialResult;
          break;
        case "+":
          result = result + partialResult;
          break;
      }
    }
  }

  // Multiply or divide two factors.
  void EvalExp3(out double result)
  {
    string op;
    double partialResult = 0.0;

    EvalExp4(out result);
    while((op = token) == "*" ||
          op == "/" || op == "%") {
      GetToken();
      EvalExp4(out partialResult);
      switch(op) {
        case "*":
          result = result * partialResult;
          break;
```

```
        case "/":
          if(partialResult == 0.0)
            SyntaxErr(Errors.DIVBYZERO);
          result = result / partialResult;
          break;
        case "%":
          if(partialResult == 0.0)
            SyntaxErr(Errors.DIVBYZERO);
          result = (int) result % (int) partialResult;
          break;
    }
  }
}

// Process an exponent.
void EvalExp4(out double result)
{
  double partialResult, ex;
  int t;

  EvalExp5(out result);
  if(token == "^") {
    GetToken();
    EvalExp4(out partialResult);
    ex = result;
    if(partialResult == 0.0) {
      result = 1.0;
      return;
    }
    for(t=(int)partialResult-1; t > 0; t--)
      result = result * (double)ex;
  }
}

// Evaluate a unary + or -.
void EvalExp5(out double result)
{
  string  op;

  op = "";
  if((tokType == Types.DELIMITER) &&
      token == "+" || token == "-") {
```

```
      op = token;
      GetToken();
    }
    EvalExp6(out result);
    if(op == "-") result = -result;
  }

  // Process a parenthesized expression.
  void EvalExp6(out double result)
  {
    if((token == "(")) {
      GetToken();
      EvalExp2(out result);
      if(token != ")")
        SyntaxErr(Errors.UNBALPARENS);
      GetToken();
    }
    else Atom(out result);
  }

  // Get the value of a number or variable.
  void Atom(out double result)
  {
    switch(tokType) {
      case Types.NUMBER:
        try {
          result = Double.Parse(token);
        } catch (FormatException) {
          result = 0.0;
          SyntaxErr(Errors.SYNTAX);
        }
        GetToken();
        return;
      case Types.VARIABLE:
        result = FindVar(token);
        GetToken();
        return;
      default:
        result = 0.0;
        SyntaxErr(Errors.SYNTAX);
        break;
    }
```

```
  }

  // Return the value of a variable.
  double FindVar(string vname)
  {
    if(!Char.IsLetter(vname[0])){
      SyntaxErr(Errors.SYNTAX);
      return 0.0;
    }
    return vars[Char.ToUpper(vname[0])-'A'];
  }

  // Return a token to the input stream.
  void PutBack()
  {
    for(int i=0; i < token.Length; i++) expIdx--;
  }

  // Handle a syntax error.
  void SyntaxErr(Errors error)
  {
    string[] err = {
      "Syntax Error",
      "Unbalanced Parentheses",
      "No Expression Present",
      "Division by Zero"
    };

    throw new ParserException(err[(int)error]);
  }

  // Obtain the next token.
  void GetToken()
  {
    tokType = Types.NONE;
    token = "";

    if(expIdx == exp.Length) return; // at end of expression

    // skip over white space
    while(expIdx < exp.Length &&
          Char.IsWhiteSpace(exp[expIdx])) ++expIdx;
```

```
    // trailing whitespace ends expression
    if(expIdx == exp.Length) return;

    if(IsDelim(exp[expIdx])) { // is operator
      token += exp[expIdx];
      expIdx++;
      tokType = Types.DELIMITER;
    }
    else if(Char.IsLetter(exp[expIdx])) { // is variable
      while(!IsDelim(exp[expIdx])) {
        token += exp[expIdx];
        expIdx++;
        if(expIdx >= exp.Length) break;
      }
      tokType = Types.VARIABLE;
    }
    else if(Char.IsDigit(exp[expIdx])) { // is number
      while(!IsDelim(exp[expIdx])) {
        token += exp[expIdx];
        expIdx++;
        if(expIdx >= exp.Length) break;
      }
      tokType = Types.NUMBER;
    }
  }

  // Return true if c is a delimiter.
  bool IsDelim(char c)
  {
    if((" +-/*%^=()".IndexOf(c) != -1))
      return true;
    return false;
  }
}
```

To try the enhanced parser, you can use the same program that you used for the simple parser. Using the enhanced parser, you can now enter expressions like these:

A = 10/4
A – B
C = A * (F – 21)

Syntax Checking in a Recursive-Descent Parser

In expression parsing, a syntax error is simply a situation in which the input expression does not conform to the strict rules required by the parser. Most of the time, this is caused by human error—usually typing mistakes. For example, the following expressions are not valid for the parsers in this chapter:

```
10 ** 8
((10 – 5) * 9
/8
```

The first contains two operators in a row, the second has unbalanced parentheses, and the last has a division sign at the start of an expression. None of these conditions is allowed by the parser. Because syntax errors can cause the parser to give erroneous results, you need to guard against them.

As you studied the parser code, you probably noticed the **SyntaxErr( )** method, which is called under certain situations. Unlike some other types of parsers, the recursive-descent method makes syntax checking easy because, for the most part, it occurs in **Atom( )**, **FindVar( )**, or **EvalExp6( )**, where parentheses are checked.

When **SyntaxErr( )** is called, it throws a **ParserException** that contains a description of the error. As **Parser** is currently written, this exception is caught in **Evaluate( )**. Thus, the parser immediately stops when an error is encountered. You can, of course, change this behavior to suit your own needs.

Some Things to Try

As mentioned early on in this chapter, only minimal error checking is performed by the parser. You might want to add detailed error reporting. For example, you could highlight the point in the expression at which an error was detected. This would allow the user to find and correct a syntax error.

As the parser now stands, it can evaluate only numeric expressions. However, with a few additions, you can make it evaluate other types of expressions, such as strings, spatial coordinates, or complex numbers. For example, to allow the parser to evaluate string objects, you must make the following changes:

1. Define a new token type called **STRING**.

2. Enhance **GetToken( )** so that it recognizes strings.

3. Add a new case inside **Atom( )** that handles **STRING** type tokens.

After implementing these steps, the parser could handle string expressions like these:

```
a = "one"
b = "two"
c = a + b
```

The result in **c** should be the concatenation of **a** and **b**, or "onetwo".

APPLYING C#

Here is one good application for the parser: Create a simple, pop-up mini-calculator that accepts an expression entered by the user and then displays the result. This would make an excellent addition to nearly any commercial application.

Finally, try converting **Parser** into a component. This is easy to do. First, have **Parser** inherit **Component**. Then, implement **Dispose(bool)**. That's it! If you do this, you will have a parser available to any application you write.

Appendix A

XML Comment Quick Reference

C# supports three types of comments. The first two are // and /* */. The third type is based on XML tags and is called an *XML comment*. (XML comments are also called *documentation comments*.) Each line of an XML comment begins with ///. XML comments precede the declaration of such things as classes, namespaces, methods, properties, and events. Using XML comments, you can embed information about your program into the program itself. When you compile the program, you can have the XML comments placed into an XML file. XML comments are also able to be utilized by the IntelliSense feature of Visual Studio.

The XML Comment Tags

C# supports the XML documentation tags shown in Table A-1. Most of the XML comment tags are readily understandable, and they work like all other XML tags with which most programmers are already familiar. However, the **<list>** tag is more complicated than the others. A list contains two components: a list header and list items. The general form of a list header is shown here:

```
<listheader>
  <term> name </term>
  <description> text </description>
</listheader>
```

Here, *text* describes *name*. For a table, *text* is not used. The general form of a list item is shown next:

```
<item>
  <term> item-name </term>
  <description> text </description>
</item>
```

Here, *text* describes *item-name*. For bulleted or numbered lists, or tables, *item-name* is not used. There can be multiple **<item>** entries.

Tag	Description
<c> *code* </c>	Specifies the text specified by *code* as program code.
<code> *code* </code>	Specifies multiple lines of text specified by *code* as program code.

Table A-1.   *The XML Comment Tags*

Tag	Description
<example> *explanation* </example>	The text associated with e*xplanation* describes a code example.
<exception cref = *"name"*> *explanation* </exception>	Describes an exception. The exception is specified by *name*.
<include file = *'fname'* path = *'path* [@*tagName* = *"tagID "*]' />	Specifies a file that contains the XML comments for the current file. The file is specified by *fname*. The path to the tag, the tag name, and the tag ID are specified by *path*, *tagName*, and *tagID*, respectively.
<list type = *"type"*> *list-header* *list-items* </list>	Specifies a list. The type of the list is specified by *type*, which must be either bullet, number, or table.
<para> *text* </para>	Specifies a paragraph of text within another tag.
<param name = *'param-name'*> *explanation* </param>	Documents the parameter specified by *param-name*. The text associated with e*xplanation* describes the parameter.
<paramref name = *"param-name"* />	Specifies that *param-name* is a parameter name.
<permission cref = *"identifier"*> *explanation* </permission>	Describes the permission setting associated with the class members specified by *identifier*. The text associated with e*xplanation* describes the permission settings.
<remarks> *explanation* </remarks>	The text specified by *explanation* is a general commentary often used to describe a type, such as a class or structure.
<returns> *explanation* </returns>	The text specified by *explanation* documents the return value of a method.
<see cref = *"identifier"* />	Declares a link to another element, specified by *identifier*.

Table A-1.   *The XML Comment Tags* (continued)

Tag	Description
<seealso cref = "*identifier*" />	Declares a "see also" link to *identifier*.
<summary> *explanation* </summary>	The text specified by *explanation* is a general commentary often used to describe a method or other class member.
<value> *explanation* </value>	The text specified by *explanation* documents a property.

Table A-1. *The XML Comment Tags* (continued)

Compiling XML Documentation

To produce an XML file that contains the documentation comments, specify the **/doc** option. For example, to compile a file called **DocTest.cs** that contains XML comments, use this command line:

```
csc DocTest.cs /doc:DocTest.xml
```

To create an XML output file when using the Visual Studio IDE, you must use the Property Pages dialog box, which is activated by selecting View | Property Pages. Next, select Configuration Properties | Build. Then, specify the name of the XML in the XML Documentation File property.

An XML Documentation Example

Here is an example that demonstrates several XML comments:

```
// A XML documentation example.

using System;

/// <remark>
/// This is an example of XML documentation.
/// The Test class demonstrates several tags.
/// </remark>
```

```
class Test {
  /// <summary>
  /// Main is where execution begins.
  /// </summary>
  public static void Main() {
    int sum;

    sum = Summation(5);
      Console.WriteLine("Summation of " + 5 + " is " + sum);
  }

  /// <summary>
  /// Summation returns the summation of its argument.
  /// <param name = "val">
  /// The value to be summed is passed in val.
  /// </param>
  /// <see cref="int"> </see>
  /// <returns>
  /// The summation is returned as an int value.
  /// </returns>
  /// </summary>
  static int Summation(int val) {
    int result = 0;

    for(int i=1; i <= val; i++)
      result += i;

    return result;
  }
}
```

Assuming the preceding program is called **XmlTest.cs**, the following line will compile the program and produce a file called **XmlTest.xml** that contains the comments:

```
csc XmlTest.cs /doc:XmlTest.xml
```

After compiling, the following XML file is produced.

```
<?xml version="1.0"?>
<doc>
    <assembly>
```

```
            <name>t</name>
        </assembly>
        <members>
            <member name="T:Test">
                <remark>
                This is an example of XML documentation.
                The Test class demonstrates several tags.
                </remark>
            </member>
            <member name="M:Test.Main">
                <summary>
                 Main is where execution begins.
                </summary>
            </member>
            <member name="M:Test.Summation(System.Int32)">
                <summary>
                Summation returns the summation of its argument.
                <param name="val">
                The value to be summed is passed in val.
                </param>
                <see cref="T:System.Int32"> </see>
                <returns>
                The summation is returned as an int value.
                </returns>
                </summary>
            </member>
        </members>
    </doc>
```

Notice that each documented element is given a unique identifier. These identifiers can be used by other programs that use the XML documentation.

Appendix B

C# and Robotics

lthough I haven't written about it much, my hobby is robotics. Actually, many years ago it was also my job, because I designed and implemented industrial robotic control languages. Robots are exciting because they animate the logic of the programs that we write. They also interface to the real world. Even though I have not been actively involved with robotics on a professional level for quite some time, it has always remained an important area of interest. The reason that I bring this up is that C# offers some advantages to the robotics programmer.

Normally, when one thinks of robotics control code, one thinks of high-performance routines written in C++. However, C# may cause some to rethink that assumption. The reason is that robotic control programs can be quite large, containing many subsystems, such as guidance, vision, pattern recognition, motor control, and so on. These subsystems can be organized into (and implemented as) a collection of C# components. Taking a component approach to robotics code helps manage the complexity involved with robot control. It also enables a subsystem to be easily changed or upgraded.

If you are interested in robotics—especially if you are interested in creating your own robot for experimentation—you might find the robot shown in Figure B-1 of interest. This is my current test robot. Several things make this robot interesting. First, it contains an on-board microprocessor that provides basic motor control and sensor feedback. Second, it contains an RS-232 transceiver that is used to receive instructions from the main computer and return results. This approach enables a remote computer to provide the intensive processing that is necessary in robotics without adding all that weight to the robot, itself. Third, it contains a video camera that is connected to a wireless video transmitter.

Figure B-1. *A simple yet effective experimental robot*

The robot is built on a Hobbico M1 Abrams R/C tank chassis. (I have found that the chassis of R/C model tanks and cars often work well as a robot base.) I removed most of the internals from the tank, including the receiver and speed controls, but I kept the motors. The Hobbico tank is well suited for a robotics platform because it is quite strong, the motors are good, it can carry a lot of weight, and its tank treads don't fall off. Also, by using tank treads, the robot has a zero turning radius and can run on uneven ground. The chassis is about 18 inches long and about 8 inches wide.

Once the chassis was empty, I added the components. To provide on-board control, I used a BASIC Stamp 2, which is a simple, yet powerful microprocessor manufactured by Parallax, Inc. (www.parallaxinc.com). The RS-232 transceiver is also from Parallax, as is the video camera and transmitter. Both the wireless RS-232 transceiver and the video transmitter have a range of about 300 feet. I also added electronic speed controllers for the tank motors. They are of the type used by high-performance R/C cars. They are controlled by the BASIC Stamp microprocessor.

Here is the way the robot works. The remote computer runs the main robotic control program. This program handles all "heavy-duty" processing, such as vision, guidance, and spatial orientation. It can also learn a series of moves and then replay them. The remote computer transmits motion-control instructions (via the wireless RS-232 link) to the robot. The BASIC Stamp receives those instructions and puts them into action. For example, if a "move forward" command is received, the BASIC Stamp sends the proper signals to the electronic speed controllers connected to the motors. When the robot has completed a command, it returns an acknowledgement code. Thus, communication between the remote computer and the robot is bi-directional, and the successful completion of each command can be confirmed.

Because the main processing for the robot occurs on the remote computer, there are no severe limitations to the amount of processing that I can do. For example, at the time of this writing, the robot can follow an object by using its vision system. This capability requires a fair amount of processing that would be difficult to carry on board.

At the time of this writing, most of the robotic control code is still written in C++. However, I plan to begin migrating pieces of it to C# as soon as I get some free time. The first subsystem I will be converting is the one that replays a series of instructions. This is a list-based task that can be handled easily by a C# collection.

Index

M

N

INTERNATIONAL CONTACT INFORMATION

AUSTRALIA
McGraw-Hill Book Company Australia Pty. Ltd.
TEL +61-2-9417-9899
FAX +61-2-9417-5687
http://www.mcgraw-hill.com.au
books-it_sydney@mcgraw-hill.com

CANADA
McGraw-Hill Ryerson Ltd.
TEL +905-430-5000
FAX +905-430-5020
http://www.mcgrawhill.ca

**GREECE, MIDDLE EAST,
NORTHERN AFRICA**
McGraw-Hill Hellas
TEL +30-1-656-0990-3-4
FAX +30-1-654-5525

MEXICO (Also serving Latin America)
McGraw-Hill Interamericana Editores S.A. de C.V.
TEL +525-117-1583
FAX +525-117-1589
http://www.mcgraw-hill.com.mx
fernando_castellanos@mcgraw-hill.com

SINGAPORE (Serving Asia)
McGraw-Hill Book Company
TEL +65-863-1580
FAX +65-862-3354
http://www.mcgraw-hill.com.sg
mghasia@mcgraw-hill.com

SOUTH AFRICA
McGraw-Hill South Africa
TEL +27-11-622-7512
FAX +27-11-622-9045
robyn_swanepoel@mcgraw-hill.com

**UNITED KINGDOM & EUROPE
(Excluding Southern Europe)**
McGraw-Hill Education Europe
TEL +44-1-628-502500
FAX +44-1-628-770224
http://www.mcgraw-hill.co.uk
computing_neurope@mcgraw-hill.com

ALL OTHER INQUIRIES Contact:
Osborne/McGraw-Hill
TEL +1-510-549-6600
FAX +1-510-883-7600
http://www.osborne.com
omg_international@mcgraw-hill.com